Pivot of Civilization

or

Rivet of Life?

Conflicting Worldviews and Same-Sex Marriage

CARMAN BRADLEY

TRAFFORD

Canada • England • Ireland • United States of America

Printed in Victoria, Canada

Note for Librarians: a cataloguing record for this book that includes Dewey Classification and US Library of Congress numbers is available from the National Library of Canada. The complete cataloguing record can be obtained from the National Library's online database at: www.nlc-bnc.ca/amicus/index-e.html
ISBN 1-4120-1900-1

TRAFFORD

This book was published *on-demand* in cooperation with Trafford Publishing.
On-demand publishing is a unique process and service of making a book available for retail sale to the public taking advantage of on-demand manufacturing and Internet marketing. **On-demand publishing** includes promotions, retail sales, manufacturing, order fulfilment, accounting and collecting royalties on behalf of the author.

Suite 6E, 2333 Government St., Victoria, B.C. V8T 4P4, CANADA

Phone	250-383-6864	Toll-free	1-888-232-4444 (Canada & US)
Fax	250-383-6804	E-mail	sales@trafford.com
Web site	www.trafford.com		

TRAFFORD PUBLISHING IS A DIVISION OF TRAFFORD HOLDINGS LTD.

Trafford Catalogue #03-2278 www.trafford.com/robots/03-2278.html

10 9 8

Dedicated to the survival
of the traditional family – a societal model
based on monogamous, life-long, heterosexual marriage,
and child-rearing remaining the responsibility of the biological parents.

For the love of
Mom, Dad, Gill, Mary, Lucy and Amy.

TABLE OF CONTENTS

Name Mary Date Dec 20

Guest Speaker Evaluation and Response

I was/ was not present

10

1. Name of speaker. (1 mark) ______

2. Topic of the presentation. (1 mark) Sexual assault.

3. List 5 things you learned from this presentation. (5 marks)

- sexual violenece continuum — thoughts – actions: sexism, racism, homophobia, ableism; sexual harrasment; homicide, suicide.
- sexual assault can even be rating people.
- Being "gay" is part of your genes you have no choice.
- Your only choice is whether you practice this or not
- greater chance [80–90%] of sexual assault if you are a girl with a developmental dissability

4. Select one thing that struck you as most powerful and discuss how it has affected you personally. (3 marks) The thing that struck me most "powerfully" was that the speaker seemed to think that being gay was scientifically decided in your genes. I really disagree. It says in the ~~the~~ bible that being gay is a sin. So why would God allow people to be gay if he didn't make them that way?

This topic is discussed later in the course. Please see me today re: this topic.

INTRODUCTION

Why this Book? Why Now?

Two and a half years into my research and writing, after an infinite number of two finger key strokes and endnotes, I asked myself: Why this book? Why this time? It may seem an odd confession, but I started this project without any idea of where it would end, led by an earnest desire to study the subject matter. Foremost, this book details the secular, feminist, humanist, free love worldview, which I have called "Pivot of Civilization" and the orthodox Christian paradigm, labeled "Rivet of Life." With the recently heightened issue of same-sex marriage, I now see the research as timely and the book contents as a constructive contribution to the debate.

The inspirational spark for this effort came in the form of a guest speaker evaluation, which my oldest daughter literally tossed into my lap one evening in December 2000. Mary, then sixteen, had attended a guest speaker presentation on "sexual assault" at High School. When she was asked in the evaluation (opposite page) to "select one thing that struck you as most powerful and then to discuss how it affected you personally," Mary wrote:

The thing that struck me most 'powerfully' was that the speaker seemed to think that being gay was scientifically decided in your genes. I really disagree. It says in the Bible that being gay is a sin. So why would God allow people to be gay if he didn't make them that way?

The "gay gene" issue bothered me a lot. I felt that my daughter's and thus my family's "space" was willfully invaded. Like a previously dormant immune system, now alerted, I found I had become animated in a quest for answers and explanations. Here was a clash of life beliefs, which I felt had to be addressed. I wrote to the High School (Appendix 1) seeking clarification on school curriculum and policy. A passage, which describes the situation as I saw it reads:

Every voice in the debate speaks from some sort of value system. There can be no 'neutral' answers to most social issues. The problem is, while claiming only to discourage scapegoating, gay-affirming programs do much more. In reality, they promote a particular worldview; complete with truth claims those students are expected to adopt. These programs promote the value systems of a particular social group and denigrate the views of another, while at the same time, distorting science.[1]

In the months following, I determined that the School did not hold the view that homosexuality was genetic. More important, according to the host teacher, "the guest speaker was only giving her personal beliefs." Equally as shocking, the School Board could not show me in the curriculum where any guidance was given for instruction on homosexuality; nor did they respond to questions 2-5 posed in my original letter (Appendix 1). The questions were as follows:

The 'homosexual orientation' or 'homosexual identity' does not itself cause medical problems; only typical homosexual behaviors can. What steps does XXXX School take to portray the health risks of a gay lifestyle?

During teaching on homosexuality, is any effort made to portray the heterosexual family unit as the optimum model for raising children?

Could you outline when formal teaching about homosexuality is given to students over their time with the Calgary Board of Education? What are the objectives of the education at each stage?

When teaching about homosexuality, is there any discussion on how this subject is viewed by Christians, Jews and students of other religions?

The School Board representative did say that a new curriculum was under development but she could not speculate on its guidance for teaching about homosexuality.

Since Mary's class was slated for a further presentation on the subject of homosexuality, I met with the next guest speaker to decide if Mary should attend. Julia (assumed name) was then a member on staff at the Calgary Birth Control Association (CBCA). Since 1996, CBCA has been providing comprehensive sexual education to high schools within the Public School System. Over 4300 students had already participated in CBCA's anti-homophobia education classes, designed to challenge stereotypes surrounding gay (G), lesbian (L), and bisexual (B) youth and to decrease factors leading to isolation of GLB youth. CBCA, a pro-choice agency, is also a "strong supporter of the feminist analysis of women's issues."

During our discussion at the abortion clinic, I showed Julia the guest speaker evaluation and asked what her position was on the "gay gene" theory. Her response remains indelibly etched in my memory. "Oh we would never say that. We don't discuss philosophy, just rights." Said with such conviction, this statement strengthened my resolve to do something, since all one hears about these days are "rights." Everyone wants constitutional (guaranteed) rights to do as they wish. Rights-based arguments are not just a problem for heterosexuals, but even homosexual and pro-gay theorists complain about the strategy. Jeffery Weeks writes, "The inadequacy of rights-based arguments lies not in the claim to the right in itself, but in the absence of a wider social context in which the notion of rights becomes meaningful."[2] Valerie Lehr also gives a sharp critique of "rights talk," suggesting "the extension of rights depoliticizes issues that need to be subject to public debate and discussion." She states that conceptualizing freedom in terms of rights "keeps us from asking what 'freedom' means"[3] and prevents us from understanding the importance of our collective decision making and the societal consequences.

This idea of avoiding philosophy is fundamental to the misunderstanding and division between people. There can be no simple appeal to "rights" or isolated "facts," for these cannot be considered apart from a philosophy by which the "rights" or "facts" are interpreted. For example, High School students (or anyone for that matter) do not need more raw sexual "facts" without a context upon which to decide on their relevance. Yet under the title "OUR PHILOSOPHY," the Calgary Birth Control Association web site states:

At CBCA we believe that sexuality is a natural and healthy part of life. Healthy sexual relationships are based on trust, respect and equality. We work for the right of all people to get information that helps them make choices and decisions about their sexuality...In our work we want to give clear information without passing judgment.[4]

This is not really a philosophy. It is more of a customer service standard. On the other hand, their pamphlet "What Everyone Should Know About Lesbian, Gay, Bisexual, Two-Spirited & Transgendered Youth" (which was referenced in a pamphlet Mary brought home from school) comes closer. Under the title "WHAT IF YOU DON"T KNOW FOR SURE?" it reads:

Our sexuality develops over time. Don't worry if you aren't sure. The teen years are a time of figuring out what works for you, and crushes and experimentation are often part of that. Over time, you'll find that you're drawn mostly to men or to women – or to both – and you'll know then. You don't have to label yourself today.[5]

Germaine Greer writes, "The sex-knowledge so-called is actually sex belief and includes a system of values." She goes on to say, "The sex reformers, who exhibit no respect for traditional values and address themselves to sexuality without interest in or comprehension of the whole personality, are the bawds of capitalism."[6] Under the topic "Birth Control/Contraception," on the CBCA web site, is listed a link to the Coalition for Positive Sexuality. The CBCA advisory caption reads: "Teen-oriented with down-to-earth, easy-to-understand language. Several, but not all, methods of birth control are discussed." The site reads:

[And I apologize in advance for some passages you will be obliged to read here and elsewhere – these descriptions are intended only to inform.]

Sex is everywhere — on beer commercials, billboards, and in music lyrics. But most messages we get tell us that sex is something dirty that we shouldn't talk about, or an act of violence. Most of us learn that our bodies, and our sex, are things to be ashamed of. Most of us learn that sex means a man on top of a woman, and that the only other choice is abstinence. But sex can be lots of things ... Women have sex with women, men have sex with men, women have sex with men — and sometimes the best sex is with yourself!

There are lots of safe and fun ways to get off, which you probably won't learn in school. You can do many of these things all by yourself as well as with others, and you can talk about them even if you don't want to do them. Don't feel like you have to do everything on the next page, but don't feel like anything is automatically off limits either. The important thing is that everyone involved clearly says what they want and can make it stop when they want.

Just remember, sex is only fun if everyone agrees on what they're going to do. You could...suck, kiss, touch, bite, fondle, nibble, squeeze, and lick someone's body, nipples, calves, toes, neck, ass, dick or vagina ... jerk yourself or each other off, dry or using lots of lubricant...kiss for a long time, using lots of tongue...have sex in front of mirrors, or watch each other jerking off...get into role play (for instance, tie someone up and pleasure them) ...look at sexy pictures and videos...make up or act out fantasies, talk dirty, dress up, strip down, or cross-dress (dressing in the clothes of the other gender)...If you're putting something into a butthole, make sure it has a flared base and looks something like the picture. That way it can't go all the way in and get stuck.[7]

Does CBCA really provide "comprehensive sex-ed" to our Calgary Public School children? Clearly the answer is yes, if the measure is breadth of sexual variety. But are our children, after bombardment with all and I mean "all" the facts, any further ahead in making sound life decisions? Is the "postmodern era" giving our children, adolescents, single adults, married or co-habitating couples, and parents a satisfactory moral compass? This book seriously responds to these questions. Agencies like CBCA and the Coalition for Positive Sexuality see little need for a moral compass – let your sex drive do the navigating! A lesson taken from *Don Juan*, illustrates my perspective. The Devil asks, "What is the use of knowing [a philosophy]?" To this question Don Juan responds:

Why, to be able to choose the line of greatest advantage instead of yielding in the direction of least resistance. Does a ship sail to its destination no better than a log drifts nowhither? The philosopher is Nature's pilot. And there you have our difference: to be in hell is to drift: to be in heaven is to steer.[8]

The secular world uses "religion" as a pejorative term for those who have a spiritual foundation to their lives. Jesus Christ also held disdain for "religious" people – when their practice was caught up in ritual, piety, legalism and false righteousness. However, the real issue before us is not *individual conduct*, but the societal clash of secular and faith-based life philosophies – competing *worldviews*. The decision to be an atheist is a choice of beliefs. The decision to act out gay (G), bisexual (B), lesbian (L), transgendered (T) and queer (Q) (GBLTQ) behaviors is predicated on a choice of beliefs and behind that belief system is an underlying philosophy. Not always in subtle ways, many secularists attack religion at every turn. The prevailing assumption of postmodernity is that we are now in a post-Christian era. The war is won say many with pride! Yet not all secularists or homosexuals are prepared to declare total victory. Activist Torie Osborn, argues in the gay magazine *Advocate*, "we have virtually no helpful objective or clear strategy on the long-term war, which grapples with deep-seated sexphobia as well as heterosexism."[9] Author Paul Monette sees America as the "Christian Reich" and themselves as members of the queer equivalent of the "French resistance."[10] Obscuring and contorting the battle lines of competing life paradigms are *professed* Christians claiming either a "liberal" interpretation of the Bible or a more radical opinion that the historical Christ was *probably* a "lower class, fully human orphan, who became a celebrity sage." Most of these "unorthodox believers" profess gay-Christian and pro-gay Christian theologies.

Books in general are informative, but very few become incitements to action. I have called this book "Pivot of Civilization or Rivet of Life?" with the intention of equipping and leading the reader to face his or her philosophy of life first before deciding on such issues as same-sex marriage. This book will open people's eyes to a very complex, multi-faceted, and threatening set of issues. I believe mankind is not intended to operate in a value vacuum or to navigate without a moral compass. An "adrift-lifestyle" is irresponsible. A society without moral boundaries is equally reckless. Thus secularist (Pivot of Civilization) and Christian (Rivet of Life) worldviews will be developed in this book and their relative merit, in facing key issues of the day, will be studied. The institutions of marriage and family will be cast in far reaching perspective.

The task ahead is partially one of understanding terminologies, unraveling rhetoric and exposing falsehood. I have researched well over a thousand sources in pursuit of the proverbial truth. Robert and Katherine Baird describe the challenge in *Homosexuality: Debating the Issues:*

When gays speak about themselves, they are speaking one language; when most straight people speak about gays, they are speaking another...There's only one way to get past the feeling of confusion: tireless, meticulous, dedication to study. You can't learn a foreign language over night, and you can't teach it by screaming it at people. You teach it word by word, until bit-by-bit they feel comfortable speaking it.[11]

In *Christianity, Social Tolerance and Homosexuality* (1980), John Boswell studied the relationships of homosexual peoples to their societies from the beginning of the Christian era to the fourteenth century. In the book he argues two main points: the Christian Church has not always disapproved of homosexuality, and the Bible verses assumed to condemn homosexual sex do not refer to homosexuality at all. Of the New Testament, he wrote:

In general, only the most pressing moral questions are addressed by its authors. Details of life appear only to illustrate larger points. No effort is made to elaborate a comprehensive sexual ethic: Jesus and His followers simply respond to situations and questions requiring immediate attention.[12]

Boswell's view makes the Bible look almost incidental – a good but incomplete book, inadequate to answer the questions of life. One must deduce that he views the Apostle Paul's comments to Timothy as falsehood or at best the musings of an unenlightened individual. Paul said:

All Scripture is given by the inspiration of God, and is profitable for doctrine, for reproof, for correction, for instruction in righteousness: That the man of God may be perfect, thoroughly furnished unto all good works (2 Timothy 3:16-17).

Boswell wrote of homosexuality:

The belief that they [GBLTQ] constitute some sort of threat is still so widespread that an assumption to the contrary may appear partisan in some circles, and those who subscribe to the notion that gay people are in some way dangerous may argue that for this very reason they are not typical victims of intolerance.[13]

Here Boswell goes on to explain his standard for "homophobia":

It should be noted that whether a group actually threatens society or not is not directly relevant to the issue of intolerance unless the hostility the group experiences can be shown to stem from a rational apprehension of that threat....The claims about the precise nature of the threat posed by gay people have varied extravagantly over time, sometimes contradicting each other directly and almost invariably entailing striking internal inconsistencies.[14]

The year before Boswell's book came out, CBS did a documentary on the Buena Vista sex park in San Francisco, called *Gay Power, Gay Politics*. In the film CBS reporter-producer George Crile talked with gay activist Cleve Jones. "So, what's the message today?" Crile asked. "The message is 'Look out, here we come!'" answered Jones.[15] One year later the first purple lesions of Kaposi's sarcoma (signaling AIDS) appeared on gay men in San Francisco and New York.

In response to gay activism, Kristi Hamrick, Press Secretary for Family Research Council, makes an astute point:

This is why lines must be drawn, standards discussed, and battles fought. Because when people push the envelope of morality and get away with it, they don't sit back to enjoy the sensation. They reach further – touching the lives of the people around them – touching the lives of your children, and someday, mine.[16]

The gravity of the ongoing clash of worldviews, and at this time, the same-sex marriage debate, goes well beyond the AIDS threat. Yet unfortunately, Mr. Boswell shall never read this orthodox Christian apology. The distinguished gay historian died of AIDS on Christmas Day in 1994, at age 47. In one sense, this book strives to reveal what lessons and wisdom should be taken from his death and such tragedies. I have painstakingly collected and analyzed the wisdom and thoughts of others, that I might articulate in common and convincing language what I previously accepted by faith as truth.

In preparing this book, considerable emphasis has been placed on determining historical facts along with understanding the personalities and beliefs of key historical figures. I uphold Solomon's conviction that little is new under the sun. Historian Denis Stairs expressed it this way:

History does not in detail repeat itself, but a knowledge of historical cases gives one a sense of being 'at home' in the presence of certain types of phenomena, and provides a kind of 'understanding' or 'wisdom' which tends if nothing else to bring one's expectations more closely in line with the probable.[17]

Vignettes, testimonies and quotes are used throughout to bring image and emotion to a broad array of subject matter. Since portrayal of competing worldviews is a comprehensive challenge, a holistic approach has been taken; one in which the study ranges, from cosmology to ecology to psychology to theology to biology, and so forth.

Regarding the question of the timing of this book, I believe three factors have come together. First, after some forty years of sexual liberation with its embodiment in Second Wave Feminism and the GBLTQ liberation movements, it is now possible to look back in hindsight and separate the truth from the rhetoric and ideological claims. Moreover, the science and psychology once employed to advance these movements now has much to say in contradiction to them. Second, the longstanding deliberate assault on the "heterosexual family" is now in its final phase. This text will reveal the amazing irony that after decades of viciously deriding and undermining the so-called "patriarchal institution of marriage," all in the name of free sex and liberation from pervasive heterosexism, the GBLTQ community now asks for membership. Third, the advent of genetic engineering and human cloning has ushered humankind to the edge of a radically new future. Although we have been sliding down a slippery biotechnological slope for years, the future bodes like a giant cliff. Biochemist turned philosopher, Leon Kass, warns that the impact of cloning is more than just another improvement in infertility treatments:

The stakes are very high indeed. [Until now] we have benefited mightily from the attitude let technology go where it will and we can fix any problems that arise later....that paradigm is open to question....What we have here is not business as usual, to be fretted about for a while and then given our seal of approval, not least because it appears to be unusual...the future of humanity may hang in the balance....This is really one of those critical moments where one gets a chance to think about terribly important things. Not just genetics and what is the meaning of mother and father and kinship, but also the whole relationship between science and society and attitudes toward technology.[18]

The structure of the book is as follows:

Part One – Elements of Free Will: boundaries, choice, consequences, politics, ideologies, cognitive dissonance and paradigms.

Part Two – Two Mutually Exclusive Paradigms: the secular worldview (Darwinism, humanism, feminism, GBLTQ, and free sex,) and the Christian worldview (monotheism).

Part Three – Unorthodox Christianity – The "Compromise" Paradigm: debunking gay and pro-gay Christianity and studying the paradox of sexual reorientation.

Part Four – The Practicality of Competing Worldviews: in application to babies, children, adolescents, single adults, couples, marriage, parenting and family.

Part Five – Pivot of Civilization or Rivet of Life?: deciding your life philosophy and facing its implications for same-sex marriage.

Most proponents of same-sex marriage argue that including GBLTQ in the long established definition will have little impact upon the heterosexual institution of marriage and its associated traditional family unit. Some suggest the impact will be positive, indeed *liberating*. Others believe the further distancing of God (and religious values) from the affairs of state will make the nation stronger. The following analysis and conclusions in this book contend that these conjectures are categorically misleading and will in the end be proven false, should same-sex "marriage" be adopted.

In reality the decision on same-sex marriage is a test of where the individual and the nation, as a whole, lie in belief. This book takes the issue out of its "rights-based" context and looks at the decision from a broader perspective – within the framework of what Diana Alstad calls the "planetary battle" or the "morality wars" over "Who has the right to decide what's right?"[19] Acceptance of same-sex marriage will symbolize state approval of secular, humanist, and free sex ethos, over traditional theistic-based values. Moreover, the resulting laws will legislate the union of GBLTQ *space* into heterosexual *space* and will imply (inappropriately!) that the GBLTQ lifestyle is the "same" culturally, morally, and ecologically, as the heterosexual way of life. The book will defend this interpretation and detail many of the harmful ramifications of such a huge move away from theism.

On the other hand, the book also reveals the societal benefits, should the state decide to legislate a separate definition of same-sex union, in keeping with a unique and separate recognition of the GBLTQ minority lifestyle.

PART ONE

ELEMENTS OF FREE WILL

[Jennie Ruby, came out as a lesbian and discovered the lesbian community in the mid 1980s. She discovered feminism at the same time. She chose to see herself as a lesbian radical feminist instead of transgendered.]

I made daily choices in matters large and small that expressed an androgynous persona...It was very clear that 'identity' was also 'politics.' Seeing myself as transgendered would have influenced my choices about what to wear and how to act, and ultimately would determine my politics. I would go to drag-king shows and glory in how masculine I could look or act. I would not confront the internalized misogyny that made me neglect housework, hate children, and avoid making my home warm and comfortable. I could easily come to the conclusion that I was really a man; and simply embrace masculinity whole heartedly. And instead of having a feminist critique of patriarchy, I would simply be seeking an individual accommodation with it. But I believe that who I am is a process, not a product. I am a string of decisions and choices made to prefer one thing over another, to spend more time on some things and less time on others. I am part consciousness; part feelings; part intellect; part practice. Oh, yeah, and part biology.[1]

Jennie Ruby, 1980s

The problem [of sexual preference] is, after all, part of a broader problem of choices in general: the choice of the road one takes, of the clothes that one wears, of the food that one eats, of the place in which one sleeps, and the endless other things one is constantly choosing. A choice of a partner in a sexual relation becomes more significant only because society demands that there be a particular choice in this matter, and does not so often dictate one's choice of food or of clothing.[2]

Alfred Kinsey, 1948

CHAPTER ONE

CHOICE, BOUNDARIES AND CONSEQUENCES

A college student, responding to the question 'If you had to say what morality meant to you, how would you sum it up?' replies: When I think of the word morality, I think of obligations. I usually think of it as conflicts between personal desires and social things, social considerations, or personal desires of yourself versus personal desires of another person or people or whatever....In a situation of social interaction, something is morally wrong where the individual ends up screwing a lot of people. And it is morally right when everyone comes out for the better.[1]

The essence of a moral decision is the exercise of choice and the willingness to accept responsibility for that choice.[2]

Carol Gilligan

Choice and Ecology

In *Sexual Ecology: AIDS and the Destiny of Gay Men*, Gabriel Rotello describes ecology as the science of connections. Ecology seeks to describe the vast web of interrelationships that tie living things to their environments. Its fundamental premise is that a change in any part of one of the "tangled banks of life," which we call "ecosystems," can have broad and often unexpected implications for any living thing seeking to survive within them. Rotello writes:

From an ecological perspective, human cultures are far more than just 'lifestyles' comprised of rituals and rules with symbolic meanings for their members. Cultures are adaptive strategies for survival, ways of life that allow their members to cope with the complex obstacles that nature, and other people, place in their way.[3]

The value in addressing the ecology of sexual relationships, be they heterosexual, homosexual, bisexual, or other is that it takes the focus away from "why" people make their choices and highlights instead the consequences of these choices. Seen in this context, it becomes little comfort to the dying AIDS patient to know, for example, that the existence of a "gay gene" has just been scientifically proven. Ecology focuses on the end result and is illustrated, for example, in society's disdain for child abuse. When we (both straights and gays) address the issue of pedophilia, little sympathy is offered to "why" the person chooses this course of action. Only the consequences of the behavior are important. Here, Edward Stein, author of *The Mismeasure of Desire: The Science, Theory, and Ethics of Sexual Orientation*, is in agreement that the causes of sexual orientation have "few ethical, legal, and political implications":

It is the choices they make about how to live their lives, not the origins of their sexual desires that are most important for lesbian and gay rights. Regardless of whether sexual orientations are directly chosen, indirectly chosen, or not chosen at all...people choose with whom they have sex, people choose whether to be open about their sexual orientations, people choose whether or not to enter romantic relationships, and whether or not to build families...Such choices should be the centerpiece of gay and lesbian rights...Neither question [biology or environment] is, however, relevant to settling ethical, legal, and political questions about sexual orientations...[4]

Some activists think regardless of what causes homosexuality, calls for equal rights for the GBLTQ community should be based on what they do as public citizens rather than on how they express themselves in their private lives. However, in advocating choice as the basis for gay rights, Stein and like minded gay activists miss the importance of the ecological consequences of choice, which do have enormous ethical, legal and political importance. The first prerequisite for a choice in favor of something should be a collective vision of what the choice involves. Fully disclosed, choice happens in a context of options, interests, life paradigms, tangible and intangible boundaries, relatives, friends, and others impacted by the consequences. When combined these considerations outline an ecosystem.

Natural Boundaries

In *Boundaries: When to Say YES, When to Say NO, To Take Control of Your Life*, Dr. Henry Cloud and Dr. John Townsend have refined the idea of boundaries, particularly as they apply to individual relationships. They introduce the concept of physical and intangible boundaries. A physical boundary helps us to distinguish our property so that we can take care of it. According to these clinical psychologists we need to keep things that will nurture us inside our boundaries and keep things that will harm us outside. They write:

The most basic boundary that defines you is your physical skin. People often use this boundary as a metaphor for saying that their personal boundaries have been violated: 'He really gets under my skin.' The skin boundary keeps the good in and the bad out. It protects your blood and bones, holding them inside and all together. It also keeps out germs, protecting you from infection. At the same time skin has openings that let 'good' in, like food, and the 'bad' out, like waste products.[5]

Victims of physical and sexual abuse often have a poor sense of boundaries. Early in life they come to believe from experience that their property does not really begin at their skin. Others could invade their property and do whatever they wanted. As a result, they have difficulty establishing boundaries later in life. Here responsibility for the boundary violation rests with others but the consequences fall on the victim. In the case of voluntary sexual behavior, we have much greater control over how we treat our bodies. Regardless of one's perspective – by God's design or by millions of years of Darwinian evolution, our bodies are seen as marvels of biological engineering for defence against bacterial and viral diseases, as long as they are properly maintained. An unfortunate fact of our natural skin boundary is that any exchange of bodily fluids, whether blood or semen, breaches our defense. From the body's vantage the "how" is irrelevant; whether by scratch, blood transfusion or sexual act, the result is the same. The "how" only becomes relevant when considering intangible boundaries.

Cloud and Townsend say intangible boundaries are often defined in domains such as spirituality, truth, maturity, politics and relationships. In the intangible world our fences and markers are invisible, existing in thoughts and language, or coming through divine revelation. Howard Bloom refers to "memes," in a similar context – as intangible habits (implicit behavioral memes) and thoughts (explicit verbal memes), which migrate from mind to mind, network and impact our thinking.[6] Spirituality can embody a range of boundaries. The most basic boundary setting word is "No!" It lets others know that you exist apart from them and that you are in control of you. No is a confrontational word. Christians are obliged to confront people we love, saying, "No, that behavior is not okay. I will not participate in that." "That action is wrong in Christ's eyes." The word no is also important in setting limits on abuse. The words we choose let people know where we stand and thus gives them a sense of the "edges" that help identify who you are.[7]

Truth is another invisible boundary. It is to be hoped this book will challenge the reader to ask the questions: Am I the property of God or am I on my own? Do I define myself in relation to my Creator or to money, material, work, sexual pleasure or something else? The state of willfully or inadvertently ignoring the truth is often diagnosed as denial or living in some other form of cognitive dissonance. Seeking the truth in life can be complicated by incomplete information (errors of omission and commission) and a lack of depth of analysis. Furthermore, seeking the truth can have limitations placed by level of maturity and mental development. Immaturity can be a boundary to discernment. A fourteen-year-old might not see the truth in a circumstance to the degree that a twenty-one-year-old might, or a parent, teacher or counselor. For this reason youth often rely on trust over straight reason, although as we try to create "adults" earlier and earlier, this is becoming less common. When facts come in a vacuum of context, it is hard to discern the truth.

Politics creates intangible boundaries expressed by ideology, strategy, alliance, membership criteria and group solidarity. Choice of language and terminology can be widely constrained by political considerations. For example, in the middle of the AIDS crisis in San Francisco, public health officials, anxious gay politicians, and the burgeoning ranks of AIDs activists created AIDSpeak. To speak in public a new lexicon was devised. Under the rules of AIDSpeak, AIDS victims could not be called victims. Instead, they were called People With AIDS, PWAs, as if contracting this uniquely brutal disease was not a victimizing experience. "Promiscuous" became "sexually active," because gay politicians declared "promiscuous" to be "judgmental," a major cuss word in AIDSpeak. The most used circumlocution in AIDSpeak was "bodily fluids," an expression that avoided troublesome words like "semen."[8]

Last, relationships instill intangible boundaries. There are always other stakeholders in the choices one makes. At a personal level there are friends, spouses, partners, family, relatives, neighbors and fellow workers to mention a few. At the aggregate or collective level there are communities, alliances, societies, nations and indeed genders to consider. The institution of "marriage" is a potent example, representing societal boundaries within which heterosexual males and females have traditionally committed to union, with or without the intent to procreate.

Because of "boundary" considerations, choice often comes with complications. There are always consequences for trespassing on other people's property or violating a boundary. Here is where choices and consequences are intertwined. The Apostle Paul wrote that behaviors have individual consequences in his letter to the Christian churches:

Do not be deceived: God cannot be mocked. A man reaps what he sows. The one who sows to please his sinful nature, from that nature will reap destruction; the one who sows to please the Spirit, from the Spirit will reap eternal life.

Galatians 6:7-8

Cloud and Townsend also speak of a natural axiom they call "The Law of Sowing and Reaping" or "The Law of Cause and Effect." Typically, an alcoholic or drug addict ruins his own life and often that of his spouse and family. People can interfere with the Law of Cause and Effect by stepping in and rescuing irresponsible people. Rescuing a person from the natural consequences of his behavior enables him to continue an irresponsible behavior. However, the Law of Sowing and Reaping has not been repealed. It is still operating. But the individual is not suffering the consequences, someone else is. We refer to this person who continually rescues another person as codependent. In effect, codependent people "co-sign the note" of life for the irresponsible person. Then they end up paying all the bills – physically, emotionally, and spiritually – and the spendthrift continues out of control with no consequences.[9] [Later in this chapter we will come to see so-called "free sex" behavior has a codependency upon pharmaceutical, medical technologies and "safe-sex practices."]

Taking responsibility for our choices leads to self-control. Paul outlined for the Galatians, the consequence of sinful choices and the fruits of responsible behavior:

The acts of the sinful nature are obvious: sexual immorality, impurity and debauchery; idolatry and witchcraft; hatred, discord, jealousy, fits of rage, selfish ambition, dissentions, factions and envy; drunkenness, orgies, and the like. I warn you, as I did before, that those who live like this will not inherit the kingdom of God. But the fruit of the Spirit is love, joy, peace, patience, kindness, goodness, faithfulness, gentleness and self-control. Against such things there is no law.

Galatians 5:19-23

Cloud and Townsend point out that a common boundary problem is disowning our choices and trying to lay responsibility for them on someone else. Think for a moment how often we use the phrases, "I had to" or "She (he) made me" when explaining why we did or did not do something. These phrases betray our basic illusion that we are not active agents in creating our circumstances. We think someone else is in control, thus relieving us of our basic responsibility. We need to realize that we are in control of our choices, no matter how we feel.[10]

Setting and living by boundaries involves taking responsibility for our choices. You are the one who makes them. You are the one who must live by the consequences. Associated with responsibility is integrity, which is living honestly in applying your values in the choices you make. Values are what we love and give importance to. Often we do not take responsibility for what we value and believe.[11] From a different angle, integrity is seen as the measure of one's ability to take responsibility for the consequences of one's actions. When we are caught up in valuing the approval of others, power, riches or sexual pleasure over the approval of God, we miss out on life. When things go wrong we often blame others. We miss out because these values do not satisfy our deepest longing, which is really for love (intimacy and relationship).

Another key matter of boundaries, central to effecting choice, is respect. We need to respect the boundaries of others in order to command respect for our own preferences. This is often called respecting each other's "space" in GBLTQ parlance. We need to treat their boundaries the way we would like them to treat our own. If we love and respect people who tell us no, they will love and respect our no. Respect begets respect. But what if the neighbor's goal is to dismantle all boundaries?

Free Sex?

Orthodox Christian culture has embodied very clear boundaries for sexual behavior. Sexual relations are only to take place inside the bounds of monogamous heterosexual marriage. Some fifty-five years after Jesus' resurrection, the Christian congregation in Corinth was boasting that they had a right to do as they pleased. In reply, Apostle Paul wrote:

Everything is permissible for me – but not everything is beneficial. Everything is permissible for me – but I will not be mastered by anything....The body is not meant for sexual immorality, but for the Lord, and the Lord for the body...Flee from sexual immorality. All other sins a man commits are outside his body, but he who sins sexually sins against his own body. Do you not know that your body is a temple of the Holy Spirit, who is in you, whom you have received from God? You are not your own; you were bought with a price. Therefore honor God with your body.

1 Corinthians 6:12, 18-20

Proponents of boundariless, liberated or free sex, choose to demolish these Creator-inspired safety parameters, and do so under terminology such as "positive sex" or "sex positive" ethos. The Coalition for Positive Sexuality, referred to in the Introduction, is a typical example. So too is CBCA. When the Calgary Birth Control Association states in its philosophy, "Healthy sexual relationships are based on trust, respect and equality," they are addressing a much greater set of sexual circumstances than found in the boundaries of marriage. No notion of age, quantity of lovers (simultaneous or serial), gender, sex, depth of relationship (intimacy), commitment, or responsibility is implied. None is intended. Sex positive philosophies set no boundaries other than trust, respect and equality. Regrettably, without violating either of these three tenets, it is possible to have multiple encounters, in a bathhouse cubical, with people to whom you never speak or know. There is a philosophical aversion in the sex positive ethos to address matters of right or wrong. CBCA's position is "In our work, we want to give clear information without passing judgment." Everything is relative and the basis for their guidance remains illusive. Their direction is individual-centered, anchored in liberation from perceived sexual oppression.

Free sex ideology says "define oppression as you wish and you can free yourself by escaping these boundaries." Universally valued terms for virtuous love, like "fidelity," are re-worded in positive sexuality jargon to "serial-monogamy" or "multipartnerism." "Promiscuity" slips into "sexually active lifestyle." The few times that boundaries are defined, terms like "closed" or "open" are used. A closed relationship aspires to maintain fidelity, at least until the relationship is over. An open relationship allows for parallel sexual relations. The application of such terminology is shown in these examples of how bisexuals describe their ideal sociosexual arrangements to researchers:

A deep relationship with a man and a woman...It would not be a live-in situation. I would not want the man and the woman to be sexual with each other...I would want them to be friends, but I am not looking for them to be bisexual. (F)

I would like to live with a male and female who each had their own bedroom in a large house. We would all have sexual and emotional relationships with each other, as well as others outside of the house. (M)

A good wife, a family, and a younger man for an athletic companion – it would include sexuality. (M)[12]

In these free sex models, jealousy and time management are coordinated by designating one relationship as "primary" and any others as "secondary." If one or both partners in a marriage are bi-sexual, their married relationship could be the primary commitment. In an "open" marriage, the same-sex relationships would be termed secondary; or vice versa. At a rap session for married bisexuals a researcher recorded:

Researcher: Jill, you have what, three primary relationships?

Jill: No, I do not. I have one primary relationship. My primary relationship is with Rob.

Researcher: Okay, so what are these others?

The man that I see, I see – oh, every couple weeks. As the sexual intensity has diminished the friendship and the caring has increased. We have more contact over the phone and Valentine cards and that type of thing. He's also living with a woman who's in another relationship with a man, which was a primary requisite for my willingness to get involved with him. I am unwilling at this point to be involved with anybody who is not already either partnered or clearly the kind of person who likes three or four multiple partners at a time and has no interest in getting involved in a primary relationship. I don't have that to offer. I also have eliminated through trial and error people who are deceiving their partners. I got really burned on that one, one time. And I'm not willing to be in that situation again. I'm real clear about those who are possible partners for me. That doesn't mean I wouldn't go, and if I met someone that turned on to me, have casual sex with them. It means that I wouldn't probably continue or entertain it as a possibility for any kind of ongoing relationship.

[Two years after the interview Jill and Rob divorced] – 'What they really needed, according to him [Rob], was to be monogamous for awhile.'[13]

Such terms and boundariless lovemaking are completely wrong in the traditional Christian way of thinking. But this behavior must be regarded as flawed by any civilized secular measure. In these relationships openness and freedom must collide with security, trust and intimacy. Weak and inconsistent boundaries, seemingly designed for violation, are too easily trespassed. In Chapter 3, the personal tragedy of the "mother" of sexual freedom, Emma Goldman, will be studied. While publicly proclaiming the philosophy of free sex, privately she was consumed with hurt and jealousy over the "free" wanderings of her most intimate and erotic male lover. In *Dual Attraction*, Weinberg et al. offered the following conclusions about bisexual relations:

Many of the respondents never achieved their ideal arrangement. Only about one-third felt they actually had, and half of these respondents said it lasted for just six months or less. Since such ideals are not easy to establish or maintain, bisexuals, like anyone else, often settle for something less.[14]

Weinberg found the most frequently cited potential cause of their relationship ending was relationship stagnation – not growing together any more, growing apart in general, not meeting each other's emotional or sexual needs any more, emotional, intellectual, spiritual lethargy, just not making each other happy, interests waning and changing to other things, no excitement in the relationship, not being fun any more, being tired of each other. The second most common potential cause for breakups was said to be finding someone else more satisfying, someone who had more to offer, someone more ideal, someone who met more of their needs, or finding a more permanent replacement. A third potential reason was geographic: one partner moving out of the area. The fourth was another relationship getting in the way, a competing primary partner, another relationship becoming too involved, another partner becoming more primary, falling seriously in love with someone else, becoming involved with someone the primary partner doesn't approve of, putting more time into another relationship, the primary partner not liking the idea that someone else is becoming equally primary. Finally, another potential reason was conflict over the openness of the relationship, the partner wanting to be monogamous, the partner wanting to be nonmonogamous, jealousy over outside sex, wanting fewer sexual restrictions than the partner does, or the partner getting too possessive and wanting them to cut back on outside sex.[15]

Wellness Doctrine for Promiscuity

Alcohol and other depressants – heroin, marijuana (grass, weed, spliff, blunts, ganja, etc,), poppers, cocaine – snorted, smoked or applied locally, other stimulants, and prescription drugs are often suggested as ways to help ease the pain or tension or embarrassment or discomfort related to receptive anal intercourse. If the drug is being used so that the experience is tolerable, then there is no problem.[16]

Robert E. Penn, 'The Gay Men's Wellness Guide'

The human body is capable of marvelous pleasure from orgasms excited through a great variety of mock (non-vaginal) sexual acts. Such imitation sexual activities are not mutual but can be reciprocal. A partner, trained to overcome gag reflex, accidental biting, distaste for semen and odor can service his or her mate well. *The Gay Men's Wellness Guide* devotes four pages to gag reflex and biting.[17] The guide also devotes six pages to handling the pain of anal penetration. Seven tips are offered in the *Guide* to help the penetrated partner relax:

(1) 'get to know your anus;' (2) 'practice contracting and relaxing your muscles;' (3) 'become aware of your breathing;' (4) 'practice insertion;' (5) 'try giving yourself an enema;' (6) 'let someone lick you;' (7) 'if you want to, try having anal sex with a man you like. He doesn't have to be your lover or even someone you love, but before you start there should be at minimum agreement of mutual respect; agreed-upon roles, if any; a designated sign for stopping in the event of pain... Remember to gently dilate yourself or let your partner dilate you before penetration and use plenty of lubrication both during the dilation and intercourse.'[18]

In free sex ideology, any comment against "positive sex" is turned into a sex negative statement. Any attempt to moralize on lifestyle choices is often interpreted as erotophobia or sexphobia. Moreover, to the sexually liberated, a lifestyle that contains sexual experience only within marriage, is seen as "sex negative," notwithstanding, that frequency and total quantity of sexual activity in a lifetime tremendously favors the married couple, and that the "ecosystem" for monogamous sex within marriage is benign, indeed better than good, it is very healthy. As long as body parts are used for their designed purpose, the frequency of sex has no correlation with contracting sexually transmitted diseases (STDs).

On the other hand, while sitting inside the CBCA "Wellness Clinic" (formerly called "Abortion Clinic"), I witnessed a rack filled with pamphlets on every sexually transmitted disease imaginable. On my left in the waiting area is a huge punch bowl full of condoms. Here are the prescribed health aids for those adherents to free and positive sex. Tragically, terms in the Wellness lexicon like safe sex, safer sex, sensible sex, smart risk sex, risk-reduction guidelines, and the Condom Code, expose the myth of free safe sex.

The opposite of wellness is "illness." One has no meaning without the other.

What is often not said to schoolchildren, at least in a way they can comprehend and recognize in the form of a choice, is that sex outside of marriage is inescapably dangerous. Operating outside of the boundary of marriage brings one head-on with disease – the raison d'etre of "Wellness" philosophy. Developed initially in the 60s and 70s with STDs, and amplified in the 80s with the addition of AIDS, is the awareness that sexual freedom comes with the implicit cost of disease. Sexually active gay men and promiscuous heterosexuals, in particular, face the continual threat of death from AIDS. The infection can happen on first and sole contact.

Risk of getting a STD depends on three factors. First, is "infectivity"- the likelihood that a particular microbe will be transmitted under particular circumstances. Second, is "prevalence" – the percentage of a population that is currently infected. Last, is "rate of partner change" – the contact rate. The last factor is really the only one in the individual's control. Simply put, without partner change no STD can spread. Partner A may infect Partner B, but things will end there. In a thoroughly monogamous population there would be no STDs at all, no matter how infectious certain microbes might theoretically be. Conversely, the higher the level of partner change, the more likely that even microbes that are relatively hard to transmit will have an opportunity to spread.[19] Gabriel Rotello explains the transmission process in this example:

...the students at the local university mostly date each other, and in general their sexual activity is characterized by fairly high levels of casual partner exchange...Because they mostly have the same sexual relations within the same pool of partners, their sexual ecosystem is characterized by relatively high levels of fast-moving STDs like syphilis and gonorrhea, which have an opportunity to spread in an environment where people often switch partners before they discover they are infected and get treatment....For the fortysomething married professionals on the other side of our hypothetical town, partner change occurs mostly in the form of occasional adultery, divorce, and remarriage. Since the social costs of adultery, divorce and remarriage are far more onerous than the casual partner switching among college students, there is understandably less of it. Fewer that half of all partners engage in even a limited episode of adultery during their marriage, and fewer than 5 per cent engage in a continuous pattern of adultery with multiple partners. As a result, in this ecosystem there is less opportunity for short-term, curable STDs like syphilis or gonorrhea to gain a foothold. Most STDs here will consist of lifelong and incurable infections such as herpes and HPV, diseases that most people acquired when they were college age and have never gotten rid of.[20]

A second foundation of Wellness doctrine is avoidance of the naturally intended consequence of heterosexual sex – pregnancy. The challenge: How to utilize a biological process, perhaps millions of years in refining, and not have it function as designed. Where this design can not be drugged, deceived or blocked from expressing itself, abortion becomes the ultimate liberator. That all heterosexual sex is inherently pro-creative is muzzled under Wellness terms like "planned parenthood." [More on abortion in Chapter 7.]

In Wellness and positive sex philosophies the ethics of one sexual behavior over another are never discussed. Dialogue on the meaning of sex is embalmed in safeguards for disease and elevation of erotica. "Good sex doesn't result in disease, but disease proves the existence of bad sex."[21] What is taboo in Wellness and positive sex dialogue is whether a sexual behavior, in of itself, is wrong. AIDS activists, for example, say "sex does not cause AIDS, a virus does," or "there are no risk groups, just risk behaviors," or "it's not who you have sex with or where you have it that counts, it's what you do." Indeed, it is viewed as homophobic to implicate aspects of gay behavior in the AIDS epidemic. Wrongly, many believe straight people's behavior is essentially the same. Rotello writes:

In fact twenty years after HIV began its relentless decimation of the gay population, it remains largely confined to the same heterosexual groups in the developed world that it infected at the start: hemophiliacs, intravenous drug users, and their female sexual partners and children. The only self-sustaining heterosexual HIV epidemic in the United States appears to be among crack cocaine addicts, who share many factors of sexual ecology with gay men.[22]

While some Gay activists may concede the above to be true, they avoid the issue by pointing out that in the less developed world, HIV is a heterosexual disease, proving that gay behavior is irrelevant. However as Rotello contends, this conclusion is ill founded:

In fact, HIV is spreading in an extremely selective way in the wider world, causing disastrous epidemics in places where heterosexual ecology favors its spread, and causing no epidemic at all in places where heterosexual behavior is less conductive. If anything, the highly selective spread of HIV around the world shows that AIDS is neither a gay nor a straight epidemic, but an ecological epidemic that exploits certain behaviors, chief among them the practice of having large numbers of partners, straight or gay.[23]

In some southern African countries, more than 30 per cent of the adult population is infected. By contrast, in North America, less than 1 per cent of the adult population is HIV-positive. Of these North American HIV-positive adults, about 80 per cent are still men.[24] The fact that AIDS is sustained by promiscuity is further evidenced in the rise of HIV infection in seniors! Patricia Pearson reports that seniors are flocking to retirement retreats for "non-younger citizens only" in Florida and Arizona. "They are also falling in love again, and again, and making prodigious use of Viagra." Seniors now account for 13 per cent of new HIV diagnosis in the United States.[25]

Any hint of judgmental talk is seen as opening up past "sex negative" patterns, homophobia, erotophobia, patriarchy, germophobia or oppression. Indeed, as Cindy Patton, records in *Sex & Germs: The Politics of Aids,* it doesn't matter whether the source is gay or straight, even safe sex policy can be seen as sex negative:

In the 1960s another category of diseases was discovered to be sexually transmitted...Many are, quite literally, diseases resulting from contact with contaminated feces...Despite the common social aversion to feces, it is not the feces themselves that are "dirty," but rather that they provide an amenable environment for various microbes. The relationship of these new sexually transmitted diseases to feces makes them equally offensive markers of illicit sexual activity. Not only are they untidy diseases of the digestive tract, but they are proximate to that most ambivalently regarded point of human anatomy, the asshole. These STDs imply the active involvement of 'unnatural acts' in their transmission...In explaining STDs, and the activities supposedly implicated in AIDS, the generalized conflation of sexual acts and sexual diseases creates innumerable problems.[26]

Conveying "sensible sex" information has been received as cultural erotophobia. Despite the best intentions of AIDS activists, guidelines are often perceived as judgmental and limiting. Numerous men have experienced the sense that modifying or eliminating a central practice means they "are no longer gay." Sex is often perceived as the cement in the gay male community: gay men fear that if sexual ties are reduced or de-emphasized the community as a whole will disintegrate. Without community institutions and support for sexual practice and political action, some men fear the identity they struggled to create will be destroyed.[27] Patton tries to finger germs and microbes as the "boundary" transgressors and not the sexual acts. Moreover, she implies that the medical profession is somehow guilty for not congratulating the individual upon contracting his or her latest disease or killing her unwanted fetus:

The pervasive and systematic use of penalties like disease and pregnancy [among heterosexual women] to inhibit sexual activity is felt by the transgressors as a profound and physical terror. The threat of consequences for sex is much more frightening and successful than physical retributions for theft. The idea that you 'can't be just a little pregnant [or infected]' rules out the possibility of calculated risk, and disempowers the sexual 'transgressors.'[28]

Magic Bullet – Codependency on Technology

Technology provides the viability of Wellness doctrine. To operate sexually in a boundary-free lifestyle, men and women have a codependency on technology. Over the years mankind's inventions have provided: sex drive enhancements, longevity drugs to delay the impact on sex from aging, intervention drugs to overcome erectile difficulties, abortificants to stop a pregnancy, and birth control drugs to prevent pregnancy. Drugs come in jells, foams, pills and injectable forms. There are various implants and rubber covers such as condoms and dams. There is surgery for both sexes. Some of which is reversible. Writing on *The Pill* (1995), Bernard Asbell said, "Millions today embrace the Pill as a salvation, while other millions shun it as sinful or as a time bomb of dormant cancers." He goes on:

As it was intended to, the Pill has disconnected fear of pregnancy from the pursuit of sexual pleasure. But, intended or not, it has done more. The Pill has led each of us, women and men alike and in a most personal sense, into a new era of potential mastery over our bodies and ourselves. As the first systematic contraceptive, it altered the routine functioning of the healthy human body. It opened the gateway to what I shall call the Era of Biointervention, which is already taking us beyond medicine into an eventual ability to modify – genetically – other body functions as well as our physical form itself.[29]

When mastery of the female body fails there is the ultimate biointervention called "abortion." Moreover, only seven years after publication of *The Pill* evidence of a 400 per cent elevated risk of cervical cancer was confirmed among women taking birth control pills and infected with the human papilloma virus, one of the most prevalent sexually transmitted diseases in Canada. Says Dr. Jack Cuzik, head of epidemiology at Cancer Research UK in London, "...oral contraceptives may actually be promoting the rate at which it [HPV infection] progresses to cancer."[30] Magic bullets also exist for infection. Drugs are the sole line of defence against STDs caused by bacteria, virus or parasites. Bacterial diseases can usually be cured with antibiotics. Once cured, these STDs will not reoccur unless the person continues the same at risk behavior. Bacterial STDs include Chlamydia, Shigella, Campylobacter, Salmonella, Giardia, Entamoeba Gonorrhea, Syphilis and Chancroid. Parasitic STDs can also be cured, but may reappear under continued at risk behavior. These include Scabies, Lice and Crabs. Finally, viral STDs are resistant to medical intervention, and can not be cured. There are forms of treatment that can help alleviate and manage the discomfort and overt symptoms of viral STDs. Although treatments may be very effective, a viral STD may recur in the individual from time to time. Included in this category are Herpes, Genital Warts, Hepatitis B and C and HIV.

In February 2002, Tom Blackwell reported that the incidence of Syphilis had doubled per capita since 1997. Says Dr. Ian Gemmill, a spokesman for the Canadian Public Health Association:

It really is a bit of a disappointment because we thought we were about to conquer the first sexually transmitted disease. Authorities blame the spike on complacency about contraception prompted by new treatments for HIV, ignorance and 'safe sex burnout.'[31]

Ecological Consequences of Gay Lifestyle

Don't take down a fence until you know why it was built.

Robert Frost

Take this thing on homosexuality. I think the view we take here is that there's no place for the state in the bedrooms of the nation. I think what's done in private between adults doesn't concern the criminal code. When it becomes public this is a different matter, or when it relates to minors this is a different matter...

Justice Minister, Pierre Elliott Trudeau
December 22, 1967

Some traditional authors express alarm that any let-up of legal discipline might result in a marked increase in homosexual behavior. But first of all, such legal reforms will certainly not contribute to any increase in the homosexual condition.

There is no evidence that the legal status of homosexuality in any way influences the number of those who share this condition. However, there is good reason to believe that the healthier climate that would result from such a legal reform could reduce the social pressures and consequent emotional disorders for those who share this condition. Secondly, there is no evidence that homosexual practices have increased in those societies where no such legal penalties exist or where they have recently been reformed. All these considerations lead to the conclusion that the Church has a serious moral responsibility out of both justice and charity to work for the reform of laws concerning homosexuals and do everything in its power to educate the faithful to the need of such a reform.[32]

John J. McNeil, 'The Church and the Homosexual,' 1976

In line with Trudeau's *enlightened* and *liberated* spirit, John McNeil advocated a theological experiment – hypothesis testing for the will of the God of all Creation. McNeil wrote in 1976:

Peter Fink, S.J., in the same issue [Commonweal] proposed what he called 'A Pastoral Hypothesis.' He points out that pastoral activity cannot be left in abeyance until complex theological questions are resolved with total clarity. In fact, pastoral activity itself is the source of essential data needed for theological reflection. Fink's hypothesis is that the Church should explore the possibility that homosexual love is a valid form of human love, and, consequently, can also mediate God's loving presence. In the absence of any definitive condemnation of all homosexual activity a priori, it is a valid theological method, Fink argues, to explore this hypothesis and judge its validity on the basis of its consequences. 'If homosexual love is sinful this will show itself as destructive of the human and disruptive of man's relation with God.'...'All I ask here is that the Church employ all its resources in an honest effort to lead gay people to love, to the human and to God through their homosexuality.'[33]

The 60s and 70s were "pivotal" times for initiating changes in homosexual rights, abortion rights, and women's rights, not to mention minority rights. The period was hailed by Trudeau as the era of the "Just Society." He was going to liberate society from archaic religious taboos and free homosexuals from hypocritical and unfair civil laws. Just prior to political life, Trudeau had been an enthusiastic civil libertarian and had a seat on the board of the Montreal Humanist chapter.[34] As hoped, traditional legal and psychological boundaries started to fall like dominoes under the force of a new sexual revolution. Many priests, pastors and theologians, like John McNeil, embraced the new-age revolution with alacrity.

The gay liberation movement in the U.S officially started in June 1969, when the police raided a Greenwich Village gay bar called the Stonewall, and patrons especially the fringe groups, the transvestites and the effeminate types, fought back.[35] In this liberation struggle, collateral damage (boundary clashes) to various stakeholders and institutions in traditional society were inevitable. Dennis Altman writes:

The new self-assertion of homosexuals, particularly of male homosexuals, has made sexuality itself a political issue; the new gay culture represents an affirmation of sexual play and experimentation that goes beyond the repressive norms most people in this society, including many homosexuals, have internalized. The constant linkage in the New Right rhetoric of homosexuality and abortion, the ERA [Equal Rights Amendment], drugs, pornography, and 'secular humanism' reveals deep-seated fear that the social fabric is being threatened by an assertion of sexual diversity, or even by the search for sexual pleasure.[36]

By 1983, in the face of an AIDS crisis, gay physicians resisted with costly impact announcing needed policies targeted at *re-regulating* "what's done in private between adults." Contrary to Trudeau's tenet of liberation ideology, the state learned the hard way; it does have an interest in what goes on in the "bedrooms of the nation." In the midst of a raging epidemic, pro-gay and gay theologians chose to live in denial, rejecting any notion that AIDS was the "experimental consequences" of their "Pastoral Hypothesis." Many doctors, activists and politicians reacted with their versions of denial:

AAPHR released its tepid proposals for 'healthful gay male sexuality.' Sensitive to the concerns that the group not be 'sex negative,' the guidelines assured gay men that there was nothing wrong with having sex, but that they should check their partners for KS [Kaposi's sarcoma] lesions, swollen lymph nodes, and overt symptoms of AIDS. It might be a good idea to have fewer partners, the guidelines also suggested tentatively. The Gay Men's Health Crisis in New York had put the accumulated wisdom of homosexual physicians in one phrase: 'Have as much sex as you want, but with fewer people and HEALTHY people.' Complicated considerations of asymptomatic carriers – the people who looked perfectly healthy while they deposited a dose of AIDS virus – were not weighted for the guidelines; even though they were well documented in medical literature. In San Francisco, the more cautious Bay Area Physicians for Human Rights was still holding committee meetings to wrangle over every phrase of risk-reduction guidelines. Some doctors were squeamish about the very idea of telling people what to do in bed.[37]

By August 1984, San Francisco politicians and lawyers were wrangling over closure or regulation of bathhouses:

The groups that wanted to keep open the baths got support from San Francisco's Human Rights Commission, which voted unanimously to oppose 'any action by the City....to close bathhouses or prohibit or regulate private consensual sexual activity in any bathhouse or sex establishment, absent a showing that it is a necessary and essential public health measure supported by a clear and convincing medical and epidemiological evidence.'

'From a legal perspective, such drastic government intervention to control sexual conduct would set a precedent in endangering the fundamental right to privacy of all gay people irrespective of where such conduct occurs,' Meriel Burtle, one of the attorneys representing the baths, was reported as saying. 'How do we stop the...prohibition of consensual sexual activity in one location [from becoming a prohibition of] ...such activities in all locations?'[38]

On October 25, 1985, New York State Health Commissioner, David Axelrod said, "there is no doubt that AIDS was spread by anal and oral sex." He asked the state Public Health Council to vote on a sixty-day emergency regulation, which would allow local health officials to close gay bathhouses and other places, like peep shows, porno theaters, and adult bookstores, where people engaged in high-risk sex.[39] Spokesman for the National Gay Task Force, Ron Najman, responded, "We think that some state action is welcome, but we still have serious reservations regarding essential civil liberties. We cannot condone the state prohibiting private behavior between consenting adults. It's a regulation of shocking overbreadth," Tom Stoddard, the legislative director of the New York Civil Liberties Union, was reported as saying:

This regulation purports to outlaw any form of nontraditional sex between any people outside the home. It goes way beyond the issue of AIDS.[40]

In 1990, the U.S Public Health Service projected that by the end of 1994, in the United States, "the cumulative number of diagnosed AIDS cases would be in the range of 415,000-535,000, with 320,000-385,000 deaths.[41] By 1990, Larry Kramer, one of a few gays to foresee the potential, had the following well rehearsed speech:

There is one new HIV infection in the United States every fifty-four seconds. There are 267 new cases of AIDS every day. That amounts to some eight thousand cases every month. There is one AIDS death every nine minutes. At least four in every thousand college kids are now infected. That means at least two or three or four of you here tonight are now infected. Don't feel safe. Please the rest of you don't feel safe.[42]

British sociologist Jeffery Weeks, in *AIDS and Contemporary History,* in 1993 wrote:

It was an historic accident that HIV disease first manifested itself in the gay populations of the east and west coasts of the United States.[43]

This view has been almost universal among gay and AIDS activists even to this day. The movement's inability to recognize its own responsibility for the disease in North America, keeps silent the good that can be learned from the crisis. Previously quoted, gay journalist and author, Gabriel Rotello, stands among only a few in claiming accountability:

Yet there is little 'accidental' about the [gay] sexual ecology...Multiple concurrent partners, versatile anal sex, core group behavior centered in commercial sex establishments, wide spread recreational drug abuse, tourism and travel – these factors were no 'accidents.' Multipartner anal sex was encouraged, celebrated, considered a central component of liberation. Core group behavior in baths and sex clubs was deemed by many the quintessence of freedom. Versatility was declared a political imperative. Analingus was pronounced the champagne of gay sex, a palpable ges-

ture of revolution. STDs were to be worn like badges of honor, antibiotics to be taken with pride.[44]

Michael Callen is another outspoken AIDS activist. His self-reported medical history was typical of gay men in the most active core group in New York's sex scene. Not until forced to confront his own AIDS infection, did he acknowledge how much sex and disease he had. He wrote in *Surviving AIDS*:

I calculated that since becoming sexually active in 1973, I had racked up more than three thousand different sex partners in bathhouses, back rooms, meat racks, and tearooms. As a consequence, I had also had the following sexually transmitted diseases, many more than once: hepatitis A; hepatitis B; hepatitis non-A/non-B [now called hepatitis C]; herpes simplex types I and II; venereal warts; amebiasis, including giardia lamblia and entamoeba histolytica; shilgella flexneri and salmonella; syphilis; gonorrhea; nonspecific urethritis; chlamydia; cytomegalovirus and Epstein-Barr virus mononucleosis; and eventually cryptosporidiosis.[45]

Randy Shilts describes his version of the ecological consequences of gay sex in his landmark narration of the life of AIDS Patient Zero:

By the time Bill Darrow's research was done, he had established sexual links between 40 patients in ten cities. At the center of the cluster diagram was Gaetan Dugas, marked on the chart as Patient Zero of the GRID [Gay-Related Immune Deficiency] epidemic. His role truly was remarkable. At least 40 of the first 248 gay men diagnosed with GRID in the United States, as of April 12, 1982, either had had sex with Gaetan Dugas or had had sex with someone who had. The links sometimes were extended for many generations of sexual contacts, giving frightening insight into how rapidly the epidemic had spread before anyone knew about it. Before one of Gaetan's Los Angeles boyfriends came down with Pneumocystis, for example, he had had sex with another Angelino who came down with Kaposi's sarcoma and with a Florida man who contracted both Kaposi's and the pneumonia. The Los Angeles contact, in turn, cavorted with two other Los Angeles men who later came down with Kaposi's, one of whom infected still another southern California man who was suffering from KS. The Floridian, meanwhile, had sex with a Texan who got Kaposi's sarcoma, a second Florida man who got Pneumocystis, and two Georgia men, one of whom got Pneumocystis and another who soon found the skin lesions of KS. Before finding these lesions, however, the Georgian had sex with a Pennsylvania man who later came down with both Pneumocystis and KS....A CDC statistician calculated the odds on whether it could be coincidental that 40 of the first 248 gay men to get GRID might all have had sex either with the same man or with men sexually linked to him. The statistician figured that the chance did not approach zero – it was zero.[46]

What went wrong and what lessons can be learned from the AIDS crisis? To begin to answer this question we need to further develop the prevailing gay philosophy and understand the medical implications of their behavior.

Ian Young wrote in *The Stonewall Experiment*, his pyscho-history of gay culture:

Centuries of sexual repression and distortion are not quickly or simply overcome, though they can be easily repackaged and labeled Pleasure or Freedom. A society that had made heterosexuality into an absolute had provided no rules, no guidelines, no ways for men to relate affectionately and erotically with one another...Only an insistent sexual need persisted.[47]

Yet in the context of some thirty plus years of hindsight, the "integrity" of this analysis – the measure of one's ability to take responsibility for the consequences of one's actions, must be questioned. Today, the gay movement has not birthed a revised philosophy, which has unified all their hard won rights and privileges into a more healthy sustainable culture. While staring in the face of death (AIDs), against a backdrop of socially sanctioned equal rights, the only exception being marriage and acceptance in the military, thousands of young gay men continue to engage in high risk sex. A Health Canada study of gay men showed that in 2000, gays were "increasingly practicing unsafe sex and putting themselves at risk for contracting HIV and AIDS." Gay men made up half the new AIDS cases, an increase of 10 per cent over 1999. Between 1996 and 1999, there was a 30 per cent increase in the number of gay men who tested HIV positive. This figure spiked another 10 per cent in 2000.[48] Contrary to Young's psycho-historic theory, it is as if many homosexual men are driven by some intangible force best labeled a "death wish."

This suicidal sexual compulsion, according to Jim Geary, director of the Shani Project, at the Pride Center, has a psychological basis independent of social stigma. Author David Black records:

'We work a lot with the issue of sexuality and the changes that our clients need to make,' Geary said. That is a hot topic. It divides itself into two key issues: compulsive sexuality and safe sex. Compulsive sexuality...you need a constant series of sexual adventures, each one upping the ante of the others, in order to nourish your sense of self. What happens when that need slams up against your instinct for survival? After years indulging in sex for sex's sake, it's hard to break the habit. The brain's pleasure centers are used to being stimulated; like rabid hyenas, they howl and gnash their synaptical teeth when they are not fed. But pleasure can become a taskmaster; it can be as ruthless as guilt. If the purpose of sex is pleasure, you can become obliged to have the most exquisite pleasure possible or feel you have wasted your time. If you add to that the newly revived Elizabethan notion that sex can cause death, that every orgasm brings you closer to the grave, you have the first rate compulsion as exciting as risking your life savings on one role of the dice. In fact, more exciting. The greater the stakes, the greater the risk. And the greater the risk, the greater the focus of attention. And in sex the closer the attention you pay to the moment, the greater your arousal. At the other extreme, gay men, seeking shelter from the storm of sex and disease, have taken refuge in drugs that block their sex drive. They have tried vitamins and herbs, psychoneuroimmunology counseling, and stress-reduction seminars. Or they have joined AA-type groups...The goal of

treatment is not to 'cure' the person, but rather to have him keep up his fighting spirit in the face of chronic 'illness.'[49]

Michelangelo Signorile, author of *Life Outside – The Signorile Report on Gay Men: Sex, Drugs, Muscles, and the Passages of Life,* describes a young man's quest for gay masculinity, at the same time revealing a source of sexual compulsion:

'I want to be physical perfection in the eyes of gay men – totally physically appealing, like the ultimate. The perfect tits and butt, bulbous biceps. I want to achieve symmetry, big and in proportion. I would look like the cover of an HX [Homo Xtra, a New York bar giveaway known for its covers of hot men] – lean, sculpted, muscular, virile, a stallion, a guy that should make your mouth water. I want to know what it's like to walk down the street and have everyone look at you, absolutely everyone. I want to know what it's like to really feel like an object'...What does he believe all of this will do for him?...'Honestly, and I'm embarrassed to say it, but I'm hoping it will boost my self-esteem,' he admits. 'I don't know how to boost my self-esteem now. My feeling is, 'Get a great body and people will admire you. Get a great body and everything will be okay.' There's that voice inside me that of course says that all of that is full of shit. But it's not powerful enough to overcome the magnetic pull, the promise of what the perfect body might bring. It's this belief that if I can just get the perfect body, then I wouldn't be insecure. I would feel more confident. I wouldn't be afraid in certain gay environments.'[50]

Returning to the early sexual liberation period, society saw the start of a large-scale transition in the status of homosexuality from a deviance or perversion to an alternative lifestyle or minority, as remarkable a change in the characterization of "the homosexual" as was the original invention of that category in the nineteenth century. Along with this change, homosexuals were being cast increasingly in the role of the vanguard of social and sexual change, worthy of considerable media attention. Some homosexual writers and artists had speculated that the eighties would see overt homosexuals dominating much of cultural life. And "gay chic" emerged as a phrase in newspaper columns.[51] Decreased legal and social sanctions against homosexual conduct, in conjunction with increased opportunities presented by the growth of the gay community, produced several changes in homosexual behavior. The proportion of previously married men among those who acknowledged having sex with men increased drastically, from 4 to 11 per cent between 1970 and 1988 surveys.

"It was never just about sex," said the man with AIDS, "I enjoyed sex, but going to the baths was also political." The Gay Liberation Front, which had both male and female members, was a child of the sixties, leftist, against all oppression, and committed to feminism, gay sex, and gay culture. It wanted to promote gay liberation by radical transformation of the entire social structure. On the other hand, the Gay Activists Alliance did not want to change society. It just wanted to fight for gay rights, which came to mean, writes David Black:

...fucking and sucking as much as you wanted. 'We were going to show the straight world what it was missing,' one gay leader said. 'We are going to show them how

liberating sex was. We defined ourselves by our cocks.' Morals were seen as chains to be broken; just as, in some sadomasochistic games, chains were seen as symbols of freedom, proof that one was not limited by straight, middle-class morality. The more one fucked – and the more eccentric the manner of fucking – the freer one was....As one masochist said, appropriating the language of the gym to the language of sin, "No pain, no gain.[52]

Soon the "pain" fully eclipsed the "gain." Dr. June Osborn, a National Institute of Health (NIH) researcher who was one of the first to sound the alarm about STD transmission in gay core groups, had a hard time maintaining a handle on the level of multipartnerism. She reported in 1980:

Every time we do an NIH site visit, the definition of 'multiple sex partners' has changed. First it was ten to twenty partners a year. That was nineteen seventy-five. Then in nineteen seventy-six it was fifty partners a year. By nineteen seventy-eight we were talking about a hundred sexual partners a year and now we're using the term to describe five hundred partners in a single year. I am duly in awe.[53]

The popular bestseller *The Joy of Gay Sex*, by gays, for gays, described a gay subculture that was equipped with its own rituals, its own agonies and ecstasies, its own jargon. In this book the authors in the main spoke to gays in their own language, using words and terms not accepted everywhere but natural to gays. For example, the *Joy of Sex* called rimming [anal-oral sex] the "prime taste treat in sex," while a leftist Toronto newspaper published a story on "rimming as a revolutionary act."[54]

By 1980, the sexual liberation movement had become a victim of its own success. Particularly in San Francisco, the taboos against homosexuality ebbed easily in the midst of the overall sexual revolution. The promise of freedom had fueled the greatest exodus of immigrants to San Francisco since the Gold Rush. Between 1969 and 1973, at least 9,000 gay men moved to San Francisco, followed by 20,000 between 1974 and 1978. By 1980, about 5,000 homosexual men were moving to the Golden Gate every year. The immigration now made for a city in which two in five adults were openly gay.[55]

The movement depended heavily on commercial enterprises to define itself. While the role of papers, dances, and organizations has been significant, it was overshadowed, especially for gay men, by the commercial world. Gay freedom had spawned a business of bathhouses and sex clubs. The hundreds of such institutions were a $100-million industry across America and Canada, and bathhouse owners were frequently gay political leaders as well. The businesses serviced men who had long been repressed, gay activists told themselves. It would all balance out later, so for now, sex was part and parcel of political liberation. One of the ironies of American capitalism is that it has been a major force in creating and maintaining a sense of identity among homosexuals, and so far such identity seems attainable only within existing capitalist societies.[56] Here more than anything else the bathhouse symbolized the capitalization of sex:

Going to a bathhouse was not like picking someone up in a gay bar or even a park.

Picking up in a bar only gave somebody one shot at the virus. It was haphazard. Parks were more iffy; the weather did not always cooperate and shrubs did not provide a good ambiance for anal intercourse, the riskiest sexual behavior. On the other hand bathhouses were havens for anal intercourse. The only limit to promiscuity was stamina....For this reason, Don Francis had called 'commercialized gay sex' an 'amplification system' for the disease...[57]

Dennis Altman gives us a glimpse into the new temples of gay culture:

It is not just a bathhouse, for you can eat snacks here, buy leather gear and inscribed T-shirts, even watch live cabaret performances on certain nights...Most striking is a large disco floor on the top story, surrounded by enormous soft pillows, where men dance clad only in towels, their movements jerky under the strobe lights. In the basement there is a small swimming pool, showers, and steam rooms; the main floor is largely occupied by a maze of small rooms that people hire for eight hours at a time; there is always a door or two open, with men, all-but-naked, lying inside in wait for a temporary partner. The place is strangely quiet, disturbed only by the background noise of disco music from upstairs and the constant, muted plodding of bare feet. Men in bathhouses rarely talk much, and it is quite common for sex to take place without words, let alone names, being exchanged. Yet even the most transitory encounters are part of a heightened eroticism that pervades the building; there is a certain sexual democracy, even camaraderie, that makes the sauna attractive. The willingness to have sex immediately, promiscuously, with people about whom one knows nothing and from whom one demands only physical contact, can be seen as a sort of Whitmansque democracy, a desire to know and trust other men in a type of brotherhood far removed from the male bonding of rank, hierarchy, and competition that characterizes much of the outside world. It is equally true, however, that age and physical beauty set up their own hierarchies and barriers.[58]

Because of gay culture, the fight against venereal diseases was proving, in the words of Randy Shilts, to be a "Sisyphean task":

The screening in [Dr.] Ostrow's clinic had revealed that one in ten patients had walked in the door with hepatitis B. At least one-half of the gay men tested at the clinic showed evidence of a past episode of hepatitis B. In San Francisco, two thirds of gay men had suffered the debilitating disease. It was now proven statistically that a gay man had a one in five chance of being infected with hepatitis B virus within twelve months of stepping off the bus into a typical urban gay scene. Within five years, infection was a virtual certainty. Another problem was enteric diseases, like amebiasis and giardiasis, caused by organisms that lodged themselves in the intestinal tracts of gay men with alarming frequency. In New York Gay Men's Health Project, 30 per cent of the patients suffered from gastrointestinal parasites. In San Francisco, incidence of the 'gay Bowel Syndrome,' as it was called in medical journals, had increased by 8,000 per cent after 1973. Infection with these parasites was a likely effect of anal intercourse, which was apt to put a man in contact with his partner's fecal matter, and was virtually a certainty through the then-popular prac-

tice of rimming, which medical journals politely called oral-anal intercourse. What was so troubling was that nobody in the gay community seemed to care about these waves of infection. Disease clinics had their 'regulars' who came in with infection after infection, waiting for the magic bullet that could put them back in the sack again.[59]

A Seattle study of gay men suffering from shigellosis, for example, discovered that 69 per cent culled their partners from bathhouses. A Denver study found that an average bathhouse patron having his typical 2.7 sexual contacts a night risked a 33 per cent chance of walking out of the tubs with syphilis or gonorrhea, because about one in eight of those wandering the hallways had asymptomatic cases of these diseases.[60] About 3,000 gay men a week streamed to the gargantuan bathhouse at Eight and Howard streets, the Club Baths, which could serve up to 800 customers at any given time. Gay psychologist, Dr. Joe Brewer, figured that the attraction to promiscuity and depersonalization of sex rested on issues of intimacy. These were not gay issues but male issues. The trouble was that, by definition, you had a gay male subculture in which there was nothing to moderate the utterly male values that were being adulated more religiously than any macho heterosexual could imagine, right down to the cold hard stares of the bathhouse attendants. Promiscuity was rampant because in an all-male subculture there was nobody to say "no" – no moderating role like that a woman plays in the heterosexual milieu.[61]

Boundaries of Silence

Don't offend the gays and don't inflame the homophobes. These were the twin horns on which the handling of this epidemic would be torn from the first day of the epidemic.[62]

...prescient gay men suspected they were faced with an issue that might strike at the heart of the political and sexual culture they had so carefully constructed in the face of such opposition from homophobes and moralists. Within the gay community a 'crisis of ideology is threatening to explode,' wrote Mass in the New York Native in March of 1982. 'With much confusion on all sides, advocates of sexual fulfillment are being opposed to critics of promiscuity.'[63]

According to Rotello, in the beginning voices were raised that proposed solutions that might have reduced the risks of the epidemic. Yet those voices were by and large shouted down – not by the mainstream media and government, but by the gay media and gay men themselves. Gay activists demanded absolute proof before they were willing to advise gay men to wear condoms every time, to reduce partners to one monogamous partner at a time and to close commercial sex institutions. Such proof was impossible to provide in that early period. "What if abstinence, monogamy, the shutting down of institutions like sex clubs and baths were encouraged," it was argued, "and then it turned out the AIDS wasn't sexually transmitted?"[64] AIDS physician Joseph Sonnabend not only criticized the culture of multipartnerism but extended his critique to physicians who countenanced it. Sonnabend wrote in September 1982:

A desire to appear non-judgmental, a desire to remain untinged by moralism, fear of provoking ire, have all fostered a conspiracy of silence. For years no clear message about the danger of promiscuity has emanated from those in whom gay men have entrusted their well-being.[65]

"Unless we fight for our lives we shall die. In all the history of homosexuality we have never been so close to death and extinction before." With those words, Larry Kramer declared war on gays living out the epidemic in denial. Kramer's cover story in the *New York Native*, headlined "1,112 and Counting," was an end run around all the gay leaders and Gay Men's Health Crisis (GMHC) organizers worried about not panicking the homosexuals and not inciting homophobia. Endless letters poured into the *Native*, denouncing Kramer as an "alarmist" who was rabidly "sex negative."[66]

Another voice "crying in the wilderness" was that of AIDS activist Bill Kraus. He believed AIDS could not be fought effectively if gay people continued to think in terms of the rhetoric of the old gay community. It was not anti-gay to be pro-life, he thought:

We believe it is time to speak the simple truth – and to care enough about one another to act on it. Unsafe sex is-quite literally – killing us...Unsafe sex with a number of partners in San Francisco today carries a high risk of contracting AIDS and of death. So does having unsafe sex with others who have unsafe sex with a large number of partners. For this reason, unsafe sex at bathhouses and sex clubs is particularly dangerous....If the gay movement means anything, it means learning self-respect and respect for one another. When a terrible disease means that we purchase our sexual freedom at the price of thousands of our lives, self-respect dictates it is time to stop until it once again is safe.[67]

Here Kraus drew the battle lines on which he would wage a fierce political fight.

In the crisis straight politicians felt trapped. New York's Mario Cuomo knew if he did nothing, he'd be attacked and if he did something, he'd be attacked. It had become heresy to suggest that moral questions should be publicly confronted. Herein lies a key lesson from the consequence of unfettered individual, rights-based legislation. In his book *The Plague Years: A Chronicle of Aids The Epidemic of Our Times*, David Black writes:

But why shouldn't a society confront questions of morality? The danger comes not from the debate but from the belief that moral questions are legislatable. In fact, the courts, simply by addressing a moral issue, undermine morality...Even if the law did have an effect – especially if it had an effect – it removed from the individual the burden of behaving morally. The question becomes not what is right? But what can I get away with? As morality changed from a spiritual to a legal issue, it lost its private hold over people. Courts replaced conscience. The fight over the bathhouses confused the moral question (what sex acts should someone with AIDS allow him-

self to perform?) with the legal question (what is the government's responsibility in promoting public health?)[68]

Bathhouse owners across the continent were reluctant to acknowledge their pivotal positions in helping to curb the AIDS crisis. Their aversion to remedial action in the battle against AIDS was doubly damaging to AIDS activists since no media would attack their complacency. Most of the nation's gay newspapers received substantial advertising revenues from the bathhouse and sex business. In the aftermath of a San Francisco meeting, local bathhouse owners launched a propaganda counterattack:

'If AIDS is indeed sexually transmitted, why have there been so few cases?' asked the advertisement from the Liberty Baths. 'Yes, I say few because if an estimated 20,000,000 gays have an estimated 200 contacts per year this means that in 4 _ years we have seen 1,279 cases of AIDS in 4,000,000,000 contacts, or odds of 3,127,443 to 1 against getting AIDS during a given contact. With all this gay play going on, why aren't we all getting AIDS instead of only 1,279 of us?'[69]

In response to the "gay plague," Paul Volberding, cancer chief at the melanoma clinic, San Francisco General Hospital, decided to invite the bathhouse owners to the AIDS Clinic to talk about AIDS. At the time [1984] the bathhouse owners who attended were hostile. After Volberding spoke, one of the owners of the largest bathhouse took him aside and tried to reason:

'We're both in this for the same thing,' he said. 'Money.' We make money at one end when they come to the baths. You make money from them on the other end when they are here.' Paul Volberding was speechless. This guy wasn't talking civil liberties; he was talking greed.[70]

While gay AIDS activists and political leaders were making bathhouses their top issue, support for the facilities steadily dropped within the community itself. With patronage plummeting, member clubs of the Northern California Bathhouse Owners Association joined to take out full-page ads in gay newspapers offering half-price coupons that carried a full reprint of the group's "Revolution Regarding an Objective Response to AIDS" on the reverse side.[71] November 1984, San Francisco Superior Court issued a ruling aimed at balancing public health and private rights. The bathhouses could open, but only with monitors who survey the premises every ten minutes and expel any men engaging in unsafe practices.[72]

More gay newspapers circulated in San Francisco than in any other city in the United States, but often these publications did more to cloud than to define the challenges facing gay men. *Bay Area Reporter* columnist Konstantin Berlandt attacked the Harvey Milk Club, branding club officers as "our worst enemies" for their "anti-sex" brochure on safe sex called "Can We Talk?" Berlandt wrote:

Advice of safe sex, while perhaps well meaning, is actually collaboration with the death regime that delights in blaming ourselves and would pin the blame on us. The myth of 'safe sex' fosters the finger pointing when anyone of us does come down with a disease:'You see, we told you so. We brought it on ourselves.'[73]

A week later, Berlandt followed this essay with a treatise that announced:

I love to rim. To some people, a tongue up the asshole can be relaxing, mesmerizing, even spiritually uplifting.[74]

Berlandt maintained it was society's responsibility to find the medical technology to prevent all sexually transmitted diseases, rather than the gay community's responsibility to keep sexuality in line with what medical technology could cure. As for safe sex, he wrote, "I don't mean we can't make such changes if absolutely necessary, but why must we?"[75]

A decade later, Mark Blasius, in *Gay and Lesbian Politics: Sexuality and the Emergence of a New Ethic*, argues in support of Berlandt's claim. For Blasius, "being lesbian or gay is by definition political." His idea of gay "ethos" describes a "way of life" that "emerges not so much from moral as from existential criteria," specifically the content of lived experience.[76] In this ethos, lesbians and gays "invent themselves, recognize each other, and establish a relationship to the culture in which they live." Central to the creation of self and ethos, states Blasuis, is the elaboration and defense of "lesbian and gay rights," aimed at "self-determination of one's relationships with others."[77] This right encompasses what he describes as the central "moments" in lesbian and gay rights struggles, rights for sexual freedom, equality and "equity in the cultural and social acknowledgment of one's health needs and the consequent receipt of the benefits of citizenship."[78] Blasius uses AIDS politics to elaborate his claim to an equity right, but his idea extends beyond that to a general claim for "a right of access to protection from any biological risks derived from sexual relations."[79] He assumes this right from the larger right to sexual self-determination, arguing that in an era of "biopower" and population management the government has an affirmative responsibility to ensure the health of its citizens. This point reflects his anger over his perception of the U.S. Governments (non) handling of AIDS in its initial years.

Against what has been presented thus far, and stated in layman's language, Blasius is really asking society and government to enshrine a philosophy or right that "absolutely anything goes" – any nature of relationship(s), any form of family and any partner volume, form and frequency of sexual act. Furthermore, should there be any health and safety issues arising from the sexual activity protected under these rights, the risks must be surmounted by government, apparently without obligation to the individual responsible for the choice of unsafe lifestyle. Has nothing been learned from twenty years with AIDS and the ecology of gay sex? Surely "accountability" is a word not found in the "absolutely anything goes" lexicon. In reviewing Blasius' book, Shane Phelan, highlights another weakness in this line of argument:

Do governments, even ones heavily invested in biopower and strategies of governmentality, have a responsibility to protect citizens from all health consequences of their behavior? If this holds only for sexual behavior but not for other forms of self-creation and expression (and it is not clear that Blasius would so limit it), what would justify such privileging? Blasius notes that sexual relationships are a central means through which we (gays and lesbians, at least) define ourselves. Do governments then have an obligation to support all the central ways in which we define ourselves?...What of those whose means of definition is a religion that disapproves of homosexuality? Should they be allowed to discriminate against people whose sexual tastes they abhor? If not, why exactly should sexuality be privileged over other forms of identity formation and maintenance?[80]

If there was a Hall of Fame for AIDS activists during the 80s, few would decry Larry Kramer's place. One of the few, dare one say, prophetic gay activists, Kramer saw the crisis coming before anyone else. Over the course of its growth he upheld a remarkably clear vision of what was happening and what needed to be done. This rare quality [at the time] of seeing what others could not, combined with his sharp [foul] and unbiased tongue placed him on a lonely and frustrating path during the AIDS battle. In time he exhausted himself trying to move three diverse constituencies onto a common path of AIDS prevention and resolution. By the end he would come to accuse, and indeed, hate his fellow homosexuals, the government, and the scientific and medical research communities for their complacency. Early on he fired a salvo at the researchers:

And, for the first time in this epidemic, leading doctors and researchers are finally admitting they don't know what's going on. I find this terrifying too...For two years they weren't talking like this. For two years we've heard a different theory every few weeks. We grasped at the straws of possible cause: promiscuity, poppers, back rooms, the baths, rimming, fisting, anal intercourse, urine, semen, shit, saliva, sweat, blood, blacks, a single virus, a new virus, repeated exposure to a virus, amoebas carrying a virus, drugs, Haiti, voodoo, Flagyl, constant bouts of amebiasis, hepatitis A and B, syphilis, gonorrhea.[81]

His frustration with the gay community was only surpassed by his feeling of anger towards government and white middle-class America. Kramer writes:

Politicians understand only one thing: PRESSURE...For six years I have been trying to get the gay world angry enough to exert this pressure. I have failed and I am ashamed of my failure. I blame myself – somehow I wasn't convincing enough or clever enough or cute enough to break through your denial or self-pity or death wish or self-destruction or whatever the fuck is going on. I'm very tired of trying to make you hear me.[82]

Get your stupid heads out of the sand, you turkeys!...I am sick of guys who moan that giving up careless sex until this blows over is worse than death. How can they value life so little and cocks and asses so much? Come with me, guys, while I visit a few of our friends in Intensive Care at NYU. Notice the looks in their eyes, guys. They'd give up sex forever if you could promise them life.[83] *This is a horrible illness, wasting, wretched, painful, ghastly to watch and to witness and to endure.*[84]

I have learned, during these past seven years, to hate. I hate everyone who is higher in the pecking order and in being so placed, like some incontinent pigeon, shits all over all those below. And, sadly, tragically, as more and more of my friends die – the number is way over two hundred by now – I hate this country I once loved so much. And as each day Ronald Reagan and the Catholic Church and various self-styled spokespeople for God – the Right Wing, the Moral Majority, fundamentalists, Mormons, Southern Baptists, born-agains, Orthodox Jews, Hasidic Jews, La Rouchies, Jesse Helms, Representative Dannemeyer, Governor Deukmejian, Phyllis Schlafly, Jerry Falwell, enemies all – take the law into their own hands, a law that neither the framers of the Constitution nor Christ himself, if indeed there ever was a Christ, ever envisioned would be so used to cause deaths of fellow men, I not only hate, but I know there will never be freedom, or peace on earth...[85]

I am going to tell you something you've never heard before. I am going to tell you that the AIDS pandemic is the fault of the white, middle-class, male majority. AIDS is here because the straight world would not grant equal rights to gay people. If we had been allowed to get married, to have legal rights, there would be no AIDS cannonballing through America. The concept of making a virtue out of sexual freedom, i.e. promiscuity, to use that loaded word, came about because gay men had nothing to call their own but their sexuality....The poor, black, and Hispanic have also been forced into AIDS by your oppression...AIDS, having thus been caused to seed and sprout, is allowed to grow and fester and increase a million fold. Yes, indeed, the white man made AIDS – the heterosexual white man. The heterosexual white man with money. The greedy heterosexual white man with money, who two thousand years into the so-called Christian era, is still boss and master.[86]

Regrettably, the nature of this book prevents any full and suitable witness to the great character of Larry Kramer. As with so many of his friends the virus eventually caught up to him:

I am writing these words on a lovely April day in 1994, a Sunday morning. I have just retyped the preceding two editorials so I can submit a clean manuscript to my editor. I have not slept all night, because while taking a shower at 2 a.m., I discovered a blotch on my left leg that I am convinced is a lesion...every bump and splotch is redolent with death possibilities. Only this time I am convinced I am right. After all these years I think I know an incipient lesion when I see one. I get out of bed as the sun is coming up and walk my puppy over half of downtown New York, accustoming myself to my new condition. Now I have AIDS.[87]

Lessons of AIDS and Anal Sex

By the late 1980s there were ample reasons why researchers were generally not eager to investigate complex theories about the origin of AIDS. The question had become intensely political. Defensiveness about "causing" AIDS had originally led to a bias towards fingering Africa over industrialized countries. Gay men and AIDS activists, too, were less than eager to delve for the origins of the disease in the history of AIDS. The paradox for those advocating silence on the issue, was that discovering the origin of the virus would be a pivotal link in the chain to finding a cure.

Initially, the hypothesis centered on the idea that two strains of HIV had begun in African monkeys and crossed over to humans. The idea soon became entrenched that AIDS was not just a new pandemic but a new human disease, one that passed from simians to humans in Africa, then swiftly crossed the Atlantic to America. In 1987, Randy Shilts helped popularize this concept in *And the Band Played On*, by speculating on the exact moment of arrival. His theory centered on the Bicentennial celebration of 1976, when the Tall Ships regatta brought thousands of sailors, including many from Africa, in contact with gays from New York.[88]

According to Gabriel Rotello, problems arose from the very beginning with the simian crossover hypothesis. HIV-2 is closely related to simian immunodeficiency viruses (SIVs). HIV-1, the killer virus we call AIDS is not. Rockefeller University virologist Stephen Morse told Rotello:

There is no known virus that looks even closely ancestral to HIV-1 in the wild. It's a genuine missing link.[89]

Observes Rotello, "If so, it's a whopper." If not, it's an awesome imaginary scapegoat. "After all," Rotello asks, "if HIV-1 is a monkey virus that recently jumped to humans, where are the infected monkeys?"[90]

Medical historian Mirko Grmek puts it this way:

You can suppose some kind of cross species transmission as a single event, but how can you make a theory to account for two contemporary transmissions of two completely different viruses that both cause the same disease?[91]

The idea that HIV-1 and HIV-2, only 40 per cent genetically related and therefore distant cousins from a viral point of view, both just happened to cross over accidentally to the same species (us) at the same time is, according to Grmek, "extremely improbable, even impossible, if held to be the result of chance biological mutation." Here the initial theory, as Robert Gallo wrote in 1987, in *Scientific American,* of the HIV-2 crossover from simians to humans, is now decisively debunked by genetic analyses. It is now universally held that HIV-2 could not have given birth to HIV-1.[92]

Blamed by the Right for that worst of Biblical crimes – the bringing down of plague – many felt that the stigma of causing an epidemic was so politically damaging that it rendered open discussion of the epidemic's origin extremely unwise. Rotello says, "At ACT UP meetings in New York, activists hissed when anyone raised the subject of the epidemic's origin."[93] Into this potent politicization of what remained, at the core, a medical mystery, scientists ventured at their peril. One pathfinder in particular pioneered an experiment at the Cornell Medical Center in New York City. Observing from the very beginning that most of the people with AIDS were gay, Dr. Steve Witkin decided to look at what gays did. Not what drugs they took, not what places they went to, but something in their sexual practices that might make them more susceptible than straights. Witkin said, "I personally believe that the average person" – by which he apparently meant male heterosexuals who were neither junkies, Haitians, hemophiliacs, nor people in need of transfusions -"is not at risk for AIDS."[94] His study then focused on what is the difference between the "average person" and a male homosexual? The common denominator was "semen."

According to David Black, author of *The Plague Years*, Witkin didn't have any hidden agenda, any bias to defend; he wasn't on a moral crusade. He seemed motivated simply by the desire to save lives. Since so many "sexually active" gays got AIDS, Witkin and his colleagues reasoned, it seemed logical to conclude that "the syndrome may have some relation to circulating antibodies evoked as a result of semen deposition in the alimentary canal."[95] In other words, someone else's semen, shot into your rectum, might cause your body to produce antibodies to the foreign semen, which in turn could suppress the immune system, leaving it unable to fight off infection by the AIDS-associated diseases. Witkin would test his hypothesis on rabbits.

An earlier study had found that when semen is injected intravenously into rats, antisperm antibody is produced. Witkin wanted to make sure it was the introduction of semen, not the trauma – or the semen entering the bloodstream through abrasions or cuts – that affected the immune system. Saltwater was squirted into the rectum of a group of control rabbits. "How did you get the rabbit semen?" Black asked. The surprised Witkin answered, "Just use an artificial [rabbit] vagina." The rabbits, both those buggered and those from which Witkin got the semen, were originally healthy. Just as he had suspected, "In six to eight weeks, the rabbits [who were getting the semen] developed antibodies to the sperm, antibodies that reacted with the immune system."[96] The rabbits getting the saltwater did not develop antibody to sperm.

"So is semen dangerous?" According to Witkin, sperm [typical semen, as opposed to HIV infected] was not dangerous when introduced vaginally. The cells lining the vagina are different from cells in the rectum. Heterosexual sex appears naturally safe. "But is not, anal sex, whether heterosexual or homosexual unsafe?" In Witkin's mind, not necessarily. Although there is one study done in Texas and reported in *The Journal of the American Medical Association* that suggested that women who have anal sex might respond in a similar way to men who have anal sex, developing anti-sperm antibody and having their immune system suppressed, that was not conclusive. Witkin thought that women were not at risk even if they had anal sex – or rather even if their partners ejaculated inside them during anal intercourse. "Females," Witkin said, "have evolved immunological mechanisms to deal with exposure to sperm." They had to in order for the species to continue. But men did not have to evolve immunological mechanisms to deal with exposure to sperm. The implication was that gay sex – at least gay anal sex – is biologically unnatural. Here, concluded Black, was "tentative scientific support for bigotry."[97]

In *Sexual Ecology: Aids and the Destiny of Gay Men,* Rotello describes that years after Witkin's experiment a breakthrough event occurred with the French publication of Mirko Grmek's landmark *History of AIDS*. Here one of the world's leading authorities on medical history presented the startling hypothesis that HIV has long existed in human populations, not just in Africa, but the West as well. Grmek's book was hailed by critics for its thorough scholarship, its cautious, unsensational approach to the subject. Grmek described three basic ways to test the hypothesis that HIV is old in humans: Search old medical records for retrospective diagnosis of AIDS; test old blood and tissue samples to see if they contain traces of HIV or antibodies to HIV; and genetically sequence different samples of the virus to attempt to reconstruct its past.

In the retrospective diagnosis, a breakthrough came in the form of medical records from a brilliant young Viennese dermatologist named Moritz Kaposi. In 1868, Kaposi received a visit from a middle-aged male patient who sought his help for a strange skin cancer, one neither Kaposi, nor any of his colleagues had ever seen. As this strange malignancy spread to the patient's internal organs, Kaposi kept a careful record of the unusual malady, confident he would never see another case. However, a few months after the patient died, a second patient appeared with the same condition. Then a third patient, and a fouth and a fifth, all middle-aged men, all soon dead. Via an autopsy, one of them was found to have strange lesions in his lungs which, from today's perspective, sound suspiciously like Pneumocystis carinii pneumonia, another of the most common AIDS afflictions. This cluster of KS cases – ending as abruptly as it began – provided Kaposi with the opportunity to describe the cancer that now bears his name.[98]

In the late 1870s and early 1880s another physician, Tommaso De Amicis, stumbled across another cluster of twelve cases of Kaposi's sarcoma. Except for one small child, all were Neapolitan men between the ages of thirty-nine and forty-four. A third recorded outbreak occurred among European men in the early twentieth century, and a fourth in postwar Africa. Writing in the *Journal of the National Medical Association*, researchers Harold P. Katner and George A. Pankey argued that by using KS as a "probable marker" of pre-epidemic AIDS, they were able to identify tentative AIDS cases back to 1902. It is now believed that KS is transmitted by a herpes virus, and the patterns of KS in gay men strongly suggest that this virus is, like HIV, sexually transmitted. One study suggests it may be spread in saliva. But the cancer itself virtually never appears in gay men in the absence of HIV. Whatever causes the cancer appears to require HIV's additional immune supression infection to produce disease. So it is theorectically possible that what Kaposi and others observed in decades past was quasi-epidemic clusters of HIV and the KS virus, clusters that died out for lack of the kind of multipartner sexual networks needed to rekindle a full-fledged-epidemic.[99]

The search of stored tissue samples uncovered more evidence. Perhaps the most widely known example is the case of "Robert R." He was a fifteen-year-old African-American youth who checked into St. Louis City Hospital in 1968 with edema of the lower body and various other afflictions and died the next year, beset with Kaposi's sarcoma, Chlamydia trachomatis, STDs, and intestinal disorders. After he died physicians collected and froze samples of his blood and lymph nodes for future study. In 1987, the samples were examined by microbiologist Robert Garry at Tulane University, who published his results in the *Journal of the American Medical Association*. To the surprise of the AIDS medical community, Robert R. had tested HIV-antibody positive, two decades after his death.[100] An even earlier case provides the first confirmed example of transmission from a husband to his wife, and from the wife to their infant child. In 1966, a twenty-year-old Norwegian man checked into Oslo's Rikshospitalet complaining of recurrent colds, lymphadenopathy, and Kaposi's-like dark spots on his skin. He did not improve, and the next year his wife came down with candidiasis, cystitis, and other afflictions. A child born to the couple that same year seemed healthy at first, but by age two was suffering from severe bronchial candidiasis. They all died within months of each other, and serum samples were collected and frozen. In 1988, the long-dead family all tested HIV seropositive.[101]

The third area to study was genetic sequencing. Writes Rotello:

By analyzing the genetic structure of HIV, geneticists believe they can estimate how far and for how long its various strains have evolved away from a common ancestor....Researchers at a 1996 International AIDS Conference in Vancouver presented data indicating that instead of evolving away from each other, some global strains of HIV are evolving toward each other, joining together in a process researchers call recombination.[102]

This refers to the unique and frightening ability of retro-viruses to fuse together. When a person is infected with two or more strains of a retrovirus like HIV, those strains can literally merge, fusing characteristics of both into a wholly new strain. In collecting samples of HIV from around the world in the nineties and comparing them to earlier samples, the researchers discovered that some of the most troublesome strains on the planet, including virulent subtype E, are recombinants that have only recently emerged. Writes Rotello:

While the researchers did not say so in their paper, their discovery provided evidence that AIDS is an old disease in humans. The reason is simple. If, under the jet-age conditions of the modern world, the different global strains of HIV are combining with each other, then how and under what conditions could those strains have evolved separately in the first place? A logical answer, some say the only logical answer, is that their evolution must have occurred before the jet-age conditions of the modern world, when Africans, Asians, Americans, and Europeans lived in relative isolation from each other. Under those conditions, the theory goes, HIV was able to evolve into the major subtypes that existed when the epidemic was first noticed....By analogy we see the same process in our own species, both biologically and culturally. As humans from all over the planet travel, emigrate, mix, and intermarry, the global races and global cultures are very slowly combining. If this process continues for millennia, human populations may eventually become culturally and even genetically homogenized.[103]

What is one to conclude from all this? To some anal sex will always be an unnatural act, exposing its participants to at minimum the destructive forces of nature, and for others the wrath of God. On the other hand, for adherents to Wellness doctrine and the ethos of Konstantin Berlandt, Mark Blasius and the like-minded, the verdict will be not guilty – sorry not responsible. For them, the lesson to be taken is that more "knowledge" is needed on risk reduction methodologies; more "technology" needs to be applied for protection; and society at large, is obliged to appropriate more "money" to sustain this central behavioral tenet of gay culture. Gabriel Rotello's brilliant and controversial analysis of the ecology of AIDS should be applauded for bringing all readers closer to the truth. He no doubt has paid a price for his integrity, among his activist associates in the gay community. Later in Chapter 5, in a section titled "Replacing Leviticus Code with the Condom Code," I will continue to draw on Rotello's insights to debunk the myth of the Condom Code.

CHAPTER TWO

POLITICS, ALLIANCES AND COGNITIVE DISSONANCE

The lesbian is the rage of all women condensed to the point of explosion.[1]
Radicalesbian position paper, 'The Woman – Identified Woman', 1972

To feminists who want to retain the category 'woman,' she asks: Can we redeem slave? Can we redeem nigger, negress? How is woman different?...Women are defined only in relation to men. Lesbians are not defined in relation to men. 'Lesbians are not women.'[2]
Monique Wittig, Novelist and Lesbian-feminist, 1978

Manifestations of Cognitive Dissonance

Cognitive Dissonance Theory, developed in 1957 by Leon Festinger, is concerned with the relationships between cognitions (pieces of knowledge). He found people prefer cognitions that fit together over those that do not. The feeling of imbalance (unpleasant psychological tension) when people find themselves doing things that do not fit with what they know or with the opinions that they hold is "cognitive dissonance." The theory looks at what happens to people with dissonant cognitions and contributes much to understanding the determinants of attitudes and beliefs, the internalization of values, the reaction to the consequences of decisions, the effects of disagreement among persons, and other important psychological processes.

Festinger observed that in people who have dissonant cognitions the level of psychological stress increases with the degree of discrepancy between cognitions and the number of discrepant cognitions. Thus, to cope with the dissonance, people adopt strategies like: adding or subtracting (denial) cognitions; trying to reduce the importance of dissonant cognitions; or distorting information or stimuli. The theory predicts that people will attend to information that conforms to their attitudes and values while ignoring information that is inconsistent with their beliefs. Moreover, once a decision is made, dissonance is likely to be aroused. In response people alter aspects of the decision alternatives to reduce dissonance, which leads to viewing the chosen alternative as more desirable and the rejected alternative as less desirable. This effect is called the spreading of alternatives, and the theoretical paradigm is termed the "free-choice paradigm."[3] Festinger used the following example to explain his theory:

A habitual smoker who learns that smoking is bad for health will experience dissonance, because the knowledge that smoking is bad for health is dissonant with the cognition that he continues to smoke. He can reduce the dissonance by changing his behavior, that is, he could stop smoking...Alternatively, the smoker could reduce dissonance by changing his cognition about the effect of smoking on health and believe that smoking does not have a harmful effect on health (eliminating the dissonant cognition). He might look for positive effects of smoking and believe that smoking reduces tension and keeps him from gaining weight (adding consonant cognitions). Or he might believe that the risk to health from smoking is negligible compared with the danger of automobile accidents (reducing the importance of the dissonant cognition). In addition, he might consider the enjoyment he gets from smoking to be a very important part of his life (increasing the importance of consonant cognitions).[4]

In the text ahead, much insight will be gained by viewing the subject matter from the perspective of cognitive dissonance theory. This analytical model will help explain historical phenomena such as: the rewriting of Scripture into a Women's Bible; attempts to transpose the Christian Trinity into Mother God, Female Christ, and Spirit Liberator; the denunciation of 75 per cent of the New Testament words of Christ; the slandering of Christian revelation on the equality of the sexes in marriage, in family and in bed; portrayal of safe sex under the Condom Code; projection of sexuality as a social construct; denial of heterophobia while emphasizing homophobia; use of homophobia to silence contrary argument; construction of patriarchy as oppression; fabrication of matriarchy as the ideal; portraying women with superior characteristics (tolerance) and men with inferior attributes (aggression); portrayal of all wrongs in the world – wars, environment, government, economic structures, religion etc. as male failures rather than "human" failures; reliance on gay gene theory as a loophole in morality; portrayal of gay lifestyle as healthy; seeing free sex as having no cost; contending that ecological health and biology problems associated with free sex are the state's responsibility to resolve; last but not least, the notion of the male-free "infinite orgasm" as women's natural destiny.

In the previous chapter, the focus was primarily on gay issues. Now the study will aim at lesbianism and feminism, hoping to understand their relationship, goals and impact. Lillian Faderman, in *Odd Girls and Twilight Lovers: A History of Lesbian Life in Twentieth-Century America* writes:

Lesbianism even came to be regarded as the quintessence of feminism...'There were probably more lesbians in America during the 1970s than at any other time in history, because radical feminism had helped redefine lesbianism to make it almost a categorical imperative for all women truly interested in the welfare and progress of other women.[5]

Sheila Jefferys, laments in her essay "*How Orgasm Politics Has Hijacked the Women's Movement*," that the "unreflective politics of orgasm seems to have won out" among feminists.[6] Women's liberation advocates argued that women and men should be equally free to pursue careers, care for children, initiate sex, and select social companions. Public day-care services, they contended, should be available to assume part of the responsibility previously borne solely by parents. And individuals should be free – as individuals – to determine their own lifestyle, sexual preference, occupation, and personal values.[7]

Not surprising, both the indictment of heterosexism and the proposed solutions deeply offended people who had been raised to believe that existing norms of behavior were not only functional but morally inviolate. To women who had spent a lifetime devoting themselves to the culturally sanctioned roles of homemaker and helpmate, the claim by feminists like Monique Whittig, that women had been enslaved frequently appeared as a direct attack on their personal experience. Such women did not believe that they had wasted their lives or had been duped by malevolent husbands. Many enjoyed the nurturant and supportive roles of wife and mother, believed that the family should operate with a division of labor, and profoundly resented the suggestion that the life of a homemaker somehow symbolized failure. From their point of view, the women's liberation movement was guilty of arrogance and contempt toward the majority of women, and some expressed that view by voting against the Equal Rights Amendment and by organizing their own associations – "Total Woman," "REAL Women," and "Feminists For Life" were typical movements.[8]

Many men believed the radical feminists were conducting an insidious campaign to undermine their strength, deny their authority, and destroy their self-image. Instead of helping women, many believed, feminists were intent on wrecking the family and turning the wife against the husband. From such a vantage point, "women's liberation symbolized anarchic and amoral forces at work in the society, seeking to untie all the knots and loosen the bonds that gave life its security and stability."[9] In this aspect there seemed little deception. At the Conference of Socialist Feminists in 1975, some 1500 participants all agreed that oppression, whether based on class, sex, race, or lesbianism, was inter-related. Lesbian feminists argued that homosexuality represented more than a personal sexual preference and was a political act against the institutional source of all women's oppression, heterosexuality. Within this perspective, male supremacy constituted the basic problem, and its primary instrument of control was the heterosexual relationship. Thus only a direct attack on the source of male oppression could bring liberation for women; for that reason, all feminists had to identify, politically at least, with the lesbian struggle.[10] The prototypical American woman, wrote Vivian Gornick, was perceived as "never taking, always being taken, never absorbed by her own desire, preoccupied only with whether she is desired."[11] Hence, by feminist logic, to develop a new autonomous and positive self-image required separation from the bonds of dominance – men.

According to Cynthia Eller, author of *The Myth of Matriarchal History*, feminist matriarchalists claim "there is a feminine nature captured within women that is struggling to be free of the cultural doctoring of patriarchy" and "it is the task of women living now to find out what the nature is." As we shall see this radical liberation ideology motivates adherents to ignore the countless voices of satisfied mothers and wives, as if they were Borg on *Star Trek*. It would hardly be of any utility speaking to a Borg until she has been disconnected from her control source and deprogrammed [liberated]. Vicki Noble explains the challenge:

Women do not know how to be feminine. We may think we have a corner on the market, since we were born with feminine bodies, but it's just as new to us as if we were men. We have to create feminine.[12]

What these feminist matriarchalists didn't say was why women have to create the feminine. In response to asking, "Why can't we just ignore it and see if it goes away?" Eller writes:

In the absence of any gendered expectations, presumably men would continue to grow beards; why would women not as easily continue to evince traits of nurturance and relationality, whatever they were taught to the contrary, if this is in fact our biological nature? The feminist matriarchalist answer to this is undoubtedly that women do evince these traits, over and over again, across all cultures, all the way back to prehistoric times. But if this is so, why can't they leave it at that? Let women become who they naturally are, but don't suggest to any individual woman that she's not doing a good job of being female, and that therefore she must learn to be feminine[13]

Feminist theories argue that gender is "not a fact or an essence, but a set of acts that produce the effect or appearance of a coherent substance." "Gender is not embodied," they say, "but performed, over and over again."[14] Yet there is a dichotomy in this constructionist paradigm. How can feminists criticize the way women are perceived and treated and simultaneously insist that there is no such thing as femaleness per se. Obviously there is, or it wouldn't be possible to know who the mistreated are. Eller observes:

There is a deep and compelling desire among feminists to have it both ways: we are women, and there are things about femaleness that we treasure and want to celebrate; yet we will not be limited in our choices and actions just because we happen to fall into a category you have labeled 'woman.' Without femaleness – the category of women – feminism 'would be lost for an object, despoiled of a fight'; but with this category firmly in mind, it is too easy to forget that 'femaleness' serves sexist interests, was possibly created to do so, and will always threaten to continue to do so.[15]

Perhaps as feminist scholar Denise Riley suggests, females should "stand back and announce there aren't any 'women.'"[16] And yet there are. We see them on the street every day, and they know that they are women and that that has no small effect on what sort of lives they are able to live.

In *Heteophobia: Sexual Harassment and the Future of Feminism,* Daphne Patai ponders how some women appear to remain "devoted" wives and yet rally for the feminist banner. She asks:

What, for example, is a heterosexual woman to do when she is told that male potency is a threat? That the penis is an instrument of domination? That her own sexual fantasies may be betraying her 'indoctrination' into patriarchal norms? How many hetero feminists feel guilt over 'sleeping with the enemy?' How many fail to challenge heterophobia out of a belief that lesbian feminists are the 'real thing'?[17]

Two lesbian feminists, Sue Wilkinson and Celia Kitzinger, show the politically correct apologetics for such questions:

Mary Crawford: 'I use heterosexual privilege to subvert heterosexism.'

Sandra Bartky: 'The felt impossibility of changing one's sexual orientation is not an argument for the desirability of this orientation.'

Sandra Bem's explanation that though she has lived with the man she loves for twenty-six years, she has not and has never been a 'heterosexual,' her sexuality being 'organized around dimensions other than sex.'[18]

Lesbian feminists rarely challenged the presupposition that there need be, and actually is, a conflict between feminism and heterosexuality. Heterosexual feminist Shulamit Reinharz, tried to strike a balance, allowing that "we cannot dismiss heterosexual women as having 'false consciousness.'" Yet she goes on to say, "It would be good for us also to empower women to understand their lesbian potential," while making no comparable suggestion to lesbians.[19] Nonetheless, decades later, Arlene Stein found that a high percentage of feminist lesbians did eventually turn straight, including Gloria Steinem.[20]

The anthology *Lesbianism and Women's Movement*, first published in 1972-73 by a lesbian-feminist collective in Washington, D.C, revealed they had not yet created an alternative vision of men's and women's relations. The change that contributor Margret Small desired did not require all women to become lesbians – just the end of heterosexuality as we know it:

The question, I think, is rather how all women will understand themselves. If the ideology of heterosexuality can be attacked and exposed and an alternative ideology can be developed, I'm not sure how important it is that all women stop being heterosexual. Because the way a woman would understand what it would mean to be heterosexual, would be totally different.[21]

A critique of heterosexual ideology ultimately reduces heterosexuality to an act at the moment of impregnation. If you're going to have a baby, there is a role for heterosexuality. If we develop other ways to have babies, then what heterosexuality is becomes irrelevant.[22]

The new *Houghton Mifflin Reader's Companion to U.S. Women's History* contains an entry by E. Kay Trimberger on "Heterosexuality." While failing to note that heterosexul intercourse is the means by which the species has been propogated all these years and that it corresponds to the wishes of some 97 per cent of the global population, the *Companion* trumpets feminist dogma unproblematically:

Sexuality is not private, but is political and related to power. 'Compulsory heterosexuality' is part of a power structure benefiting heterosexual males at the expense of women and homosexuals. This inequity is justified by an ideology that sees heterosexuality as natural, universal, and biologically necessary, and homosexuality as the opposite. The system also is reinforced by legal sanctions and violence against women (rape, battering, incest, and murder) and against lesbians, gays, and transgendered persons (verbal harassment, physical assault, and murder).[23]

In this entry Trimburger also asserts that "if our sexuality is socially constructed it can also be de- and re-constructed." To help women organize and create their new liberated reality required the leadership of activists such as Sonia Johnson. In *Wildfire: Igniting the She/volution*, she writes:

The vision that has flown into my mind is of women coming together in small groups all over the world, pooling our resources, building communities of many different sorts and living together in them in a conspicuously feminist (i.e. woman-like) way.[24]

How and when will such communities come into being? Who will build them and where? What will they look like? How will they function?[25]

When women ask me 'What shall we do?' I don't think they are really asking me to tell them what to do; they know I can only answer 'Live today as you want the world to be.' None of us knows for certain how we will act when we are free; the only thing we can be sure of is that none of us will be doing the same things we did before, and that there will be much more variety...the women who are asking that question know that absolutely nothing is working for women 'out there,' that all the passion and effort, all promises, all the hopes have essentially come to nothing for women as a global caste.[26]

I ask the reader to ponder this notion that heterosexuality is a social construct in the way Small and like-minded feminists articulate the theory. What is their rationale for this contention? After considerable study, the only logic in the idea, is found in the application of Festinger's cognitive dissonance theory and the "free-choice paradigm." First, legitimizing lesbian space is impossible without declaring heterosexuality a cultural construct. Second, once a decision is taken in favor of lesbianism the phenomenon of "spreading of alternatives" occurs. This can be shown in Sonia Johnson's vision of the new lesbian "space" and her view of the realities of women in heterosexual society:

My dream is that women will create the world again, that we will be 'original' women, originating now what we need for ourselves.[27]

When enough lesbians create such a space inside and around ourselves, when enough of us feel free of the imperatives of this system, moment by moment, freedom will become reality for all women in the world. The principle that the means are the ends provides more – and more conclusively – evidence that resistance is not only futile, but that it literally and actively strengthens the things resisted.[28]

The bumper sticker says it all: "What if they threw a war and nobody came?" The men are still throwing the age-old, all-out, global, gynecidal war against women, but I'm not going, and if I don't go, they can't use my resistance to keep the war going. If enough of us don't go, they can't throw the war at all. I want women everywhere not to go to the war anymore. I want us not to turn up on the battlefield thinking we can win when we can only be slaughtered. For this reason, I no longer think of myself as a 'woman warrior' as I once did. I am not fighting anything or anyone anymore, not mimicking men's old deadly pattern. I think of myself and other like-minded women now as the goddess, creating a new pattern, creating the world afresh.[29]

Tragically, more than three decades later, we find that radical feminism has had exactly the opposite impact that Johnson envisaged and longed for. We will see in Chapters 7 and 8, that feminism has not resulted in a more "original" woman, but rather the outcome has been labeled (by critics) the "masculinization of the female gender," where for example, careerism has replaced motherhood, and women have abandoned traditional feminine virtuosity and fidelity for the long-established (in feminist analysis) masculine ethos of free sex and promiscuity. The radical feminist solution to the sexual double standard – join the male model.

Perhaps lesbians have come nearer to their utopian social "space," but many heterosexual women have been misled under feminism and are now wounded and fighting upon a different battlefield, one that is more hostile, has fewer support mechanisms and offers less hope of peace. In this battlefield "liberated" men take no responsibility for their lover's pregnancy and hold little economic obligation to their abandoned wives and children. Examining the characteristics of this new battlefield and the extent of the damage done to heterosexual relations and institutions makes up a majority of the remainder of this book.

That the feminist separation strategy was unsound and in trouble from the very start is evidenced in the early introduction of the strategy of "matriarchal supremacy." Like the leader of a floundering army caught in a protracted war and faced with desertion, spiritual collapse, and manifest poor morale, Johnson goes on to create myth and misinformation to rally lesbian converts, create hope and a sense of eventual peace. Johnson writes:

In Albuquerque at Wiminfest in 1988 when Alix talked to Susan and me about meeting the aboriginal Australian women she was especially excited about their rituals. Believing that at the beginning of time and for hundreds of thousands of years thereafter all Earth's people were women, in their sacred rituals these women now invoke that time and their ancient counterparts. By holding it firmly in memory, they keep their history dynamic and continuous, they know their place in the scheme of things, they retain the vision of themselves as characters in a human saga of what to us would be unthinkable antiquity...Imagine women whose sense of self has not been nearly obliterated by men's violence! Such women have existed for millennia before us, still exist in small pockets such as this. Imagine how we would be, what we would do, if we were such women.[30]

Gloria Steinem had been speculating about the origins of patriarchy as early as 1972, when she told the readers of *Wonder Woman* this story:

Once upon a time, the many cultures of this world were all part of the gynocratic age. Paternity had not yet been discovered, and it was thought ...that women bore fruit like trees – when they were ripe. Childbirth was mysterious. It was vital. And it was envied. Women were worshipped because of it, were considered superior because of it...Men were on the periphery – an interchangeable body of workers for, and worshippers of, the female center, the principle of life.

The discovery of paternity, of sexual cause and childbirth effect, was as cataclysmic for society as, say, the discovery of fire or the shattering of the atom. Gradually the idea of male ownership of children took hold...Gynocracy also suffered from periodic invasions of nomadic tribes...The conflict between the hunters and the growers was really the conflict between male-dominated and female-dominated cultures...women gradually lost their freedom, mystery, and superior position. For five thousand years or more, the gynocratic age had flowered in peace and productivity. Slowly, in varying stages and in different parts of the world, the social order was painfully reversed. Woman became the underclass, marked by their visible differences.[31]

Phyllis Chesler, adds to this her own embellished version of the above:

Amazon society, as both mythology, history, and universal male nightmare, represents a culture in which women reign culturally supreme because of their sexual identity...In Amazon societies, women were mothers and their society's only warriors; mothers and their society's only hunters; mothers and their society's only political and religious leaders. No division of labor based on sex seems to have existed in all-female societies. Although Amazon leaders existed and queens were elected, the societies seem to have been classless ones, or at least ones in which any woman could aspire to and achieve full human expression.[32]

The more radical [Amazon] kind of administration, in Chesler's fantasy, did not send any babies away but crippled the newly born boys and rendered them innocuous for life through the twisting of one hand and one hip out of their sockets. Despised slave cripples, never touched erotically by the Amazons, were used for the rearing of children, the spinning of wool, and domestic service. According to Helen Diner, author of *Mothers and Amazons: The First Feminine History of Culture* (1965), in the most extreme anti-male society, the male offspring was always killed, and sometimes the fathers too...Children, were brought up on mare's milk and given to men to rear.[33]

Myths are simple but powerful explanations, providing an escape from historically complex situations. They allow us to grasp not so much what is true but what we believe, or would like to believe, to be true. Women who respond enthusiastically to matriarchal myth do so at least in part because it offers them a new, vastly improved self-image. It teaches them about their "innate goodness," their "own natural majesty." It has, says Charlene Spretnak, "reframed our conceptualization of femaleness" and given us "the gift of ourselves." Martha Ann and Dorothy Myers Imel set it out in the dedication to their massive reference work, *Goddesses in World Mythology*:

To all the women in the world who were unaware of their heritage. You are descended from a long line of sacred females who have been respected and honored for thousands of years. Remember and make it so.[34]

Johnson describes the impact of matriarchy on her attitude:

Once to a group of friends, I talked about how, with my current understanding of my role in perpetuating patriarchy and because of my love for myself and women and all life, I had to let go, to detach, to cut the umbilical cords of belief and feeling:[35]

'Oh, Sonia,' one of them sighed, 'that's just not practical!' 'Practical,' I repeated thoughtfully, 'Isn't that an interesting word.' I thought to myself how for 5,000 years women have been resisting patriarchy in all the ways that have been called practical...Some say that women weren't always aware enough to resist or didn't know anything was wrong. But I say that if we want to know how women were down through the centuries, all we have to do is look at ourselves. We are how women have been: brilliant, brave, strong – magnificent. All through history women have known, intuitively when not cerebrally, that patriarchy was deadly to everything we loved, and we have always resisted it in everything we loved, and we have always resisted it in every way, overt and covert, private and public, that presented itself – most creative, inventive, imaginative ways possible on all levels. Women have resisted patriarchy with unsurpassed cunning, craft, and passion for at least 5,000 years. I don't want to be hasty, but it seems to me that 5,000 years is long enough to try any method, particularly one that doesn't work. Women want above all else to be fair, and we have given resistance a fair trial. In all fairness then, it is time to try something different.[36] *[lesbianism]*

In her study, Eller finds only misguided utility in matriarchal myth. Feminist matriarchalists justify their commitment to origin stories by claiming that since "our analysis of causes affects strategies for change," we cannot usefully proceed without knowing where sexism came from. This makes a lot of intuitive sense, especially for those who were told in every history class they ever took that if we don't learn from history we are doomed to repeat it. Says Eller:

There is only one wrench in the works, if sexism had an origin – that is, if it were not always present from the beginning of hominid evolution – then we need to know how it came into being. But when it comes to detecting ideological developments in prehistory, we can't learn the relevant facts; they are 'in principle unobtainable.'[37]

Ironically, for peddlers of myth, the lost past is ideal. Feminist matriarchalists, like other myth-makers, begin with a vision of the world as they would like it to be, project it into the past, and then find a way (narratively speaking) to make present conditions emerge from ideal ones.[38] If they are not going to discover history at the end of the day, but simply create myth, then the only grounds upon which feminist origins thinking can be justified is that it serves feminist political purposes. Matriarchal myth addresses one of feminist movement's most difficult questions: How can women attain real power when it seems we have never had it before? How can women hope that sex egalitarianism is possible, that male dominance can be ended, when it has been a mark of who females are as a species from time immemorial? Feminist matriarchal myth attempts to answer these questions in an emotionally compelling, inspiring way. However, Eller has many concerns for feminists following this tact:

Insofar as strong theories of sex difference are an unavoidable component of matriarchal myth, we should be suspicious about the myth's feminist utility from the start. But it is problematic on another level too. As Archaeologist Sarah Taylor remarks, 'I for one do not find it very comforting to think that once, in a very distant and 'primitive' society, women held power, especially if we have been moving away from that condition ever since.'[39]

...it raises new questions, equally difficult to answer: Why did matriarchy collapse – and not just in one place or time, but everywhere, all around the world? And how can we hope to get it back, under conditions so radically different from those which supposedly fostered it in the first place? If male dominance followed naturally on the discovery of biological paternity, is the only way to reclaim matriarchy to ensure that no one knows who the fathers of individual children are? Though this could be easily achieved through artificial insemination or promiscuous sex, no one who puts the patriarchal revolution down to the discovery of paternity seriously advocates this as a desirable public policy. Others have pinned male dominance to the development of agriculture, but we cannot return the world to a sustainable foraging technology without euthanizing 99 per cent of the world's population.[40]

Why is it that feminist matriarchalists continue to cling to the edict of gender difference, when other feminists argue for gender sameness? The best explanation, according to Eller, is that there is no escape. Whether "femininity" is produced by the possession of two X chromosomes or by a lifetime of culture; indoctrination is beside the point. Either way, gender is a reality against which everyone – but particularly women – must contend. Given this reality, Eller suggests:

The best we can do is to see how the facts of femaleness can be negotiated to serve women's interests...Feminist matriarchalists are not imagining that sex differences exist; they do exist, and they legislate life choices with a sometimes frightening force.[41]

When the matriarchal ideal does not win over all women, radical feminists are forced to take on a second dissonance strategy – discrimination against alternative views. The most effective device for maintaining internal group discipline and silencing contradictory perspective is to ostracize those who do not conform. Two examples of this phenomenon come from the relations between REAL Women (discussed two sections from now) and the National Action Committee on the Status of Women (NAC). Both cases illustrate the hypocrisy of feminist "tolerance and inclusiveness." The first example is a striking (excuse the pun) case of women's violence to women. In its 1996 application for funding, the Vancouver Status of Women, identified "women living in violence" as one of its top priorities. The offices of the Status of Women advertised for women to attend a meeting at their premises in November to help organize for the next year's International Women's Day event. The invitation specifically mentioned that "all women" were welcome.

Two REAL Women members arrived around 7:30 p.m. that day. There were approximately 30 women crowded into a back room, which was closed off with glass windows. A woman attending the meeting asked Margaret and Gail (REAL representatives) who they were and which groups they represented. As soon as Margaret and Gail were identified as "anti-abortion" representatives, they were asked to leave. The two women refused to leave and stayed in a room just outside the meeting room where they were still able to hear and see what was going on. The feminists in the meeting room boarded up the windows, closed the door and stationed a woman at the door as a guard.

Margaret, who had a camera with her, decided to take some pictures of the boarded up windows and the woman guard at the door. When the feminists noticed the camera, she was told to surrender it. She refused.

At approximately 8:30 p.m. some of the feminists were leaving. Margaret and Gail remained in the hallway, looking at the bulletin board and taking a last picture. At that point four to five feminists lunged at Margaret who had the camera, throwing her to the ground on top of her camera. One had her arm around Margaret's neck, choking her. Because of the fall, Margaret dropped her wallet and cell phone, both of which were picked up by one of the feminists who had attacked her. The feminists threatened that the items would only be returned if Margaret surrendered the camera. When Gail tried to come to her aid, she was pushed, shoved, and punched. Gail had a swollen face and needed medical attention while Margaret was severely bruised and had a broken camera. A man arrived at the scene and called the police, but before the police arrived, the wallet and phone were returned. Charges were laid.[42]

The second example of discrimination and silencing occurred at a Conference titled "Consultation on Gender Equality" held December 1999 in Aylmer, Quebec. The Status of Women Canada was hosting the event and wanted "to ensure representation of a diversity of perspectives, interests and expertise." However, as long as the feminist National Action Committee (NAC) was claiming to represent all Canadian women, the association of REAL Women had to fight for recognition. Cecilia Forsyth, REAL Women's Representative at the Conference, relates her story:

The feminists were threatening to boycott the consultation if I did not leave....It was also clear that they had decided that no one would speak to or sit at the same table with me during...the meeting, for not a single woman did after that point...

The lesbian caucus at the Conference (their own label) then passed a resolution demanding that REAL Women never be invited to a Status of Women Conference again. Little did these women know, however, that I come from a line of strong and determined women. If my maternal grandmother had the courage to homestead in the territory of New Mexico as a young (then), unmarried woman, I could sit by myself for three days at the Chateau Cartier Hotel...

Later that day, REAL Women issued a press release... The silencing of women with a differing viewpoint by radical feminists...is an insult to the intelligence, integrity and dignity of all Canadian women and makes a mockery of 'gender' equality, when there is no equality among women.[43]

In spite of the harassment, Forsyth did manage to address two areas during the workshop discussion: the farm crisis in Saskatchewan and the discrimination against single-income families in the tax system.

In closing this topic on cognitive dissonance in the feminist movement, the issue of finances for the single-income family raises an important feminist makeover of history, which should not be missed. In the early 70s, lesbian activist Margret Small, wrote that "heterosexual ideology" was support to male supremacy. She pointed to "unnamed, unpaid, undervalued work that women perform for men within marriage."[44] A few years later two groups, "Lesbian Mother's Defense Fund" and "Wages for Housework" were seeking to become involved in NAC. The former was approved; however, much controversy ensued over housework as a policy issue. For the first time, NAC refused a group admission. The application of Wages for Housework was rejected because, according to the minutes from 24 February 1979, "the principles of wages for housework have been explicitly rejected by NAC." One month later, socialist feminist Lynn Macdonald was elected NAC President.[45]

Over a decade later, in *Moving Beyond Words*, Gloria Steinem claimed pay for homemakers as a feminist challenge.[46] In Canada, Carol Lees, a homemaker in Saskatoon, looked at a 1991 census question about "number of hours worked in the past week," realized she would have to answer "zero" by census definitions, and decided to celebrate March 8, International Women's Day, by writing a letter to the minister-in-charge saying:

Since I have worked full-time within the home for the past 13 years raising three children, I take exception to the fact that my labor is not defined as productive...As a result of the exclusion of women's labor from information gathering and dissemination, we are denied proper access to programs and policy at every level of government...The government will not show well if it levies a fine on a mother of three with no income because she is refused recognition for her labors in raising her children.[47]

Sublimely, Steinem notes:

In anticipation of the 1996 census, she [Lees] and other Canadian women have organized a group called Work Is Work Is Work and they are circulating test questions for inclusion in the census. As she says, 'A lot of us are never going to give up until we're counted.'[48]

In February 2000, Joan Cummings, President of NAC, reiterated the Committee's anti-homemaker position: "We need a national childcare program and an extension and enhancement of parental leave benefits...so as not to punish women for their decision to have children." Where was NAC during the twenty year battle of a Calgary homemaker, named Beverly Smith? In December 1998, Smith went to the UN over the issue of unfair tax discrimination. In response, Finance Minister, Paul

Martin finally took action to study the issue of unpaid work in the home. Martin's request was prompted by news that the UN would rule on the matter. Under Canada's Income Tax Act, a provision called the Child Care Expense Deduction (CCED) allowed families that use paid day care to lower their taxable income by up to $7,000 per child under age seven and by $4,000 for children age seven to sixteen. By contrast, families where one parent stayed home to care for children received a Child Tax Benefit of only $213 per child six years old or younger.[49]

The overall message of this section – beware of feminist truth. The last word on matriarchy is Cynthia Eller's:

Whether patriarchy is our history, or merely one history, we are not in either case bound 'to clone the past....One could choose to interpret this [cultural sex role diversity] as evidence that male dominance has many cunning tools in its toolbox, but one could easily read the sheer amount of ethnographic variety in matters of gender and sex as proof that we have a lot more latitude in setting up gender relations than any amount of sorrowful recounting of the sins of Western patriarchy would lead us to believe.[50]

Lesbianization of a Women's Movement

In a 1971 resolution, National Organization for Women (NOW) identified lesbians as the frontline troops of the women's movement and accepted the lesbian-feminist analysis that the reason lesbians had been so harassed by society was that they were a significant threat to the system that subjugated women – the very system that heterosexual women were trying to challege and destroy by their feminism. The 1971 resolution acknowledged the inherent feminism of lesbianism and the anti-feminism of lesbian persecution.[51] One needs to ask, particularly if you are heterosexual female, was this resolution prudent? In the 70s and 80s, both Canadian and American feminists would wrestle with this question in different ways, in the end, both arriving at the same answer – yielding to full alliance with their counterpart lesbian movements.

The American decision was made earlier than in Canada with results more significantly detrimental to the integrity of the women's movement. Jeri Dawn Wine, a founder of the Canadian National Lesbian Forum, maintains that:

NAC avoided the split over lesbian participation that the National Organization for Women suffered in the United States only at the cost of a decade of silence on the part of Canadian lesbians.[52]

Heterosexual women feared the negative ramifications of a public commitment to lesbian issues. It would take until 1985 for NAC to include lesbian issues on its agenda – after entrenchment of the Charter of Rights and Freedoms. Soon lesbians would come to represent more than 50 per cent of the membership in NAC.

Under the title, "Outside Agitator: Why was Betty Friedan ostracized by the movement she founded?" Judith Shulevitz writes:

These days the mother of [North American] feminism is mostly written off as obsolete – too bourgeois for the left-wing feminists, too feminist for the family-values right and too kooky for everyone else.[53]

However, she defends Friedan's pragmatic and less dogmatic approach to feminism:

Biographer Daniel Horowitz account of Friedan's early years establishes several links between the Old Left...and the second-wave feminism of the 1960s... Horowitz's main objective appears to be to wag his finger at Friedan for the sin of not writing 'The Feminine Mystique' as a member of the American left – for hedging 'her discussion of a capitalist conspiracy,' 'for failing to explain the feminine mystique' as an example of 'consciousness,' for offering 'psychological insights' rather than 'institutional solutions.' This is simply obtuse. It is precisely because Friedan abandoned the vocabulary of Marxism for that of bourgeois psychology that she was able to dismantle the reigning discourse about women. If she'd merely rehashed the theories of Frierich Engels, no one would have paid the slightest attention.[54]

There should have been some dissonance over the realization that although capitalism was implicated in the problem, male supremacy also existed in socialist countries like Cuba, where homosexuals were still oppressed and "macho" values remained largely intact. William Chafe, suggests for this reason only a direct attack on heterosexuality could bring liberation for women; thus all feminists had to identify, politically at least, with the lesbian struggle.[55]

Betty Friedan could boast of being as good a mother as the archconservative Phyllis Schlafly and at the same time of having won women the right to enter any profession or bar in the country. Unlike the radically chic New York feminists, she spoke for the mainstream: the women of Peoria, women like her mother! Lesbians alienated these women, endangering the movement.

Friedan co-founded, in 1966, the National Organization for Women (NOW). She tells her story:

At the luncheon we each chipped in a dollar. I wrote the word 'NOW' on a paper napkin; our group should be called the National Organization for Women, I said, 'because men should be part of it.' Then I wrote down the first sentence of the NOW statement of purpose, committing ourselves to take action to bring women into full participation in the mainstream of American society now, exercising all privileges and responsibilities thereof, in truly equal partnership with men.[56]

The founding vision of an equal heterosexual partnership lasted four years. A key part of the puzzle of Friedan's downfall comes from, the NOW Lesbian Summit titled "Feminist Strategies and Lesbian Issues," April 1999. At this conference NOW presented "Women of Courage Awards" to Del Martin and Phyllis Lyon, a couple who have been long-term activists in the lesbian and feminist movements. When Lyon said, "We've been involved with NOW off and on since 1967," the audience broke out in laughter because of the well-known difficult history of NOW and lesbians. Lyon described the couple's early activism in Daughters of Bilitis, a lesbian organization which they helped found because of sexism they found in gay male groups. Martin and Lyon's involvement with NOW began in 1967, when the couple saw NOW's offer of special couple memberships – designed by Betty Friedan to encourage husbands to join the organization – and wrote in to join as a couple. They were refused. "The couples offer (to husbands and wives) soon disappeared," said Lyon, when the 1971 NOW National Conference declared discrimination against lesbians as a feminist issue. Friedan, a national leader of NOW, told the media that lesbians would destroy the organization. However, by 1973, the lesbian caucus had become a regular part of the NOW governance.[57]

In *The Feminine Mystique (Twentieth Anniversary Edition)*, Friedan records her perspective on the lesbianization of the women's movement:

I never did see it [the women's movement] in terms of a class or race: women, as an oppressed class, fighting to overthrow or take power away from men as a class, the oppressors. I knew the movement had to include men as equal members, though women would have to take the lead in the first stage...The changes necessary to bring about that equality were, and still are, very revolutionary indeed, they involve a sex-role revolution for men and women which will restructure all our institutions....[58]

To Friedan, women also had to confront their sexual nature, not deny it. Society had to restructure so that women, who happen to be the people who give birth, would not be barred thereby from participating in society in their own right. She could not define "liberation" for women in terms that denied the sexual and human reality of our need to love, and even sometimes to depend upon, a man. What were obsolete were feminine and masculine sex roles that dehumanized sex. Says Friedan, "Weren't men as well as women still locked in lonely isolation?" To her, men weren't really the enemy – "they were fellow victims, suffering from an outmoded masculine mystique that made them feel unnecessary when there were no bears to kill."[59]

By 1970, it was beginning to be clear to Friedan and others that the women's movement was more than a temporary fad; it was the fastest-growing movement for basic social and political change of the decade. She felt at this time that someone was trying to take over the movement, to stop it, immobilize it, splinter it, under the guise of radical rhetoric and a similar fetish against leadership and structure. She wanted the women's movement to get out of the sexual politics:

I thought at first it was a joke – those strangely humorless papers about clitoral orgasms that would liberate women from sexual dependence on a man's penis, and the 'consciousness raising' talk that women should now insist on being on top in bed with men.[60]

She was never sure what motivations were behind the "exhibitionist, down-with-men, down-with-marriage, down-with-childbearing rhetoric and actions." Some of the disrupters seemed to come from the extreme left groups, some seemed to be using the women's movement to proselytize lesbianism, others seemed to be honestly articulating the legitimate and too-long-buried rage of women into a rhetoric of sex/class warfare, which she considered to be based on a false analogy with obsolete or irrelevent ideologies of class warfare or racism.[61] The man-haters were given publicity far out of proportion to their numbers in the movement because of the media's hunger for sensationalism. She observed that many women in the movement went through a temporary period of great hostility to men which she termed, "pseudo-radical infantilism."[62] Although she admired the flair of the young radicals when they got off the rhetoric, those who preached the man-hating sex/class warfare threatened to take over the New York NOW and the national NOW and drive out the women who wanted equality but who also wanted to keep on loving their husbands and children.[63]

In May 1970, on the first night of the second Congress to Unite Women, just after the assembly had settled down for a panel discussion the lights went out. A minute later, when the lights came on, twenty-five women with T-shirts identifying them as Lavender Menaces were assembled at the front stage. Alluding to Betty Friedan, one of them explained:

We have come to tell you that we lesbians are being oppressed outside the movement and inside the movement by a sexist attitude. We want to discuss the lesbian issue with you.[64]

Copies of "The Woman-Identified Woman" were distributed to members of the audience. At the end of the congress, the assembly voted to adopt the set of resolutions put forward in the name of "The Lavender Menance: Gay Liberation Front Women and Radical Lesbians":

Be it resolved that Women's Liberation is a lesbian plot.

Resolved that whenever the label lesbian is used against the movement collectively or against women individually, it is to be affirmed, not denied.

In all discussions of birth control, homosexuality must be included as a legitimate method of contraception.

All sex education curricula must include lesbianism as a valid, legitimate form of sexual expression and love.[65]

Chief among the so-called "takeover feminists" was Kate Millett, author of *Sexual Politics*, which was hailed in its day, as the ideology of sex/class warfare by those who claimed to be radicals of the women's movement. Advance copies of this Ph.D thesis had been circulating among magazine and newspaper editors during the spring of 1970. Millett's editor, Betty Prashker had been impressed. "I felt the scales drop from my eyes," she would remember. *Sexual Politics* was the most exciting stuff she had seen in years.[66]

Spurred on by her editor's enthusiasm, Millett had roared forth in a sustained burst of creativity, working up to eighteen hours a day, the cultural analysis developing into an indictment of thousands of years of "the patriarchy," the rule of men over women. Freud was the archvillian, romantic love a trap, chivalry a "sporting kind of reparation." Millett would eventually tell a reporter:

I was really afraid to write this book so much. I used to go crazy with terror about it.[67]

The fiftieth anniversary of women's suffrage was coming up that summer, perfect timing for full-scale pieces on the women's movement.

Sexual Politics cited that a sexual revolution would require, perhaps first of all, an end of traditional sexual inhibitions and taboos, particularly those that most threaten patriarchal monogamous marriage: homosexuality, "illegitamacy," adolescent, pre- and extra-marital sexuality. The negative aura with which sexual activity has generally been surrounded would necessarily be eliminated, together with the double standard of sexual freedom, and one uncorrupted by the crass and exploitive economic bases of traditional sexual alliances. Primarily, however, a sexual revolution would bring the institution of patriarchy to an end, abolishing both the ideology of male supremacy and the traditional socialization by which it is upheld in matters of status, role and temperament.

It seems unlikely, if Millett's thesis took effect, that all this could take place without drastic effect upon the patriarchal family. The abolition of sex role and the complete economic independence of women would undermine both its authority and its financial structure. An important corollary would be the end of the present chattel status and denial of rights to minors. The collective professionalization (and consequent improvement) of the care of the young, also involved, would further undermine family structure while contributing to freedom of women. Marriage might generally be replaced by voluntary association, if such is desired. Were a sexual revolution completed, the problem of overpopulation might, through the emancipation of women, cease to be the insoluble dilemma it now appears.[68] Millett responded to her new publicity with wit:

'I wrote it with a bang, bang, bang. Like wow! A triple orgasm.'

'My mother had a college degree and do you know what she was offered for her first job? Demonstrating potato peelers.'

'You go around feeling neurotic and then, Christ, you find out that you are not alone.'

Yes of course she belonged to a full range of women's liberation groups, from NOW to the Radicalesbians. 'You don't want me to print that, surely?' asked one sympatheitic reporter. 'No?'[69]

All the attention was heady stuff for the obscure, thirty-five year old academic and wife. All Millett could think about was how proud her mother must be. Helen Millett, who valued literacy above all, could see her daughter's book stacked high and bold in the front windows of the St. Paul bookstores, her talent extolled in all the magazines. *Time* planned to do a cover story about the movement and asked Kate questions on the book. Full of enthusiasm, Millett even shared ideas for the magazine's cover, suggesting a picture of Betty Friedan or a crowd of women. This was the big issue that she (along with every other feminist she knew) was counting on to carry the message of the movement to women all over the country, to every elite person on earth.

However, when *Time* hit the stands, there was no picture of Betty Friedan or a mass of joyously united women Millett had expected. Instead, was an artist's rendering of her – "with a smoking, biblical rage in her dark eyes, a deathless fury that could have pulverized the temple of the Philistines into dust." The article announced:

Until this year, with the publication of a remarkable book called Sexual Politics, the movement had no coherent theory to buttress its intuitive passions, no ideologue to provide chapter and verse for its assault on patriarchy.[70]

Suddenly, there she was – Kate Millett, the new "high priestess," the "Mao Tse-tung of Women's Liberation," as *Time* called her.

Upset that *Time* had now declared her to "stardom" to the detriment of everyone else, the wrath of all manner of feminists descended on Millett's head. This was the least of her concerns. The media wanted answers:

How the patriarchy that had ruled the world for so many centuries was directly responsible, not only for all power imbalance, for the domination of one human being over another, but for the slaughter then raging in Southeast Asia, and for all the wars that had afflicted humanity since the dawn of time.[71]

Unlike the feminist Virginia Woolf before her, Millett did not merely suggest that male hegemony might be the major cause of war. Millett was sure. "Always sure...a quality that would lose her several potential admirers in the years to come."[72] Was *Time* right? Perhaps Millett, not Friedan – more precisely illustrated the latest, hottest wave, the movement that would demand as its philosophical province not just the arena of women's rights but the entire history of the world.[73]

In November, an anonymous underground pamphlet appeared, accusing Millett of damaging lesbians on her "media trip." It was provoked, she was sure, by a comment attributed to her in a *Life* magazine article. When questioned about her membership in Radicalesbians, Millett, according to the magazine, responded: "I'm not into that." She would be absolutely positive that she never said such a thing to the *Life* reporter.

This issue came back to Millett with a vengeance at Columbia University, where she was one of three presenters. The topic of discussion was sexual liberation and Millett had been asked to address the subject of bisexuality. She planned to deliver a fairly standard moderator's speech, sandwiched, as she was between a representative of the still mostly underground homosexual community and someone who would express the feminist point of view. "They're going to zap us tonight," a friend whispered as Millett climbed up onto the stage. After she spoke the floor opened for questions. Teresa Juarez, a member of the Radicalesbians, shouted a question directly for Millett:

'Bisexuality, as we all know...' The woman chiseled the words.

*"Bisexuality is a cop-out!' 'Are you a lesbian?'
Silence. 'Say it. Are you?'*[74]

In the years that followed, Millett would insist again and again that she had never denied being a lesbian, that within her circles, within the openly lesbian Daughters of Bilitis, for instance, she had spoken of it several times – often, as she was sure was the case, when reporters were present. She was in fact living a bisexual life. "Noticeable, privileged, crowned," she had been photographed in *Life* kissing her husband, just as if she were an ordinary, conventional, happy housewife![75]

'Are you a lesbian? Say it!'

At that awful moment, Kate Millett could not have imagined what the ugly consequences of her answer would be. She knew that most everyone in the women's movement was nervous about accusations of lesbianism. Many feminists – Betty Friedan and Susan Brownmiller among them – feared that the taint of homosexuality could destroy whatever progress had been made. And what if Kate Millett, now heralded far and wide as the new leader (priestess), was to make a public "confession of lesbianism?" With the last strength that she had she answered:

'Yes, I am a lesbian.'

In December, *Time* offered their readers a "second look" at women's lib. The most extensive attack on *Sexual Politics* and on Millett was by the famous critic Irving Howe. He ripped into the book as "a farrago of blunders, distortions, vulgarities and plain nonsense." Millett was guilty of "historical reductionism ...crude simplification...middle class parochialism...sexual monism... methodological sloppiness...arrogant ultimatism...comic ignorance."[76] Another article read:

The disclosure is bound to discredit her as a spokeswoman for her cause, cast further doubt on her theories and reinforce the views of those skeptics who routinely dismiss all liberationists as lesbians.[77]

To some feminists, many of them wives and mothers, these were words that reached beyond the pale.

An emergency meeting was held in NOW member Dolores Alexander's apartment, where Betty Friedan also lived. But Friedan wasn't present at the session. "I guess we all knew," Dolores would recall, "where Betty stood on the lesbian issue." That night 25 women thrashed out a press statement for a news conference. "This is a real test of sisterhood," as Ivy Bottini, president of New York NOW, put it. "We've got to stand behind Kate."[78] But before the scheduled press conference the issue hit the front pages provoked by radical lesbians.

It happened in New York on Saturday, December 12, at a march held in freezing sleet in support of abortion and child-care centers. It had been called by a new group, the Women's Strike Coalition, organized by Betty Friedan. Friedan, Gloria Steinem, Flo Kennedy, and Kate Millett were slated to speak. They had just climbed up on the flatbed truck parked infront of Gracie Mansion, the mayor's residence, when a speckling of pale purple – like pointillist dabs of paint – began to glow here and there in the crowd. Some women – no one was sure how many – were wearing and distributing lavender armbands to the entire crowd. They were also handing out leaflets. Marcia Cohen describes the event:

'We're ALL wearing lavender lesbian armbands today. It is not one woman's sexual experience that is under attack,' the leaflet said. 'It is the freedom of all women to openly state values that fundamentally challege the basic structure of patriarchy. If they succeed in scaring us with words like 'dyke' or 'lesbian' or 'bisexual,' they'll have won.

AGAIN. They'll have divided us. AGAIN. Sexism will have triumphed. AGAIN....They can call us all lesbians until such time as there is no more stigma attached to women loving women. SISTERHOOD IS POWERFUL!!' [79]

Betty Friedan was handed an armband:

They then watched her carefully as Betty's deep-brown eyes gazed at the flimsy lavender cloth in her hand. Ivy saw her thoughtfully consider the symbol – its implications – and then make her decision. Betty let the piece of purple cloth fall through her fingers to the floor of the flatbed truck. To Ivy, who had helped engineer the lavender display and who would go on to play an active role in gay rights, this was the turning point, the moment when the women's movement took on a life of its own, moved beyond Betty Friedan's 'civil rights' structure, leaving the creator of NOW – respected, admired, feared, and sometimes hated – behind.[80]

Friedan had already declared in the magazine *Social Policy*:

Sexual politics is highly dangerous and diversionary, and may even provide good soil for fascist, demagogic appeals based on hatred...we cannot permit the image of women to be developed by the homosexual. [81]

At that moment, Friedan did more than let that "lavender herring" drop. This coalition – her coalition – had never asked her permission to make that pro-lesbian statement. Immediately, she phoned the offices of the coalition and resigned. If ever they used her name again, she informed them in no uncertain terms, she would sue. Friedan hauled Millett into the nearest bar and told her, "You blew it."[82]

Less than a week later, the feminist remnant held a press conference in front of the Washington Square Methodist Church, with banners and posters decorating the event – "Kate is Great," "We Stand Together as Women Regardless of Sexual Preference," "Is the Statute of Liberty a Lesbian Too?" In a trembling voice, Millett read her statement:

Women's liberation and homosexual liberation are both struggling towards a common goal: a society free from defining and categorizing people by virtue of gender and/or sexual perference. 'Lesbian' is a label used as a psychic weapon to keep women locked into their male-defined 'feminin role.' The essence of that role is that a woman is defined in terms of her relationship to men. A woman is called a lesbian when she functions autonomously. Women's autonomy is what women's liberation is all about.'[83]

Infinite Orgasm

Sex is the lubricant of the consumer economy, but in order to fulfill that function the very character of human sexuality itself must undergo special conditioning. Its connection with reproduction, which is potentially disruptive, must be severed. Its anti-social aspects, human susceptibility to passion, obsession, jealousy, and guilt must be purged. Sexuality which is a feature of the whole personality must be localized and controlled. Fantasy, on the other hand, must be expanded, elaborated and exploited. The promotion of sex which had begun with De Sade has reached its apogee in a civilization which gives tangible expression to every form of human sexuality, every perversion, every paraphilia – except passion... The new opiate of the people...is the discipline of the orgasm, not just any orgasm but the perfect orgasm, regular, spontaneous, potent and reliable. The cathartic function of sex has replaced all other rituals of purification. The blessed are laid-back, into their bodies, in touch with themselves. They shrink from no penetration, they feel no invasion of self, they fear nothing and regret nothing, they defy jealousy. The regular recurrence of orgasm provides proof that they are in the state of grace. To object that orgasm is itself inadequate to this high purpose is to expose oneself as orgastically impotent, for sex religion, like all others, relies on self-fulfilling prophecies. To the faithful, who believe that orgasm will release tension, make all potentialities accessible, dissipate discontent and aggression and stabilize the ego in its right relation to the world, all these are achieved when the sacred duty is discharged. Those who rise from orgasm sad and angry, disappointed or bored, are themselves at fault. They have held something back, harbored deep skepticism: they are the self-destructive.[84]

Germaine Greer, 'Sex and Destiny: The Politics of Human Fertility'

A great deal of information has recently been circulated regarding the political basis of female frigidity; women are sexually repressed by patriarchal institutions which enforce fear, dislike, and confusion about female sexual and reproductive anatomy in both men and women. Phallus-worship is well represented in myth, painting, sculpture, and modern bedroom practices: clitoris-worship and/or non-reproductive vagina-worship is not.[85]

Phyllis Chesler, 'Women and Madness,' 1972

According to Phyllis Chesler, clinical case histories, psychological and sociological surveys and studies – and women's lives – have documented the extent to which most twentieth-century women have not been having orgasms. She refers to psychoanalyst, Marie Robinson, who has characterized the proper female orgasm as one in which "the woman may be rendered unconscious for up to three minutes."[86]

In *Sexual Politics*, Kate Millett, quotes from Masters and Johnson:

If a female who is capable of having regular orgasms is properly stimulated within a short period after her first climax, she will, in most instances, be capable of having a second, third, fourth, and even a fifth and sixth orgasm before she is satiated. As contrasted with the male's usual inability to have more than one...[87]

The average female with optimal arousal will usually be satisfied with three to five manually-induced orgasms; whereas mechanical stimulation, as with the electric vibrator, is less tiring and induces her to go on to long simulative sessions of an hour or more during which she can have twenty to fifty consecutive orgasms. She will stop only when totally exhausted.[88]

Millett cites Dr. Mary Jane Sherfey's findings:

No doubt the most far reaching hypothesis extrapolated from these biological data is the existence of a universal and physically normal condition of woman's inability ever to reach complete sexual satiation in the presence of the most intense, repetitive orgasmic experiences, no matter how produced. Theoretically, a woman could go on having orgasms indefinitely if physical exhaustion did not intervene. Given women's extraordinary biological potentiality for sexual arousal and pleasure, no form of sexual association would have satisfied it less than monogamy.[89]

Chesler sees women's sexual appetite varying from "insatiable" to "not really needing orgasms as much as they need love, maternity, and fine silverware." She cites that psychoanalytic tradition has viewed "neurosis" and even "psychosis" as stemming from sexual repression and that most clinicians have tried hard to help their female patients "achieve" heterosexual orgasms – usually by counselling a joyous acceptance of the female role as envisioned and enforced by men: as Madonna-housewife and mother, or as Magdalene Earth Goddess. Showing disdain for all things male, she points out that even sexual liberationist pioneers, such as Wilhelm Reich, have posited the primacy of vaginal eroticism, and viewed bisexuality and lesbianism as "regressive" or "infantile." Moreover, according to Chesler:

...most clinicians have not thought deeply about the sociopolitical – or the psychological – conditions that are necessary for female sexual self-definition. Women can never be sexually actualized as long as men control the means of production and reproduction. Women have had to barter their sexuality (or their capacity for sexual pleasure) for economic survival and maternity. Female frigidity as we know it will cease only when such bartering ceases. Most women cannot be 'sexual' as long as prostitution, rape, and patriarchal marriage exist, with such attendent concepts and practices as 'illegitimate' pregnancies, enforced maternity, 'non-maternal' paternity, and sexual deprivation of 'aging' women. From a psychological point of view, female frigidity will cease when female-children are surrounded by and can observe non-frigid female adults.[90]

In contrast to feminist ideology, Adrian Forsyth, writes in *A Natural History of Sex*, "equality is not a biological design." Sexual behavior almost inevitably entails substantial conflicts of interest between males and males, females and females and males and females. The sexes differ markedly and fundamentally. A woman may produce 400 eggs in a lifetime, but she may rear at most a few dozen children at an exhaustive physiological cost. A man can produce millions of sperm every day and sire, in theory at least, thousands of offspring at an exceedingly small physiological cost. A woman is almost certain of her genetic relationship with her children; a male is never completely certain. Such fundamental asymmetries in the costs and benefits of sexual behavior are responsible for the complex array of tactical and strategic relationships that characterize interaction within and between sexes.[91]

Many (perhaps all feminists) have wondered why males exist! By definition, a male is nothing more than an individual that produces small sex cells, the gametes used to make a new individual. No other masculine excrescence's are necessary or sufficient to distinguish him from the female, the one that produces large gametes. The average male gamete, or sperm, is usually dwarfed by the female egg, and to some, it seems as if the male is a parasite on the female. Both sexes get the same genetic return from fertilization, but the material contribution of the male to the new offspring is a fraction of that of the female. This fundamental dimorphism in investment often extends into the realm of parental care, the cost of pregnancy and child-rearing being largely a female responsibility. Females bear the burden. Says Forsyth, "This is vexatious to those who believe that nature is just."[92]

In considering the biological role of orgasm, Forsyth observes that at the rate sperm swim, they would take five to six hours to traverse to the female egg, but usually sperm are present in the fallopian tubes within one to two hours. Here sperm is aided in its journey by seminal fluids produced in the seminal vesicles. Prostrate and Cowper's glands, also add alkaline secretions, which buffer the sperm against the acidity of the vagina and stimulate the sperm into activity. They make up the bulk of the fluid in the ejaculate.[93] In the case of humans, few of the sperm ever make it to the egg. Half of them may swim up the wrong fallopian tube, and there is attrition along the way; of some 300 million sperm in the ejaculate, only 2,000 are likely to contact the egg. On the tip of the sperm is an enzyme that must dissolve a way into the egg. As soon as one sperm has penetrated, the egg changes its physiology and bars entry of all others.[94]

Semen in humans and other animals is full of prostaglandins, hormonal compounds that serve many functions in different parts of the body. The rich concentrations of prostaglandis in male semen cause muscular contractions of the uterus that move the sperm toward the egg. This explains why sperm travel faster than they can swim. Prostaglandin-induced contractions must pump the sperm ahead. A high portion of males who are infertile have a low concentration of prostaglandins in their sperm.[95]

Thus orgasms are motivational devices. For males, the adaptive payoff is obvious. Males that are self-rewarded by orgasm in frequent copulation will in general have a higher fitness than those that lie around and sleep. Biologists, however, have had difficulty in applying this simple logic to females. The conundrum is this: if males are more than capable of inseminating all females, then a female presumably does not require a device that causes her to seek out many copulation's. Indeed, since too many or inappropriately timed pregnancies could reduce the total fitness of a female, then orgasms might even be maladaptive.[96] Biological anthropologist, Donald Symons, who has researched the female orgasm, concluded that the female orgasm is not an adaptation of females per se. It is merely a by-product of intense selection for the male orgasm. This selection and the neural information required by the act of copulation have led to a condition of genital sensitivity in both sexes. Given enough stimulation, Symons argues, any female primate can experience orgasm simply as a building and release of neural stimuli. In his words, "The human female's capacity for orgasm is no more an adaptation than the ability to read."[97]

Forsyth, further claims there is no evidence in favor of the idea that female orgasm and increased sexual activity are important in maintaining a pair bond. Mammalogist, Devra Kleiman analyzed the phenomenon of mammalian monogamy and concluded that sexual activity "occurs infrequently and thus must play a minor role in pair-bond maintenance, and also that "there are no more intense sociosexual interactions in species exhibiting long-term pair bonds than in polygamous forms."[98] Possibly in the same sense that male orgasm motivates males to copulate, we might assume (perhaps incorrectly) that orgasm also evolved to increase a female's interest in, and thus her rate of, copulation. How could increased female copulation enhance fitness? The effect of increased female copulation on polygeny could increase paternity uncertainty in multimale troops. Males would be less able to ascertain which offspring were their own and thus less able to discriminate selectively against unrelated infants. The net result would be to raise the average female's fitness. It has been suggested that this explains why lions copulate so frequently.[99]

To support the argument that orgasm is a motivational device designed to increase a female's tendency to copulate, orgasm should be most developed in species which copulate frequently and females in such species should initiate sexual activity. In species with very low female copulation rates and little variation in male quality or both, we expect less solicitation and less orgasm. Frequent sex was not expected in and, indeed, is not a feature of the lives of tamarins, marmosets, titis or night monkeys, all of which are known for monogamy and high male parental care. It is in promiscuous monkeys such as various macaques and chimpanzees, that orgasmic behavior was first documented and shown to be most comparable to that of human females. But says Forsyth:

...this correlation is weak at best and would be hard to establish, since it is difficult to quantify female orgasm in other species. The report of female orgasmic behavior in gorillas argues against orgasm and increased copulation rate as being ways to test males.[100]

These are all complicated scenarios, and none of them seems to capture any generalizations about female orgasm. A more mechanical explanation may turn out to be more general. Experimenters have found that orgasm in human females results in a sharp change in air pressure in the uterus. Before orgasm, the air pressure in the uterus is positive, but at orgasm, it reverses, and suction is created. This would have the effect of drawing sperm up into the uterus and increasing the chance of fertilization. In other words, orgasm would be a form of female mate choice, allowing the female to exert some control over who fertilized her eggs. Since the uterus can be a formidable barrier to sperm, orgasm under female control could be an effective device for enabling her to decide the fate of the male ejaculate according to her interests.[101]

Concludes Forsyth:

So it may all come down to something as prosaic and simple as suction. But that does not diminish the true evolutionary import of the female orgasm: In orgasm, females may take a proximate pleasure in achieving an ultimately adaptive goal.[102]

Not that orgasm by male stimulation was what either Chesler or Millett had in mind. Imagine the dawning of a new sexual era where human intimacy is replaced by the mechanical vibrator. In this self-autonomous feminist utopia, who would be foolish enough to want a husband?

REAL Women and Feminists for Life

A group called "Women Interested in Toppling Consumption Holidays" (WITCH), mostly targeted marriage and traditional family values. In *Why We Lost the ERA*, Jane Mansbridge, labeled them a "guerrilla theater group." At one metropolitan bridal fair, WITCH distributed a pamphlet beginning, "Marriage is a dehumanizing institution – legal whoredom for women."[103] On a Mother's Day, WITCH solemnly incanted these stanzas from a "card by Hellmark":

Every year we set aside a very special day to remind you, Martyr Dear that home is where you stay. While hubby challenges the world his wonders to perform, you cook his meals, clean his home and keep his bedside warm. Now look upon your daughter will she too be enslaved to a man, a home, and family or can she still be saved?[104]

Such rhetoric, combined with the lesbianization and radicalization of feminism, made the splintering of the women's movement highly probable. The inclusion of abortion on demand as a central ideological tenet made breakup inevitable. Established in 1972, Feminists for Life (FFL) is an American, nonsectarian, nonpartisan, grassroots organization that seeks equality for all human beings and champions the needs of women. They see themselves as "women and men who support justice and equality." They oppose all forms of violence and "proudly continue in the pro-life tradition of their feminist foremothers, who recognized abortion as the ultimate act of violence against women and children." FFL is allied with the 1.3 million members of the anti-abortion group National Coalition for Life.

In Canada, by 1982, the new NAC president had acknowledged that the Committee was split into two camps: "expansionists" were accused of left-wing political union domination; the other group was considered old liners and more business women.[105] From NAC's vantage, "female anti-feminist groups" claimed neither of these camps served them. Thus groups, such as REAL Women, grew to challenge the whole criteria for Women's Program funding in Canada.[106]

REAL (Realistic, Equal, Active for Life) Women of Canada is a non-partisan, inter-denominational organization, which believes the social and economic problems of women should be resolved by taking into consideration the effects on family life and society as a whole. They see themselves as an alternative:

We're filling a need that has long existed. None of us has a corner on the truth. Thus, the diversity of views and approaches should be regarded as an advantage to women, as well as an indication of our tremendous diversity, independence and resourcefulness.

While supporting women's equality, they however, critique radical separationist feminists – "we seem to have overlooked one very important fact – namely our need, which has remained unchanged over the years, for family, children and other relationships."[107] As Canada moves forward, REAL Women claims to be in the vanguard of change for a fairer, more compassionate, caring, pro-family society:[108]

WE PROMOTE...equality for all women including homemakers. WE BELIEVE...the family is the most important unit in society. WE SPEAK...for traditional values of marriage and family life. Our view is that the family, which is now undergoing serious strain, is the most important unit in Canadian society. We believe that the fragmentation of the Canadian family is one of the major causes of disorder in society today.

REAL Women's objectives are as follows:

To reaffirm that the family is society's most important unit, since the nurturing of its members is best accomplished in the family setting.

To promote the equality, advancement and well being of women, recognizing them as interdependent members of society, whether in the family, workplace or community.

To promote, secure and defend legislation which upholds the Judeo-Christian understanding of marriage and family life.

To support government and social policies that make homemaking possible for women who, out of necessity, would otherwise have to take employment outside the home.

To support the right to life of all innocent individuals from conception to natural birth. Before women can have equality with men, we must first have equality among ourselves and this means a tolerance and respect for the differing views of other women. This also means a recognition, not only of the dignity of the individual, but also of the fact that women have always required more than just one voice to speak for our concerns.

REAL Women speaks for women who support traditional family values. Society may change, but society's need for strong, stable families remains.

Jane Mansbridge writes that beginning around 1976, the STOP ERA movement acquired a third constituency, as fundamentalist groups began to enter politics and focus on "woman's issues" like the Equal Rights Amendment. Many of these fundamentalist women were full-time homemakers. But unlike most homemakers, their church activities had given them experience in public speaking and approaching strangers. Their churches and their own convictions demanded an interventionist, missionary stance toward anyone who had not accepted Jesus Christ as Savior. While most Americans confronted with someone who does not share their religious or political views avoid the subject, missionary fundamentalists deliberately bring the controversial subject into conversation, challenge the unbeliever, present personal testimony, and work actively for conversion. These skills and the evangelical enthusiasm that gave them life made it relatively easy for such women to enter the political arena. Moreover, the churches were already organized. They had pre-existing meeting places, buses, and claims on their member's time and money.[109] The actions of REAL Women representatives (described earlier), when ostracized by NAC, epitomize this principled determination.

By briefly looking at a few reasons for the failed ERA, we can get a better understanding of the mobilized power of these "homemaker-inclusive," "feminist" organizations and of changing perceptions among men. Mansbridge raises three factors. First, while the ERA would not have had any direct negative effect on family life, it was nonetheless a by-product of a movement that was profoundly opposed to traditional conceptions of how families should be organized. Second, homemakers as a group were ripe for such an appeal because they had recently lost considerable status in society. Third, the ERA would in fact have deprived homemakers of some traditional protections and benefits (like the tender years presumption). While feminists intended to raise new and presumably better protections in place of the old, these were not strictly mandated by the ERA. Homemakers could feel, therefore, that they were being asked "to relinquish tangible benefits in exchange for a vague promise of dubious value".[110]

Although, NOW's final founding statement of purpose, in 1966, stated: "We believe that true partnership between the sexes demands a different concept of marriage, an equitable sharing of the responsibilities of home and children and of the uneconomic burdens of their support,"[111] the word "equitable" was not nearly as strong as the more radical groups' demands for "equal" sharing. NOW's "different concept" of marriage still implied an androgynous division of labor, in which men took half the responsibility for child care and housework and women took half the responsibility for bringing in money. This position became not just an implication but an article of faith for later "homemaker-exclusive" feminists. This was not the case for NOW in its beginnings. We have seen the fall of Betty Friedan and the rise of Kate Millett, in 1971, and all that this entailed. Prior to what I call the "lesbianization" of NOW, its founding members were careful not to take a formal position against the homemaker. In using the phrase "equitable sharing," they had made provision for a 100/0 per cent division if sufficient "credit" were given the person who did the 100 per cent of the childcare and housework. Also they laced the founding statement with other phrases and sentences that gave support to the full-time homemaker.[112] However, in the 60s NOW was one of the more conservative feminist groups and the ERA debate of the 80s mostly focused on other groups that gave the life of a homemaker a shorter shrift.

Students for a Democratic Society (SDS), first organized in 1967 to work towards "women's liberation," suggested that the Society "work on behalf of all women for communal child care, wide dissemination of contraceptives, easily available abortions, and equal sharing of housework."[113] Most other women's groups also pushed for reforms – like day-care centers, shared housework, and legal abortion – that would help women cast off their traditional role of full-time homemaker and join the paid labor force.[114] The conflict between feminists and homemakers was a genuine conflict of interest, which could not easily be resolved by compromise. The very existence of full-time homemakers was incompatible with many goals of the women's movement, like the equal sharing of political and economic power. Mansbridge summarized the dilemma as follows:

Women can never hold half the economically and politically powerful positions in the country if a greater proportion of women than men withdraw from competition for those positions. More important, if even 10 per cent of American women remain full-time homemakers, this will reinforce traditional views of what women ought to do and encourage other women to become full-time homemakers at least while their children are very young. If women plan to drop out of the labor force while their children are young, they will choose careers that are interruptible, that convert easily to part-time work, that do not demand either long hours or geographic mobility, and that whenever possible have some connection to the tasks of motherhood (like teaching or nursing). Occupations that have these characteristics will remain stereotyped as 'women's occupations,' and for the foreseeable future they will pay less than men's occupations that require comparable training. As we have seen, about half the difference between men's and women's wages is due to the sex segregation of occupations, age (women are in the paid labor force when they are young or old, not in their prime productive years), and interrupted careers. If women disproportionately take time off from their careers to have children, or if they work less hard than men at their careers while their children are young, this will put them at a competitive disadvantage to men whose wives do all the homemaking and child care. This will show up especially clearly in the most powerful and best positions in the society. Thus, the more full-time homemakers there are, the harder it will be to break traditional expectations that homemaking ought to be a woman's career. This means that no matter how any individual feminists might feel about child care and housework, the movement as a whole had reasons to discourage full-time homemaking.[115]

Most feminists also had personal reasons for rejecting the notion that women should "specialize" in housework and childcare. Typically, college-educated, very few of these women saw homemaking as their primary identity. Focusing on images of marriage permeated by scenes of male domination and female subordination, they concluded that married life would always be shaped by this legacy. An "egalitarian marriage" was thus a contradiction in terms. No matter how "liberated" she was, a woman who defined herself as "married" would inevitably slide into roles that carried an inegalitarian heritage, and would adopt, without fully thinking them through, symbols like the bridal veil, or lingerie at the "shower," that reinforced the inegalitarian tradition.[116] In this analysis, if a married woman were to have any hope of developing self-respect or self-confidence, she would have to be at least as independent of her husband as he was of her. This meant having a job as interesting, as demanding, and as well paid as his, not being his unpaid housekeeper and baby-sitter. Gaining economic and political power, as thus strategized, made antagonism between homemakers and feminists almost inevitable.

Opponents of the ERA were acutely aware that its sponsors were generally opposed to homemaking as a career. Phyllis Schafly's very first salvo against the ERA, "What's wrong with 'Equal Rights' for Women?" identified the ERA with *Ms.* magazine, which she characterized as:

...anti-family, anti-children, and pro-abortion. It is a series of sharp-tongued, high-pitched, whining complaints by unmarried women. They view the home as a prison, and the wife and mother as a slave. To these women's libbers, marriage means dirty dishes and dirty laundry. One article lauds a woman's refusal to carry up the family laundry as 'an act of extreme courage.' Another tells how satisfying it is to be a lesbian...Women's lib is a total assault on the role of the American woman as wife and mother, and on the family as the basic unit of society...Women's libbers are trying to make wives and mothers unhappy with their career, make them feel that they are 'second-class citizens' and 'abject slaves.' Women's libbers are promoting Federal 'day-care centers' for babies instead of homes. They are promoting abortions instead of families.[117]

In Illinois, one argued that the ERA is:

...really an attack on the home. It is an attack on motherhood. It says that for a woman to have to be a mother and have to be a housewife is somehow degrading.[118]

In 1977, 42 per cent of American women saw the women's movement as a major cause of family breakdown.[119] By the late 1970s, many full-time homemakers had come to see women who worked for pay as "the enemy," regardless of whether those women were feminists or not. It reflected the fact that the social respect once accorded to homemakers was eroding. While this erosion may have been partly traceable to feminist attacks on housework, Mansbridge concludes, "its primary cause had nothing to do with ideology. Full-time homemaking lost status primarily because high-status women abandoned it."[120]

In 1962, only 37 per cent of all wives worked for pay outside the home. The wives of high school and college-educated men were hardly more likely to work for pay than the wives of men with only a grade school education. Between 1962 and 1978 the proportion of wives working for pay rose from 37 to 58 per cent. This growth was among wives with highly educated husbands, for whom the economic pressures to work were the lowest. Among women whose husbands had only a grade school education, 34 per cent worked for pay both in 1962 and 1978. Among women whose husbands had attended college, 38 per cent worked for pay in 1962, but this had grown to 65 per cent by 1978.[121]

The growing class divergence in whether married women worked for pay was matched by a growing class divergence in how women felt about housework. Between 1957 and 1976 there was no change in the percentage of homemakers with a grade school education who said they "enjoyed" housework. In both years it was about 76 per cent. Among those who attended high school, the per cent who said they enjoyed housework fell from 66 to 54 per cent. Among homemakers who had attended college it fell from 67 to 38 per cent. The same pattern emerged when one looks at career aspirations. Among grade-school educated homemakers, the percentage who said that they had at some point wanted a career actually fell from 30 per cent in 1957 to 15 per cent in 1976. Among high school educated homemakers it rose only slightly, from 37 to 40 per cent. Among college-educated homemakers it rose from 48 to 60 per cent.[122]

The rise of careerism and the declining attraction of housework among educated women was partly a response to changes in job opportunities. For a woman with only a grade school education, homemaking was usually a more pleasant, autonomous, growth-inducing profession than waitressing, cleaning other people's houses, or working as a factory operative, and these alternatives did not improve during the 60s, 70s or 80s and 90s. For women with a college education, homemaking was often more attractive than teaching school or being a secretary, which were the main alternatives in 1960. But homemaking was often far less attractive than the options that had opened up by the late 1970s.

These changes meant that women became less likely to share the same common experiences. At the beginning of the Second Wave women's movement, in 1968, women of all classes found themselves in something like the same boat. Their structural positions either as homemakers or as lower-level employees were similar, and they expressed much the same feeling about their work and their home lives. By 1982, when the ERA went down to defeat, one of the bonds of sisterhood – common experience in the home – was breaking. Says Manbridge:

When employers opened good jobs to women, the beneficiaries were highly educated women who had decided not to become full-time homemakers. The more educated a woman was, the more she benefited from these changes. For less-educated women, homemaking remained the job of choice, but it lost social standing as high-status women abandoned it.[123]

The decision of most college-educated women to pursue careers other than homemaking raised to public consciousness the many disadvantages of work in the home. Highly educated women were trendsetters for their sisters. In the 1950s, to preserve their own self-esteem, they extolled the virtues of work in the home. By 1980, they saw matters quite differently. A job once perceived as noble now seemed distinctly plebeian. Thus, homemakers suffered a tremendous loss in social prestige in two decades. Sociologists call this phenomenon "status degradation." It had happened to these homemakers through no fault of their own. As the paid labor force offered urban, educated women attractive options, the more rural, less educated women found that the world judged the traditional job of homemaking as being less attractive. Middle-class women who chose to stay in the home began to feel declasse. Women's magazines began to print outraged letters from homemakers who now found that they had to describe themselves as "only" a housewife, not only to men but to other women.[124]

Homemakers not only lost a lot of status in the course of the decade preceding the ERA struggle, they lost a number of their traditional protections as well. The divorce rate was increasing, and alimony was decreasing. Many states had instituted "no-fault" divorce laws, which reduced social blame on the husband who tired of his family, and even put pressure on some nurturant women to go along with their husbands' desire to abandon ship. A new ethic had arisen for men, in which hedonistic egotism was no longer encumbered by responsibility. Society was beginning to condone a man leaving his family on the sole grounds that living with them and providing for them made him unhappy.[125] As Barbara Ehrenreich put it:

What was at stake in the battle over the ERA was the legitimacy of women's claim on men's incomes, and for this there was reason enough to fear – and to judge from the intensity of the opposition, fear enough to abandon reason.[126]

It was the ERA's symbolic meaning that frightened the opposition. When Phyllis Schafly said of loveless marriages, "Even though love may go out the window, the obligation should remain, ERA would eliminate that obligation," any reader would assume she meant the ERA's legal impact. But she spelled out her concerns more clearly when she insisted that the ERA would say, "Boys, supporting your wives isn't your responsibility anymore," and then they could no longer see it as their duty. It is what the ERA would "say," not what it would do, that really concerned Schafly and the rest of the opposition. In this deep sense the struggle over the ERA was indeed a "struggle over symbols." When a proponent of the ERA argued on a televised debate with Schafly that the idea that a woman can sit home and be supported by her husband has long died out, she was not only wrong as a matter of fact but was reinforcing doubts about the ERA among the millions of women whose husbands were supporting them.[127]

Furthermore, on interracial marriage, homosexuality, and abortion, the gap between homemakers and working women increased markedly over these years. These concerns meant that homemakers were less likely than working women to join feminist organizations like NOW. When NOW did a sample survey of its members in 1974, only 17 per cent described themselves as homemakers, whereas 52 per cent of all women over 18 in the US described themselves that way in that year.[128] Schlafly directed her pitch to homemakers, pointing out that the Civil Rights Act of 1964 already guaranteed equal pay for equal work. She concluded by describing the "two very different groups of women lobbying for ERA":

One group is the women's liberationists. Their motive is totally radical. They hate men, marriage and children. They are out to destroy morality and the family. They look upon husbands as the exploiters, children as an evil to be avoided (by abortion if necessary) and the family as an institution which keeps women in 'second-class citizenship' or even 'slavery'.[129]

The second group was business and professional women "who have felt the keen edge of discrimination in their employment." Citing her own experience with discrimination, Schlafly said she supported this group in their effort to eliminate injustice, but she argued that everything necessary could be done through the Civil Rights Act and the Equal Employment Opportunity Act, which would not "take away fundamental rights and benefits from the rest of women." Just as an exaggeration of the ERA's effect on working women became the major argument for the proponents, because it appealed not only to the general public but to a particular large and angry constituency, so an exaggeration of the ERA's effect on homemakers became, for the same reasons, the first major argument of the opponents.[130]

Regarding the current same-sex marriage dispute, much can be learned from the ERA struggle. A huge lesson is the importance of symbolism to both sides. The same-sex marriage issue cannot be isolated from the past forty years of marriage bashing and attempted separation strategy, by the very lesbian movement that is now demanding inclusion. Against the forty plus year history of Second Wave feminism, it now appears untenable that the radical feminist lesbian interests have anything positive to contribute to heterosexual women's interests. Much more will be raised in defense of this conclusion. However, for the remainder of the book, unless stated otherwise, the terms feminist, women's liberationist and radical feminist will be used interchangeably to connote the pro-lesbian, post Betty Friedan, women's movement. The National Organization For Women (NOW) and the National Action Committee on the Status of Women (NAC) are typical agencies falling under this generic feminist label. Where *feminism* is associated with other "women's organizations," such as REAL Women and Feminists For Life, the term will be qualified to appropriately differentiate these organizations by ideology and goals from radical feminism.

Politics of Oppression and Patriarchy

In *The Miracle of Lesbianism*, Sally Gearhart states that "Exclusive heterosexuality has to be understood as a perversion of [humanities] natural state." She quotes with approval Janis Kelly's contention that "...where women are concerned, highest development of the ability to love can occur only in a homosexual context." Her attitude toward men is openly hostile:

We are tired of being buffer states of conciliation between men; they can either find love and care within themselves for each other, or they can continue without us down their accelerating conveyor belt to destruction.[131]

She interprets the church's emphasis on the nuclear family as an expression of hatred toward lesbians and women:

The churches are our most up-front pushers of the sex-role habit, of daddy-mommy-baby habit. They peddle the drug daily.[132]

She rejects the authority of the church as a form of patriarchal oppression, which is reinforced by doctrinal formulations of worship, sin, charity, heaven, judgment, and grace. Gearhart says:

Ultimately the church as we know it cannot be reformed; it must die. So must the Trinitarian theology on which it is based.[133]

Although I have a yearning to debunk the "miracle of lesbianism" right here, an analysis of the roles of females and males as described in Scripture will be delayed to Chapter 4 and the issues surrounding gay Christian theology will be addressed in Chapter 5.

In the anthology *Lesbianism and Women's Movement*, mentioned before, Margret Small claims:

Men justify this male-beneficent organization of women's labor through the creed, the 'ideology of heterosexuality,' which 'says it is natural for women to ...take care of men.' Heterosexuality is 'not merely an act in relation to impregnation, but the dominant ideology' which defines women as 'appendages of men.' It is not 'reproduction itself' which determines the social organization which places men above women. 'The ideology of heterosexuality' does that, 'not the simple act of intercourse.'[134]

Seeing heterosexuality as an "ideology" – an influential, political idea – was important in the move to question it. And distinguishing a socially defined heterosexuality from women and men's acts of reproductive intercourse is central to the feminist analysis of heterosexual history.

"Lesbians," writes Small, "are outside of the reality which heterosexual ideology explains." Lesbians therefore "have the potential for developing an alternative ideology, not limited by heterosexuality." She stresses:

Heterosexual ideology limits our vision of any alternative sexed, erotic community, just as 'bourgeois ideology' naturalizes the social organization of capitalism, thwarting any sense of a possible, viable alternative to that system of production. And since the 'assumptions of heterosexual ideology,' have existed far longer than bourgeois ideology, hetero assumptions are even more difficult to question. You have to create the space that stands outside of all the boundaries of heterosexuality – assumptions about the family, about marriage, about motherhood, about housework, about childrearing, about rape, about illegitimacy, about spinsterhood – about everything that has to do with the relationships between men and women. To stand outside of heterosexual ideology and to develop an alternative way that male-female relationships could exist is an incredibly creative act.[135]

Phyllis Chesler, further describes this "creative" act as a "sex war":

To the extent to which feminism is conceived of as a cooperative rather than a competitive ideology; to the extent to which it is ritual, tribal, and pleasure-oriented, rather than unique, individual, and heroic-death-oriented – it is feared as 'barbaric' and 'primitive,' or 'fantastic,' by women as well as men. Certainly I fear it, if the 'rituals' are anything less than bold and true, if rituals concern mediocrity and defeat, rather than power, pleasure, and self-defined works of the imagination.[136]

Chesler asks:

Is the American feminist movement a 'return of the repressed,' is it an old religion, an old polity, whose time has mysteriously, impersonally, come round again? Or is it genuinely new mythology, technologically rendered, whose consequences are un-

foreseen? Will the structures of human psychology remain unchanged if women should 'win' the sex war – should directly control the means of production and reproduction? Or if men should become social and biological mothers? Or if women ceased being the psycho-biological representations of birth – and, consequently, of death? Or if women became biological mothers and social fathers? Or if a communist-sexual revolution really succeeded? Or if sexual gender ceased to exist as a significant, identifying dimension? Can women 'win' the sex war, or banish such a war entirely, without becoming the dominant sex? If women were to dominate, would biological men then be oppressed as biological women have been – and if so, why should this matter to women? There must be some good or at least some overwhelming reasons why the injustice of female oppression has never mattered enough to men for them to banish it.[137]

Finally, Chesler gets to the feminist bottom line:

What is the feminist method? Given our conditioning as women, can we ever become feminist revolutionaries (or human beings), without becoming lesbians?[138]

For Chesler, women cannot wage any sort of revolution if they are "psychosexually bound to men or marriage or full-time child care." She concludes, "As women, we will never be allowed full emotional and sexual expression unless we control the means of production and reproduction."[139] Although abortion is central to this vision of *liberation*, we will find in Chapter 7 that the majority of women who have abortions do so *against* their personal wish, but do so in *subservience* to an unwilling potential father or grandparent. The sad irony of feminism is the extent to which heterosexual women have been duped by the feminist-defined "oppression of patriarchy" and then sold in exchange a societal package of greater "oppression" (uncommitted sexual partners and husbands) and "violence" (undesired abortions).

A glimpse of "psychosexual bondage" and "oppression of patriarchy" as seen by feminists is described by Sonia Johnson:

All women are battered women in patriarchy. Every woman born is in an abusive relationship with men as a class and with their system since the raison d'etre of all men's institutions – political, legal, educational, religious, economic, and social – is to achieve and perpetuate the slavery of women and dominion of men.[140]

A man intent on dehumanizing a woman, for instance, often tries to isolate her, to control what she does. He may harass her economically by trying to prevent her from getting or keeping a job, making her ask for money, giving her an allowance, or taking any money she makes. He is likely to force her into sexual acts against her will, attacking the sexual parts of her body, raping her, and generally treating her as a sex object. And, of course, physical abuse is standard: he beats her, throws her down, twists her arm, trips, bites, pushes, shoves, slaps, chokes, pulls her hair, punches, kicks, grabs, and/or uses a weapon against her. [141]

In the final analysis, Johnson sees the patriarchal wife, by this time in our history, as almost genetically bred to be emotionally and mentally subservient to men.

The wife "finds this view of herself and of her situation all too reasonable." She has deeply internalized this propaganda, is profoundly brainwashed to believe it all. So she placates, praises, pleads, grovels and denies the dangerousness of her situation. Self-proclaimed revolutionist, Johnson tells her readers:

As grim as this is, it is only a surface picture...Some understanding of why women under terror merge so completely with their torturers and so strongly resist awareness of men's perfidy and gynocidal intent helps explain why women as a class the world over bond with and support men's woman-hating, woman-destroying governments, institutions, values, ideologies, and cosmologies. Why, in short, we vote, go to church, believe in male gods, follow male gurus and channeled entities, attend and teach at universities, send our children to school, become lawyers and corporation servers, marry, and work for male-defined 'women's rights.'[142]

How does one, particularly of the male sex, respond in this "sex war?" Most would agree that parts of these polarized negative perspectives exist in all marriages, although the number, frequency, magnitude and end result may be grounds for debate. Typical of anarchist ideology, whether Johnson sees herself as one or not, is a rallying call to dismantle <u>all</u> institutions and offer no replacement, as if mankind works better disentangled from so-called "civilized institutions" and empowered by primal instincts. In Chapter 3 the connection of Second Wave feminism and anarchism will be established. Moreover, in the course of this book, the life-organizing tenet of an insatiable and empowering primal sex drive that needs Wellness doctrine to be harnessed will be debunked.

Before leaving this section on the politics of oppression and patriarchy, a male's view of man's historical position in this "sex war" may level the feminist rhetoric considerably. As much as feminists wish to bury biology, it keeps its own rules and boundaries. Under the subject "Expendable Males," Howard Bloom writes:

In nearly every society, men alone are canon fodder...Males in animal groups and primative societies may seem rather glorious creatures, accorded the privileges of gods, but in reality, they are treated by nature like the biological equivalent of paper plates, creatures whose prime feature is their disposability.[143]

When it gets tough for the Karamojong in Uganda, they save their scraps of food for their girls and allow the boys to die. In 1979, when Uganda was starving in the grip of civil war, the Karamojong tossed the stiffened bodies of their male children out of the village each night. The only creatures growing fat were the hyenas, who feasted on the discarded corpses.[144]

According to Bloom, male expendability starts in the womb. The egg of the female inches, in solitary splendor, down the fallopian tube, inviting impregnation. It has no competition. On the other hand, the sperm – the male's contribution in procreation – vigorously swim the lengthy course up the vagina and uterus, beating their long, thin tails in an effort to outrace the millions of their brothers heading for the solitary egg. Only a single spermatozoon – one literally "chosen" by the ovum –

manages to finally penetrate the egg's outer membrane and achieve the grand prize of impregnation. The losers die.

But that is merely a preview of the casual manner in which Nature tosses male lives away. Male fetuses are the primary victims of natural abortions, miscarriages and stillbirths. In tough times, Nature shows her preference by hiking rates of spontaneous abortion for males to higher than normal but continuing her tendency to preserve her embryonic daughters. As James V. Neel of the University of Washington says, for males "in utero it's a jungle."[145]

Things don't get any better after birth. In their first few years of life, male babies have a higher death rate than their sisters. Then the nasty habits built in to the male genes begin to take their toll. Even in a nice, civilized spot like Alameda, California, where researchers performed a longitudinal study of five thousand adults, males were nearly four times more likely to lose their lives to homicide than females. And they were twice as likely to be accident victims. Their own aggression and bravado did them in. But cockiness is not the only thing that eliminates men. They are twice as likely to be victims of lung cancer, suicide, pulmonary disease, cirrhosis, and heart disease. The immune systems of females work far more efficiently than those of males. How can you encourage the male immune apparatus to function at a higher level? There is a way, says Bloom, "but I wouldn't recommend it: castration." The single trick that kicks the male defensive system into high gear is the elimination of maleness.[146] Expendability is built into the very genes of males. One result of these myriad handicaps: in every industrialized country, women live four to ten years longer than men. But why does Nature treat the lives of males with such abandon? Says Bloom:

The reasons are simple. If you did away with the vast majority of men on the planet but preserved the women, you would scarely even dent our species' reproductive capabilities. One man kept around as a stud could easily provide a hundred women with the wherewithal to become pregnant whenever they pleased. Every nine months a one-man, one-hundred-woman collective could produce a hundred babies.

The lives of women, on the other hand, cannot be so casually disposed of. Pare humanity down to one woman for every hundred men, and you will have one hundred very horny and bellicose guys slicing each other to ribbons or slashing themselves in dispair. What's worse you will cut the number of babies down from one hundred every nine months to one, dooming the human race to extinction. The result? We send our men to war but keep women safe at home. When ships are sinking, it's women and children to the lifeboats first. Let the men founder in the sea. You need each precious woman as a vessel for procreation.[147]

Just how disposable males are becomes obvious in the light of statistics revealed by anthropologists William Divale and Marvin Harris in 1976. The pair scrutinized data from 561 primitive social groups. They found that societies constantly engaged in war are very selective about the babies they allow to live. They want boys – male children who can grow up to be warriors – so they weed out the female infants, killing them outright or undernourishing and over working them. The result is that they end up with 128 male children for every 100 females. So far, it sounds like the males have made out quite well. But when the "treasured" young boys pass the age of fifteen, their fate becomes less rosy. They are sent off to war. And there, they die. On average, 28 out of every 128 never make maturity. Their lives are simply tossed away.[148]

Today men are more expendable than ever. Writes Bloom:

If the women's movement were to decide that the night had come when all women of the world would sneak into the bedroom and eliminate their snoring burden who insists on drinking beer, smoking cigars and watching Sunday football, the time would be now. Save up enough semen in communal refrigerators, and it would seem the species could move along quite well without males.[149]

Indeed, observes Bloom, an increasing number of lesbian women are turning to artificial insemination when they want to have a child. In Chapter 8, I discuss the desire to use human cloning as the basis for "alternative" family planning within the lesbian community, i.e. without the use of male sperm.

No doubt feminists will continue to see no utility for the human species in the unfairness of human biology and sex destiny. Indeed, they will do everything in their power to avoid such a conclusion. At its core the feminism, which evolved after Betty Friedan's resignation from NOW, has nothing to contribute to bettering the pro-creational dynamics of the heterosexual female and male. It was not intended for such a purpose. Lets not kid ourselves that including lesbian union in the institution of heterosexual marriage is going to somehow white wash, unify or otherwise correct what are acute cultural, ideological, biological and pro-creational differences, indeed, incompatibilities.

Lesbian and Gay Bigotry

During the course of the so-called "liberation wars," all combatants have stooped to bigotry. As evidenced in the ousting (and assault) of REAL Women representatives at a National Status of Women meeting and the outing of Kate Millett, clashes of ideology, agenda, and interest can act as catalysts for intolerance. What is remarkable in reflection over the past forty years is the singular success of a well articulated public relations campaign to portray the GBLTQ community as the victimized minority, needing protection from a homophobic, sexist and bigoted heterosexual majority, while simultaneously masking public awareness of intolerance and bigotry applied to heterosexuals, Christians and indeed, members within their own GBLTQ community. In this section some of this GBLTQ bigotry shall be unmasked.

First, what is the fine line between upholding a conviction and bigotry? For example, in the early 1930s, Lucy Maud Montgomery found herself pursued by a young woman named Isobel, a schoolteacher who wrote her passionate love letters and visited the author's home. Excerpts of Isobel's letters were preserved in Montgomery's journals, including the passages where Isobel pleaded to be allowed to kiss her passionately and sleep with her. "You're the dearest thing in the world to me," Isobel wrote in one letter. "I'll die without you...To die for the love of Lucy Maud Montgomery!" Puzzled at first, Montgomery headed to the Toronto library to read up on homosexuality and then recorded in her journal in 1932, "Faugh! I am not a Lesbian." "I understand her 'special need for me' only too well – much better than she understands it herself. It is the horrible craving of the Lesbian." Later Montgomery called Isobel's sexual orientation a "curse."[150]

Is Montgomery a bigot? Greg Bahensen advises that "Contrary to a common retort, disagreeing with homosexuals about their rights and disapproving of their behavior does not automatically make someone a bigot."[151] Montgomery's opposition is not a violent hatred or exaggerated fear, rooted in unfair and irrational attitudes based on blanket preconditions. She had not blindly developed her opinion. Opposition to homosexuality need not be motivated by a prejudiced and insulting attitude toward a group of people as such. A fair and dispassionate examination of the evidence relevant to an ethical evaluation of homosexual acts and affections can very well support a negative moral conclusion held with principled conviction. Viewing something as immoral is not the same thing as being bigoted; for example, it is not customary to look upon a pro-life advocate as a bigot towards abortions.

Bigotry applied to the heterosexual majority can be subtle, but it is nonetheless intolerance. If a father asks his son's school to not acknowledge Mother's Day because his son's biological mother is not at home and the father's partner is another man, is this bigotry? When Rodeph Sholom Day School, in the Upper West Side of New York, received a complaint, the school's management decided to cancel a tradition of having its students make Mother's Day cards. Cindi Samson, director of the lower elementary division, explained in a letter to parents, that these holidays [including Father's Day] served no educational purpose and that the school had decided that "recognition of these holidays in a social setting may not be a positive experience for all children." One wonders where the mother is in this boy's life. Many adopted children have invisible biological parents, yet they have not asked for the end of Mother's Day. Is it easier to bring an end to a tradition for 97 per cent of the students, than explain an existing family circumstance? Perhaps the logic in this complaint is political, directed at more social engineering.

Less subtle, Marilyn Frye, author of *Willful Virgin, or Do You Have to Be a Lesbian to Be a Feminist?* (1992), continued the vision started by Solanas in the 1960s, MacKinnon and Dworkin in the 1970s, and Gearhart and Trebilco in the 1980s:

I believe that all feminist theory and practice eventually conveys one to this proposition: that a central constitutive dynamic and key mechanism of the global phenomenon of male domination, oppression and exploitation of females, is near-universal female heterosexuality... The point is that virtually all women in patriarchal cultures are rigorously required to be sexual with and for men...For females to be subordinated and subjugated to males on a global scale, and for males to organize themselves and each other as they do, billions of female individuals, virtually all who see life on the planet, must be reduced to a more-or-less willing toleration of subordination and servitude to men. The primary sites of the reduction are the sites of heterosexual relation and encounter – courtship and marriage-arrangement, romance, sexual liaisons, [intercourse], marriage, prostitution, the normative family, incest and child abuse.[152]

To any feminist imagining herself capable of consciously choosing a male partner with whom to share her life, Frye offers this advice: If you wish to "embody and enact a radical feminism," you can't be heterosexual in any "standard patriarchal meaning of the word." You must learn to be "a heretic, a deviant, an undomesticated female, an impossible being. You have to be a virgin."[153] Biology is irrelevant to Frye, whose argument denies that heterosexuality has any biological roots:

A vital part of making generalized male dominance as close to inevitable as a human construction can be is the naturalization of female heterosexuality. Men have been creating ideologies and political practices which naturalize female heterosexuality continuously in every culture since the dawns of the patriarchies.[154]

In a few sentences Frye trashes all things heterosexual and elevates lesbianism to perfection:

Female heterosexuality is not a biological drive or an individual woman's erotic attraction or attachment to another human animal which happens to be male. Female heterosexuality is a set of social institutions and practices defined and regulated by patriarchal kinship systems, by both civil and religious law, and by strenuously enforced mores and deeply entrenched values and taboos. Those definitions, regulations, values and taboos are about male fraternity and oppression and exploitation of women. They are not about love, human warmth, solace, fun, pleasure, or deep knowledge between people.[155]

Is Frye a bigot? Her opinion is full of hatred and exaggerations, not to mention universal in application. According to Daphne Patai, "If homophobia is still a problem for society at large, heterophobia is now feminism's own predictable reversal of the problem."[156] This phenomenon has been honed over the past forty years, a current that has been "theorized" explicitly by feminist scholars and agitators alike as they attack men and heterosexuality. Patai defends her contention that radicalized feminism bears the hallmarks of what has been called a "manic" theory – that is, one that does not know its own limitations. In everyday form, heterophobia occurs as "male bashing." The rage was so manifest that even gay men bore its wrath. In *Odd Girls and Twilight Lovers: A History of Lesbian Life in Twentieth-Century America*, author Lillian Faderman described the 1970s:

Because a general disenchantment with and suspension of all males was central to lesbian-feminist doctrine, the gay man was naturally seen as being no less an enemy than any other human with a penis, and lesbian-feminists could make no lasting coalition with the gay men in a gay revolution.[157]

In 1994, Karen DeCrow, former president of NOW (National Organization For Women) stated, "God knows, in the last twenty-five years, man as 'the enemy' has certainly emerged" within feminism.[158] But heterophobia is not merely the work of lesbian separatists, since they, vastly outnumbered by heterosexual women, could never have imposed such an agenda were it not acceptable to heterosexual feminists as well. As discussed earlier, after the departure of Betty Friedan from NOW, the feminist organization identified lesbians as the frontline troops in the movement and accepted the lesbian-feminist analysis that the reason lesbians had been harassed was that they were a significant threat to so-called "patriarchy."

The British lesbian separatist Sheila Jefferys, in her 1991 book *Anticlimax*, gives a clear account of the attitude Patai calls "heterophobia" and I claim is bigotry:

The 'sexual revolution,' Jefferys argues, is positively detrimental to women. The aim of women's liberation, and particularly of lesbian liberation (which seeks to go beyond 'heterofeminism'), is 'the destruction of heterosexuality as a system.' Heterosexual desire, Jefferys affirms...is 'eroticised power difference'...Far from being grounded in biology, heterosexual desire 'originates in the power relationship between men and women' – though, she grants, power differences can also exist in same-sex relationships. But where sadomasochism or role-playing occurs in a homosexual relationship, Jefferys explains, they must be labeled 'heterosexual desire.' The institution of heterosexuality is, to Jefferys, founded upon the ideology of 'difference': 'Men need to be able to desire the powerless creatures they marry. So heterosexual desire for men is based upon eroticising the otherness of women, an otherness which is based upon a difference of power.' What sort of sexuality does Jefferys approve of? 'The opposite of heterosexual desire i.e. the eroticizing of sameness, a sameness of power, equality and mutuality. It is homosexual desire.'[159]

Jefferys views, according to Patai, illustrate the two strands of heterophobia: the fear and antagonism toward male sexuality, especially heterosexual males; and the turn toward "sameness," understood as the only kind of authentic relationship possible. Marilyn Frye expresses her anti-male bigotry this way:

Without (hetero)sexual abuse, (hetero)sexual harassment and the (hetero) sexualization of every aspect of female bodies and behaviors, there would not be patriarchy.[160]

Bigotry was not solely directed at men, although they were never out of the feminist sights. Compliant heterosexual women became targets. Valerie Solanas, author of the Society for Cutting Up Men (SCUM) Manifesto, in 1968, opened her landmark feminist document:

Life in this society being, at best, an utter bore and no aspect of society being at all relevant to women, there remains to civic-minded, responsible, thrill-seeking females only to overthrow the government, eliminate the money system, institute complete automation, and destroy the male sex.[161]

Foreshadowing the intense animosity between many feminist women and their nonfeminist sisters, Solanas pinpointed the real conflict as not between females and males, but between SCUM (women who are dominant, secure, proud, independent) and those contemptuously labeled "approval-seeking, Daddy's Girls." Records Patai, "SCUM will 'couple-bust,'" Solanas ominously announced. "It will barge into mixed (male-female) couples, wherever they are and bust them up."[162] When Solanas was charged with attempted murder of Andy Warhol (he had refused to show interest in her film script "Up Your Ass"), she was accompanied in court by representatives of NOW, Ti-Grace Atkinson and attorney Flo Kennedy. Atkinson said on that occasion that Solanas would go down in history as "the first outstanding champion of women's rights." Kennedy called her "one of the most important spokeswomen of the feminist movement."[163] Solanas was declared incompetent to stand trial and was committed to a mental institution and later sentenced to three years for reckless assault with intent to harm.

Something perhaps worse than the garden variety bigotry is hypocritical intolerance. Jane Gallop, a distinguished Professor of English at the University of Wisconsin-Milwaukee, was a major feminist theorist and in the early seventies was an outspoken lesbian. She and her longtime boyfriend, photographer and filmmaker Dick Blau, parent their son. Gallop has the no longer completely rare distinction of being accused of sexual harassment by two lesbian graduate students. In addition, one of the accusers faulted her for "pretending to be a fashionable lesbian."[164]

What is one to make of a professor who dedicates a scholarly book: "To my Students: The bright, hot, hip (young) women who fire my thoughts, my loins, my prose. I write this to move, to please, to shake you?" How would we react to such a dedication if we knew it to be by a man? In fact, it was written by Jane Gallop, in a book she published, *Around 1981: Academic Feminist Literary Theory*. According to Patai, the flamboyance of her words is vintage Gallop, and it therefore causes little surprise to learn that at just about the time she was finishing the book, Gallop found herself accused of sexual harassment.

In *Feminist Accused of Sexual Harassment*, her response to the accusation, Gallop both critiques and endorses what Patai calls the "Sexual Harassment Industry." According to Patai, she openly declares that only male-against-female aggression can count as harassment. Gallop begins *Feminist Accused of Sexual Harassment* by calling attention to its "tabloid" title, the "newsworthy anomaly" (rather like "Man bites dog") of a feminist finding herself accused of sexual harassment. Alas, says Patai, this is no longer as unusual an event as she imagines. There have been a number of such cases – some very well publicized (such as that of Elizabeth Fox-Genovese, former director of women's studies at Emory University); others less so (such as the charges against the director of women's studies program at the University of Alabama by her ex-lover, a forty-year-old woman who thereafter became a man); still others having thus far attracted hardly any attention nationally. All have in common that the women so accused not only were feminists but were actively involved in women's studies and that their accusers were other women also involved in these programs.[165]

Most notable in Gallop's tale is her failure to empathize with men accused of harassment, although herself distraught over the allegation. She accurately notes, "Most people take an accusation for a finding of guilt. Simply to be accused of a sexual crime is to be forever stigmatized." Says Patai:

But no where in Feminist Accused does she acknowledge that it is above all the inflated hostile sexual harassment environment that has swept men, in particular, into a vortex of accusations, stigmatization, disrepute, and – in some cases – broken careers.[166]

Patai details the feminist strategy of portraying a continuum of male sexual dominance of women, at the low end of which lie mere clumsy overtures and passes and at the high end (progressing through more unsavory grabbing and threats) of which loom, rape, battery, and even murder. Their reason is evident. [See Mary's notes in the guest speaker evaluation at the start of the book.] Once one agrees to this proposition, it is very hard to make light of the charges at the lower extreme. It is true that some men rape and batter. It is also true that most do not. How can one do justice to both of these assertions? Patai asks, why is there so much literature on both the comprehensive range and significance of sexual harassment? A key element in the construction of a social problem is, of course, its size (range). The larger the problem, the greater the attention it can legitimately command. Range claims are intended to suggest that the problem at issue pervades the entire social structure. Range claims are useful because they allow activists to depict their problem as having reached, or being about to approach, "epidemic proportions." This serves to create the impression that all citizens need take some action. As the reach of sexual harassment claims is extended, charges of wrongful behavior move from employers and professors to peers and even to the school yard. Not long ago, the country was treated to the spectacle of a six-year-old North Carolina boy being suspended from his first-grade classroom for a day because he had kissed a female classmate on the cheek. We must now be grateful to the U.S. Department of Education for having reassured us officially, through its Office of Civil Rights 1997 Guidance that "a kiss on the cheek by a first grader does not constitute sexual harassment." Patai points out this particularly absurd case highlights the antiheterosexual (male) bias imbued in the "sexual harassment industry." Surely a six-year old girl kissing another little girl would not have been the target of such vigilance.[167]

On the other hand, evidently tired of the game Gallop was playing, students accused her of attempting to extort sexual favors from them and then retaliating after they turned her down – classic quid pro quo harassment. One of the students pointed to an event Gallop could not deny but certainly would subject to her own interpretation: a very public French kiss at a 1991 gathering, the First Annual Graduate Student Gay and Lesbian Conference. This conference was by her own words an exhilarating experience:

Once again I was surrounded by bold young women, exploring the possibilities of a new mix of political, intellectual, and sexual liberation.

Compared to other professional meetings, 'Everyone seemed so clever and sassy [that] I wanted to rise to the occasion.' Hence Gallop's announcement at one of the conference sessions that 'graduate students are my sexual preference,' followed by the long kiss.[168]

The evidence was sufficient that she had violated a university policy prohibiting "consensual amorous relations" between professors and students.

The most interesting aspect of this saga, at least for the purposes of this book, is Gallop's disingenuous self-defense against the charge of sexual harassment. "Female sexual harassment seems like a contradiction in terms," she wrote. After all, "feminism invented sexual harassment." "Sexual harassment," Gallop explains in an earlier article dealing with her case, "is a way men obstruct women from doing work." In saying this, Gallop is merely following the line laid down by feminists in the 1970s. Not sex but sexism is the issue in sexual harassment. It is, Gallop writes, "criminal not because it is sex but because it is discrimination." But if "sexism" is discrimination or "disadvantaging" on the basis of sex, why can't women's negative treatment of women on the basis of sex, be sexism? Only the false tautology that to be feminist is never to be sexist (at least against women) can defend this claim. Patai argues that the notion that women never discriminate against other women is pious fiction.[169]

Gallop claims it is a mistake to confuse sex with sexism, and erotics with discrimination. For a feminist to be accused of sexual harassment is, to Gallop, the mark of "an issue drifting from its feminist frame." Gallop contends that only men are capable of abusing power; hence, only men are capable of harassing; only "male heterosexuality in our culture connotes power."[170] In this she is evidently in complete agreement with NOW, which on its web site, presents interesting information regarding sexual harassment. The very first words reveal that the feminist line, articulated twenty-some years ago, has undergone no refinement – "Sexual harassment is a form of violence against women, used to keep women 'in their place.'" How then, one might well ask with Gallop, could a women ever be guilty of sexual harassment. Contends Patai, Gallop's double standard becomes quite explicit here, "she is attempting to defend her own particular behavior by hiding behind men's social and institutional power, which must make any behavior of hers necessarily innocent, lacking power and unactionable. This is a patently dishonest and illogical analysis. What it reveals writes Patai, "is how far Gallop goes to retain her own autonomy while still being politically correct."[171]

Let us consider more closely some of the implications of the rhetoric of sexual harassment, in which even verbal expressions of sexual interest are transformed into exercises of power. When gay men pursue other men for casual encounters, is this an expression of "power" or of the search for "pleasure?" When lesbians pursue other women, how is this to be construed? Unless sex reformers want to open themselves to accusations of being antisex (not to mention homophobic), they would have to admit (along with Jane Gallop) that their analyses of sex-as-power are intended to apply, above all, to the world of heterosexual relations. And in fact, early "radical feminists" did openly admit this. Ti-Grace Atkinson, for example, is credited with the comment, "Feminism is the theory, and lesbianism the practice."[172] Do feminists seriously wish to claim that gay men may pursue other men out of desire while straight men pursue women only out of a wish to oppress them and demonstrate male power?

Last, let us look at bigotry within the GBLTQ community. In the background studies recorded in *Dual Attraction: Understanding Bisexuality*, Martin Weinberg observed that twice as many bisexual women as men (about 80 per cent compared with 40 per cent) said they had experienced problems with homosexual women. They reported that many lesbians complained that bisexual women related more emotionally and sexually to men and therefore could not be trusted. During a rap session one bisexual woman complained of the shame she felt admitting to homosexual women that she was "bi" and that in San Francisco it was harder to "come out" to homosexual women than to heterosexual women or even claim to be a bisexual feminist. Complaints bisexuals listed in relations with lesbians included:

They see a woman who is still having sex with a man as a traitor. (F)

They don't think it is politically correct to be bisexual; they don't trust women who are involved with men. (F)

Accusations of sitting on the fence, of being traitorous, of being just in a stage of lesbianism, 'You sound just like me when I was twenty-two.' Sometimes I don't even dress politically correct. (F)

The relationship is really limited with my lesbian friends – it would be more open if I were gay. But the "bi" is threatening. They are much more guarded and everything has to be clear with no ambiguity. Otherwise sexual overtones are always suspected in expressing affection. (M)

Mainly I experience a sense of hatred for men. They are not willing to give a man a chance to do anything. I don't like the attitude that some have that they would like the whole opposite sex eliminated from the world. (M)[173]

Majorie Garber, author of *Vice Versa* writes that the appearance of "biphobia," a word coined on the model of homophobia, suggests that the opposition to bisexuality is a mode of social prejudice. Straight people may stereotype bisexuals as closeted men who deceive their wives with a series of randomly chosen male sex partners, but some gays and lesbians also stereotype bisexuals as self-indulgent, undecided "fence-sitters" who dally with affections of same-sex partners, breaking their hearts when they move on to heterosexual relationships.[174] Garber notes, "Here too, was a paradox. The more borders to patrol, the more border crossings." And if, as she believes, the act of crossover is itself, as the word implies, a "transgression," the exciting guilty pleasures of transgressing, of intruding and spying and misbehaving, can be added to the eroticism of the occasion.[175]

Weinburg wrote of surprise to find the level of dislike many gays and lesbians felt for bisexuals and vice versa. The communities were divided by conflict. Many gays felt that bisexuals were really homosexuals who were afraid to admit it. On the other hand, bisexuals felt that gays and lesbians ignored the fact that bisexuals also faced discrimination for engaging in same-sex behaviors:

We all know what homophobia is – the fear of same-sex feelings/relationships, the fear of people who feel that way and do those things. What about biphobia? Biphobia, to me, is homophobia. Oppression is oppression is oppression. And bis are a minority within a minority. We all know how minorities are treated. (Eleanor: A bisexual-identified Woman)[176]

The majority of lesbians, heterosexuals, and gay men still believe that bisexuality is a phase or bi's are really gay or do not exist. Over the years Weinberg talked to a lot of lesbians who were devastated because the woman they loved returned to the "safe space" of the man they were with before. He writes:

These lesbians transferred their sense of betrayal and bitterness to other women. This has a lot to do with the myth that bi women are not to be trusted. Many lesbians believe that bi's use the label to avoid stigma. Lesbians feel that although a bi woman lives with a woman she fantasizes about men and keeps open the option to return to men if her woman relationship dissolves. There's resentment that bi's can appear to be heterosexual when it's convenient. They are seen only to want a sexual, not an emotional, commitment.[177]

Whereas both men and women complain of a lack of sexual frequency, women are more likely to desire homosexual sex – and this deficiency is defined as much more serious by the women. Bisexual women's limited entree to the lesbian subculture (their rejection by many lesbians on account of their bi-sexuality) reduces opportunities for meeting same-sex partners. There is a certain concern with sexually transmitted diseases since bi women are seen to be having sex with men. And with the AIDS epidemic there is a fear of coming in contact with bi women who have contact with bi men. Many politically active lesbians are now defending women's rights to choose bi-sexuality as a lifestyle. But there is a danger in assuming that bisexuality is the "ideal state" for humans. There is a tendency on the part of some bi's to push that concept to the extreme and put down others.[178]

Weinberg concluded that the belief that bisexuals are confused about their sexual identity is quite common. This conception has been promoted especially by those lesbians and gays who see bisexuality as being in and of itself a pathological state. From their point of view, "confusion" is literally a built-in feature of "being" bisexual. As expressed in one study:

While appearing to encompass a wider choice of love objects...[the bisexual] actually becomes a product of abject confusion; his self-image is that of an overgrown young adolescent whose ability to differentiate one form of sexuality from another has never developed. He lacks above all a sense of identity...He cannot answer the question: Who am I?"[179]

When asked to provide details about this uncertainty, the primary response was that even after having discovered and applied the label "bisexual" to themselves, and having come to the point of apparent self-acceptance, they still experienced intermittent doubt and uncertainty regarding their sexual identity. One reason was the lack of social validation:

While the heterosexual world was said to be completely intolerant of any degree of homosexuality, the reaction of the homosexual world mattered more. Many bisexuals referred to the persistent pressures they experienced to relabel themselves as 'gay' or 'lesbian' and to engage in sexual activity exclusively with the same sex. It was asserted that no one was really bisexual, and that calling oneself 'bisexual' was a politically incorrect and inauthentic identity.

Sometimes the repeated denial the gay community directs at us. Their negation of the concept and the term bisexual has sometimes made me wonder whether I was just imagining the whole thing.

My involvement with the gay community. There was extreme political pressure. The lesbians said bisexuals didn't exist. To them, I had to make up my mind and identify as lesbian...I was really questioning my identity, that is, about defining myself as bisexual...[180]

For the women, the invalidation carried over to their feminist identity (which most had). They sometimes felt that being with men meant they were selling out the world of women:

I was involved with a woman for several years. She was straight when I met her but became lesbian. She tried to 'win me back' to lesbianism. She tried to tell me that if I really loved her, I would leave Bill. I did love her, but I could not deny how I felt about him either. So she left me and that hurt. I wondered if I was selling out my woman identity and if it [being bisexual] was worth it.[181]

Weinberg recorded that one woman said her bisexuality was the result of '"acculturation,' a social dimension to her homosexual component:

There was one period when I was trying to be gay because of the political thing of being totally woman-identified rather than being with men. The Women's Culture Center in college had a woman's studies minor, so I was totally immersed in women's culture.[182]

Both gays and lesbians claimed that those who adopted the label "bisexual" did so because they feared the stigma attached to defining themselves as "gay" or "lesbian." Additionally, gays and lesbians saw bisexuality as a transition to becoming homosexual. In other words, they often rejected the bisexual identity in and of itself. Such attacks were said to come especially from politically active homosexuals who deplored the political fragmentation they saw caused by bisexuals who refused to fight the common enemy of "heterosexism." Bisexuals could exercise "heterosexual privilege" – i.e., they could always revert to a comfortable identity rather than suffer the consequences of standing up for their gay rights.[183]

These beliefs, writes Weinberg, affected personal interactions between bisexuals and homosexuals. Bisexuals were accused of being unable to sustain long-term relationships because of their continued desire for and contact with the opposite sex. Homosexual women, who complained that they had to compete with men for their female lovers, particularly voiced this criticism. It was especially an anathema to lesbian feminists, who saw any female heterosexuality as "sleeping with the enemy." Generally speaking, bisexuality was equated with "promiscuity." As one homosexual man said to Weinberg, "Bisexuals are erotic gluttons."

Bisexuals confronted these accusations with dismay. What they had initially perceived as a potential source of support – the homosexual community – turned out to be another avenue of rejection. Despite seeing themselves as victims of the same type of prejudice as homosexuals, they found themselves victims of further discrimination. A sense of isolation and anger grew toward homosexuals in general:[184]

...because lesbians, as a result of the AIDS crisis, are more frightened of anyone who touches sperm. I've had some lesbian women, when I tell them I'm bisexual, just get up and walk away. They see me as a potential disease spreader. (F)

I've been bashed by lesbians. Just hear them putting down bi's – they're conduits for AIDS, bi women will leave them for men, bi women claim heterosexual privilege, and so on. (F)[185]

Straight men feel more threatened now as they see bisexuals as a potential source of AIDS. There has been homophobia among straights and this just fuels their alienation towards bi's. (M)[186]

Third Wave Feminists

In *Manifesta: young women, feminism and the future*, one can get a foreshadow of the so-called "Third Wave" of feminism. The co-authors Jennifer Baumgardner and Amy Richards threw a party on 5 August 1999, during which the future of feminism was discussed and a new manifesto developed. Baumgardner, a former editor of *Ms.* and writer for *The Nation*, *Jane*, *Nerve*, and *Out*; and Amy Richards, contributing editor at *Ms.* and co-founder of the Third Wave Foundation, an activist group for young feminists, documented the resulting Third Wave conversation to demonstrate "how feminism invigorates" their lives. In *Manifesta*, they note:

Obviously, this random sample of friends (who live in New York City and mostly work in the media) can't represent all women. But this group of feminists who are observing and reporting on their generation, combined with conversations we have with young women across the country...gave us an idea of what a present-day political movement must tackle. [187]

Baumgardner and Richards go on to describe the invited guests. What follows is a synopsis of the party. At 8 p.m. the doorbell rang and Amaryllis Leon, a thirty-six-year-old executive assistant and serious student of belly dancing, arrived, sangria in hand. Baumgardner hadn't seen Amaryllis much since she stopped working at *Ms.* two years ago, but since then she had separated from her husband and taken up bicycling, flamenco dancing, and smoking. Dancing had become a way to express the rage she felt toward her dependent husband, her emotionally manipulative ex-lover, and herself for continuing to let these men lead when they are capable only of following.

Becky Michaels arrived on her bicycle from her job at the book publisher Little, Brown and Company. Flopping into a chair, she said that she had just been promoted (literally an hour before) to assistant director of advertising and promotion. Michaels has had two stepfathers, has one stepmother, and five siblings, only one of whom is biologically related to her. From chaos, Michaels is committed to creating order. Married to a musician, she is the stable moneymaker. She also runs a support group for battered women at Victim Services. The next guest to arrive was Hagar Scher, twenty-seven, clad in one of her trademark Charlie's Angels outfits. Hagar, originally from Israel, had been an intern at *Ms.* and is now a popular magazine writer. On the night of the party, she was coming off of a hard six months since she and her husband had separated and she had recently begun dating a couple of other men.

Elizabeth Wurtzel, a thirty-two year old author of two books (*Prozac Nation* and *Bitch*), attained early notoriety as a talented and exhibitionistic writer. Having just graduated from a successful rehab program in the city, Wurtzel was reorganizing her life as a sober and single person. Workaholic Farai Chideya showed up, announcing that she would have to leave a bit early due to her 5 a.m. call at *Good Morning America*, where she was a correspondent. (Soon after the dinner, Farai became a host of *Pure Oxygen*, a morning show on *Oxygen*, the new women's network.) Forever a non-monogamous worker, Farai also has a column in *Vibe*, has written two books about race, hosts her own web site called *Pop and Politics*, and is a syndicated political columnist. On this night, she was full of tales of the first dates she had gone on recently. Finally, Sabrina Margarita Alcantara-Tan, the twenty-nine year old creator of the feminist magazine *Bamboo Girl*, arrived. She was running late from her job at *Women Make Movies*. (Soon after the dinner, she quit her job.) Both of Sabrina's arms and her entire back are fully tattooed. She is a political, omnisexual (a term she prefers to the "too-limiting" bisexual), punk-rock feminist who is also proficient in Filipino martial arts. She recently married a traditional Filipino man.[188]

Together these women drafted this "Third Wave MANIFESTA":

To out unacknowledged feminists, specifically those who are younger, so that Generation X can become a visible movement and, further, a voting block of eighteen to forty-year-olds.

To safeguard a woman's right to bear or not bear a child, regardless of circumstances, including women who are younger than eighteen or impoverished. To preserve this right throughout her life and support the choice to be childless.

To make explicit that the fight for reproductive rights must include birth control; the right for poor women and lesbians to have children; partner adoption for gay couples; subsidized fertility treatments for all women who choose them; and freedom from sterilization abuse. Furthermore, to support the idea that sex can be – and usually is – for pleasure, not procreation.

To bring down the double standard in sex and sexual health, and foster male responsibility and assertiveness in the following areas: achieving freedom from STDs; more fairly dividing the burden of family planning as well as responsibilities such as child care; and eliminating violence against women.

To support and increase the visibility and power of lesbians and bisexual women in the feminist movement, in high schools, colleges, and the workplace. To recognize that queer women have always been at the forefront of the feminist movement, and that there is nothing to be gained – and much to be lost – by downplaying their history, whether inadvertently or actively.

To liberate adolescents from slut-bashing, listless educators, sexual harassment, and bullying at school, as well as violence in all walks of life, and the silence that hangs over adolescents' heads, often keeping them isolated, lonely, and indifferent to the world.

To pass the Equal Rights Amendment so that we can have a constitutional foundation of righteousness and equality upon which future women's rights conventions will stand.[189]

Gloria Steinem endorsed *Manifesta* claiming: with wit and honesty, *Manifesta* shows us the building blocks of the future of this longest revolution.

PART TWO

TW0 MUTUALLY EXCLUSIVE PARADIGMS

(Pivot of Civilization or Rivet of Life?)

The common morality seems to reject any notion of deliberately selecting kinds of love-making [natural kinds] in order to avoid pregnancy, at the same time as it ordains the maximum use of creativity and versatility in sex. We might ask what the point of all the versatility is if not to avoid unwanted pregnancy; the answer seems to be that it is an end in itself...Sex may be debased by using extraneous aids to stimulate flagging desire, by inviting third parties, by substituting instruments and other limbs for the flagging penis, but not by reverence for the power of sperm and ovary. Couples may dress up, play roles, manipulate and abuse each other, but they may not treat the vagina as dangerous. Our culture obliges us to abandon all attempts to control our own fertility by using our polymorphous potential for pleasure, and to give that control up to external agencies on the grounds that they are both more efficient and less harmful...the efficacy of traditional methods has never been studied because they were invariably assumed not to exist...Our preference for mechanical and pharmacological agents of birth-control is irrational. Our position with regard to the function of sex is absurdly confused...There is no logic in a conceptual system which holds that orgasm is always and everywhere good for you, that vaginal orgasm is impossible, that no moral opprobrium [shame] attaches to expenditure of semen wherever it occurs, that considerable opprobrium attaches to the bearing of unwanted children, and at the same time insists that 'normal' heterosexual intercourse should always culminate in ejaculation within the vagina. These are the suppositions which underlie our eagerness to extend the use of modern contraceptives into every society on earth, regardless of its own set of cultural and moral priorities. As the basic premises of the position are incoherent, the position itself is absurd.

Another name for this kind of mental chaos is evil.[1]

Germaine Greer

Jesus said, 'Come to me, all you who are weary and burdened, and I will give you rest.'

Matthew 11:28

CHAPTER THREE

PIVOT OF CIVILIZATION

Man arose from the ape and inherited his passions, which he can only refine but dare not attempt to castrate unless he would destroy the foundations of energy that maintain civilization and make life worth living and the world worth beautifying.[1]

The only weapon that women have, and the uncivilized weapon that they must use, if they will not submit to having children every year and a half, is abortion. We know how detrimental abortion is to the physical side as well as the psychic side of women's life. It is a woman's instinct, and she knows herself when she should and should not give birth to children, and it is more natural to trust this instinct and to let her be the judge then it is to let her judge herself by some unknown God. I claim it is a women's duty and right to have for herself the power to say when she shall and shall not have children.[2]

Its central challenge is that civilization, in any true sense of the word, is based upon the control and guidance of the great natural instinct of Sex.[3]

Margaret Sanger, 'Pivot of Civilization.'

This chapter outlines the secular, humanist and free love worldview by studying some of the founding ideologies, tenets and pioneers associated with the atheist paradigm. The chapter title, "Pivot of Civilization," is taken from a book written by Margaret Sanger. She is credited with the creation of Planned Parenthood, a global multi-agency alliance grounded in free sex, pro-sex, pro-abortion and Wellness philosophies, all of which have much in common with feminist and GBLTQ value systems. A guest speaker on homosexuality, who was a staff member with the Calgary Birth Control Association, an affiliate of Planned Parenthood Canada (thus connected directly to the International Organization and its late founder Margaret Sanger), brought these philosophies into my daughter's Grade 10 class.

Although difficult to give a strict (all inclusive) definition of the term "atheist," it is probable that the expression characterizes Margaret Sanger. For her the universe is empty of spiritual authenticity or is at best silent. She denies the existence of any god; certainly not one that you can have a relationship with. In her world, mankind is alone, except for the chance visit of extraterrestrial life forms, similar in Darwinian development process to us, although by random evolution unlikely to be remotely the same. Carl Sagan and Peter Singer illustrate key aspects of the Pivot of Civilization worldview:

To discover that the Universe is some 8 to 15 billion years and not 6 to 12 thousand years old improves our appreciation of its sweep and grandeur; to entertain the notion that we are a particularly complex arrangement of atoms, and not some breath of divinity, at the very least enhances our respect for atoms; to discover, as now seems probable, that our planet is one of billions of other worlds in the Milky Way Galaxy and that our galaxy is one of billions more, majestically expands the arena of what is possible; to find that our ancestors were also the ancestors of apes ties us to the rest of life and makes possible important – if occasionally rueful – reflections on human nature.[4]

Carl Sagan, 'Demon Haunted World: Science as a Candle in the Dark'

When we reject belief in a God we must give up the idea that life on this planet has some pre-ordained meaning. Life as a whole has no meaning. Life began, as best available theories tell us, in a chance combination of gases; it then evolved through random mutations and natural selection. All this just happened; it did not happen for any overall purpose. Now that it has resulted in the existence of beings who prefer some states of affairs to others, however, it may be possible for particular lives to be meaningful. In this sense atheists can find meaning in life[5]*....If the fetus does not have the same claim on life as a person, it appears that the newborn baby does not either, and the life of a newborn baby is of less value than the life of a pig, a dog, or a chimpanzee...In thinking about this matter we should put aside feelings based on small, helpless and – sometimes – cute appearance of human infants...If we can put aside these emotionally moving but strictly irrelevant aspects of the killing of a baby we can see that the grounds for not killing persons do not apply to newborn infants.*[6]

Peter Singer, 'Has Life a Meaning?'- 'Practical Ethics'

Before reviewing the lives and beliefs of a few of the more influential initiators of modern secular, sex-positive and humanistic philosophy, it will be valuable to briefly consider the psychology of atheism. Psychological motives and pressures that one is generally unaware of frequently lie behind unbelief. Moreover, it is reasonable to propose that people vary greatly on the extent to which these factors are present in their lives. Some of us have been blessed with an upbringing, temperament, social environment, and other circumstances that have made belief in God much easier than for others who may have suffered more; or have been raised in a spiritually impoverished environment. Here the life circumstances of activists like Mary Wollstonecraft, Charlotte Perkins Gillman, Emma Goldman, Margaret Sanger, Alfred Kinsey and Henry Morgentaler will provide excellent examples.

Scripture makes it clear that many children (even into the third or fourth generation) may suffer in their lives from events and circumstances of previous generations, regardless of whether past relatives may or may not have been Christian. What is the point therefore? It is this – some people have much more serious psychological barriers to Christian belief than others. Most people studied in this chapter detest "religion" and include Christianity at the top of their hate list. The roots of their hatred are often not intellectual or scientifically based, but more often the causes are anchored in depths of experienced abuse, deceit and hypocrisy. Usually terrible Christian example and witness fuels the sense of hypocrisy and experienced harm. Regrettably, this abuse has existed as a historical and continuing appendage to Christianity from the start. Saying one is a Christian and behaving in a Christ-like fashion are regrettably, often two very different things. In the chapters ahead a goal is to differentiate true faith in Christ and in the Word of God (Scripture) from religiosity, especially religiosity found in judgmental attitudes, legalism, pious behaviors and hypocrisy.

In looking at the personalities and experiences of these few key activists, we are searching for a general understanding of their beliefs, motivations and experiences. How did their life experiences impact their worldview? How well did their life experiences validate their worldview? The last section of this chapter, titled "Humanistic (Modern Gnostic) Civilization," deals with the humanistic idea of eugenic utopia, the related concept of secular bioethics, and the likely future of humankind organized according to the values and philosophies of the "Pivot of Civilization."

Mary Wollstonecraft 1759-1797

According to Alice Rossi, Mary Wollstonecraft's book, *Vindication of the Rights of Woman*, "burns with indignation." Rossi says:

Given to exaggeration as it was, by taking exceptional abuses as though they typified the experiences of all women, it had rhetorical power and persuasiveness, and for its time it was a remarkably fearless book.[7]

Writing in *The Feminist Papers*, Rossi says Wollstonecraft felt both the cause and the solution to women's oppression lie in education. In this view there are no innate racial, sexual, or social class differences among men and women; all differences are rooted in the social environment and can thus be eradicated. Women would learn (or could be taught) their true interest, the root of their subjection, and similarly fight for true equality of the sexes. According to Rossi, Wollstonecraft was as much a daughter of the Enlightenment as were Fuller and Stanton later in the nineteenth century, or Millett in the 1970s.[8]

In 1792, at age 33, she had a foolish infatuation with a white-haired, temperamental artist, Henry Fuseli, which she presented as a platonic enthusiasm for the man; the episode peaked when Wollstonecraft sought permission of the Fuselis to live with them – a request Mrs. Fuseli turned down in no uncertain terms. Shortly thereafter she left for France and there met Gilgert Imlay, a tall, awkward young American. From an initial dislike her feelings changed until she found herself in a passionate affair. What seems to have been a passing matter for Imlay was quite otherwise for Wollstonecraft. She became pregnant, give birth in Havre in 1794 to a daughter she named Fanny, after an early close friend. She pursued Imlay for months in a vain hope of establishing their relationship on firmer grounds. Less than two months after her flaming *Vindication of the Rights of Woman*, she wrote to Imlay:

Cherish me with that dignified tenderness, which I have only found in you; and your own dear girl will try to keep under a quickness of feeling, that has sometimes given you pain.[9]

Painful months of protest, hopes raised and then dashed, and an attempt at suicide by drowning occur before she accepted the fact that the relationship had ended as far as Imlay was concerned. In fact, he was already established with her successor in a London apartment. Woolstonecraft next met William Godwin, her intellectual and ideological match. Godwin, the first philosophical anarchist in English history, opposed marriage and many other institutional patterns. According to Rossi, "...he was the butt of no little humor from his contemporaries when it became known that he and Woolstonecraft married in the spring of 1797. The decision to marry took place after it was clear that Mary was pregnant." Commenting before discovering the second pregnancy, Godwin expressed their views on the institution of marriage:

We did not marry. It is difficult to recommend any thing to indiscriminate adoption, contrary to the established rules and prejudices of mankind; but clearly nothing can be so ridiculous upon the face of it, or so contrary to genuine march of sentiment, as requiring the overflowing of the soul to wait upon ceremony.[10]

Like most sexual liberationist thinking, their intellectual horizon includes only articulation of the freedom to indulge sexual pleasure. Potential adverse consequences of such behavior are kept out of sight. Here the notion that marriage was created as a societal institution to license reproduction and instill protective responsibilities for offspring remained lost in the urgency of the sexual moment. Wollstonecraft had learned nothing from her abandonment by Imlay, although this time she was fortunate her lover stayed. For those who had no intention of reproducing and desired only early sexual gratification, marriage would seem oppressive. However, for young children it was essential that adults (mostly biological fathers) take legal responsibility for raising them to the age of maturity. Wollstonecraft died ten days after the birth of her second daughter.

Charlotte Perkins Gilman, 1860 –1935

Gilman's fragmented personal experience impacted her views on marriage. Her father walked out when Charlotte was young. Although she described her own husband as a tender, devoted man, she ended up in a depression after the birth of their child. Divorce followed. She recovered and devoted her life to an assault on the middle-class marriage and family. Gilman described the economics of marriage in the language of biology: "The female of the genus homo is economically dependent on the male. He is her food supply." Marriage was a "sexuo-economic relationship," in which men paid money for the personal services performed by women, and paid ironically, in inverse relation to the work performed. "The women who do the most work get the least money, and the women who get the most money do the least work." Typical of most feminist analysis, heterosexual romance was not part of Gilman's marriage equation. She was dismayed that in modern industrial society, which was supposed to have freed personal relationships from the bonds of economic necessity, women were still dependents of men.[11] Indeed, the industrial revolution had made some prosperous, but in doing so many families had become double income with no economic, parental or marital dividends.

The American economy, by the early twentieth century, was based on the principle of the family wage: a male worker should be paid enough to support a family. The principle, as Louise Kapp Howe observed, applied to everyone: as a goal for personal upward mobility a man took pride in the fact that his wife didn't "have" to work. This was a social ideal. By illustration, the following extract from Margeret Sanger's *Pivot of Civilization*, depicts the status of "double-income" families at the lowest social rung:

In her report of living conditions among night-working mothers in thirty-nine textile mills in Rhode Island, based on exhaustive studies, Mrs. Florence Kelley describes the 'normal' life of these women: 'When the worker, cruelly tired from ten hours' work, comes home in the early morning, she usually scrambles together breakfast for the family. Eating little or nothing herself, and that hastily, she tumbles into bed-not the immaculate bed in an airy bedroom with dark shades, but one still warm from its night occupants, in a stuffy little bedroom, darkened imperfectly if at all. After sleeping exhaustedly for an hour perhaps she bestirs herself to get the children off to school, or care for insistent little ones, too young to appreciate that mother is tired out and must sleep. Perhaps later in the forenoon, she again drops into a fitful sleep, or she may have to wait until after dinner...The midday meal is scarcely over before supper must be thought of. This has to be eaten hurriedly before the family are ready, for the mother must be in the mill at work, by 6 P.M....A Polish mother with five children had worked in a mill by day or by night, ever since her marriage, stopping only to have her babies. One little girl had died several years ago, and the youngest child, says Mrs. Kelley, did not look promising. It had none of the charm of babyhood; its body and clothing were filthy; and its lower lip and chin covered with repulsive black sores....They are driven to it by the low wages of their husbands.[12]

Socialists advocated the family wage, trade unions fought for it, and most feminists, by the turn of the century, either approved or did not oppose it. But, as historian Heidi Hartmann has explained, the fight for the family wage helped establish the historic gender-based occupational hierarchy. As it turned out, the other side of the principle that a man should earn enough to support a family has been that a woman doesn't need to earn enough to support even herself.[13]

Continuance of the family wage system depended on two things, one a fact, the other an assumption. The fact is that men, on average earn more than women. The assumption is that men use their higher wages to support women and hence that most women are at least partly supported by men. It is easy to see how the assumption has reinforced the fact, and vice versa. If it is assumed that men already support most women, then they can, in good conscience, be paid less than men. And if women cannot expect to earn a decent wage on their own, they will indeed seek financial support from men. This in turn reinforces the assumption that men, as supporters of women, deserve higher wages than women. Hence the basic asymmetry of need that shaped the "battle of the sexes," particularly impacting feminist ideology.

The contemporary feminist reaction to "wages for housework," discussed in the previous chaper, tells us that NAC and NOW care little for the modern mother. These organizations prefer both parents working in the so-called "textile mills," regardless of the impact on the mother's health, the children's up-bringing, the marriage success and the family's welfare. The status of the modern "double income" family will be studied in Chapters 7 and 8.

Emma Goldman 1869-1940

Emma Goldman (Red Emma), anarchist, activist and organizer, lecturer and agitator, feminist, spokesperson for anti-war topics, advocate of birth control, free speech and free love, was also a staunch advocate for liberalizing homosexuality. In her autobiography, Goldman describes the "indignation" she felt at the conviction of Oscar Wilde. She "had pleaded his case against the miserable hypocrites who had sent him to his doom." In *Living My Life* (1934), she mentions that, while studying to be a nurse-midwife in the period before World War I, she became acquainted with the subject of "Urnings" and "Lesbians" through the lectures of Professor Bruhl (co-author with Freud on some of his early works). She adds that for the first time "I grasped the full significance of sex repression and its effect on human thought and action."[14] According to Marjorie Garber, a number of recent bisexual-feminist writers have chosen Goldman as a model, even though Goldman's own writings and speeches, like her relationships, were overwhelmingly heterosexual. In a letter to a lifelong friend Alexander Berkman, Goldman declared: "lesbians are a crazy lot. Their antagonism to the male is almost a disease with them. I simply can't bear such narrowness."[15] Although Goldman may have felt a profound ambivalence about lesbianism, she unquestionably was a champion of homosexuality. She enthusiastically participated in a verbal "battle royal about inversion, perversion, and the question of sex variation" at the turn of the century. For contemporary feminists, Emma Goldman has become something of a cult figure. Her ideas have struck a sympathetic cord among those who see sexual liberation and women's liberation as inextricably linked.[16]

Emma Goldman's destiny appears to spiral from a bitter chaotic start, to more agony in early marriage, to anarchy and free love, ending in the worst agony and loneliness. Although adamant that one's public life should mirror one's personal life, the testimony from her prolific letter writing (most are on historic record) and her autobiography bears witness to an extreme contradiction in principle and practice. Her life was manifest with cognitive dissonance. More than any of her numerous ardent beliefs, faith in a philosophy of "free love" haunted her from youth to old age. Typical of anarchists, normalcy was not common. She is famous for advocating and living an extremely unconventional lifestyle.

In a paper titled, *Minorities Versus Majorities*, Goldman equates the masses to "quantity." The multitude, the mass spirit, dominates everywhere, destroying "quality." She wrote, "The majority can not reason, it has no judgment. Lacking utterly in originality and moral courage, the majority has always placed its destiny in the hands of others." She quoted from Dr. Stockman:

The most dangerous enemies of truth and justice in our midst are…the dammed compact majority. Without ambition or initiative, the compact mass hates nothing so much as innovation. It has always opposed, condemned, and hounded the inno-

vator, the pioneer of truth....It is absurd to claim that ours is the era of individualism...every effort for progress, for enlightenment, for science, for religious, political and economic liberty, emanates from the minority, and not from the mass.[17]

Surprisingly, she cites Jesus Christ as a example of minority power:

The principle of brotherhood expounded by the agitator of Nazareth preserved the germ of life, of truth and justice, so long as it was the beacon light of the few. The moment the majority seized upon it, that great principle became a shibboleth and harbinger of blood and fire, spreading suffering and disaster.[18]

What Stockman and Goldman reveal through their "minority-majority" analysis is the anarchist foundation to their thinking. Emma Goldman explained much of this ideology in *Anarchism: What it Really Stands For.* Citing Oscar Wilde she explains:

A practical scheme, says Oscar Wilde, is either one already in existence, or a scheme that could be carried out under the existing conditions; but it is exactly the existing conditions that one objects to, and any scheme that could accept these conditions is wrong and foolish. The true criterion of the practical, therefore, is not whether the latter can keep intact the wrong or foolish; rather it is whether the scheme has vitality enough to leave the stagnant waters of the old, and build, as well as sustain, new life. In the light of this conception, Anarchism is indeed practical.[19]

Adhering to the anarchist viewpoint, Goldman blames theism for the "storm raging within the individual, and between him and his surroundings." Primitive man, unable to understand his being, much less the unity of all life, felt himself absolutely dependent on blind, hidden forces ever ready to mock and taunt him. Out of that attitude grew the religious concepts of man as a mere speck of dust dependent on superior powers on high, which can only be appeased by complete surrender. According to Goldman, all the early sagas rested on "biblical tales dealing with the relation of man to God, to the state, to society." The state, society, and moral laws all sing the same refrain: Man can have all the glories of the earth, but he must not become conscious of himself." [Twisted from Matthew 6:33, "seek first His kingdom and His righteousness, and all these things well be given to you as well."] Thus the ideology says that anarchism is the only philosophy that brings to man self-consciousness. Anarchism maintains that God, the state, and society are non-existent, that their promises are null and void since they can be fulfilled only through man's subordination. Anarchism is the teacher of the unity of life; not merely in nature, but in man. For Goldman there is no conflict between the individual and the social instincts. She quoted Emerson:

The one thing of value in the world is the active soul – this every man contains within him. The soul active sees absolute truth and utters truth and creates.[20]

In other words, for Goldman, the individual instinct is the thing of value in the world. It is the true soul that sees and creates the truth alive, out of which is to come a still greater truth, the reborn social soul. Anarchism is the great liberator of man from the phantoms that have held him captive; it is the arbiter and pacifier of the two forces for individual and social harmony. To accomplish that unity, Anarchism has declared war on the pernicious influences which have so far prevented the harmonious blending of individual and social instincts. These are religion, the dominion of the human mind; property, the dominion of human needs; and government, the dominion of human conduct. Each represents enslavement. Of these religion was particularly foul:

How it dominates man's mind, how it humiliates and degrades his soul. 'God is everything, man is nothing,' says religion. But out of that nothing, God has created a despotic, tyrannical, cruel and terribly exacting world. Anarchism rouses man to rebellion against this black monster. 'Break your mental fetters,' says Anarchism, 'for not until you think and judge for yourself will you get rid of the dominion of darkness, the greatest obstacle to all progress.' [21]

Advocating free love insured the institution of marriage was dominant on Goldman's demolition list. She saw the wife as a "parasite" and an "absolute dependent." Marriage incapacitates the woman for life's struggle, annihilates her social consciousness, paralyzes her imagination, and then imposes its gracious protection, which is in reality a snare, a travesty of human character. She writes:

If motherhood is the highest fulfillment of woman's nature, what other protection does it need save love and freedom? Marriage but defiles, outrages, and corrupts her fulfillment. Does it not say to woman, only when you follow me shall you bring forth life? Does it not condemn her to the block, does it not degrade and shame her if she refuses to buy her right to motherhood by selling herself? Does not marriage only sanction motherhood, even though conceived in hatred, in compulsion? Yet if motherhood be of free choice, of love, of ecstasy, of defiant passion, does it not place a crown of thorns upon an innocent head and carve in letters of blood the hideous epithet, Bastard? Were marriage to contain all virtues claimed for it, its crimes against motherhood would exclude it forever from the realm of love.[22]

One might ponder (hypothetically) whether Mary Wollstonecraft, lying in her post-natal deathbed with two dependent children, would have agreed. That Goldman's hatred of marriage is based on many life experiences is clear; however, if one's experiences are statistically rare and thus represent only a small minority of the population, how legitimate is it to call to anarchy the so-called "damned compact majority." There are at least two problems with Goldman's activist approach. First, is the assumption that her life occurrences might somehow be a valid basis for advocating a new life philosophy to others. Like many radical feminists, Goldman takes wretched parenting, unhappy marriages and poor social-economic experiences and concludes institutional marriage and the family structure are at fault. Second, it is evident that Goldman's opinion of her publicly declared free love ideology changed over time. With age and maturity, she fell victim to her own politics and faced a continual crisis between her public reality and her personal experience. The tenacity with which she held to her principles in the face of overwhelming contrary evidence is intriguing. In the end there was no integrity between what she said in public and what she did in private. She was a proverbial "false prophet." She went on to deny "herself" and deaden her "authentic soul" for a few more moments of free love ecstasy. In her autobiography, she characterized her decision to rejoin Reitman with the Russian expression:

'If you drink, you'll die, and if you don't drink, you'll die. Better to drink and die.' To be away from Ben meant sleepless nights, restless days, sickening yearning. To be near him involved conflict and strife, daily denial of my pride. But it also meant ecstasy and renewed vigor for my work. I would have Ben and go with him on tour again, I decided. If the price was high, I would pay it; but I would drink, I would drink![23]

Goldman's memories of her childhood experiences clouded her attitudes toward sexuality. Her mother had been quick to exhibit disapproval when she discovered Goldman masturbating. When Goldman informed her mother of her first menstrual cycle she was greeted with a slap in the face. Her mother said sternly, "this is necessary for a girl, when she becomes a woman, as a protection against disgrace."[24] Biographers Theresa and Albert Moritz describe Goldman's angry and disappointing years of youth. Although she wanted an education, in her father's view she did not require one and the family needed her earnings from sewing in a corset factory in St. Petersburg. Emma wanted love, but she was destined for an arranged marriage. Biographer, Richard Drinnon wrote:

Emma's independent views were highly dangerous. The Jewish community looked upon the adolescent girl as little more than a chattel, and, more specifically, as property of the father...When Abraham Goldman exercised a father's right by making arrangements to have her marry at fifteen, Emma boldly rejected.[25]

Her father beat her when she refused the match. Her autobiography captures her independent spirit and her hatred of marriage and religion:

...no 'really intelligent man' believed in the divinity of Christ, and that the church and state have no business interfering in relations between the sexes: 'Why should a man and a woman...have to go through a ridiculous ceremony mumbled by a priest or preacher before they can live together? If they love and love purely that is sufficient.'[26]

In New York, Goldman was once again a seamstress working long hours in a factory. After only a few weeks of work, she complained that $2.50 for a 6 day week of 10 hour days left her with no extra money for a book or even a flower, and with no time for a life outside work, was an outrage. When the owner replied that her tastes were too extravagant for a factory girl, Goldman quit.

According to Candice Falk, it was not long before Goldman met a textile worker named Jacob Kershner. At seventeen, Goldman began to think of marriage to the handsome twenty-one year old. He would be her ticket to escape the oppressive drudgery of work. On her wedding night in February 1887, Goldman learned of a new kind of loneliness and isolation, when Jacob failed to consummate their marriage. In time it became clear that Kershner was impotent. The revelation left Kershner so humiliated that he fell into a deep depression. His interest in books and dancing, which gave common ground with Goldman evaporated. He retreated into long hours of card playing with his companions. Within two years, not yet twenty years old, Goldman gathered enough courage to announce that she was divorcing him.[27]

Only two months later Kershner met with her at her sisters, begging her to return, threatening to commit suicide if she did not. Goldman badly in need of care herself could not resist. Her family (now in America) was relieved that their daughter had reformed after her act of youthful rebellion. Goldman actually remarried Kershner. Once reunited their destructive patterns began again. When Goldman left the second time she was spurned by the Jewish community. Her parents, who had disapproved of the original divorce, now disowned her for what seemed to them her utter disregard of her societal responsibilities. Their lack of sympathy hurt.[28]

Near this time Goldman was diagnosed with an "inverted womb," which was a catch all term for menstrual and fertility problems. Her friend Dr. Hillel Solotaroff took her to a physician who told her she could never bear children with this condition. The same doctor (incorrectly) suggested that an operation could cure her monthly pain and make it possible to conceive. Goldman decided to forgo the operation and any "instinctive" desire for a child, attributing this decision to the memory of her own brutal childhood, her awareness of the numbers of unwanted and impoverished children in the world, and her new dedication to the cause.[29]

In 1889, at age twenty, Goldman moved to New York and joined an anarchist commune where she met Alexander Berkman, who later became her lifelong companion and lover. A decade later, at the age of thirty-nine, she met her "Great, Grand Passion," an uninhibited hobo-turned-physician from Chicago, one Ben Reitman, who was ten years younger than she. He would strain severely her commitment to free love with his compulsive unfaithfulness and promiscuity. On the plus side, Reitman's gynecological knowledge made him a fund of information few others possessed. Goldman wrote that he robbed her of her reason:

I would put my teeth into your flesh and make you groan like a wounded animal. You are an animal and you have awakened lust in me.[30]

Their relationship was an intense and emotionally charged one in which the two combined their professional and private lives. Reitman drew her sexually as no other man had, and taught her the meaning of an erotic love more intense than she had ever imagined. Yet not even her nine year obsession with Reitman, which ended when he left her to marry another woman, weakened her devotion to Berkman, who also turned to younger women when he emerged from prison in 1906.[31]

In 1910, Goldman published her first volume of essays entitled *Anarchism and Other Essays*, which contained treatises on women's emancipation, marriage and love, female prostitution, anarchism, education and "Puritanism." In many of her essays Goldman advocated "free love" and marriage based on mutual affection rather than property relations. Unlike her more proper suffragette opponents, she advocated sexual experimentation (engaging in "varietism" or heterosexual variety), rather than chastity. She followed this principle in her associations with men, carrying on a number of sexual relationships with a variety of fellow anarchists.[32]

Although Goldman wished for a seamless union of her public persona with her private life, believing that the "way one lived one's life everyday was an individual's most important political statement," the contradiction between the strong anarchist-sexual libertarian and the weak child-like lover was not lost. On July 26, 1911, she wrote to her lover Ben Reitman:

Years ago I read The Life of Mary Wollstonecraft. Her weak and humiliating love life with Imlay was the most terrible thing to me. Mary Wollstonecraft, the most daring woman of her time, the freest and boldest exponent of liberty, of free love, the slave of her passions for Imlay. How could anyone forgive such weakness? Thus I reasoned many years ago. Today? E.G., the Wollstonecraft of the 20th century even like her great sister, is weak and dependent, clinging to the man no matter how worthless and faithless he is. What an irony of fate.[*33]

Goldman, conveying her jealous rage, wrote of Reitman, "His promiscuity tears my vitals, fills me with gall and horror and twists my being into something foreign to myself." She demanded that he explain what his love for her meant to him. Somewhat in dissonance, Goldman said that she could imagine giving one's love freely, but not when it was as powerful as the love she felt for him.[34] Reitman's promiscuity rapidly became the central issue in their relationship. Although Goldman's championship of the idea of free love kept her from condemning his behavior on political grounds, her letters revealed a tortured effort to reconcile her bitter disappointment and anger with her ideology. She tried to deny her jealousy, but it gnawed at her. In the midst of her work in the *Mother Earth* office she still had uncontrollable cravings to see Reitman:

And there is that other thing, the thing so abhorrent, so utterly impossible to endure – your irresponsible unscrupulous attitude towards women – your lack of honesty with them, with yourself, with myself. Oh, I know you will ascribe it to jealousy. But it's not. I have told you over and over again, if you really care for a woman, if you love her, no matter how much that may grieve me, I should have strength to face it. Or if you were honest in your dealings with women, openly and plainly telling them, 'I want you for a sex embrace and no more,' that too, I could stand. But your complete lack of justice, of common humanity, of consideration for the rights of another, is simply killing me.[35]

Once, after discovering that Reitman had gone almost immediately from her to another woman, she wrote:

All is blank before me, all is dark and dreary, nothing is left behind. Oh, Ben, Ben! Fate is hard and cruel – 38 years I walked through life with a burning and insatiable longing in my heart for the unknown. I could reason, then, oh so clearly on all human subjects, on every secret string of the human heart. The miracle came, in a most glorious color. It enveloped me, took possession of me, crept into my soul and body and robbed me of all reason. It's but 24 hours ago, the miracle lifted me to a dazzling light, with the world all puny and insignificant at my feet. Now all is dark, I cannot see, nothing is left of life. Oh, Ben, Ben, Ben! I am so chilled and pained, I am struggling the bitterest struggle of my life and if I succeed, I fear I will never be able to see you again. Yet, if I fail, I shall stand condemned before the bar of my own reason.[36]

Emma's bitterness about "the modern woman" (free lover, independent, unmarried) was further reflected in her own feelings of loneliness and loss when Alexander Berkman, aged 52, fell in love with Emmy Eckstein, in her early twenties. In stoic fashion the three continued a life long relationship. Eckstein would be jealous of Berkman's relationship to Goldman and Goldman would be bitter over Berkman's relations with Eckstein. Goldman was particularly angry that Berkman could form "satisfying, long-term relationships with much younger women while she the great champion of free love, suffered endlessly from unsatisfied longing." According to Alice Wexler, "Drifting apart from Berkman, with no compelling activity to claim her energies, Goldman felt more bereft and abandoned than ever, viewing her life as a complete 'debacle.'"[37]

Goldman reflected on her life in the summer of 1925:

...tragedy of the emancipated woman, myself included, particularly the older single woman, who found herself getting on in age without anything worthwhile to make life warm and beautiful, without a purpose.[38]

Goldman felt that people need someone who really cares. She believed that women need a caring person even more and that women find it impossible to meet anyone when they have reached a certain age. Goldman described the dilemma to Berkman:

No matter how 'modern' she was, as a woman growing older, she was likely to feel more painfully the absence of a husband, children, a home, economic security, and companionship...[39]

She concluded one of her letters to Berkman:

Ah well life is one huge failure to most of us. The only way to endure is to keep a stiff upper lip and drink to the next experience.[40]

In spite of her personal tragedy, Goldman continued to attack "Puritanism" as a source of oppression. Human sexuality and reproduction were constrained, in Goldman's view, by norms of behavior grounded in religious, moral or civil doctrine rather than governed by "natural" or "instinctual" criteria. The further that individuals moved away from "nature" towards "culture" and the "state," the more repressed and sublimated their desires would become. Goldman placed issues of sex and reproduction on the instinct side of the line, as did Sanger.[41]

According to Haaland, Goldman argued that women's participation in the intellectual sphere of civil society imposed "artificial" modes of behavior and beliefs which have "isolated woman and have robbed her of the fountain springs of that happiness." The "emancipation" which brought women into public sphere activity as teachers, doctors, lawyers, architects and engineers did not equip them with the "necessary strength to compete with man." As a result, Goldman thought a woman "is compelled to exhaust all her energy, use up her vitality and strain every nerve in order to reach the market value." Goldman stated that in very few cases are women able to achieve professional equality with their male counterparts; and if and when they do achieve equal recognition, either in the form of remuneration or confidence conferred on them by their male colleagues, they "generally do so at the expense of their physical and psychical well-being." These professional women – teachers, physicians, lawyers, engineers, etc. – possess in Goldman's words, "a dignified, proper appearance while their inner life is growing empty and dead."[42]

Goldman's rejection of women's involvement in the public sphere can be better understood in the context of the contemporary debates over women's apparent "equality" versus "difference." Ruth Pierson and Alison Prentice have set out the issues associated with "the coexistence of the demand for equality with the acceptance or celebration of difference." Pierson and Prentice suggest that in order for women to be as "autonomous and self-determining" as men, they must be able to participate in the public realm.[43] An attendant problem of this goal, according to the authors, is one which could lead to a further "atomizing" of society:

The self-sufficient woman, living alone, unencumbered by intimate ties to or responsibilities to other human beings, however, is not necessarily a feminist goal. Feminists insist, rather, that women have a human need equal to men's for affection and emotional support but that for satisfaction of this need women should not have to make a greater sacrifice of autonomy than men.[44]

Yet, Goldman places women's choices into "rigid categories and dichotomies, positing irreconcilable conflict between two solutions."[45] Goldman suggests that women's "difference" is best expressed in the realm of the private and the instinctual, while women's "equality" as expressed through public realm activity is a hollow and artificial goal. Haaland observes that contemporary debates on the so-called dilemma of "equality" versus "difference," which Goldman faced earlier in this century, are increasingly "integrative."[46] Pierson and Prentice state:

We argue that it is possible and desirable to pursue both goals ['equality' and 'difference'] at once, despite their apparent contradiction...it [feminism] must go further and insist on full complexity of human lives and possibilities..."[47]

Goldman, like Havelock Ellis, saw motherhood as providing a source of "natural" fulfillment for women and, like Ellis, she expressed concern over modern movements which purported to advocate "equality" for women. Smith-Rosenburg notes that "feminism, lesbianism, equality for women, all emerge in Ellis's writings as problematic phenomena."[48] Goldman's belief that women need to give and receive love, preferably from a man as well as a child, was consistent with prevailing gender ideology which defined women's nature as based in a need to nurture a child and to have a heterosexual relationship. Sex and love, for Goldman, were gender-specific experiences in which women and men do not share common emotions and sensations. Her view of the "relational" nature of women was set out in a letter she wrote to Alexander Berkman, in 1925, in which she expounded upon the tragedy of "all us modern women." She writes:

It is a fact that we ['modern women'] are removed only by a very short period, of our transitions, the transitions of being cared for, protected, secured, and above all, the time when women could look forward to an old age of children, home and some-one to brighten their lives...most modern women begin to feel the utter emptiness of their existence, the lack of a man whom they love and who loves them, the comrade-ship and companionship that grows out of such a relation, the home, a child.[49]

Notwithstanding her position on the naturalness of motherhood and the draw-backs of the "modern woman," Goldman would reject Ben Reitman's and Ed Brady's request to marry and settledown. Ironic from a contemporary feminist perspective (i.e. the reversed gender roles) Goldman chose career over the desires of at least two suitors, who wished for a more "secure" relationship.

Working with Reitman at *Mother Earth* and living with his mother was the straw that broke the camels back. Candice Falk records:

The desire seized me to make an end of Ben as far as I was concerned, to do some-thing that would shut out forever every thought and every memory of this creature who had possessed me all these years. In blind fury I picked up a chair and hurled it at him. It whirled through space and came crashing down at his feet. He made a step towards me, then stopped and stared at me in wonder and fright. 'Enough!' I cried, beside myself with pain and anger, 'I have had enough of you and your mother. Go, take her away – today, this very hour!' He walked out without a word.[50]

She would rejoin Reitman. In her autobiography, Goldman characterized the decision as choosing ecstasy over reason.[51] But by the end of the tour he made clear to Goldman his desire for domestic security:

If I can't have a home with you, I want a home alone with my mother...I have lived alone with my mother all my life and I have no desire to make a change. ...I feel full of life but I am insecure with you. Oh, God, my lover, I know you much better than you think I do, and often I think that you are either not honest with me, or with yourself.[52]

Reitman was finally facing the obstacles to his personal well-being imposed by the triangles in his life – among Goldman, his mother and himself; and among Goldman, Berkman and himself. The fact that Reitman and Berkman were not get-ting along made for more conflict between Reitman and Goldman.[53] Goldman made her views clear. She had chosen work as her family and her chosen child was *Mother Earth* magazine. Reitman decided that what he wanted now was a real wife and family. Since he and Emma could not see their way clear to such a stable future, he arrived in New York with a somewhat cold-blooded resolve to search for a woman with whom he could settle down. Thus he leaped at the opportunity to renew his acquaintance with Miss Martindale, a tall blonde Englishwoman, who had attracted his attention in the *Mother Earth* office the previous winter, when he and Goldman were splitting up.

He married and became a father to a son, he named Brutus. As Brutus had betrayed Cæsar, Reitman felt he had betrayed Goldman by choosing marriage and family over the cause. While Goldman was awaiting an appeal over retaining American citizenship, a farewell banquet was held for Reitman. He stood up at the dinner and announced that despite ten years as Emma's co-worker, he was now through with anarchism:

Emma came into my life years ago and seduced me from the old world. I dropped my old ideas. I dropped Jesus Christ. But today I'm thanking God I've learned the right road – and I learned it when I came back to Jesus.[54]

Goldman was infuriated. There would be many more free lovers in Goldman's life, however, she failed to turn one of them into the "positive" experience her speeches had declared they should be.

Important in the study of Goldman is her relationship to Margaret Sanger. Goldman proclaimed that only perfect freedom and communication make a true bond between man and woman, meeting in the open, without lies, without shame, free from the bondage of duty. Regarding a woman's duty, Goldman was in support of the demand that woman must be given means to prevent conception of undesired and unloved children; that she must become free and strong to choose the father of her child and to decide the number of children she is to bring into the world and under what conditions. In her estimation this is the only kind of motherhood which can endure. The new fervor of Goldman's work for birth control came partly from her ties with Margaret Sanger, whose magazine *The Woman Rebel*, had been banned in the U.S. mails as containing "obscenities." Literature from Sanger's birth control offices included: a technical manual on *The Limitation of Offspring* and pamphlets on *What Every Mother Should Know* and *What Every Girl Should Know*. Goldman wrote Sanger:

I know you will be amused to learn that most of the women are up in arms against your paper; mostly women, of course, whose emancipation has been on paper and not in reality. I am kept busy answering questions as to your 'brazen' method.[55]

Sanger was put on trial for the pamphlets. Ultimately, she decided to enter a plea of not guilty in order to separate the idea of prevention of conception and birth control from the sphere of pornography.[56] Goldman continued to speak on the birth-control issue and to raise money for the Sanger case. *The New York Times* of January 17, 1916, reporting on the talk she gave, headlined the article: TEDDY ROOSEVELT WRONG: SAYS ANARCHIST – EMMA GOLDMAN ASSERTS CHILD HAS A RIGHT NOT TO BE BORN.

Margaret Sanger 1879 – 1966

Margaret Sanger, in *The Pivot of Civilization*, detailed her prophesy on the impact of birth control:

I look, therefore, into a Future when men and women will not dissipate their energy in the vain and fruitless search for content outside of themselves, in far-away places or people. Perfect masters of their own inherent powers, controlled with a fine understanding of the art of life and of love…they will unafraid enjoy life to the utmost. Women will for the first time in the unhappy history of this globe establish a true equilibrium and 'balance of power' in the relation of the sexes… Interest in the vague sentimental fantasies of extra-mundane existence, in pathological or hysterical flights from the realities of our earthliness, will have through atrophy disappeared, for in that dawn men and women will have come to the realization, already suggested, that here close at hand is our paradise, our everlasting abode, our Heaven and our eternity. Not by leaving it and our essential humanity behind us, nor by sighing to be anything but what we are, shall we ever become ennobled or immortal. Not for woman only, but for all of humanity is this the field where we must seek the secret of eternal life.[57]

Margaret Sanger was born on September 14, 1879, the sixth of eleven children. Her father, Michael Higgins, was an Irish Catholic immigrant who fancied himself as a freethinker and a sceptic. Margaret's mother, Anne Purcell, was a second generation American from a strict Catholic family. Frail with tuberculosis she was utterly devoted to her atheist husband. The family suffered cold, privation, hunger, scorn, shame, and isolation because of the father's radical Socialist ideas and activities. Margaret would later describe her family's life together as "joyless and filled with drudgery and fear."[58]

In spite of her non-believing father's efforts to undermine Margaret's young and fragile faith, her mother had her baptized in St. Mary's Catholic Church on March 23, 1893. A year later, on July 8, 1894, she was confirmed. Both ceremonies were held in secret – her father would have been furious had he known. For some time afterward she displayed a keen devotion to spiritual things, but gradually her father's cynicism snuffed out any flame. By the time she was seventeen her passion for Christ had collapsed into a hatred of the Church, which became her spiritual hallmark for the rest of her life.[59] She wrote:

I never liked to look at Jesus on the Cross. I could not see any good it did to keep looking at him. We could not help him, as he had been crucified long ago.[60]

Margaret moved away as soon as she could to a boarding school, Claverack College of the Hudson River Institute, where she got her first taste of freedom. According to biographer, Madelaine Gray, she plunged into radical politics, suffragette feminism, and unfettered sex.[61] And after a failed trial marriage at 18, in 1897, she escaped from the harsh "bondage" of labor by entering into another marriage to William Sanger in 1902. He was a young man of great promise. An architect with the famed McKim, Mead, and White firm in New York City, he had already made a name for himself working on the plans for Grand Central Station and the Woolworth building.

The Sangers settled into a pleasant apartment in Manhatten's upper east side and set up housekeeping. But the housekeeping had little appeal to Margaret. She quickly grew restless and soon engaged in extramarital affairs while encouraging her husband to do the same. She pronounced the marriage bed to be "the most degenerating influence in the social order" and advocated a "voluntary association" between sexual partners.[62] Her doting husband began casting about, trying to find a way to satisfy her passions. He sent her off for long vacations in the Adirondacks. He hired maids and attendants. He bought her presents. He even built her an extravagant home in the suburbs. In short order they had three children, two boys and a girl. After nearly a decade of undefined domestic dissatisfaction, Margaret convinced William to sell all they had and move back into Manhattan hubbub and fast-paced social life. Meanwhile, William began to renew old ties in radical politics by attending Socialist, Anarchist, and Communist meetings in Greenwich Village. "Occasionally attending with her husband," says Gray, "Margaret plunged headlong into the maelstrom of rebellion and revolution."[63]

While William was happy that Margaret had finally found a cause that satisfied her restless spirit, he gradually became concerned that she was taking on too much, too soon. Their apartment was in a perpetual state of disarray. Their children were constantly being farmed out to friends and neighbors. And their time alone was nonexistent. But when Margaret fell under the spell of the militant utopian Emma Goldman, William's husbandly concern turned to disapproval. Margaret had gone from an archetypal "material girl" to a revolutionary firebrand almost overnight. And now she was taking her cues from one of the most controversial insurrectionists alive.

According to Gray, Margaret was completely overwhelmed. She hung on Goldman's every word and began to read everything in Goldman's library including the massive seven volume *Studies in the Psychology of Sex* by Havelock Ellis, which stirred her in a new lust for adventure. She told William she needed emancipation from every taint of Christianized capitalism, including the strict bonds of the marriage bed.[64] Divorce was narrowly averted, when William rented a cottage on Cape Cod and took Margaret and the children on a long vacation.

In the time following, Margaret occupied herself by dabbling in midwifery by day and at night by speaking to intellectuals, radicals, artists, actors, writers and activists, who gathered at Mabel Dodge's Fifth Avenue apartment, to mingle, debate and conspire. Margaret's topic of discussion was always sex. When it was her turn to lead an evening, she held Dodge's guests spellbound, ravaging them with intoxicating notions of "romantic dignity, unfettered self-expression, and the sacredness of sexual desire."[65] Free love had been practiced for many years by avant-garde intellectuals in New York. Eugene O'Neill took on one mistress after another, immortalizing them in his plays. Edna St. Vincent Millay "hopped gaily from bed to bed and wrote about it in her poems." As shown, Emma Goldman enjoyed unrestrained sexploits. Says Gray, "But no one championed sexual freedom as openly and ardently as Sanger."[66] Mabel Dodge would write in her memoirs:

Margaret Sanger ...introduced us all into the idea of birth control, and it, along with other related ideas about sex, became her passion. It was as if she had been more or less arbitrarily chosen by the powers that be to voice a new gospel of not only sex-knowledge in regard to conception, but sex-knowledge about copulation and its intrinsic importance. She was the first person I ever knew who was openly an ardent propagandist for the joys of the flesh. This, in those days was radical indeed when the sense of sin was still so indubitably mixed with the sense of pleasure…Margaret personally set out to rehabilitate sex…She was one of its first conscious promulgators.[67]

Everyone seemed delighted by Margaret's explicit and brazen talks. Everyone except her husband. According to Gray, William began to see the Socialist revolution as nothing more than "an excuse for a Saturnalia of sex." He took her and the children to Paris. After two weeks, she begged him to return to New York. He refused, so she abandoned him there, and returned with the children.[68] She wrote in her 1931 book, *My Fight for Birth Control*:

My first marriage failed, not because of love, romance, lack of wealth, respect or any such qualities which are supposed to be lacking in broken ties, because the interest of each widened beyond that of the other…From the deep waters into which I had been swept by the current of events it was impossible to return to the shallow pool of domesticity.[69]

Without great financial support, she started writing and published a paper called *The Woman Rebel*. It was an eight sheet pulp with the slogan "No Gods! No Masters!" emblazoned across the masthead. The first issue denounced marriage as a "degenerate institution," capitalism as "indecent exploitation," and sexual modesty as "obscene prudery." The next issue, the article entitled "A Women's Duty" proclaimed that "rebel women" were to "look the whole world in the face with a go-to-hell look in the eye." Another article asserted that "rebel women claim the following rights: the right to be lazy, the right to be an unmarried mother, the right to destroy…and the right to love." In later issues she published several articles on contraception, several more on sexual liberation, three on the necessity for social revolution, and two defending political assassination.[70]

Charged with three counts of lewd and indecent articles, she eventually fled on a false passport to England to escape prosecution. Before departing she released in the mail a pamphlet called *Family Limitation*. It was lurid and lascivious, designed to enrage the postal authorities and titillate the masses. But worse it was dangerously inaccurate, recommending such things as Lysol douches, bichloride of mercury elixirs, heavy doses of laxatives, and herbal abortifacients. Margaret's career as the "Champion of Birth Control" was now well underway.

Once in England she started attending lectures on Neitzsche's moral relativism, anarchist lectures on Kropotkin's subversive pragmatism, and communist lectures on Bakunin's collectivistic rationalism. But she was especially interested in developing ties with the Malthusians. In his magnum opus, *An Essay on the Principle of Population*, published in six editions from 1798 to 1826, Malthus wrote:

All children born, beyond what would be required to keep up the population to a desired level, must necessarily perish, unless room be made for them by the deaths of grown persons...Therefore...we should facilitate, instead of foolishly and vainly endeavoring to impede, the operations of nature in producing this mortality; and if we dread the too frequent visitation of the horrid form of famine, we should sedulously encourage other forms of destruction, which we compel nature to use. Instead of recommending cleanliness to the poor, we should encourage contrary habits...but above all, we should reprobate specifically remedies for ravaging diseases; and restrain those benevolent, but much mistaken men, who have thought they were doing a service to mankind by projecting schemes for the total expiration of particular disorders.[71]

Malthusians believed that if Western civilization were to survive, the physically unfit, the materially poor, the spiritually diseased, the radically inferior, and the mentally incompetent had to be eliminated. Malthusianism gave Sanger the "high ground" upon which to argue her case for birth control (and co-associated sex liberality), using scientifically verified threat of poverty, sickness, racial tension and overpopulation as the backdrop. But even more important, Sanger's exile in England, gave her the chance to make some critical interpersonal connections as well. Writes Gray:

Her bed became a veritable meeting place for the Fabian upper crust: H.G. Wells, George Bernard Shaw, Arnold Bennett, Arbuthnot Lane, and Norman Haire. And of course, it was then that she began her unusual and tempestuous affair with Havelock Ellis.[72]

Ellis was the iconoclastic grandfather of the Bohemian sexual revolution. The author of nearly fifty books on every aspect of concupiscence from sexual inversion to auto-eroticism, from the revolution of obscenity to the mechanism of detumescence, from sexual periodicity to pornographic erotism, he provided the free love movement with much of its intellectual apologia. Much to his chagrin however, he himself was sexually impotent, so he spent most of his life in pursuit of new and more exotic sensual pleasures. He staged elaborate orgies for his Malthusian and Eugenicist friends; he enticed his wife into innumerable lesbian affairs while he quietly observed; he experimented with mescaline and various other psychotropic and psychedelic drugs; and he established a network for both homosexual and heterosexual encounters.[73] To Sanger, Ellis was a modern day saint.

By 1922 her fame and fortune were unshakably secure. *The Pivot of Civilization* had become a best seller. On morality Sanger wrote:

The moral justification and ethical necessity of Birth Control need not be empirically based upon the mere approval of experience and custom. Its morality is more profound....It gives us control over one of the primordial forces of nature, to which in the past the majority of mankind have been enslaved, and by which it has been cheapened and debased. It arouses us to the possibility of newer and greater freedom. It develops the power, the responsibility and intelligence to use this freedom in living a liberated and abundant life. It permits us to enjoy this liberty without danger of infringing upon the similar liberty of our fellow men, or of injuring and cur-

tailing the freedom of the next generation. It shows us that we need not seek in the amassing of worldly wealth, not in the illusion of some extra-terrestrial Heaven or earthly Utopia of a remote future the road to human development. The Kingdom of Heaven is in a very definite sense within us. Not by leaving our body and our fundamental humanity behind us, not by aiming to be anything but what we are, shall we become ennobled or immortal. By knowing ourselves, by expressing ourselves, by realizing ourselves more completely than has ever before been possible, not only shall we attain the kingdom ourselves but we shall hand on the torch of life undimmed to our children and the children of our children.[74]

Writing on her views of the role of science, she quoted R.G. Ingersoll:

There is but one hope. Ignorance, poverty, and vice must stop populating the world. This cannot be done by moral suasion....This cannot be done by religion or by law, by priest or by hangman. This cannot be done by force, physical or moral. To accomplish this there is but one way. Science must make the woman the owner, the mistress of herself. Science, the only possible savior of mankind...[75]

According to Sanger, science likewise illuminates the whole issue of genius. Hidden in the common stuff of humanity lies buried this power of self-expression. Modern science is teaching us that genius is not some mysterious gift of the gods, some treasure conferred upon individuals chosen by chance. Nor is it, as Lombroso believed, the result of a pathological and degenerate condition, allied to criminality and madness. Rather is it due to the removal of physiological and psychological inhibitions and constraints that makes possible the release and the channeling of the primordial inner energies of man into full and divine expression. The removal of these inhibitions, so scientists assured her, makes possible more rapid and profound perceptions, – so rapid indeed that they seem to the ordinary human being, practically instantaneous, or intuitive. The qualities of genius are not, therefore, qualities lacking in the common reservoir of humanity, but rather the unimpeded release and direction of powers latent in all of us. This process of course is not necessarily conscious.[76] Here Sanger is echoing tenets common to anarchist, humanist and Gnostic paradigms, which will be studied throughout this book.

Sanger went on to embrace current medical discoveries as heralding a new and unprecedented era of mastery of the human body. She writes:

For a clear and illuminating account of the creative and dynamic power of the endocrine glands, the layman is referred to a recently published book by Dr. Louis Berman. This authority reveals anew how body and soul are bound up together in a complex unity. Our spiritual and psychic difficulties cannot be solved until we have mastered the knowledge of the wellsprings of our being.[77]

Her cause seemed unstoppable now. The revolution had truly begun. Even so, writes Gray, Sanger was miserable. Her private life was in utter shambles. Her marriage had ended. Her daughter caught cold and ultimately died of pneumonia. Her boys were neglected and forgotten. And her once ravishing beauty was fading with age and abuse. Desperate to find meaning and happiness, she lost herself in a profusion of sexual liaisons. She went from one lover to another, sometimes several in a single day. She experimented with innumerable erotic fantasies and fetishes, but satisfaction always eluded her grasp. She began to dabble in the occult, participating in séances and practicing Eastern meditation. She even went so far as to apply for initiation into the mysteries of Rosicruciansim and Theosophy.[78]

She continued her sordid and promiscuous affairs even after old age and poor health had overtaken her. Her attraction to occultism deepened. And perhaps worst of all, by 1949 she had become addicted to both drugs and alcohol. Although Planned Parenthood was well launched by this time, according to Gray, its success did little to ease her perpetual unhappiness.[79] Like her mentors Emma Goldman and Havelock Ellis, Sanger was not content to keep her lascivious and concupiscent behavior to herself. She was a zealous evangelist for free love. Even in her old age, she persisted in proselytizing her sixteen year old granddaughter, telling her that kissing, petting, and even intercourse were fine as long as it was "sincere," and that having sex about "three times day" was "just about right."[80] That Planned Parenthood (and Calgary Birth Control Association) is committed to undermining the moral values of teens is evident in virtually all its literature. It teaches kids to masturbate. It endorses premarital sex. It approves of homosexuality. It encourages sexual experimentation. It vilifies Christian values, prohibitions, and consciences.[81] In *The Pivot of Civilization*, Sanger explains her philosophy of "sex drive":

Restraint and constraint of individual expression, suppression of individual freedom 'for the good of society' has been practiced from time immemorial; and its failure is all too evident. There is no antagonism between the good of the individual and the good of society. The moment civilization is wise enough to remove the constraints and prohibitions which now hinder the release of inner energies, most of the larger evils of society will perish of inanition and malnutrition....Free, rational and self-ruling personality would then take the place of self-made slaves, who are the victims both of external constraints and the playthings of the uncontrolled forces of their own instincts.[82]

The great central problem, and one which must be taken first is the abolition of the shame and fear of sex. We must teach men the overwhelming power of this radiant force. We must make them understand that uncontrolled, it is a cruel tyrant, but that controlled and directed, it may be used to transmute and sublimate the everyday world into a realm of beauty and joy. Through sex, mankind may attain the great spiritual illumination which will transform the world, which will light up the only path to an earthly paradise. So must we necessarily and inevitably conceive of sex expression. The instinct is here. None of us can avoid it. It is in our power to make it a thing of beauty and a joy forever: or to deny it, as have the ascetics of the past, to revile this expression and then to pay the penalty, the bitter penalty that Society today is paying in innumerable ways.[83]

Sanger's other passion was Eugenics, which unashamedly espoused Northern and Eastern European White Supremacy. This supremacy was to be promoted both positively and negatively. Through selective breeding, the Eugenicists hoped to purify the bloodlines. The "fit" would be encouraged to reproduce prolifically. This was the positive side of Malthusian Eugenics. Negative Malthusian Eugenics on the other hand, sought to contain the "inferior" races through segregation, sterilization, birth control and abortion. The "unfit" would be slowly winnowed out of the population as chaff is from wheat.[84] The great Christian apologist G.K. Chesterton, aimed biting critiques at the Eugenicists accusing them of "a hardening of the heart with a sympathetic softening of the head," and for presuming to turn "common decency" and "commendable deeds" into social crimes. "If Darwinism was the doctrine of 'survival of the fittest,' then Eugenics was the doctrine of 'the survival of the nastiest.'" In 1922, he released a remarkably visionary book *Eugenics and Other Evils.* Chesterton pointed out, for the first time, the link between Neo-Malthusianism and Fascist Nazism. He argued:

It is the same stuffy science, the same bullying bureaucracy, and the same terrorism by tenth-rate professors, that has led the German Empire to its recent conspicuous triumphs.[85]

Here, the reader would do well to remember Chesterton's warnings when we further examine the humanist doctrines of unfettered biogenetics, pharmaceutics and what John Gilder critiques as the new "technocracy" – man's means to utopia on Earth.

Margaret Sanger was especially mesmerized by the scientific racism of Malthusian Eugenics. Part of the attraction for her was surely personal: her mentor and lover, Havelock Ellis, was the beloved disciple of Francis Galton, the brilliant cousin of Charles Darwin who first systemized and popularized Eugenic thought. Moreover, she was convinced that the "inferior races" were in fact "human weeds" and a "menace to civilization." She believed that "social regeneration" would only be possible when the "sinister forces of the hordes of irresponsibility and imbecility" were repulsed. She had come to regard organized charity to ethnic minorities and the poor as a "symptom of a malignant social disease" because it encouraged the proliferation of "defectives, delinquents, and dependents." She yearned for the end of the Christian "reign of benevolence" that the Eugenic Socialists promised, when the "choking human undergrowth" of "moron and imbeciles" would be "segregated" and "sterilized." Her goal was "to create a race of thoroughbreds" by encouraging more children from the fit, and less from the unfit.[86]

To build the work of the American Birth Control League, and ultimately, of Planned Parenthood, Margaret relied heavily on the men, women, ideas, and resources of the Eugenics movement. Virtually all of the organization's board members were Eugenicists. Financing for the early projects – from the opening of birth control clinics to publishing of the revolutionary literature – came from Eugenicists. The speakers at the conferences, the authors of the literature and the providers of the services were almost without exception avid Eugenicists.[87]

Margaret's first birth control clinic was opened in 1916, in an impoverished and densely populated area of Brooklyn. The neighborhood offered the ideal clientele: "immigrant Southern Europeans, Slavs, Latins, and Jews." As her organization grew in power and prestige, she began to target several other "dysgenic races" – including Blacks, Hispanics, Amerinds, and Catholics – and set up clinics in their respective communities as well. By their estimation as much as seventy per cent of the population fell into this "undesirable" category. In 1939, they designed a "Negro Project" in response to "southern state public health officials" – men not known for their racial equanimity. "The mass of Negroes," the project proposal asserted, "particularly in the South, still breed carelessly and disastrously, with the result that the increase among Negroes, even more than among Whites, is from that portion of the population least intelligent and fit."[88]

Again and again Planned Parenthood has asserted that its birth control programs and initiatives are designed to "prevent the need for abortion."[89] However, its claim that contraceptive services lower unwanted pregnancy rates is entirely unfounded. A number of studies have demonstrated that as contraception becomes more accessible, the number of unwanted pregnancies actually rises, thus increasing the demand for abortion.[90] And since minority communities are the primary targets for the contraceptive services, Blacks and Hispanics inevitably must bear the brunt of the abortion holocaust. A racial analysis of abortion statistics is quite revealing. As many as forty-three per cent of all abortions are performed on Blacks and another ten per cent are on Hispanics. This despite the fact that Blacks make up eleven per cent of the total U.S. population and Hispanics only about eight per cent.[91]

As already seen from the Calgary Birth Control Association philosophy and web site, Planned Parenthood-style sex education is intentionally lurid. As its founder intended, it is designed to break down sexual inhibitions and bring us into "higher self-consciousness." But in reality, Sanger's philosophies are leading our youth down the garden path of experimentation, and then deserting them in a brier patch of disease, unplanned pregnancy and emotional trauma. This study of Margaret Sanger is concluded with a current "Eugenics Manifesto":

Evolution is the development of the energy of the universe in such a way that it has an increasing ability to consciously control itself and the universe around it. It is a progressive change from the unconscious to the conscious. We are the universe trying to comprehend itself. Man is the corporeal manifestation of the universe trying to control its own destiny. Man is God in the process of coming into existence.[92]

Alfred Kinsey 1894 – 1956

The author of *Sexual Behavior in the Human Male* (commonly called *The Kinsey Report*) grew up at the turn of the century, in Hoboken, a town of 60,000. As a child, Kinsey felt emotionally confined by the pressure of his family's religious practices. The Kinsey's were Methodist – evangelical Protestants of the Victorian era, who's God was a "jealous and vengeful God." After 25 years of study, biographer James H. Jones wrote of the Kinsey spiritual environment, "He was the God of the Old Testament."[93] More important for Alfred, was the example of his father Alfred Seguine Kinsey, who dominated the spiritual life of the household. Weekly, they would follow a strict ritual of attending Sunday school, Sunday morning services and the Sunday evening prayer meeting. No one could ride to church; they had to walk. A neighbor claimed the father would not allow the family to do anything but "go to the church and eat" on the Sabbath. Not untypical, Kinsey remembered his father ordering his aunt to leave the house for playing the piano one Sunday afternoon. If suffering under this regimen was not enough, Kinsey's father also strictly played God's spokesman for the family.[94] In the pew, much of what Kinsey heard was mean-spirited, hate-filled, and fearful, calculated to produce feelings of dependence and submission, rather than love and trust. He must have suffered terribly. Theologically confused and spiritually alone, the fear of impending judgment always hovering over his consciousness. Jones claims the energy Kinsey found for his research drew upon a well of emotion "created in his private life, in the fearful things he kept hidden from the world."[95]

From early youth there were two sides to Kinsey. Publicly he attended with other adolescent boys, his church, his schools, the YMCA, and the Boy Scouts. Privately, according to Jones, Kinsey practiced high levels of voyeurism and exhibitionism after he reached adulthood, likely the result behaviors developed in camps, change rooms or in settings of Kinsey's own making. In an interview (1984), Harvard anthropologist and Kinsey's associate Paul Gebhard, explained the likely genesis of Kinsey's inner most turmoil as a youth. Like all children he was curious about sex and wanted to explore others and himself. "The only homosexual thing that he ever mentioned in this early part [of his life] was in his childhood when there was preadolescent sex play with a neighborhood group."[96] In reaction to a more detailed depiction, Jones writes, "Gebhard's characterization of the basement incident as 'homosexual' strongly suggests that Kinsey used this term to describe the incident to him."[97] According to Jones:

What is clear is that this pious boy lost his ongoing battle with masturbation and was consumed by guilt for doing so. Given how badly he wanted to control his urges, Kinsey must have been tough on himself, especially as seems likely, masturbation was accompanied by homosexual fantasies.[98]

From a number of evidences, Jones concluded, "In secret, Kinsey found pleasure through pain" and "by late adolescence, his masochism was well advanced."[99]

Hard work and keen intellect made Kinsey the valedictorian of the Columbia High School class of 1912. Writes Jones:

By this time Kinsey was trapped within two separate and conflicting identities: a public boy who met his parent's every wish, and a private boy who secretly violated their most basic moral strictures and punished himself for doing so. Although it must have taken enormous energy to keep these identities in equilibrium, Kinsey accomplished this with remarkable success. Still it was a precarious balancing act, requiring constant reinforcement by success in the public world and rigid control over the self he showed others.[100]

Regarding the former, Kinsey had to be the best at everything he did. Throughout his life, he showed a passion for complex and difficult activities, he could never be satisfied with being merely good at something. As Gebhard observed:

This man had a real demon on his back. He had to excel, and if he couldn't excel in an area, he wouldn't have anything to do with that area...he had this real obsession he had to excel.[101]

In high school, the class prophecy predicted he would become "a second Darwin." But his father had other plans. The "great 'I' man" ordered his son to attend the Stevens Institute to study mechanical engineering. Kinsey's wife Clara, later remarked in sarcasm, "everybody except his father knew he wanted to be a biologist." A self-trained engineer, the father wanted his elder son to follow in his footsteps. Jones observed:

It was predictable that Alfred Seguine Kinsey would dictate his son's occupation because the issue of control colored every aspect of their relationship. Telling a son what to do with his life came easy to a man who placed little premium on independence of his children.[102]

Alfred Seguine Kinsey saw his son as an extension of himself and although he had achieved much in his lifetime, he intended to use his son to complete his own unfinished business.

For Kinsey, the thought of becoming an engineer was abhorrent. Despite his passion for biology and his desperate need for independence, Kinsey obediently entered Stevens Institute in the fall of 1912. A lifetime of feeling suffocated by parental domination expressed itself in poor marks, which was out of character for Kinsey. Says Jones, "He simply chose not to succeed." For the first time in his life education became an ordeal. He endured for two years until commencement day, June 1914. After the ceremony, Kinsey withdrew from Stevens and asked to have his transcripts sent to Bowdoin College, an institution known for its strong biology department. As Clara Kinsey put it, "Finally, he just rebelled. He said he absolutely wouldn't go anymore."[103] Alfred Seguine Kinsey, was shocked, stunned and furious. How could a boy who had always been so obedient, so perfect in every way, suddenly turn into a rebel?

Showing his true colors, if he could not control his son's life, he would neither finance his freedom. From that day on, Kinsey's father refused to put another penny into his son's education. Leaving home for college, all the support he got from his parents was a new suit worth twenty-five dollars. Never again would Kinsey ask his father for assistance, and never again would he seek permission or approval for anything.[104] A nasty divorce between his parents ended what remained of Kinsey's relationship with his father. In August 1931, Kinsey's father went to Reno, Nevada where he filed for a "quickie" divorce. Alfred Seguine Kinsey simply abandoned his wife and never returned. Facing the "Dirty Thirties" on her own, virtually uneducated, sixty years old, with no marketable skills, she pleaded for reconciliation, but her husband refused. Soon after he started dating an attractive woman who was many years his junior. Eventually he remarried.[105] For Kinsey, the episode was bittersweet:

...Kinsey despised his father, as only a person who has been deeply wronged can, and the divorce freed him to act accordingly. Perhaps even Kinsey took a perverse satisfaction at seeing his father exposed as a hypocrite. While attitudes were changing, divorce still carried a stigma in the United States. Public opinion did not look kindly on a man who abandoned his wife, especially one who had given him three children and had stood by him for nearly forty years. At any rate, Kinsey walled his

father off completely. Without ranting and raging, he reduced the old man to a psychological status of a nonentity.[106]

Separated in spirit, Kinsey and his father never solved the basic conflicts that fathers and sons must resolve in order to see each other as autonomous individuals. Instead, they stood hostage to their old roles as antagonists.[107] Kinsey went on with his life, completing his education, marrying Clara McMillen and joining the faculty of Zoology at Indiana University.

Jones writes of Kinsey's private life:

His inner turmoil surfaced most clearly in his strident rejection of the twin touchstones of his childhood – religion and sexual repression.[108]

Each was connected to the other; each was a source of ongoing conflict. As head of the family, Kinsey rejected the intense religiosity of his childhood. Daughter Joan, recalls:

Daddy felt very strongly about...the need for no religion....It was not a passive attitude toward it...He really had no use for it. It was an active, almost on occasions aggressive dislike for religion.[109]

A former graduate student, recalled Kinsey's animosity toward religion:

He wouldn't go to church, and he didn't believe in God, and he believed that this was it....If there was any heaven you'd better make it right now, and you could make it a hell also.[110]

More than religion, sexual repression was the issue on which Kinsey broke most dramatically from the past. Recognizing the role religion played in his childhood guilt-repression-trauma-expression cycle, he thought the best way to produce well-adjusted adults was to rear children who did not feel guilty about their sexuality. He placed his hopes on sex education to mold individuals and reform society.[111] He no longer felt self-inhibited or constrained in his expression of sexuality, other than prudent secrecy. Even here he delighted in exhibitionism and living on the "edge."

By the mid-1930s, Kinsey was involved with numerous male students, taking great risks as "a sex-obsessed man would take in exchange for a modicum of erotic satisfaction." Jones brings evidence of a number of student conversions to homosexual behavior, while on field camps with Kinsey:

For four and a half months, Kinsey did not see his wife, just as the young men who accompanied him did not see their girlfriends...Repeating the behavior that had upset Rainwater [student], Kinsey initiated a series of graphic discussions about sex. Judging from Breland's diary, he knew which buttons to push...Breland's diary suggests that the three engaged in sexual activity, with Kinsey and Breland showing Coon [another student] the way....Breland described what happened one evening: 'After supper told 'bedtime' stories & initiated Jim. Some party!'[112]

Not only was he able to suffuse his field trips with sexual discussions and sexual behavior, but he managed to keep two students, Voris and Breland, in his orbit long after they finished their degrees. Nellie Breland hated Kinsey. More than a half a century after her husband finished his Ph. D. at Indiana University, she adamantly refused to be interviewed about Kinsey. Jones recorded part of her short conversation over the telephone:

He was a dirty old man. He really hurt us. We were just kids from Mississippi. We didn't know anything.[113]

Kinsey denounced sexual prejudices and superstitions for inflicting untold damage on people. He pointed to religion stating:

There is abundant reason for placing the breakdown of our modern home at the door of the Christian Church, through its relentless hostility to passion and its strident efforts to control sexuality.[114]

Kinsey attempted to stand conventional morality on its head. "The great distortions of sex are the cultural perversions of celibacy, delayed marriage, and asceticism."[115] Kinsey asserted the irreducible fact that human beings are animals, an argument he would make over and over again throughout his life. He held that as certain behaviors occur in the animal kingdom, society was wrong to expect human beings to be held to some artificial higher behavioral standard. By insisting that humans shared certain patterns of sexual behavior common with other mammals, he was arguing that biology had to be reckoned with when people formulated sexual mores and codes of conduct. Following from his biology-based prescription, Kinsey felt religion had to be deposed as the arbiter of sexual conduct. In its place he offered science. He wanted the public to consult science to discover "the biological bases of society." Science alone would reveal the truth about human sexuality, allowing people to satisfy their needs as nature intended. [116]

Kinsey, frustrated at not having enough statistical material for his lectures, began collecting his own data by surveying students in his marriage class. Finding that data insufficient, he distributed questionnaires to students and the faculty at large, conducting interviews when he could. As he told one young man, "I am interested in discovering the fact(s) and believe the world's thinking can be made more tolerant only if the facts are known."[117] Soon Kinsey was arguing his interpretation of sexual identity to a gay interviewee:

In essence, Kinsey argued that sexual identity was largely the result of how people, responded to their early sexual experiences. 'After one has a pleasurable first experience, of either sort,' he explained, 'he looks forward to a repetition of the experience with such anticipation that he may be aroused by the sight or mere thought of another person with whom he can make contact.' Reminding the young man of his own history, Kinsey argued that 'unsatisfactory experience, of either sort, will (as in your early contact with the heterosexual) build up a prejudice against any repetition of that experience.' Therefore, it seemed clear that sexual identity followed the pleasure principle. 'Whether one builds a heterosexual pattern or a homosexual pattern depends, therefore, very largely upon the satisfactory or unsatisfactory nature of his first experiences,' Kinsey declared.[118]

The beauty of sex research, for Kinsey, was that it allowed him to transform his voyeurism into science. Over time Kinsey built up a remarkable network of individuals who were prepared to perform while people watched. Once *Sexual Behavior in the Human Male* was released to the public Kinsey experienced a heightening of pressure and stress publicly and growing risk and fantasy privately. As a last testimony to Kinsey's inner life, Jones reveals:

Kinsey attempted to build a private world that would provide the emotional support he needed. Within the inner circle of his senior staff members and their spouses, he endeavored to create his own sexual utopia, a scientific subculture whose members would not be bound by arbitrary and antiquated sexual taboos…Although he excluded children categorically…Kinsey decreed that within the inner circle men could have sex with each other, wives would be swapped freely, and wives, too, would be free to embrace whichever sexual partners they liked...a handful of trusted outsiders would be…given full membership privileges.[119]

Bringing in outsiders was absolutely essential for Kinsey to achieve sexual satisfaction, as no other member of the inner circle could fulfill his masochistic or homosexual desires, though Pomery [married staff member] was willing to play act to meet Kinsey's needs. The problem, though, was that the sex between Kinsey and Pomeroy had gradually lost its erotic charge. A man who knew both Kinsey and Pomeroy intimately declared, 'Wardell [Pomeroy] is fundamentally not s/m; he's experimental.' Thus…Kinsey had to look elsewhere…'Kinsey thought sadomasochists were the most frustrated people in the world because of their difficulty in finding each other,' wrote Pomeroy.[120]

Kinsey had a preference for coworkers with certain behavioral items in their sexual histories. Homosexual experience was a definite plus.[121] Throughout the time of the Institute he would court some of the staff for his own sexual relationships. Jones drew from a reliable source who knew both Kinsey and a staff member [Martin]:

Kinsey relied upon guilt and covert pressure to woo young Martin into bed, which proved to be far more effective than bullying. 'Sweet fatherly figure sort of expects it and you don't want to disappoint him and you don't want to make waves and so on.' Was how the friend described Kinsey's approach. Not that he blamed Kinsey for lusting after Martin. 'Martin was a very good-looking boy in those years,' the friend declared.[122] *For a time, Martin was able to be sexually responsive, but homosexuality was not his inclination. He was much more interested in women. Kinsey got Martin to do all sorts of things, but Martin didn't like it…Kinsey stayed 'after him for years.'* [123]

There was something grim in the way Kinsey was approaching sex, not only in his private life but in his research. In both areas, he was becoming more compulsive, like a man who had become addicted to risk taking. The sexual escapades of his staff and others in his home attic were political dynamite. If the press had gotten wind of what was happening, Kinsey's career and credibility would have ended then and there, particularly with the advent of McCarthyism. Yet not only did he go right on staging these sessions but he compounded the danger by creating a visual record on film.

Initially he had the attic episodes filmed without the participants' knowledge, but in March 1949, Kinsey hired William Dellenback, as a permanent camera man and staff member of the Institute. "Open" live filming in the attic started almost immediately. Dellenback recalled the tight security, noting the filming was done "on the q.t." and that copies of the staff films were "kept under lock and key."[124] One staff wife complained of the "sickening pressure" she was under to have sex on film with her spouse and other staff members. She told an interviewer, "I felt like my husband's career at the Institute depended on it."[125] Stewart ("privileged" outsider) recalls as the sessions unfolded, various members of the inner circle dropped in to watch the performance. Among the spectators, he was particularly impressed by Kinsey's wife, Clara, whom he described was "a true scientist to the end," noting that "she sat by and once in a while calmly changed the sheets upon the work bench." This was typical Clara noted Gebhard:

At the conclusion of a filming session, Mac [Clara] would suddenly appear, literally with persimmon pudding or milk and cookies or something. [She would] simply come in absolutely blasé about the nude individuals...Some...were simply dumbfounded by this.[126]

In theory, the ideology that underpinned Kinsey's study and report was "to accumulate an objectively determined body of fact about sex which strictly avoids social or moral interpretations of that fact." Yet in sex there is hardly space for what might be called "neutral ground." His approach to what he delighted in calling "the human animal" was "agnostic."[127] Learning from his past mistakes, particularly the assault by the medical and psychiatric professions during his marriage and family course, Kinsey took great pains to come across as impartial. However, the final report showed his true intent. In reality, Jones concludes, "He had definite ideas about how people should behave sexually, and these preferences were only too transparent in his writing." Gebhard recalled, "Underneath there was this powerful streak of crusading humanitarianism."[128] Kinsey applauded every kind of sexual activity, and he disapproved of abstinence. Gebhard notes:

I think he felt the human animal, as he would say, was basically pansexual – that everybody would be a mixture of hetero and homosexuality, about a two on the Kinsey scale.[129]

For Kinsey, labels such as homosexual and heterosexual did not make sense. People engaged in homosexual acts; they were not homosexuals. Therefore the only proper use for the word was as an adjective, not as a noun. Pressing his point, he declared:

It would encourage clearer thinking on these matters if persons were not characterized as heterosexual or homosexual, but as individuals who have had certain amounts of heterosexual experience and certain amounts of homosexual experience.[130]

And he felt that neither male nor female was inherently monogamous.[131]

Kinsey's report, *Sexual Behavior in the Human Male* offered a plea for further liberation. For example, when he discussed young boys who had somehow found the courage to defy the sexual morality of their parents, Kinsey spoke not of wicked, rebellious children but of youngsters who "triumph over the parents."[132] Kinsey saw civilization as the enemy of sex, particularly the "prohibition on youth-aged sexual activity." His only regret was that children did not have more sex, and he blamed society for making it hard for youngsters to explore their sexuality. He went even so far as to argue that "half or more of the boys in an uninhibited society could reach climax by the time they were three or four years of age, and that nearly all of them could experience such a climax three to five years before the onset of adolescence."[133] Kinsey referred to pre-marital sex as a "triumph over morals." "They may 'know that intercourse is wrong,' but 'they expect to have it anyway, because it is human and natural to have it.'"[134] This was Kinsey's language of defiance, hope and redemption.

When the *Kinsey Report* hit the street it was an immediate public relations success. Rocketing to the top of the bestseller list, where it stayed for 27 weeks, the report introduced facts and statistics into America's dinner table conversations that dramatically altered perception of sexual behavior in America. The statistics shocked and scandalized: 86 per cent of men said they had engaged in premarital sex; 50 per cent said they had committed adultery before turning 40; 37 per cent of men reported at least one episode of homosexual sex; and 17 per cent of men who had grown up on farms claimed to have had sex with animals. The *Kinsey Report* blew the lid off the container in which sexual experience had been sealed. The following magazine examples give a taste of media approval:

Many of our most deep-rooted concepts of sex and marriage are about to be blasted by a soberly documented report of a group of University of Indiana [sic] scientists, following a nine year survey of sex habits of the American people. – Harper's

[Kinsey's facts showed] a great schizophrenic split, a chasm between what Americans do and what they believe they do, what they practice and what they preach. – Science Illustrated

Implicit in the revolutionary Kinsey report is a plea for greater public and private tolerance of the vast differences in the sex habits of Americans. Such terms as abnormal, unnatural, oversexed, and undersexed, as used in our legal and moral codes, have little validity in light of Professor Kinsey's revelations. There is a tremendous variety in the frequency and type of sexual behavior in normal Americans. – Harper's[135]

In *Time* critical commentary came from a number of professional fields. The most scathing commentaries took longer to rally. According to Jones, debate stratified along a number of issues: poor statistics of data collected; unrepresentative sampling technique; faulty interview technique; treatment of humans as animals; rank biological reductionism, blatant behaviorism, ignored psychology; ignored social and emotional context of sex – "love" was never discussed; ignored culture and its role; and finally, he was a crypto-reformer who promoted permissiveness under the guise of science.[136] Had these objections come from minor people in obscure journals and magazines, Kinsey could have relaxed, but his critics read like the Who's Who of American intellectual life.[137]

Succumbing to Kinsey's tenet that numbers rendered behavior normal, young people wondered if there was no longer a place for the word "abnormal" in a scientist's vocabulary. Norman Vincent Peale argued against this idea in *Reader's Digest*: "No matter how many murders there are, murder will never be normal."[138] Geoffrey Gorer, a British anthropologist, challenged Kinsey's data. Gorer would have instigated random "stratified sampling" correlating data with other criteria like age, education, religion, region, economic level etc. Instead, "Kinsey had relied upon volunteers at college lectures" and "on personal introductions from interested individuals, which were obviously statistically invalid; and consequently distorted."[139] Margaret Mead, one of America's most distinguished cultural anthropologists, broadened the attack. She criticized Kinsey for upsetting the balance between ignorance and knowledge upon which social restraint depended, for atomizing sex by taking "sexual behavior out of its inter-personal context" and "reducing it to a simple act of elimination." What most disturbed her, however, was Kinsey's failure to offer young people guidance. As she put it caustically, "the book suggests no way of choosing between a woman and a sheep."[140]

Kinsey had asked Lawrence Kubie, one of the nation's most prominent psychoanalysts, to write a review. Kubie sent Kinsey a copy, along with a warning, "It was a two-fisted review, I am afraid." Weaving back and forth between technical criticisms and theoretical objections, Kubie attacked Kinsey for faulty statistical procedures that inflated the incidence of taboo behavior, for failing to comprehend and correct for bilateral deceptions and other psychodynamics inherent in oral interviews, for his blind faith in, and imperfect understanding of human memory, for consistently ignoring or discounting the importance of psychological forces in human sexuality, for his biological definition of normality that was elastic to include a variety of sexual perversions, and, last but not least, for his gratuitous, ignorant, and wrongheaded criticisms of psychological theory and his demeaning characterizations of the psychiatric profession. *Time* magazine gave Kubie's review big play, calling his criticisms "the most devastating scientific attack on the *Report* yet."[141]

Lionel Trilling, attacked Kinsey from a cultural flank. He took Kinsey to task for his view of human nature, which never transcended the argument *de animalibus*; for atomizing sex (failing to comprehend that sex involves the whole of an individual's character); for allowing the notion of the natural to develop into the idea of the normal; and for advancing his own peculiar views while simultaneously proclaiming his objectivity. Trilling further argued, "it is full of assumptions and conclusions; it makes very positive statements on highly debatable matters and it editorializes very freely." Above all, he criticized Kinsey for oversimplified thinking and reliance on absolute concepts. He saw Kinsey for what he was: a biologist who could not transcend narrow, materialistic thinking. On the positive, Trilling viewed the *Report* as "a recoil from the crude and often brutal rejection which society has made of persons it calls aberrant" and as a way to habituate "its readers to the idea of sexuality in all its manifestations, to establish, as it were, a democratic pluralism."[142]

In time, the American Statistic Association conducted a full review of Kinsey's work. Regarding the most serious issue, the reliability of the results, they commented that "there was no way Kinsey could have avoided a nonrandom sample." In their judgment, "the peculiar problems associated with sex research made statistical analysis extremely difficult." Even with the most reliable sampling techniques, they declared, "there will be a certain percentage of the population who refuse to give histories." In sum the inspectors refused to give a definitive straight answer on the accuracy of the *Report*.[143]

In 1953, Kinsey finished the sequel, *Sexual Behavior in the Human Female*. However, by the time of the second study his beloved Institute for Sex Research was near to closure. Claims that 2 per cent of females identified themselves as exclusively homosexual, and 13 per cent of women had had homosexual activity at least once, no longer caught the public's imagination. By the end of the summer 1954, Kinsey finally faced the reality that the Rockefeller Foundation would never renew his grant. Dejected and bitter, he did the unthinkable. For years, he had boosted the pain he inflicted on himself with urethral insertions by tying a rope around his scrotum and tugging hard while he masturbated. On this particular August evening, his anxiety must have been worse – much worse Jones writes:

Too strong to be resisted, the compulsion could only be obeyed. Doing as his inner demons demanded, Kinsey threw a rope over the pipe…Skillfully, he tied a strong, tight knot around his scrotum with one end of the rope dangling from the pipe overhead. The other end he wrapped around his hand. Then, he climbed up on a chair and jumped off, suspending himself in midair…the only way he could vent his anxiety was through self-torture and debasement.[144]

Immediately after this tragedy, Gebhard and Kinsey flew to Peru. There Kinsey took ill and spent weeks in a Peruvian hospital. As a cover story, Kinsey attributed his illness to a throat infection that had spread to his pelvis en route to Peru.[145] A physician friend witnessed that Kinsey's illness was orchitis, pinpointing the testicles as the site of infection.[146] In the remaining two years of his life, Kinsey tried to keep his Institute alive. On August 1, 1956, the government had filed suit against the Institute. Congress had investigated his research and all but accused him of being a communist. Kinsey died a broken man, on August 25, 1956, at sixty-two years of age.

Though the data is now 50 years old, and though most experts believe its findings of sexual activity to be grossly inflated, the Kinsey reports remained the standard source for information about sexual activity until at least 1994. Various academic studies contradicted aspects of Kinsey's findings, but these studies were of much narrower scope. Broad studies of society that captured some data about sex, such as the General Social Survey (GSS), found quantities and varieties of sexual activity much lower than what Kinsey found. Would-be analysts of the sexual revolution and its aftermath were left with a morass of conflicting and outdated information. In 1994, the University of Chicago researchers announced the findings of their *National Health and Social Life Survey*. Their conclusion – Our sex lives are dull, very, very dull.[147]

"Americans, we find, are not having much partnered sex at all," the authors wrote. The survey said Americans are largely monogamous. Over a lifetime, a typical man has only six partners; a woman, two. Married people have more sex than singles. Hardly anyone goes in for kinky stuff; vaginal sex was far and away the most popular brand (favored by 96 per cent of respondents), followed by a sex act so mild it can be performed through eyeglasses: "Watching a partner undress." Seventy-five per cent of the men and 85 per cent of the women said they had never cheated on their spouses. And forget what you've seen on the bumper stickers, the homosexual population is nowhere near one in ten. Only 2.7 per cent of the men and 1.3 per cent of the women reported that they had had gay sex in the preceding year.[148]

More than 300 newspapers ran the story on the front page. "Turns Out," one headline read, "We Are Sexually Conventional." The Chicago team even collaborated with a journalist to produce a companion book, *Sex in America*, that attempted to break down all the stuffy scientific rhetoric. We learn that 10 per cent of the men and 9 per cent of the women had had anal sex in the preceding year; that 23 per cent of the men and 11 per cent of the women bought X-rated movies; that 27 per cent of the men and 19 per cent of the women had had oral sex; and that 63 per cent of the men and 42 per cent of the women masturbated. We learn that 6.2 per cent of men and 4.2 per cent of women said they were sexually attracted to people of the same gender, though fewer than half that number had actually engaged in homosexual sex in the preceding year. We read that Roman Catholics were the most likely to say they were virgins (4 per cent) and that Jews had had the most sex partners (34 per cent had had ten or more). Protestant women had the most orgasms (32 per cent had one every time), but Catholics had more intercourse. For the most part, the study was well received, although not in the gay community, where many thought their numbers had been undercounted. Laumann and Michael predicted that AIDS would not become an epidemic that infected huge portions of the heterosexual community. Stay away from gay men and drug users, the authors comforted us, and you should be fine.[149]

Billy Graham would accuse Kinsey of doing more harm to undermine morality than any other American.

Henry Morgentaler 1923 -

According to biographer Catherine Dunphy, it was through the "pro-choice cause" that Henry Morgentaler was able to live up to the legacy of his Jewish socialist-martyr father, Josef Morgentaler, and to the stern ideals of his remote, artistic mother, Golda. The abortion crusade in Canada gave him meaning and rescued him from despair. It let him be brave. It provided the enemies he needed, the media attention he sought, the adulation he craved and a platform with which he, a survivor of Auschwitz and Dachau, could fight the state and win.[150] Abortion on demand fit well the morality of his atheist and humanist belief system. He was not seen as a feminist but as a humanist; he loved many women and couldn't be monogamous.

His first wife, his childhood sweetheart, with whom he survived five brutal and tense years in the Lodz ghetto during the war, refuses to speak about her former husband and has as little as possible to do with him. Just months before a tribute to Morgentaler his second wife bolted from Montreal to Chile, taking their son, Yann, with her. Yann has said this was what he himself wanted. Morgentaler's eldest child and only daughter, Goldie, cut off communications with him many years before.[151] He is not a family man in any traditional sense of the term.

Henry Morgentaler is a Polish-born Jew raised as an atheist. When thinking about the ten year abortion battle, he credited his mother for his "strength of character, steadfastness in adversity and artistic sensitivity," and his father for "gentleness, compassion, idealism and a commitment to social justice."[152] He was first president and founder of the Humanist Association of Canada (HAC). This humanist philosophy, in "spirit" placed him in company with Charles Darwin; Albert Einstein; Margaret Atwood; John Kenneth Galbraith; Pierre Trudeau; Sue Rodriguez; Carl Sagan and Benjamin Spock, to mention a few.

According to the HAC web site, humanism is a life-stance dedicated to the betterment of society through the use of reason and ethics from a non-religious viewpoint. Humanists look to scientific inquiry, reason and compassion for the solutions to human problems. Humanists do not believe in any deity and consider notions of an afterlife and rewards and punishment after death by a supernatural god meaningless. The movement supports equality between the sexes and promotes a non-violent approach to resolving conflicts. Statistics Canada records that about 3 million people are without religious beliefs [all are not necessarily humanists]. For adherents, humanism is an alternative to organized religion. The first funeral service conducted by an HAC celebrant was held in March 1995, the first HAC wedding ceremony was held in August 1996, and in June 1998, HAC performed its first "undoctrination" ceremony.[153]

Humanism, although not yet identified as such in Poland, was Morgentaler's heritage. His father, Josef was a Jewish socialist and union-activist, who Henry worshipped, although he rarely saw him. Josef helped establish the Textile Workers' Union and began protesting for an end to sixteen-hour days, improved working conditions and better pay. He earned the reputation of revolutionary and troublemaker. According to Dunphy, the Jewish socialist Labor Bund was never just a political party. It was central to the lives of thousands of secular Polish Jewish families. Its dogma was their faith, its heroes their saints. There were celebrations, a secular society's replacement for religious holidays and rituals. Morgentaler's parents were attracted because the Bund broke with the fatalistic Jewish religious tradition of wait, hope and adapt as a way of overcoming problems.[154] Golda Nitka Morgentaler intimidated Henry, and he has always felt she didn't love him. His had been a painful breech birth; she had been ill for the first six weeks of his life and he was cared for by a wet nurse. More to the point, says Dunphy, he was pale and awkward, always underfoot, as well as sickly.[155]

Walking home, he would pass a Polish Roman Catholic school just as its students were getting out for the day. They poured from the building, blond kids, faces reddening as they screamed, "Jew! You killed Jesus Christ," then surrounding him and beating him up. Soon Henry began to detour through the fields, giving a wide berth any time he saw a group of Polish boys, no matter how far away they were. It was the prudent thing to do. Dunphy says, today, it still gnaws at him: "Walking around, walking away, avoiding those Polish boys gave me a feeling I was a coward. I had to battle against that feeling for a long time. And later on I had to prove to myself I wasn't." [156] Four years later in 1936, when Henry was thirteen, the Morgentalers moved back to the ghetto. Anti-Semitism by then was rampant; violence was increasing. It was no longer possible for a even a nonreligious Jewish family, to live in the Polish parts of the city.

By the time the Germans had officially taken over the city, a sixteen year old Henry was already on his way to Warsaw. Henry could not understand why Josef had returned from his hiding place in the country. He did not want to think his heroic father might have given up, but Josef Morgentaler was subdued and depressed, and looked very much a broken, disheartened man those last days he spent with his family. There was no laughter, no more fist pounding politics or earnest confessions of simple dreams. When the military police knocked on their apartment door the afternoon of September 21, 1939, they were very polite as they requested that Josef Morgentaler accompany them. He was taken to a detention camp in Radogoszcz, a suburb of Lodz, where he was interrogated and tortured. Golda managed to visit her husband and bring him some food once or twice before he disappeared, but Henry never saw his father again.[157]

The "Final Solution" was adopted on January 20, 1942. Henry managed to maintain a semblance of his former life until then. The Morgentaler family was soon rounded up and sent to Auschwitz. Although only fifty, Golda Morgentaler had probably been ordered straight to the gas chamber. Just twenty-five, like many others including his brother Mike, Henry worked twelve hours of excruciating labor every day to survive. Surrounded by death and starvation he still wanted to live, but his strength was ebbing away. He thought, "Maybe I should believe in God." Writes Dunphy:

But how could a God let such a thing happen to his people? To people who believed in him? All around were the faithful praying to their God, and then dying wretchedly the next day. How could millions of people be so sinful that they would be punished by this horrible death by degradation? So he picked a star in the sky, an active one that zigged, then zagged with brio. That's what he would believe in.[158]

When Morgentaler was rescued, he weighted 70 lbs. Says Dunphy:

At some stage he decided to become a doctor, a healer, a Saviour, a man like Louis Pasteur. He would never be afraid again. He would never play by anyone else's rules. That was for his father. The Nazis had not beaten Henry Morgentaler. Anything was possible again.[159]

In February 1950, Henry and wife Chava (3 months pregnant) arrived in Montreal to create a new life. Memories of his father's achievements left Morgentaler with a nagging sensation that he did not deserve a comfortable life, until he had attained a level of heroism like that of his father. And he had always known what he wanted. From the moment he'd walked off the boat into Montreal's chilled February air, he has been in charge of his life. Observes Dunphy:

Most everything in the years that followed had gone according to plan, his plan and his goal, the one he had decreed for himself in the camps.[160]

Goldie Morgentaler was born August 8, 1950, and was named after the mother Henry was never sure loved him. By 1953, he had received his medical degree at Cardinal Léger. He worked summers as camp doctor in a Hebrew-speaking camp until gaining Canadian citizenship, along with his license to practice in the province of Quebec, in 1955. From 1960 to 1964, Morgentaler underwent therapy for nightmares. The alternating blue lights and siren of the snow removal equipment triggered flashbacks. Some psychiatrists believed it was impossible ever to recover from the Holocaust, even for a survivor like Henry, who believes it was luck, not any divine guidance, that let him live.[161] Therapy had given him an understanding: "It opened up a lot of energy." In 1963 Henry happened to read a small newspaper announcement of a Montreal talk by a member of the Ethical Cultural Society from New York City. It was sponsored by the Humanist Fellowship of Montreal, an organization Morgentaler had never heard of; however, that night everything Jerome Nathanson said Mongentaler believed. Suddenly his ideas and experiences were coming together into a coherent framework. He joined the Humanists that night.

With humanism, Henry finally thought he was home. A philosophy and lifestyle that is not only nonreligious but antireligious, it advocated bettering society through reason, scientific inquiry and humanitarian compassion. Here was everything Josef Morgentaler believed in – social justice, brotherhood and the belief that people are inherently good and society's institutions cause much of the evil in our culture. In Montreal's Humanist Fellowship, Henry believed he had found a place where Jews were equal partners in social activism with Unitarians, atheists, intellectuals and other humanitarians from far-flung and varied ethnic origins. This would be where Henry would keep his father's faith – and rejuvenate his own, which had been battered by the brutality he encountered from the Third Reich. In 1964, Henry became president of the Montreal Humanist Fellowship and when the Montreal Humanists decided to present a paper to a special government standing committee of health and welfare looking into abortion law reform, Morgentaler's destiny fell into place. Writes Dunphy:

Here was an issue he knew something about, a medical matter that spilled over into society and into real people's lives. It provided an unprecedented chance to mesh his work with his philosophical and value systems, and gave Humanists the opportunity to rally around an idea central to their beliefs. It was also an issue on which all the Fellowships could agree. (The brief was endorsed by Humanists in Victoria, BC, and in Toronto, and Henry believed it served to instigate the formation the following year of the Humanist Association of Canada. Henry was its first president.) But first he had to convince his fellow Humanists to take a more radical position from the one they referred, which mirrored the Canadian Medical Association's middle-of-the-road stance that abortions be granted when a committee of three doctors decreed a woman's life or health was in danger.[162]

He was in a state of heightened anticipation, happier than he had felt in years. In recommending that women have abortion on demand, he knew he was going to make Canadian history. During the presentation, Liberal MP Warren Allmand, asked why a fetal age of five months should be a cut-off point for allowing abortions (as recommended by the Humanists), when science should be able to keep a child alive outside the womb after three months. "I think that is a very interesting question," Morgentaler replied. "I also think I will have trouble answering it…"[163] Soon women from all over Canada started calling Morgentaler, women who thought they had finally found someone who would perform abortions on demand. "Oh, God, what did I do? What did I do ?" he moaned.[164]

In 1967, Canada appeared to want to follow Britain's lead in liberalizing abortion and homosexuality. Justice Minister Pierre Trudeau (previously a member of the Board of the Montreal Humanist Chapter)[165] tabled an omnibus bill reforming the Criminal Code. It became law in 1969 when he was Prime Minister. Homosexuality was decriminalized and so was the dissemination of contraceptives or contraceptive information, after a long campaign spearheaded by Planned Parenthood founders Barbara and George Cadbury.[166] Prior to legal reform in 1969, abortion was the leading cause of death to women in their maternal years. Despite social condemnation, legal barriers and dangerous conditions, many women sought out abortions. A police chief complained long and bitterly in a *Toronto Telegram* article about the many women going to Cuba for abortions and those using the dubious talents of local abortionists. "Most abortionists are unskilled persons who do their work in the client's home or in their own home with no regard for sanitation," noted reporter Helen Allen. The motive was age-old and it wasn't noble. "It's the money that gets people into this business," said Detective Sergeant William Quennell, whom Allen described as head of Metro Toronto police's abortion squad.[167]

As early as 1960, the United Church of Canada was the first religious body to publicly advocate abortion for women whose health or life was in jeopardy because of pregnancy. But it was only when medical professional bodies joined the fray that legislators were convinced it was time to come out of hiding on this issue. In *The Politics of Abortion*, professors Janine Brodie, Shelley Gavigan and Jane Jenson estimated that thirty-three thousand abortions were performed in Canada in 1959 alone.[168] Here a need to address the safety issue seemed practical and sensible. Certainly more sensible than the headline-grabbing notion being touted by a Dr. Morgentaler that there should be no value judgments, just abortions for whoever asked for one.[169] Says Dunphey:

Perhaps, but it was 1969. Society was in extreme flux, and the boundaries between medicine and mores were blurred and shaken. To Morgentaler the opportunity was clear and in east-end Montreal, he decided to fold up his family practice and specialize in abortion.[170]

Only once did he tell a journalist that his wife Eva had had an abortion. In the mid eighties, Ian Brown, then a feature writer for the *Globe and Mail*, reported that "Eva has endured a 'very illegal; and very painful abortion in the early 1950s – no anesthetic was used." Henry admitted he felt helpless and demeaned. They had been ordered to use the servants' back entrance into the imposing stone Westmount mansion of the abortionist. The nurse there was brusque and disdainful; Eva had been ill and shaken.[171] In his ground-breaking article in the *Humanist*, he wrote of a patient of his who had needed an abortion and who committed suicide when he didn't help her. [Since then he has admitted that the reference to the suicidal patient was not entirely accurate.] Said Morgentaler, "I wanted to make my point. I don't think I ever had a patient who committed suicide, although I had lots of women who threatened to commit suicide if they didn't get help."[172]

Morgentaler amazed himself:

Here I was for the first time in my life doing my most daring thing in my life, really, defying the law of the new country that had adopted me, basically, and playing for very high stakes, risking prison, possibly my medical license, the security of my family.[173]

Comments Dunphy:

He felt uplifted, mythic; finally he had reached for and embraced his destiny. Now that his cause had his total commitment, now that he was an action hero, it was more than a cause – it was a crusade.[174]

He never asked Eva what she thought of his decision to perform abortions. He spoke with no one about it – "Why didn't I discuss it with Eva? I don't know. At the time we were pretty much apart in our lifestyles."[175]

Morgentaler went on the campaign trail across Canada. As Bobbie Spark, one of the women on the Abortion Caravan, told the *Socialist Worker* magazine years later:

You have to understand that patriarchy is a system of control, that those who control my body and my womb and those who control the courts are all linked... I think it's important to understand that when you take on what appears to be, in the public eye, a single issue, in fact if you really follow it through you find that they all interlock and dovetail. It puts you up against capitalism, against the church and against the state, and against all the structures that support these institutions, and they all have a vested interest in opposing women's rights to abortion.[176]

Dr. Heather Morris, who headed a Canada-wide organization, Alliance for Life, became a bitter foe. Morgentaler described her:

[She] was the worst. She was very religious. Once I debated her in front of a labor movement group and she took out a recording of a fetal heart. It filled the room. Boom, boom. Boom, boom. On 'Canadian AM' I asked her if she would allow a fourteen year old who had been raped to have an abortion and I took by her silence that she would not even allow an abortion in this type of case. Afterwards, as we were leaving the studio, she said, 'I know you are a good doctor, a good technician. Hitler also was technically proficient, you know.' I was so shocked I almost slapped her face. She just left. To this day I hate her for that.[177]

The result of conducting some 5,000 illegal abortions by the early 70s, meant Morgentaler needed help managing his financial success. He hired his brother to administer a couple of apartment buildings he had bought. With Mike's advice, he eventually bought five more buildings, all of them with small down payments, most of them before 1972, when income tax laws allowed depreciation on apartment buildings to be deducted against professional income.[178] In 1982, Right to Life president, Laura McArthur claimed Morgentaler had performed some 116,000 abortions at $225 per procedure.[179] Moreover, in 1988, when Henry Soucy learned and applied Morgentaler's technique, in a Toronto clinic, he started charging $50 a procedure (Morgentaler charged $250). In three increments Soucy raised his charge to $175. "I lowered our rates to match his," said Morgentaler. He had to. Soucy had spread the word in Montreal that he was using "Henry's" technique.[180]

Continuing on the theme of money – by 1988, the issue was no longer access to abortion, but the quality of the process. Members of his own staff wished to raise the customer care bar. "Henry was warm and caring, but it was the way the whole thing was set up," said clinic worker Janet Mawhinney. "You couldn't see twenty-five women a day and offer them more than six or seven minutes for counseling, including a description of the procedure." Some of the newly hired doctors were "fabulous." Others were in it for the money, which at $100 per doctor per procedure, became some $1,800 in a day.[181]

In 1973, fellow humanist Pierre Trudeau became Liberal Prime Minister. Encouraged by the U.S. Supreme Court decision with Roe vs Wade, of January, Morgentaler chose to reveal that he had performed 5,641 successful abortions by vacuum suction curettage. Wright Pelrine, an abortion rights activist and author of *Morgentaler: The Doctor Who Wouldn't Turn Away* was at the event:

The meeting erupted in pandemonium. Enthusiastic feminists and civil libertarians went wild. They gave Henry Morentaler a standing ovation….But from the press, a deafening silence.[182]

That spring, Pelrine convinced CTV to have Morgentaler appear on the television public affairs program "W5" actually doing an abortion. CBC had earlier turned the proposal down. Morgentaler thought it would "demystify" the procedure. They had even found a woman willing to participate:

Slim and attractive, Petra Hartt was married and the mother of a toddler. She and her husband wanted to have more children, but first they were building a house and expected to be in Mexico all winter. She wanted to be identified.[183]

CTV aired the segment on May 13, Mother's Day. Hartt was about five weeks pregnant; the abortion took about five minutes. It was obvious the procedure was safe and "pain free."

Charged with performing illegal abortions, Morgentaler went to trial in the fall of 1973. In October a letter went out from the Toronto Committee to Defend Dr. Morgentaler. Organizations endorsing his defence included: the Canadian Union of Public Employees and the National Action Committee on the Status of Women (NAC). The trial lasted six weeks and ended in his acquittal. After the trial Morgentaler entered an affair with Mireille Lafortune, a university psychology professor who had written him a short note after his acquittal. As an abortion rights activist, she was thrilled by his win. At this time Morgentaler's wife was often in Australia with her lover.[184]

In the spring of 1975, the Supreme Court upheld Quebec Court of Appeal's decision that Morgentaler was guilty of performing an illegal abortion. He went to jail. Soon appeals for amnesty came from NAC and the American Humanist Association. Although Prime Minister Trudeau had personally known Morgentaler for over twenty years, he refused to consider any action. The authorities also wouldn't release him from jail to allow him to receive the American Humanist Association award for the Humanist of the Year (He was to share the honors with Betty Friedan). Friedan, one of the founders of the National Association for Abortion Rights, came to Montreal the day of the final court appearance, along with some Humanists, in a foiled attempt to present Mongentaler with his Humanist of the Year award in the courtroom.[185]

Once allowed day passes from the prison, Morgentaler decided to visit his Barton Street address. He was happy with Mireille and accepting that Eva was equally content in her new relationship. But when he found the locks to the doors had been changed, he felt so insulted and angry; he instituted divorce proceedings on the basis of Eva's adultery. They were easy to prove, since her Australian lover had been living with her in what was still officially the Morgentaler matrimonial home. Later Henry reconsidered. "I had committed adultery many times before, so it was a bit sneaky and hypocritical that I should accuse her of adultery." He subsequently changed the grounds to marriage breakdown out of respect for both of them, and the childhood sweethearts were officially divorced in 1977.[186]

By September 1976, Morgentaler was involved with Joyce Yedid, a young articling law student. Henry had met her through his friend Muriello when she'd told the psychiatrist she admired Henry and supported his cause. She visited Henry at Villa Mount Royal as an acolyte, and their relationship progressed from there. On December 10, the Quebec government halted all prosecution against Henry and recommended that the federal government amend the abortion law.

According to Dunphy:

With this news he grew restless. Winning had meant he had lost his cause, and without his cause he no longer had an identity. He was a private citizen without a purpose, living safe and flat; he was ordinary.[187]

Always a lover of women, he pursued them now with pent-up, redirected passion. There had been, and would continue to be many women in his life, and with one exception – criminologist and Le Dain Commission member Marie-Andree Bertrand – Henry was always the one who left. "I think each woman would believe she was the final stop, but the train had a lot further to do," said Gertie Katz. "Once he left Chava he got on that train and it just kept going. For a long time there was no stopping." His breakups with women were often abrupt and careless. Many times his liaisons overlapped, making women feel betrayed as well as abandoned. In Toronto and Montreal, there was talk that Henry Morgentaler was a chauvinist, insensitive to individual women.[188]

Soon after the anti-climactic opening of a Manitoba clinic, Henry left for Oregon to follow a guru Baghwan Shree Rajneesh, labeled "Sex and Saran Wrap Swami" by the media. He had set up an earthly paradise in Oregon and managed to amass thousands of red-robed devotees, most middle class professionals "who changed partners as often as a square dance."[189] "Rajneesh was ahead of his time about AIDS and diseases," Henry explained. "He had his followers wear rubbers. He even had married couples wear condoms and rubber gloves during sex. I thought that was stupid." Morgentaler liked the guru's brand of dynamic meditation; he approved of the advice he heard others get in some of the counseling sessions; he liked chanting, the massages; he agreed with them that sex was important; he figured all the Rolls-Royces weren't.[190] Ma Anand Sheela, the guru's principal advisor, had to officially announce to the women followers they were not obligated to have sex on request. Two years later, Rajnesh was arrested on board a plane he had chartered with some followers, trying to avoid some immigration charges. He was fined $400,000 and ordered never to return to the US; his fleet of ninety-three Rolls-Royces were put up for auction.

Some 1.5 million abortions are now performed annually in Canada and the United States. Abortion is one of the most common medical operations.

Humanistic (Modern Gnostic) Civilization

Evolution is the development of the energy of the universe in such a way that it has an increasing ability to consciously control itself and the universe around it. It is a progressive change from the unconscious to the conscious. We are the universe trying to comprehend itself. Man is the corporeal manifestation of the universe trying to control its own destiny. Man is God in the process of coming into existence.[191]

Eugenics Manifesto

'When you make the two one, and when you make the inmost as the outermost and the outer as the inner and the above as the below, and when you make the male and female into a single unity, so that the male will not be only male and the female will not be only female, when you create eyes in the place of an eye, and create a hand in the place of a hand, and a foot in the place of a foot, and also an image in the place of an image, then surely will you enter the kingdom.' (Gnostic gospel, Thomas 22)[192]

Tertullian long ago, before modern investigation gathered together the numerous groups and movements of the heresy of the period under the general designation 'gnosis,' had grasped their essential elements. For him Gnosis is a 'declining syncretism' such as the natural spirituality of mankind loves, a spiritual and idealistic overestimate of the self which blurs the fixed limits that separate the creature from the deity; and it is at the same time the 'nihilistic' hostility against God of reality who has created the world and has revealed himself concretely in the flesh.[193]

Kurt Rudolph, Professor – History of Religion

This last section on the Pivot of Civilization paradigm gives further insight into a world void of the Holy Spirit and God-fearing people; a potential civilization run on the philosophy of humanism. Imagine the world in a global genetics and cloning race, fulfilling Margaret Sanger's wildest eugenics dream.

The concept of gene therapy is so inherently simple, says Kevin Davies, that it is hard to believe that it will thwart researchers much longer. If the technology does become successful, there will be those who will advocate using gene therapy to modify genes in the germ-line (sperm and egg cells) so the errant gene can be prevented from being passed down to future generations. Some scientists even harbor dreams of enhancing memory or postponing aging.[194] These intentions to alter our natural gene pool have "boundary" implications with the baby, surrogate mother, biological parents, actual parents, society, subsequent generations, and also with medical, religious and other social institutions. Thinking of such scientific prospects a few scientists offer their comments.

James Watson, co-discoverer of the DNA double helix, says:

Dare we be entrusted with improving upon the results of several million years of Darwinian natural selection? Are human germ cells Rubicons that geneticists may never cross? Yes [do not cross].[195]

Eric Lander, director of the American Genome Center at the Whitehead Institute, warns against germ-line intervention:

One reason is the dire possibility of something going awry. The prospect of a 'product recall' from the human gene pool is too surreal to contemplate.[196]

Kevin Davies, author of *Cracking the Genome*, also writes against germ-line intervention:

Another reason is that we will never know what we might miss. Some of the most famous figures in history suffered serious genetic diseases: Abraham Lincoln had Marfan's syndrome, Van Gogh epilepsy, Albert Einstein dyslexia, Lou Gehrig and Stephen Hawking amyotrophic lateral sclerosis...[197]

Cautious as Watson, Lander and Davies may be, their opinions are not entirely representative of the "science community" and their views do not fully assess the potential mankind has for using science for selfish and ultimately evil purposes. It only takes one obsessive zealous researcher to alter forever human evolution. And in an essay titled "What's Wrong With Cloning?" Richard Dawkins beckons for the research:

'But do you whisper to yourself a secret confession? Wouldn't you love to be cloned?'...'I find it a personally riveting thought that I could watch a small copy of myself, 50 years younger.' [198] *'My feeling is founded on pure curiosity.'*[199]

The International Academy of Humanists proclaims:

The potential benefits of cloning may be so immense that it would be a tragedy if ancient theological scruples should lead to a Luddite rejection of cloning.[200]

Steen Willadsen, representing the British Agricultural Research Council states:

The role of the scientist is to break the laws of nature, rather than to establish, let alone accept them.[201]

As a humanist, evolutionist and hierarchical reductionist, Dawkins has little reservation about experimenting with creation. He prefers to follow the laws of physics and atheism:

There is no reason to think that the laws of physics are violated in living matter. There is nothing supernatural, no 'life force' to rival the fundamental forces of physics.[202]

In human life, start to finish, as Dawkins proclaims, there appears to be essentially no breach in the application of the laws of physics as commonly understood. However, many things appear to happen outside the boundaries of physics, in the time period between conception and death, which are unique, distinctive, measurable and of no small influence. Human life is a phenomenon inseparable from magnetism, gravity and chemical-molecular processes, but in experience is so much more. We have virtually no personal consciousness of the minute-to-minute functioning of our organs or our various involuntary bodily systems and we are not self-aware of how we see and think. Neither do we normally have consciousness of the molecular, cellular and atomic level events occurring in our bodies. The physics of these things are usually the assumed in life, after which any description of one's life would tend to reveal measurements of experiences such as joy-depression, pleasure-pain, company-loneliness, hope-despair, evil-goodness; and descriptions of character and beauty. When Dawkins contends there is nothing supernatural, no "life force" to rival the forces of physics he speaks of a self-constrained and very shallow, indeed hollow, view of life.

Steve Grand, author of *Creation: Life and How To Make It*, observes that our division of the world into the categories "living" and "non-living" seems to be one of the most fundamental judgments we make.[203] We treat each category in very different ways. Our application of morals and concepts of "right" and "wrong" are only applicable to living things. Says Grand, "We never accuse an avalanche of being a murderer, and we never campaign for the rights of hurricanes." However, the more we reduce our biology to "inanimate" laws of physics, the closer we come to classifying mankind's existence as purposeless as the avalanche. Grand asks, "If life is reduced to mere clockwork, where does that leave our sense of morality?" In responding to this question, he writes:

In fact, as life has indeed begun to be reduced to clockwork, and especially as we have gained mastery over that clockwork, so has our moral certainty declined. Today we face difficult moral judgments...Life is not made of atoms, it is merely built out of them. What life is actually 'made of' is cycles of cause and effect, loops of causal flow. These phenomena are just as real as atoms – perhaps even more real. If anything the entire universe is actually made from events, of which atoms are merely some of the consequences.[204]

The reason why we esteem the material world more than we do the intangible one is fairly obvious – it is the world that our senses tell us is really out 'there.'...On the other hand, we do not have any direct sensory confirmation of intangible things. We don't have poverty sensors, we cannot touch a society, and our only evidence for the existence of other people's minds is the visible or auditable motion of their physical bodies. Consequently, we come to believe that the things we can directly sense are real, while the things we cannot sense are more like figments of our imagination or convenient labels, rather than about anything absolute, independent and genuine.

And yet despite all this, the things we really care about are largely intangible. 'Life' is an intangible concept, as is 'mind.' We care about suffering in a way that we never do about mass. This has led to some strange and almost perverse logic errors in the past.[205]

When sacred human life begins in the humanist paradigm is one of these perverse logic errors. It is toward this intangible, and therefore, highly unscientific notion called "life," that we must turn our attention. Against a cultural background of postmodernity – individualism, liberalism, materialism and secularism – we must examine the idea of a utopian humanistic civilization. We must ask, where the ethical boundary lies separating the Josef Mengeles' from the Louis Pasteurs, in helping the species achieve perfection? Where is the boundary protecting vulnerable human life from the powerful?

Ian Wilmut, an embryologist with impeccable credentials, was fifty-two years old when the cloned sheep Dolly was born. Gina Kolata writes:

By the time of Dolly, he had worked at the Roslin Institute for twenty-three years, laboring for nine hours a day, leaving the lab at six each night and, more often than not, bringing work home. The cloning work was long and tedious. It required infinite patience and an ability to work long hours hunched over a microscope in a tiny room heated to the internal temperature of a sheep.[206]

Wilmut entered Darwin College in Cambridge in 1971 and received a Ph.D. in only two years. He holds no *religious* belief and considers himself an agnostic. Wilmut says:

I am not a fool, I know what is bothering people about this. I understand why the world is suddenly at my door. But this is my work. It has always been my work, and it doesn't have anything to do with creating copies of human beings. I am not haunted by what I do, if that is what you want to know. I sleep very well at night.[207]

To clone Dolly, Wilmut used methods his research group and others had been developing for more than a decade. His colleague Keith Campbell sucked the nucleus out of an egg that had been removed from a ewe, creating an egg that had no genes at all, an egg that would soon die if it did not get a new nucleus. Then he began the process of adding the nucleus of an udder cell to the bereft egg. Campbell slipped an udder cell under the outer membrane of the egg. Next, he jolted the egg for a few microseconds with a burst of electricity. This opened the pores of the egg and the udder cell so that the contents of the udder cell, including its chromosomes, oozed into the egg and took up residence there. Now the egg had a nucleus – the nucleus of an udder cell. In addition, the electric current tricked the egg into behaving as if it were newly fertilized, jump-starting it into action. After 277 attempts to clone an udder cell, Wilmut's group succeeded and Dolly was created.[208]

Perhaps to Wilmut's surprise, approximately a half decade later, Brigitte Boisselier, president of CLONAID, announced the birth of a third baby – a boy, born of a surrogate mother, in Japan. The DNA for the baby – she didn't know his name – was obtained from the dead son of a couple – whom she refused to identify – after he died 18 months previous in an accident. Boisselier said the parents of the dead child who's DNA was used for the cloning called CLONAID. "We rushed over there and had time to take cells, to culture them, to develop them."[209] Because the mother was 41 years old, it was decided that there was a risk of miscarriage and a surrogate mother was chosen to carry the baby. Boisselier said the second cloned baby girl, born to a lesbian couple in Holland on January 3, 2003, was doing well. So far none of the couples had paid for the treatment. The first 20 cloned babies, according to Boisselier, were being funded by two investors who were hopeful of being cloned themselves. After the 20th baby, the many thousands of couples who want cloned babies will be expected to pay. Says Boisselier, "This is how the investors see this, as a capital risk investment."[210]

A few years before CLONAID's announcements, Britain's Human Fertilization and Embryology Authority, in a joint report with the Human Genetics Advisory Commission, gave its blessing to the notion that cloning technology could be employed to culture human tissues that could later be used for repair. Cells from a person would be used to create an embryo, as with Dolly; then cells from the young embryo would be cultured to provide tissue that was genetically identical to the donor. The embryo itself would of course be "sacrificed," but various ethical committees in Britain have broadly agreed that human embryos up to fourteen days (long before they acquire any distinctive nervous tissue) have not yet acquired the status of personhood.[211] Here Britain's Human Fertilization and Embryology Authority, the Human Genetics Advisory Commission, the International Academy of Humanists, and indeed the pro-abortion movement, are content with a particular secular-humanist ethical gymnastic. The cognitive maneuver (perversity to Christians) has been described in one of two ways.

One approach argues that a zygote is not a human being, although all human beings were zygotes. The notion further implies that human embryos are not human beings; although all human beings were embryos. This notion of a *sub-human* status for what typically occurs in the womb has been argued for the *non-rights* of the fetus. Therefore the killing of a human zygote, embryo or fetus is considered ethical. In writing about ethical and legally valid "informed consent" for stem cell research, Dianne Irving, Ph.D., notes that decision-makers: donors, recipients, legislators and voters, need an explanation of "what" these early human entities are. Here she asks:

Are they prawns, cabbages, fish, frogs, chickens, monkeys, or human beings? Are they just 'eggs' such as those used in fertilization, skin cells, 'bunches of stem cells,' 'pre-embryos,' or merely the earliest stages of 'the evolving human species?'[212]

In answering these questions Irving chooses to use "absolutely no subjective 'religious,' 'theological,' 'political,' or 'personal' opinions." Rather she sticks to the objective scientific facts documented by the experts in the field of human embryology – "the only scientists who have the academic credentials to answer the question, 'When do human beings begin to fully exist?'" Speaking of sexual human reproduction, Irving states:

Scientifically, then…there is no question or confusion whatsoever that the immediate product, and all continuous, contiguous, growth and developmental stages thereafter through adulthood, involves an already fully existing unique living human being.[213]

Thus the fusion of the sperm (with 23 chromosomes) and the oocyte (with 23 chromosomes) at fertilization results in a live human being, a single-cell human zygote, with 46 chromosomes – the number of chromosomes characteristic of an individual member of the human species. Irving draws a similar conclusion about cloning:

Human beings can also be reproduced a-sexually, without the use of sperm or oocytes – as we know empirically happens in human monozygotic twinning…Just as the single-cell organism produced sexually at fertilization is a human being, the single-cell organism produced a-sexually at cloning is also a human being.[214]

Therefore, this first ethics approach – the contention of killing the life form while in some "sub-human" biological state has been debunked and is generally not raised in defense of abortion, genetic engineering, or cloning.

The second approach concedes that a zygote, embryo or fetus is truly a human being, hence the ethical grounds for destroying human life are framed differently – through the hypothesis of "personhood." Obviously the fetus is biologically human, genetically human and a distinct member of the species homo sapiens. So the "personhood" argument has to distinguish between human beings and persons, must say that embryos are human but not persons, and say that all persons, but not all humans, are sacred and inviolable. According to Peter Kreeft the crucial issue is this:

Are there any human beings who are not persons? If so, killing them might be permissible, like killing warts. But who might these human non-persons be? Many of the more radical humanist pro-abortion advocates (Peter Singer) include severely retarded, genetically deficient and handicapped humans, or very old and sick humans, as non-persons.[215]

Margaret Sanger (and Adolf Hitler) would no doubt applaud Peter Singer for his views. Kreeft believes no one ever conceived of this category before the abortion controversy. It looks very suspiciously like the category was invented to justify the killing. To humanists the Christian paradigm seems to confuse the sanctity of life with the greater moral construct – the sanctity of the person. To the humanist not all human life is sacred. Not even all human beings; not all individual members of the human species, are sacred. But all human persons are sacred! According to Kreeft, humanists contend that the Christian bioethics paradigm:

...commits the intellectual sin of biologism, idolatry of biology, by defining persons in a merely biological, genetic, material way. Membership in a biological species is not morally relevant, not what makes persons sacred and murder wrong.[216]

For the humanist, it seems to be an obvious mistake to claim that personhood begins abruptly, at conception, for personhood develops gradually, as a matter of degree. Every one of the characteristics we use to identify personhood arises and grows gradually rather than suddenly. The Christian seems to be the victim of simplistic, black-or-white thinking, but reality is full of greys. Potential persons should not be confused with actual persons. The zygote, embryo or fetus is potentially a person, but it must grow into an actual person.

Kreeft says there is a common premise hidden behind all of these life-terminating arguments. He writes:

It is the premise of Functionalism: defining a person by his or her functioning or behavior. But common sense distinguishes between what one is and what one does, between being and functioning, thus between 'being a person' and 'functioning as a person.' One cannot function as a person without being a person, but one can surely be a person without functioning as a person. In deep sleep, in coma, and in early infancy, nearly everyone will admit there are persons, but there are no specifically human functions such as reasoning, choice, or language. Functioning as a person is a sign and an effect of being a person. It is because of what we are, because of our nature or essence or being, that we can and do function in these ways.[217]

Functionalism arises with the modern erosion of the family. Half of our families break up. But the family is the place where you learn that you are loved not because of what you do, your function, but because of who you are. What is replacing the family, where we are valued for our being is the workplace, where we are valued for our functioning.[218]

Where Steve Grand finds the notion of life and its morality eroded by scientific reductionism, Kreeft sees the old "Sanctity of Life Ethic" eroded by the new "Quality of Life Ethic," which reflects the shift from family and parenting values to increased careerism in society. Now a human life is judged as valuable and worth living if and only if the judgers decide that it performs at a certain level – e.g., a functional I.Q. of 60 or 40; or an ability to relate to other people; or the prospect of a fairly normal, healthy and pain-free life. If someone lacks the functional criteria of a "quality" life, he lacks personhood and the right to life. It would logically follow that a severely autistic person does not have enough "quality" in his life to deserve to live, and thus active euthanasia, or assisted suicide, is justified.

The Functionalism that is the basis of the "Quality of Life Ethic," which underpins the path to humanistic utopia, is morally reprehensible for at least three reasons. Writes Kreeft:

First, it is degrading, demeaning and destructive to human dignity; it treats persons like trained dolphins.

Second, it is elitist; it discriminates against less perfect performers.

Third, it takes advantage, it is power play, it is might over right rationalized.[219]

Kreeft contends, if personhood is only a developing, gradual thing, then we are never fully persons, because we continue to grow, at least intellectually and emotionally and spiritually. Albert Schweitzer said, at 70, "I still don't know what I want to do when I grow up." But if we are only partial persons, then murder is only partially wrong, and it is less wrong to kill younger, lesser persons than older ones. If it is more permissible to kill a fetus than to kill an infant because the fetus is less of a person, then it is for exactly the same reason more permissible to kill a seven year old, who has not yet developed his reproductive system or many of his educational and communications skills, than to kill a 27 year old. This absurd conclusion follows from defining a person functionally.

For more than a century we have called this mode of thinking Darwinism – survival of the fittest. Also called the "Quality of Life Ethic" the concept places no intrinsic value on human life, rather real value has to be earned and maintained through demonstrated function (life must have demonstrated utility). Diane Irving, sees the rise of the "personhood" ethic as dangerous. She expresses the controversy as follows:

To claim that these innocent and vulnerable living beings can be used and destroyed in order to help other human beings – especially when there are viable alternatives, such as the use of umbilical cord and adult stem cells – is to legislatively create a subcategory of human beings who may be exploited as a mere commodity for the use of other human beings – and we've been there before. The argument is that some human beings are not 'persons,' and other human beings are 'persons,' and is based on a theory about active 'functionality,' rather than on the empirical facts about a thing's nature.

Such is the position of many of those in bioethics, e.g., Peter Singer, Director of Human Values at Princeton University (Princeton, New Jersey). Singer opines that 'personhood' is defined only by the active exercising of 'rational attributes' (e.g., willing, choosing, knowing, relating to the world around one, etc.) or 'sentience' (e.g., the feeling of pain and pleasure) – a philosophical claim inherently based on passé 17th and 18th century Cartesian, rationalist, and empiricist philosophical systems.[220] *…One reason for their indefensibility is simply that if there are two separate and different things, such as a 'mind' or 'soul' thing, and a 'body' thing, there is no possible way to explain any interaction between these two different and separated things. In philosophical parlance, this is known as the myth of the 'mind/body' split – or chorismos….Finally, 'pushing the logic' of those bioethics definitions of 'person' leads to extraordinarily bizarre conclusions – and it would be wise, I respectfully suggest, not to cement them into legislation. Peter Singer, for example,* *opines that some human beings are not 'persons,' and some animals are 'persons.' Indeed, this is the basis for Singer's recent defense of 'bestiality.'*[221] *But think about it: if only those who are actively exercising 'rational attributes' and 'sentience' are 'persons,' then the following list of adult human beings are not 'persons,' and thus not ethically or legally protected as real 'persons': Alzheimer's and Parkinson's patients, the mentally ill and mentally retarded, the frail elderly, the emotionally ill, drug addicts and alcoholics, literally all mentally and physically disabled, – even all of us when we are sleeping.*[222]

Alas the genetic scientist "sleeps well at night" under a *cognitive* security blanket, which says that there is a difference between human beings and human persons – a proverbial "window of experimental opportunity" in between "being" fully human and "being" fully a person. Ian Wilmut describes this totally anti-Christian notion with the curious twist to the "experimental window":

Zygotes are intrinsically more difficult to work with, yet efficiency clearly has to be much higher, for zygotes are precious commodities...zygotes are transient – racing to become embryos [and embryos are racing to become babies] – while cells may live and multiply in a culture for many weeks or months, plenty of time to make the necessary manipulations and to monitor the results.[223] *[my insert]*

Content in their secular moral judgment, British law-makers also say that frozen human embryos should not be stored for more than five years without the express request of the genetic parents.[224] Many see these laws as calling for state-sponsored mass abortion. Most fail to recognize the potential for humanitarian abuses starting in the petrie-dish and ending in our home. Corroborating the notion of a war between the "Pivot of Civilization" and the "Rivet of Life," Irving explains that bioethics has two virtually exclusive paradigms from which to draw moral and ethical conclusions:

Secular bioethics generally considers the following as ethical: contraception; the use of abortifacients; prenatal diagnosis with the intent to abort defective babies; human embryo and human fetal research; abortion; human cloning; the formation of human chimeras (cross-breeding with other species); human embtyonic stem cell research; 'brain birth;' 'brain death;' purely experimental high risk research with mentally ill; enthanasia; physician-assisted suicide; living wills documenting consent to just about anything; and, withholding and withdrawing food and hydration as extraordinary means.[225]

In contrast, Roman Catholic medical ethics...considers all of these unethical – with the exception of the use of 'brain death' criteria...[226]

How is it that these two different ethical systems lead to such opposite and contradictory moral conclusions? The answer is predictable – every ethical theory has foundational ethical principles; deducing from different world paradigms necessarily leads to different ethical conclusions. We can now visualize a future civilization, unfettered by theism and spurred-on by humanism, secularism, libertinism and hedonism.

For example, at the conference, "Great Issues of Conscience in Modern Medicine," held at Dartmouth College in 1960, the Chairman was Rene Dubois, a scientist at Rockerfeller Institute. Dianne N. Irving writes of his views:

Rene Dubois called 'prolongation of the life of aged and ailing persons' and the saving of lives of children with genetic defects ' the most difficult problem of medical ethics we are likely to encounter within the next decade...To what extent we can afford to prolong biological life in individuals who cannot derive either profit or pleasure from existence, and whose survival creates painful burdens for the community?...It will be for society to redefine these ethics, if the problem becomes one that society is no longer willing or able to carry.' Geneticists worry that the gene pool was becoming polluted because early death of persons with certain genetic conditions was now preventable; in addition to antibiotics, insulin for diabetes and diet for phenelkytonuria were frequently mentioned. A unique solution was offered by Nobelist Hermann J. Muller, who promoted his concept of a bank of healthy sperm, together with the 'new techniques of reproduction' to prevent otherwise inevitable degeneration of the race.'[227]

A similar theme was repeated at the conference titled, "Man and His Future," sponsored by the Ciba Foundation in London in 1962. Themes included genetics and brain science. Of special note were the similar concerns with evolution, eugenics and population control:

Sir Julian Huxley opened the conference with a wide-ranging lecture entitled, 'The Future of Man – Evolutionary Aspects.' He painted a picture of evolution that for the first time had become conscious of itself in human kind and thus was responsible for its population, economics, education, and above all, for the exploration of 'inner space – the realm of our own minds and the psychometabolic processes at work in it.' The problems of overpopulation and the dysgenic effects of progress had to be overcome to assure the realization of human fulfillment: 'Eventually, the prospect of radical eugenic improvement could become one of the mainsprings of man's evolutionary advance.' Man was, he triumphantly proclaimed, 'the trustee...of advance in the cosmic process of evolution.'[228]

Writes Irving, "scientists took sides for and against programs of eugenics and thought control." J.B.S. Haldane described a vision of his own utopia, imagining the biological possibilities in the next ten thousand years. His utopia included broad control of physiological and psychological processes, achieved largely by pharmacological and genetic techniques, including cloning and deliberate provocation of mutations, to suit the human product for special purposes in the world of the future.[229] At the first Nobel Conference in 1965, named "Genetics and the Future of Man," Dr. William Shockley, who had won the Nobel prize for physics, presented his views on eugenics. According to Irving, he suggested that, since intelligence was largely genetically determined, serious efforts to improve human intelligence should be pursued by various means, including sterilization, cloning, and artificial insemination. He praised Hermann Muller's advocacy of sperm banks.[230]

Bentley Glass, the outgoing president of the American Association for the Advancement of Science, echoed similar thoughts in a speech in December 1970 to the nation's largest professional association of scientists. Writes Gina Kolata:

According to Glass, the looming problem for humanity was a population explosion that would force people to sharply limit their family sizes. And so, he said, when parents will be able to have no more than two children, they will want to be sure that those children are perfect. Science, he said, will come to the rescue.

'No parents in that future time will have a right to burden society with a malformed or a mentally incompetent child,' Glass said. 'Just as every child must have the right to full educational opportunity and a sound nutrition, so every child has the inalienable right to sound heritage.'

Glass predicted that parents will have their fetuses screened for a myriad of genetic defects, and will abort those fetuses that are imperfect or will use gene therapy to change the genes of their unborn children. He predicted that young people, at an age when their sperm and eggs would be the healthiest, will store their gametes for use when they are older. He predicted that embryos that are especially desirable, because of their perfect genetic inheritance, might be frozen for use by couples who want ideal babies, a process he called 'embryo adoption.' And he had no serious qualms about advocating these eugenic practices. 'The Golden Age toward which we move will soon look tawdry as we no longer see endless horizons. We must, then, seek a change within man himself. As he acquires more fully the power to control his own genotype and direct the course of his own evolution, he must produce a Man who can transcend his present nature,' he said.[231]

Even Linus Pauling, the Nobel laureate from California Institute of Technology, spoke unhesitatingly about using science to improve the human race. In a paper published in 1968 in the *UCLA Law Review*, Pauling proposed in all seriousness that we tattoo the foreheads of people who carried one copy of recessive, disease-causing genes so that they would not accidentally have children with someone else who carried the same gene.[232] He explains:

It is my opinion that legislation along this line, compulsory testing for defective genes before marriage, and some form of public or semipublic display of this possession, should be adopted.[233]

These humanists, eugenicists and secularists start with the legal license to kill *tiny* zygotes and *forgotten* frozen embryos and end up proposing wholesale killing, sterilizing and cloning based on some *self-conscious gnosis* of utopian functionality.

American values have been seen as products of alternately, heavy dependence on the liberal tradition (with its emphasis on individual self-determination and freedom) and a fundamental consensus on the value of individual human life. Writes Blank:

Social and political institutions have proved remarkably resilient and adaptable, given the diverse population and tradition of individualism; still, cultural pluralism has produced a large number of potential lines of stress in society.[234]

These new technologies are bringing the old liberal tradition, with emphasis on the "individual," in conflict with "public good." In explaining the challenge of developing governmental policies on the application of technology, Blank cites Daniel Callahan:

It cannot handle those problems where people with diverse values must work together to deal with common problems, cannot create a necessary sense of trust which must undergird community and cannot, in particular deal with those problems of technology where, because of their implications and consequences are communal, the values by which they are judged and controlled must be communal.[235]

The most committed proponents of direct genetic intervention tend to be biologists and geneticists who focus their attentions on human survival. Others are humanists, certain religious sects (Raelians of CLONAID for example), and others who uphold a utopian wish to perfect the species and society. Some scientists and secularists are like Richard Dawkins, just "curious." Key proponents outside the scientific and religious communities are those of the GBLTQ community. Some civil libertarians and various members of GBLTQ declare an individual "right" to reproductive self-determination. [More is presented about these homosexual interest groups under the section titled "Clones: Alternative Family Planning," in Chapter 8]

Ignoring for the moment the problem of risk, another large quandary remains – the ethical dilemma arising from the allocation of constrained resources and coordination of the benefits in a less than perfect scenario. A modest gauge of the complications of implementing technological utopia is found in the history of kidney dialysis. The medical ethics movement had its roots in this era. The problem was that dialysis machines were in short supply, so not everyone could be saved. The question was, who should live and who should die? According to Kolata, the medical community in Seattle turned to a committee of volunteers to make the choices:

The committee, a group of upright citizens who later became known as a 'God squad,' earnestly formulated the rules. They gave priority to breadwinners, family men who were fine upstanding members of the community. People who did not have a job, those who seemed unstable or who lived in the margins of society, were denied the lifesaving treatment. Men were favored over women, married over single.[236]

We like to believe that Nazi-style medical experimentation on humans is rare and required fanatical if not psychopathic doctors operating under sanction by an equally obsessive government. However, the treatment of humans as guinea pigs or as disposable fetuses was historically only a matter of a slight paradigm shift, where society moved from God-fearing to becoming God. We have seen how Margaret Sanger and associated eugenicists developed a new, anti-Christian worldview, which encouraged abortion, endorsed eugenic manipulation of societies for mankind's evolutionary good and proclaimed racial Darwinism. More recently, bioethicist Peter Singer was quoted declaring:

When the death of a disabled infant will lead to the birth of another infant with better prospects for a happy life, the total amount of happiness will be greater if the disabled infant is killed.[237]

Terry Golway quotes from Singer's book *Practical Ethics*:

...the right to life movement 'is misnamed. Far from having concern for life...those who protest against abortion but dine regularly on the bodies of chickens, pigs and calves, show only a biased concern for the lives of members of their own species.' ...'I have argued that the life of a fetus...is of no greater value than the life of a nonhuman animal at a similar level of rationality [and] self-consciousness...If the fetus does not have the same claim to life as a person, it appears that the newborn baby does not either.'[238]

Golway says Singer urges us to "put aside feelings based on the small, helpless and-sometimes-cute appearances of human infants." Laboratory rats, after all, are "innocent in exactly the same sense as the human infant." According to Golway, Singer complains that prohibitions against killing "deformed or sickly" infants are "a product of Christianity." Moreover, now that many assume a post-Christian era, Singer says:

Perhaps it is now possible to think about these issues without assuming the Christian moral framework.[239]

In the last section of Chapter 8, we will see that same-sex couples and elderly single female heterosexuals, wishing to overcome inherent biological incompatibilities in their unions or singleness, do not view biotechnology as negative, risky or morally wrong. Indeed, many gay and lesbian couples see access to human cloning technologies as a fundamental human right, no different than the current applications of fertility enhancements for heterosexual married or co-habitating couples.

Not surprising, Alvin Toffler, a futurist, sums-up a growing public phenomenon:

A lot of perfectly fine and decent and humane people now think that technology is negative.[240]

CHAPTER FOUR

RIVET OF LIFE

And He is before all things, and in Him all things hold together (Colossians 1:17).

If chance exists in any size, shape, or form, God cannot exist. The two are mutually exclusive. If chance existed, it would destroy God's sovereignty. If God is not sovereign, he is not God. If he is not God, he simply is not. If chance is, God is not. If God is, chance is not.[1]

R.C. Sproul, Orthodox Christian Theologian

No servant can serve two masters. Either he will hate the one and love the other, or he will be devoted to the one and despise the other (Luke 16:13).

Two Sides in a Binary Decision

In a free society, most will agree that one has the choice to either believe in Jesus Christ as one's personal Savior or reject Him, as secularists do, as myth, a false lunatic, an overly zealous sage or something else. According to Scripture, if we do not accept Christ for who He claims to be, we are, by our own choice or by indecision, lost. In Christian theology ignoring Christ equals rejecting Him. Acceptance of Christ requires an act of personal will and faith. According to Scripture (and the witness of millions of Christians), this decision initiates a relationship with God, which takes on greater meaning now and for eternity.

There are only two choices: accept or reject. The implications of the choice one faces can be stated as follows: either the "secular, anarchist, humanist, sex positive, boundariless, feminist, and pro-gay belief system" espoused by people like Emma Goldman, Margaret Sanger, Alfred Kinsey, Henry Morgentaler, and agencies like Planned Parenthood and CBCA, best represents the truth; or the reality revealed in Scripture and through a commitment to Jesus Christ is right. The obvious exclusivity of either paradigm makes belief in one, by corollary, rejection of the other. As stated before, logic dictates that one (or both) could be false, but both cannot be true.

As much as some may wish to find a compromise position or an intermediate interpretation, it simply does not exist. This duality might be illustrated in the daily operation of an electrical light switch. There are only two possibilities. The light is either on or it is off. One is either married or not. Never can reality be both nor some intermediate settlement. Similarly, Christ is either God in the flesh or Scripture is an epic hoax. At death your name is either in the Book of Life (Revelation 3:5) or it is not.

Many of the historical divisions between these opposing worldviews are summarized in the following table:

Subject	Pivot of Civilization	Rivet of Life
abortion	pro-choice	anti-abortion
feminism	pro-lesbian	pro-heterosexual
gender	social construct	roles by divine and biological design
sex	GBLTQ free, recreational multipartner sexually active – safe sex	male and female designed to procreate monogamous marriage illicit sex
person	self-centered what can I do?	Christ-centered what is God's will for me?
marriage	basis of oppression	basis of family unit
family	any arrangement	by divine design, one wife, one husband, with children
sexual orientation	fixed GBLTQ	fixed male – female reorientation to heterosexual
mankind	survival of fittest	the first shall be last
pornography	civil liberty eros	sin lust
life	evolved by chance	created
death	end	beginning

Note: GBLTQ - Gays, Bisexuals, Lesbians, Transgendered and Queers

The polar opposite, mutually exclusive, and zero-sum nature of the two worldviews demands the advocacy of one along with simultaneous denunciation of the other. The Christian paradigm, according to orthodox interpretation, comes as an interlocking package of values and guidance, which is not discretionary. And here lies a cognitive flaw among those proclaiming a personal theistic faith or a culturally religious heritage that professes Christ's sovereignty in their lives, but who choose to only adhere to their value system outside of Parliament or Congress. Paradoxically, some self-proclaimed *Christian* politicians see no need to heed their Lord in a legislative decision (same-sex marriage) that so directly impacts the long-standing pillars of one's stated faith. These inconsistent Christians are either closet secularists or bamboozled by the very humanists who would never dare abandon their beliefs in state affairs. An editorial in the *Calgary Herald* illustrates the cerebral error of separating God and state:

The original historical purpose of separating religion and state as advanced by the framers of the American republic in their foundational documents was that there ought to be no institutional control of the organs of government by a particular denomination or any religion, or vice-versa...Then as now, the Church of England was established as the official state religion in both Great Britain and its American colonies....This had critical implications in matters of worship for people of other faiths, and when the colonists had a chance to separate the church from the state, they took it.[2]

That separation, however, was never intended to compel politicians with *faith* to set aside their convictions in the conduct of state affairs. The same editorial claims:

...if one were to banish religious impulses from decision-making in politics, why not banish irreligious convictions that originate in feminism, environmentalism or atheism?... Finally, insofar as politicians with faith are concerned, there is a risk of great personal hypocrisy if they do not follow at least some teachings of their church in matters of state, presumably ones that are grave....Setting aside deeply-held convictions for the sake of political expediency does not constitute the proper separation of church and state, but the separation of one's conscience from one's deeds. It is in fact intellectual and spiritual suicide.

Either God is master in your life or He is not. This principle of duality was explained when the Apostle Luke recorded Christ's words regarding the sin of serving money ahead of God (Luke 16:13). Nothing is to come between a Christian and his worship of God. Anything that does: work, lustful sexual desire, drug addictions, pornography, homosexuality, even a man-made charter of rights and freedoms becomes an idol when it takes priority over and diminishes God's intent. [This issue of God in our Constitution, including the Charter of Rights and Freedoms, is studied in the last chapter, titled "Theistic Boundaries to Rights and Choice."]

God is not a rheostat, by which you adjust his guidance and impact to suit a desired situation. The idea of a spectrum of right and wrong depending on contextual preconditions like consent, love and utility, defiles holiness and the idea of one truth before God. Those who claim to be Christian and choose to treat the Word of God in a rheostatic fashion will be studied in Part 3 – Unorthodox Christianity: The "Compromise" Paradigm. Christians and non-Christians, who promote unbiblical norms in ethics in the name of "authentic personality," are in reality against Jesus Christ. Such critics usually propose to set aside explicit biblical teaching and substitute secular alternatives. The obvious result of this line of thinking is the attitude that explicit biblical teaching is often "reprehensible," "repugnant," and "irrelevant;" that enlightened men must take "discriminating" approaches to what the Bible teaches, and that those who do not are guilty of "bibliolatry." The choice before Christians is a bona fide zero-sum dynamic:

Either we will discriminate against homosexuals, or we will discriminate against the Word of God. We will either aim to convert the homosexual and have him transformed into the image of Christ, or we will aim to convert the church's thinking about God's Word and transform the Christian ethic into the image of homosexual values.[3]

In response to Philip asking, "Lord, show us the Father and that will be enough for us," Jesus answered:

Don't you know me, Philip, even after I have been among you such a long time? Anyone who has seen me has seen the Father…If you love me, you will obey what I command. And I will ask the Father, and he will give you another Counselor to be with you forever – the Spirit of truth. The world cannot accept him [Holy Spirit], because it neither sees him nor knows him. But you know him, for he lives in you and will be with you (John 14:8-18).

For Christians, "Fear of the Lord is the beginning of wisdom, and knowledge of the Holy One is understanding" (Proverbs 9:10). This "understanding," like the infilling presence of the Holy Spirit is a free gift of grace by God's initiative and not a reward earned upon graduation to some measured level of knowledge (*Gnosis*). Notwithstanding this providential aspect of receiving Christ's grace, the following defense of Christianity is done in the prayerful hope that more may open their eyes to see the Christian paradigm.

Before looking at some key Christian tenets in the following sections, a short illustration by N. T. Wright powerfully reveals the dilemma in communication between theists and atheists, Christians and secularists, as a consequence of divergent world paradigms:

When I was a professor at McGill University, Montreal, in the early 1980s, I taught a sixth grade Sunday-school class in our local church. I once began a class by asking them the question: 'Why did Jesus die?' They thought about it with no conferring, and we then went around the room and collected single-sentence answers. The interesting thing was that about half of them gave me historical reasons: he died because he upset the chief priests; he died because the Pharisees didn't like him; he died because the Romans were afraid of him. The other half gave me theological answers: he died to save us from our sins; that we could go to heaven; he died because God loves us.

We spent a fascinating hour putting those two sets of answers together. I do not know if any of those children remember that session, but I certainly do. I still believe that this putting together of the two sides of that great question – the historical dimension and the theological one – is one of the most important tasks we can engage in when we study Jesus.[4]

In recognition of this theistic-secular communication challenge, the next three sections, which address creation of the universe, initiation of life on earth and the making of the human species, are all predominantly scientific and historical analyses. Sections on the basics of Christianity, pagan and Gnostic threats to the faith, Greek and Roman sexism around the time of Christ, and an introduction to Christian teaching on patriarchy follow. The chapter ends with a study of the legacy of hypocrisy in the Christian Church. Most of this chapter is a historical, scientific and academic-theological report. I would have liked to include my personal testimony to the saving grace of Jesus Christ; however, the book length and integration of my witness became obstacles. Indeed, in earlier drafts I tried. I can but hope that this book creates a "seeker" out of each reader. Christ is alive and restoring lives, marriages and families. Perhaps at another time I will have occasion to tell a marvelous personal redemptive story.

Creation of the Universe

Einstein once asked the question, 'How much choice did God have in constructing the Universe?' – If the no-boundary proposal is correct, he had no freedom at all to choose initial conditions. He would, of course, still have had the freedom to choose the laws that the Universe obeyed. This, however, may not really have been all that much of a choice; there may well be only one, or a small number of complete unified theories...Even if there is only one possible unified theory, it is just a set of rules and equations. What is it that breathes fire into the equations and makes a Universe for them to describe?...Why does the universe go to all the bother of existing? Is the unified theory so compelling that it brings about its own existence?[5]

Stephen Hawking

A no-boundary model of the Universe 'really underlies science because it is really the statement that the laws of science hold everywhere.' However, if the Universe is self-contained, do we not need to explain how it got there in the first place. Stephen Hawking's answer is that we do not – 'It would just BE.'[6]

Moses said to God, 'Suppose I go to the Israelites and say to them, 'The God of your fathers has sent me to you' and they ask me, 'What is his name?' 'Then what shall I tell them?' God said to Moses, 'I am who I am! This is what you are to say to the Israelites: I AM has sent you.'...'This is my name forever, the name by which I am to be remembered from generation to generation.'

Exodus 3:13-15

In answer to the question, 'Who do you think you are?' Jesus replied: 'If I glorify myself, my glory means nothing. My Father, whom you claim as your God, is the one who glorifies me. Though you do not know Him, I know Him. If I said I did not, I would be a liar...I tell you the truth before Abraham was born, I am!

John 32-58

Ironically, most "science-based" authors like Richard Dawkins, well grounded in the wisdom of physics, reductionism, evolution, and holding vehemently to an anti-Christian worldview, stop short of explaining how our universe came into existence. How can the supposedly *sound* reductionist theories of these scientists not deal with the very birth of the universe? No doubt the now archaic *steady-state* model of the universe, which assumed away a moment of creation, would offer less of a cognitive flaw. Like a belief of faith from the Apostle's Creed to a Christian, the scientific community clings to their own founding tenet, proclaimed by Stephen Hawking – the Universe "would just BE." In layman's terms this is the equivalent of saying "we do not know how things got started, but we're not concerned. Just accept the creation moment on *scientific* faith (but never *religious* faith!)

Is this a so-called "show-stopper?" Yes! Nowhere do evolutionists, cosmologists or hierarchical reductionists take their theories of mechanism, random chance, gradualism and the "blind" laws of physics back to the very birth of our universe. Is the reality of our universe the first accidental chance event? Who believes this? The Big-Bang theory stops well short of answering the question of existence and certainly does not give evidence against God. Getting something from nothing is still mathematically impossible and the current scientific model *assumes* the existence of "something" measuring light years across at time zero. If the universe is self-contained, how did it get here? There is a certain cognitive incoherence when pubic schools confidently proclaim to our children an assumed miraculous (chance?) birth of the universe, an equally marvelous (chance) start of life on earth and an extraordinary (chance) evolution to mankind from some tree-hugging apes, who through incremental (chance) decisions choose to forage for (chance) hard nuts in the nearby (chance) open savannas. All of this the students are told *without any chance* of the deliberate hand of God. Moreover, when you come to accept the teachings of this secular curriculum, argue many anti-Christian groups, remember the virgin birth and bodily resurrection of one named "Jesus Christ" are preposterous improbabilities. We may not know absolutely how the universe was actually created or how life got started or now humankind came into being, but we know for sure there is no Creator or God. Indeed, the absurdity of teaching all this evolutionary randomness to the preclusion of God, is magnified by the fact that our constitutions, charter of rights and freedoms, oaths of allegiance, national anthems, and in the U.S. the currency, all acknowledge the existence of God. A lot of people are either blind or in denial when it comes to life's purpose.

Michael White offers a modern definition of Darwin's theory of evolution:

To Darwin, the individual organism is utterly meaningless, and Darwinian evolution shows that all things are solely at the mercy of two factors, the random shuffling and mutations of genes and the forces of natural selection. In Darwin's universe there is no guiding hand inside or outside the individual because there is no plan, no objective other than the drive for survival. Nature is mindless, ungoverned, a free spirit, and because of this, Darwin tells us, life is cruel, violent, and utterly meaningless. This then is a model for all of Nature. Thomas Hobbes touched upon this truth some two centuries earlier when he said of the human condition (a tiny element of Nature's grandeur) that it is 'solitary, poor, nasty, brutish, and short.'[7]

Either mankind is alone (but, for the chance encounter with another chance extraterrestrial in a chance overlap of the time-space continuum, as Carl Sagan theorizes); or there is a God who is our Creator and who wants to enter into a relationship with each of us. The tug-of-war over such conflicting beliefs deserves far greater attention than most give in their lifetime. More important for the purpose of this book, the paradigm you choose has a decisive impact on your view of GBLTQ culture and subsequently same-sex marriage. To a great degree the orthodox Christian's assertion of God's "divine condemnation" of GBLTQ sex practices, is constrained within a context of the reader's willingness to accept monotheism.

Prayerfully, this chapter and the entire book will help open your eyes to the Christian worldview.

[Note: One does not have to become a Christian or a devoted humanist to make an informed choice between the merits of one worldview over that of the other. Jesus Christ, Margaret Sanger, and Charles Darwin all share a human birth; however, their divergent life purposes and proclamations for the "way" to happiness and peace give everyone two distinct paradigms of choice.]

Agnostics, like others who ignore God's existence, have a public and political advantage in society. Unlike "religious" people, they are not expected to censor their personal beliefs in such *secular* milieus as public schools, universities, courthouses and parliament. This diminution of theism has been a humanist goal for many years. At a meeting of the Metaphysical Society in 1869, Thomas Huxley invented the term agnostic as a play upon the Gnostics. Here Huxley chose not just to claim *"I do not know,"* but he preferred the negative view *"One cannot know."* And it is this strictly universal negative judgment that permeates much of the scientific and academic communities.

Ironically, the evolution of science is now contributing more to the credibility of God amongst non-believers than to the Creator's discredit. Regrettably most scientists seem trapped within choices from only a non-Christian worldview: (1) agnostic – doubting God's tangible existence, or (2) Gnostic – acknowledging an "unknowable deity." Most scientists are either ignoring God or trying to become God, but seldom are they submitting to God. Humanism is the ultimate anti-Christian worldview, which includes agnosticism and Gnosticism. Humanism adheres to the ancient idea that we are our own masters and that we in a sense become God through acquired and applied wisdom. However, logic argues that we cannot be both creator and the created; hence the hard fought humanist anti-Christian theory of a meaningless random universe. Let us look first at the existence of our universe from both paradigms.

For Christians the model for creation of the universe, earth and humankind is found in Genesis 1 and 2. We believe God created it all and did so in the sequence detailed in the Book of Genesis.

On the other hand, Steven Weinberg, describes the "Big Bang" theory in *The First Three Minutes: A Modern View of the Origin of the Universe*.[8] Prior to this theory, which is also called the "standard model," many scientists of cosmology, had hitched their beliefs to the notion (theory) that the universe was infinite and had for all intents and purposes existed much as seen for an eternity. In 1917, a year after the completion of his general theory of relativity, Einstein tried to find a solution of his equations that would describe the space-time geometry of the whole universe. Einstein looked for a solution that would be homogeneous, isotropic, and truly static. However, no solution could be found. Writes Weinberg:

Einstein was forced to mutilate his equations by introducing a term, the so-called cosmological constant, which greatly marred the elegance of the original theory.[9]

By the late 1940s, a theory called the "steady-state model," was proposed by Herman Bondi, Thomas Gold, and Fred Hoyle. With a slightly different formulation, they proposed that the universe has always been just about as it is now. As it expands, new matter is continually created to fill up the gaps between galaxies.[10] Here, the problem of the early universe is banished; there simply was no early universe. Today, according to Weinberg, the prevailing theory is the standard model, which can be described as follows:

In the beginning there was an explosion. Not an explosion like those similar on earth, starting from a definite center and spreading out to engulf more and more of the circumambient air, but an explosion which occurred simultaneously everywhere, filling all space from the beginning, with every particle of matter rushing apart from every other particle. 'All space' in this context may mean either all of an infinite universe, or all of a finite universe which curves back on itself like the surface of a sphere. Neither possibility is easy to comprehend, but this will not get in our way; it matters hardly at all in the early universe whether space is finite or infinite.

At about one-hundredth of a second, the earliest time about which we can speak with any confidence, the temperature of the universe was about a hundred thousand (1011) degrees Centigrade. This is much hotter than in the center of even the hottest star, so hot, in fact, that none of the components of ordinary matter, molecules, or atoms, or even the nuclei of atoms, could have held together. Instead, the matter rushing apart in this explosion consisted of various types of so-called elementary particles, which are the subject of modern high-energy nuclear physics.[11]

Says Weinberg:

The standard model sketched above is not the most satisfying theory imaginable of the origin of the universe....there is embarrassing vagueness about the very beginning, the first hundredth of a second or so. Also, there is the unwelcome necessity of fixing initial conditions, especially the initial thousand-million-to-one ratio of photons to nuclear particles. We would prefer a greater sense of logical inevitability in the theory.[12]

Can we really be sure of the standard model? Will new discoveries overthrow it...or even revive the steady-state model? Perhaps. I cannot deny a feeling of unreality in writing about the first three minutes as if we really know what we are talking about.[13]

Using the Hubble constant of 15 kilometers per second per million light years, the age of the universe must be less than 20,000 million years.[14] Previously (1930-40), the Hubble constant was believed to be 170 kilometers per second per million light years, which predicted a universe of 2,000 million years or less. But this calculation conflicted with radioactivity studies by Lord Rutherford, which indicated the earth was much older; it is now thought to be about 4,600 million years old. Says Weinberg:

It may be that the removal of the age paradox by the tenfold expansion of the extragalatic distance scale in the 1950s was the essential precondition for the emergence of the big bang cosmology as a standard theory.[15]

The strongest support for the "Big Bang" cosmology comes from the confirmation that the universe is expanding and the measurement of the cosmic microwave radiation background discovered in 1965.[16] Weinberg explains in more detail the early start:

Eventually, as we look farther and farther back into the history of the universe, we come to a time when the temperature was so high that collisions of photons with each other could produce material particles out of pure energy....Therefore, in order to follow the course of events at really early times, we are going to need to know how hot the universe had to be to produce large numbers of material particles out of the energy of radiation, and how many particles were thus produced.[17]

...The temperature of the universe is 100,000 million degrees Kelvin (1011 °K). The universe is simpler and easier to describe than it ever will be again. It is filled with an undifferentiated soup of matter and radiation.[18]

It is natural to ask how large the universe was at the very early times. Unfortunately we do not know, and we are not even sure that this question has meaning....the universe may well be infinite now, in which case it was infinite at the time of the first frame, and always was infinite. On the other hand, it is possible that the universe now has a finite circumference, sometimes estimated to be about 125 thousand million light years....this gives a first-frame circumference of about four light years. None of the details of the story of cosmic evolution in the first few minutes will depend on whether the circumference of the universe was infinite or only a few light years.[19]

The law of energy conservation is an empirical law of science, also known as the First Law of Thermodynamics, states that while energy can be converted from one form to another, it can neither be created nor annihilated. According to Isaac Asimov:

It is considered the most powerful and most fundamental generalization about the universe that scientists have ever been able to make.[20]

Both scientists and Christians have grounded their worldview in specific facts, beliefs and faith. Secularists have no difficulty believing in the "miraculous" creation of the universe, i.e. ignoring the dictates of the First Law of Thermodynamics. Either something came from nothing or for a very tiny instant at the start of the standard model, there was an egg 3-5 light years in circumference. Modern physics now confirms what Christians have known by faith all along. There was a miraculous creation moment.

Einstein supplied the relationship between matter and energy[21] and later the Heisenberg uncertainty principle supplied a possible relation between energy and time. Scientists are now quite willing to concede that a moment of creation was possible. Other evidence even dictates the necessity of a creation. The famous Second Law of Thermodynamics (Boltzmann/Kelvin) establishes that the universe must not have always existed or it would have run down to dead stop before now.[22] Hubble's correlation between red shifts and distances to stars, and the consequent rate of expansion for the universe, even indicates a rough estimate for the time of its creation.[23]

Atheists will attempt to present the moment of creation as if it were a completely "random accident" – one which, by "lucky coincidence," started a chain reaction of cause and effect that ultimately fell together into the Sistine Chapel and Marilyn Monroe among other wonders. Those who are uncomfortable with a moment of creation (and hence a Creator) have proposed the hypothesis that the universe goes through endless cycles of "Big Bang" followed by "Big Crunch" where it collapses again only to be re-exploded in a subsequent "Big Bang." Even if this hypothesis proves to be true, it does not eliminate the need for a moment of creation.[24]

Creation of Life

Nothing makes sense in biology except in the light of evolution.[25]
Russian-American biologist Theodosuis Dobzhansky

Scripture states that God created life on earth and secularists argue life came about by accident. Cornelius Hunter cites that the Universal Genetic Code leads evolutionists to conclude that all life shares a single origin.[26] Virtually all living organisms, from primitive bacteria to plants to animals, make use of the same code. Notwithstanding the intricacies of deoxyribonucleic acid (DNA) macromolecule and its universal application, evolutionists view the code as the result of a historical event, what DNA codiscoverer and Nobel laureate Francis Crick called a "frozen accident." The code, they say, originally evolved as the result of blind forces, but once established, it was strongly maintained. It is difficult to overestimate evolutionists' confidence in biochemical homologies. According to the National Academy of Sciences, the "evidence for evolution from molecular biology has opened up dramatic new veins of support" for evolution, and the theory is "now beyond a reasonable doubt."[27]

Let us return to the micro-challenge of proving spontaneous generation here on earth before succumbing to the temptation of a macro-hypothesis, popularized by Carl Sagan and proclaimed by the National Academy of Sciences. Dr. Francis Crick, who received the Nobel Prize for discovering the DNA double-helix structure, is a credible authority on the extraordinary complexity of the living cell. Crick and his associate, Leslie Orgel, at California's Salk Institute, are quite committed to the theory of evolution, yet they cannot accept the usual explanation that the first self-replicating cell came together spontaneously by chance. Ian Taylor explains:

They concede that statistically it would just never happen. In 1973 Crick and Orgel seriously proposed that life initially appeared on earth as a direct act of 'seeding' by intelligent life from another planet, and they call their theory directed panspermia.[28] *As far out as this may be, and it is distinctly Lowellian Darwinism, the proposal is based on two observations: First, life as we know it depends on traces of the rare element molybdenum, and it is argued that it would more likely have evolved on a planet in which the element was more abundant. Second, there is but a single genetic code to all life, and, if it had developed by chance in 'some primordial ocean,' then with multiple chance beginnings, more than one genetic code would be expected. The idea that life could have arrived by meteorite is rejected, because of the radiation damage during its long space journey. The field of possibility, therefore, has been narrowed to the choice between miraculous supernatural creation and life having been deliberately brought to earth by intelligent extraterrestrial beings in the remote past. Crick has placed his bet on the unprovable idea that somewhere in time and space there existed conditions on another planet more conducive to the spontaneous generation of life on our planet under any possible conditions.*[29]

It has been discovered more recently, principally by Crick, that the DNA spiral-helix molecules found within the nucleus of every cell are the "blueprints" for cell building, but these molecules, work in a symbiotic relationship with the RNA molecules, which transfer the information from within the nucleus to various parts of the cell. Only by this relationship can molecules derived from food be directed to where they are needed for cell building. In this case the theory requires that we believe that two extremely complicated molecules, DNA and RNA, which must fit together perfectly, have each evolved separately and then appeared at the same time and in the same place in order to work together. Evidently, this was seen to be an appeal to the miraculous and went beyond Crick's credulity.[30]

Sir Bernard Lovell, the British astronomer, makes the following statement in his book *In the Centre of Immensities* (1919):

The operation of pure chance would mean that within half a billion year period the organic molecules in the primeval seas might have to undergo 10^{50} (one followed by fifty zeroes) trial assemblies in order to hit upon the correct sequence. The possibility of such a chance occurrence leading to the formation of one of the smallest protein molecules is unimagibably small. Within the boundary conditions of time and space we are considering it is effectively zero.[31]

In 1981, Sir Fred Hoyle wrote in his article "The Big Bang in Astronomy," for *New Scientist*:

Anyone with even a nodding acquaintance with the Rubik cube will concede the near impossibility of a solution being obtained by a blind person moving the cube faces at random. Now imagine 10^{50} blind persons (standing shoulder to shoulder, these would more than fill our entire planetary system) each with a scrambled Rubik cube and try to conceive of the chance of them all simultaneously arriving at the solved form. You then have the chance of arriving by random shuffling (random variation) of just one of the many biopolymers on which life depends. The notion that not only the biopolymers but the operating program of a living cell could be arrived at by chance in a primordial soup here on Earth is evidently nonsense of a high order. Life must plainly be a cosmic phenomenon.[32]

Mathematically, there appears to be two belief options – Creation or Extraterrestrial Seeding – although a visitor from outer space must in the end answer for its origin. One wonders why an extraterrestrial species (which by "chance" had assumed the evolutionary lead in the then 9 billion-year-old universe) would leave their planet, discover ours in its then primordial soup state (some 4.6 billion years ago) and then choose to deposit apparently "one" replicating cell (a tiny protozoan) and leave. This is not to diminish the complexity of such a cell or its value as a gift to earth. Michael Denton describes the complexity behind even the simplest bacteria:

Although the tiniest bacteria cells are incredibly small, weighing less than 10-12 gms, each is in effect a veritable micro-minaturized factory containing thousands of exquisitely designed pieces of intricate molecular machinery, made up altogether of one hundred thousand million atoms, far more complicated than any machine built by man and absolutely without parallel in the non-living world.[33]

Furthermore, the DNA strands in each cell are tightly coiled and condensed thousands of times inside the nucleus. The space between each letter in the genetic code (each rung in the double helix) is 0.34 nanometer, less than one billionth of a meter. The DNA in a human cell is squeezed into a nucleus about 0.005 millimeter in diameter, and yet fully extended, the DNA of a single cell would stretch to about 2 meters, or 6 feet. The period at the end of this sentence would encompass about 200 cells, or 400 meters of DNA. The total amount of DNA in the 100 trillion cells in the human body laid end to end would run to the sun and back about twenty times.[34]

The process of converting the instructions carried by a gene into the corresponding protein relies on an intermediary called RNA. In any given cell, only a small proportion of genes are turned on at any one time. An enzyme called RNA polymerate reads along the sequence of the gene, producing a complementary strand of RNA that is escorted out of the nucleus and into the body of the cell. Molecular machines called ribosomes clasp the RNA strand and read the base code in triplets, or codon. At each codon, the appropriate amino acid is carried to the ribosome by an adaptor RNA molecule that specifically recognizes each codon. One by one, the string of amino acids that constitute the protein are linked until the complete protein is assembled.[35]

If extraterrestrials were hoping for and seeking other intelligent life with which to communicate, 4.6 billion years seems a long gestation period. This is not like making an investment with an amortization for the grandchildren. Imagine NASA asking for funding for a project with a payoff in four billion years. Moreover, if we believe as most evolutionists do, that the whole natural selection endeavor (which created mankind) has historically hung upon the random act of some primates consistently choosing over hundreds of millennia to eat hard nuts and seeds (requiring technology to crack) while roaming the savannas (searching on foot) rather than choosing, as their relatives the chimpanzees have, to uphold the easy life based on the soft fruits of the forest, the theory becomes mind-boggling. Who and what are we to believe?

This theory of human life originating from outer space was seen by most as removing the problem rather than providing a solution. Says Taylor:

It was almost taboo to speak of spontaneous generation occurring on earth, and yet philosophically it raised the awful specter that if life didn't arise spontaneously, then it must have been purposefully created. There was no third alternative.[36]

For secularists, this conclusion leaves only the "seeded" option:

The stark reality of mathematical probability, however, dashes even this slim hope, because it is, after all, the origin of life and not the intergalactic carrier that is crucial. Two of England's leading scientists, Hoyle and Wickramasinghe (1981),[37] *working independently of each other came to the conclusion that the chance of life appearing spontaneously from nonlife anywhere in the universe was effectively zero. Surprisingly, these authors, respectively an agnostic and a Buddhist, concluded the origin of life demands the existence of God to have created it. The London Daily Express (14 August 1981) headlined their conclusion: 'Two skeptical scientists put their heads together and reach an amazing conclusion: There must be a God.' As far as the dedicated humanist is concerned, this answer to life's riddle is totally unacceptable…*[38]

James Coppedge estimates after speeding up the rate of bonding a trillion times:

The probability of a single protein molecule being arranged by chance is 1 in 10^{161}*, using all atoms on earth and allowing all the time since the world began…For a minimum set of the required 239 protein molecules for the smallest theoretical life, the probability is 1 in* $10^{119,879}$*. It would take* $19^{119,841}$ *years on the average to get a set of such proteins. That is 10,119,831 times the assumed age of the earth and is a figure with 119,831 zeroes.*[39]

Carl Woese, a physicist turned evolutionary biologist at the University of Illinois, placed another nail into the evolutionist model by advocating that life has three domains and not two. After surveying the genetic similarities of bacterial species he claimed that two of these domains belonged to microbes, which was Darwinian heresy. His results published in 1977, were widely reported in the popular press. Editorial writers proclaimed that Woese had revealed a third kingdom of life on earth, a strange alien organism that appeared to be neither animal nor vegetable. Writes Kevin Davies:

By contrast the reaction of the established evolutionary experts was hardly fit to print. According to one observer, Woese's fanciful proposition 'was greeted with wrath and ridicule, not to mention abuse.' It was bad enough that Woese was an outsider practicing an obtuse technique that few others could master. Worse, he was essentially arguing that the alleged experts in the field of evolution had completely overlooked a huge limb of the tree of life.[40]

Woese's theory is rooted in a discovery found in 1982, when a research submarine named *Alvin* combed the floor of the Pacific Ocean off the coast of Baja California, in search of new forms of life. Two miles beneath the surface, *Alvin* rummaged around the base of a thermal vent known as a white smoker – a torrid emanation from the netherworld. The prize catch from the plutonic depths of the Pacific was a methane-producing microbe that thrived in temperatures around a balmy 85° C, 200 atmospheres of pressure, and no traces of oxygen. This curious organism, which had never been seen before, was named *Methanococcus jannaschii*, in honor of its chief waste product and the expedition leader, Holger Jannasch.

Genomic pioneer and entrepreneur Craig Venter was fascinated by the controversy between Woese and orthodox evolutionists. He could identify with Woese's plight:

...a researcher brave enough to risk ridicule by challenging evolution's central dogma while yearning for the respect and recognition of his peers.[41]

Venter knew that his sequencing technology could settle this contentious debate by comparing genome to genome. And so, in collaboration with Woese, he selected the genome of *M. jannaschii* as the next contestant for the genome sequencing treatment. The results complicate the Darwinian hypothesis:

The first archaea genome sequence vindicated Woese's long insistence that the archaea represent a third limb of the tree of life. According to this view, life traces back some 3.5 billion years to LUCA – the last universal common ancestor. LUCA divided into two nonnucleated cells, the bacteria and the archaea. Millions of years later, the archaea gave rise to cells with a nucleus – the eukaryotes. By a process of endosymbiosis ('endo' meaning internal, 'symbiosis' meaning a mutually beneficial relationship), these cells took up small bacteria that serve as mitochondria (the energy-producing factories) and chloroplasts (sites of photosynthesis in plants), vital cogs in the evolution of animals and plants. Richard Fortey put it like this: 'We are one tribe with bacteria that live in hot springs, parasitic barnacles, vampire bats and cauliflowers. We all share a common ancestor.'

However, even Woese concedes that the tree of life is not quite this straightforward. The branches of the evolutionary tree are much more gnarled than we might expect. As we have seen, archaea possess bacterial genes, eukaryotes possess bacterial genes, and bacteria possess archaea genes. This was borne home when Venter's group sequenced the genome of Thermotoga maritima, a rod-shaped bacterium first discovered in Vulcano, Italy, in a 80° C marine sediment. The sequence of this genome revealed a surprisingly archaea-like organization, with about a quarter of its genes related to archaea. This example, and many others, suggests that in addition to vertical transfer of genes from generation to generation, a high degree of lateral gene transfer – the process by which bacteria can spread genes for antibiotic resistance – has occurred during evolution. It suggests that life may have evolved from a small population of primitive cells with shuffling genes. To some, this is an unwelcome complication in evolutionary theory. Observes evolutionary biologist Ford Doolittle, 'It is as if we have failed at the task that Darwin set for us: delineating the unique structure of the tree of life.' [42]

Even the Raelian Movement, whose corporation CLONAID, has declared the first few cloned humans, claim "Evolution: a myth," quoting scientific evidence for their claim. Their web site states:

Curiously, during the month of January 1996, a prestigious French magazine 'La Recherche' published an article titled 'The Drawbacks of Darwinism.' Following this the magazine published a virulent debate on the question confirming the fact that many scientists question evolution. Some even went so far as to say that the theory is not scientific, and that 'it rests on a sophism, a circular reasoning: the environment selects animals most apt to survive, and we call the most apt animals those which survive!'[43]

Under the title "An anti-evolutionist system in our genes," Raelians argue for the vision of what they call "scientific creationism":

Perhaps the most awkward question today for the theory of evolution is the one raised by...the DNA repair mechanism. This has been found to be common to all mammals and repairs damaged DNA. If the damage is too great to repair, it organizes the cell's self-destruction.

Therefore if any defect in the transcription of the genetic code arises, (the foundation on which evolution is based) then this repair or programmed cell death mechanism will remove such a mutation. If not, then the organism as a whole will die of cancer.

This control system is clearly present to avoid all mutation. Thus, if this system is common to all mammals, according to the theory of Evolution, it should also be present in the common ancestors of mammals.

If it were present in our ancestors, how were they able to diversify in order to render so many different species? This is clearly a major contradiction which can only put a serious doubt on the theory of evolution.[44]

The credibility of the model of unprompted generation of life on earth followed by chance micro-mutations driving macro-evolutionary processes has been under continuous controversy since its genesis. Two centuries before, Reverend William Paley refuted the notion of a Godless universe. A theologian and author of *Natural Theology – or Evidences of the Existence and Attributes of the Deity Collected from the Appearances of Nature,* published in 1802, he is the best-known early defender of the "Argument from Design" and thus the existence of God. Richard Dawkins, author of *The Blind Watchmaker*, challenges Paley's notion of natural theology with his own humanist, evolutionist belief system:

Paley's argument is made with passionate sincerity and is informed by the best biological scholarship of his day, but it is wrong. The analogy between telescope and eye, between watch and living organism, is false. All appearances to the contrary, the only watchmaker in nature is the blind forces of physics, albeit deployed in a very special way. A true watchmaker has foresight: he designs his cogs and springs, and plans their interconnections, with a future purpose in his mind's eye. Natural selection, the blind, unconscious, automatic process which Darwin discovered, and which we now know as the explanation for the existence and apparently purposeful form of life, has no purpose in mind. It has no mind and no mind's eye. It does not plan for the future. It has no vision, no foresight, no sight at all. If it can be said to play the role of watchmaker in nature, it is the blind watchmaker.[45]

The reader should be wary of accepting Dawkins' level of conviction as an indication of proof from scientific facts. First, his notion that "a *true* watchmaker has foresight" is a reflection of his own assumptions about a God and his own interpretation of what life should really be. He is contending that a *true* watchmaker should have done a better job of life on Earth. In the section "Gnostic Cancer," in this chapter, the idea that the world is too chaotic, evil and "fallen" to have been a divine creation, is linked to Gnosticism. Such negative theology was a consistent theme for Darwin, and it remains popular with today's evolutionists. For illustration, Darwin thought orchids seemed to be made of spare parts rather than individually created. Evolutionist Stephen Jay Gould sums up the argument as follows:

Orchids manufacture their intricate devices from the common components of ordinary flowers, parts usually fitted for very different functions. If God had designed a beautiful machine to reflect his wisdom and power, surely he would not have used a collection of parts generally fashioned for other purposes. Orchides were not made by an ideal engineer; they are jury-rigged from a limited set of available components. Thus, they must have evolved from ordinary flowers.[46]

Cornelius G. Hunter, author of *Darwin's God: Evolution and the Problem of Evil*, observes:

Notice how easy it is to go from a religious premise to a scientific-sounding conclusion. The theory of evolution is confirmed not by a successful prediction but by the argument that God would never do such a thing. Evolutionists have no scientific justification for these expectations, for they did not come from science. They are part of a personal religious belief and as such are not amenable to scientific debate.[47]

Darwin did not liberate biology from metaphysical thought as sometimes claimed – he merely switched the metaphysics. What was right is now wrong, and vice versa. The evolutionist use of homology as an argument against creation requires evolutionists to place their own interpretation on the metaphysical realm.[48]

In further defending Creationism, I shall now pursue the negative-evidence tactic of Darwinists (highlighted above by Hunter). In the remainder of this section five evolutionist theories, which have been proven false and have lead to a general, although under-publicized, rejection of original Darwinism and neo-Darwinism, will be studied. Furthermore, in the next section the falsified hominid evidence linking mankind to the ape is exposed. In order the erroneous evolutionist theories are: speciation, spontaneous generation, life on Mars, embryology/homology, vestigial organs, and mutation theory. The latter topic includes discussion of living fossils, genomics and the currently popular theory called "punctuated equilibria."

According to G. Ledyard Stebbins, the acceptance of Darwin's theory of natural selection reached it's lowest ebb around 1926. At the time biology students were often asked to read the most authoritative history of biology, by Erik Nordenskiöld. He wrote:

To raise the theory of natural selection, as often been done, to the rank of a natural law, comparable to the law of gravity established by Newton is, of course, completely irrational, as time has already shown; Darwin's theory of the origin of species was long ago abandoned. Other facts established by Darwin are all of second-rate value.[49]

Instead of small changes accumulating and resulting in large changes, the small changes appear to be bounded. One can successfully bring about all sorts of features in a population of pigeons, dogs, horses, and the like, but there seem to be definite limits – one cannot modify pigeons to become dogs or horses. If breeders found that change had limits, how did evolution produce it so copiously? According to Hunter, Darwin argued that natural selection can produce all sorts of change that had eluded the breeders. "Man selects only for his own good: Nature only for that of the being which she tends."[50] Darwin triumphantly concluded:

As man can produce, and certainly has produced, a great result by his methodical and unconscious means of selection, what may not natural selection effect?[51]

Darwin did the best he could to elevate the powers of natural selection over the breeder's artificial selection, but in the end we are left with a mere possibility. Experiments in mutation theory further undermined the concept of speciation. The radioactive bombardment of fruit flies over a fifty year period only produced deformed and grotesque variations of fruit flies.

In 1988 Ernst Mayr wrote:

In spite of all the advances in genetics we are still almost entirely ignorant as to what happens genetically during speciation.[52]

In his book *The History of Creation* [1876], Professor Ernst Haeckel wrote of the crucial need for "spontaneous generation" to support Darwin's theory:

This hypothesis is indispensable for the consistent completion of the non-miraculous history of creation.[53]

Science on this matter has "evolved" over the years, however, as discussed at the start of this section the hypothesis still remains unproven and doubtful. In 1861, only two years after Darwin's *Origin*, Louis Pasteur dealt a severe blow to the idea of spontaneous generation, by proving that microbes, previously believed to have spontaneously developed, were in fact the result of airborne bacteria. In 1864, only five weeks after Pasteur had delivered a particularly spirited and widely reported defense of divine creation as the only possible initiator of life, a meteorite fragment *purportedly* containing possible evidence of life from outer space was reported to have fallen at Orgueil in southwestern France. The fragment was analyzed and said to show evidence of once living organisms.[54] In 1871 Sir William Thomson, president of the British Association, told the assembly that life had come to this planet from outer space, carried on "countless seed-bearing meteoritic stones."[55]

The Orgueil meteorite is technically referred to as a carbonaceous chondrite and is kept at the American Museum of Natural History. In 1961 it was subjected to a mass spectroscopy. The characteristics of the hydrocarbons detected very closely matched those of butter and terrestrial sediments.[56] Notwithstanding, the investigators concluded the mass was definitely a meteorite. As recently as 1964, the popular *Life Science Library* series in its book *The Cell* declared that "cell-like fossils have been found in meteorites [Orgueil]" and concluded that this was a "startling indication that life might have been much more prolific on other worlds."[57] Taylor has determined that the image of the "cell" shown in the *Life Science* series was taken from a 1963 book by Brian Mason, titled *Organic Matter From Space*. Even though, in his book Mason had explained that this supposed elemental life-form found in the Orgueil meteorite resembled nothing more than an hexagonal crystal of iron sulfate.[58] At the time many claimed the Orgueil life-form was a hoax and in the end they were proved right. Another chondrite fell in Australia in 1969. This sample was more thoroughly investigated and found to contain twenty-three aromatic hydrocarbons of abiotic origin, i.e. they were not from anything living.[59]

Italian astronomer Schiaparelli reignited the faith among many evolutionists in extraterrestrial life in 1877. He claimed to have discovered "canali" on the planet Mars. Schiaparelli's work was continued in 1894 by Percival Lowell who developed a Martian life theory based on the discovery of some seven hundred canals which he named and published.[60] This life on Mars thesis gained science fiction notoriety when H.G. Wells wrote *War of the Worlds* in 1898. More recently, the torch sustaining the theory of extraterrestrial life had been taken up by Carl Sagan. The basis for the current hope derives from a statistical hypothesis that contends – given chance life on Earth and the size of the universe; the mathematical probability of extraterrestrial life elsewhere is near certainty. The theory says given a very large number of stars in each galaxy; given the enormous number of galaxies in the universe; given some greater than zero probability that a star has a so-called "solar system;" given some measurable probability that a portion of these solar systems may contain another planet similar to earth (conducive to life); and factor in billions of potentially "creative" years, extraterrestrial intelligent life then becomes a certainty.

Adherents now search the universe awaiting contact. Interestingly, the lack of contact and the scarcity of life forms on nearby planets has not diminished evolutionist enthusiasm. In any case, one must wonder if discovery of some extraterrestrial life form need diminish creationist zeal. Critical to the secular worldview is the absence of a divine Creator, dabbling in the unfolding events of time. Predictably, the premise that God is absent, that the start of life was a chance event, and evolution a series of random purposeless events, has lead scientists such as Francis Crick to theorize that the biological patterns behind DNA found on earth would likely be unrelated to those elsewhere:

The principles enshrined in the periodic table are truly universal, signifying the invariant properties of chemical elements dispersed throughout the universe. But if life exists on other planets, there is little reason to believe that the genetic code adheres to the same pattern as it does on earth, for chance played a major part in the origin of life as we know it.[61]

One wonders what would be the science community's response to the discovery of life elsewhere, micro-biologically organized as ours. Would an alien with 40 per cent primate DNA or a microorganism off a meteorite with 80 per cent similarity to a terrestrial species silence the "random chance, purposeless universe" apostles? I doubt it.

Tim M. Berra, described "embryology" in his 1990 book *Evolution and the Myth of Creationism: A Basic Guide to the Facts in the Evolution Debate*:

Comparative embryology is another field of study that reflects evolution. There are many features of embryonic development common to related animals, and the closer the relationship, the more similar the development. The early embryos of all vertebrate classes (fishes, amphibians, reptiles, birds, and mammals) resemble one another markedly. The embryos of vertebrates that do not respire by means of gills (reptiles, birds and mammals) nevertheless pass through a gill-slit stage complete with aortic arches and a two chambered heart, like those of a fish. The passage through a fishlike stage by the embryos of the higher vertebrates is not explained by creation, but is readily accounted for as an evolutionary relic. The higher vertebrates, including humans, carry a number of ancestral genes that are switched on and off during ontogeny (the developmental process from a fertilized egg to adult).[62]

Many evolutionists claimed homologies in the developing stages of life where organisms construct themselves. This self-construction process can be quite elaborate. Very different animals have similar embryos that apparently are not designed for their respective unique requirements. Darwin concluded that the resemblances were homologous. He claimed they reveal the structure of evolutionary ancestors:

As the embryo often shows us more or less plainly the structure of the less modified and ancient progenitor of the group, we can see why ancient and extinct forms so often resemble in their adult state the embryos of existing species of the same class. Agassiz believes this to be a universal law of nature; and we may hope hereafter to see the law proved out.[63]

What a boon this would be for evolutionists. If true, the law could yield a plethora of data. Where the ancient fossil record had its gaps, perhaps modern embryos could fill in the picture. This notion set the stage for Haeckel's famous dictum "ontogeny recapitulates phylogeny," otherwise known as the biogenetic law.[64] In its strong form, it states that the early development of an individual is a brief and rapid review of its evolutionary history. In *Ontogeny and Phylogeny* Harvard professor Stephen Jay Gould points out that the German scientist Wilhelm His exposed such "shocking dishonesty" on the part of Ernst Haeckel that it rendered him unworthy "to be counted as a peer in the company of earnest researchers."[65] Sir Gavin de Beer of the British Natural History Museum was quoted as saying:

Seldom has an assertion like that of Haeckel's 'theory of recaptitulation,' facile, tidy, and plausible, widely accepted without critical examination, done so much harm to science.[66]

Haeckel not only utilized deceptive data but also used doctored drawings to delude his devotees.[67] His dishonesty was so blatant that he was charged with fraud by five professors and convicted by a university court at Jena.[68] His forgeries were subsequently made public with the 1911 publication of *Haeckel's Frauds and Forgeries.*

Writes Hank Hanegraaff:

Today the 'recapitulations' most commonly referred to by educators and evolutionists are the 'gill slits' in the 'fish stage' of human embryonic growth. Dr. Henry Morris notes several reasons why this supposed recapitulation is entirely superficial. First, the human embryo never at any time develops gill slits and therefore never goes through a 'fish stage.' Furthermore, a fetus does not have fins or any other fish structures. Finally, every stage in the development of an embryo plays a crucial role in embryonic growth. Thus, there are no redundant vestiges of former evolutionary phases.[69]

Although Haeckel's frauds and forgeries were exposed more than half a century ago, modern studies in molecular genetics have further demonstrated the utter absurdity of the recapitulation theory. The DNA for a fetus is not the DNA for a frog and the DNA for a frog is not the DNA for a fish. Rather the DNA of a fetus, frog, fish, or falcon, for that matter, is uniquely programmed for reproduction after its own kind.[70]

Incredibly, such facts have not stopped men like humanist Carl Sagan from affirming recapitulation. In his 1977 book *The Dragons of Eden*, he wrote:

Haeckel held that in its embryological development, an animal tends to repeat or recapitulate the sequence that its ancestors followed during their evolution. And indeed in human intrauterine development we run through stages very much like fish, reptiles, and non-primate mammals before we become recognizably human. The fish stage even has gill slits, which are absolutely useless for the embryo who is nourished via the umbilical cord, but a necessity for human embryology: since gills were vital to our ancestors, we run through a gill stage in becoming human.[71]

Writes Hanegraaff:

In The Dragons of Eden Sagan stated that determining when a fetus becomes human 'could play a major role in achieving an acceptable compromise in the abortion debate.'[72] *In his estimation the transition to human 'would fall toward the end of the first trimester or near the beginning of the second trimester of pregnancy.'*[73]

Shortly before Sagan died, Hanegraaff watched him reiterate this odd predilection. Without so much as blushing, he communicated his contention that a first-trimester abortion does not constitute the painful killing of a human fetus but merely the termination of a fish or frog. Thus in Sagan's world, Roe v. Wade provided the legal framework for the slaughter of multiplied millions of creatures rather than children.[74]

I challenge the reader to check out your child's biology book or visit the nearest high school to see what our children are reading in their textbooks. My middle daughter's textbook (*Biology*, Ritter, Robert John, Nelson Canada, 1993) for grade eleven, in June 2003, introduces fossil evidence supporting "evolution" and then offers the following under the title "Indirect Evidence: Living Organisms":

Direct evidence provided through fossils is not the only evidence that supports the theory of evolution. Other evidence is readily observable in living organisms, which like fossils, show the links between existing forms and their ancestors....Embryology, the study of organisms in the early stages of development, offers valuable insight into the process of evolution. During the late 1800s, scientists noted a striking similarity between the embryos of different species (see Figure 4.7) [here is seen the classic imagery of salamander, chicken, pig and human embryological development.] *At the time, a German embryologist, K.E. von Baer, wrote that because he had not labeled the two similar embryos he had in his possession, he was unable to identify whether they were the embryos of lizards, birds, or mammals....Around the same time, another German biologist, E.H. Haeckel, advanced the theory of recapitulation, more commonly expressed as 'ontogeny recapitulates (repeats) phylogeny.' In other words, every organism repeats its evolutionary development in its own embryology. The theory is applicable only in a very broad sense. Scientists believe that many structures in an embryo are similar to those found in common ancestors.*[75]

If one glaring error of commission is not enough, the same *Biology* text raises the homology argument in combination with embryology in defense of evolution:

When the anatomies of various organisms are studied and compared, the suggestion that organisms with similar structures evolved from a common ancestor becomes increasingly obvious. For example, the flipper of a seal, the leg of a pig, the wing of a bat, and the human arm all have the same basic structure and the same pattern of early growth. These homologous structures in some cases serve different functions. However, they are sufficiently similar to suggest that they have the same evolutionary origin. Many other examples of homologies can be found in living organisms. For example, the Eustachian tube, which leads from the middle ear to the mouth of humans is homologous to one of the gill slits of fish, and the middle-ear bones of humans are homologous to certain jawbones of fish.

The homology argument is quite general, for it says that any pattern found in nature was produced by evolution. Hunter refutes this theory:

Evolution is supposed to have created all this diversity. It seems to be capable of designing and implementing every conceivable biological design. Yet on the other hand, when a pattern is found – a similarity between species – this is supposed to be an example of how stingy evolution can be. Evolution we are told, favors practicality over optimality. Instead of designing the perfect species, it uses spare parts that are available from ancestral species. On the one hand, evolution seems to have tremendous creative powers, bringing forth the millions of species with all their diversity; yet on the other hand, it is pragmatic. It exerts its creative powers only to the extent that is necessary, often settling for less than optimum designs in the name of expediency.[76]

Consider the streamlined torpedo shapes, tall dorsal fins, and broad tails found in sharks, swordfishes, and dolphins. None of these are closely related, because they belong in disparate groups (sharks with the cartilaginous fishes, swordfishes with the bony fishes, dolphins with the mammals). Therefore evolutionists believe they are only distantly related, and so their similarities must be analogous, not homologous. Hunter cites Futuyma in further explanation of evolutionist rejection of any possibility of God's hand in nature:

The facts of embryology, the study of development, also make little sense except in the light of evolution. Why should species that ultimately develop adaptations for utterly different ways of life be nearly indistinguishable in their early stages? How does God's plan for humans and sharks require them to have almost identical embryos?

Take any major group of animals, and the poverty of imagination that must be ascribed to a Creator becomes evident.

When we compare the anatomies of various plants or animals, we find similarities and differences where we should least expect a Creator to have supplied them.[77]

Here again one sees scientific pre-supposition and negative theology. Evolutionists further believe that certain homologous structures have, over the course of evolution, lost their original purpose. The list of such organs in humans might include wisdom teeth, coccyx (tail vertebrae), ear-wiggling muscles, and the appendix. Says Hunter, at the molecular level, evolutionists also believe they have identified vestigial structures in the form of *pseudogenes* – DNA sequences that resemble genes but appear to be nonfunctional. Evolutionists believe pseudogenes are the remnants of ancient genes, no longer in use but carried along as access baggage.[78] [More on DNA later in this section.]

Like the vagueness of homologies, the argument from vestigial organs appears persuasive, yet it too suffers from the lack of objective measure. According to Hunter, the problem is that in order to identify an organ as vestigial, we need to measure its adaptive value. When we find that an organ makes a positive contribution to fitness, then we disprove the vestigial claim. It is not surprising that the history of vestigial organs involves shrinking lists:

In 1895 Ernst Weidersheim published a list of eighty-six organs in the human body that he supposed to be vestigial. The vast majority of items on Weidersheim's list are now known to be functioning organs. The pineal gland, for example, is now known to be part of the endocrine system...Weidersheim also claimed the coccyx, a short collection of vertebrae at the end of the spine, was vestigial. But the coccyx is the attachment point for several important muscles and ligaments. And Weidersheim claimed the thyroid and thymus glands and appendix were vestigial, but important functions for all three have since been discovered.[79]

In 1981 zoologist S.R. Scadding analyzed Weidersheim's claims and had difficulty finding a single item that was not functional, although some are so only in a minor way.[80] Hunter said Scadding concluded that the "vestigial organs" provide no evidence for evolutionary theory. Furthermore, Hunter argues:

When evolutionists identify a structure as vestigial, it seems that it is the theory of evolution that is justifying the claim, rather than the claim justifying the theory of evolution.[81]

If a penguin's wing is highly efficient for swimming, then why should we think it is vestigial, aside from simply presupposing it was formed by evolution? The idea that vestigial structures can in fact be perfectly useful makes the argument subjective. A character trait that is fully functional for one observer may only partially function for another observer, and may be considered inefficient by yet another observer. And so we are again left with evidence for evolution that is subjective.

The strategy in presumptions about what God should or should not do, is that if opposing theories can be falsified (in this case Creationism), then the credibility of the alternative (evolutionism) is enhanced by the process of elimination. Gould puts it this way:

Odd arrangements and funny solutions are the proof of evolution – paths that a sensible God would never tread but that a natural process, constrained by history, follows perforce. No one understood this better than Darwin. Ernst Mayr has shown how Darwin, in defending evolution, consistently turned to organic parts and geographic distributions that make the least sense.[82]

In presenting his theory, Darwin made a serious mistake in characterizing natural selection as a "struggle for life" or "struggle for existence." Natural selection acts as different individuals of the same population display different rates of survival and reproductive capacity. Between such individuals, struggles to the death are rare. In most species of fishes, insects, and plants, which constitute the majority of known organisms, active struggle between individuals belonging to the same population is completely absent.[83] A further misconception was the mistaken idea that mutations can establish the rate and direction of evolution and that bursts of rapid evolutionary change are produced by increases in the rate of mutations. Some population geneticists have sought out "hot spots" on the earth's surface where radiation intensities are unusually high, hoping to find evidence of rapid evolutionary rates caused by the effect of radiation increasing the mutation rate. One particular spot for these investigations has been certain radioactive sands along the south coast of India. The results of these investigations have been negative; increased rates of evolution have not been observed. According to G. Ledyard Stebbins, this is no surprise. These results are to be expected on the basis of the "interaction-selection" hypothesis – another mutation of Darwinism:

Rapid evolution results from a strong challenge generated by a rapidly changing environment and the presence of organisms with gene pools capable of meeting the challenge.[84]

About the turn of the century, a Dutch botanist named Hugo de Vries proposed his mutation theory as the mechanism of evolving one species into another. However, de Vries' theory was short-lived and by 1914 was discredited by Edward C. Jeffery who showed that all he had discovered in his experiments with primroses was a previously unknown variety within the species.[85] He thought that the new variety was a "mutant" or new species.

The idea of "mutations" did set the stage for further work. During the 1920s it was discovered that emissions from radioactive substances, such as radium, X rays, and even ultraviolet light, sometimes caused mutant offspring when parents had been exposed to this kind of radiation. The word "mutant" in this sense usually meant a change for the worse; de Vries, however, used the word to mean a change for the better. A number of scientists saw this as a possibility for producing new species and set about to prove this using the common fruit fly, *Drosophilia melanogaster*, which reproduces fairly rapidly and enables mutants to be studied over many generations in a short time. After half a century of work on fruit flies bombarded with all kinds of radiation, many mutant types have been produced with different colored eyes, with different sizes of eyes, with no eyes, and with variations in wings, but throughout, the creatures have steadfastly remained fruit flies. No new species has ever been produced, while mutants have invariably been deformed or in some way are less than normal. This is perhaps not too surprising when one thinks of the lead-shield protection given to our reproductive organs when we have an X ray examination, since this is specifically to prevent mutant or damaged offspring. There is a tendency in biological textbooks to make supposition appear as fact by suggesting that some mutations have been for the better by increased wing muscles, etc., and the reader should be careful to understand what has, in fact, been observed and what is being supposed.[86]

By the 1930s the classical Darwinian theory was being supplanted by the neo-Darwinian theory in which it was thought that mutant genes of a favorable type played a decisive part. The mutant genes were believed to be produced by radiation such as cosmic rays rather than X rays. In 1942 Julian Huxley coined the term modern synthesis for the same idea, and it is the neo-Darwinian theory or synthetic theory that has dominated evolutionary thinking for the past forty years. The theory proposes that there is the infrequent appearance of a mutation where by chance the individual is more favorably suited to its environment. While admitted to be rare, the mutant then finds an exactly matching mate; since they are slightly better fitted to the environment, it is supposed they tend to have more offspring than normal variants. This chance process is repeated over countless generations, and the small mutant changes accumulate and eventually lead to the appearance of an entirely new species.[87]

The neo-Darwinian school began to have its dissenters in the 1960s. The feeling at the time was marked by the Wistar Institute Symposium held in Philadelphia, in April 1966, where the chairman, Sir Peter Medwar, made the following opening remarks:

The immediate cause of this conference is a pretty widespread sense of dissatisfaction about what has come to be thought as the accepted evolutionary theory in the English-speaking world, the so-called neo-Darwinian theory. [88]

By 1980 the neo-Darwinian theory was struggling for survival in the battle of belief against a rising new theory for the mechanism of evolution. The latest theory is the preferred choice of paleontologists Niles Eldredge and Stephen Gould, which they call "punctuated equilibria. Taylor writes:

In 1980 an historic conference was held in Chicago's Field Museum and attended by 160 of the world's top paleontologists, anatomists, evolutionary geneticists, and developmental biologists. The content of the conference directly challenged the uncertain position of the neo-Darwinian theory, which had dominated evolutionary biology for the previous decades....The most important outcome of the meeting on which most were agreed was that the small changes from generation to generation within a species can in no way accumulate to produce a new species. This was a radical and major departure from the faith and, in principle, as much a departure as the Vatican's Second Council (1962-65) decision to allow Roman Catholics to eat meat on Friday! Yesterday, a man could fail an exam or lose a job for not subscribing to the neo-Darwinian mechanism. Today that unbelief is no longer worthy of excommunication. The punctuated equilibria theory took a rather prominent position at this conference and, although not accepted by the die-hard neo-Darwinists, was generally well received and will undoubtedly occupy tomorrow's textbooks as the new faith.[89]

Taylor also questions evolutionary explanations for extinction in the fossil record. Why did many creatures die out when it seems that many like creatures have survived unchanged to present day. Examples of "living fossils" include bats (who are exactly the same as their fossilized counterpart); the peccary; the Okapi (formerly known as *Paleotragus*); and the *Coelacanth* (a fish discovered to be living unchanged for as much as 100 million years). Says Taylor:

It is no wonder that many of these discoveries cause controversy since their very existence challenges the faith in a theory that is based upon the assumption of enormous lengths of time.

Clearly, the problem of survival of some and not others, the extinction of many but not all, is a matter that has baffled evolution scientists ever since Darwin's day, and there has yet to be a satisfactory explanation.[90]

Today there also exists a genomic variant of vestigial hypothesis. For evolutionist Kenneth R. Miller, pseudogenes, which he believes are nonfunctional, reveal a designer who "made serious errors, wasting millions of bases of DNA on a blue-print full of junk and scribbles."[91] Evolutionists also argue that "God" would never use a universal pattern to create life. Science in their eyes can only reveal the absence of a divine dynamic. Hunter writes:

The genetic code and the DNA molecule are often cited as homologies that provide strong evidence for evolution....but there is a nonscientific interpretation of this evidence to which evolutionists often appeal. They see the genetic code and DNA molecule as evidence against the doctrine of divine creation. For example, Ridley claims that whereas the genetic code is preserved across species, it would not be if the species had been created independently.[92] Apparently Ridley believes that if there is a Creator, then he is obliged to use different genetic codes for the different species. Similarly, Berra claims that the theory of evolution is 'the only reasonable explanation' for the fact that virtually all organisms carry their genetic information in the DNA molecule.[93] In other words, this homology is not positive evidence in favor of evolution but rather negative evidence against the competition....It seems that for Ridley the notion of a 'common architech' does not support divine creation. Of course, Ridley is entitled to whatever metaphysical view of God and the world he prefers, but he is using that view to support the theory of evolution, and this is the point.[94]

Evolutionists also claim they find supporting evidence in molecular biology. But DNA reveals complexity, not evolution:

The existence of a code implies that two distinct entities – the sender and receiver – must know the code before the message is sent. Therefore the existence of the DNA genetic code requires elaborate and coordinated sending and receiving machinery to be in the cell when a new individual is first conceived.

One might think that the twentieth century's discovery of the genetic code and the associated cellular machinery might have cast some doubt on the theory of evolution. For whereas earlier Darwinists might have hoped for simple beginnings, biology now knows that the cell not only is highly complex but also shows no signs of intermediate or abbreviated forms. In a letter Darwin speculated of a warm little pond with a protein compound ready to undergo more complex changes. Darwin's credulous acceptance of a spontaneous increase in complexity set the tone for evolutions response to the twentieth century's findings. The immense complexity of the cell, including the genetic code and DNA molecule, were seen not as a challenge to evolution but as supporting evidence, despite the fact that evolution could not explain how such complexity could have originated...

Given the complexity of the cellular machinery and genetic code, it is not surprising that evolutionists do not have any detailed hypothesis about how it could have originated or evolved. Instead they have a wide variety of speculative ideas. Some evolutionists believe that the genetic code arose as a result of interactions with clay minerals. Others try to explain it as a result of nonenzymatic chemical reactions, and yet others have tried stereochemical approaches. An entirely different set of hypoth-

eses holds that the genetic code arrived on earth from outer space, on meteors, comets, or spores driven by radiation pressure or even deliberately planted by extra-terrestrial beings.[95]

In addition to the origin of the code, there are a variety of hypotheses about how the modern code could have evolved from a simpler code. Perhaps fewer amino acids were originally coded for, or perhaps the code distinguished between classes of amino acids rather than specific amino acids. Perhaps the alphabet was originally binary, or perhaps the words were only two letters long. Perhaps the original machinery was imprecise, so that a given gene did not always code for the same protein.[96]

One thing evolutionists do agree on is that there is a great deal of uncertainty about how the genetic code came about.[97] *All the various hypotheses are grappling with the problem of finding a neo-Darwinian mechanism for the genetic code. Because the code is chemically arbitrary, it holds no apparent competitive advantage over any other code. Swap in another code and things would work just as well, and therefore Darwin's law of natural selection is powerless to help explain the origin of the code…. The different hypotheses reveal fundamental differences of opinion.*

It is natural for science to go through this stage in the early development of a theory. The problem here is that evolutionists are claiming the genetic code as evidence for their theory when the code's very existence remains unexplained. We have no idea how the genetic code originated; therefore we can hardly appeal to its existence as evidence for evolution.

There is yet another reason that the universality of the genetic code is not strong evidence for evolution. Simply put, the theory of evolution does not predict the genetic code to be universal (it does not, for that matter, predict the genetic code at all). In fact, leading evolutionists such as Francis Crick and Leslie Orgel are surprised that there aren't multiple codes in nature.[98]

Let us return to the latest evolutionary theory. Stebbins in *Darwin to DNA, Molecules to Humanity*, explains the "punctuated equilibria" theory:

Traditionally, paleontologists have supported the hypothesis of gradual change, as did Darwin, the founder of modern evolutionary theory. In recent years, however, a group of younger paleontologists, particularly Niles Eldredge, Stephen J. Gould, and Steven Stanley, have compiled a large body of evidence in support of the hypothesis of punctuated equilibria, or sudden bursts….These paleontologists maintain that, for many groups of organisms, the fossil record is now so well known that it is very unlikely to contain long gaps unrepresented by fossils…In addition, Eldredge and Gould have studied fossil sequences of snails in Bermuda in which gaps in a sequence are so recent that they are difficult to explain on the assumption that they represent periods during which no fossils were formed.

Steven Stanley has presented an even stronger argument against the hypothesis of extremely slow, gradual evolution. He points out that the Darwinian theory of natural selection, which is accepted by most evolutionists...will not work unless a fairly rapid rate of evolution is postulated with reference to the geological time scale.[99]

Stebbins asks, "if evolution is not continuous but is confined to periods of activity separated by long intervals of stability, then the next obvious question is, why?" The answer Stebbins developed:

...populations do not evolve beyond the differentiation of races or closely related species unless they are faced with an environmental challenge. Populations of organisms are basically conservative; if they can survive by staying in the habitat that they have always occupied and by exploiting it in the same way their ancestors did, they will do so. They evolve new characteristics only when a changing environment forces them either to evolve or become extinct.[100]

Stephen Gould estimates that "more than 99.9 per cent of species are not sources of great future diversity." Stebbins believes:

Evolution is not a universal property of life, like self-reproduction, growth, and individual response to the environment. Its most significant changes result from unusual combinations of events.[101]

Many evolutionists, especially those who emphasize internal genetic changes or mutation probability rates as the primary limiting factors, look for a built-in "clock" that governs evolutionary rates. However, George G. Simpson, the first paleontologist to apply careful statistical methods for interpreting the fossil record, showed that quantum bursts of evolution have taken place and that some species have remained constant during tens or hundreds of millions of years. Says Stebbins:

Punctuated equilibrium is an extension of Simpson's ideas that, if accepted, renders the search for generalized rates of evolution meaningless.[102]

He goes on to give his theory on the evolutionary variance:

Although at all times some populations are evolving somewhere in the world, evolution is not a continuous, inevitable property of all populations at all times and in all circumstances. Most evolution, particularly of striking new adaptive types, occurs in quantum bursts that are triggered by challenges of a changing physical and biotic environment. When such a challenge occurs, the populations exposed to it respond in one of three ways. Most populations become extinct; some adjust to the new environment with minimal change in their hereditary makeup and thus persist with little evolution over millions of years; a few populations respond by evolving entirely new adaptive mechanisms. Such newly adapted organisms may spread widely, evolve further, and evolve adaptations to still other new habitats.

What determines whether a population responds to a particular challenge by becoming extinct, continuing with little change, or evolving in a new direction? Briefly, a population's response depends on the nature of its hereditary variation, or gene pool, at the time of the challenge, and on the resulting kinds of interactions between the population and environment.[103]

Whether by punctuated equilibria (a few steps) or by neo-Darwinian explanation (many steps), evolution still demands that the transition from one species to the next be in graduated steps. This being so, there is still a major problem with the transition creatures who are really neither one species nor another. Changing from reptile to bird, for example, would involve untold generations of reptiles with imperfectly formed scales in process of transition to birds with imperfectly formed features, and, in either case, the creatures would be vulnerable and certainly not the fittest to survive. Darwin's own natural selection would then be working against rather than for such imperfections ever evolving to become another, more perfect, kind of creature. In spite of this evident drawback, general textbook descriptions usually lead the reader to believe that a reptile's scales somehow got ragged at the edges, and, after many generations, became feathers.[104]

This kind of argument, generally known as the argument from perfection, was well known to Darwin, who recognized that an organ was not only useless but an outright handicap if it was not close to being perfect. However, he wrote confidently in the *Origin*:

If it could be demonstrated that any complex organ existed which could not possibly have been formed by numerous successive slight modifications my theory would absolutely break down.[105]

Shortly after he wrote this, he confided in a letter to American botanist Asa Gray:

I remember well [the] time when the thought of the eye made me cold all over.[106]

The idea that some intermediate state of two-eyed "partial" blindness (a work-in-process lasting millions of years) or a cyclopic link connecting the no-eyed model with the standard two-eyed model did not constrain Darwin's enthusiasm for natural selection. In *Origin* Darwin wrote:

To suppose that the eye...could have been formed by natural selection, seems, I freely confess, absurd in the highest possible degree. Yet reason tells me, that if numerous graduations from a perfect and complex eye to one very imperfect and simple, each grade being useful to the possessor, can be shown to exist; if further, the eye does vary ever so slightly, and the variations be inherited, which is certainly the case;...then the difficulty of believing that a perfect and complex eye could be formed by natural selection, though insuperable by our imagination, can hardly be considered real.[107]

Says Taylor:

What Darwin has actually done in this statement is to use natural selection to justify natural selection and dismiss the difficulty as not real[108] .

Taylor likens Darwin's approach to accepting the evolution of complex organs on faith:

By definition, faith is being sure of what we hope for and certain of what we do not see; in short, it is the same stuff that makes religion.[109]

Reductionist Richard Dawkins presents his analysis of the "evolution" of the eye through a series of questions:

[Question 2] Could the human eye have arisen directly from something slightly different from itself, something that we may call X?

...If the answer to Question 2 for any particular degree of difference is no, all we have to do is repeat the question for a smaller degree of difference sufficiently small to give us a 'yes' answer to Question 2.

X is defined as something very like a human eye, sufficiently similar that the human eye could plausibly have arisen by a single alteration in X. If you have a mental picture of X and you find it impossible that the human eye could have arisen directly from it, this simply means that you have chosen the wrong X. Make your mental picture of X progressively more like a human eye, until you find an X that you do find plausible as an immediate predecessor to the human eye. There has to be one for you, even if your idea of what is plausible may be more, or less, cautious than mine!...By interposing a large enough series of Xs, we can derive the human eye from something not slightly different from itself but very different from itself. We can 'walk' a large distance across 'animal space,' and our move will be plausible provided we take small-enough steps.[110]

[Question 3] Is there a continuous series of Xs connecting the modern human eye to a state with no eye at all?

It seems to me clear that the answer has to be yes, provided only that we allow ourselves a sufficiently large series of Xs. You might feel that 1,000 Xs is ample,...if 10,000 is not enough for you, allow yourself 100,000, and so on. Obviously the available time imposes an upper ceiling on this game...Given, say, a hundred million Xs, we should be able to construct a plausible series of tiny graduations linking a human eye to just about anything!

[Question 4] Considering each member of the series of hypothetical Xs connecting the human eye to no eye at all, is it plausible that every one of them was made available by random mutation of its predecessor?

...My feeling is that, provided the difference between neighboring intermediates in our series leading to the eye is sufficiently small, the necessary mutations are almost bound to be forthcoming. We are, after all, always talking about minor quantitative changes in an existing embryonic process. Remember that, however compli-

cated the embryological status quo may be in any given generation, each mutation change in the status quo can be very small.[111]

[Question 5] Considering each member of the series of Xs connecting the human eye to no eye at all, is it plausible that every one of them worked sufficiently well that it assisted the survival and reproduction of the animals concerned?

...to quote Stephen Jay Gould, the noted Harvard paleontologist, as saying: 'We avoid the excellent question, What good is 5 per cent of an eye? By arguing that the possessor of such an incipient structure did not use it for sight.

An ancient animal with 5 per cent of an eye might indeed have used it for something other than sight, but it seems to me at least as likely that it used it for 5 per cent vision. And actually I don't think it is an excellent question. Vision that is 5 per cent as good as yours or mine is very much worth having in comparison with no vision at all. So is 1 per cent vision better than total blindness. And 6 per cent is better than 5, 7 per cent better than 6, and so on up the gradual, continuous series.[112]

Notwithstanding that Dawkins' gradualist approach can "connect the human eye to just about anything," the term "punctuated equilibrium" was invented by German geneticist Richard Goldschmidt, after he conceded there was scant compelling evolutionary evidence for vertical transitional forms in the fossil record. In his book *The Material Basis of Evolution*, he states:

The major evolutionary advances must have taken place in single large steps....The many missing links in the paleontological record are sought for in vain because they have never existed: 'the first bird hatched from a reptilian egg.'[113]

Now according to Gould's interpretation of punctuated equilibrium:

...a species does not arise gradually by the steady transformation of its ancestors; it appears all at once and 'fully formed.'[114]

Moreover, he confesses:

The extreme rarity of transitional forms persists as the trade secret of paleontology.[115]

In sum it takes huge myopic insensibilities to confidently proclaim faith in evolution at the expense of creationism, knowing that it provides little more concrete evidence. Francis Collins, a Christian and Director of the National Human Genome Institute supports this viewpoint:

When a scientist discovers something that no human knew before, but God did—that is both an occasion for scientific excitement and, for a believer, also an occasion for worship. It makes me sad that we have slipped into a polarized stance between science and religion that implies that a thinking human being could not believe in the value of both. There is no rational basis for that polarization. I find it completely comfortable to be both a rigorous scientist, who demands to see the data before accepting anybody's conclusions about the natural world, and also a believer whose life is profoundly influenced by the relationship I have with God.[116]

When are we going to level the educational playing field at schools so that our children can make their own informed choices? One-sided instruction on "homophobia" and "Darwinian evolution" serves only humanist and secularist beliefs and agendas.

Again, to illustrate what I consider as unfair handling of the evolutionism-creationism issue in our public schools, I can cite family experience as recent as June 2003. Lucy, our 17 year old (middle daugther), knowing that I have been investigating among many things, Darwinism for some two and a half years, asked for some help with a biology assignment. One week before the end of the school year, she had one evening to respond to nine questions on evolution, four of which were:

(1) How does the theory of natural selection explain the development of long-necked giraffes? (2) Why is the study of evolution important? (3) Write a paragraph that would defend the creation account of Scripture or discredit the theory of evolution. (Your personal belief may or may not be the same). (4) Write a paragraph that would be the best defense of the theory of evolution or discredit the arguments of a creationist? (Your personal belief may or may not be the same).

My wife takes the optimistic view that at least creationism and "Scripture" were mentioned at school. She is likely correct that this inclusion is a curriculum concession in response to Christian activism of yore. Lucy's teacher may be well intending, however, I think reducing creationism to one paragraph, one evening, with one week before the end of the year is a sham. Much more challenging and enlightening questions might be:

(1) Explain how the universe came into existence, if not miraculously; (2) After experiencing your eyesight blindfolded to 1 per cent effectiveness, explain how an unbroken chain of random mutations continuously improved humankind's prospects for survival and evolved our eyes from no sight to their present state; (3) Given the mathematical improbability of spontaneous generation (and Francis Crick's conclusions on the origin of life on earth), explain how life did get started; (4) Given that Francis Collins, Director National Human Genome Institute, is a Christian, do you think his religious beliefs in anyway weaken his credibility as a scientist?

These questions should be posed at the beginning of the term and the students given the entire term to respond. The answers should be discussed in the last week!

The next section will reveal considerable illogic in the evidence for humankind's primate connection and the regretful legacy of hoax in sustaining its popularity over the decades. We start with a hypothesis built upon the discovery of a single tooth with extra thick enamel common to *Ramapithecus and Australopithecines.*

Creation of Humankind

Gorillas are like us in so many ways. They live and die, copulate and reproduce like us. They get sick from the same diseases as those we suffer from. They belch, cough, hiccup, sneeze, pick their noses and break wind just as humans do. They love, protect, care for and discipline their children. They like and love one another. Mother love, in particular, is very pronounced, as it is with all mammals. Love is an essential emotion in the lives of these animals.[117]

W. Baumgartel, Anthropologist

And God said, Let us make man [humankind] in our image, after our likeness.

Genesis 1:26

Christianity cannot lose the Genesis account of creation like it could lose the doctrine of geocentricism and get along.[118]

G. Richard Bozarth, Atheist

Since every human being is made in God's image, every human being is worthy of honor and respect. Each life has intrinsic worth bequeathed by the Creator's intent – He knew us before our parents did. When Christians think of being made in God's image they are not thinking of anatomical parts. The Almighty is a Spirit, and therefore, the facets of "likeness" and "image" include characteristics such as righteousness, holiness, knowledge and moral judgment. Starting with the disobedience of Adam and Eve, God established that there is a right and a wrong way to do things and that He will hold each of us accountable.

On the other hand, secularists contend that Adam and Eve, indeed the whole Creation-Genesis story, is myth. In their evolution paradigm our existence is owed to a lengthy sequence of chance primate mutations and selective pressures. And when humankind is thus framed apart from the image of God, only the rules of the evolutionary "survival game" need apply. The implications are huge. If *right and wrong* have no application in the animal kingdom, why should moral and ethical issues apply to the crown of evolution's gestation – humankind? Sir Julian Huxley long ago said they should not apply. He gives us a revealing reason why people quickly embraced Darwinism:

It is because the concept of a Creator-God interferes with our sexual mores. Thus, we have rationalized God out of existence. To us, He has become nothing more than the faint and disappearing smile of the cosmic Cheshire cat in Alice in Wonderland.[119]

More recently, Bioethicist Peter Singer essentially said there should be no significant distinctions between man and the animal kingdom. He writes:

I have argued that the life of a fetus...is of no greater value than the life of a nonhuman animal at a similar level of rationality [and] self-consciousness.[120]

Much is at stake. The scientific credibility of either evolution or creation theory lies in the presence or absence of "missing link(s)" – a half-man half-ape species. In this competition of worldviews (including morality wars), the truth of the origin of man is central. The consequence of what you believe on this point will establish unequivocally which paradigm you have chosen and likely establish your thinking on gay rights and same-sex marriage. Richard Bozarth (quoted above) is correct, there is absolutely no provision for the reality of a hominid in Christian theology. One can see that the claim to a free sex "Pivot of Civilization" paradigm for both heterosexuals and homosexuals rests on the premise of no Creator and, therefore, no divine accountability.

Thinking about evolution theory applied to humankind, one might expect to find, in light of the general theory's legacy of falsehoods, conjectures and revisions, a similar legacy of deception and speculation in substantiating hominid existence. In this section we will examine what the evolutionists are saying of humankind's creation and the hominid evidence they have unearthed to support their argument. Where beliefs compete in a zero-sum dynamic, evidence against hominid existence or proof of evolutionist fraud only strengthens the creationist paradigm.

Although contradicting the current theory of "punctuated equilibrium," humanist and hierarchical reductionist Richard Dawkins explains the crucial nature of intermediary or transitionary species to the Darwinian model:

A complicated thing is one whose existence we do not feel inclined to take for granted, because it is too 'improbable.' It could not have come into existence in a single act of chance. We shall explain its coming into existence as a consequence of gradual, cumulative, step-by-step transformations from simpler things, from primordial objects sufficiently simple to have come into being by chance. Just as 'big-step reductionism' cannot work as an explanation of mechanism, and must be replaced by a series of small step-by-step peelings down through the hierarchy, so we explain a complex thing as originating in a single step. We must again resort to a series of small steps, this time arranged sequentially in time.[121]

Dawkins describes what he calls the "gradualist" approach to evolution – chronological sequences of fossils, exhibiting evolutionary trends with fixed rates of change. In his words:

If we have three fossils, A, B and C, A being ancestral to B, which is ancestral to C, we should expect B to be proportionately intermediate in form between A and C. For instance, if A had a leg length of 20 inches and C had a leg length of 40 inches, B's legs should be intermediate, their exact length being proportional to the time that elapsed between A's existence and B's.[122]

As an example of gradualism, he cites the swelling of the human skull from an *Australopithecus*-like ancestor, with a brain volume of about 500 cubic centimeters (cc), to modern *Homo sapiens's* average brain volume of about 1,400 cc. This increase of about 900 cc, nearly a tripling of the brain volume, has been accomplished in no more than three million years. By evolutionary standards this is a rapid rate of change. The caricature of the gradualist is supposed to believe that there was a slow and inexorable change, generation by generation, such that in all generations sons were slightly brainier than their fathers, brainier by 0.01 cc. Presumably the extra hundredth of a cubic centimeter is supposed to provide each succeeding generation with a significant survival advantage compared with the previous generation.[123]

At the genetic level, the evolution of the human brain can be described as an increase in the frequency of genes that code for larger numbers of neurons in certain parts of the brain, particularly those known to be most important for making associations between different sense impressions and learned ideas. At the level of natural selection of phenotypes, however, at least the later stages of this evolution depended on the superior adaptive value of both new combinations of genes and the kinds of cultural influences that interacted with the brain to produce functioning minds. So can we believe that the biological basis of the complex attributes we see in humankind today derives predominantly from quantitative changes in the size and structure of our brains?

According to the August 2002 issue of *National Geographic* the answer is no. Rick Gore reports that a new skeletal find in a medieval town called Dmanisi in the Republic of Georgia, had a tiny brain:

This is the face that's changing a thousand minds. It could be the first human to leave Africa. And it's not what anyone expected. This 1.75-million-year-old pioneer…had a tiny brain, not nearly the size scientists thought our ancestors needed to migrate into new land. And its huge canine teeth and thin brow look too apelike for an advanced hominid, the group that includes modern humans and their ancestors. Along with other fossils and tools found at the site, this skull reopens so many questions about our ancestry that one scientist muttered: 'They ought to put it back in the ground.'[124]

Until the Dmanisi find, scientists thought hand axes allowed early humans to effectively butcher and process meat, enabling migrants to take more energy-rich fat, grow bigger brains, and build taller bodies. But the tools found to date at Dmanisi are all simple choppers and scrapers like those that *Homo habilis* used in Africa to cut small pieces off carcasses or pound marrow from bone. Concludes Rick Gore, "Maybe scavenging provided all the nutrients a migrant needed." Regarding the tiny brain of the Dmanisi skull, Gore writes:

Scientists may be forced to reexamine the connection between brain size and intelligence. 'There's no reason to downgrade these early Georgians on the IQ scale,' says Philip Rightmire. 'They took a long hike, and they made it.' Maybe, says Rightmire, brain size by itself doesn't matter, and instead the ratio of grey matter to the rest of the body that determines intelligence. In other words, these small-brained humans might have done more with less.[125]

Philip Rightmire of Binghamton University, who has spent his career measuring the bumps on skulls and spaces between eyes of a hodgepodge of fossils known as *Homo erectus*, is pronouncing a paradigm shift. He no longer believes *Homo erectus* (tall, large brain) was the first hominid to walk out of Africa. Perhaps it was really *Homo habilis* (short legs, small brain).

Clearly, Dawkins-style gradualism applied to hominid history is not as fulfilling in practice as in theory. G. Ledyard Stebbins, professor emeritus, University of California, writes in his book *Darwin to DNA, Molecules to Humanity* that with respect to human origins, the discoveries made during the past fifteen years present a complex picture. The facts do not support the hypothesis of a simple progression *Ramapithecus – Australopithecus – Homo habilis – H. erectus – H. sapiens*. Instead, they are best interpreted as reflecting a series of radiations. Most of the radiant lines became extinct; only a few led to more advanced forms. The nature of the transitions between H. erectus, Neanderthals, and modern humans (as exemplified by Cro-Magnon man) is still a matter of debate. He writes:

What selective pressures caused certain apelike animals, about 5 million years ago, to evolve in the direction of tool-making [technology], culture-dependent humans, while contemporaneous related animals that apparently lived in very similar habitats evolved into forest-loving apes, highly specialized but without a tool-based culture?...

The separation may have begun when ancestors of apes and humans adopted different evolutionary strategies for surviving in forests and savannas. This speculation is based on the fact that both Ramapithecus and the Australopithecines had similar tooth enamel. Anthropologist Clifford Jolly suggests that this thick enamel was acquired as a result of selective pressure to cope with a diet of seeds and nuts. Jolly emphasizes grass seeds rather than nuts as the crucial factor, but I would emphasize nuts, for several reasons. First, nuts grow on trees and undoubtedly would have been eaten by forest-dwelling primates along with fruits, which are the principle food of modern chimpanzees. Second, nuts have to be cracked. Fashioned tools are not necessary for this purpose, but dexterity in handling unfashioned pebbles or stones would have great adaptive value for the nut-eater. In addition, nuts can be stored. Perhaps the ancestors of Ramapithecus or the Australopithecines acquired the habit of hunting nuts in caches and saving them for dry seasons when food was scarce. Such a habit would place a premium on ingenuity in finding good hiding places and on memory to recall them. Finally, some nuts are sweet, others are bitter; some nuts are good to eat, others are poisonous. The ability to distinguish between good and bad nuts would have been a matter of life and death....

Once a race of apes had become dependent on using rocks to crack nuts and grind up grass seeds, bulbs, and tubers, they would be ready to abandon the practice (still characteristic of chimpanzees and gorillas) of crossing open country only to get from one tree or forest to another. Instead, they would have spent most or all of their time in open country, going from nut trees to rock piles and caves where caches of food were kept. Their main problem would then be predators. Being adept at handling rocks for preparing their food, and being capable of running for at least short distances on their hind legs, they could have used rocks as missiles to ward off or kill predators. As their aim improved, more access to animal meat could have brought about a change in diet. A greater dependence on meat could have raised the adaptive value of fashioning rocks with a more lethal impact....In short, it appears that hominids increased in intelligence while apes did not because ancestors of humans relied on hard foods and on the tools that made these foods easier to prepare and eat. In this way they became better adapted to life in open savannas, while ape ancestors lived in areas that provided soft fruits and plant shoots, for which no tools were needed.[126]

Well before Philip Rightmire's suggested paradigm shift, zoologist and evolutionist Tim M. Berra, in his book *Evolution and the Myth of* Creationism, explained the Darwinian "gradualist" dogma applied to man's evolution:

The accelerating pace of hominid fossil discoveries is truly dazzling. In Darwin's time, only a few Neanderthal remains were known, and they were misunderstood. Today we have a whole cast of characters in the drama of human evolution. These fossils are hard evidence of human evolution. They are not figments of scientific imagination. If the australopthecines, Homo habilis and H. erectus, were still alive today, and if we could parade them before the world, there could be no doubt of our relatedness to them. It would be like attending an auto show. If you look at a 1953 Corvette and compare it to the latest model, only the most general resemblances are evident, but if you compare a 1953 and a 1954 Corvette, side by side, then a 1954 and a 1955 model, and so on, the descent with modification is overwhelmingly obvious. This is what paleoanthropologists do with fossils, and the evidence is so solid and comprehensive that it cannot be denied by reasonable people. There are quibbles about individual relationships, but each new discovery helps fine-tune our increasingly detailed knowledge of human evolution.[127]

As far as we can tell from the fossils at hand, Homo erectus was the first hominid to leave the African continent and was widely distributed in Africa, Europe, and Asia...H. erectus persisted until about 250,000 years ago in China and Java.

It is difficult to determine exactly when Homo erectus gave rise to our species, Homo sapiens. Some anthropologists put the transition as early as 500,000 years ago...[128]

The Neanderthals (named after the Neander Valley in Germany) emerged about 150,000 years ago and persisted until about 32,000 years ago. Homo sapiens neanderthalensis is a member of our own species, but has been portrayed in a poor light in the older literature as a beetle-browed, shambling subhuman...The 'classic' Neanderthal, which ranged widely in Europe and North Africa, had a large skull with heavy brow ridge and weak chin, and prognathous (protruding) jaws. Progressive Neanderthals from the Middle East showed less massive features and more rounded skulls. Specimens from Mount Carmel Israel and Shanidar in Iraq were intermediate between 'classic' Neanderthals and modern humans....

Whether Neanderthals evolved into modern humans, or whether modern humans displaced Neanderthals or interbred and genetically swamped them, is not clear, but by about 32,000 years ago fully modern human fossils had replaced the Neanderthals everywhere.[129]

Stebbins corroborates Berra's interpretation of the fossil record of primate-human ancestry:

Australopithecines lived throughout eastern and southern Africa, and evidence in the form of tools similar to those associated with East African fossil bones suggests that Homo habilis ranged as far as northwestern Africa, western Europe, China, and South-east Asia.

Contemporaneous with and following the latest Australopithecines, the species Homo erectus spread through Eurasia and Africa. First discovered by the Dutch physician Eugene Dubois on the island of Java in 1898, the remains were first called Pithecanthropus erectus – the Java ape man. A somewhat later and more extensive series of skulls and skeletons was discovered by anthropologist Davidson Black in a cave near Peking, China, and called Sinanthropus pekinensis – the Peking man – a name that persisted until careful analyses showed that Java and Peking man differed from each other no more than do different races of modern humans. A fossil jaw found near Heidelberg, Germany, could also be placed in the same species, and further remains of H. erectus were found by the Leakey's in East Africa.[130]

Skeletons of humans belonging to the subspecies called Neanderthal have been unearthed in many parts of Eurasia and Africa – France, Germany, Yugoslavia, the Middle East, Central Asia (Uzbekistan), South China, South Asia, and South Africa. Neanderthal humans existed for about 60,000 years – from 100,000 years ago to 40,000 years ago. Although the skeletons from Europe have many primitive features, they resemble those of modern humans more than they do those of Homo erectus. Skulls from the Middle East, particulary Israel, are even more modern in appearance. [131]

Careful analysis by anthropologists Lewis and Sally Binfold suggests that Neanderthals used Mousterian-type tools for a variety of purposes – hunting game, scraping and boring holes in hides, preparing food from plant materials, and suspending meat over an open fire....Some of the remains associated with Neanderthal-type bones show that these people had acquired some of the most distinctively human qualities – reverence and spirituality. They apparently buried their dead with ritual and ceremony.[132]

With gradualist theory and this zoological-anthropological version of our hominid legacy as background, let us further review the scientific evidence. Although archaeological proof shows when the Neanderthals disappeared from Europe, it now appears clear the species had no hominid evolutionary relationship to modern humans. In 1997, a team of investigators led by Svante Pääbo, a leading molecular anthropologist, painstakingly sandblasted a few grams of the arm bone of the original Neanderthal skeleton. Pääbo found that there were twenty-seven differences between the Neanderthal sequence and a standard human mitochondrial DNA sequence. According to Kevin Davies:

This strongly suggests that Neanderthals did not contribute any DNA to the current human gene pool and that Neanderthals and humans diverged some 500,000 years ago. The cover headline accompanying Pääbo's article in Cell emphatically declared, 'Neanderthals Were Not Our Ancestors.'[133]

What does this do to the credibility of the graduated evolutionary chain? Three years later, a team led by William Goodwin, of the University of Glasgow, provided indispensable verification of Pääbo's findings. Goodwin extracted and sequenced DNA from a 29,000-year-old Neanderthal fossil recovered from the Mezmaiskaya cave in the northern Caucasus in Southern Russia, nearly 2,000 miles to the east of the Feldhofer cave (Pääbo's fossil). The resulting sequence, obtained by amplifying DNA extracted from a rib bone, differed in twelve positions (3.5 per cent) from the original Neanderthal specimen, but in twenty-two positions with a reference human sample. The proof of evolutionary sequencing, what Tim Berra describes as a 1953 Corvette followed by a 1954 model, stumbles with the verification of *neanderthalensis* as a proverbial "truck;" although the truck is still a member of the automobile family – both have front bumpers and four tires. Pääbo, an evolutionist, follows gradualist dogma by adding more time to the transition. He now believes that humans and Neanderthals last shared a common ancestor roughly 500,000 years ago. Kevin Davies suggests the true figure could be anywhere from 300,000 to 700,000 years ago.[134]

One author not surprised with Pääbo's discovery is Ian Taylor. He had been researching the evidence surrounding so-called "missing-links." In his book *In The Minds of Men: Darwin and the New World Order,* he refutes the claims of *Java Man (Pithecanthropus Erectus), Nutcracker Man (Zinjanthropus)*; *The '1470' Man (Australopithecine)*; *Lucy (Australopithecus afarensis)* and the others discussed here. According to Charles Oxnard of University of Chicago, multivariate statistical analysis of a series of *Australopithecus* bones, shows that *Australopithecus* was not intermediate between man and ape but uniquely different; as different from both man and the apes as each is from the other.

Such a finding reveals the challenges in the classification of difference. Taylor points out that the ape has forty-eight chromosomes and man has forty-six. This raises the questions of at what point in the transition from ape to man the two chromosomes became lost, and how they produced fertile offspring when this loss occurred randomly to some and not to others. In all my readings on Richard Dawkins and gradualism, I never found a discussion of this glitch. To take another example, the ape has a bacculum or *os penis* (a bone in the penis) and man does not. It might be asked, therefore, at what point in the line of transition the bone was replaced by the fluid mechanism, bearing in mind that it had to work flawlessly the first time in order to propagate the race.[135]

According to Taylor, by 1900 Darwin's theory of natural selection was found to be deficient, principally because there was absolutely no evidence that one species could become another by the accumulation of minute variation. Breeding experiments had shown time after time that the species barrier could not be permanently crossed. The gradualist appeal to untold millions of years simply evaded the possibility of proof, while the abundant evidence expected in the fossil record turned out to be conspicuously absent. At the same time, Darwinian evolution was more difficult to explain in terms of Mendel's genetics. And as the principles of inheritance were beginning to be understood by the next generation of scientists, the time was ripe for a replacement theory to explain the mechanism of evolution.[136] Not surprising, the time to find a hominid to redeem the theory was equally urgent.

In 1908, a Neanderthal skeleton was discovered at La Chapelle-aux-Saints in France. Marcellin Boule, Darwinist and professor of L'Institut de Palaeontologie Humaine, in Paris, envisaged *Homo neanderthalensis* as evidence of the transition between ape and man. He described an imagined creature, half ape, half man, head thrust forward, knees slightly bent, while the numerous reconstructions that were subsequently modeled, drawn and painted depicted this creature naked and hairy in a cave setting. Says Taylor:

It should be born in mind that only bones had been found; all the rest of the reconstruction was speculation based on preconception; for all we know, Neanderthal man may have worn clothes and lived in houses.[137]

Unlike the first Neanderthal, of whom only the skullcap was found, the La Chapelle-aux-Saints skull was almost complete, and Boule's measure of the volume gave a surprisingly high figure of 1,600 cubic centimeters, significantly more than the average person today. This aspect was all but ignored at the time because it did not fit into the preconceived view of early man, but as more Neanderthal-type skulls were discovered, it was found that on average all were slightly larger than that of man today. Taylor notes:

To this day, the best explanation put forward for a race of ancient men having larger heads than modern man is that it is brain quality that counts rather than quantity – an unproved assumption.[138]

Reductionist (and now revisionist) Richard Dawkins, ironically favors quality, citing examples in his defense:

Anatole France – a Nobel prizewinner – had a brain size of less than 1,000 cc, while at the other end of the range, Oliver Cromwell is cited for having a brain of 2,000 cc.[139]

Coincidental with an ebbing tide of support for Darwinism, the Piltdown remains were discovered during the period from 1908 to 1912 and only a few miles from Darwin's old home. Parts of a human skull, together with most of the jaw of an ape, had been stained to look aged and placed in the Piltdown gravels in the country just outside London, which was known to interest an amateur fossil hunter, Charles Dawson. These remains were brought to the attention of Authur Smith Woodward, keeper of the department of geology at British Natural History Museum and a personal friend of the fossil hunter.[140] Writes Taylor:

Arthur Keith, the anatomist, was called into the investigation. Soon the team was joined by Grafton Elliot Smith, a renowned brain specialist. The team consisted of some of the very best men of science; their collective credentials were not only impressive but impeccable...When Piltdown man was formally announced at the

Geographical Society in 1912, it was warmly welcomed by the press as a sensational missing link...Needless to say, objections to man's ape ancestry made in the pulpit were effectively silenced. A whole generation grew up with Piltdown man in their textbooks and home encyclopedias; who in their right mind would question the veracity of the Encyclopaedia Britannica?[141]

Dawson, who died in 1916, had received his glory when formal scientific recognition was given to his discovery – classified *asoanthropus dawsoni* (Dawson's Dawn man). Keith, Woodward and Smith were later knighted. Unfortunately for Darwinists, in 1953, Joseph Weiner and Kenneth Oakley conducted a recently developed fluorine test on the original Piltdown material and discovered that the bones were in fact relatively recent. The suspected hoax was finally revealed. Piltdown man was a fraud. The jaw of an ape was stained to make it appear as though it matched a human skull; the Piltdown fossils along with accompanying bones were not only stained but reshaped.[142] Marvin Lubenow explains:

The file marks on the orangutan teeth of the lower jaw were clearly visible. The molars were misaligned and filed at two different angles...The canine tooth had been filed down so far that the pulp cavity had been exposed and then plugged.[143]

According to Taylor, the science behind Peking Man is no more credible than *asoanthropus dawsoni.* Two characters emerged to lead the search for man's early origins in China. The first was a Canadian physician, Davidson Black. Enthusiastic over the prospects of finding the elusive missing link, Black went to England in 1914, to study under Grafton Elliot Smith [Knighted after Piltdown man]. The second character was the Jesuit priest Teilhard de Chardin, who was banished by his superiors to China, for his radical views on evolution and Christianity. Stephen J. Gould and M. Bowden, both concluded that Teilhard was the culprit in the Piltdown scandal.[144] Teilhard, had since studied under Marcellin Boule, who was responsible for the false impressions of Neanderthal man. In 1927, just as finances were running out, a tooth was discovered at Chou K'ou Tien, and Black considered that it had characteristics intermediate between ape and man. He announced the discovery of *Sinanthropus pekinensis*. In 1929, after two years of digging and again just as funds were running out, an almost complete brain case was discovered fossilized and embedded in rock; there was no face, jaw, or base. Black fervently believed that this was indeed the skull of *Sinanthropus pekinensis*, the name he had previously coined on the basis of a single tooth. Black estimated the brain capacity to be just under 1,000 cubic centimeters, which happens to be midway between ape and man.[145]

Black died of a heart attack at the age of forty-nine, in 1934, after having received many international honors for his discovery and publication of *Sinanthropus pekinensis.* His place was taken by Franz Weidenreich, who subsequently reconstructed Peking man's skull from all the bits and pieces that had been found. Plaster models of Weidenreich's composite reconstruction are what we see in textbooks today, labeled "Peking man." He is said to be half a million years old and is held to be a hominid. Soon after Weidenreich (1948) and Teilhard (1955) died, the scientific community renamed "Peking man" *Homo erectus pekinesis*, lumping it together with Java man, classified as a man-like ape. According to Taylor, every one of the fourteen fossil "skulls" and all the remaining fossil pieces listed by Weidenreich in 1943 disappeared during the confusion of World War II.

Taylor describes the scientific evidence indicating *Homo erectus pekinesis* was really primate dinner for fully modern humans. In 1931, Professor Henri Breuil of the College of France and L'Institut de Palaeontologie Humaine, a world-renowned expert on the Stone Age, spent nineteen days at Chou K'ou Tien site, at the request of Teilhard:

Breuil found abundant evidence there of a large-scale human operation. A great number of antler bones had been worked, stone tools imported to the site from more than a mile away. Chippings eighteen inches deep in places indicated some kind of stone 'industry.' There was also evidence of a furnace operation of some kind. Breuil described this as an ash heap seven meters (twenty-three feet) deep that had been kept going continuously for some time because the minerals in the surrounding soil had fused together with the heat.[146] *However, the picture that is conveyed to the outside world...describe this furnace operation as 'traces of artificial fire' and dismiss the matter in a few lines. Bowden*[147] *shows that efforts were made to suppress Breuil's report, and virtually every textbook and popular book on ancient man since has used the expression 'traces of fire'...This conveys the impression intended, that this was man in his earliest stages having just learned to use fire. For, example, Pilbeam, in his book The Evolution of Man, says 'From Chou K'ou Tien too came signs of the first use of fire.'*[148] *To emphasize the point further, in 1950 the British Museum commissioned Maurice Wilson to paint a cave scene showing Peking man. The resulting picture shows a naked individual chipping away at some stones and squatted before a small fire consisting of three or four sticks. This is not representative of the facts...*

Breuil also collected a number of bone and stone items that bore the evident signs of human workmanship and left them on display at the local museum. These have subsequently disappeared, however.[149] *Were it not for Breuil's 1932 report, which has survived, it is certain that the only evidence available would be that which supports the view that Peking man was a hominid. As it was, more damaging counterevidence came to light in 1934 by the discovery of the parts of six truly human skeletons, including three complete skulls that were found in what was described as the 'upper cave.'...Evidently, the human remains caused difficulties for the imagined scenario especially as evidence for links between the two sites began to appear. It took Weidenreich*[150] *five years to finally break the news of the discovery of the true humans, and that it was confined to the relative obscurity of the Peking Natural History Bulletin. Even so, the popular books and most textbooks today never mention the appearance of true human beings at the site of Peking man.*[151]

Marcellin Boule, when he actually saw *Sinanthropus pekinensis*, was angry at having traveled halfway around the world to see a battered monkey skull. He pointed out that all the evidence indicated that the skulls found were those of monkeys. It was further suggested at the time that the skulls were the result of the monkey brains having been eaten by the human workers. Boule concluded with the comment:

We may therefore ask ourselves whether or not it is over-bold to consider sinanthropus [now called homo erectus pekinensis] the monarch of Chou K'ou Tien when he appears in its deposit only in the guise of a mere hunter's prey, on a par with the animals by which he is accompanied.[152]

No objective study would be complete without looking at hominid *Cro-Magnon* man. Writes Stebbins:

About 30,000 years ago, Neanderthals were replaced in Europe and southwestern Asia by people who in every detail of their skeletons were indistinguishable from ourselves. Their best known remains consist of several such complete skeletons found in central France. They bear the name Cro-magnon, a locality of that country. The nature of the transition from the Neanderthal to the Cro-Magnon race of Homo sapiens is somewhat in doubt. A common theory is that Cro-Magnon invaders from some unknown part of Eurasia displaced the less efficient Neanderthals, causing them to become extinct, presumably by conquest and slaughter. Others postulate that one race was gradually transformed into the other by natural selection of new gene complexes. Skeletons were found in a cave on Mount Carmel in Israel that are intermediate between Neanderthal and Cro-Magnon races. They have been variously interpreted as transitional forms that support the genetic replacement hypothesis, hybrids resulting from contact between two distinct races, and self-perpetuating race of hybrid origin containing a mixture of Neanderthal and Cro-Magnon characteristics. The exact sequence of events that gave rise to modern human races may never be known, but the superficial nature of differences between modern human races has been biochemically established.[153]

Contradicting Stebbins account of the Cro-Magnon/Neanderthal hybrid is a more recent hypothesis, which to a lay Christian observer closes the circle to the Adam and Eve account. On New Years Day, 1987, Allan Wilson, Rebecca Cann, and Mark Stoneking published a paper in *Nature*, which heralded evidence that mankind descended from a single woman, the so-called "African Eve." Wilson conducted a thorough comparison of mitochondrial DNA sequences from 147 people representing five geographic populations: African, Asian, Australian, Caucasian, and New Guinean. By comparing sequence differences he concluded most ancestral sequence rose in Africa. Moreover, by assuming that mutations accrue at a constant rate [a poor assumption – see punctuated evolution in the previous section] of 2 to 4 per cent per million years, Wilson's group came to the dramatic conclusion: "All these mitochondrial DNAs stem from one woman who is postulated to have lived about 200,000 years ago, probably in Africa."[154] One can only wonder what to do about the Dmanisi hominid dating back to 1.75 million years ago. What theory is one to believe?

Regarding the "African Eve" hypothesis, Davies writes:

This is not to say that there was only one woman alive at the time; more likely, there was a small population of a few thousand people, but the progeny of only one woman successfully thrived.[155]

Interestingly, analogous studies performed using markers on the Y chromosome produce remarkably similar results, agreeing to a reasonable approximation on both the date (up to 200,000 years ago) and the location (Africa) of the earliest ancestor. But the comparisons of data from mitochondrial DNA and the Y chromosome point to some interesting differences. If anything, "Y-chromosome Adam" lived somewhat later than 'mitochondrial Eve.'[156]

Over the past few years, Douglas Wallace, a prominent mitochondrial geneticist, systematically catalogued the diversity of mitochondrial DNA sequences in the world's populations. These results suggest that mitochondrial Eve had eighteen 'daughters,' each with a distinct mitochondrial DNA sequence that spread to different regions of the globe.[157]

One ponders, given the legacy of self-supporting conceptualizations and the variance (indeed contradiction) between the mentioned theories of humankind's origin, whether it might be time to concede that the location, genesis process and event timings now scientifically support Biblical interpretation. Just speed-up the muta tion rate and adjust the location only slightly from Africa to the Middle East?

Indeed, it appears that Old Testament records have recently received full vindication. A most remarkable application of Y-chromosome markers has been made to Jewish populations in the Middle East and beyond. The Book of Exodus describes the sanctification of Moses's brother Aaron and his sons, "so that their anointing will make an eternal hereditary priesthood for all generations." Aaron thus became the first Jewish priest, or *cohen*, a tradition that has since been handed down from father to son. Michael Hammer, Karl Skorecki, David Goldstein, and colleagues studied Y markers from three hundred Jews, including more than one hundred *cohanim*, and found that half of the Jewish priests shared the same genetic signature, compared to less than 5 per cent in the lay Jewish population. Moreover, the origin of this chromosome dates back some 3,000 years, in agreement with biblical history.[158]

Have we descended by chance after the accidental start of the universe; from a freak random spark of life; and from chance curious nut-loving primates; and by continuous selective random mutations; or are we unique creatures of God, with intrinsic worth and purpose?

Christianity 101

The event and nature of the death of Jesus Christ is well established in pagan records and chronicled in Scripture. Normally, condemned men were forced to carry a beam of the cross to the place of the crucifixion. Jesus started out with his cross (John 19:17), but he was so weakened by public flogging that Simon from Cyrene, a passer-by, was pressed to carry it to the place called Golgotha. It was the third hour when they crucified Him. The written notice of the charge against Him read: *The King of the Jews.* Two other men, both criminals, were also executed with Jesus – one on His left and one on His right. Those who passed by hurled insults at Him, shaking their heads and saying, "So! You are going to destroy the temple and build it in three days, come down from the cross and save yourself!" Jesus said, "Father, forgive them, for they do not know what they are doing" (Luke 23:34). The people stood watching, and the rulers even sneered at Him. They said, "He saved others; let Him save Himself if He is the Christ of God, the Chosen One." One of the criminals who hung there hurled insults at Him: "Aren't you the Christ? Save yourself and us!" But the other criminal rebuked him. "Don't you fear God," he said, "since you are under the same sentence? We are punished justly, for we are getting what our deeds deserve. But this man has done nothing wrong." Then he said, "Jesus, remember me when you come into your kingdom." Jesus answered him, "I tell you the truth, today you will be with me in paradise" (Luke 23:43). At the sixth hour darkness came over the whole land until the ninth hour, when Jesus cried out, "My God, my God, why have you forsaken me?" By now the sun stopped shining. Jesus called out, "Father into your hands I commit my spirit" (Luke 23:46). When He said this He breathed His last.

For the orthodox believer to fully appreciate Jesus Christ's death as depicted here, he must accept three key associated cognitive pre-conditions. First, we accept that every Christian receives a spirit, but it is never said that she or he is a spirit.[159] This "spirit" like that which Jesus commits to God at His death is an incorporeal aspect of human nature. When the Bible speaks of the origin of the spirit, it invariably ascribes it to God. In both Testaments it is the human's individual spirit which is the "spring of his innermost thoughts and intentions," and the child of God must be renewed in spirit if he is to serve God acceptably. The following passages help illustrate the intricate relationship of our spirit and the Spirit of God:

Create in me a pure heart, O God, and renew a steadfast spirit within me. Do not cast me from your presence or take your Holy Spirit from me. Restore to me the joy of your salvation and grant me a willing spirit, to sustain me. (Psalm 51:10)

Jesus declared, I tell you the truth, no one can see the kingdom of God unless he is born again...no one can enter the kingdom of God unless he is born of water [flesh] *and the Spirit. Flesh gives birth to flesh, but the Spirit gives birth to spirit. (John 3:3-6)*

The spirit is not something which has mass or tangible image. Nor can it be put into a bottle. It exists nonetheless:

But the fruit of the Spirit is love, joy, peace, patience, kindness, goodness, faithfulness, gentleness and self-control...Those who belong to Christ Jesus have crucified the sinful nature with its passions and desires. Since we live by the Spirit, let us keep in step with the Spirit (Galatians 5:22).

Second, is the pre-condition of believing in heaven and hell. Upon death one of the criminals is going with Jesus to "paradise." The other criminal is obviously going somewhere else. Those who do not turn themselves over to Christ, accepting Him as Lord and Savior, do not go to "paradise." The so-called "hell" is the alternative, spiritual state of the ungodly. The Apostle Matthew refers to "the fire of hell" (Matthew 5:22) as the final place of punishment. The Apostle Luke wrote about a rich man who was dressed in purple and fine linen and lived in luxury everyday. At his gate was a beggar named Lazarus, covered with sores and longing to eat what fell from the rich man's table. Even the dogs came and licked the beggar's sores. The time came for their deaths. Angels carried Larazus to Paradise and the rich man went to torment in hell:

[The rich man called] Father Abraham have pity on me and send Lazarus to dip the tip of his finger in water and cool my tongue, because I am in agony in this fire. But Abraham replied, 'Son remember that in your lifetime you received your good things, while Lazarus received bad things, but now he is comforted here and you are in agony. And besides all this, between us and you a great chasm has been fixed, so that those who want to go from here to you cannot, nor can anyone cross over from there to us.' He answered, 'Then I beg you, father, send Lazarus to my father's house for I have five brothers. Let him warn them, so that they will not also come to this place of torment.' Abraham replied, 'They have Moses and the Prophets; let them listen to them.' 'No, father Abraham,' he said, 'but if someone from the dead goes to them, they will repent.' He said to him, 'If they do not listen to Moses and the Proph ets, they will not be convinced even if someone rises from the dead' (Luke16: 19-31).

Many "liberal" Christian churches have all but smothered the issue of laws, judgment and consequences under some universal notion that God's infinite and unconditional love assures all a place in Heaven. This "cheap grace" heresy flies in the face of the developments in Chapter 1, where the use of rules, boundaries and consequences are seen as fundamental for successful relationships and avoidance of ecological disasters. God did not excuse Pharaoh in the time of Moses, nor the mocking criminal at the crucifixion. Scripture tells us He will not receive us other than with a repentant heart and the accepted blood of Jesus Christ.

Third, and the most vital cognitive pre-condition, is acceptance of Jesus as the divine Son of God. Jesus believed he was the Messiah and his actions reflected this. His response to the believing criminal, demonstrates His authority, "I tell you the truth, today you <u>will</u> be with me in paradise." Throughout His short life, He consistently conducted Himself as God's divine Son. Therefore, in summary, before addressing the Resurrection, the description of Christ's death tells us: (1) His Spirit was placed in God's hands; (2) there is a heaven and hell; and (3) Jesus has Divine authority on earth.

The Resurrection of Jesus lies at the heart of Christian faith. Did God raise His Son or is this a hoax? The great second century Christian apologist, Origen, faced pagan critics on this issue in his day (245 A.D.). The debate has always been part of post crucifixion history. The Apostle Mark recorded (50-60 A.D.) Christ's reprimand of his own disciples in the days following His resurrection:

Later Jesus appeared to the Eleven as they were eating: he rebuked them for their lack of faith and their stubborn refusal to believe those who had seen Him after He had risen. He then said to them, 'Go out into the world and preach the good news to all creation. Whoever believes and is baptized will be saved, but whoever does not believe, will be condemned (Mark 16:14-16).

Another Christian belief is the devil, who is never viewed as a scapegoat for the sinner in Scripture. The archenemy of God [but in no ways equal], Satan is a created, but not human being. He is referred to as "the ruler of the kingdom of the air, the spirit who is now at work in those who are disobedient" (Ephesians 2:2). Satan is also "prince of the demons" (Matthew12:24). The Apostle Paul referred to the devil and his works, "The god of this age has blinded the minds of unbelievers, so that they cannot see the light of the gospel of the glory of Jesus Christ" (2 Corinthians 4:4). The Apostle John spoke of the devil, "We know that we are children of God and that the whole world is under the control of the evil one" (1 John 5:19). For the conversion of Paul along the road to Damascus, Jesus demonstrated the nature of the Kingdom of God (light) and the kingdom of satan (darkness). He said, "I am sending you [Paul] to them [Jews and Gentiles] to open their eyes and turn them from darkness to light, and from the power of satan to God, so that they may receive forgiveness of sins and a place among those sanctified by faith in me" (Acts 26: 17-18). In differentiating children of God from the lost, Jesus explains:

If God were your Father, you would love me, for I came from God, and now am here. I have not come on my own, but He sent me. Why is my language not clear to you? Because you are unable to hear what I have to say. You belong to your father the devil, and you want to carry out your father's desire. He was a murderer from the beginning, not holding to the truth, for there is no truth in him. When he lies, he speaks his native language, for he is a liar and the father of lies. Yet because I tell the truth, you do not believe me! Can any of you prove me guilty of sin? If I am telling the truth, why don't you believe me? He who belongs to God hears what God says. The reason you do not hear is that you do not belong to God (John 8:42-47).

Pagan Slander

Anti-Christian movements of today display little originality in their attacks over the pagan slander of the first and second centuries after Christ's resurrection. Much can be learned by studying the nature of these anti-Christ arguments and examining the most eloquent defense of Christianity by the third century apologist Origen. In reply to the work of a pagan named Celsus, who had written *The True Doctrine,* Origen wrote eight treatises. The identity of Celsus is uncertain, but Origen knew that the man had been dead a long time and that Celsus was an Epicurean, flourishing in the latter half of the second century. Historian Henry Chadwick says, "to call a person an Epicurean, from a Christian perspective was symbolic of the modern materialist, infidel or hedonist."[160] Moreover, according to Chadwick, Origen was frequently incensed that Celsus confused the tenets of orthodox Christianity with beliefs held by Gnostic sects.[161]

The non-believer's slander invariably is directed at denying the divinity of the "Rivet of Life" – Jesus Christ. How could a poor Jew be elevated to monotheistic worship? How could Christ be born of a virgin? The miracles He preformed were those of a magician. His apparent inability to save Himself from crucifixion discredits His claim to divinity. Celsus finally argues that there is a fixed amount of sin in the universe. Implicit in his premise is the notion that humankind will not be held morally accountable on an individual basis, that there is no devil promoting evil, and that there is no need for a Savior or Redeemer.

Celsus has little to say for Christian monotheism:

As all pagans knew, Moses was an expert magician. And so, the goat herds and shepherds who followed Moses as their leader were deluded by clumsy deceits into thinking that there was only one God called the Most High...The Christians are even worse. They reject the worship of daemons [other deities] and quote the saying of Jesus, 'No man can serve two masters.'

[Christianity is]...a rebellious utterance of people who wall themselves off and break away from the rest of mankind. What is more, the fantastic respect shown by the Christians for this Jew who was crucified a few years back shows just how seriously they take all their talk about serving one master. If these men worshipped no other God but one, perhaps they would have had a valid argument against the others. But in fact they worship to an extravagant degree this man who appeared recently, and yet think it is not inconsistent with monotheism.[162]

Let the Christians return to take their stand upon the old paths and abandon this newly invented absurdity of worshipping a Jew recently crucified in disgraceful circumstances. Let them return to the old polytheism, to the customs of their fathers. Christianity is a dangerous modern innovation and if not checked it will be a disaster for the Roman Empire.[163]

In formulating his critique of Christianity Celsus represented a Jew [imaginary character] as having a conversation with Jesus Christ himself and claiming many falsehoods in Christ's story: that he fabricated his birth from a virgin; that he came from a Jewish village and from a poor country woman who earned her living by spinning. Celsus accuses Christ, claiming Mary was driven out by her husband, who was a carpenter by trade, as she was convicted of adultery. Then he says while she was wandering about in a disgraceful way she secretly gave birth to Jesus. Origen replied:

Among men of noble birth, honorable and distinguished parents, an upbringing at the hands of wealthy people who were able to spend money on the duration of their son, and a great and famous native country, are things which help to make a man famous...But when a man whose circumstances are entirely contrary to this is able to rise above the hindrances to him... brought up in meanness and poverty, who had no general education and had learnt no arguments and doctrines by which he could have become a persuasive speaker to crowds and a popular leader and have won over many hearers, could devote himself to teaching new doctrines and introduce to mankind a new doctrine which did away with the customs of the Jews while reverencing their prophets, and which abolished the laws of the Greeks particularly with the worship of God? How could such a man, brought up in this way, who received no serious instruction from men (as even those who speak evil of him admit), say such noble utterances about the judgment of God, about the punishments for wick-

edness, and rewards for goodness, that not only the rustic and illiterate people were converted by his words, but also a considerable number of the more intelligent.[164]

To Origen the mythical degradation of Mary was concocted "to get rid of the miraculous conception by the Holy Spirit." He writes:

It was inevitable that those who did not accept the miraculous birth of Jesus would have invented some lie. But the fact that they did not do this convincingly, but as part of the story that the virgin did not conceive Jesus by Joseph, makes the lie obvious to people who can see through fictitious stories…Is it reasonable that a man who ventured to do such great things for mankind in order that, so far as in him lay, all Greeks and barbarians in expectation of divine judgment might turn from evil and act in every respect acceptably to the Creator of the universe, should have had, not a miraculous birth, but a birth more illegitimate and disgraceful than any?[165]

Origen quotes the prophecy of Isaiah, from around 700 B.C.:

Therefore shall the lord give you a sign. Behold a virgin shall conceive in her womb and bring forth a son, and thou shalt call his name Emmanuel, which is interpreted 'God with us' (Isaiah 7:14).

He argues that Celsus, however, did not quote this, either because he did not know it, or he willfully said nothing of it to avoid appearing unintentionally to support the doctrine, which is opposed to his purpose. Origen choses to refute any attempt to muddle with the correct translation of Isaiah 7:14:

But if he [Celsus] should ingeniously explain it away by saying that it is not written 'behold a virgin' but, instead of that, 'behold a young woman,' we should say to him that the word Aalma, which the Septuagint translated by 'parthenos' (virgin) and others by means (young woman), also occurs, so they say, in Deuteronomy applied to a virgin. The passage reads as follows: 'If a girl that is a virgin is betrothed to a man, and a man find her in a city and lie with her, ye shall bring both out to the gate of the city and stone them with stones that they die, the young woman because she did not cry out in the city, and the man because he disgraced his neighbor's wife'. And after that: 'If a man finds a girl that is betrothed in the country and the man forces her and lies with her, ye shall kill only the man that lay with her, and ye shall do nothing to the young woman; there is no sin worthy of death in the young woman.[166]

Recognizing the importance of this fundamental tenet, Origen continues:

Lest we appear to depend on a Hebrew word to explain to people…that this man would be born of a virgin…let us explain the affirmation from the passage itself. The lord, according to the scripture, said to Ahaz: 'Ask thee a sign from the lord thy god, either in the depth or in the height.' And then the sign that is given is this: 'behold a virgin shall conceive and bear a son.' What sort of a sign would it be if a young woman not a virgin bore a son? And which would be more appropriate as the mother of Emmanual, that is 'God with us,' a woman who had had intercourse with a man and conceived by female passion, or a woman who was still chaste and pure and a virgin? It is surely fitting that the latter should give birth to a child at whose birth it is said 'God with us.' If, however, he explains this away by saying that Ahaz was addressed in the words 'ask thee a sign of the Lord thy God,' we will say; Who was born in Ahaz's time whose birth is referred to in the words 'Emmanuel, which is God with us?' For if no one is to be found, obviously the words to Ahaz were addressed to the house of David because according to the scripture our Savior was 'of the seed of David according to the flesh.' Furthermore, this sign is said to be 'in the depth or in the height,' since 'this is he who descended and who ascended far above all heavens that he might fill all things. I say these things as speaking to a Jew who believes the prophecy. But perhaps Celsus or any who agree with him will tell us with what kind of mental apprehension the prophet speaks about the future, whether in this instance or in the others recorded in the prophecies. Has he foreknowledge of the future or not? If he has, then the prophets possessed divine inspiration. If he has not, let Celsus account for the mind of a man who ventures to speak about the future and is admired for his prophesy among the Jews.[167]

Origen also refuted Celsus' accusation that Christ was a magician:

He [Celsus] says: He was brought up in secret and hired himself out as a workman in Egypt, and after having tried his hand at certain magical powers he returned from there, and on account of those powers gave himself the title of God. I do not know why a magician should have taken the trouble to teach a doctrine which persuades every man to do every action as before God who judges each man for all his works, and to instill this conviction in his disciples whom he intended to use as the ministers of his teaching. Did they persuade their hearers because they had been taught to do miracles in this way, or did they not do any miracles? It is quite irrational to maintain that they did no miracles at all, but that, although they had believed without any adequate reasons comparable to the dialectical wisdom of the Greeks, they devoted themselves to teaching a new doctrine to any whom they might visit. What inspired them with confidence to teach the doctrine and to put forward new ideas? On the other had, if they did perform miracles, is it plausible to suggest that they were magicians, when they risked their lives in great dangers for a teaching which forbids magic?[168] *[Most of the 12 disciples died a martyr's death.]*

Celsus attacked the crucifixion event and Christ's divine authority writing, "But if he really was so great he ought, in order to display his divinity, to have disappeared suddenly from the cross." Origen describes such thinkers as opposed to belief in providence. But more important, he shows that disappearing physically from the cross was "not to the greater advantage of the whole purpose of the incarnation":

...Thus in this way his crucifixion contains the truth indicated by the words 'I am crucified with Christ' (Galatians 2:20), and by the sense of the words 'But God forbid that I should glory save in the cross of my Lord Jesus Christ, by whom the world is crucified unto me and I unto the world' (Galatians 6:14). His death was necessary because 'in that he died, he died unto sin once,' and because the right-

eous man says that he is 'being conformed unto his death', and 'for if we die with him, we shall also live with him.' So also his burial extends to those who are conformed to his death and crucified with him and dying with him, as Paul also says; 'For we are buried together with him by baptism,' (Romans 6:4) and we have risen together with him.[169]

Last, Celsus asserts:

In the existing world there is no decrease or increase of evils either in the past or in the present or in the future. For the nature of the universe is one and the same, and the origin of evils is always the same.[170]

Origen refuted this statement, citing the philosophers who have examined the question of good and evil:

They have shown from history that at first prostitutes hired themselves out to those who desired them outside the city and wore masks. Then later they disdainfully laid aside their masks, though as they were not allowed by the laws to enter the cities, they lived outside them. But as perversion increased every day they ventured even to enter the cities. This is said by Chysippus in his 'Introduction to the subject of Good and Evil.' It is possible to argue that evils do increase and decrease from the fact that the so-called 'doubtful' men were at one time prostitutes, being subject to and arranging for and serving the lusts of those who came to them; but later the public authorities expelled them, and concerning the countless vices which have entered human life from the flood of evil, we can say that earlier they did not exist. At any rate, the most ancient histories, even though they make innumerable criticisms of those who went astray, know nothing of people who committed unmentionable enormities.[171]

Celsus' notion that persons, communities, societies, cultures and nations somehow draw from a fixed reservoir of sin, evil, or wrong-doings is amiss, yet many unwittingly indulge in such thinking. There is no First Law of Conservation for evil. If there was such a Law, it would lead to a trade-off whereby one side in war is the recipient of all "good," offset by a proportionate amount of evil consumed by the enemy. If only life could be so simple. What happens when the wrong side wins? Can the bad side ever have a replenishment of good? How does one rid oneself of accumulated evil? If anything, evil tends to feed upon itself in an increasing spiral of wrongs or, as Origen recorded, by an ever-eroding sense of virtue through errant decisions over a period of time.

Worse than the "fixed reservoir" theory, for dealing with the fact of evil, is the "non-judgmental" philosophy. This line of thinking contends that either there are neither wrongs nor rights; or when there are, they are self-defined; or when they exist, they draw from a reservoir of sin which is so close to empty that the indiscretions may be ignored; or they happen under the mitigating circumstances of experimentation. Such relativistic thinking implies there are no moral consequences to choices at individual or aggregate levels. It is not surprising that secularists have trouble articulating the notion of evil and sin. The formula that mutual consent is all that is required for ethical sexual relations, allows many to be at ease or to acquiesce morally with the lifestyles of men like Gaetan Dugas (AIDS Partner Zero), entering their seven hundredth cubical for the delights of anonymous sex. They argue, if he is not bothering anyone else who cares? Believing that we evolved into existence at the end of a long and random sequence of mutations, secularists conclude we operate in a vacuum of moral standards. Moreover, for many the problems of sin and guilt are only social constructs rooted in the attempts by mostly religious societies to set moral standards. As a result secularist philosophies refrain from judgment, avoid guilt and discourage setting boundaries and rules. Ironically, while stressing a unified theory of mathematics and physics for explaining our material universe, secularists have no unified theory for dealing with the very tangible realities of evil. Most attempts hide the problem under the veil of biology, theories of "selfish genes" or other Darwinian models rooted in the idea of survival of the fittest.

The notion that a multipartner same-sex lifestyle might be intrinsically wrong never enters the "non-judgmental" mind. On the other hand the bathhouse scene brings tears to Christian's peering from the vantage of "graced" eyes. What causes one to see right and another to see wrong? Once again, in his letter to the Christians at Corinth, Paul speaks of those who cannot see their wrongdoings:

The god of this age [devil] has blinded the minds of unbelievers, so that they cannot see the light of the gospel of the glory of Christ (2 Corinthians 4:4).

Christianity exists very much in a dynamic struggle for the truth. Christ brings light and evil serves the prince of darkness. As evidenced in these few exchanges between Origen and Celsus, the themes for attempting to slander Christianity have changed little over the centuries. In Chapter 5, "Debunking Gay and Pro-gay Christian Theology," self-proclaimed pro-gay and gay theologians will be shown unwittingly raising the same arguments as Celsus, even going so far as embracing Gnostic tenets in pursuit of a "rheostatic" or "self-fulfilling" theology. The next section explains the genesis of orthodoxy in Biblical interpretation during the early period of the Church. Origen blamed Gnostic influences for much of the slander pagans like Celsus directed toward genuine Christianity. Studying Gnostic cults will demonstrate further the paired dynamics of truth-deception and blindness-sight. The next section will also reveal the huge embodiment of Gnosticism in Darwinism and postmodern secularism.

Gnostic Cancer

Orthodoxy, the English equivalent of Greek *orthodoxia* (from *orthos*, "right," and *doxa*, "opinion") means right belief, as opposed to heresy or heterodoxy. The term is not Biblical; no secular or Christian writer uses it before the second century, though *orthodoxein* is used by Aristotle. The word expresses the idea that certain statements accurately embody the revealed truth content of Christianity, and are therefore in their own nature normative for the universal church. This idea is rooted in the New Testament insistence that the Gospel has a specific factual and theological content and that no fellowship exists between those who accept the apostolic standard of Christological teaching and those who deny it.[172] The Apostle Paul, for example, wrote in 1 Corintians 15:1-2:

Now, brothers, I want to remind you of the Gospel I preached to you, which you received and on which you have taken your stand. By this gospel you are saved, if you hold firmly to the word I preached to you. Otherwise, you have believed in vain.

The idea of orthodoxy became important in the Church in and after the second century, through conflict with Paganism and most important Gnosticism. Later the Church would need to deal with other Trinitarian and Christological errors and in the seventeenth century Protestant theologians, especially Lutherans, stressed the importance of orthodoxy in relation to teachings on salvation in the Reformation creeds. In summary, the Church has continuously faced a struggle to maintain unity and orthodoxy over diverse geographic, national, linguistic and cultural barriers. Theological diversity, denominational chaos, and Christian disunity have too often served the interests of anti-Christian groups. However, on the positive side, debating, defending, clarifying and canonizing Christian thought over time has reaffirmed the power and majesty of God's Word, and in particular the orthodox Gospel of Jesus Christ. This section will reveal the danger of Gnostic thinking to the early Church and thus its equivalent harm today. Herein lie the seeds of libertinism and Darwinism.

One of the earliest Church struggles (not related to Gnosticism) came from a division between conservatives and universalists (including Gentiles), resulting in a general conference in Jerusalem (Acts 15). The outcome was in some respects a compromise but one which in all decisive points favored universalists. The Gentile converts were recognized as truly within the covenant by the mother-church at Jerusalem even if they were uncircumcised.[173] From here on in, the unity of the scattered Christian communities depended on two things – on a common faith and a common way of ordering their life and worship. They called each other "brother" and "sister." Whatever differences there might be of race, class or education, they felt bound together by their focus and loyalty to the person and teaching of Jesus. Church leaders were challenged well into the third century finding where intellectual deviation should lead to censure. Translation of the Gospel into the religious language of the Hellenistic world was a task of great intricacy and Christian missionaries were not operating in a metaphysical vacuum. Henry Chadwick described the era:

The moment they moved outside of the ambit of synagogues of the Jewish dispersion and their loosely attached Gentile adherents, the missionaries were in a twilight world of pagan syncretism, magic, and astrology. The pagan world was quite accustomed to myths of great heroes elevated to divine rank. Nonetheless they were amazed at the extraordinary claim that the divine redeemer of the Christian story had lately been born of a woman in Judea, had been crucified under Pontius Pilate, had risen again, and at last would judge the world.[174]

Among his Gentile converts Paul soon met groups needing doctrinal correction. At Corinth a spiritual aristocracy formed that was inclined to pride itself on the possession of a more profound wisdom and deeper mystical experience than brethren or even the apostle Paul, himself. At Colassae in Asia Minor, Paul met with graver heresy, a syncretistic blending of Christianity with theosophical elements drawn partly from the mystery cults and partly from heterodox Judaism. According to Chadwick, both of these types of heresy, belong to the general category commonly labeled "Gnosticism," which is a generic term used primarily to refer to theosophical adaptations of Christianity propagated by a dozen or more rival sects which broke with the early church between 80-150 A.D..[175] The term Gnosticism is derived from the ordinary Greek word for knowledge (gnosis). The second century sects claimed to possess a special "knowledge" which transcended the simple faith of the Church. The Gnostic initiate was taught to acknowledge no responsibilities. Much time was devoted to learning correct magic passwords and the most potent amulets, which would assist the elect soul to transverse a perilous journey through the planetary spheres back to its heavenly home. The rival sects hated one another as much as they hated orthodoxy, with each group claiming to possess the authentic path for man's soul.[176] According to Kurt Rudolph, the traditional Church accused the Gnostics of deceit, falsehood and magic, declaring the supernatural cause of gnostic teaching to be Satan himself, who in this fashion sought to corrupt the Church.[177]

Gnostic tradition frequently drew its material from varied existing traditions, attached itself to them, and at the same time set it in a new frame by which this material took on a new character and a completely new significance. Seen from the outside, the gnostic documents were often compositions and even compilations from the mythological or religious ideas of the most varied regions of religion and culture: from Greek, Jewish, Iranian, Christian, Manicheism, also Indian from the Far East. To this extent Gnosis, is a product of hellenistic syncretism, that is the mingling of Greek and Oriental traditions and ideas subsequent to the conquests of Alexander the Great.[178] Today, Freemasonry and the Masonic Lodge embodies similar syncretism. Albert Pike, Sovereign Grand Commander of the Southern Supreme Council, A.A, Scottish Rite, for 32 years, wrote in *Morals and Dogma of Masonic Doctrine*:

Masonry is the legitimate successor from the earliest times, the custodian and depository of the great philosophical and religious truths, unknown to the world at large, and handed down from age to age...We belong to no one creed or school. In all religions, there is a basis of truth...All teachers and reformers of mankind we admire and revere. Masonry has her mission to perform...She invites all men of all religions to enlist under her banner.

It sees in Moses, the law giver of the Jews, in Confucius and Zoroaster, in Jesus of Nazareth, and in the Arabian iconoclast, great teachers of morality, and eminent reformers, if no more, and allows every brother of the Order to assign to each such higher and even divine character as his creed and truth require....Masonry is a worship, but one in which all civilized men can unite...

The first Masonic teacher was Buddha...[179]

This "anything goes" theology is an anathema to the Christian Church today, as in the past. The period between 150 and 250 A.D., was evidently a high point in the debate between the Christian church and the Gnostics. Of this period the anti-heretical works of Tertullian (previously quoted at the start of "Humanistic (Modern Gnostic) Civilization," Chapter 4) were prominent. H. von Campenhausen writes:

For him Gnosis is a 'declining syncretism' such as the natural spirituality of mankind loves, a spiritual and idealistic overestimate of the self which blurs the fixed limits that separate the creature from the deity; and it is at the same time the 'nihilistic' hostility against God of reality who has created the world and has revealed himself concretely in the flesh.[180]

According to Kurt Rudolph, the external variety of Gnosis is naturally not accidental but evidently belongs to its very nature. There is no gnostic "church" or normative theology, no gnostic rule of faith nor any dogma of exclusive importance. No limits were set to free representation and theological speculation so far as they lay within the frame of the gnostic worldview. Hence we find already in the heresiologists the most varied systems and attitudes set out under the common denominator "gnosis." In all but one sect, there was no gnostic canon of scripture. The gnostics seem to have taken particular delight in bringing their teachings to expression in manifold ways.[181] In libertine sects they find fault with providence and its Lord, in that (as a consequence of their hostility to the world) they disregard all the legality of this world:

...they make our human discipline into a mockery – in this world there may be nothing noble to be seen – and thereby they make discipline and righteousness of no importance.[182]

H. Jonas has stated decisively that "libertinism" was a form of expression which by its very nature applied to the adherents ("pneumatics"), because it expressed in the best way possible their self-esteem and sense of freedom (i.e. from every kind of cosmic coercion):

The whole idea revolves around the conception of a pneuma as the noble privilege of a new kind of man who is subjugated neither by the obligations nor the criteria of the present world of creation. The pneumatic in contrast to the psychic [orthodox Christian] is free from the law – in a quite different sense from that of the Pauline Christian – and the unrestrained use of this freedom is not just a matter of a negative license but a positive realization of this freedom itself. This 'anarchism' then was stamped by a 'determined resentment against the prevailing rules of life,' and by 'obstinate defiance of the demands of the divine cosmic powers who are the guardians of the old moral order.'[183]

Gnosticism culminates in the assumption of a new *unknown* God, who dwells beyond all visible creation and is proclaimed the real lord of the universe. The counterpart to this highest being who can be described only in negative terms – the *unknown* God, is the revelation of his secret through intermediate beings to the elect, who are thereby enabled to attain to the "knowledge" of the (hitherto) unknown one. The gnostic idea of God is therefore not only the product of dualism hostile to this world, but it is at the same time also a consequence of the esoteric conception of knowledge: "Gnosis" mediates the secret and leads men out of their ignorance concerning the true God.[184]

Gnosticism is a religion of self-redemption. It is the act of self-recognition that introduces the "deliverance" from the situation encountered and guarantees humankind salvation. For this reason the famous Delphic slogan "know thyself" is popular also in Gnosis. The Gnostic is already redeemed, although the completion of the redemption is still outstanding. The laying aside of ignorance guarantees his freedom:

Truth is like ignorance: when it is hidden it rests itself. But when it is revealed and recognized it is praised, inasmuch as it is stronger than ignorance and error. It gives freedom...Ignorance is a slave. Knowledge is freedom. When we recognize the truth we shall find the fruits of the truth in us. If we unite with it, it will bring our fulfillment.[185]

The Gnostic redemption is a deliverance from the world and the body, not as in Christianity from sin and guilt.[186]

That the Christian gnostics considered themselves to be Christian and not pagan, and were using the name, severely vexed their ecclesiastical rivals. The Valentinians, for example, were the "Disciples of Christ," a term seldom used in their time. As we have seen, the shrewd opponent of Christianity, Celsus made no distinction between the two.[187]

The symbolic transformation of gnostic wisdom into cultic practice indirectly led in some branches to quite scandalous practices. Here the oldest informant is Epiphanius of Cyprus. In the section on the so-called Ophites (the "snake people") in his *Medicine Chest* he gives the following account of a ceremonial feast held by his community:

They have a snake which they foster in a particular box; at the hour when they perform their mysteries they coax it out of the hole, and whilst they load the table with bread, they summon forth the snake. When the hole is opened, it comes out...crawling onto the table and wallowing in the bread: this, they claim, is the 'perfect offering.' And that is also why, so I heard from them, they not only 'break bread' (an old Christian expression for the Lord's Supper) in which the snake has wallowed, and offer it to the recipients, but everyone also kisses the snake on the mouth, once the snake has indeed been charmed by sorcery...They prostrate themselves before it (in worship) and call this the 'thanksgiving' (eucharist) which originates from its (the snake's) wallowing (in the bread), and furthermore with its help they raise up a hymn to the Father on high. In this manner they conclude their mystery feast. Supposing it was actually performed like this the ceremony bears a closer resemblance to older Greek and Hellenistic secret cults...in which the snake was worshipped as a symbol of the chthonic [spirits of the underworld] deity and fertility. For the Ophites or Naassene gnostics the snake was a medium of revelation and mouthpiece of the most sublime God.[188]

Epiphanius, invoking eyewitnesses, presents further insights into the gnostics whom he introduces as "Stratiotici" (i.e. "soldier-like, war-like'), "Phibionites" (meaning unknown) or "Borborites" (i.e. dirty). What is told about their cultic celebration has pornographic features.

[I must warn you that perseverance will be needed to get through a few more heinous descriptions of Gnosis. At the risk of sickening the reader I have chosen to include additional testimonies, thereby developing a feel for the magnitude of evil aimed at the genuine Church. You will come out with an understanding of why "orthodoxy" and the canonization of Scripture is necessary for the preservation of the truth.]

In ideology explains Rudolph, the Gnostics theorize about speculations on the collection of the seed of light, which in the form of the male semen and female menstrual blood must be allowed to escape, to get back to God. Bound up in this is the liberal interpretation of all earthly laws, which extend to their negation (libertinism). They refuse to give birth to children because this only prolongs the sorrowful lot of the seed of light and only serves the purpose of the disdainful creator of the world.[189]

Epiphanius stated that after they have "filled their stomachs to satiety" the actual love-rite (*agape*) commences. Apparently, the purpose of sleeping together is to present the women who are seduced to the Archon [rulers or commanders]. Since this allies respectively to the 365 Archons and is to be practiced in ascending and descending series, 730 "immoral unions" ensure, at the end of which the man in question is made one with Christ.[190] Other gnostic texts include references of a censorious kind that are clearly made about such rites. The Pistis Sophia curses in the name of Jesus the people "who take male semen and female menstrual blood and make it into a lentil dish and eat it;" they will in the "outer darkness be destroyed." Child bearing is to be avoided. If pregnancy ensues the infant embyro is forcibly removed and – this quite certainly belongs to the realm of perverted phantasy – is consumed after being torn apart and duly prepared. Epiphanius also calls this their "Passover."[191]

One Gnostic text presents the remarkable view that one of the sacred dwelling places of the men of Seth (the "Great Savior") was Sodom and Gomorrah, i.e. the cities condemned by biblical tradition have for the Gnostics a positive ring:

Then came the great Seth and brought his seed, and it was sown in the ages (aeons) which have come to be [in the transitory world], whose number is the measure of Sodom. Some say that Sodom is the pasture [for the seed] of the great Seth, which is Gomorrah. Others on the other hand [say] that the great Seth took his planting from Gomorrah and planted it in the second place, to which he gave the name Sodom.[192]

Irenaeus mentions that one gnostic movement considered itself descendants of Cain, Esau and the Sodomites. Says Rudolph, such transmutations of Jewish history in various forms is a result of the rejection of the biblical creator, as a lower and hostile being.[193]

Church Fathers commented on the "Carpocrations":

[They] are so abandoned in their recklessness that they claim to have in their power

and to be able to practice anything whatsoever that is ungodly (irreligious) and impious. They say that conduct is good and evil only in the opinion of men...according to their scriptures they maintain that their souls should have every enjoyment in life, so that when they depart they are deficient in nothing...[194]

Freedom must therefore be gained by a complete demonstration of it on earth, like a task that has to be accomplished – maximum consumption of pleasure. In what way this was put into effect in the cult is demonstrated to us by the Phionites. "Polluted with their own shamefulness," Epiphanius recalls, "they pray with their whole bodies naked, as if by such a practice they could gain free access to God."[195] Says Rudolph, "Nakedness as a sign of restored freedom, of the paradisiacal innocence of Adam, was also practiced at a later date in gnostic or gnosticizing movements, like the Mediaeval 'Adamites.'"[196] Epiphanius elaborated on the Gnostic cult:

When they thus ate together and so to speak filled up their veins from surplus of their strength they turn to excitements. The man leaving his wife says to his own wife: 'Stand up and perform the agape with the brother.' Then the unfortunates unite with each other...I will not be ashamed to say those things which they are not ashamed to do, in order that I may cause in every way a horror in those who hear about their shameful practices. After they have had intercourse in the passion of fornication they raise their own blasphemy to heaven. The woman and the man take the fluid of the emission of the man into their hands, they stand, turn toward heaven, their hands besmeared with uncleanness, and pray as people called stratiotikoi and gnostikoi, bringing to the father the nature of all that which they have on their hands, and they say: 'We offer to thee this gift, the body of Christ.' And then they eat it, their own ugliness, and say, 'This is the body of Christ and this is the Passover for the sake of which our bodies suffer and are forced to confess the suffering of Christ.' Similarly also with the woman when she happens to be in the flowing of the blood they gather the blood of menstruation of her uncleanness and eat it together and say: 'This is the blood of Christ.'[197]

Subsequently, the Fathers of the Church simply traced back the rise of Gnosis to the devil. The classic formulation of this view was made by the father of ecclesiastical historiography, Eusebius of Caesarea (ca. 264-339) in his *Ecclesiastical History*:

Like brilliant lamps the churches were now shining throughout the world, and faith in our Savior and Lord Jesus Christ was flourishing among all mankind, when the devil who hates what is good, as the enemy of truth, ever most hostile to man's salvation, turned all his devices against the church. Formerly he had used persecutions from without as his weapon against her, but now that he was excluded from this he employed wicked men and sorcerers, like baleful weapons and ministers of destruction against the soul, and conducted his campaign by other measures, plotting by every means that sorcerers and deceivers might assume the same name as our religion and at one time lead to the depth of destruction those of the faithful whom they caught, and at others, by the deeds which they undertook, might turn from the path to the saving word those who were ignorant of the faith.

According to Chadwick, the Church's defense against these anti-Christian forces was threefold. The first defense against Gnosticism was developed in the idea of orthodoxy through succession from the apostles. Against any heretical claim to possess secret traditions of what Jesus had told the apostles in the forty days after the resurrection, there was a clear argument that the Apostles Peter and Paul could not have failed to impart such doctrines to those whom they had set over the churches, and that by the line of accredited teachers in those churches of apostolic foundation no such heretical notions had been transmitted. The succession argument carried the implication that the teaching given by the contemporary bishop of, say, Rome or Antioch was in all respects identical with that of the apostles. This was important for two reasons:

In the first place, the faithful were thereby in some sense assured that revelation was not only knowable by retrospective historical knowledge...but had in the bishop a contemporary authority, able and authorized to speak God's word in the present.

In the second place, it enabled the defenders of orthodoxy, especially Irenaeue of Lyons, to oppose the proliferating Gnostic sects, none of which agreed with one another and all of which were continually modifying their views, with the concept of the monolithic church, universally extended in space and with unbroken continuity in time, unanimous in its possession of an immutable revelation.[198]

Heresy was born of the desire for something new; from innovation and dangerous speculation. It came of "curiosity," which meant prying into matters which the human mind had neither capacity to know or authority even to think about. The second weapon of orthodox defence was the gradual formation of the New Testament canon. The controversy with the Gnostics gave sharp impetus to control the authentic tradition which a written document possessed and which oral tradition did not. Justin Martyr, who probably knew all the four canonical gospels, seems to have used Matthew, Mark, and Luke in a gospel harmony, to which his pupil Tatian added St. John to form his Diatessaron. The Gospel of John caused some controversy because of its evidently discrepant account compared with the other three Gospels, but it was fully defended by Irenaeus as being the work of John son of Zebedee, to whom he also ascribed the Revelation.[199] Naturally enough, orthodoxy and apostolicity were equated. This made it difficult to detect non-apostolic authorship of orthodox documents like the Second Epistle of Peter. Other disputed and eventually successful documents were the Revelation of John, the Epistles of James and Jude, and the second and third Epistles of John. Likewise disputed but unsuccessful candidates on the orthodox side were the Acts of Paul and Thecla and the Apocalypse of Peter. Sometimes modern writers wonder at the disagreements. Chadwick noted, "The truly astonishing thing is that so great a measure of agreement was reached so quickly."[200]

The third and last weapon against heresy, according to Chadwick, was the "Rule of Faith," a title used by Irenaeus and Tertullian to mean a short summary of the main revelatory events of the redemptive process. Irenaeus declares that the whole Church believes:

...in one God the Father Almighty, maker of heaven and earth and the seas and all that is therein, and in one Christ Jesus the Son of God, who was made flesh for our salvation, and in the Holy Spirit who through the prophets preached the dispensations and the comings and the virgin birth and the passion, and the rising from the dead and the assumption into heaven in his flesh of our beloved Lord Jesus Christ, and His coming from heaven in the glory of the Father...to raise up all flesh.[201]

The crux of this creed for polemical purposes lies in its assertion of the unity of the divine plan from Old Testament to New, a theme which Irenaeus developed in his doctrine of "recapitulation" or the correspondence between Adam and Christ. The heretics did not believe the supreme God to be maker of heaven and earth and, with their low valuation of the Old Testament, were not interested in the fulfillment of prophecy.[202]

To implement this defense, Church structure was needed not only for administration but for maintenance of orthodoxy. The apostles had derived their name and purpose from the fact of being sent by the Lord as missionaries. Within seventy years of this initial period, Ignatius was speaking of Antioch and the Asian churches as possessing a monarchical bishop, together with presbyters and deacons. In his time there were neither apostles nor prophets. The exact history of this transition within two generations from apostles and prophets to bishops, presbyters and deacons is lost in obscurity, though sources give occasional glimpses of the process. Chadwick claimed the churches established by the traveling missionaries soon came to have local, stationary clergy, subordinate to the general oversight of mobile apostolic authority. For a generation or more the apostles and prophets coexisted with this local ministry of bishops and deacons.[203]

This study of the "Gnostic Cancer" of early times is fittingly closed with a letter likely written by Apostle Peter, near 65 A.D. He is trying to teach members how to deal with false teachers and evildoers who have come into the Church:

But there were also false prophets among the people, just as there will be false teachers among you. They will secretly introduce destructive heresies, even denying the sovereign Lord who bought them – bringing swift destruction on themselves. Many will follow their shameful ways and will bring the way of truth into disrepute. In their greed these teachers will exploit you with stories they have made up. Their condemnation has long been hanging over them, and their destruction has not been sleeping. For if god did not spare angels when they sinned but sent them to hell...if he condemned the cities of Sodom and Gomorrah by burning them to ashes, and made them an example of what is going to happen to the ungodly; and if he rescued Lot, a righteous man, who was distressed by the filthy lives of lawless men...if this is so, then the Lord knows how to rescue godly men from trials and to hold the righteous for the day of judgment. This is especially true of those who follow the corrupt desire of the sinful nature and despise authority. Bold and arrogant, these men are not afraid to slander celestial beings...these men blaspheme in matters they do not understand. They are like brute beasts, creatures of instinct, born only to be caught and destroyed, and like beasts they too will perish...Their idea of pleasure is to carouse in broad daylight. They are blots and blemishes, reveling in their pleasures while they feast with you. With eyes full of adultery, they never stop sinning; they seduce the unstable... They have left the straight way and wandered off to follow the way of Balaam...Blackest darkness is reserved for them. For they mouth empty, boastful words and, by appealing to the lustful desires of sinful human nature, they entice people who are just escaping from those who live in error. They promise them freedom, while they themselves are slaves of depravity – for a man is slave to whatever has mastered him. If they have escaped corruption of the world by knowing our Lord and Savior Jesus Christ and are again entangled in it and overcome, they are worse off at the end than they were at the beginning...Of them the Proverbs are true: 'A dog returns to its vomit,' and 'A sow that is washed goes back to her wallowing in the mud' (2 Peter 2).

The study of Gnosticism in contemporary times, starts with Carl Jung in this section, and carries over to Chapter 5, with a analysis of the heresies of the pro-gay theologian Rev. Dr. John Shelby Spong. Stephan A. Hoeller, author of *The Gnostic Jung* and *Jung and the Lost Gospels* writes on Jungian psychology. Hoeller is an associate professor of comparative religions at the College of Oriental Studies in Los Angeles and director of the Gnostic Society in Los Angeles. The latter is an organization interested in Jungian thinking, the Kabalah, Tarot, classical Gnosticism, myth and literature.[204] Dr. Hoeller writes that not long before his death in 1961, C.G. Jung had a series of visions of a future great catastrophe around 2010. In an earlier book *Aion* (1951), Jung predicted the coming of the age of the Antichrist (a personified rejecter of Jesus Christ), placing its culmination within or possibly soon after the termination of the twentieth century. Apparently, the cosmic sychronicities outlined by Jung in *Aion* concerned the progression of the so-called "zodiacal ages."[205]

According to Hoeller, the discovery of the Gnostic collection of scriptures at Nag Hammadi plays an important role in Jung's prediction. Hoeller writes, quoting from these Gnostic texts:

Risen from the sleep of the centuries and emerging into the focus of consciousness, the other, alternative reality beckons to us with its vision of transformative redemption. We have nothing to fear but unconsciousness. The Antichrists, Behemoths, and Leviathans threatening us are but the creatures of our unconscious projections, which may vanish like a nightmare when the process of individuation becomes operative. The kingdom, the reconstituted world of wholeness, opens its gates to us as the words of the archetype of the individuated Self of humanity receive their final vindication. Destruction and its alternative, liberation from form and redemption within form:

'When you make the two one, and when you make the inmost as the outermost and the outer as the inner and the above as the below, and when you make the male and female into a single unity, so that the male will not be only male and the female will not be only female, when you create eyes in the place of an eye, and create a hand in

the place of a hand, and a foot in the place of a foot, and also an image in the place of an image, then surely will you enter the kingdom' (Gnostic gospel Thomas 22).[206]

Jung's visions of future upheaval and this verse from the Gnostic gospel of Thomas could certainly purport of the era of genomics and cloning, or on the other hand, the prophecies could prove totally false. Once more the reader must decide who and what to believe. In the face of life's chaos, and particularly in times of increasing catastrophes, each person will search for a worldview, which offers tangible security. The anti-Christian worldview, proclaimed by Jung, asserts an "alternative reality" with "its vision of transformative redemption." Humankind has only to achieve a greater level of self-consciousness. And "Antichrists are but the creatures of our unconscious projections, which will vanish like a nightmare when the process of individuation becomes operative." Like the central tenet of Margaret Sanger's ideology and the creed of first and second century Gnostics, *self-knowledge* is seen as the real source of salvation. And in the postmodern era this self-knowledge manifests itself in science and technology.

Cornelius G. Hunter, author of *Darwin's God: Evolution and the Problem of Evil*, points out Gnostic presuppositions about God inherent in current naturalistic evolutionist thought. He writes:

There is, to be sure, plenty of evidence supporting evolution, but there is plenty of evidence for all sorts of discarded theories. In fact, one can formulate arguments against evolution, often using the same evidence, that are more persuasive than the supporting arguments. But there is, as we shall see, a line of nonscientific – metaphysical – reasoning that is consistently used to support evolution. It uses scientific observations to argue against the possibility of divine creation. Such negative theology is metaphysical because it requires certain premises about the nature of God....There is a profound yet subtle religious influence in the theory of evolution. Darwin as well as today's modern evolutionists appeal to these metaphysical arguments.[207]

Hunter continues:

Two important themes are discernible in the writings of Darwin and his fellow naturalists: Gnosticism and natural theology.[208]

Where as the Bible says that God made the world, Gnosticism holds that God is separate from the world. Gnostics acknowledge evil, but it is far removed from God. God is separate and distinct from the world and not responsible for its evils. In Darwin's time the world was increasingly seen as controlled by natural laws. God may have instituted these laws in the beginning, but he had not since interfered; the laws were now his secondary causes. Natural phenomena were not interpreted as results of divine providence. A clean separation of God and creation made for an even purer God, just as the Gnostics had found that the spirit could be good when it was opposed to matter. In 1794 Darwin's grandfather Erasmus Darwin wrote this Gnostic-oriented statement of how natural history should be viewed:

The world itself might have been generated, rather than created; that is, it might have been gradually produced from very small beginnings, increasingly by the activities of its inherent principles, rather than by a sudden evolution by the whole by the Almighty fiat. What a magnificent idea of the infinite power of the great architect! The Cause of Causes! Parent of Parents! Ens Entium! For if we may compare infinities, it would seem to require a greater infinity of power to cause the causes of effects, than to cause the effects themselves.[209]

The ancient Gnostics were also antihistorical. Whereas the Bible presents a history of God's activity in the world, including dates and historical figures, the Gnostics believed that God's revelation was not open but secret – revealed from within rather than in public documents such as Scripture. Furthermore, whereas the Bible says that the heavens declare the glory of God, the Gnostics believed that one should not look for signs of God in nature.[210] In Darwin's day, a parallel view developed that urged the separation of religion and science.

According to Hunter, Victorians in Darwin's time, could not believe that Christ the Savior could become involved with creation any more than the Gnostics could. One historian of Gnosticism wrote:

If Christ is to be taken seriously as the Savior how can he actually be part and parcel of this material cosmos?[211]

The Gnostics could not believe God became a man for the same reasons they could not believe God directly created the world – they could not envision God involved in a world so fraught with misery. Similarly, the Victorians in Darwin's time had trouble with the idea that God created a natural world that often seems devoid of His divine presence. Philosopher Michael Ruse explained the tenet this way:

Darwin was obviously no traditional Christian, believing in an immanent God who intervenes constantly in His creation. Most accurately, perhaps, Darwin is characterized as one held to some kind of 'deistic' belief in a God who works at a distance through unbroken law: having set the world in motion, God now sits back and does nothing.[212]

Contemporary evolutionist Stephen Jay Gould continues these Gnostic tendencies with a acronym he calls "NOMA," or "non-overlapping magisteria." He writes:

I do not see how science and religion could be unified, or even synthesized, under a common scheme of explanation or analysis.[213]

Gould is not the only recent evolutionist with Gnostic sympathies. Niles Eldredge takes the position that "religion and science are two utterly different domains of human experience."[214] Bruce Alberts, writing for the National Assembly of Sciences, says:

Scientists, like many others are touched with awe at the order and complexity of nature. Indeed, many scientists are deeply religious. But science and religion occupy two separate realms of human experience. Demanding that they be combined detracts from the glory of each.[215]

Hunter asks, "Where did Alberts learn that combining science and religion detracts from the glory of each?" The answer of course is that God did not create the world, at least not directly – the world evolved.[216] The historian's assessment of Gnosticism could just as easily apply to evolution:

The cardinal feature of Gnostic thought is the radical dualism that governs the relation of God and world....The deity is absolutely transmundane, its nature alien to that of the universe which it neither created nor governs and to which it is the complete antithesis....The world is the work of lowly powers.[217]

The Gnostic's belief in "lowly powers" was fulfilled in evolution's natural selection. The acceptance of evolution, in turn, reinforced Gnosticism in modern thought. Darwin gave form to the Gnostic's vision, but that brought with it a movement toward Gnosticism. The influence of Gnostic thought today is not often acknowledged or understood. It is, according to Harold Bloom, the most common thread of religious thought in America. He calls it the "American Religion" and finds it "pervasive and overwhelming, however it is masked." Bloom concludes:

...even our secularists, indeed even our professed atheists, are more Gnostic than humanist in their ultimate presuppositions.[218]

It is perhaps one of the great ironies in religious thought that one can profess to be an agnostic, skeptic, or even atheist regarding belief in God yet still hold strong opinions about God. Evolution may breed skepticism, but its adherents have continued to make religious proclamations. Theodicies for both natural and moral evil push God into the background. Taken to the extreme, this leads to atheism and materialism, with the universe as nothing but matter and motion. Moreover, in our one-track Western culture we can see that exclusive, purely scientific and technological thought allows whole areas of our humanity to die out or become stunted, and precisely in so doing alienates man from himself. It is illuminating that the man who does not worship a divine God automatically prostrates himself before a non-divine God. The truth about man in his encounter with the world is not exhausted by his purposeful control of the world in science and technology.[219]

In such a worldview there is no authority that supplies our sense of morality, and therefore judgments regarding evil arise only from personal feelings. In this paradigm, Darwinism became the non-theistic explanation for the reality of evil. Darwin wrote to a friend:

There seems to me too much misery in the world. I cannot persuade myself that a beneficent and omnipotent God would have designedly created the [parasitic wasp] with the express intention of their feeding within the living bodies of caterpillars, or that the cat should play with mice.[220]

To Darwin, "Nature seemed to lack precision and economy in design and was often 'inexplicable on the theory of creation.'"[221] Darwin observed that different species use "an almost infinite diversity of means" for the same task and the different species use similar means for different tasks. He argued that this evidence does not fit into the theory of divine creation.[222] Says Hunter:

Evolutionists use negative theological arguments that give evolution its force. Creation doesn't seem very divine, so evolution must be true. By Darwin's day the list of such explanations was growing. One strategy was to try to show that God was somehow disconnected from creation. Natural evil arose not from God's direction but from an imperfect linkage between Creator and creation.[223]

In such thinking, God was constrained to benevolence and was distanced from evils of creation through the imposition of natural laws. Positioning natural selection operating in an unguided fashion on natural biological diversity was Darwin's unique solution. He distanced God from creation to the point that God was unnecessary. One could still believe in God, but not in God's providence. God may have created the world, but ever since that point it has run according to impersonal natural laws that may now and then produce natural evil. After reading *The Origin of the Species*, geologist Adam Sedgwick wrote to Darwin. He believed that exploring the created order is a privilege for naturalists, which they should not abuse by denying the divine hand behind creation:

There is a moral or metaphysical part of nature, as well as a physical. A man who denies this is deep in the mire of folly. Tis the crown and glory of organic science that it does through final cause, link material and moral; and yet does not allow us to mingle them in our first conception of laws, and our classification of such laws, whether we consider one side of nature or the other. You have ignored this link; and, if I do not mistake your meaning, you have done your best in one or two pregnant cases to break it.[224]

The split in approach between Sedgwick and Darwin developed from Sedgwick's concern with morality, while Darwin was concerned with explaining evil. Darwin summarized the argument which underlies evolution in his autobiography:

Suffering is quite compatible with the belief in Natural Selection, which is not perfect in its action, but tends only to render each species as successful as possible in the battle for life with other species, in wonderfully complex and changing circumstances....A being so powerful and so full of knowledge as a God who could create the universe is to our finite minds omnipotent and omniscient. It revolts our understandings to suppose that his benevolence is not unbounded, for what advantage can there be in the sufferings of millions of lower animals throughout almost endless time? This very old argument from the existence of suffering against the existence of an intelligent First Cause seems to me a strong one; and the abundant presence of suffering agrees well with the view that all organic beings have been developed through variation and natural selection.[225]

Darwin's reconciliation resolved the metaphysical dilemma that bothered him – the problem of evil; but now, with one metaphysical dilemma gone, another stepped in to take its place – the one that bothered Sedgwick: the problem of morality. What is the source of our moral law? The existence of evil seems to contradict God, but the existence of our deep moral sense seems to confirm God. What morality was heralded by the so-called "enlightenment?" In addition to the development of the "Pivot of Civilization" philosophy of Margaret Sanger, the era witnessed the advent of social Darwinism and plans for a humanistic-eugenic civilization, similar to the utopia described in Chapter 3. You review what the prophets of the period had to say and decide if they spoke the truth:

The more civilized so-called Caucasian races have beaten the Turkish hollow in the struggle for existence. Looking to the world at no very distant date, what an endless number of the lower races will have been eliminated by the higher civilized races throughout the world.[226]

Charles Darwin 1881

...no rational man, cognizant of the facts, believes that the average Negro is the equal, still less the superior, of the white man...It is simply incredible [to think] that...he will be able to compete successfully with his bigger-brained and smaller jawed rival, in a contest which is carried on by thoughts and not by bites.[227]

Thomas Huxley, Agnostic

If the unfit survived indefinitely, they would continue to 'infect' the fit with their less fit genes....The concept of evolution demands death. Death is thus as natural to evolution as it is foreign to biblical creation. The Bible teaches that death is a 'foreigner,' a condition superimposed upon humans and nature after creation.

Marvin Lubenow, 'Bones of Contention'

For myself, as no doubt, for most of my contemporaries, the philosophy of meaninglessness was essentially an instrument of liberation. The liberation we desired was simultaneously liberation from a certain political and economic system and liberation from a certain system of morality. We objected to the morality because it interfered with our sexual freedom....The supporters of these systems claimed that in some way they embodied the meaning (a Christian meaning), they insisted of the world. There was one admirably simple method of confuting these people and at the same time justifying ourselves in our political and erotic revolt: we could deny that the world had any meaning whatsoever...[228]

Aldous Huxley, Brother of Julian

What follows is the study of the "depravity" found in the sexual freedom of ancient Roman and Greek cultures. To measure the good in the Christian Gospel one needs to witness the bad. This next section also serves as a reminder of what unfettered hedonism and free love on a national scale would look like. Consider this Roman and Greek era of study the Dark Age before the advent of Jesus Christ. Oxford zoologist Richard Dawkins generalizes the worldview, which prolongs darkness:

The universe we observe has precisely the properties we should expect if there is at bottom no design, no purpose, no evil and no good, nothing but pointless indifference.[229]

Greek and Roman Sexism

According to Cynthia Eller, Greek literature paints a picture that is not at all favorable to women. Aristotle, writing in the fourth century B.C., put it unequivocally:

The male is by nature superior, and the female inferior; and the one rules and the other is ruled. Greek poetry, drama, and myth are full of the 'problem' of women. The eight-century B.C. poet Hesiod describes woman as a drone who 'sits within the house and reaps the fruits of others' toil to fill her belly,' saying that even a 'good wife' will bring misfortune upon a man. Indeed, the myth of Pandora suggests that women were regarded as a breed apart, not truly human. Pandora, the first woman, is created as a punishment to men. And although Greek literature recognizes it as an (unfortunate) fact that women are involved in reproducing all human beings, Pandora is named only as the origin of 'the race of women.'[230]

The misogyny evident in Greek literature permeated Greek society. Women in classical Athens were under the guardianship of one male or another for their entire lives. Married free-born women were confined to their houses - actually to one portion of the house designated for women, the gynaecaeum. Fathers had the right to discard their new born children, and more girls than boys were left to die in this manner. Heterosexual sex was understood as an "unequal transaction by which woman steals man's substance," and so men were better advised to have sexual relations with one another. As Eva Keuls summed up classical Athens:

In the case of a society dominated by men who sequester their wives and daughters, denigrate the female role in reproduction, erect monuments to male genitalia, have sex with the sons of their peers, sponsor public whorehouses, create a mythology of rape, and engage in rampant saber-rattling, it is not inappropriate to refer to a reign of the phallus.[231]

According to Elaine Pagels, within the capital city of Rome, three quarters of the population were either slaves – persons legally classified as property – or were descended from slaves. Besides being subjected to their owner's abuses, fits of violence, and sexual desires, slaves were denied such elementary rights as legitimate marriage, let alone legal recourse for their grievances. Clement attacked the widespread Roman custom of exposing abandoned infants on garbage dumps, or raising them for sale: "I pity the children owned by slave dealers, who are dressed up for shame," says Clement, and trained in sexual specialties, to be sold to gratify their owners sexual tastes. Justin in *Defense of Christians*, complained that "not only the females, but also the males" were commonly raised "like herds of oxen, goats, or sheep," and as a profitable crop of child prostitutes. Many Christians were themselves slave owners and took slavery for granted as unthinkingly as their pagan neighbors. But others went among the hovels of the poor, the illiterate, slaves, women, and foreigners – with the good news that class, education, sex, and status made no difference, that every human being was essentially equal to any other "before God," including the emperor himself, for all mankind was created in the image of the one God.[232] There is intrinsic worth in each individual bequeathed by God.

John Boswell (presented in the Introduction) observed there were no laws in Rome condemning homosexuality as such until the sixth century A.D.. He notes there were a number of cases involving pederastic relationships but Boswell argued, that the crime was never homosexuality. His conclusion is worth citing at length:

Homosexual acts could hardly have been illegal in Augustine Rome, where government not only taxed homosexual prostitution but accorded boy prostitutes a legal holiday; and it is virtually impossible to imagine any law regulating homosexual activities in Rome in which Martial wrote: not only does he mention by name numerous prominent citizens having homosexual affairs, often listing their partners, but he frankly admits to engaging in such activities himself.[233]

Vern Bullough, in *Homosexuality: A History*, writes that the whole Greek idea of beauty is masculine. In Greek art, particularly in vase paintings, boys and youths are portrayed more frequently and with greater attention than girls. Even the most erotic of females, such as the legendary Sirens, look boyish. Exclusive homosexuality, however, was discouraged among the Greeks. Homoerotic feelings were not to threaten the family. Instead the Greeks permitted, if they did not encourage, homosexuality during a brief period in a young man's life, from the time he had his hair cut at age sixteen through his military training until he became a fully accepted citizen. Then he was supposed to marry and beget children, although later in life he was supposed to take a young adolescent under his protective custody, repeating the cycle. The Greek word *paiderastia*, anglicized as "pederasty," is derived from *pais*, boy, and *erastia*, love and in its ideal sense denoted the spiritual and sensual affection felt by an adult for a boy who had reached puberty.[234]

In spite of Aristotle's belief that homosexuality might possibly be habit-forming, pederasty was institutionalized within both the military and educational system in Greece. Plato believed that the most formidable army in the world would be one composed of lovers, inspiring one another to deeds of heroism and sacrifice. Adding to the acceptance of homosexuality was the institutionalization of pederasty within the educational system. According to Plato the purpose of homosexual love was to "educate," and so the dedicated teacher and true boy lover were one and the same. This was accentuated in Greece, as it was later in the English public schools, because the Greek educational system was a closed masculine society excluding women, not only physically but ideologically. After the primary grades education implied an intimate relationship, a personal union between a young student and the elder who was at once his model, guide and initiator – a relationship in which passion played an important part.[235]

Robin Scroggs, argues in *The New Testament and Homosexuality* that the Greco-Roman culture of homosexuality was markedly different from today and, therefore,

"Until we know what the biblical authors were against we cannot begin to reflect on the relevance of Scripture for contemporary issues. Arguments assume the identity of homosexuality then is as now."[236] In his book he described the society starting with education.

In the classical Greek period, while primary schools might see boys and girls studying together, the secondary schools – the gymnasia – were certainly mostly for males. In this period the military training was giving way to athletics, and youths studied music, poetry, and writing. H.I. Marrou concluded: "Such was the old Athenian education – artistic rather than intellectual." In the gymnasium the youths exercised in the nude, the aim being to create a strong and beautiful body. The sexual possibilities virtually inherent in the gymnasia are indirectly reflected in Alcibiades' narration of his attempts to seduce Socrates:

After that I proposed he should go with me to the trainer's, and I trained [literally to train in the nude] with him, expecting to gain my point there. So he trained and wrestled with me many a time when no one was there.[237]

Aeschines outlines a law pertaining to pederasty in a speech against Timarchus:

The teachers of the boys shall open the school-rooms not earlier than sunrise, and they shall close them before sunset. No person who is older than the boys shall be permitted to enter the room while they are there…If anyone enter in violation of this prohibition, he shall be punished with death. The superintendents of gymnasia shall under no conditions allow any one who has reached the age of manhood to enter the contests of Hermes together with the boys…Every choregus who is appointed by the people shall be more than forty years of age.[238]

Thus according to Scroggs, the ethos of the gymnasium is all-male. After completion at the gymnasium the Athenian youth served two years in the army, which only strengthened his inclinations to view the world as essentially a male reality. After military service, those who wished might attend private schools, which, if these were not exclusively all-male clubs, they were nearly so.[239]

In adult public life there were important, if occasional, male voices of intercession on behalf of women, as when Plutarch argued for the superiority of marriage over pederastic relationships. Nevertheless, these voices are mostly a concession. One hears them saying, "women are not so bad," or "they do have the potential of becoming respectable companions."[240] Ischomachos described how he trained his wife in the duties he assigned her: "Your duty will be to remain indoors and send out those servants whose work is outside, superintend those who are to work indoors…"[241] No women performed important roles that affected the public life; it is, rather, that when one looked around at the voters, the court cases, the meetings of the city officials, the larger political organizations, the local "city councils," or the Senate of Rome, one would see nothing to suggest that the "men's club" was not in complete control.[242]

The ideal of beauty was masculine dominant. Ancient pin-ups were much more likely to be male figures than female. And it is crucial to realize that it would be the adult male who would be interested in such pin-ups. The primary word to describe such beautiful youths was the Greek adjective, *kalos*. K.J. Dover succinctly describes the meaning of the word:

It means 'beautiful,' 'handsome,' 'pretty,' 'attractive,' or 'lovely' when applied to a human being, animal, object or place...It must be emphasized that the Greeks did not call a person 'beautiful' by virtue of the person's morals, intelligence, ability and movement.[243]

Dover concluded that one is "justified in treating the quantity of the materials [inscriptions, epigrams, vases] as evidence of Greek male society's preoccupation with the beauty of boys and youths and...of the characteristic Greek conception of sexuality as a relationship between a senior and a junior partner.[244] Thus in this all-male society the beauty of the male youth was, perhaps, the key symbol and organizing center for adult male eroticism. "Beautiful" – *kalos* – refers to physical beauty with the inevitable "aura" of eroticism that had come to accompany it.[245]

R. Flaceliere wryly commented on the accuracy of the highest ideal behind pederasty: "It may well be objected, however, that since not all young Athenians were handsome, the education of the less attractive must have suffered." Furthermore, the frequent assertions that lovers should retain permanent relations with the merging adult probably suggests that the opposite happened – as seems indeed to have been customary in more explicitly sexual relationships.[246] The older adult was the active partner, the *erastes* (lover), usually seeking out the relationship, provoking the sexual contact, and in one way or another obtaining orgasm by the use of the boy's body. The younger person, on the other hand, was the passive partner (at least normally) and was called the beloved, the *eromenos*. Apparently the beloved did not desire, or at least did not expect, sexual gratification from his older lover. According to Dover, if a youth did feel pleasure he was considered no better than a prostitute. At any rate there is no evidence that he was given the chance to be satisfied. His bodily activity was only to provide sexual satisfaction for his lover.[247]

The age of the younger partner varied. He may be called *pais*, "boy," which might point to an age prior to puberty, or at least not beyond it. He may also be identified as *meirakion*, an older youth past puberty. If it is correct that youths were the more desirable the more they looked like a woman, then the appearance of facial hair could signal the end of the adult's interest in the youth. Aeshines, at age 45, claims by that time to have had several lovers, which suggests a rapid rate of turnover. Lysias (fifth-fourth century B.C.) by his own admission was in his late fifties when such a fierce competition arose between another adult and himself over a beloved that resulted in altercations and eventually ended in court.[248]

With the exception of male prostitutes, Scroggs claimed to know of no suggestions in the texts that homosexual relationships existed between same-age adults. The basic inequality in the typical age is characteristic. The older, active partner enjoyed orgasm with the youth's body but did not reciprocate. How this orgasm is achieved may have varied. Dover, basing himself primarily on fifth century vase paintings, argues that in proper relationships (i.e. with consenting free males) intercourse was "intercrual," that is "between the thighs." Anal intercourse, on the other hand, is that forced on prostitutes, slaves (and women!), and is indicative of an improper relationship and a dominating position taken by the active partner.[249]

Scroggs claimed if intercrural sex is true for the early period, it does not seem to hold for the later period. He holds to pederasty as sexual and anal in nature.[250]

Scroggs summarized Classical Greek pederasty as inequality; impermanency and humiliation. How could a youth not often be close to feeling that he was being abused and dehumanized? This might especially be the case where anal intercourse was the favored form of gratification. Two texts, widely separated in time, poignantly illustrate contemporary judgments (or remembrances?) of this humiliation. One is from Plato. In the *Phaedrus* Socrates is speaking of the feelings of the beloved in the midst of pederastic intercourse:

But what consolation or what pleasure can he [the lover] give the beloved? Must not this protracted intercourse bring him to uttermost disgust, as he looks at the old, unlovely face, and other things to match, which it is not pleasant even to hear about, to say nothing of being constantly compelled to come into contact with them [i.e. physically to have to handle]?

The second is from Plutarch, four centuries later:

[Young men] not naturally vicious, who have been lured or forced into yielding and letting themselves be abused, forever after mistrust and hate no one on earth more than the men who served them and, if opportunity offers, they take a terrible revenge.[251]

Now men's intercourse with women involves giving like enjoyment in return. For the two sexes part with pleasure only if they have an equal effect on each other. But no one could be so mad as to say this is the case of boys. "No, the active lover, according to his view of the matter, departs after having obtained an exquisite pleasure, but the one outraged suffers pain and tears at first…but of pleasure he has none at all." [252]

Children fell into slave prostitution by: being born to a slave mother, captured in warfare (and then sold), picked up as an exposed baby while still alive, being sold by one's family. There were brothel houses filled with boys for sexual services. Many were household servants. Perhaps the most poignant example is given by Seneca. He describes one slave, now an adult, who is a wine-server at banquets, there forced to wear women's clothes, kept beardless by hair removal, dividing his time between his master's drunkenness and his lust. In the chamber he must be a man (*vir*), at the feast a boy (*puer*). It was not uncommon to castrate such beautiful youths, in order to prolong their youthful appearance and therefore their usefulness for pederastic activities. The most famous case (but not the least typical) was Nero's treatment of his favorite boy-slave, Sporus. He had the slave castrated, dressed in women's clothes, given a women's name, and then married to Nero as his wife.[253]

The effeminate call-boys were free (i.e. nonslave) youths, or adults, who sold themselves for providing sexual gratification. Perhaps the most famous case is Mark Anthony, the great lover of Cleopatra. In his youth he was a male homosexual prostitute. Or at least this is the view held of him not only by Cicero, but also Josephus, the Jewish historian. When such youths decided the practice was attractive and remunerative enough, they could essentially make their living this way, often by getting taken into someone's house as a "mistress" for varying periods of time. As they grew older, many of them gave added emphasis to the charge of effeminacy by trying to prolong their youthfulness and at times by imitating the toilette of women. Coiffured and perfumed hair, rouged face, careful removal of body hair, and feminine clothes are often part of the descriptions of such prostitutes.[254]

In a later text Dapnaeus, in Plutarch's *Eritikos*, contrasted union with women with that between males:

But the union with males, either unwillingly with force and plunder, or willingly with weakness (malakia) and effeminacy (thelutes), surrendering themselves, as Plato says, 'to be mounted in the custom of four-footed animals and to be sowed with seed contrary to nature' – this is entirely ill-favored favor (charis), shameful, and contrary to Aphrodite.[255]

Plato contrasted heterosexuality with homosexuality:

When male unites with female for procreation, the pleasure experienced is held to be due to nature (kata phusin), but contrary to nature (para phusin) when male mates with male or female with female.[256]

According to Daphnaeus in *Erotikos*, pederasty is a "union contrary to nature" (*he para phusin omilia*), in contrast to the natural heterosexual relationship. One example Gryllus gives is the natural sexual intercourse of animals in comparison with that of humans. "Since animals are wholly concerned with nature (again *phusis*), until now the desires of animals have involved intercourse neither of male with male nor female with female." He concludes that "even men themselves acknowledge that beasts have a better claim to temperance and the non-violation of nature in their pleasures."[257] Plutarch concludes in *Erotikos*:

There can be no greater pleasures derived from others nor more continuous services conferred on others than those found in marriage, nor can the beauty of another friendship be so highly esteemed or so enviable as [quoting Homer] when a man and wife keep house in perfect harmony.[258]

Christian Patriarchy

There is some evidence that fertility cults in ancient society at some point took a turn toward patriarchy, displacing and downgrading female function in procreation and attributing the power of life to the phallus alone. Patriarchal religion could consolidate this position by the creation of a male God or gods, demoting, discrediting, or eliminating goddesses and constructing a theology whose basic postulates are male supremacist, and one of whose central functions is to uphold and validate the patriarchal structure.[259]

Kate Millett, Sexual Politics

Many adherents to the feminist-rallying creed – "oppression by patriarchy," wrongly count Christianity as part of man's seditious stratagem. Believing that Christianity's God is male and therefore irredeemably sexist, some women have left the church. This group often called "post-Christian feminists," are strictly speaking, "pre-Christian feminists," because in many cases they find inspiration from goddesses in pre-Christian mythology, who are not even mentioned in the Old Testament. For them, Christianity is being replaced with a woman-centered, matriarchal religion in which men have no part.[260]

Yet against the highly sexist cultures and historic realities at play during the time of Christ and after His death, large numbers of both men and women chose to lay claim to the New Covenant. They came to Christianity regardless of their sex, age, nationality, social status; and in spite of a frightening probability of martyrdom. Leaving the initiative of the Holy Spirit, and the influences of men aside, the women embraced Christianity as a truly egalitarian faith. All were equal in the eyes of God. The Church was also universal – anyone willing could join. Christianity offered hope and optimism in an unforgiving empire and social existence. There was a spirit of mutuality among brothers and sisters; an obligation to help each other. Most important, Christianity specified a wholesome purpose, design and operation of what we currently call the "traditional family unit." Christian Scripture laid out the guidelines and boundaries for courtship, marriage, sexual relations, parent-child dynamics and wife-husband relations. Before interpreting some of this guidance we should start with the radical feminist contention with "Father God."

Feminism has often stereotyped and wrongly interpreted genuine Christianity. Elizabeth Cady Stanton's reformulation of the Trinity in her Women's Bible replaced the Holy Spirit with Mother. Yet the Holy Spirit is never described anthropomorphically. The Spirit is symbolized by breath, oil, water, wind, fire, a dove and a seal; all non-personal, genderless images.[261] The Church of Scotland had a rude awakening at the 1982 Annual General Meeting of the Woman's Guild, when Anne Hepburn, the National President, prayed to "God our Mother" and "Dear Mother God." In April 1984 the Episcopalian Cathedral of St. John the Divine in New York became newsworthy when it displayed Edwina Sandy's bronze of a female figure on a cross.[262]

According to Ann Brown, author of *Apology to Women*, it was not until the nineteenth century that Elizabeth Cady Stanton and the women who worked with her to produce *The Women's Bible* articulated the ideological significance of addressing God as Mother. Stanton argued that "the first step in the elevation" of woman is the recognition "of an ideal Heavenly Mother, to whom prayers should be addressed, as well as a Father."[263]

A draft version of a new United Church book of services sparked protest from conservatives in Canada's largest Protestant denomination, who complained the proposal reflected radical feminist ideology and a gay and lesbian agenda. The draft – titled *Celebrate God's Presence* – refers to Mother and Father God. It changes Father, Son and Holy Spirit into Creator, Liberator and Healer. It also suggests a good alternative to the term "husband and wife" is "life partners." To orthodox Christians adoption of the book would give the World Council of Churches ammunition to eject the United Church:

We will break ourselves away from other denominations, we will divide our own church, we will in fact become an isolated cult.[264]

Biblical feminists (like REAL Women); however, attempt by careful exegesis to give fuller appreciation to the neglected passages of maternal imagery without abandoning the Father, and without implying that God is sexual. The God of Scripture is depicted as mothering and being motherly. In some poignant and beautiful passages, God is compared to a woman crying out, gasping and panting in childbirth and to a mother nursing, quieting and consoling a child. In the New Testament, too, God is compared to a woman. In the parable of the woman and the lost coin, Jesus portrayed God as a woman who has lost one of her ten silver coins and searches carefully until she finds it (Luke 15:8-10). This female imagery is striking because it denies the myth that only male imagery can be used to describe God. At the same time, these passages of female imagery do not make God female any more than the male analogies make God male. It can help us to understand God's character and our relationship to God, but it does not make God literally male or female. God is not limited or defined by the imagery. Summarizes Brown, "All the mothers in the world put together reflect only in part the limitless love of God."[265]

God comforts his people as a mother comforts her child (Isaiah 66:13). However, God is never actually addressed as Mother. But Jesus did command us to pray to our Father, and in his personal prayers he prayed exclusively to God as Father. But can we ignore the precedent set by Jesus? Virginia Ramey Mollenkott argues that we can. According to her, it was for cultural reasons that Jesus did not command us to pray to God as mother. She argues that he would have been misunderstood, and that, had he prayed to our mother, it would have been mistaken for some kind of pantheism. This is not very convincing. Jesus was misunderstood for most of his ministry, but he taught regardless of the opposition that he created. Repeatedly, he challenged the mores of his first-century culture. Jesus caused cultural shock waves by calling God his Father. If he had wanted to pray to God as Mother, cultural considerations alone would not have prevented him.[266] The choice of Mother God would have further confused the manner and origin of His birth.

Brown says adding "Mother to Father gives the impression that divine maleness must be supplemented by divine femaleness or replaced by divine androgyny. This completely changes the biblical view of God as non-sexual and beyond gender." To change the way we address God is ultimately to talk about a different god. Some feminist theologians are determined to change gods. Rosemary Radford Reuther insists it is not enough to change words and speak of Mother as opposed to Father, but that the whole concept of God must change. She replaces God with the symbol "God/ess". "God/ess" is defined as the "primal Matrix, the ground of being – new being." Many of the revisionist reinterpretations, like Ruether's, are colored by theologians like Tillich. They conceive of God in mystical, pantheistic terms, beyond personality, as with Gnosticism – God becomes distant, impersonal, unknowable. Prayer is replaced by meditation. Jill Tweedie, who describes herself as an inquiring atheist, comments on the current trend of feminizing God:

Recently, we have shown a little audacity. We have drawn cartoons of a man run-

ning out of the stable and shouting 'It's a girl.' Worth a giggle but the laughter springs from nervousness at blasphemy against God.[267]

Dale Spender, the Australian feminist writer, states as one of her articles of faith, "Man made God in his own image and not the other way around." The Christian God is , therefore, rejected as being a projection of male ideas and ideals, created by men because they need him. As the projection of the patriarchal head of the family, "God the Father" is used to legitimize the oppression of women.[268] Thus sayeth feminist rhetoric.

Replies Brown:

Questions of truth belong to epistemology, not to the domain of psychology. God's self-revelation in and through the person of Jesus Christ, makes the projection tenet hard to believe. It is inconceivable that the person of Jesus Christ is the product of finite minds. From whatever angle we care to look at Jesus' life as recorded in the New Testament, he is above reproach and bears His own claim to be God. If we look at Him from the point of view of women, we discover that Jesus' behavior as God in the flesh is so distinctive in its freedom from any hint of sexism that it is impossible to believe that he has been fabricated by men's minds in the first century.[269]

Interestingly, the Bible specifically repudiates the theory of projection in that we are told not to make images of God in our own likeness. The second commandment makes this explicit (Exodus 20:4). Throughout the Old Testament God is contrasted with man-made idols, the creations of men's hands and minds (Isaiah 44). It is true that the Old Testament writers denounced the fertility cults and the veneration of deities. Their aim was not to replace these goddesses with a male god. In fact they condemned the Baals and other male gods as vehemently as the goddesses. Unlike the fertility cults which attributed male or female sexuality to their deities, the prophets emphasized God's transcendence. God is maker, creator, savior, redeemer, Holy One.[270]

The Judaeo-Christian God is above sexual categories and sexual differentiation. Sexuality is a characteristic of God's creatures but not of the Creator. God as spirit is neither male nor female, but is beyond gender, or genderless. The Bible insists that God is not to be depicted by making male or female figures. Deuteronomy gives a strong warning:

You saw no form of any kind the day the Lord spoke to you at Horeb out of the fire. Therefore watch yourselves very carefully, so that you do not become corrupt and make for yourselves an idol, an image of any shape, whether formed like a man or a woman (Deuteronomy 4:15-16).

Paul condemned the folly of those who "exchanged the glory of the immortal God for images made to look like mortal man" (Romans 1:23). Neither sex is to make God in its own image. In the image of God "male and female he created them" (Genesis 1:27). At the deepest level man and woman do resemble God. But this does not mean that God is male, female or bisexual. God embraces and transcends male and female.

Brown points out, when we read, Psalm 23, beginning, "The Lord is my Shepherd," we understand immediately that we are not meant to think of God literally as a shepherd with crook in hand and sheepdog at heel. In the same way, to say God is our Father does not imply that he shares the physical characteristics of human fathers. At the same time, the fatherhood of God is more than an analogy. God is not just like a father, as in the parable of the prodigal son, but he actually is our Father, if we are Christians. As theologian Tom Smail puts it: "We have to live in the light of Jesus' revelation of God and not in the darkness of our own caricatures." Jesus' revelation of God the Father forces people to think again, whatever negative connotations the word "father" may have for them. In the Gospels Christ paints a picture of perfect fatherliness: of a heavenly Father who knows and responds to his children's needs, is always available, sets limits [boundaries] and loves unconditionally. No wonder Jesus told his followers to pray to "Abba" ("Daddy," "Papa").[271] In Judaism God is never addressed as Father. Jesus did the unthinkable when he prayed to God as Abba.

We have to relearn the meaning of the word "father." The Apostle John writes that adoption into God's family depends on spiritual rebirth, not on a sexual act:

Yet to all who received him, to those who believed in his name, he gave the right to become children of God – children born not of natural descent, nor of human decision or a husband's will, but born of God (John 1:12-13).

In another example, God is portrayed as a father who guides, cares for and has compassion on his children. The object of these comparisons is never to make the point that God is male, but to emphasize some aspect of God's character and the way he relates to his people. Jesus was careful to stress that God far transcends human fatherhood. In the contest of teaching about prayer, he said that if even evil men respond to their children's requests for food, "how much more will your Father in heaven give good gifts to those who ask him?" (Matthew 7:11).[272]

To continue a defense against the radical feminist notion of Christ-sponsored "patriarchal oppression" we need to specifically see what Scripture states about marriage. That legitimate "oppression" attached to the historic Church, has happened cannot be disputed or undervalued. However, just as priests have unacceptably molested young girls and boys throughout history, this should not be translated into a cognitive notion that Christ or Scripture sanctions sexual abuse. Nor does oppressive behavior among "Christians" mean Christ approves of "oppression." I realize not all will allow one to differentiate the messenger or adherent from the message, but I am asking you to focus on the message first. This is not unprecedented as even Susan B. Anthony drew upon Scripture in her war against oppression. The following table highlights much of the code and philosophy upon which Christians stand.

Be very careful, then, how you live...be filled with the Spirit. Speak to one another with psalms, hymns and spiritual songs. Sing and make music in your heart to the Lord, always giving thanks to God the Father for everything, in the name of our Lord Jesus Christ. Submit to one another out of reverence for Christ (Ephesians 5:15-21).

Wives, submit to your husbands as to the Lord. For the husband is the head of the wife as Christ is the head of the church, his body, of which he is the Savior. Now as the church submits to Christ, so also wives should submit to their husbands in everything (Ephesians 5:22-24).

Husbands, love your wives, just as Christ loved the church and gave himself up for her to make her holy, cleansing her by the washing with water through the word, and to present her to himself as a radiant church without stain or wrinkle or any other blemish, but holy and blameless. In the same way, husbands ought to love their wives as their own bodies. He who loves his wife loves himself. After all, no one ever hated his own body, but he feels and cares for it, just as Christ does for the church – for we are members of his body. For this reason a man will leave his father and mother and be united to his wife, and the two will become one flesh. This is a profound mystery – but I am talking about Christ and the church. However, each one of you also must love his wife as he loves himself, and the wife must respect her husband (Ephesians 5:25-33).

... whether in word or deed, do it all in the name of the Lord Jesus, giving thanks to God the Father through him. Wives, submit to your husbands, as is fitting in the Lord. Husbands, love your wives and do not be harsh with them. Children, obey your parents in everything, for this pleases the Lord. Fathers, do not embitter your children, or they will become discouraged (Colossians 3:18-19).

...each man should have his own wife and each woman her own husband. The husband should fulfill his marital duty to his wife, and likewise the wife to her husband. The wife's body does not belong to her alone but also to her husband. In the same way, the husband's body does not belong to him alone but to his wife. Do not deprive each other except by mutual consent and for a time, so that you may devote yourselves to prayer. Then come together again so that Satan will not tempt you because of your lack of self-control. I [Paul] say this as a concession, not as a command. I wish that all men were as I am. But each man has his own gift from God...Now to the unmarried and the widows I say: It is good for them to stay unmarried, as I am. But if they cannot control themselves, they should marry, for it is better to marry than to burn with passion. To the married I give this command (not I, but the Lord): A wife must not separate from her husband. But if she does, she must remain unmarried or else be reconciled to her husband. And a husband must not divorce his wife (1 Corinthians 7:2-11).

You shall not commit adultery (Exodus 20:14).

Christianity seems to have been especially successful among women. It was often through the wives that it penetrated the upper classes of society in the early history of the Church. Christians believed in the equality of men and women before God, and found in the New Testament commands that husbands should treat their wives with such consideration and love as Christ manifested for his church. Christian teaching about the sanctity of marriage offered a powerful safeguard to married women. The Christian sex ethic differed from the conventional standards of pagan society in that it regarded unchastity in a husband as no less serious a breach of loyalty and trust than unfaithfulness in a wife. The apostle's doctrine that in Christ there is neither male nor female (Galatians 3:28) was not taken to mean a program of political emancipation, which in antiquity would have been unthinkable. The social role of women remained that of the home-maker and wife. At the same time, Christianity cut across ordinary social patterns more deeply than any other religion, and encouraged the notion of the responsibility of individual moral choice in a way that was quite exceptional. Christianity did not give political emancipation to either women or slaves, but it did much to elevate their domestic status by its doctrine that all are created in God's image and all alike are redeemed in Christ; and they therefore must be treated with sovereign respect.[273]

Much has been made of the Scriptural account of Adam's creation first and Eve's creation second, indeed, from Adam's rib. Christian sexists and those wishing to vilify Scripture have both ignored very rational interpretations. The issue is whether this chronology means that women are of less significance. Here Lillie Devreux Blake, one of the contributors to *The Woman's Bible*, argued that applying the order of creation principle, one would have to conclude either that animals are of a higher creation than man or woman is the crowning creation.[274] Phyllis Tribe, plays down the order in creation and argues that male and female were created simultaneously, to relativize sexual differences.[275] In layman's language, Adam was created anatomically matched to Eve. Consider the creation of a door lock. Is there any value in claiming an order of design for the key and the lock? Neither could be made independent from the other. Both have intended functions which are both essential to meet the creator's purpose. We cannot evade the fact that man and woman have the same origin. There are no grounds for a contemptuous attitude to woman. A solitary man was not self-sufficient. The creation of woman was a necessity. Woman is indispensable; she is not an afterthought. From the beginning human beings were created for heterosexual relationship.

According to Brown, woman is not so much the opposite sex or the second sex as the neighboring sex. She is uniquely like man. The whole Genesis account stresses the interdependence and complementarity of man and woman rather than man's independence or woman's inferiority.[276] There is no discrimination in creation. But this does not mean that man and woman are the same. It is just as wrong to insist on the sameness of the sexes or on an androgynous beginning as it is to argue for the superiority of the male. Sexual differentiation existed from the beginning. The Bible neither absolutizes nor relativizes sexual differentiation. Adam and Eve were created in God's image and shared the same place in the created order. They were made of the same essence and created for unity. They resembled each other more than they resembled any other creature, but they were not mirror images of each other. As well as unity there was diversity in their relationship. This differentiation means that the sexes complement and correspond to each other.[277]

Elizabeth Cady Stanton, writing at a time of great ferment about women's rights, explained the equality of the sexes beautifully:

Equal dominion is given to woman over every living thing, but not one word is said giving man dominion over woman. Here is the first title deed to this green earth given alike to the sons and daughters of God.[278]

Everywhere Jesus went he made the headlines. People were prepared to die for him, or plotted to kill him; they rarely remained indifferent. His teaching was radical, his behavior unconventional. He was accused of blasphemy, and of mixing with the wrong people, many of whom were women. These women joined his following, received important teaching, and witnessed miracles. They are visible throughout the gospel records. One piece of evidence that deals a death-blow to the idea that Jesus encouraged women to be passive is an intriguing passage in Luke. Brown records:

After this, Jesus traveled about from one town and village to another, proclaiming the good news of the kingdom of God. The twelve were with him, and also some women who had been cured of evil spirits and diseases: Mary (called Magdalene) from whom seven demons had come out; Joanna the wife of Chuza, the manager of Herod's household; Susanna; and many others. These women were helping to support them out of their own means (Luke 8:1-3). This was revolutionary. Women left their homes, took to the road and followed Jesus. Professor Jeremias, writing about the social position of women in New Testament times, comments that this was 'an unprecedented happening in the history of that time. John the Baptist had already preached to women and baptized them; Jesus, too, knowingly overthrew custom when he allowed women to follow him.'[279]

The total inclusion and equality of women is further witnessed in the Gospel by the fact that women were the first witnesses of the resurrection. They were the first to discover the empty tomb and to hear the news of the resurrection. This is astonishing. According to first-century Judaism, a woman could not act as a witness in a court of law because it was assumed that her evidence was unreliable. Yet women were chosen as the first witnesses to the resurrection, and were told to take the good news of the risen Lord to the other disciples. Along with the other arguments for the historicity of the resurrection, the report about the women points to the reliability of gospel accounts. It would have been quite outside the mindset of a first-century man to invent a story in which women were first on the scene. Such a story would have been beyond his wildest imaginings. According to the Gospels, the male disciples "did not believe the women, because their words seemed to them like non-sense" (Luke 24:11). Mark records that Jesus rebuked the Eleven for "their lack of faith and their stubborn refusal to believe those who had seen him after he had risen" (Mark 16:14).[280]

Mary of Bethany presents another demonstration of the equal status of women in Christ's eyes:

As Jesus and his disciples were on their way, he came to a village where a woman named Martha opened her home to him. She had a sister called Mary, who sat at the Lord's feet listening to what he said. But Martha was distracted by all the preparations that had to be made. She came to him and asked, 'Lord, don't you care that my sister has left me to do the work by myself? Tell her to help me!' (Luke 10:38-42).

We might expect Jesus to have responded by saying, "Mary go and give your sister a hand." Instead, he defended Mary's right to enjoy his teaching. He replied, "Martha, Martha…you are worried and upset about many things, but only one thing is needed. Mary has chosen what is better, and it will not be taken away from her." Here Jesus credited Mary with having "chosen what is better," while he cautioned Martha about her preoccupation with her domestic role. By sitting at Jesus' feet, Mary was adopting what was the traditional male role of a student sitting at the feet of a rabbi. In the case of the Christian gospel, there was no closed circle of men around Jesus. Jesus attitude contrasts with the sentiments of the rabbis. In the Talmud, Rabbi Eliezer declared, "There is no wisdom in a woman except with the distaff." One version adds, "It is better that the words of the Law should be burned, than that they should be given to a woman."[281]

Brown further cited the foot washing incident in arguing against any de-valuing of women in Christian Scripture:

Now one of the Pharisees invited Jesus to have dinner with him, so they went to the Pharisee's house and reclined at the table. When a woman who had lived a sinful life in that town learned that Jesus was eating at the Pharisee's house, she brought an alabaster jar of perfume, and as she stood behind him at his feet weeping, she began to wet his feet with her tears. Then she wiped them with her hair, kissed them and poured perfume on them (Luke 7:36-50).

When the Pharisee who had invited him saw this, he said to himself, "If this man were a prophet, he would know who is touching him and what kind of woman she is – that she is a sinner." Many contemporary women are scandalized, for they interpret this account to mean that Jesus relegated the woman to a servile position. Says Brown, both first- and twentieth-century onlookers have misinterpreted the foot washing. Jesus interprets the encounter for us.[282]

Jesus answered him, "Simon, I have something to tell you." "Tell me, teacher," he said. "Two men owed money to a certain money-lender. One owed him five hundred denarii, and the other fifty. Neither of them had money to pay him back, so he canceled the debts of both. Now which will love him more?" Simon replied, "I suppose the one who had the bigger debt canceled." "You have judged correctly," Jesus said. Then he turned towards the woman and said to Simon, "Do you see this woman? I came into your house. You did not give me any water for my feet, but she wet my feet with her tears and wiped them with her hair. You did not give me a kiss, but this woman, from the time I entered, has not stopped kissing my feet. You did not put oil on my head, but she has put perfume on my feet. Therefore, I tell you, her many sins have been forgiven – for she loved much. But he who has been forgiven little loves little." Then Jesus said to her, "Your sins are forgiven." The other guests began to say among themselves, "Who is this who even forgives sins?" Jesus said to the woman, "Your faith has saved you; go in peace" (Luke 7:40-50).

On the subject of foot washing, it is worth noticing that on the evening before his crucifixion, Jesus himself washed the disciples' feet. The key to the Christian lifestyle is self-giving. Warns Brown, foot washing is to be the model for both *male and female* followers of Jesus.[283] She also refutes the notion of strictly patriarchal inheritance, which is often cited by feminists as an outrage. It is true that the sons usually inherited their father's property as a means of ensuring that each tribe retained its own tribal land. But when a man died without sons, his daughters inherited providing they married within their own tribe so that land was not passed from tribe to tribe (Numbers 27-11; 36:1-12).

The Apostle Mark records the episode in which the woman with the hemorrhage came up behind Jesus in the crowd, touched his cloak and was healed. According to Levitical law this woman was ritually unclean (Luke 15:19-30), and her touch made Jesus ceremonially unclean. But Jesus did not treat her as defiling; he made no attempt to cleanse himself and he did not command her to offer the sacrifice required in Leviticus. Clearly the ceremonial law is fulfilled in Jesus and no longer applies.[284] Thus any apparent discrimination against women before the law of the Old Testament comes to an end with Jesus. He was teaching in the temple courts, with all the people gathered around him, when the teachers of the law and the Pharisees brought in a woman caught in adultery. They made her stand before the group and said to Jesus, "Teacher, this woman was caught in the act of adultery. In the Law Moses commanded us to stone such women. Now what do you say?" They omitted to say that the law of Moses also commanded that the man found sleeping with the woman was to be put to death (Deuteronomy 22:22-24). Jesus replied, "If any one of you is without sin, let him be the first to throw a stone at her." As he stooped down and wrote on the ground the woman's accusers melted away until Jesus and the woman were left alone. Then Jesus asked her, "Woman, where are they? Has no one condemned you?" "No one, sir," she said. "Then neither do I condemn you," Jesus declared. "Go now and leave your life of sin" (John. 8:2-11).

Brown found that Jesus never used women as negative examples, as was so common in rabbinical teaching. He referred to women positively and used illustrations from their everyday lives to teach spiritual truths. A widow repeatedly presenting her case before a judge is powerful reminder of the need for persistence in prayer (Luke 18:1-8); a woman adding yeast to flour to make dough depicts hidden growth of God's kingdom (Matthew 13:33); and a woman rejoicing over the discovery of her lost silver coin is used to explain the rejoicing in heaven over one sinner who repents (Luke 15:8-10). The patient bridesmaids are examples of how to wait for the return of Jesus (Matthew 25:1-13), and the moving story of the widow and her mite illustrates that God assesses gifts not by their size but by the commitment on the part of the giver (Mark 12:41-44). In the Sermon on the Mount, Jesus came down hard on the way women are reduced to sexual objects. In the context of teaching that thoughts are as important as actions he said: "You have heard that it was said, 'Do not commit adultery.' But I tell you that anyone who looks at a woman lustfully has already committed adultery with her in his heart" (Matthew 5:27-28). Mary Evans regards this statement as perhaps the key to understanding Jesus' attitude to women:

Jesus, in contrast to the rabbis, completely dismisses the suggestion that lust is inevitable. He does not warn his followers against looking at a woman, but against doing so with lust. Women are to be recognized as subjects in their own right, as fellow human beings, fellow disciples, and not just the objects of men's desires.[285]

With Jesus self-control comes as a gift with His daily grace and the faithfulness of continuous prayer. Like the rabbis above, secular humanists in the philosophical heritage of Margaret Sanger and Alfred Kinsey concede the inevitability of the animal sex drive and its pivotal force in civilization. Sanger's life contention was that encouragement of the libido through positive, free, adulterous and homosexual behavior was key to happiness and that containment of the biological consequences by technology was worth the cost. There is no place for such a concession in Christianity.

Jesus' teaching on marriage and divorce was also original, and must have sounded most unusual to his first century hearers. In contrast to the rabbis, who allowed only the husband to divorce, Jesus put both partners on the same footing (Mark 10:1-12). He also made it clear that the only acceptable reasons for divorce are marital unfaithfulness and abandonment by an unbelieving spouse (Matthew 19:3-8). And unfaithfulness was already covered under the commandment to not commit adultery (Exodus 20:14). Many fundamentalist orthodox churches claiming a hard line on homosexuality would be well served to measure their hypocrisy in upholding unscriptural policies on divorce and remarriage. Much more will be said on Christian sexual relations and marriage in Chapters 5 and 8; however, this next and last section of Chapter 4 serves to acknowledge a self-made cancer wreaking havoc within the Church body.

One of the goals of this book is to equip the reader to distinguish God-inspired Christians from "cultural" Christians, contemporary Pharisees, or indeed religious subversives. Once again the central issue is one of choice, primarily between two paradigms of values and philosophy. It is the message of the Bible that the reader should focus on in this decision. The historical conduct of the Church adherents should be a secondary consideration. Christian history is rich with examples of God raising individuals to rebuke and restore His faithful. The following describes a few examples.

Christian Hypocrisy: A Self-made Cancer

In the early nineteenth century, Jeremy Bentham took delight in the contrast between the Son of Man who had no where to lay his head, and the fat and corrupt Anglican dean or prependary with his enormous state revenues:

In the sight of Jesus, if any credit be due to Gospel history, all men are equal. The claim of the poor was, in the eyes of Jesus, superior to that of the rich. Not so in the eyes of Dean Andrews...In his stall at Canterbury, chief of a set of idlers, paid for doing nothing under the name of Prebendaries...To the sportive genius of the Receiver of the Holy Ghost,...by this Dignitary of the Daughter church...men who are neither so rich, nor so wedded to wine as to loath all cheaper liquors will be seen marked out as the objects of scorn, and their health as an object of just regard, under the name of Ale-drinkers….[286]

Experiences will vary from individual to individual, but anti-Christian fears and criticism are too often rooted in painful or hypocritical encounters with so-called "Christians." Sometimes these Christians are such in name only. Often the term "cultural Christian" best embodies how a third party sees the conduct. Alfred Kinsey's father's religiosity and treatment of his son and wife offers an example of Christian culture without the Holy Spirit. Moreover, the number of unrepentant lay and ordained "proclaimed" Christians acting in blatant contradiction to Scripture stand as a formidable counter-witness to the Gospel. Whether in divorce, child abuse, fraud or whatever, their unholy actions defile God and discredit His Church and His Word.

I once overheard a man cursing at the photocopier. Using the Lord's name in vain momentarily relieved his frustration. Most of us have in a lifetime committed a similar offense in a fit of pain or rage. The astonishing thing about this instance is that the person felt nothing wrong and yet claimed he was Christian. I asked, "Do you know what you just said?" "No, what?" he replied. "You just used the Lord's name in vain?" "Really, I didn't even notice." "I recommend you stop saying that, if you are a Christian. It's against Scripture and it can't be helping." He was more embarrassed for apparently offending my religious "space" then in accountability before God.

You may well think my actions invaded his space, but I was offended. However, the point is that the name of Jesus Christ meant nothing to this person, yet he felt he was a breathing, walking Christian. This day and age the term Christian is too diverse to have accurate meaning in a universal sense; spanning "Gnostics" to "all inclusive liberals" to "cultic fundamentalists" and so on.

As recorded by the early Christian apologists and Gospel writers, the need for discernment and testing of the authenticity of Christ's presence in individuals (clergy or lay), groups, churches, denominations and organizations is as old as the Church itself. Apostle Matthew records Jesus saying:

Enter through the narrow gate. For wide is the gate and broad is the road that leads to destruction, and many enter through it. But small is the gate and narrow the road that leads to life, and only a few find it. Watch out for false prophets. They come in sheep's clothing, but inwardly they are ferocious wolves. By their fruit you shall recognize them...Not everyone who says to me, 'Lord, Lord,' will enter the kingdom of heaven, but only he who does the will of my Father who is in heaven. Many will say on that day, 'Lord, Lord,' did we not prophesy in your name, and in your name drive out demons and perform many miracles? Then I will tell them plainly, 'I never knew you. Away from me you evildoers!' (Matthew 7:13-23).

Jesus Christ detested the pretense of piety during His life. It is unlikely He is more patient with hypocrisy now. That the Church has been guilty of manifest hypocrisy now and in the past is clear. However, just as a poorly built house could be the result of either poor design or faulty construction, it is important to determine whether the source of the hypocrisy is faulty Scripture or the willful decisions and actions of adherents. The Christian sanction of African slavery will serve to illustrate the designer-builder paradigm and the need to carefully assign responsibility appropriately where it is due – man or Scripture.

Consider the historic fact of slavery and how it was ended. Fredric Douglas wrote:

I assert most unhesitatingly, that the religion of the South is a mere covering for the most horrid crimes – a justifier of the most appalling barbarity, a sanctifier of the most hateful frauds, and a dark shelter under which the darkest, foulest, grossest and most infernal deeds of slaveholders find the strongest protection. Were I again reduced to the chains of slavery, next to that enslavement, I should regard being the slave of a religious master the greatest calamity that could befall me...I...hate the corrupt, slaveholding, women-whipping, cradle-plundering, partial and hypocritical Christianity of this land.[287]

In his letter to Colossians, Paul outlined appropriate conduct between slave and master:

Slaves, obey your earthly masters in everything; and do it, not only when their eye is on you and win their favor, but with sincerity of heart and reverence for the Lord... anyone who does wrong will be repaid for his wrong, and there is not favoritism. Masters, provide your slaves with what is right and fair, because you know you also have a Master in heaven (Colossians 3: 22-25, 4:1).

To the Ephesians he wrote:

Slaves, obey your earthly masters with respect and fear, and with sincerity of heart. Just as you would obey Christ...And masters, treat your slaves in the same way. Do not threaten them, since you know that he who is both their Master and yours is in heaven, and there is no favoritism with Him (6: 5-9).

Here the equal value of the slave in Christ's eyes is clear, not to mention the higher dictate to love one another and to treat all, including enemies in a Christ-like manner.

In 1784 Wilberforce, at age twenty-five, became converted to Evangelical Christianity. While on tour in Europe, he saw in the luggage of a traveling companion, William Law's book, *A Serious Call to a Devout and Holy Life*. He asked his friend, "What is this?" and received the answer, "One of the best books ever written."[288] After reading the book, he joined a form of Protestantism which had emerged in Britain in the late 1780s. The conversion of John Wesley in 1738 is often regarded as the beginning of the movement, which insisted on rigorous standards of personal conduct, frequent examination of conscience, the infallibility of the Bible, detailed Bible study and lay activity. Most unwelcome in Church of England pulpits, Wesley was forced to preach out of doors and to eventually develop an organization of his own.

As a result of this conversion, Wilberforce became interested in social reform and was eventually approached to use his power as an MP to bring an end to the slave trade. The Society of Friends in Britain had helped form the Society for the Abolition of the Slave Trade. Of the twelve members on the committee nine were

Quakers (Christians). As a member of the Evangelical movement, Wilberforce was sympathetic to the cause. Soon he was seen as one of the leaders of the anti-slave trade movement. When he presented his first bill to abolish the slave trade in 1791 it was easily defeated by 163 votes to 88. He continued to fight for an end to slavery. William Wilberforce died on 29 July, 1833. One month later, Parliament passed the Slavery Abolition Act that gave all slaves in the British Empire their freedom.

What is the truth? The sin and hypocrisy Fredric Douglas observed still stands as historic fact. On the other hand, one observes a Christian revival which brought about conversions (including Wilberforce) and a revived enthusiasm to do God's work. Wilberforce, the Society for the Abolition of the Slave Trade and the Evangelical Movement in Britain helped put an end to slavery.

One of two brothers accused of killing a gay couple in July 1999, told a newspaper he shot the men because he believed their homosexuality violated God's law. "I'm not guilty of murder, I'm guilty of obeying the laws of the creator," Benjamin Matthew Williams, 31, told *The Sacramento Bee* in a jailhouse interview "Suspect in slayings cites 'creators law.'"[289] We don't know if this man claimed to be a Christian. If Williams is acting in God's will, we need to discover what god. Jesus Christ makes no provision for such murder? This man's actions are sinful in a double-deed manner. First, the worst evil is perpetrated upon the gay couple. Second, the inappropriate association of the murder to fulfilling God's will, serves to smear all religions and Christianity in particular, building greater distrust in the non-believer. The importance of separating "false prophets" (false spirits) from the genuine is critical to finding Christ's light within the breadth of doctrines and number of Christian denominations.

Nowhere was the contrast between the misconduct of the church and the will of God more evident than in the matter of the translation of the Bible into English for lay people in the 16th century. Here the Church is represented by Cardinal Wolsey and the true representative of the "will of God" is personified in an obstinate translator, William Tyndale. At the heart of the crisis was a simple question, What does the Bible say? For the first time in more than a thousand years, a majority of people gained the opportunity to read the Bible and see for themselves. J. F. Mozley, recorded a description of Tyndale in his 1937 biography:

Such was the power of his doctrine and the sincerity of his life, that during the time of his imprisonment, which endured a year and a half, he converted his keeper, the keeper's daughter, and others of his household. Also the rest that were with Tyndale conversant in the castle, reported of him, that if he were not a good Christian man, they could not tell whom they might take to be one.[290]

In Tyndale's last letter to his friend, John Frith, written a few months before he was strangled and burned at the stake, the translator had this advice:

Fear not men that threat, nor trust men that speak fair: but trust him that is true of promise, and able to make his word good. Your cause is Christ's gospel, a light that must be fed with the blood of faith. The lamp must be dressed and snuffed daily, and that oil poured in every evening and morning, that the light go not out.[291]

Before his death in 1536, he cried out: "Lord! Open the King of England's eyes."[292] Within one year of Tyndale's death Henry VIII granted licenses for the production of Bibles. Within two years, the decision was taken that every parish church in England make a copy of the Bible available for public reading.

Hypocrisy has never characterized the Lord's will and in the area of sexual ethics the double-standard within the "church fold" only weakens our witness. Many Christians seem to be saying that the world has absolutely nothing to teach them. Regarding homosexuality, we believe that any way of life that accepts or encourages sexual relations for pleasure or personal satisfaction alone turns away from the disciplined community that marriage is intended to engender and foster. Rightly, many outsiders looking in see our rigid application of Scripture against homosexuality and have to wonder what is different about divorce, contraception and for some abortion. Religious communities that have in recent decades winked at promiscuity (even among clergy), that have solemnly repeated marriage vows that their own congregations do not take seriously, and that have failed to concern themselves with the devastating effects of divorce upon children cannot with integrity condemn homosexual behavior unless they are also willing to reassert the heterosexual norm more believably and effectively in their pastoral care. In other words, those determined to resist the gay and lesbian movement must be equally concerned for the renewal of integrity, in teaching and practice, regarding "traditional sexual ethics."[293]

Here in a direct challenge to Christians, *The Nation*, a journal for mostly gay readers, asserts (May 3, 1993):

All the crosscurrents of present-day liberation struggles are subsumed in the gay struggle. The gay movement is in some ways similar to the movement that other communities have experienced in the nation's past, but it is also something more, because sexual identity is in crisis throughout the population, and gay people – at once the most conspicuous subjects and objects of the crisis – have been forced to invent a complete cosmology to grasp it. No one says the changes will come easily. But it's just possible that a small and despised sexual minority will change America forever.[294]

This is fair warning. However, it is just as possible that a small and despised group of God-fearing Christians may be all that is needed to uphold the lamp of light showing the path to a better Canadian and American society. God willing! Anita Bryant describes well the Christian calling:

Neutrality is our worst enemy. Two major mistakes can be made during a lifetime. One is to make the wrong decision and the other is to make no decision. Some wish to be neither fish nor fowl. They just float along with the tide. To take sides means to have enemies and friends. To not take sides means a lack of respect from all sides. Neutrality is not in the vocabulary of a Christian. You are for everything God is. You are against everything He declares displeasure with in His Word.[295]

PART THREE

UNORTHODOX CHRISTIANITY: THE "COMPROMISE" PARADIGM

The well-nigh total victory, within the universities and among the chattering classes, of the gay movement…make it extraordinarily difficult to speak what many homosexuals… still believe to be the truth: that the man who is sexually attracted only to those of his own sex suffers from an unfortunate…condition from which he deserves pity…That gays today, full of hubris at the success…can spare no sympathy for 'wavering' children is understandable. Having persuaded themselves that gay and straight are co-equal, it would be quite inconsistent to deplore the fact that some young people will move into the gay life when they might happily live straight. It is astonishing, however, that heterosexuals – few of whom actually believe one orientation is as good as another – contentedly accept changes in society that are likely to have that result.[1]

E.L. Pattulo

…having known many homosexuals personally, and having done a good deal of reading on the subject, I do not doubt that some young boys are so driven by the lust for other men, and so erotically repelled by women, that for all practical purposes the only choice they have is between homosexuality and chastity. Nor do I doubt that a biological or genetic factor is at work here. Of course it does not follow from this that homosexuality is healthy; after all, many disabilities, diseases, and self-destructive tendencies are genetically transmitted. Still less does it follow that there is no room for free will, as witness the many people (including those with powerful homosexual inclinations) who have successfully struggled against inborn predispositions.

Yet if I do not doubt that some young boys are in effect doomed from the beginning to a choice between homosexuality and chastity, neither do I doubt that other young boys are what E.L. Pattullo has characterized as 'waverers' who are capable of going either way. They can yield to the temptation of homosexuality if they are encouraged or seduced into it…Such boys, however, are no longer helped by the world around them to resist the homosexual temptation and to overcome their fears of a normal life. They are instead being abandoned to the ministrations of a culture that not only legitimizes homosexuality but glorifies and glamorizes it, even to the point of representing those who die of AIDS as martyrs and heroes and even as angels.[2]

Norman Podhoretz

CHAPTER FIVE

DEBUNKING GAY AND PRO-GAY CHRISTIAN THEOLOGY

Being gay, lesbian or bisexual is a normal and healthy way to be. It's one more part of who you are – like being tall or short, black or white, Asian or Native, left-handed or right-handed. It takes time to know who you are. It's okay to be confused, it's okay to be unsure whether you're gay or straight and it's okay to take your time figuring it out. There's no need to rush....At some point, almost everybody gets a 'crush' on someone of the same sex...Almost everybody's 'best friend' is of the same sex. This doesn't mean that you are gay, lesbian or bisexual as other feelings are involved than just these. One or two sexual experiences with someone of the same sex may not mean you're gay, either – just as one or two sexual experiences with someone of the opposite sex may not mean you're straight....Our sexuality develops over time. Don't worry if you aren't sure. The teen years are a time of figuring out what works for you and crushes and experimentation are often part of that. Over time, you'll find that you're drawn mostly to men or to women – or to both – and you'll know then....Telling friends and family AT THIS POINT is premature. This is not to suggest being gay, lesbian or bisexual is something to be ashamed of and to hide (it isn't) but our society doesn't really understand homosexuality and, right now, you probably don't need the hassle of dealing with any negative stuff that telling might bring.

Think of it as a range or 'sexual continuum'...Wherever you are on that continuum, you've got plenty of company....Ann Landers, the advice columnist, wrote: 'It never ceases to amaze me that in this day and age, so many people fail to understand that homosexuality is not a lifestyle that is chosen. That 'choice' was made at birth.'...If you're gay, lesbian or bisexual, you're going to run into prejudice. Our society has a 'heterosexual assumption.' We're taught – by our families, our schools, our religions and the media – to assume that everyone is straight and we're often influenced to discriminate against those who aren't. That 'assumption' has begun to change only recently.

– 'BE YOURSELF: Q & As for Gay, Lesbian, Two-spirited and Bisexual Alberta Youth' [a pamphlet by Planned Parenthood Alberta and PFLAG, referred to in the CBCA presentation on homosexuality to my daughter's Grade 10 class.]

God's Truth

In 1998, 54 per cent of Americans believed homosexuality to be a sin, and even more – 59 per cent – believed it to be morally wrong; 44 per cent believed that homosexual relations between consenting adults should be illegal.[1] For orthodox Christians the notion (as declared above by PFLAG and CBCA) that one can find his or her individual comfort zone along a self-declared continuum of sexual preference and behavior, is patently unscriptural. Moreover, professing Christians who advocate an "all-inclusive" theology are seen by the orthodox as compromised at best, otherwise fully deceived. Whether the "halfway" application of Scripture or "full" rejection of the Word (Bible) happens by national denominational decree, presbytery plebiscite, or some decentralized and individual parish wish, makes little difference. The bending of God's truth or rejection of His Word creates a hot bed for growing falsehoods and opportunity for further misinterpretation of Scripture.

Much is at stake here. The observance of spiritual compromise in one of His Churches, literally made Jesus sick:

I know your deeds, that you are neither cold nor hot. I wish you were either one or the other! So, because you are lukewarm – neither hot nor cold – I am about to spit you out of my mouth...you do not realize that you are wretched, pitiful, poor, blind and naked. I counsel you to buy from me... salve to put on your eyes, so you can see (Revelation 3:15-18).

Some versions of Revelation 3:15 use "spew" in place of spit – literally to vomit. Jesus declared that the church in Laodicea supplied neither healing for the spiritually sick nor refreshment for the spiritually weary. Their compromised teachings lead Him to want to throw-up. Although they thought of themselves as Christians and their congregation as blessed, Jesus had not entered their church in Spirit. Addressing the self-deluded members of the church, Christ called:

Here I am! I stand at the door and knock. If anyone hears my voice and opens the door, I will come in...

Secular readers put aside your worldview while reading the next two chapters. The premise of these chapters is that we are all professed Christians wishing to serve God's will. And given our commitment to Christ, we seek a legitimate interpretation of Scripture. What is at issue in this chapter is the Scriptural truth. Here, the "Christian" reader faces the difficult challenge of deciding which churches bring truth and which, like the church at Laodicea, offer nothing spiritually. In a world filled with counterfeit faiths only the truth brings spiritual life; untruth brings death. Although the Laodicean congregation was happy, full of pride, and likely flourishing, membership in the church put the individual's salvation at risk.

Looking back over more than forty years of debate on homosexual issues in the predominantly heterosexual Christian Church, one finds three general positions adopted. The orthodox position, states that homosexual acts defile God and His creation. Adherents proclaim that Scripture is unequivocal in condemnation of homosexual fantasies and activities. On the other hand, the pro-gay position divides into two camps. One camp, the conservative side of so-called "liberal" Christians, contends that Scripture has been wrongly interpreted on issues of homosexuality all these years, and therefore theology should be revised to affirm homosexual relationships as blessed within God's design. To put forth its case, this group usually argues that the Bible is not fully God's Word and that key verses are no longer valid in light of postmodern wisdom. In *What the Bible Really Says About Homosexuality,* Danial A. Helminiak, Ph.D., outlines this postmodern-liberal position:

We now know that homosexuality is a core aspect of the personality, probably fixed by early childhood, biologically based, and affecting a significant portion of the population in virtually every known culture. There is no convincing evidence that sexual orientation can be changed, and there is no evidence whatsoever that homosexuality is in any way pathological....in biblical times there was no elaborated understanding of homosexuality as a sexual orientation....Our question today is about people and their relationships, not simply about sex acts...Our question is about spontaneous affection for people of the same sex and about the ethical possibility of expressing that affection in loving relationships. Because this was not a question in the minds of the biblical authors, we cannot expect the Bible to give an answer.[2]

Call this first "liberal" group the "compromised." The second and more radical pro-gay camp advocates the full revamping of traditional Christian theology. In essence these groups advance many of the Gnostic heresies recorded by the first and second century Christian apologists. Best typified in the articulations of Episcopal Bishop John Shelby Spong, these radicals advocate unfettered acceptance of homosexuality in a revised theology, which rejects among other things the virgin birth, Christ's divinity, the bodily resurrection of Christ, and the significance of His atoning sacrifice. Drawing virtually the same conclusions as Spong, under the guise of a "quest for the historical Jesus," another radical pro-gay organization, the Jesus Seminar, has concluded that at least 75 per cent of New Testament sayings of Christ are false. Spong gives us a glimpse of the radical new pro-gay Christianity:

To build a new basis for ethics, we must learn to look in a different place. We look, I believe, not outside of life for some external and objective authenticating authority, but rather at the very center and core of our humanity. We can get to that core by asking a totally different series of questions. These are not God questions but human questions, such as: What gives us life? What lifts us into wholeness? What enhances our being? What introduces us to transcendence? What calls us beyond our limits? What do we ultimately value? These questions will force us to search, not the empty heavens, but the depths of our own being for answers....Morality, in any area of life, will not be achieved by threats and negativity. The repression of sexual energy, for example, which marked traditional ethics for so long, did not lead to the fullness of life. It only created the backlash of an uninhibited exercise of sexual energy, which was also destructive to our essential humanity. When the value of human sexuality is repressed, it returns as pornography. When we try to take sex away from love, we succeed only in taking love away from sex.[3]

The conclusion of this humanistic search for ethical norms is that something like ethical objectivity begins to emerge. There is an 'objective' wrongness to seeking cause or to increase the pain of another life....So the freedom to be myself is in dialogue with the need to enhance the being of others....Such virtues do not come, however, from an external God. They come, rather, from our human depths, where I suggest the meaning of God must finally be sought. A second ultimate but still human value emerges upon the heels of this freedom. It is the objective value of knowledge.[4] *...When a homosexual orientation is revealed by the development of the science of the brain and its neurochemical processes to be a normal part of the sexual spectrum of human life, a given and not a chosen way of life, then it becomes inhumane to use a person's sexual orientation as the basis for a continuing prejudice. Therefore, the kind of judgment that compromises the worth and well-being of a homosexual person or places limits on the opportunities of that person becomes the activity of ignorance. Since that is so, then a third ultimate human value emerges. It is objectively wrong to act in such a way....*[5]

Call this second radically "liberal" group the "fully deceived." Along with these two groups of pro-gay Christians is another group of mostly gay Christians. These gays and lesbians have chosen to join mostly homosexual congregations in relatively new churches espousing a hybrid mix of Christian tenets, gay affirmations and self-sustaining ideologies. The Metropolitan Community Church (MMC) is representative of religious institutions developed specifically to suit the GBLTQ Community.

Beset by this smorgasbord of orthodox, pro-gay and gay theologies, and wanting to come out from twenty-three years of genuine homosexuality, Ann Phillips describes her difficulties in finding and following the *true* path. Over several months she had found a multitude of books, organizations and even pastors who told her that homosexuality was acceptable for a Christian. "It simply isn't sin," they told her. "God made you gay, and he doesn't make mistakes." Phillips recalled her reaction:

Try as I might, I was never satisfied with their answers. The attitudes, activities and rhetoric of the pro-gay theology movement never seemed to line up with what I was reading in Scripture and hearing in my heart. So many of their positions seemed to be motivated by self-interest and anger. No one appeared to be particularly concerned that they or anyone else move closer to Christ. The focus was all about getting our acceptance and affirmation of our homosexuality from the church, regardless of cost...

Of course, I also read books and listened to pastors on the other side who said the life I had lived for almost twenty-three years was sinful and had to stop. Their words terrified me. In response it seemed as though God had hunted me down, and I was backed into a corner. Every fiber of my being had cried out to know the truth, but who could I believe when even the church seemed to disagree? The pressure I felt within me was incredible and unbearable...

People all around me were saying things like, 'I didn't ask to be gay' and 'I was born this way.' These were statements I had made all my adult life. Then a woman seated right next to me made another comment I'd said many times, 'And no one can change me.'

Within my mind I heard these words crystal clear: But God can do anything. There it was again God's truth. He had a way out for me even if I couldn't imagine how this was possible. As much as I couldn't face leaving my partner and my gay identity there was no alternative as far as I could see.[6]

The importance of differentiating between truth and counterfeit is evident in specific references to "the truth," made some 186 times in the New Testament alone. This matter of "the truth" must be seen in the context of a crucial spiritual battle for one's mind. As Richard Strauss points out:

Man's will can only choose what his mind has first grasped. Freedom of choice is restricted to the information one has in his mind. So if our minds are shielded from the truth of the Gospel, this effectively keeps us from getting to know God and from fulfilling God's purpose for creating each of us.[7]

To those who believed in Him, Jesus said:

If you hold to my teaching, you are really my disciples. Then you will know the truth, and the truth will set you free (John 3:32).

The truth Jesus Christ is referring to is not philosophical truth or scholarly truth in the sense of freedom from temporal ignorance; but rather He is speaking of the truth that leads to salvation – the truth that leads to freedom from the consequences of sin. Here Jesus reveals a central Christian tenet – we cannot break free from sin by our own strength:

I tell you the truth, everyone who sins is a slave to sin. Now a slave has no permanent place in the family, but a son belongs to it for ever. So if the Son sets you free, you will be free indeed (John 3:34).

One should bear in mind that moral and spiritual truth is as much truth as mathematical, scientific, and historical truth; and it is all equally "intellectual." And Christians cannot talk of the truth apart from the Gospel of Jesus Christ. As important, Christians cannot see, nor understand the truth apart from the infilling of the Holy Spirit. Christ says:

But I tell you the truth: It is for your good that I am going away. Unless I go away, the Counselor will not come to you; but if I go, I will send Him to you. When He comes, He will convict the world of guilt in regard to sin and...when He the Spirit of truth comes, he will guide you into all truth (John 16:7).

Charging Timothy with spreading "the truth," the Apostle Paul advises:

All Scripture is useful for teaching, rebuking, correcting and training in righteousness, so that the man of God may be thoroughly equipped for every good work (2 Timothy 3:16-17). In the presence of God and of Christ Jesus, who will judge the living and the dead, and in view of His appearing and His kingdom, I give you this charge: Preach the Word; be prepared in season and out of season; correct, rebuke and encourage – with great patience and careful instruction. For the time will come when men will not put up with sound doctrine. Instead, to suit their own desires, they will gather around them a great number of teachers to say what their itching ears want to hear. They will turn their ears away from the truth and turn aside to myths (2 Timothy 4:1-4).

As he observed the libertine practices of Gnostics (described in Chapter 4) the Apostle John wrote to first century Christians with the purpose of exposing false doctrines:

Dear friends, do not believe every spirit, but test the spirits to see whether they are from God, because many false prophets have gone out into the world. This is how you can recognize the spirit of God: Every spirit that acknowledges that Jesus Christ has come in the flesh is from God, but every spirit that does not acknowledge Jesus is not from God. This is the spirit of the antichrist, which you have heard is coming and even now is already in the world. You, dear children, are from God and have overcome them, because the one who is in you is greater than the one who is in the world. They are from the world and therefore speak from the viewpoint of the world, and the world listens to them. We are from God, and whoever knows God listens to us; but whoever is not from God does not listen to us. This is how we recognize the Spirit of truth and the spirit of falsehood" (1 John 4:1-6).

The danger from deception in the spiritual realm needs still further clarification. In the Book of Matthew, Christ warns of the many who will think they are safe, only to find they have been mistaken:

Many will say to me on that day, 'Lord, Lord, did we not prophesy in your name, and in your name drive out demons and perform many miracles?' Then I will tell them plainly, 'I never knew you. Away from me, you evildoers!' (Matthew 7:13-23).

In highlighting the issue of the right "Spirit," Emil Brunner comments on ignoring the Law and the inerrancy of the Bible:

The Gospel came into the world as the obedience-commanding message of the dominion of God. But the human heart with its egoistic desire for freedom asserts itself everywhere….The individualistic enthusiast….insists that everything depends on the free rule of the Spirit. 'The Spirit bloweth where it listeth' – hence there is nothing fixed, nothing divinely given, no rule and authority, no established doctrine and institution. Nothing is binding but the free, ruling Spirit of God, who enlightens everyone, when and how He pleases. This enlightening through the Spirit takes place, according to this point of view, from moment to moment, without established rules, without being bound to the fixed, given Word or to historical facts.[8]

A common sentiment is that, since God's ideal cannot always be achieved in the present sinful world, concessions or exceptions must be made in line with man's circumstances and proclivities. If a man finds himself possessed of a homosexual passion, is there not some appropriate – albeit less than ideal – sense in which he can exercise it. Must he be frustrated with unfulfilled physical desires, or is there a possible exception that can be granted? James P. Hanigan argued homosexuals should not be turned away to burn in unrighteous sexual passion. Is the only choice Christian sexual ethics can offer the choice to burn with unfulfilled desire? He says, "Something better than 'You are a sinner; repent,' or 'Tough luck; that's the way things are,' or 'Resign yourself to a life of sexual abstinence,' or 'The rules do not apply to you,' has to be said."[9]

Yet how much of this so-called "desire" is truly Spirit inspired. What does God say to: the young Christian separated from his or her spouse by necessities such as years of imprisonment, lengthy war or a distant career posting; the person living a vowed celibate life; the person married to a spouse who is physically or mentally so ill that no hope of recovery and no normal marital relationship is possible? There is no provision made for temptations of the flesh in these situations, so why should homosexuality be granted unfettered sexual expression? The rub of the matter as Hanigan, himself proclaims is this:

And if there are other choices open to homosexuals, why should not these options be available to heterosexuals as well? Thus, homosexuality may well serve as the 'test-case' of Christian sexual ethics since it poses the clearest challenge to the universal and evangelical character of that ethic.[10]

What if a man cannot quell a burning desire for a daughter or son? What of a burning desire between sisters? The assumption underlying questions such as Hanigan's, is that man's imperfections and personal limitations call for lowering of God's requirements; it is assumed that secondary moral demands are suitable enough in Christian ethics when circumstances beyond an individual's control prevent him from full obedience to God's revealed will. This indicates a critical failure to understand the nature of God, whose eyes are too pure to approve evil and who cannot look on wickedness with favor (Habakkuk 1:13). God demands throughout the Bible that men be holy in all of their behavior: "You shall be holy, for I am holy" (Leviticus 11:44, Peter 1:1). Christ settles for no lowering of this unqualified standard of holiness, no rationalizations, no exceptions to God's high demand: "You are to be perfect, even as your heavenly Father is perfect" (Matthew 5:48).[11]

Another frequent polemic maintains that those who criticize homosexuality are guilty of having a judgmental attitude. It has been said that "surely it is neither the Christian's responsibility nor prerogative to judge other people's lifestyles." One self-professed "evangelical" study of homosexuality goes so far as to accuse its opponents of false witness and blasphemy against the Holy Spirit! If meant to be taken seriously, these are misguided remarks. What advice do these so-called pro-gay, non-judgmental Christians offer AIDS activists like Larry Kramer? What Spirit of truth has he trespassed, when he says the following:

We brought AIDS upon ourselves by a way of living that welcomed it. You cannot F— —indiscriminately with multiple partners, who are also doing the same, without spreading disease...We have made sex the cornerstone of gay liberation and gay culture, and it has killed us.[12]

What cognitive process chooses to overlook the impact of AIDS on both straight and gay free love lifestyles and asserts: Who are we to judge? What Spirit of truth is served by allowing pro-gay agencies to tell our children homosexuality is healthy, indeed, a blessed lifestyle? The pagan Larry Kramer has shown more integrity and honesty in facing the following facts on gay lifestyle:

A study by Cameron (1992) of 16 gay publications over an 11 year period (1981-92) found that the median age of death was only 39. Excluding AIDS deaths improved the picture to a small degree, and for non-AIDS deaths the median age was 42.

A male homosexual has as much as a 50 per cent chance of acquiring HIV by middle age. In 1995, AIDS was the leading cause of death among all Americans aged 25 to 44, and homosexual men, who make up less than two per cent of the population, accounted for 50 per cent of all new AIDS cases in 1995 and 1996...Even Sullivan agrees. Consider what he wrote in The New York Times Magazine: 'Suddenly, it seemed, as my 20s merged into my 30s, everyone was infected'...Sullivan has 'lost friend after friend' in 'a health crisis as profound as any in modern American history.' Male homosexuals are 'a group of men who have witnessed a scale of loss historically visited upon war generations.' 'What AIDS has done to homosexuals is a 'horror.' A 'veil of terror,' and a 'natural calamity.' Such apocalyptic language is not invoked because AIDS is killing lots of 73-year-old men; it is because, as Sullivan wrote, AIDS is 'visiting death upon so many, so young.'[13]

Paul Cameron...I sampled over 6,500 obituaries in 18 different homosexual journals. Sullivan was a tad dishonest when he said, 'As any student of these papers knows, the obit sections – which scarcely existed before AIDS – are primarily ways to commemorate openly gay people who have died early deaths.' Not only were many old homosexuals' deaths recorded in these obits, but a considerable number of deaths of gays who were married to women were also recorded. I also reviewed a large number of studies of those engaging in homosexuality going back to 1858 and found a similar paucity of old homosexuals in just every such study. Additional supportive information about my findings can be found in the University of Chicago's 'definitive' sex survey of Americans. While 2.9 per cent of men aged 18-29 and 4.2 per cent of men aged 30-39 claimed that they were bisexual or homosexual, for those aged 40-49 the proportion declined to 2.2 per cent, and for those 50-59 it declined to 0.5 per cent. Another study found that 75 per cent of gays in Colorado who got HIV tests were aged 39 or younger and only one per cent of gays getting tested were old....Why do so few old gays show up in these studies? The answer seems to be because not very many gays become old.[14]

To be true to God and His Word we cannot be uncritical of or neutral toward those things Scripture prohibits. People must be warned against attitudes and behaviors that are displeasing to a holy God. Those who have been redeemed by the mercy of God are called to conscious separation from sin and emulation of God's character. This would be impossible without identifying some things as sinful and ungodly – which is patently judgmental. The fact is that Scripture does not forbid judging in itself, but judging which is ill-motivated, hasty, unfair, or according to unbiblical standards. Indeed, God in His Word requires us to judge actions (Matthew 7:15-23, John 7:24) and to reprove the unfruitful works of darkness (Ephesians 5:11, Timothy 5:20, 4:2, Titus 1:13; 2:15) – but without partiality (1 Timothy 5:21), hypocrisy (Matthew 7:1-5), or attempting to determine inward matters pertaining to the individual's heart (1 Samuel 16:7). It is the "spirit of this age" that demands the general suppression of discernment, encourages unprincipled tolerance, and criticizes anyone who would dare to criticize. The Holy Spirit exhorts us to "prove all things; hold fast that which is good; abstain from every form of evil (Ezekiel 11:19-20, Romans 3:31, 6:1-7:6, 8:1-4, 2 Corinthians 5:14-15, Titus 2:11-14).

In the following sections of this chapter we will weigh interpretations from orthodox and liberal perspectives. Furthermore, we will study the initiatives to find a different Jesus and to invent a new Christianity.

Bailey's Pervert – The False Homosexual

A piece in the British journal Gay Times announced that 'Sex between gay men and lesbians is coming out of the closet' ...Now people talk openly of their opposite-sex-same-sexuality lovers and at the party after the SM Pride March a gay man and a lesbian had sex on the dance floor, but it wasn't heterosexuality. 'You can tell.' As critic Jo Eadie points out, what 'you can tell' here above all is that bisexuality is being edited out of consciousness, or disavowed. 'Opposite-sex-same-sexuality' enshrines 'gay' and 'lesbian' as the real, identifying, and in this gay context reassuring sexualities of the participants. That 'it wasn't heterosexuality,' and that 'you' (the insider) can know that and 'tell' it, whether to yourself or to like-minded others, is presented as a boundary-keeping consideration, a border guard against permeable and politically dangerous transgression.[15]

What about the famous rallying cry "Feminism is a theory, lesbianism is a practice?" These days the tendency of shifting sexual preferences manifests itself in a label like "L.U.G.," for "Lesbian Until Graduation." The description that implies "She was oh-so-close with her dorm-mates," magazine *10 Per cent* comments sardonically of the typical L.U.G., "But that was then, and this is...adulthood." If women who are frequently attracted to men and frequently have sex with them are "lesbians," then it becomes quite clear that, in these women's eyes at least, "lesbian" is a cultural and political designation rather than – exclusively – a narrowly drawn sexual one. "Our clumsy categories of gay, bisexual and straight are political divisions, primarily, much more than descriptive categories."[16] Elizabeth Reba Weise said as much at a National Bisexual Conference in 1990, where she was "a bit uncomfortable" declaring herself a bisexual. "The label doesn't seem as solid as the lesbian label. Because to declare yourself bisexual is to declare, really, that labels don't mean anything. So it seems paradoxical to declare this as an identity."[17]

When Derrick S. Bailey published *Homosexuality and the Western Christian Tradition*, in 1955, the notion of the bisexual was classified as "very doubtful," indeed; the idea of a continuum of sexual orientation, as developed by Alfred Kinsey, was problematic to his premise. Bailey wanted to establish a revolutionary idea of fixed, innate sexual orientations, freeing homosexuality from moral judgment. His invert construct gained a large following in spite of contradictory scientific evidence. After all, what sense does it make to call all of the activities and fantasies around same-and-other-sex relationships by a single name? Is it really appropriate to include in the same category:

(1) a man who after ten years of marriage declares that he is gay, moves to San Francisco, and takes up a lifestyle of multiple male partners, phone sex with men, and gay activism; (2) a woman who was politicized by the feminist movement in the seventies and becomes a lesbian because she believes that real intimacy in a patriarchal culture is only possible with other women; (3) a couple who, like Vita Sackville-West and Harold Nicolson in the earlier part of this century, or like Time magazine's featured pair and hundreds of others today, remain happily married to one another and each have affairs with members of their own sex; and (4) young men and women who 'come out' as bi rather than gay or straight in high school, without passing through a 'phase' of gay or straight identity?[18]

Moreover, if Bailey had accepted the Kinsey format, he would have to acknowledge that the continuum is limiting in its inability to handle other important dimensions of sexual preference. Notably by itself, the continuum fails to capture how bisexuality may take different forms:

There is simultaneous bisexuality (having separate relations with one man and one woman during the same period of time), and serial or sequential bisexuality (having sex with just men or just women over a period of time, and just the other sex over another period of time). This shows the danger, of relying on relatively simple scales to capture the complexity of people's siociosexual relations.[19]

Contemporary gay author Gore Vidal contends there are no inverts:

There is no such thing as a homosexual person, any more than there is such a thing as a heterosexual person. The words are adjectives, describing sexual acts, not people. Those sexual acts are entirely natural; if they were not, no one would perform them....The human race is divided into male and female. Many human beings enjoy sexual relations with their own sex, many don't; many respond to both. The plurality is the fact of our nature and not worth fretting about...The dumb neologisms, homosexual and hetero-sexual, are adjectives that describe acts but never people.[20]

At the time, Bailey was a member of a small informal group of Anglican clergymen and doctors, studying homosexuality, who reported in *The Problem of Homosexuality*, which was produced for the Church of England Moral Welfare Council by the Church Information Board, in 1954. He disclaimed that others in the group agreed with "his" thoughts, which were that societal attitudes to homosexuality were set in the Middle Ages, anchored in Christian dogma of the period and had changed little. He said:

It is important to understand that the genuine homosexual condition, or inversion, as it is often termed, is something for which the subject can in no way be held responsible; in itself, it is morally neutral. Like the normal condition of heterosexuality, however, it may find expression in specific sexual acts; and such acts are subject to moral judgment no less than those which may take place between man and woman. It must be made quite clear that the genuine invert is not necessarily given to homosexual practices, and may exercise as careful a control over his or her physical impulses as the heterosexual; on the other hand, those who commit sexual acts are by no means always genuine inverts. This suggests a rough but serviceable distinction between the invert proper, and those who may be described as perverts. The pervert, as the term implies, is not a true homosexual, but a heterosexual who engages in homosexual practices. ...The pattern of 'perversion' is thus one of remarkable complexity, from which some have concluded that there exists a third type, the so-called 'bisexual;' but this is very doubtful. ...An invert can often engage in heterosexual acts (though to some these are abhorrent), just as a heterosexual can act as a pervert; but in each case the condition of the person concerned is unambiguous.[21]

In order to move society from a "Middle-age" attitude towards homosexuality, Bailey had to discredit or overcome internalized letter and verse of Christian Scripture. The most prominent feature in the tradition, being that God declared his judgment upon homosexual practices once and for all time by the destruction of the cities of Sodom and Gomorrah. Overlooking thousands of years of consistent Biblical hermeneutics Bailey concluded the destruction of Sodom and Gomorrah had nothing whatever to do with such homosexual practices. He wrote:

...the interpretation of the Sodom story generally received by Western Christendom turns out to be nothing more than a post-Exilic Jewish reinterpretation devised and exploited by patriotic rigorists for polemical purposes. Thus disappears the assumption that an act of Divine retribution in the remote past has relieved us of the responsibility for making an assessment of homosexual acts in terms of theological and moral principles. It is no longer permissible to take refuge in the contention that God himself pronounced these acts 'detestable and abominable' above every other sin, nor to explain natural catastrophes and human disasters as his vengeance upon those who indulge in them. It is much to be hoped that we will soon hear the last of Sodom and Gomorrah in connection with homosexual practices – though doubtless the term 'sodomy' will always remain as a reminder of the unfortunate consequences which have attended the reinterpretation of an ancient story in the interests of propaganda.[22]

Having dismissed in his estimation, Sodom and Gomorrah as irrelevant, Bailey turned to the rest of the Scriptural material relating to homosexual practices. Regarding the Old Testament, he argued:

They stand as a witness to the conviction shared by the ancient Hebrews with other contemporary peoples that homosexual practices are peculiarly disreputable, and deserve exemplary punishment as unnatural indulgences, incompatible with the vocation and moral obligations of the People of God.[23]

After this conclusion he advised:

This view may not greatly assist the legislator or the sociologist for whom the sanctions of religion are not absolute, but it cannot be lightly dismissed by the Church – although it may eventually need some qualification by the moral theologian in light of further scientific discovery and of a reconsideration of the morality of sexual acts as a whole.[24]

It is really with the New Testament that Bailey tries to silence Scripture with his invert-pervert paradigm. He explained his view this way:

St Paul likewise denounces homosexual practices as inconsistent with membership of the kingdom of God, but our knowledge of life in the social underworld of the first century enables us to set his words in their correct context. He specifically mentions the arsenokoitai or active sodomists, and the malakoi or passive sodomists (who were often prostitutes or exsoliti), both of whom are familiar enough from the pages of Petronius and others; and it can hardly be doubted that he also had such types in mind when writing to the Romans of those men who, 'leaving the natural use of the woman, burned in their lust one toward another, men with men working unseemliness' – the last a phrase sufficiently wide in meaning to cover every kind of homosexual indulgence practiced by the vicious of that or any other age. Although St. Paul does not expressly refer to corrupters of youth or paidophthoroi, we may be certain that he intended his condemnations to include them.[25]

Here, then, we have decisive Biblical authority for censoring the conduct of those whom we may describe as male perverts, such as the depraved paederasts and catamites of the Satyricon; but do the Apostle's strictures apply also to the homosexual acts of the genuine invert, and in particular to those physical expressions of affection which may take place between two persons of the same sex who affirm that they are 'in love'? To such situations it can hardly be said that the New Testament speaks, since the condition of inversion, with all its special problems, was quite unknown at that time. ...As we survey the development of this tradition it becomes evident that the effect of the reinterpreted Sodom story upon the mind of the Church was in fact more profound than that of either the Levitical laws or the teaching of the New Testament.[26]

Nevertheless it has at least been established beyond controversy that in many cases sexual inversion is an inherent and apparently unalterable condition – though its causes and character still need careful and detailed investigation....What principles ought to direct our moral judgments upon the sexual conduct of the genuine invert? Here the Christian tradition affords us little guidance, for it knows only one kind of sexual behavior – that which would be termed perversion; thus to one of the most perplexing ethical questions of our time it has at best but an indirect and dubious relevance.[27]

The male invert, whether practicing or not, generally maintains that homosexual acts are, for him, entirely 'natural,' and that coitus with a woman would be nothing less than a perversion. Hence he would claim that it is unjust and illogical to deny him, should he so desire, the right to express himself and to seek physical satisfaction and relief in acts appropriate to his condition – provided no harm accrues to society or to any individual as a result.[28]

Bailey was instrumental in inaugurating a committee which published a document in 1957 called the *Wolfenden Report* after its chairman. The report recommended that homosexual behavior between consenting adults, in private, be no longer a criminal offence. Bailey's thesis that the Christian tradition has misread the account of the judgment on Sodom in Genesis 19 undercut the popular notion that toleration of homosexual behavior was a sign of national decay, and helped to lay a theoretical basis for the adoption of the Wolfenden recommendation by Parliament in 1967. His handling of Genesis 19 argues that the inhabitants of Sodom did not intend a homosexual rape of the angels accompanying Lot, and that the real sin of Sodom was its violation of the duty of hospitality to strangers, which was part of a general pattern of wickedness described elsewhere in Scripture as including pride, gluttony, adultery, deception and injustice.[29]

Again, as in the case of Bailey's distinction between inversion and perversion, few interpreters who are not themselves homosexuals have adopted his view on the judgment of Sodom and Gomorrah. A simple reading of the Sodom story in Genesis 19 is enough to refute Bailey's thesis that inhospitality was the sole and major sin of the Sodomites. When Lot offers hospitality to the two "men," the evil males of Sodom encompass the house to try to force Lot to send the guests out crying: "Bring them out to us, that we may know them" (19:5). Lot tries to divert their intention to his two daughters, virgins "who have not known man" (19:8). The evil men persist, however, in wanting the male guests, hence sealing the doom of Sodom. Since the Hebrew verb "to know" can be used in the sense "to have sexual intercourse with," and since the use of that word with regard to Lot's daughters demand a sexual meaning, it has traditionally been thought that the men of Sodom intended to violate the bodies of the male guests. Most recent interpreters who defend some forms of homosexual activity stress that the only sin we can be sure of here is rape, but this is also a very unreliable argument.

Although, acknowledging that the Hebrew terms used for rape do not appear in the account, Robin Scroggs says:

Any claim, however, that the story is a blanket condemnation of homosexuality in general is unjustified. The attempt on the bodies of the guests is but an example of the general evil, which has already caught God's attention. It is, furthermore, an attempt at rape. The most that can be said is that the story judges homosexual rape to be evil and worthy of condemnation.[30]

However, the Israelite who was acquainted with Leviticus would view the use of force simply as aggravation of a practice which was in itself condemned by God as sinful.[31]

Jerry Kirk, author of *The Homosexual Crisis in the Mainline Church*, writes, "The central question in interpreting the passage is, what were the men of Sodom seeking when they called upon Lot to bring out the men – "that we may know them" (Genesis 19:5)? Kirk writes:

Virtual unanimous interpretation of this passage for over twenty centuries has been that the motivation of the men of Sodom was homosexual lust linked with murderous hostility. This overwhelmingly predominant position has been held by John Calvin; Martin Luther; Karl Barth; The Westminster Study Bible; the New English Bible; Brown, Driver, and Briggs (authors of the Hebrew Lexicon of the Old Testament); Gerhard von Rad; Bruce Metzger; William Everett Harrison; Paul Jewett; and Donald Williams.

Bailey teaches that since Lot was a sojourner he had no right to extend hospitality to these foreigners. The men of Sodom, by their inhospitality, were sinning against the ancient practice of hospitality. Bailey ultimately concludes that the Sodom story has no reference to homosexual practice at all….David Barlett of the Chicago Theological Seminary, a supporter of gay theology, disagrees with Bailey directly. 'The integrity of the story indicates that what is at issue in each instance is intercourse, and not just getting acquainted.'…After all, unless all modern biology is amiss, Adam went far beyond 'getting acquainted' with Eve to populate planet Earth. For the Scripture tells us, Adam knew his wife.[32]

Scroggs explains in *The New Testament and Homosexuality*, that only with the codification of the Priestly code in the fifth-fourth centuries B.C. does an explicit law emerge which deals with male homosexuality in general (Leviticus 18:22; 20:13). Scroggs noted that Leviticus 18 has a clear literary structure. At the beginning and end are warnings against practices of the Egyptians and Canaanites. In between are listings, presumably, of what these abhorred practices were, with prohibitions against doing them:

Do not give any of your children to be sacrificed to Molech [god of Ammonites] for you must not profane the name of your God. I am the Lord (21).

Do not lie with a man as one lies with a woman; that is detestable (22).

Do not have sexual relations with an animal and defile yourself with it. A woman must not present herself to the animal to have sexual relations with it; that is a perversion (23).

Scroggs says there is no technical term for homosexuality in Hebrew:

Nevertheless the meaning is clear. Shakav is frequently used to denote sexual intercourse; thus the sentence is a general prohibition of male homosexuality.[33]

There is more to note than the lack of a technical term and the use of a euphemism (shakav) for intercourse. What is critical is the general word for 'male' is used, without any qualification of age. This lack of qualification will determine the lan-

guage of all future Jewish discussions, no matter what forms of homosexuality are being attacked....Paul is no exception to this rule.[34]

Writing on "Homosexuality as a Gentile Vice" Scroggs discovered that for rabbis of the period, homosexuality is certainly a Gentile, not a Jewish sin. He writes:

We have already noted that the reply to the opinion that two Jewish males should not sleep under the same cloak is that 'Israel is not suspected' of such activities. In an interpretation of Leviticus 18:3, where Moses warns the Israelites not to imitate the vices of Egypt and Canaan, one vice attributed to the pagans is both male and female homosexual marriage. Occasionally this attitude reaches into legal or quasi-legal discussions. One tradition warns against sending a Jewish youth to a Gentile to study, learn a trade, or even to be alone with – obviously for fear the youth will be used for pederastic purposes....According to a later rabbi, one [decree] was designed to protect Jewish youths from Gentile homosexual lust. All Gentile youths were declared by the Shammaites to be legally ill with gonorrhea so that Jewish youths could not be tempted to associate with them for homosexual purposes (although this shows the temptation was feared to be a real possibility).[35]

On "Jewish Homosexuality" Scroggs writes:

The question has to be raised about evidence for homosexual activity among the Jews themselves of this period, however much 'Israel is not suspected.' To the best of my knowledge, there is only one story in the literature about an event contemporary to the rabbis themselves, and this is reported of a rabbi from the later period. Judah ben Pazzi once climbed to the upper story of a beth midrash (the Jewish schoolhouse) and discovered two males having intercourse with one another. They said to him, 'rabbi, take note that you are one and we are two.' The point of the retort is that two witnesses who agree are necessary in a Jewish court to prove wrongdoing. The men could falsify their witness and the rabbi's single affirmation could not overrule theirs, no matter how false theirs was. The point for us, however, is that the rabbi discovered two males, doubtlessly Jewish and knowledgeable about the legal niceties, having homosexual intercourse.[36]

From his search of other historical sources Scroggs concludes:

Jewish culture in its official form was entirely opposed to male homosexuality and, presumably, to female as well....The discussion is entirely directed toward the sexual act and its culpability. Nothing is ever said about any other possible dimension of the relationship. Indeed, from discussion alone, one would assume a homosexual encounter to be only for purposes of sexual gratification, as if other qualities of a possible friendship either were irrelevant, unimportant, or perhaps non-existent.[37]

Scroggs comments on Leviticus 18:22, 20:13 translated faithfully:

It is important to see the words the translator chose....With a male [arsen] you shall not lie the intercourse [koitē:lit. 'bed'] of a woman' (18:22)....And whoever lies with a male [arsen] the intercourse [koite¯] of a woman. Both have committed an abomination; they shall be put to death, they are guilty (20:13).[38]

Turning to the New Testament writings I shall continue to draw primarily from Robin Scroggs studies. Under the title "Homosexuality and Idolatry," Scroggs cited a text which likely predates the Christian era. In this early correspondence, the *Letter of Aristeas*, which purports to describe the origin of the Greek translation of the Bible, the unknown author contrasts the piety and sexual righteousness of the Jews and their legal code with the activity of "the majority of other people." Among the sins of the Gentiles are male homosexuality and incest.[39] In the *Wisdom of Solomon* there is a possible reference to homosexuality, which if it should prove to be the case, would signal an early linkage in Jewish thought between idolatry and homosexuality, a relationship that Paul knows and describes in Romans 1. In this treatise the author claims that idolatry is the cause of all Gentile sins. He first makes a specific reference to sexual sins: "For the beginning of sexual evil is the invention of idols." Later, he broadens this: "For the worship of unspeakable idols is the beginning, cause, and end of every evil."[40]

Writes Scroggs:

Under the guise of oracular utterances of ancient prophets, a Jewish literature arose which passed judgment on Gentiles and gave comfort to the Jewish community. In these writings, called The Sibylline Oracles, several passages refer to pagan pederasty, sometimes in relation to idol worship. In one the 'prediction' is made that Roman culture will permit males to draw near to males and that boys will be placed in shameful brothels.[41]

In another the rise of the pious nation of the Jews is "predicted;" in contrast to pagans they will not worship idols, and shall preserve sexual purity, not "having unholy union with male children" as do many other nations (several are named explicitly).[42] God will punish these nations for this sin and for the worship of idols. Clearly sexual crime and idol worship are closely united, although it is not clear which is cause and which effect. Relationship between the two is indicated in still another passage. The reader is exhorted to flee unlawful worship and to worship the living God, to abstain from adultery, child exposure, and unceasing (or confused) intercourse with males.[43]

Another text, *The Testaments of the Twelve Patriarchs*, (if it is indeed Jewish) may possibly give further evidence of the relationship Jews felt between idolatry and sin. Scroggs writes:

The patriarch Naphtali counsels his children to remain true to God's will. Then abruptly he adds a warning. Sun and moon and stars do not change their order; thus also you must not change the law of God in the disorder of your deeds. Deceived Gentiles who left the Lord changed their order and followed stones and trees, following spirits of deceit. Be not like this, my children, knowing in the firmament, earth, and in sea, and all things made, the Lord who makes all of these, that you become not like Sodom, which changed the order of its nature. Likewise the watchers changed the order of its nature[44]*....The phrase, 'to change one's order,' is curi-*

ous and seems here equivalent to leave what is true and subvert it into a false reality.[45] *For the Gentiles to change their order means to leave their proper relationship to the deity and live in a false world with false deities. To remain in true relation with the creator God is thus a defense against that changing of the order of nature which is attributed to the Sodomites. Although the phrase is strange and unparalled in our other references to Sodom, I do not see to what other fact the author could be alluding except the homosexual inclinations of the Sodomites. If so, then not to change the order of relationship to God will mean not to violate one's heterosexual nature. The association of homosexuality with idolatry is thus well respresented in Hellenistic Judaism prior to Paul.*[46]

Scroggs concludes that the early Christian Church echoed the Jewish tradition. The clearest text is found in Romans 1: 18-28:

The wrath of God is being revealed from heaven against all the godlessness and wickedness of men who suppress the truth by their wickedness, since what may be known about God is plain to them.

For although they knew God, they neither glorified him as God nor gave thanks to him, but their thinking became futile and their foolish hearts were darkened. Although they claimed to be wise, they became fools and exchanged the glory of the immortal God for images made to look like mortal man and birds and animals and reptiles.

Therefore God gave them over in the sinful desires of their hearts to sexual impurity for the degrading of their bodies with one another. They exchanged the truth of God for a lie, and worshipped and served created things rather than the Creator – who is forever praised. Amen.

Because of this, God gave them over to shameful lusts. Even their women exchanged natural relations for unnatural ones. In the same way the men also abandoned natural relations with women and were inflamed with lust for one another. Men committed indecent acts with other men, and received in themselves the due penalty for their perversion.

Furthermore, since they did not think it worthwhile to retain the knowledge of God, he gave them over to a depraved mind, to do what ought not to be done.

According to Scroggs three points of clarification need to be made. The first is that the phrase, "God gave them up," means that people now living in the false reality do what they choose. God does not force them into such false actions; his judgment lies in his leaving them where they want to be, in actions which, as already suggested, they think to be good and right. This is the ultimate irony of their fate. The second, is that Paul heaps up anthropological terms – heart, body, passions, mind – apparently to indicate that this false reality permeates a person's entire existence. All dimensions of one's self are distorted by false reality in which he or she lives. The third relates to the use of the illustrations Paul chooses. The structure of the passage shows that for heart-body Paul gives no illustration. That which illustrates passion (emotions) is a traditional Hellenistic Jewish judgment on homosexuality. For the third, the unfit mind (i.e. that which cannot judge between what is true and what is false) Paul inserts the most detailed and vigorous vice catalogs in all his letters (Romans 1:29-32).[47]

Scroggs explains that although Paul makes judgment on homosexuals, he is "not out to get them" anymore than other sinners. In considering the text applied to women, which reads, "For not only did their females exchange natural intercourse for that which was against nature…," Scroggs writes:

Taken independently of the verse directed at men, it would not be certain that this clause referred to female homosexuality at all. Indeed some have suspected it could refer to various positions of heterosexual intercourse deemed deviate by pious Jews. It could as well be hinting at artificial phalli, which we know were used by women of the day to stimulate themselves – although such stimulation could take place in the context of homosexual encounters. Since the following verse is without question an attack on male homosexuality, however, and since the two verses are so closely linked in the Greek, it is virtually certain that Paul and the tradition on which he is dependent had lesbianism in mind.[48]

Scroggs also draws attention to the phrase:

Receiving the punishment (literally reward) within themselves, which their falsehood necessitated.

He observes that there have been two interpretations. Either Paul is hinting at physical disease (perhaps venereal) which homosexual intercourse could cause, or he counts the distortion of homosexuality itself as the punishment. The latter seems to Scroggs the most likely, given the reference in that phrase to the false reality in which people now live.[49]

In conclusion Scroggs asks, "What can we learn from these verses about Paul's reflections on homosexuality?" He responds:

First, Paul's primary purpose in this entire section is to describe the fall of humanity into false reality in which it now lives….He does say at the end of the entire section that those who live this way 'deserve to die;' doubtless this culpability includes the price of homosexuality and all of the other sins listed in the vice catalog. Yet one would be hard put to find in the Old Testament specific injunctions against all the items in the catalog, much less statements of liability to the death penalty for all of them. Thus what Paul probably has in mind, in reference to the death penalty, is the basic sin of the refusal to acknowledge God as God. This is the root of sin and thus is the root of the life that is displeasing to God, which ultimately results in death.[50]

Scroggs also says that:

Paul is dependent for his judgment that it [homosexuality] is against nature ulti-

mately on Greek, not Jewish sources. There it rests not on some doctrine of creation or philosophical principles, but on what seemingly is thought to count as common-sense observation.[51]

He found no Greco-Roman text that attempts to explain why homosexuality is against nature. Thus contends Scroggs, Paul makes no attempt either:

For him idolatry results in a false world with a false self, that is, unnatural. The false self finds homosexuality pleasing and sees nothing wrong in what is for the Apostle a deflection of desire from opposite sex to same sex. Thus for Paul passions directed toward people of the same-sex are illustrative of the false self. Paul, no more than the Greeks and Jews, attempted not to explain his argument. Perhaps he could not. Perhaps it seemed obvious to him, given his Jewish presuppositions.[52]

After presenting his analysis, Scroggs asks "Does this data suggest Greek authors knew of a non-pederastic male homosexuality? Answering yes, he cites three examples:

When male (arsen) unites with female (thelus) for procreation, the pleasure experienced is held to be due to nature, but contrary to nature when male mates with male or female with female (Plato, Laws I, 636C).

Whence until now the desires of animals have involved intercourse neither of male [arsen] with male nor of female [thelus] with female. But [there are] many such among your noble and good [classes] (Plutarch, Beasts are rational 999D).

Do not transgress the beds of nature for unlawful passion. Male [arsen] beds do not please even the beasts. Nor shall females [here a derivative from thelus is used] imitate the beds of males (Pseudo-Phocylides, Maxims, lines 190-92).[53]

These statements have in common with Paul several features: they are general, nonspecific judgments; they use the terms for male and female which are not age-differentiated; they all make negative judgments on homosexuality. To this should be added that Plato explicitly and Plutarch implicitly share with Paul the argument from nature. Seen in this regard, Romans 1:26-27 could be seen as a commonplace of Greek moral wisdom.[54] Tertullian writes:

All other frenzies of lusts which exceed the laws of nature and are impious toward both bodies and the sexes we banish, not only from the threshold, but also from all shelter of the Church, for they are not sins so much as monstrosities.[55]

Yet in the end, Robin Scroggs chooses to believe Scripture is unclear on homosexuality! This interpretation lies in the obstinate belief (notwithstanding the contrary evidence) that there is a substantial difference in the nature of homosexual relations today over those addressed in the Bible. Let us therefore look at GBLTQ Christianity to see how gay-theology fits with Scripture.

Queer Christianity

The attempt of gay men to merge their Catholicism with homosexuality has always seemed to me touching but doomed. I used to walk past the church on Sixteenth Street in New York where I knew Dignity – an organization for gay Catholics – was meeting, but I never went in. I felt sorry for the men inside, sympathetic to their attempt, and superior to what seemed to me their naiveté. Don't even try, I thought, as I walked past, on the way from the gym to the bath (my new church), you're just kidding yourselves. There can be no commerce between, no conflation of, these two things. Fellatio has nothing to do with Holy Communion. Better to frankly admit that you have changed gods, and are now worshipping Priapus, not Christ.[56]

Andrew Holleran

Naturally the gay Christian movement looks so appealing to the woman or man struggling with homosexuality. It offers them acceptance and understanding that they may never have found in congregations adhering to orthodox Christian truths. In 2 Timothy 3:16-17, the Scripture states:

All Scripture is God-breathed and is useful for teaching, rebuking, correcting and training in righteousness, so that the man of God may be thoroughly equipped for every good work.

Raised before, but it also bears repeating, in the same letter to Timothy, Paul exhorts us:

...I give you this charge: Preach the Word; be prepared in season and out of season; correct, rebuke and encourage – with great patience and careful instruction. For the time will come when men will not put up with sound doctrine. Instead, to suit their own desires, they will gather around them a great number of teachers to say what their itching ears want to hear. They will turn their ears away from the truth and turn aside to myths (2 Timothy 4:1-4).

The term "cult" really came to many people's attention for the first time with the Jonestown Mass Suicide (913 people), in November 1978. *Time* magazine told the story of the "cult of death," about a man named Jim Jones, who had begun as a proclaimed Christian minister in Indiana. He came to San Francisco and like the Gnostics Marcion and Simon Magus, set himself up as the voice of God on earth. Then he started what he called "The People's Temple" and eventually led his followers to Guyana in South America. One wonders how this could happen. Dr. Ron Carlson and Ed Decker offer this warning:

The commander of the U.S. forces who was responsible for going to Jonestown, cleaning the camp out, and bringing the bodies back for burial was a Christian. When he returned with the bodies to Dover Air Force Base he held a press conference. We'll never forget one of the things he said: 'The thing that interested me most about Jonestown is that when we cleaned the camp out, we did not find a single Bible in all of Jonestown. Jim Jones had so effectively replaced the Bible with his own man-made teaching and theology, he had so convinced those people that he was God's voice on earth, that when he told them to drink poison, they did it.'[57]

Ron Rhodes, author of *The Culting of America* makes a good observation on the draw of cults:

A person does not usually join a cult because he has done an exhaustive analysis of world religions and has decided that a particular cult presents the best theology available. Instead, a person generally joins a cult because he has problems that he is having trouble solving, and the cult promises to solve these problems.[58]

Psuedo-Christian cults are religious organizations or movements that claim to be Christian and claim to believe in the Bible, but instead of building their theology and teaching on God's Word – the Bible, they claim some "new revelation" or man-made teaching as superior to the Bible. By interpreting the Bible through the grid of their particular revelation or teaching, these movements and churches end up denying central doctrines of historic, orthodox, biblical Christianity. The key perversions of the cults always relate to the central issues of theology, specifically the doctrines of God, Jesus Christ, and salvation. For example, the "non-divinity" of Jesus Christ is often an open or hidden tenet in Psuedo-Christian organizations. These groups are considered cults because they seek to counterfeit biblical Christianity. Counterfeits deceive by their outward appearance. Like counterfeit money, the cults want to look and sound like the genuine thing without having their bogus nature detected. Such cults use Christian terminology to sound Christian, but then redefine the terms to fit their own man-made theology. The pseudo-Christian cults have essentially emptied biblical Christianity of all of its content theologically. They have replaced the content with a perverted theology of their own making, then sprayed it over with Christian words and terminology to make it look and sound Christian.[59]

Minister and religious scholar, Reverend Dr. William Johnson, explains some of his reasons for believing in queer Christian theology:

...we need to acknowledge that the Gospel writers and the missionary Paul did not possess the psychological, sociological, and sexological knowledge which now inform our theological reflections about human sexuality....We know that homosexuality is part of the created order, same-gender sex acts having been observed in a multitude of species from sea gulls to porcupines.[60]

One of the legacies of the Protestant tradition is the conviction that each of us has the freedom to evolve spiritually and to nurture our own biblical understanding and theology....Jesus proclaimed the imperative of fundamental equality of women and men and illuminated the primacy of love and forgiveness in sexual and all other matters. He was clearly not an ascetic, being known for his drinking and acquaintance with persons from every strata of society.[61]

In our visibility, we are also personifying the viability of our Christian faith. Our lives give evidence that the 'argument from scripture' historically used to condemn homosexuality is a smokescreen for prejudice. It is, in fact, an 'argument from homophobia' that justifies itself through an intellectually dishonest abuse of scripture.

According to Joe Dallas, author of *A Strong Delusion: Confronting the "Gay Christian" Movement,* the body of Christ will suffer immeasurably because sound doctrine – and even the Bible itself – will have to be taken less seriously if pro-gay theology is widely accepted. He writes:

You cannot tamper with one part of Scripture (in this case, a very significant part) without dismantling its authority in general. And when the authority of the Bible is denigrated, the church of Jesus Christ, the light of the world, will be without clear guidance of its own. When I belonged to Metropolitan Community Church (MCC) I saw this dilemma firsthand...One minister wrote in the MCC's official publication that it was idolatry to worship Jesus as God. Another stated in print her discomfort with the cross, implying a link between references to the blood of Christ and sadomasochism. And on at least one occasion I spoke with a pastor who said he wasn't sure what being born again meant, so he had no intention of encouraging people to do it.

When conservatives in the MCC argued for a return to biblical authority, their liberal opponents reminded them that the position they all shared on homosexuality was at odds with Christian tradition and conservatism, so how could they (conservatives) now push for biblical literalism? That was an argument I never heard a convincing rebuttal to.[62]

A lesbian minister asserts, "It is inconceivable to me that God would create someone like me who is unable to change and then condemn that person to hell."[63] A familiar theme – God's standards seem unfair; therefore, they must not really be God's standards. In studying Queer Christianity, we might consider the diminished respect for biblical authority and the lowering of standards in the actions of its founders. Gay author and minister Mel White (formerly of Fuller Theological Seminary), for example, described his first homosexual encounter (which he had while he was still married) as "inevitable." He described his partner in adultery/homosexuality as "one of God's gifts."[64] Troy Perry, the founder of MCC, takes a similar view of adultery. Recounting a tryst he had with another man (while his own wife was in the next room), he recalls: "Eventually, I came to realize that what we were doing seemed right for me. It stopped short of being love, but it was a marvelous education."[65] The first openly gay Episcopal priest to be ordained, Robert Williams, goes further than Perry and White by declaring in *Newsweek* magazine, on the subject of monogamy:

If people want to try, OK. But the fact is, people are not monogamous. It is crazy to hold up this ideal and pretend it's what we're doing, and we're not.[66]

Williams ends his remarks with an unusually tasteless flourish when he suggests, in the most vulgar terms, that Mother Theresa ought to have a sexual experience.[67]

Joe Dallas asks: "Can such low moral standards among people naming the name of Christ reflect anything but a diminished view of Scripture?" A look at some statements from the Queer Christian movement betrays the truth:

What influences lead us to new ways of understanding Scripture? New scientific information, social change, and personal experience are perhaps the greatest forces for change in the way we interpret the Bible and develop our beliefs. – Troy Perry[68]

[In reference to the apostle Paul's views on homosexuality.] So what? Paul was wrong about any number of other things, too. Why should you take him any more seriously than you take Jerry Falwell, Anita Bryant, or Cardinal O'Connor? – Robert Williams[69]

I can no longer worship in a theological context that depicts God as an abusive parent and Jesus as the obedient, trusting child. This violent theology encourages the violence in our streets and nations. – Lesbian author Virgina Mollenkoot[70]

Jane Spahr, cofounder of CLOUT (Christian Lesbians Out Together) and lesbian evangelist for the Downtown Presbyterian Church of Rochester, claimed her theology was first of all informed by 'making love with Coni,' her lesbian partner.'[71]

I know in my heart that the canon is not closed – I know this because the Bible does not reconcile me with earth and the Bible does not reconcile me with my sexual self. – Melanie Morrison, cofounder of CLOUT[72]

The founder of the Universal Fellowship of Metropolitan Community Churches, Troy Perry, recounts in his books *The Lord Is My Shepherd* and *Don't Be Afraid Anymore*, his life experiences and how they led to starting UFMCC. The oldest of five boys, he was raised by a doting mother Edith in a religious environment. After his father's death in a car accident, he survived abuse from a violent stepfather who battered Edith and evidently arranged for one of his friends to rape 13-year-old Troy as punishment for coming to his mother's defense.[73] He found refuge in church and was especially attracted to Pentecostalism. His ministerial gifts showed up early. By age 15 he was a licensed Baptist preacher; by his late teens he was a paid evangelist with the Charismatic Church of God. Shortly thereafter he married and took a pastorate in the latter denomination. Having been aware of homosexual attractions the better part of his life, Perry involved himself with other young men, both before and after his marriage, and was eventually excommunicated from the Church of God and divorced from his wife. Years later, after joining the gay subculture, he was moved by the distress of one of his friends who had been jailed for simply being in a gay bar (a common occurrence at the time). His friend was convinced God had abandoned him. That night he conceived of a church for gay people to show them that God did indeed care. Along with the scattered support of a handful of liberal churches, gay Christianity grew under the addendum:

God loves and accepts us just as we are; and homosexuality is ok with him.[74]

Said Troy:

I knew I would have few if any problems with the so-called liberal churches. Liberal churches do not usually deeply involve themselves with Scripture.[75]

With its wobbly Scriptural base, the Queer Christian movement created its own creed, which could be paraphrased as follows:

Whereas we have been mistreated and misunderstood, and whereas much of our mistreatment has come from the Christian people, and whereas we tried to resist our homosexual desires but were unable to, and whereas psychologists recognize us as normal, and whereas we know God loves us and we want to continue in fellowship with Him, therefore, be it resolved that God does not condemn homosexuality.[76]

Gay, lesbian, bisexual, and transgender Christians see their very lives as presenting a theological challenge to the traditional Christian Church:

It is a challenge to honor our rights as baptized Christians: the right to equality within the household of faith; the right to all of the sacraments and rites (including marriage) of the church; the right to equity at the table that Christ sets before us at which we experience and affirm God's love and grace for all people.[77]

Queer Christianity, knowingly or not, attempts to erase a very intricate, but clear set of boundaries for sexual behavior and replace it with the same freedoms expounded in libertine Gnosticism. The boundary-free theology trumpets tenets of "inclusiveness" and "flexibility," whatever is needed to suit a particular community. We have already discussed some feminist constructionist theories on the "evolution" of gender. In queer ideology, some theorists speak of transsexuality from a poststructuralist feminist model. Transsexual Susan Stryker contends there is no essential reality to either the body or gender: both sex and gender are constructed by discourse. Viewed from this angle, "trans" identity can be seen as socially constructed in the same way that male and female identities are. The provision of surgery and hormonal treatment is simply an extension of the social construction of gender. Thus, transsexual practices are seen as the instrumentation by which the body is discursively produced. Transsexual Sandy Stone described transsexuality as a genre and suggests that bodies act as "screens on which academic and medical struggles are projected."[78]

The challenges and complications of queer Christianity have expanded well beyond any simplistic notions of an Invert-Pervert that Derrick Bailey foresaw. GBLTQ politics now eclipse the importance of Scripture in queer Christian theological development. The strength and impact of queer politics and community in development of Church doctrine, rests in the value of the social space. Queer Christianity provides for people with non-conventional gender or sexual orientations, a source of pride in being different and a means of social change based on lesbian, gay, bisexual and transsexual alliances. The term "Queer" is flexible, in the sense that people can be fluid with their sexualities and their gender. Surya Monro explains:

Transgender and transsexual people who envisage going beyond the gender binary system to allow for longer-term fluidity, third-sex or androgynous identities form a significant minority of the wider trans communities…I think it could easily be and will be gotten rid of (male-female). I think like in the past or maybe even the present it's more like a set menu 'A' or a set menu 'B' and I see the future more like an Ala Carte menu and you can make your own choice about what you have for starters, for the main course or dessert or whatever, or if you're going to have a dessert you can have your dessert for a starter or starter as a dessert or just three desserts or whatever.[79]

Although transsexualism is a rare condition, estimated to occur in 1 in 30,000 biological males and 1 in 100,000 biological females,[80] its impact on the shape of queer theology is huge. Sexual preference and gender are no longer seen as God-given gifts but rather as self-centered choices to be taken, reversed and revised as needed. With the growing awareness of AIDS, for example, more transsexuals see male sex partners of whatever sexual preference as being a higher risk. This factor, directing many of them away from a "heterosexual performance" (having men as partners) and toward becoming "lesbians" (having only women as partners), has appeared in recent years.[81] Many transsexuals also felt that a person of one's own sex was more knowledgeable about their sexual responsiveness than a person of the opposite sex:

It is like making love to yourself. All those things you know you want to have done yourself sexually – you do that for the other.[82]

Where in Scripture is there provision for self-centered (as opposed to Christ-centered) determinism? The body is a vessel for the Holy Spirit, not a "screen on which academic (indeed, ideological) and medical struggles are projected." What Godly counsel would a queer Christian theologian offer to a transgendered person such as Patrick Califia-Rice? Patrick says:

I'm 46 years old and have been uncomfortable with my body for as long as I can remember. For most of my life, the way I dealt with that was to try to be a different kind of woman. I think I have succeeded in expanding those parameters quite a bit. But when I became perimenopausal and my doctor started talking about estrogen replacement therapy, I flipped. I realized that I could not put this chemical in my body on purpose. I had dealt with puberty well enough, but that was because I didn't feel I had any choice about all the change that happened so rapidly to my body.[83]

Yet Califia-Rice doesn't see her alternative choice of testosterone therapy as a fixed track with a single goal:

I'm happy with the physical, emotional, and spiritual changes that [testosterone] has helped me to create….I currently think of myself as a transgendered person. And I am giving myself the option to change that, to go back or go forward, depending on what I need at the moment of each step in this process.[84]

Califia-Rice describes the practicalities of this notion of going backward or forward as a transgendered person:

It happened like this. I met Matt nearly 10 years ago, as one of the 'jack-booted dyke thugs of ACT-UP Chicago,' as Matt called himself then. This was before he transitioned. I was living in what was supposed to be an open relationship. But my primary partner couldn't tolerate the threat of my torrid affair, so I broke things off with Matt. We connected again three years ago, after Matt had been on testosterone for several years, had chest surgery and a beard, and was a bartender at the Lone Star, San Francisco's notorious bear bar.[85]

Califia-Rice says of the period after connecting with Matt:

At 45, I was terrified of changing my gender, afraid it would mean that I'd no longer be able to make a living, since my income was, based on being a lesbian therapist and journalist. But I didn't know what else to try, and the cognitive dissonance had worn me out. Matt started talking to me about wanting to raise a child. He had been unable to take testosterone for a couple of years because of side effects like blinding migraines. He didn't think he could adopt a child, so he wanted to have one of his own.[86]

During this time Califia-Rice's mother, a staunch right-wing Mormon died. The impact of her death on Califia-Rice's interpretation of life choices was extraordinary:

I had always believed there wasn't room for a child in my life. But when my mother passed away I realized I had also been afraid of her disapproval...she would have moved heaven and earth to prevent me from raising a kid. It seemed to me that it was part of Matt's spiritual path to be a parent. Witnessing my mother's death had opened my heart. I needed to be part of creating a new life.[87]

Since both Matt and Califia-Rice were biologically females, they needed a male sperm donor. Califia-Rice describes the search:

We didn't want to do anything that might harm the baby, so we got the best medical advice we could. We went to see a lot of doctors, who all told us that what we wanted to do was unusual, but biologically possible. So we started auditioning our betesticled friends for the role of sperm donor. That turned out to be quite a soap opera. Guys who thought nothing about throwing away their sperm daily in Kleenexes or on the floor of a sex club, got very precious with us about their sacrosanct bodily fluids.[88]

A year and a half later the couple became parents. Califia-Rice describes how the saga ended:

The only people who've gotten upset are a handful of straight-identified homophobic FTMs [females to males] online, who started calling Matt by his girl name, because real men don't get pregnant. One of these bigots even said it would be better for our baby to be born dead than be raised by two people who are 'confused about their gender.'[89]

Our large and loving chosen family made up of gay men, lesbians, bisexual people, transgendered people, and straight allies, buffers us from this kind of hostility. We are also hearing from more and more FTMs [females to males] who have had or want to have children. As Blake's dads, we have created a village to help us raise him. I started taking testosterone a couple of months before Blake was born. While he learns how to grab things, click his tongue, hold his own bottle, and walk while somebody holds his hands, I am going through my own metamorphosis. My hips are smaller, my muscle mass is growing, and every day it seems like there's more hair on my face and body. My voice is deeper, and my sex drive has given me newfound empathy with the guys who solicit hookers for blow jobs. When I think that I can continue with this process – get chest surgery and pass as male – I feel happier than at any other point in my life. And when I think that something will stop me, I become very depressed.[90]

From this testimony, one sees that Califia-Rice chose to see identity as a self-defined, pragmatic and an ultimately a mutable concept. The cliché, "What I want, when I want and how I want," comes to mind. In this worldview, there are literally no boundaries – spiritual, physiological, sexual, ethical or moral, by which Queer Christianity might say stop. Rather the role of "queer" churches is to reaffirm its membership in their life *choices*. That God made humankind male and female holds no importance in pro-gay or gay theology.

Transsexuals, people who have an emotional gender at odds with their physical sex, once described themselves in terms of dimorphic absolutes-males trapped in female bodies, or vice versa. As such, they sought psychological relief through surgery. Although many still do, some transgendered people today are content to inhabit a more ambiguous zone. A male-to-female transsexual, for instance, may come out as a lesbian. Jane, born a physiological male, is now in her late thirties and living with her wife, whom she married when her name was still John. Jane takes hormones to feminize herself, but they have not yet interfered with her ability to engage in intercourse as a man. In her mind Jane has a lesbian relationship with her wife, though she views their intimate moments as a cross between lesbian and heterosexual sex. It might seem natural to regard intersexuals and transgendered people as living midway between the poles of male and female. To all of this, Ann Fausto-Sterling says:

But male and female, masculine and feminine, cannot be parsed as some kind of continuum.[91]

Thus many in GBLTQ see sex and gender as best conceptualized as points in a multidimensional space. Fausto-Sterling, argues that the two sex system embedded in our society is not adequate to encompass the full spectrum of human sexuality. In its place she advocates the acceptance of five sexes:

...males; females; "herms" (named after true hermaphrodites, people born with both a testis and an ovary); "means" (male pseudohermaphrodites, who are born with testes and some aspect of female genitalia); and "ferms" (female pseudohermaphrodites, who have ovaries combined with some aspect of male genitalia).[92]

Here Queer Christianity must revise the two sex Genesis account to affirm "herms," "means," "ferms" and "transsexuals" as non-aberrant sexualities. The quandary is not in ministering to or affirming an individual's dignity. The catch-22 comes from modifying and revising Scripture to somehow deny, hide or overcome the fact that these psychological or physiological conditions are aberrant. It is true that people are born with a wide array of abnormalities, deafness and blindness being two examples. It is a fact that blind people are no less equal beings in God's creation. It is a fact that deaf people have an equivalent right to pursue a Godly life. And it is true that God has a purpose for all and that He has used blind and deaf persons to achieve great things. All this said, truthfully affirming the blind or deaf person does not require denial of the fact that blindness and deafness are aberrant physical states. All eyes were designed to see and all ears to hear. Non-Christians (Darwinists, for example) should agree that any physical failure or under-development of mechanisms designed over millions of years is anomalous. The history of Darwinism and eugenics tells us that evolutionists, who recognize aberrant genes, must have a notion of what the proper gene or *nature's* design should be. To contend that a person with a male body and a female emotional gender is not atypical is to rewrite God's creation. To advocate that intersexuality is not an abnormal condition is to change the Creator's intent, and therefore to change the God of Scripture. It is one thing to protect the blind, the deaf, or the disadvantaged from societal abuse, and care for them through protective and supportive government legislation. It is entirely another issue to contend that blindness is not a shortcoming with differentiating implications from those with sight. We discriminate against blind people by not giving them driver's licenses. A common sense application of the Charter of Rights and Freedoms would not obligate the National Hockey League to accept a blind goalie to achieve a sense of *sameness* and *equality*.

In all societies it is a fact that a portion of the adult population is oriented to have sex with children. This *fact* does not imply that it is God's intent that pedophiles exist or that their condition be seen as anything other than aberrant. Is there an orthodox, pro-gay or queer Christian, who is willing to dispute the fact that male and female sex organs were created for each other? To contend that other non-vaginal sexual applications of these organs are God-ordained, and not anomalous sexual experimentation is to worship a different deity than the God of Scripture. And when God's truth is subverted, spiritual darkness sets in.

In *Sex and the Church: Gender, Homosexuality, and the Transformation of Christian Ethics*, Kathy Rudy challenges the orthodox view of gender as the organizing principle of theology and the traditional family. An advocate of sex positive ideology, she argues "sex is ethical when it opens God's world to others." Unlike most Christian observers, including many queer and feminist theologians, she refuses to interpret non-monogamous queer sex practices and activities as merely desperate attempts at sexual gratification. She contends that these activities are often, although not always, essential elements in community building and that at least some queer practices of "communal sex" may be pleasing to God.[93]

Even more audacious, she makes an explicit connection between the free sex activities in the GBLTQ community and the traditional Christian emphasis on building up the body of Christ, contending that the church could learn much from a group of people who, because they are so often without family support, base their social and emotional existence on membership in a community. Despite her pro-sex attitudes, Rudy argues that identities such as "gay" or "lesbian" or "queer" – even "male" or "female" should be cast aside:

Our primary identification is and ought to be Christian; any identification that takes precedence over our baptism is to be avoided.[94]

She bases this contention on an insight articulated by queer theorists, namely that the categories "gay," "straight," and even "bisexual" are not natural and fixed. By siding with queer theory in this regard, she stakes out a position at odds with that argued by other gay Christians and pro-gay friends – namely that these categories are unchangeable and ordained by God. Accepting the fluidity of sexual categories and identities advanced in queer theory, Rudy argues that Christians are first and foremost called "to become new people, with a new and radically different ontology."[95]

Robert L. Treese follows in Rudy's footsteps and acknowledges, as concluded in the previous section, that the Pauline texts on homosexual behavior:

...indicate with no possibility of qualification that homosexual practices were considered by Paul...to be concrete sins on a par with adultery and murder, and evidence of original sin with which the human race is infected.[96]

However, Treese goes on to interpret in Galatians 3:28, that sexual relationship between members of the same sex can be a valid expression of Christian love. The passage reads:

There is neither Jew nor Greek, there is neither slave nor free man, there is neither male nor female; for you are all one in Christ Jesus.

He further suggests that:

...one can view both homosexuality and heterosexuality as perversions of the original or intended order of nature, insofar as both are conditions caused by human sin. The ideal state of humanity is thus androgynous or bisexual.

Against this background, Joe Dallas reflected upon sex positive queer theology. Writing on his experiences with gay Christian clergy and their departures from sound doctrine, he says:

During a radio debate with a UFMCC minister, when asked how he discerned God's truth, he said there were three sources he relied on, each having equal authority:

the Bible, the witness of his own heart and the witness of his community. I responded that I had no such confidence in either my heart or my community – the Bible was the ultimate authority in all matters....The church has clear guidelines for sexual behavior: Intercourse before marriage is forbidden, marriage must be monogamous, and divorce is permissible only in the event of fornication or abandonment by an unbelieving spouse.

During my involvement with the gay church, we made virtually no effort to abide by these standards. Among gay men (religious or not) it was unheard of to wait until a marriage (or 'union ceremony,' as it was called then) before engaging in sex. Indeed, sexual relations within days or even hours of meeting were not uncommon, and they were never, in my experience, criticized from the pulpit.[97]

The gospel of "acceptance" and "inclusivity" has captured many minds in liberal theology, leading not only to acceptance of homosexual practice but even to the acceptance of self-proclaimed witches ("creation spirituality"). Says Donald Faris:

The thought seems to be, no one is perfect. It is the relationship that counts...The gospel according to this logic is not 'repent, believe, and obey,' but, 'accept yourself.' A simple surrender to one's own self-centeredness and immaturity is the goal; the new obedient life in Jesus Christ is a detour to be avoided.[98]

Christian ethicist Philip Turner, author of *Sex, Money and Power* is correct in suggesting that these attempted revisions of Christian sexual ethics come from denominations that do not ask much of their membership. They see themselves as "meeting needs" rather than "making demands." Such consumer-oriented pastoral care consists of agreeing with, rather than challenging, the mind of the times.[99] Writing on "Homosexual Liberation Theologies," Faris observed that some "feminist" forms of theology reject Christian tradition in light of highly selective Gnostic variations. Not surprisingly, some followers of these variations include worshippers of the mother goddess. He writes:

They welcome homosexuality as an attack on what they see as the male dominated 'family'...Having dethroned God and rejected the Lordship of Christ, this type of feminist theologian believes that, in sexual matters, all we need is 'love.'[100]

Biblical scholar Elizabeth Achtemeier asks, "what does love mean to these people?" Her answer: "an unqualified acceptance of any lifestyle." Thus liturgies are brimming over with acceptance of extra-marital sex, of lesbian "marriage," of any divorce or abortion. Anything is acceptable if one has no standard of judgment.[101]

Whosoever is an online magazine for gay, lesbian, bisexual and transgendered Christians found at www.whosoever.org. The magazine title markets the text found in John 3:16, "whosoever believes in him [Jesus] shall not perish but have eternal life." The magazine proclaims to many gay Christians the most beautiful word in the Gospel of Jesus Christ is "whosoever" – all God's promises are intended for every human being, and this includes gays and lesbians. Orthodox Christians find no issue with this claim in and of itself. The problem arises in how many professed gay Christians and specifically *Whosoever* magazine interpret who Christ is and what is meant by taking up the Cross of Jesus. Magazine editor Candace Chellew writes under "Errancy and Insolence":

Indeed, we are assured in Romans: Neither death, nor life, nor angels, nor things to come, nor powers, nor height, nor depth, nor anything else in all creation will be able to separate us from the love of God in Christ Jesus our Lord.

Nothing. Not homosexuality, not disbelief in certain creeds, Bible passages, litanies or opinions of other believers. Not sin, not death, not anything, not even being wrong. I suspect that's good news for all of us! My fundamentalist friends, do you realize the freeing beauty of these words??? Nothing!! NOTHING! Will you take those words at heart? Will you believe the Holy Word of God when it says NOTHING separates you from God??? Or will you continue to thump your Bible and point out all those who 'you' believe have been separated from God?[102]

Under the title "Living the Way of Truth," Chellew reveals the counterfeit nature of her Christianity when she refers to approved authors. She writes:

My basic philosophy is that none of us sees the whole truth, and no one, not a religion, not a person, not a philosophy, embodies the entire truth.

In discussion, my friend made it clear that we must proclaim Jesus as Christ, if we are to claim to be Christians. That is fine. I proclaim Jesus as Christ. I truly believe he is the Son of God. Not because he says he is, however. I believe he is the son of God because he fully embodied God on earth. I believe we are all sons and daughters of God. As such, we too can become a living embodiment of God by living Christ's example. We do not embody God by only calling Jesus' name. I can praise Jesus' name all day long and it will get me nothing. Only when I take the next step, and learn to live like Jesus will my worship mean anything...By living the example of Christ, we touch the Christ within us, and we truly become sons and daughters of God.

Thich Nthat Hahn writes in 'Living Buddha, Living Christ:' When Jesus said, 'I am the way,' He meant that to have a true relationship with God, you must practice his way....To me, 'I am the way,' is a better statement than 'I know the way.'...The 'I' in His statement is life itself, His life, which is the way.

R. Kirby Godsey in his book 'When We Talk About God,' writes: ...Jesus should be no more equated with certain of his words or with certain episodes in his life than should you or I....The person of Jesus is the event in history where, for those of us who call ourselves Christian, God comes to us. It is the event where God's unconditional acceptance and embrace of us is lived out in history.

Getting stuck worshipping Jesus as a name, as a person, or even as a Messiah, distracts us from the real goal. Getting to God, becoming the living embodiment of God here on earth should be our ultimate aim. Jesus points us in the right direction.

Through Jesus we shall find the truth, and it shall set us free, but we must live to see it. Worrying about getting our dogmas right about Jesus and who he is only leads us to an idolization of Jesus.[103]

By now one can recognize the Gnostic underpinnings of Chellew's interpretation. Christ is neither divine nor resurrected in this theology. We are to model the historic being, like some important sage. Perhaps there is no heaven also. "We must live it to see it," makes me think of the crucified criminal, who said, "Jesus, remember me when you come into your kingdom." Not much time left to "live it!" According to *Whosoever,* we should doubt what Jesus said or meant by "I tell you the truth, today you will be with me in paradise." The absence of the terminology like "grace" in gay theology is critical. You don't practice grace. It's not historically frozen in the past, but is present. In one respect it is not free – it requires a repentant heart and a commitment to receive it. Grace abounds when sin is contritely confessed. The absence of grace in gay-theology results from the removal of sin from Church lexicon.

Actually, idolization of Jesus is OK! On the other hand, to not follow Scripture is to declare allegiance to another God – self, which is true idolatry. Nothing and no one may have the worship, love, and service that belong to God alone. And here sex can so easily become an idol. The following record of Armistead Maupin's testimony illustrates this point:

In the baths, he found remarkable qualities of communication with men whose names he never knew, men with whom he did not even have sex, with whom he embraced and then moved on, all of which left him with a nearly religious feeling. 'I felt very close to God,' he says. Then, perhaps mindful that our conversation is being recorded for radio broadcast, he breaks the mood and adds, 'My friends say that's because I was always on my knees.'[104]

Bruce Boone, a once devout Catholic who had entered adulthood as a Christian Brothers novice, has a Ph.D. from Berkley. He said of gay sex:

The first time you suck dick, it really is like Holy Communion. Mystical. Know what I mean?...This isn't shocking the way people think – it's about dissolving the self.[105]

According to Frank Browning:

In Boone's quest, [oral sex] was in some profound measure to find the unity that divided the dictates of his spirit from the drives of his flesh, and so ...[oral sex] became Holy Communion.[106]

Browning explored the subject of spirituality and sex for two years with homosexual and heterosexual men and women. He found the association between sex and God came to be extraordinarily common. He describes the posits of the late French writer George Bataille in explaining this phenomenon:

Most of the time we respect established taboos, abiding by the routines of social contract that protects us from chaos....Only in the transgressive moment do we solitary humans relinquish the social identities that individuate us and distinguish us from the wild, polymorphous animal force of Eros that unifies all being.[107]

The bohemian response to civic taboo is to deny the rules of convention (like the Gnostics), to declare oneself free of taboo's boundaries. But Bataille goes further, says Browning:

To deny taboo, he would say – to claim to have erased it from how we build our lives, choose our mates, seek sex – is simply to live within a different safety zone of complacency. Only by acknowledging and searching out that framework of taboo, and then by entering into its violation, by feeling its fire, is there the possibility of shattering the self and gaining rebirth – not some distant rebirth into an eventual eternity, but a continuous rebirth that comes of touching the eternal in the present.[108]

Here lies one of the problems for those who see in gay liberation a movement of liberal social progressivism, heralding a multisexual, multicultural, multierotic system of desire, a "safe space" for the celebration of diversity. For Bataille, eroticism can only be "good" insofar as it dares to penetrate and touch the "bad" that dwells within the sacredness of the self. In the call for an inclusive "safe space" wherein GBLTQ celebrate the charm of diversity, writes Browning:

We too easily blind ourselves to our own elements of darkness.[109]

Bataille would not be surprised to find sex between gay men and lesbian women coming out of the closet. The advent of "opposite-sex-same-sexuality" reveals the value of transgression in eros and the political-ideological nature of GBLTQ culture. These acts doubly defile a Holy God.

Born Again Bisexual

Dennis Altman, author of *The Homosexualization of America, The Americanization of the Homosexual*, noted the dilemma the bisexual poses for gay and lesbian theorists. Commenting on the biological basis for homosexuality, he writes:

There is a political problem here: the great advantage of the idea that homosexuals are 'born, not made' is that it suggests the condition is unalterable, and the identity innate. There is certain comfort in being able to assert, as does Alec in Mary Renault's The Charioteer, 'I didn't choose to be what I am, it was determined when I wasn't in a position to exercise any choice and without my knowing what was happening.[110]

The greater problem with the idea of a discrete homosexual identity is that it ignores the large numbers of people who are both behaviorally and emotionally bisexual and therefore ambivalent about how far to adopt a homosexual identity. This ambivalence leads to their being attacked both by gays concerned to strengthen the idea of this identity, and by "experts" who seem affronted by ambivalence. Thus the psychoanalyst Hendrik Ruitenbeck sees bisexuality as the refuge of "those people who are unwilling to face up to their sexuality as part of their whole being."[111]

Marjorie Garber, in *Viceversa,* offers an explanation for the value of the notion of orientation "conversion" in the so-called "sexuality wars." The word "conversion" seems to recur with great frequency to describe changes, or supposed changes, in people's sexual orientation. The word, recalling Paul's experience on the road to Damascus, calls up something that happens when one is already on a road, producing an inner change of direction, a reorientation, a turn. The appeal of the conversion metaphor lies in part in its narrative clarity: "I was this, but now I'm that. I was blind, but now I see." However, observes Garber:

The mutual exclusivity of the two moments, figured as blindness and truth, would seem to preclude the possibility of so called 'bisexual conversion.'

For her, in "most cases of blindness and insight, the truth may be slightly more complicated."[112] One further convenience of some conversion stories is the instant invalidation of an inconvenient past. There was "before," and then there is "now." Apparently, if you believe in conversion, the two stages need not have anything to do with each other. Writes Garber:

The fact that several mid-level figures in the Watergate scandal underwent highly publicized conversion experiences, becoming 'born again' and dedicating themselves to the pursuit of sectarian virtue, was widely seen as an appropriate cleansing gesture that wiped the moral and ethical slate clean. For related reasons conversions in prison are not uncommon, nor do I mean to imply that they are false or insincere. But conversion is, to use an overworked word, 'binary.' It draws a line. It is not interested in questioning the existence, or the moving nature, of the borderline.[113]

Elaine Pagels, author of *Adam and Eve and the Serpent*, observed that:

...converts as Justin, Athenagoras, Clement, and Tertullian all describe specific ways in which conversion changed their own lives and those of many other, often uneducated, believers, in matters involving sex, business, magic, money, paying taxes, and radical hatred. Their own accounts suggest that such converts changed their attitudes toward the self, toward nature, and toward God, as well as their sense of social and political obligation, in ways that often placed them in diametric opposition to pagan culture.[114]

One should note that Paul and many Christians did not ask to meet Christ, they were seemingly pursued as Ann Phillips had witnessed [at the beginning of this chapter] – "it seemed as though God hunted me down." However, the immediate question is: Does God convert one to bisexuality?

Against a backdrop of conversion ideologies, Garber cites the recent development of a button declaring the wearer to be a "born-again bisexual." Many persons have written memoirs or appeared on talk shows to explain how they used to think of themselves as gay or straight and now think of themselves as bisexual. But the nature of these personal adjustments does not, by and large, present itself as exclusion or denunciation, or a rewriting of the whole personal narrative. Rather it tends to take the form of inclusiveness, what a formerly gay man now involved with a woman described as "finding the other half of the human race attractive." It was not that he had lost his interest in men – not at all. But he was now involved with a woman.[115]

"I know now I'm bisexual," a woman may say. To such statements, Garber says, "But these are not conversions." Conversions are not rheostats but on-off experiences. They are often, in the secular world, motivated by considerations we could call political, such as solidarity, heterosexual privilege, a decision that certain life activities, like having children, belong to a world that is hetero- rather than homosexual. On the other hand, in the spiritual world, conversion could be motivated by issues of faith, by a belief that homosexuality and bisexuality are against God's law. Says Garber:

These days conversion narratives are often closely related to the whole question of sexual labels and of catagories of identity.[116]

The stereotypical sexual conversion narratives can go either from straight to gay, or from gay to straight. Garber concludes that the notion of legitimate bisexual conversion crashes against a power boundary – the "People's erotic investment in the institution of marriage."[117] The collateral impact on the institution of heterosexual marriage from the legalization of say bisexual marriage would be enormous. Such impact is addressed in Chapters 7 and 8. But more surprising to the heterosexual observer, are the consequences of full legitimacy of bisexuality within gay and lesbian communities. Garber writes:

'Just a phase' – it's what many parents say and hope when their children tell them they're gay, lesbian, or bisexual. But bisexuals are also accused of going through a 'phase' by many gays and lesbians, who consider that there are really only two poles, straight and gay. Once they grow up, the idea seems to be, they will know which one they are. Until that time they are waffling, floundering, vacillating, faking, posturing, or being misled by dangerous acquaintances. Bisexuality thus gets defined as intrinsically immature, as, in a way, the very sign of immaturity, and bisexuals are urged by many gays, as well as many straights, to put away childish things.[118]

Writing under the subject "Fluidity of Sexual Preference," in their book *Dual Attraction*, authors Martin S. Weinberg, Colin J. Williams and Douglas W. Pryor explain the impact AIDS has had on the orientation of bisexuals.[119] Given that AIDS has been called a "gay disease" and that bisexuals are widely thought of as carriers of the disease, could the disease change a bisexual preference? Was their dual attraction fixed, or could it be given up easily? If so, were they "really" bisexual? All these questions reflect on the wider question of the adaptability of sexual preference to environmental change. What is changeable and what is not? Weinberg found that the major change for the bisexuals was their avoidance of men – particularly bisexual men – as sexual partners. Women were especially likely to do this.

I wouldn't sleep with bisexual men at this point and I would have in the past. [Why?] Because they could possibly be carrying the [HIV] virus. It seems risky to sleep with men who have been sleeping with other men. (F)

It's been comforting to be able just to relate to females and I feel that's an easy and valid option and a safe one too. (F)

Weinberg found not only did bisexual women reject men as sex partners, but to a lesser degree bisexual men did as well.

I've stopped having sex with men. AIDS was a big reason. It was just not worth it. I was afraid that women would not want to be involved with a bisexual man. My identity as a bisexual has diminished as I don't act on my bisexual feelings. (M)

Since I feel flexible in my sexuality and can choose between genders, I've made a conscious effort to choose women and avoid the AIDS problem. (M)[120]

Thus the AIDS crisis forced many bisexuals to examine their sexual preference and to make choices. They were more aware of the flexibility of their choices, at least insofar as their sexual behavior was concerned. All aspects of the bisexuals' sexual preference seemed to be touched by the emergence of AIDS: their frequency of sex; their number and balance of same sex/opposite sex partners; their view of sexual pleasure versus intimacy; their choice of some sex acts over others, and so on. And this has occurred through factors in the social environment that Weinberg described as involved relationships, group ideologies, group support, the sexual politics of minorities, and the wider community in which they became involved. In sum, says Weinberg, "AIDS had sharply increased the importance of environmental factors."[121]

Weinberg also found many other reasons bisexuals gave for changing their orientation. He writes:

...deciding that the heterosexual label more accurately fit them; problems of self-acceptance; a result of undergoing therapy; a spiritual transformation; a desire for monogamy; wanting a traditional marriage; and having a baby. This last case is instructive as it shows how a change in sexual preference can be affected by a typical life event, which is often underrated in academic theories of sexuality.[122]

Here Weinberg speaks of the phenomenon examined in the testimony by Patrick Califia-Rice in the previous Section "Queer Christianity." Where in Scripture is lifestyle *space* given for bisexuality or flexibility in sexual preference?

Consequences of Sexual Experimentation

'When I was about 15, the six or eight boys who hung together indulged in a summer of group masturbation, oral sex, and attempts at anal sex. This passed as soon as we discovered girls'.[123]

Therefore God gave them over in the sinful desires of their hearts to sexual impurity for the degrading of their bodies with one another. They exchanged the truth of God for a lie, and worshipped and served created things rather than the Creator – who is forever praised. Amen. For this reason God gave them over to degrading passions; for their women exchanged the natural function for that which is unnatural and in the same way also the men abandoned the natural function of the women and burned in desire toward one another, men with men committing indecent acts and receiving in their own persons the due penalty of their error (Romans 1:24-27).

Some believe that one's sexual orientation is discovered, not chosen. Believing Bailey's argument for inversion, gay Christians have chosen to interpret Paul's definition of "natural" and "unnatural acts" (Romans 1: 24-27) as meaning that a lesbian or gay should not attempt to live a heterosexual lifestyle and heterosexuals should not venture outside opposite sex relations. Woe that life could be simplified into such tidy political categories and legalistic moral interpretations. Indeed, we have seen that Queer theology argues for sexual fluidity. Queer and Gay Christian notions contribute nothing but deception to the person who wonders about the consequence of sexual experimentation. How is a wavering youth to resolve his or her identity without exploring both sexual terrains? Is finding one's orientation as simple as the 15-year old boy (above) makes it out? Just experiment with the sexes – attempt some anal sex, a little oral sex, some vaginal sex, and then decide.

Albert the Great (Albertus Magnus, 1193-1280, teacher of Thomas Aquinas), in a short reference, gives five reasons to avoid indulging in homosexual behavior:

This is the most detestable of practices: it proceeds from a burning frenzy; it has a disgusting foulness; those addicted to it seldom succeed in shaking off the vice; and, finally, it is as contagious as any disease, rapidly spreading from one to another.[124]

It is to his last reason – the matter of contagion, that we need focus in this section. The more contemporary and pragmatic, Phyllis Chesler argues, as do many others, that anyone can become bisexual, if not, homosexual, just by acquiring enough experience. She cites the following passage from Gilbert D. Bartell, *Group Sex,* 1971, in illustration:

When a couple is new to swinging and the woman has never been exposed to another woman, she usually says that she would find this repulsive and cannot imagine it. After the first two or three parties where she sees women obviously enjoying each other, she is likely to modify her stand and say, 'I do enjoy having a woman work on me, but I could never be active with another women.' Then, when she has been in swinging for several months and attending many parties, she may well say, 'I enjoy everything and anything with a women, either way she wants to go.'…at large open parties we observed that almost all the women were engaged in homosexual activity with obvious satisfaction, especially if a younger group is involved.[125]

Alfred Kinsey claimed the first few sexual encounters could be crucial to influencing the direction of sexual preference. Negative experiences drove people away from particular practices and positive experiences reinforced behaviors. A pro-heterosexual web site had this to say about experimentation:

We do not recommend trying GBLTQ out. Having sex with another of the same sex will not tell you whether you are gay or lesbian! It will tell you your body is designed to respond to physical and sexual touch, indeed gross deception.[126]

In their study of bisexuals at the San Francisco Bi-center, Weinberg cites experimentation (they used "encouragement") as instrumental in leading people to initially adopt the label bisexual. The opportunity for experimentation often came from a partner who already defined himself as bisexual:

We had been together two or three years at the time – he began to define as bisexual....[He] encouraged me to do so as well. He engineered a couple of threesomes with another woman. Seeing one other person who had bisexuality as an identity that fit them seemed to be a real encouragement. (F)[127]

Women were more likely to be pressured into experimentation. Weinberg discovered that occasionally the "encouragement" bordered on coercion as the men in their lives wanted to engage in a "ménage-a-trois" or group sex:

I had a male lover for a year and a half who was familiar with bisexuality and pushed me towards it. My relationship with him brought it up in me. He wanted me to be bisexual because he wanted to be in a threesome. He was also insanely jealous of my attractions to men, and did everything in his power to suppress my opposite-sex attractions. He showed me a lot of pictures of naked women and played on my reactions. He could tell that I was aroused by pictures of women and would talk about my attractions while we were having sex...He was twenty years older than me. He was very manipulative in a way. My feelings for females were there and [he was] almost forcing me to act on my attractions...(F)[128]

Weinberg found that encouragement also came from sex positive organizations, primarily the Bisexual Center, but also places like San Francisco Sex Information (SFSI), the Pacific Center, and the Institute for Advanced Study of Human Sexuality.

After studying the development of sexual preference among bisexuals, Weinberg concludes that generally sexual attraction preceded sexual behavior regardless of same- or opposite-sex interest. However, heterosexual development appeared to be completed before homosexual development, suggesting that for many bisexuals, homosexuality is an "add-on" to an already-developed heterosexuality. Moreover, bisexuals experience a mix of feelings, attractions, and behaviors during their sexual development that they cannot satisfactorily understand by adopting the identity "heterosexual" or "homosexual." This means that they are open to the effects of further sexual experiences that these exclusive identities would tend to deny.[129]

An open gender schema allows them to react sexually to a wider range of stimuli. Developing an open gender schema seems to involve a "discovery" of attractions to the same sex. Some bisexuals experience this as the discovery of "something that has always been there," now recognized and celebrated. Others see it as a complement to their growing personalities, a new potential they have discovered – for example, in the case of exclusively heterosexual women who adopt feminism and become open to lesbianism. Various people may experience the "add-on" nature of bisexuality differently. Weinberg discovered most persons engaging in bisexual behavior do not take on the identity "bisexual." Such persons somehow temporarily set the gender schema aside to avoid the implications of their bisexual behavior. Thus we find the "heterosexual" married man who frequents public toilets for homosexual sex, the male hustler who has a girl friend, and the "heterosexual" married woman who engages in homosexual sex at a swing parties. The "add-on" nature of bisexuality may be experienced differently by various people. Weinberg suggests that for men, more widespread involvement in early same-sex behaviors makes the "add-on" experience more likely to be one of continuity. For women, more early emphasis on emotional exploration makes experiences more likely to be of personal growth.[130]

Weinberg found evidence of substantial change in an individual's sexual preference. For example, one study noted the effect of the feminist movement on women's sexuality, teaching some women that relating both emotionally and sexually to other women is an option. Another study focused on a group of women who were all heterosexual in behavior and identity before participating in swinging. As a response to their husbands' wishes and their observations of other women, they became involved in sex with other women, and all of them eventually identified themselves as bisexual. Their bisexuality, moreover, was an addition to their previous heterosexual interest, and they still preferred heterosexual sex.[131]

Based on insights into the ways in which early sexual experiences are related to subsequent sexual behavior, Weinberg says many persons have a continuing bisexual potential throughout their lives, regardless of the sexual identity they eventually adopt. Persons are born not only with a bisexual potential but the potential to eroticize – learn to give sexual meaning to – many things. What stands out is "the relationship between one's earliest sexual feelings and behaviors and one's subsequent sexual preference." Early experiences and attractions seem predictive of later sexual preference.[132] Weinberg concludes:

No theory of sexual preference should ignore the mundane feature of sexual pleasure. Unfortunately, many of them do. We believe that sexual pleasure in its various forms is ordinarily the main reason people have sex. The role of pure physical pleasure seems much clearer for men. Men, in all three preference groups in our research, had their first sexual experience much earlier than women. Men thus learn early that sexual pleasure is possible with both sexes, and that given the great difficulty of getting female partners, other men may be acceptable substitutes. This accounts for why there seemed to be a more genital focus on same-sex behavior of bisexual men.[133]

Weinberg writes that sexual identities – naming oneself or being named in terms of the sex of the partner one chooses – are crucial to sexual preference. Sexual identity gives meaning to a person's sexual feelings and behaviors by defining these as signs that the individual is a special type of person – in our culture a "heterosexual," "homosexual," or "bisexual." For persons dealing with the confusions that dual attractions can bring, a sexual identity can stabilize the sexual preference. If you know what you are it organizes what you do. And it allows for social support from others who identify similarly. Sexual identities provide the social "cement" which sets sexual preference in place.[134]

If bisexuality is a universal potential, then adopting the sexual identity of "heterosexual" ("straight") or "homosexual" ("gay" or "lesbian") can restrict a person from becoming "bisexual." That is, people who adopt an exclusive sexual identity may not even think about entering into sexual relations with both sexes, because it would violate their sense of who they are. This leads them to interact socially primarily with like-minded others, further reinforcing their sexual identity. Nonetheless, Weinberg found that there are "no watertight compartments between many 'heterosexuals,' 'bisexuals,' and 'homosexuals,' but rather overlaps." In their sexual profiles, the "somewhat mixed" heterosexual and "somewhat mixed" homosexual types were quite similar to two of their bisexual types. This traffic at the "boundaries" is enough to raise questions of identity. For such people, the *identity* they adopt explains their subsequent lives more clearly than does their behavior. Here Weinberg explained that bisexuals found it impossible to make sense of their sexuality by adopting either a heterosexual or homosexual identity. On the other hand, because the bisexual identity as a social category is not well defined or readily available to them, many experienced confusion in coming to grips with their sexuality and defined themselves as "bisexual" at a relatively late age. Weinberg writes:

We believe that the study of sexual identities – where they come from, how they are put together, how they are disseminated, how they are different among different cultures and groups, and how they change over time – is indispensable to any theory of sexual preference. Equally important is understanding how individuals relate to these social categories. For example, many of the 'bisexuals' in our study believed that they had to have regular sexual relations with both men and women to be bisexual. Ending up in an exclusive relationship, as many of them did, often called into question their identity as bisexual. Not being sexually active with both sexes contemporaneously seemed to some of them to breach the prevalent social definition of 'bisexuality.'[135]

Thus choice of sexual identity, or selection of a particular perspective (identity) not only provides a context in which to make sense of one's particular feelings and behaviors, but the identity one chooses in turn has important consequences for one's continuing sexual preference. Furthermore, Weinberg shows how "choice" of sexual preference is influenced significantly by "opportunity":

The swing club was inconspicuously located in a two story house along a neighborhood street in Oakland. While we saw many scenes worth reporting, we will describe one scene to convey the atmosphere of the setting and the relevance for our research. Three people were involved: a man was engaging in rear entry vaginal intercourse with a woman who was performing oral sex on another woman. At the same time other women were engaging in oral sex with women who had engaged in sex with men earlier. There were no men engaging in same-sex activity (which was generally not allowed in swing clubs). We subsequently found that a number of the women in our study had first engaged in bisexuality at a swing house. This clued us into the importance of different opportunities in the development of bisexuality.[136]

At this point, one wonders what gay-theology has to say to youth about experimental *opportunistic* sex and God's will. The boundaries in orthodox Christianity are clear and feasible – no sex before monogamous marriage, no sex outside of marriage, no experimental sex. For the past two to three thousand years sexual performance (eros and pleasure) in bed, in the bushes, or wherever, has never been condoned as a factor in Christian mate (partner) selection. Imagine you are the pastor at a MCC or any pro-gay "Christian" church. You are holding a boys or girls youth (12-15 year-olds) discussion group after viewing the Coalition for Positive Sexuality web site. Their interest has been tweaked. What will you tell them is permissible?

One possible MCC response – experimental sex is not God's will. "But how will we discover our orientation?" asks a youth. In time you will mature and fall in love with a man, or a woman, or both. You will choose to marry one or both. After God's matrimonial blessing you can have sex. The two or three of you will be bound for life. The two or three shall become one. [I don't think so].

A more likely MCC response – experimental sex is a natural process which allows you to find out your sexuality. God has not necessarily indicated your sexuality by the genitalia you have; therefore, only through trial and error will your true orientation be revealed. Since the ability to experiment is constrained by the "opportunities" that come along, same-sex activities usually come first. An astute youth, with no particular leanings either way, naively asks, "If same-sex experimentation gives us great pleasure, how much experimenting should we do before checking out the opposite sex?" Another adds, "I thought we had to get married before engaging in sex?" One answers before the pastor can respond, "It is okay to have pre-marital sex as long as you are honest and tell the partner you are just experimenting." "Does it matter if the trials are done in a group?" "Is it okay to get an older person to explain how and what we are to do?" "So it is permissible, even if I think at the time that I am straight, to check out gay or lesbian sex, just to make sure?" "What if we enjoy both?" "Pastor what is lust?" The pastor is just about to say something when the question is asked, "Is there anything we shouldn't do in order to please Jesus?" The pastor stays silent. Like so many doctrinal issues in an "inclusive" and "compromised" church, it is better to just not talk about them.

The English public school system offers a revealing historical insight into the ecology of elementary school boys, with little opportunity for heterosexual sex and who are operating in an internal environment where same-sex behavior is <u>not</u> taboo. Alec Waugh, author of *Public School Life: Boys, Parents, Masters,* writes:

In this environment there is nothing unnatural about the attraction exercised by a small boy over an elder one. A small boy is the nearest approach possible to the feminine ideal. Indeed a small boy at a Public School has many of the characteristics that a man would hope and expect to find in a woman. He is small, weak, and stands in need of protection. He is remote as a woman is, in that he moves in a different circle of life, with different friends, different troubles, different ambitions. He is an undiscovered country. The emotion is genuine and usually takes the elder boy by surprise.

Robert Graves, the poet and mythographer, wrote:

In English preparatory and public schools, romance is necessarily homosexual. The opposite sex is despised and treated as something obscene. Many boys never recover from this perversion. For every born homosexual, at least ten permanent pseudo-homosexuals are made by the public school system; nine of those ten as honorably chaste and sentimental as I was.[137]

Says Garber, the autobiographical description of the early-twentieth-century upper and upper-middle class English boy's school and the "pseudo-homosexual life," by Graves, is not the same as the postmodern phenomenon of the so-called "Straight Queer" or "Queer Straight;" the heterosexual who thinks it's cool to be taken for a gay. "Pseudo-homosexual" here is a technical term, introduced in the period by the sexologist Iwan Bloch to describe persons who have homosexual relations because they are in same-sex situations with no access to members of the other sex.[138]

Bloch describes in his survey of English history "an occasional apparent increase in homosexuality" that is driven by fashion and dissolute lifestyles, a "real epidemic increase in homosexual tendencies, which are sometimes manifested in a slight and uncertain fashion but, at other times are strongly roused and can lead to an apparent perversion of natural feeling." "Pseudo-homosexuality" was especially to be found in England among "sailors, schoolboys and university students, mine and street workers, footballers, athletes, members of certain men's and boys associations and the like" – in short, a large percentage of the male population. "Lack of intercourse with women, and especially indulgence in alcohol, here play an important part," Bloch adds, as does the English men's club, and "intensive cultivation of games, so like the cult of homosexuality" among the sport-loving ancient Greeks.[139]

Garber writes, "So the male-bonding society of English life, at virtually all levels, is conducive to "pseudo-homosexuality." How is the "pseudo" kind distinguishable from the real thing? Presumably because the pseudo-homosexuals turn out to be (also) heterosexuals – that is, bisexuals. Or what current sociology likes to describe as "sequential bisexuals" – people who have sex with same- and opposite-sex partners at different times in their lives.

Freud called such persons "contingent inverts," who under certain circumstances like "inaccessibility of any normal sexual object" and "imitation" are "capable of taking as their sexual object someone of their own sex and deriving satisfaction from sexual intercourse with him" (no mention of her). Inaccessibility of opposite sex partners and "imitation" (or "fashion") were key parts of Bloch's scheme, which he later renamed "secondary homosexuality." Today such persons are more frequently described as "situational bisexuals," or more accurately, as engaging in situational bisexuality.[140]

Fascination with the phenomenon of "pseudo-homosexuality" has been widespread. Magnus Hirschild enumerated three classes of what he called "spurious inverts" (males prostitutes and blackmailers; good-natured or pitying souls who permitted themselves to be loved; and the inmates of same-sex schools, barracks, or prisons), while Havelock Ellis made short work of this attempt at classification. Presuming that "the basis of the sexual life is bisexual," he noted that some people have homosexual feelings so strong that they persist even in the presence of potential heterosexual love objects, while in others the homosexual responses are "eclipsed" by heterosexual desire. "We could not, however, properly speak of the latter as anymore 'spurious' or 'pseudo' than the former," Ellis declared roundly. Desire was desire – there was nothing spurious or "pseudo" about it, despite the situation or "contingency" that had given it rise. The body could respond, the heart could break.[141]

Gore Vidal, Havelock Ellis and like minded observers may wish to declare the whole discussion of "real" and "pseudo" desire as indeed, "spurious" logic. Genuine Christians, however, can little afford such liberal-mindedness. Orthodox Christians contend that heterosexuality is the only authentic sexuality. Gay and pro-gay Christians contend that true "inversion" is also God inspired and thus divinely authentic. If for argument's sake, we briefly accept both polar extremes as authentic, the problem surrounding how Christians are to discover and nurture their "true sexual nature" remains. Nowhere in the Bible can be found support for any form of sexual experimentation. Nowhere is "space" to be granted to the wavering youth, while he or she establishes the sexual desires that lead to greatest sexual fulfillment and peace. To the contrary, Robin Scroggs has indicated the extreme provisions taken by Israel to isolate Jewish youth from the declared "abomination" of homosexuality. As God-fearing Christians, what are we to say to our children about experimentation, if not "no?"

A brief look into the life of Oscar Wilde reveals the potential outcome of wanton experimentation. Marjorie Garber, in *Viceversa,* described Oscar Wilde as this century's paradigmatic founding figure of gay style, wit, culture, and sensibility.[142] In writing about his conversion to homosexuality she described two "conversion narratives." In one, homosexuality "functions as a 'phase,' while marriage provides the narrative goal." In the second, "the marriage comes first, as a 'blindness' that is transcended by the discovery that one is 'really gay.'" Nonetheless, in characterizing Wilde's orientation experience she quoted gay author Johnathan Dollimore, who has written about Wilde extensively and perceptively. His interpretation is one of a conversion by "experiential pleasure" leading to bisexuality. Dollimore readily speaks of his own conversion narrative:

Because I'd never fantasized about that. I never desired it. When it happened it was just an incredible transformation...I can remember sitting down and thinking, look, if that degree of radical transformation in my sexual life is possible, where I become the unthinkable, anything is possible...So for me that was a conversion. It changed everything. And my life is still structured in relation to that revolutionary event. So I can understand the conversion narrative. What I would not tolerate, and what I would tease and be quite aggressive to is people who then embrace that sort of thing in the exclusionary identity politics mode. You know, of saying: 'I am now gay. My whole life is that story.' I just don't believe that desire works like that.[143]

Says Dollimore:

Oscar Wilde had that kind of conversion narrative that I was talking about. And one of the things I've argued in relation to Wilde is the tremendous power of that experience, when you identify yourself as having deviant desires. And what a tremendous energy that gives you in terms of social critique. The deviant desire of sensationality is his legacy. That is the way that Wilde resonates endlessly to me.[144]

He further explains:

Unless we restrict our definition of bisexuality to mean only the mythical; 'perfect bi,' who desires men and women equally, Wilde was bisexual in his experience. His 'sexual preference' became young men, and his marriage seems clearly to have been motivated at least in part by social and pecuniary concerns. But to use gay/straight here as an on-off switch is to underestimate both Wilde and the complexity of human sexuality. To say that Wilde was homosexual and not bisexual is to make a statement more indebted to politics than to biography. It is seductive but not true.[145]

There has been endless speculation about how Robbie Ross and Oscar Wilde first met. The contention made by one of Wilde's earliest biographers, Frank Harris, that it was in a public lavatory almost certainly hails from the wilder shores of that writer's imagination. It is unclear when Ross first met Wilde. However, in 1886, on the brink of his brilliant career as a playwright, Wilde was ripe for transgression. Constance (his wife) was pregnant with their second son and Wilde recoiled from her bloated, blotched appearance, so much at variance with his exaggerated Hellenic concept of slim-waisted beauty, she once was. Montgomery Hyde writes:

The man who said he could resist everything but temptation was simply seduced by the 17-year-old Robbie – his first 'boy.'...it was Wilde's first homosexual encounter.[146]

For Robbie, flirtation and seduction were savored as part of the spice and variety of life – something which Oscar Wilde was now determined to enjoy, with the energy of one who was making up for lost time. 'Not content to spoon among available young men in his own circle, Wilde began to frequent male brothels; he boasted that he was 'feasting with panthers.''[147]

Oscar told his friend, the journalist and wit Reggie Turner, that this was the case. Robbie himself later confirmed it to one of Wilde's earliest biographers, Arthur Ransome.[148] Hyde reflects on the domestic situation at the Wilde Household, with Constance assuming Robbie is just a good border, and asks:

One wonders what was going through each protagonists' mind as they sat down to dinner together in the evening, on those occasions when Oscar was not out of town.[149]

The fact is gay theologians, such as the founder of Metropolitan Community Church (MCC), have done the same thing – had gay sex while his unsuspecting wife was next door. Gay theology is predicated on giving no significance to the boundaries and bonds set by heterosexual marriage. This being the case, one wonders why significance would now be given to "gay marriage" (see Chapter 8, Section "Paradox of GBLTQ Marriage"). Indeed, we must ask do *judgmental* terms such as adultery and promiscuity exist in gay theology? How would a MCC pastor have dealt with Oscar Wilde. At the time of Wilde's first experiment, what is a pastor to say to a married man with children, who is 15 years older than the seductive 17 year-old living in Wilde's house? What advice is to be given Constance? What importance is to be given the heterosexual marriage bonds? Finally, what guidance is to be offered as Wilde starts a second, a third, or any number of relationships?

Near the end of Wilde's life, Bosie Douglas (his second key lover) gave this picture of a lost life:

He became a sort of show for the Bohemians of Paris; the sport and mock of the boulevard...He got his dinners on credit, and borrowed money from waiters. His health was on the down grade in consequence of the intensification by alcohol of a terrible disease he had contracted. He took to weeping and cursing at the slightest provocation, and, though his wit would flare out and his learning remained with him to the last, it was a poor wreck and shadow of himself which I saw...[150]

What shall gay theologians say to a wife, when she wakes up to the fact that her husband still holds to fantasy and behavior, first nourished in early same-sex experimentation? Most will not react with the flexibility of a Clara Kinsey. Just how experimentation contributes to lust is worth study in its own right.

The status of this term "lust" in gay theology is another cognitive feat. In a sex positive, liberated philosophy, lust has been eclipsed by the more non-judgmental term "eros." Ironically, now gay author and theologian Mel White, can be quoted in setting out the orthodox boundaries on "lust." Author of *Lust: The Other Side of Love*, White says:

...when I use the word lust, I mean any sexual thought or action that is potentially disobedient or dishonoring to God or potentially demeaning or destructive to people. And when I use the phrase 'struggle with lust,' I mean those times when we are tempted, when we know the potential for lust in our own lives but are still deciding whether we will give in to lust or resist its pressure.[151]

White widens the definition of lust to include the action as well as the thought. He writes:

It is common to define lust as something that happens only in the head. When lust goes from thought to action, it is usually called only by the action's name, for example: incest, rape, adultery, and the like.[152]

He uses the term to describe the lust process from thought through to action. White says:

Lust is the common source of all the different actions, the power that keeps the action going, and the only word we have to describe the entire process.[153] *Jesus taught His disciples not to make the dangerous distinction between lust as thought and lust as action. If we see lust only as harmless sexual fantasy, we forget that the worst sexual crimes begin as harmless sexual fantasies in someone's head. By our casual and undisciplined approach to lust in its early stages, we miss the opportunity to control lust while control is still possible.*[154]

God warns against sexual lust, not because He hates His children to enjoy each other's bodies, but because He wants to protect the marriage bed and He knows where sexual disobedience will end. White gives the following Biblical illustration of lust and its consequences before God. Taken from Numbers 25, the Israelites are on route to the Promised land:

Picture that moment when God's people stumbled into an oasis where the people of Moab lived. Boys who had been born on the march, who had grown to young manhood in the wilderness, and had never known the comforts of home and hearth were surrounded by a city with…sweet-smelling girls – wearing silken dresses, reclining on pillows, and inviting the strangers to share their hospitality.

What could be wrong with one night of pleasure after a lifetime of blistered feet and dirty bodies and parched throats? 'Tomorrow we will get back to God's journey. Tonight we will lie in the arms of the Moabite women.' And again God's warning echoed in their ears: 'Do not give in to sexual lust.' The warning seemed so unreasonable. It was the young men's one chance to experience what they might never be able to experience again….They had no intention of making it a permanent relationship. It was a sexual sin, but it could be forgiven in the morning. So they stepped outside God's circle of obedience. And at sunrise, after their night of ecstasy, the young women of Moab invited them to a special breakfast…Sleepily the young men agreed. Around the heavily laden buffet, God's children watched the curious custom of the Moabite priests' sacrificing to the stone god Baal.

Nights passed. The sun rose and set. One by one the young men joined in the breakfast sacrifice. Moses walked from the camp of Israel into the cities of Moab and found the young men living with the Moabite women, worshipping the Moabite god. His pleas to them went unheard. The young men had forgotten who they were and why they had been created….And the Lord said unto Moses, Take all the heads of [these young men] and hang them up before the Lord against the sun….And Moses said unto the judges of Israel, Slay ye every one of his men that were joined to Baal-peor (Numbers 25:4,5). Twenty-four thousand young men died before the journey could begin again.[155]

White points out a critical element conspicuously absent from gay and pro-gay theology:

It helps me to remember, when I struggle with sexual lust or any other temptation, that there is a war going on. I am neither a vegetable, a machine, nor an accidental merging of sperm and egg. I am someone special whom God made, knows and cares about. I am His child and He has dreams for me…[156]

Many liken sexual urges to one's regular appetite for nourishment. Consumption at breakfast brings energy and gastronomic peace only to be followed by a repeat craving at lunch and supper. Insatiable appetites consume where and as soon as the urge occurs. Indeed, advertising on TV or in magazines for chocolates can tempt and stimulate the uncontrolled viewer into hunger pains and entice him into a subsequent search habit leading to either depression from unfulfilled yearnings or an eating frenzy. Sexual temptation can operate like hunger. "Free love" advocate Margaret Sanger argued that the energy and power of "civilized life" has its source in our sexual cravings and, therefore, civilized society needs a worldview, which allows us to consume the pleasure of orgasm to the maximum life permits. Tacit in her claim is the premise that to stand against the urges of this biological life-force is dumb and destined to end in self-defeat. This worldview, often toted under the term "sexual liberation" really assumes that we are life-long slaves to the vagaries of our own libido. Here self-constraint is not encouraged as technology, in the form of contraception and abortion, is seen as the only successful means for harnessing sexual urges and controlling the biological consequences of our sexual activities. In Sanger's "free love" society, sexual urges require gratification where, when and with whomever they may occur. Constraint is a sex negative notion and abstinence is a term never found in the lexicon for the liberated.

If it is not uncommon for our young adolescents to feel confused about their sexual identity; if they're being encouraged during those same confusing years to experiment sexually; if they're taught that virtually all forms of sexual expression are legitimate; if pleasure begets fantasy and fantasy begets lust; and if same-sex co-experimentees are the most prevalent; when we are told, "Don't worry, we don't recruit; if your kid is not gay, these programs can't make him gay," can we really be expected to believe it?

A Scriptural Boundary for Man-Boy Sex?

If a person likes to place himself at the disposal of another because he believes that in this way he can improve himself in some department of knowledge, or in some other excellent quality, such a voluntary submission involves by our standards no taint of disgrace or servility…[157]

Plato, Symposium, 385 B.C.

The Diagnostic and Statistical Manual of Mental Disorders, Fourth Edition (DSM-IV, 1994) states the following under pedophilia:

The paraphiliac focus of Pedophilia involves sexual activity with a prepubescent child (generally age 13 or younger). The individual with Pedophilia must be age 16 years or older and at least five years older than the child. …Individuals with pedophilia generally report an attraction to children of a particular age range….These activities are commonly explained with excuses or rationalizations that they have 'educational value' for the child, that the child derives 'sexual pleasure' from them, or that the child was 'sexually provocative' – themes that are also common in pedophiliac pornography.[158]

Donald L. Faris, writes that what the homosexual lobby groups want is nothing less than a return to the pre-Christian paganism of the Greco-Roman world. They want sexual practices to be separated from moral restraint. In the name of "openness," "tolerance," "justice" and "love," they want doing whatever they want, with whomever they want, to have the same legal status in society as marriage. They want their version of "sexual orientation" (sexual behavior) to have the same sort of protection from adverse discrimination as racial origin. Specifically focusing on North American Man/Boy Love Association (NAMBLA), Faris notes the Association wants consensual sex permitted with children of any age in the name of children's rights. Recognizing NAMBLA is too often considered only a fringe element of the GBLTQ community, and therefore overlooked by the greater society, he warns:

Is this [NAMBLA's goal] really out of line with the goal of sexual liberation that is implicit in the Kinsey Report of 1948 or the kind of 'value-free' sex education that is being promoted in many education systems?[159]

Faris argues that the return to pre-Christian paganism is not only implicit in the "gay movement," it has been spelled out explicitly in a "gay manifesto for the 1990s" written by two Harvard graduates, Marshall Kirk and Hunter Madsen. Their book, *After The Ball,* concludes with a section entitled, "Gay Love Among the Pagans," in which they confess the emptiness, pathos and misery that the modern "gay lifestyle" brings to people's lives by the time they are thirty-five or forty. They are no longer attractive or sought after by younger homosexuals. Their answer to this problem – to return to the "traditional gay family" of the time of Plato. Faris relates the text of their proposal as follows:

The ancient Greek model seems to have worked something like this….As with all relationships, that of the erastes and the eromenos entailed an understood exchange: the youth would share his beauty and <u>enthusiasm</u>, the adult his strength, security, and guidance – as well as more tangible assets, including training in arms, a position in the adult's business, and so forth. Both parties would benefit to an extent beyond mere genital relief. From the point of view of the community, as well, this arrangement discharged a natural need – for homosexual gratification – in a manner advantageous to public character and morality. Similarly, it was understood that when the eromenos became a full-fledged man – and absorbed all (socially valuable) teaching that the erastes could impart – he would cease to be a lover, and would marry a woman and sire children. Neither his nor his former erastes' marriage, however, would end their friendship, nor prevent either one of them from forming a fresh alliance, in turn, with a younger male…and so on. Something like this, suitably updated (that is, without the wife and kids), is what we tentatively *recommend as a new ideal for gay men – family structure of their own.*[160] *[my underline]*

Hunter and Madsen are careful to state later in the book that they would "not advocate sex with minors," but who is a minor? Puberty, they point out, is now arriving earlier in children's lives, often in the 10 to 12 year-old range. And modern societies, under the pressure of various lobbies, are lowering the age of consent. It is 14 years now in many jurisdictions and 12 years in the Netherlands. William Gairdner points out that we are not far separated in legislation from the Netherlands. He writes:

Unbelievably, radical homosexuals have become so influential and mainstream ever since about 1960, that by 1977 the U.S. Federal Commission on Civil Rights actually called (so far unsuccessfully) for a lowering of the age of consent for all sexual acts, from the current 14 for heterosexual and 18 for homosexual acts, to age 12 for both. Such a law would have given anyone the 'right' to sexually use consenting children in any way they pleased without fear of parental interference. In other words, under such a law you could not legally prevent a 40-year-old from seducing your 'consenting' 12-year-old son or daughter. In Holland today, the age of consent for homosexual sex is 12, as long as parents do not formally object. Such laws, wherever they may arise in history, always represent a blatant retreat by the state from its traditional protections: of family, of sound parental authority, of children from bad parents, of the sexual exclusivity of the family, and of normal procreational life.[161]

Michael Swift, in *Gay Community News*, writes:

We will sodomize your sons....We shall seduce them in your schools, in your dormitories, in your gymnasiums, in your locker rooms, in your sports arenas, in your seminaries, in your youth groups, in your movie theatres, bathrooms...wherever men are together. All laws banning homosexuality will be revoked...Be careful when you speak of homosexuals because we are always among you....the family unit...will be abolished....All churches who condemn us will be closed. Our only Gods are handsome young men.[162]

For the reader, complacent in your confidence that Swift's proclamation is just rhetoric, re-read "Greek and Roman Sexism," in Chapter 4. On the one hand, "man-man" sex has become more tolerated in liberal circles, depathologized by the American Psychiatric Association, and has become increasingly decriminalized. On the other hand, "man-boy" sex has become anathemized, pathologized, and criminalized. Based on the rape and incest models advanced by the women's movement, man-boy sex was now seen as pathological because it was viewed as a form of power abuse, producing intense psychological disturbance. Consistent with this new perspective, Masters, Johnson and Kolodny drew sharp moral distinctions between man-man sex and man-boy sex in an early edition of their textbook *Human Sexuality*. They presented man-man sex (i.e. homosexuality) as normal and healthy, while viewing man-boy sex (i.e. pedophilia) as pathological and harmful. This begs the question to gay and pro-gay Christians: Where is the Scriptural boundary for man-boy sex?

Christopher Hewitt observed, in a lengthy discussion entitled "Is There a Positive Side to Pedophilia?" that Masters had critiqued an interview study conducted by Sandfort (1983) on a sample of 25 Dutch boys aged 10 to 16 involved in ongoing sexual relationships with men. Sandfort reported that the boys experienced their relationships, including the sexual aspects, predominantly in positive terms, that evidence of exploitation or misuse was absent, and that the boys tended to see the pedophile as a teacher, as someone they could talk to easily and with whom they could discuss their problems. Against Sandfort's findings, Masters argued that the study was methodologically flawed and speculated that possibly the "boys were so intimidated by their pedophile that they were afraid to say anything against him." They discounted Sandfort's conclusion that the relationships were positive, arguing that man-boy relationships are "inherently abusive and exploitive" and are always negative. They asserted that they were opposed to these relationships no matter how beneficial either party claimed them to be.[163]

According to Hewitt, Masters included in their textbook nine historical and cross-cultural examples of societies approving of male-male sex to provide perspective on homosexuality. However, all nine were relevant to the man-boy type but only two were at all relevant to the man-man type. Given their unqualified condemnation of man-boy sex in our society, it was inconsistent to use predominately man-boy examples from other times and places to inform the issue of man-man sex in our society. This bias represented an error of commission – using examples to inform issues with which they are not relevant.[164]

After reviewing 18 educational textbooks for bias, Hewitt found they all drew moral and conceptual distinctions between man-man sex and man-boy sex in our society. Man-man, labeled homosexuality, was presented as normal and acceptable. Man-boy, labeled pedophilia, was presented as pathological and harmful and was discussed along with other topics such as rape, incest, and man-girl sex. He found Ancient Greece and Sanbia were the most often used, occurring in 94.4 per cent and 66.7 per cent of the textbooks respectively. Nine of these 10 societies are most noted for their sanctioned transgenerational homosexuality (man-boy), whereas only one is most noted for its transgenderal homosexuality (man-man) – none is most noted for egalitarian homosexuality between adults. Hewitt discovered, all together, chapters on homosexuality included 21 separate societies, of which 81 per cent were transgenerational and 19 per cent were transgenderal.

Hewitt concluded it is hard to buy the logic that orientation outside of heterosexism is okay, except pedophilia, which characterized so much of historic homosexual behavior. How can one accept the cognition that all other options on the Kinsey spectrum are "natural" except pedophilia? Gay Christians who claim God made us this way, and therefore GBLTQ sexual behavior is blessed, have what evidence to privilege their innate orientation over pedophilia? Who is really the hardened invert? Surely the pedophile is driven by innate instincts more strongly than those now sanctioned in the GBLTQ community. In spite of the prohibition against pedophilia and the penalty for acting out this "orientation," men continue to desire relationships (not all mutually bad, according to Sandfort's study) with the young. Moreover, the likelihood of significantly overcoming this desire appears lower than gay reorientation to heterosexuality. This being the case, the pedophiles deserve more sympathy than the GBLTQ community presently gives. The only differentiation appears to be the age of the partner. So for gay Christians, the pedophile issue boils down to age!

In orthodox Christianity a 14 year-old-girl is allowed to have sex with a man only after a few conditions are met. First, she consents. Second, her parents and her church (including pastor) agree. Third, the understanding is that this is a lifelong union. Last, the marriage ceremony is performed and the public is made aware. It is possible, but highly unlikely, with all these conditions protecting the young adolescent's interests, that an older, more mature husband can abuse her.

What arrangements are needed to fulfill gay theological stipulations? Presumably in North America, MCC would perform a union if the boy in the man-boy partnership was fourteen. According to the DSM-IV, 1994, a marriage at age thirteen would be a pedophilic union. However, if one could go to the Netherlands and get a real homosexual "marriage," the boy could be twelve. Given the chance that "pedophilia" has been around as long as prostitution, it seems surprising that Scripture does not single out this behavior from other types of sexual sin. One can only conclude that the Apostle Paul must have considered it covered under the broader prohibition against heterosexual sex outside marriage and homosexual sex under any conditions.

Paul Waller observes the gay-rights pitch that homosexuality is biologically inborn or is essentially an involuntary condition that is "beyond the reach of moral judgment" and then argues:

The same logic would confer moral legitimation on pedophiles, who could also and did claim that they were made that way and therefore were unable to help themselves.[165]

Says Waller:

This aspect of the controversy is not peripheral. The virtual silence about male (homosexual) pedophilia and pederasty maintained by the mental health and social-work practitioners for, lo, these many years, is scandalous....'Homophobia' has been incessantly and unfavorably been contrasted with tolerance of 'alternative lifestyles.'[166]

Walker also notes that among gay-rights militants, ideological rationalizations for child sexual exploitation often take rather bizarre forms:

Many gay men acknowledge that they have initiated encounters [with young boys]. They argue that these types of relationships offer young boys the only real possibility for healthy acculturation into homosexuality...These attitudes, so pronounced and accepted in [gay] culture...allowed a Covenant House-Father Bruce Ritter case to develop and operate for twenty years...I despair of a liberal culture in which such pathological behavior, such physical and psychological traumas can be inflicted on children and adolescents, and rationalized in the name of gay rights.[167]

Once again we must ask, What keeps the "P" (Pedophile) out of GBLTQ? Moreover, the concept of gay-youth liberation hotlines should be terrifying to most in addition to all orthodox Christians. John B. Murray, in his article "Psychological profile of pedophiles and child molesters," described how pedophiles see themselves:

Ames and Houston (1990) reported in their study that 77 paedophiles saw themselves as introverted, shy, sensitive, and depressed. Personality test results tended to confirm these traits and added emotional immaturity, fear of being able to function in adult heterosexual relations, and social introversion (Levin & Stava, 1987)[168]

The justification given most often (by 29 per cent of the sample) was that the victim had consented. Having been deprived of conventional sex was the rationalization of 24 per cent. Intoxication was stated by 23 per cent, and 22 per cent claimed the victim had initiated the sexual activity.[169]

According to Murray, many acts of child molestation are single acts and are not repeated. However, pedophilia tends to be chronic, and recidivism may be more likely if the perpetrator is homosexual.[170] Some evidence indicates that perpetrators are shy, weak, passive, and non-assertive, with low self-esteem .[171]

NAMBLA vehemently denies that "consensual" sex with a child is "child sex abuse." In July 1998, the NAMBLA agenda gained official status when the APA published a study by three professors, Bruce Rind from Temple University, Philip Tromovitch from University of Pennsylvania and Robert Bauserman from University of Michigan. The report titled "A Meta-Analytic Examination of Assumed Properties of Child Sexual Abuse Using College Samples," a quantitative analysis of 59 studies, sparked vehement criticism because of its conclusion that "child sexual abuse does not cause intense harm on a pervasive basis regardless of gender in the college population." The authors want a redefinition of "child sexual abuse." If it was "a willing encounter" between "a child and an adult" or "an adolescent and adult" with "positive reactions" on the part of the child or adolescent, it would no longer be called "child sexual abuse." It would be labelled scientifically as "adult-child sex" or "adult-adolescent sex." They want society to use a "value-neutral term."[172]

The study which appeared in the 1998 issue of APA-published *Psychological Bulletin* could claim that "lasting negative effects of [child sex abuse] were not pervasive among [sexually abused] students," especially males. They recommend a redefinition [of child sex abuse] that would "focus on the young person's perception of his or her willingness to participate and his or her reactions to the experience. The APA claims that publication "does not imply endorsement," yet in no way has the APA criticized the study nor renounced its premise or recommendations. In fact, on May 14, the association's chief executive officer, Raymond Fowler, said the report has been peer-reviewed and "is a good study."

Jan LaRue, senior director of legal studies at the Family Research Council warns the reader that NAMBLA and others who want to have their way with our children will use the APA-published study to attempt to change how we protect children from sexual abuse in our public policies and laws. Such efforts need to be vigorously and consistently resisted. LaRue writes:

As a lawyer who has spent many years trying to protect children from sexual abuse and exploitation, I have more than a legal interest in doing so. Between the ages of 5 and 8, I was sexually molested by four different men. The fourth individual used his three sons to hold me down in repeated violent encounters. The authors of the APA study would agree that all of the encounters were child-sexual abuse because I did not consent and never viewed them with 'positive reactions' – quite the contrary.

What the authors need to consider is what impact the forced encounters had on my becoming sexually involved at age 16 with a man in his 40s. That relationship was not forced – it was what the authors define as consensual. If I had been asked at the time, or at college age, whether I had positive reactions to the relationship, the answer would have been a resounding 'yes.' I thought I was 'in love' and believed that he loved me, even though he never said so. I realized later that I had truly consented to sex with this man. I did what I did because it was necessary to be with him – so that he would love me back. That is coercion, not consent. The law defines it as statutory rape or unlawful sexual intercourse. Ask me now if I have 'positive reactions' to the relationship. Mental-health professionals have found that sexually abused children commonly become sexually promiscuous as children and adolescents – and many of them probably think they consented.[173]

Michael Seto, in his review of *Pedophiles and Sexual Offences Against Children*, written by Dennis Howitt, argues that defining pedophilia as:

...a generic name for sexual offenders against underage persons' conflates and therefore confuses the study of the motivations and characteristics of men who have sex with prepubescent and pubescent children (approximately 12 years old and younger) and men who have sex with adolescents.[174]

In sustaining his view, Seto writes:

Restricting the definition to prepuberal children is meaningful because the legal definitions of 'child' can vary across jurisdictions and across time, while puberty is a biological event that is nonarbitary and observable.[175]

At this point I am wondering if this man ever had children of his own. Is he actually splitting hairs over the difference between a 12 and a 14 year-old's maturity when it comes to consensual sex? Seto writes:

Also, from a evolutionary perspective, a sexual preference for sexually immature partners is anomalous, while a sexual interest in sexually maturing but legally unavailable partners, i.e. adolescents, is not.[176]

I should state at this point I do not agree with social constructionist arguments that, like consensual same-sex interactions in the past, the current legal prohibition of adult-child sex is simply moralistic and paternalistic, reflecting current attitudes, beliefs, and values about human sexuality. There is a fundamental distinction between same-sex interactions between adults and sexual interactions between adults and children, because there are empirical differences between adults, adolescents, and younger children in terms of cognitive development, moral reasoning, and experience. Most young children cannot give true informed consent to sexual interactions with an adult because they have less experience and knowledge, especially regarding sexuality, and immature abilities to refuse consent in the face of the authority of an adult figure or to appreciate the potential long-term consequences of giving consent [177]

To most readers, this is a hollow reassurance. Like Kinsey and Rind, Seto has a liberationist agenda. They all wish to release child-adult sexual activity from the closet to which it is confined. They would confine the term "abuse" to those contacts between adults and children where the child reported that she did not freely participate in the encounter or had negative reactions to it. But right and wrong for Christians is not decided by the experimentee's feelings, but by God's revelation. The Creator of this universe is defiled by the notion of a man-man man-boy sexual and moral boundary. Now we leave those I have called the "compromised" group and enter the arena of gay and pro-gay theologians bent on fully revamping Christian revelation to suit GBLTQ behavior. I call this group the "fully deceived."

The Rev. Dr. John Spong

The chief opposition to gay equality is religious. We may conduct much of our liberation efforts in the political sphere or even the 'cultural' sphere, but always undergirding those and slowing our progress is the moral/religious sphere. If we could hasten the pace of change there, our overall progress would accelerate – in fact, it would be assured.[178]

Paul Varnell, Gay Columnist

If we perform the radical surgery [on Christianity] that is required, not only will certain traditional formulations of faith fall by the wayside, but also much of the presumed content of Christianity, and rightly so. Our only consolation is that if we do not intervene radically and soon the patient will die.[179]

Thomas Sheehan, professor of religious studies, Stanford University

The Christian homosexual position when carefully examined can be exposed for what it is at its very core: an attack upon the integrity, sufficiency, and authority of Scripture, which for the Christian church is an attack upon the very nature of our Holy God.[180]

One of the more prolific, if not controversial, pro-gay theologians has been the Episcopalian Bishop, John Shelby Spong. Although defining himself "first and foremost as a Christian believer" who abhors "creedal" religions, he offers the following personal creed:

I do not define God as a supernatural being. I do not believe in a deity who can help a nation win a war, intervene to cure a love one's sickness…Since I do not see God as a being, I cannot interpret Jesus as an earthly incarnation of this supernatural deity…I do not believe that this Jesus could or did in any literal way raise the dead, [or] overcome a medically diagnosed paralysis…I do not believe that Jesus entered this world by miracle of a virgin birth or that virgin births occur anywhere accept in mythology….I do not believe that the experience Christians celebrate at Easter was the physical resuscitation of the three-days-dead body of Jesus, nor do I believe that anyone literally talked with Jesus after the resurrection moment…I do not believe that Jesus, at the end of his earthly sojourn, returned to God by ascending in any literal sense into a heaven located somewhere above the sky….I do not believe that this Jesus founded a church or that he established an ecclesiastical hierarchy beginning with twelve apostles and enduring to this day….I do not believe that human beings are born in sin and that, unless baptized or somehow saved, they will for ever be banished from God's presence….I regard the church's traditional exclusion of women from positions of leadership to be not a sacred tradition but a manifestation of the sin of patriarchy….I do not believe that homosexual people are abnormal, mentally sick, or morally depraved. Furthermore, I regard any sacred text that suggests otherwise to be wrong and ill-informed. My study has led me to the conclusion that sexuality itself, including all sexual orientation, is morally neutral and as such can be lived out either positively or negatively. I regard the spectrum of human sexual experience to be broad indeed. On that spectrum, some percentage of the human population is at all times oriented toward people of their own gender. This is simply the way life is. I cannot imagine being part of a church that discriminates against gay and lesbian people on the basis of their being….I do not believe that all Christian ethics have been inscribed either on tablets of stone or in pages of the Christian scriptures and are therefore set for all time. I do not believe that the Bible is the 'word of God' in any literal sense. I do not regard it as the primary source of divine revelation. I do not believe that God dictated it or even inspired its production in its entirety. I see the Bible as a human book mixing the profound wisdom of sages through the centuries with limitations of human perceptions of reality at a particular time in history.[181]

Theism, in Spong's line of thinking, is "a definition of God which has journeyed with self-conscious human beings from primitive animism to complex modern monotheism." Moreover, says Spong:

In every one of its evolving forms, theism has functioned as it was originally designed to do. Theism was born as a human coping device, created by traumatized self-conscious creatures to enable them to deal with the anxiety of self-awareness. It was designed to discover or to postulate the existence of a powerful divine ally in the quest for human survival and in the process to assert both a purpose to existence and a meaning to life.[182]

We human beings even accentuated our concept of God's power by developing a language of worship in which we groveled, as slaves might be expected to do before a master….We acknowledged ourselves as deserving only condemnation, for we are those 'Who stand condemned before the throne of grace,' clearly unable to please our deity without divine aid.[183]

The Eastern, Masonic and Gnostic shadows are evident in the direction Spong looks. He says, "Perhaps we can cast the Christian experience in nonthesistic images. It is certainly worth a try." He writes:

Many sources in human history encourage us to explore this new avenue. The Buddhist tradition, for example, is not a theistic religion. Nowhere in classical Buddhism do the Buddhists posit the existence of an external deity. When Buddhists experience bliss or transcendence in meditation, they do not attribute this to contact with the supernatural. They assume that such states are natural to humanity and can be learned by anyone who lives right and learns the proper spiritual techniques. Experiencing bliss involves emptying the self so as to transcend the limits of both subjectivity and objectivity to be one with Being itself, which Buddhists describe as timeless and uncreated. However, it hardly would be proper to assert that the Buddhists of the world are atheists, unless atheism can be called profoundly religious.

While visiting in China some years ago,…I stayed to pray in that temple with its statues of Buddha and its magnificent and striking colors, which called one into an intensity of consciousness. Of course I prayed to the God of my Christian experience, but in the calm of that place…I was sure that I was on holy ground…Exploring the levels of meaning that can be found in an Eastern faith tradition can help us learn to see through such limited words as theism. It also reveals that our ancient Western definitions of God do not exhaust the reality of God.[184]

Spong sees theism, "with its supernatural God ready to take care of us," as a delusion that "encourages worshipers to remain in a state of passive dependency." When he writes and speaks publicly, he hopes to demonstrate, something deeply invigorating about discovering a new maturity and realizing that God can be approached, experienced, and entered in a radically different way…not a deity who is "a being," not even if we claim for God the status of the "highest being." He speaks rather of God, "as the ground and Source of All Being" and therefore the presence that calls "to step beyond every boundary," inside which he has vainly been seeking dependent security, and now "into the fullness of life with all of its exhilarating insecurities."[185] Scoffs Spong:

Christians, for example, assert that God is a Holy Trinity, as if human beings could figure out who or what God is. The Holy Trinity is not now and never has been a description of the being of God…Twenty-first century Christians must now come to understand that God does not inhabit creeds or theological doctrines shaped with human words.[186]

From what source does Spong draw such conviction? Spong agrees with his theological ally, Robert Funk, founder of the Jesus Seminar, when Funk demands that "Jesus needs a demotion."[187] Says Spong:

An unusual and gifted scholar, Funk gives voice in this suggestion to the fact that the theistic framework in which Jesus has been captured is no longer either compelling or believable in our generation. For Christians not to face that fact is to be out of touch with reality. However, like so many critics of supernaturalism and theistic thinking, Funk also seems to assume that the only alternative to supernaturalism is naturalism and the removal from Jesus of any divine claim. If removing the theistic interpretive material from around Jesus constitutes the demotion that Funk feels to be necessary, than I am all for it. But the Jesus who remains when Funk has completed his task looks to me not like a demoted Jesus but a court-martialed Jesus, a destroyed Jesus. This approach never addresses the question of what there was about Jesus' life that caused the theistic interpretations to be thought appropriate in the first place.[188]

Fearless to criticism, Spong contends he "seeks a Christianity that preserves divinity but not supernatural theism." He writes:

The result will be a humanity so deeply and powerfully drawn that the artificially imposed barrier between the human and the divine will fade and we can recognize that these two words – human and divine – do not point to separate entities; rather, they are like two poles on a continuum that appear to be separate and distinct, yet when one travels from one to other, the discovery is made that their shadows blend into and invade each other….I seek in Jesus a human being who nonetheless makes known, visible, and compelling the Ground of All Being.[189]

Clearly there was a profound experience that caused the theistic God-interpretation to be laid upon Jesus. 'What was it?' [He warns his audience]: 'The reformation I am proposing may well kill Christianity. This is a real and enormous risk. The greater risk which motivates me, however, is the realization that a refusal to enter the reformation will certainly kill Christianity. Even though, by traveling the route I am proposing, we may not arrive at a living Christian future, I see no alternative…'[190]

Taking aim at the heart of orthodox Christianity, Spong argues:

This liturgical interpretation of Jesus' death has resulted in a fetish in Christianity connected with the saving blood of Jesus….Believers sing of being 'washed in the blood' or 'saved by the blood' of Jesus….I have always found these images to be repulsive.[191]

The deepest problem created for the doctrine of the atonement, according to Spong, is not even this, but the fact that "we" are post-Darwinian men and women. He writes:

And 'as post-Darwinians' we are in possession of a very different image of the ori-

gins of human life; and it's quite obvious that the Darwinian view, not the traditional Christian myth, has prevailed in the life of our civilization. The post-Darwinian world also recognizes that there never was a perfect man or a perfect woman who fell into sin in an act of disobedience. That account is not true either historically or metaphorically. Human beings are emerging creatures; they are a work in progress. Neither perfect nor fallen, they are simply incomplete.[192]

Down a separate path from Christ, Spong calls:

...us in invitation to enter the 'New Being' about which Tillich speaks – a humanity without barriers, a humanity without the defensive claims of tribal fear, a transformed humanity so full and so free that God is perceived to be present in it.[193]

Let me stretch the boundaries once more. To the extent that the Buddha, Moses, Elijah, Isaiah, Krishna, Mohammed, Confucius, Julian of Norwich, Catherine of Genoa, Hildegrad of Bingen, Rosa Parks, Florence Nightengale, Mahatma Gandhi, Martin Buber, Thich Nhat Hanhn, Dag Hammarskjöld, or any other holy person brings life, love, and being to another, then to that degree that person is to me the word of God incarnate. No fence can be placed around the Being of God. The suggestion that Jesus is of a different kind of substance and therefore different from every other human being in kind instead of in degree will ultimately have to be abandoned. Then the realization will surely begin to dawn that to perceive Jesus as different from others only in degree is to open all people to divine potential found in the Christ-figure. It is to invite all people to step into power of living fully, loving wastefully, and having the courage to be all that any one of us can be – a self-whole, free, real, and expanding, a participant in a humanity without boundaries.[194]

One cannot miss a huge cognitive discrepancy, after all that has been said. Spong proclaims, "Jesus will always be for me the standard by which I measure the God-presence of any other. I can view him in no other way." However, after reading many of his books, I must again ask what is the basis for his conviction, indeed, opinion?

He says he has no positive experiential witness. Rather, after a self-declared futile life waiting for contact with the "supernatural Christian God," in resignation he chose to slide into a worldview described by science, secularism, Darwinism and Gnostic cognitions. He explains his descent:

I have always wanted to be a person of prayer. I have yearned to have that sense of immediate contact with the divine. Yet for longer than I have been willing to admit, even to myself, prayers addressed to an external supreme being have had little or no meaning for me. My first presumption was that this represented the lack of some essential aspect in my own spiritual development and that all I needed to do was work harder and harder to overcome this deficiency....In the course of my life I have read every prayer manual or book on prayer on which I could lay my hands. My personal library has a shelf dedicated to once-beckoning, but now discarded books on prayer. I created a prayer corner in my study...I once even printed a cross on my watch face so that every time I glanced to establish the time of the day I would be reminded to send a prayer darting heavenward to keep me connected with the God whom I hoped might be an external compass point by which my life would be guided. My great ambition was to be one who lived in a significant awareness of the divine and could thus know the peace that comes from communing with God, the heavenly one. I really did believe that discipline and perseverance would lead me to these goals.[195]

...despite this sometimes frenzied, but at least persistent, effort I could not make prayer, as it has been traditionally understood, have meaning for me. The reason, I now believe, was not my spiritual ineptitude, but rather that the God to whom I had been taught to pray was in fact fading from my view. I suppose that I would not have been able to admit that even if I had been conscious of it. This was before I was ready to enter exile....Before one is able to raise new theological questions, one must become convinced enough of the bankruptcy of old theological solutions. I, for example, had to come to the conclusion that I could never again pray in the same manner that my ancestors in faith believed they could pray. 'Yet there must be another way,' I would say to myself again and again.[196]

By deduction, Spong has declared all Christian prayer deception, trivializing the experiences witnessed in Scripture and throughout history. Jesus Himself maintained a continuous relationship with God through prayer. To whom did He pray? Or was He deceived too? Although, upholding Christ as his *standard*, Spong offers no witness to a personal relationship with God through the saving grace of Jesus Christ. Now he is convinced that God is impersonal and Jesus is not divine. So why does Spong wish to claim membership in a Christian camp which he would level? A possible answer comes from how he describes his exile:

As a believer, I am not prepared to deny the reality of the underlying Christian experience...So while claiming to be a believer, and still asserting my deeply held commitment to Jesus as Lord and Christ, I also recognize that I live in a state of exile from the presuppositions of my own religious past. I am exiled from the literal understandings that shaped the creed at its creation. I am exiled from the worldview in which the creed was formed. The only thing I know to do in this moment of Christian history is to enter this exile, to feel its anxiety and discomfort, but to continue to be a believer. That is now my self-definition. I am a believer who increasingly lives in exile from the traditional way in which Christianity has heretofore been proclaimed. 'A believer in exile' is a new status in religious circles, but I am convinced that countless numbers of people who either still inhabit religious institutions or who did will resonate with that designation.

I see in this moment of Christian history a new vocation for me as a religious leader and a new vocation for the Christian Church in all its manifestations. That vocation is to legitimize the questions, the probings, and, in whatever form, the faith of the believer in exile...I think the time has come for the Church to invite its people into a frightening journey into the mystery of God and to stop proclaiming that somehow the truth of God is still bound by either our literal scriptures or our literal creeds.[197]

A savior who restores us to our pre-fallen status is therefore pre-Darwinian superstition and post-Darwinian nonsense....the Jesus portrayed in the creedal statement 'as one who, for us and for our salvation, came down from heaven' simply no longer communicates to our world. Those concepts must be uprooted and dismissed.[198]

Given that personal experience is not the basis for Spong's claim to Christ, what can be left but an image taken from the Scriptural record? Yet, he sees the Bible as "a human book mixing the profound wisdom of sages through the centuries with limitations of human perceptions of reality at a particular time." How does he sift the sage advice from the chaff and false testimony? If Christ, the disciples, and the Apostle Paul, received a large dose of the so-called "God presence," who is Spong to overturn their recorded Scripture? [I confess I must hold my tongue and "calmly" take you through the next few pages.] I believe Rev. Spong has no defendable basis to alter Christianity, only a deep-rooted wish to liberate the GBLTQ from Christian judgment.

On one hand Spong argues that the Gospel authors did not know what is now known of the "homosexual orientation." In this line of thinking he refutes the Apostle Paul's assertion in 2 Timothy 3:16 that Scripture is God inspired. If this is not inappropriate enough, Spong actually advocates that Paul himself was a closet homosexual. The thorn in Paul's side, according to Spong, is not epilepsy, nor poor eye sight, but rather a sexual desire for other men. In *Rescuing The Bible From Fundamentalism: A Bishop Rethinks the Meaning of Scripture*, he writes:

The apostles, including Paul, had been sent to proclaim this faith and none else...He drew, through love and grace, all people to himself as he restored them to themselves, building finally that inclusive community in which there is neither Jew nor gentile, bond nor free, male nor female. For all are one in Christ, whose love can embrace even outcasts in society, even the one pronounced depraved and called an abomination, the one who by the mandate of the Law stood under the sentence of death.

This is the way my thesis would suggest that the gospel of Jesus Christ was experienced by Paul, the man from Tarsus. To me it is a beautiful idea that a homosexual male, scorned then as well as now, living with both the self-judgment and social judgments that a fearful society has so often unknowingly pronounced upon the very being of its citizens, could nonetheless, not in spite of this but because of this, be one who would define grace for Christian people. For two thousand years of Christian history this Pauline definition has been at the very core of the Christian experience. Grace was the love of God, an unconditional love that loved Paul just as he was. A rigidly controlled gay male, I believe, taught the Christian church what the love of God means and what, therefore, Christ means as God's agent. Finally, it was a gay male, tortured and rejected, who came to understand what resurrection means as God's vindicating act...[199]

When people consider scandalous this idea that a homosexual male might have made the grace of God clear to the church, I reply, 'Yes, it is scandalous, but is that not precisely how the God of the Bible seems to work?' It is as scandalous as the idea that the Messiah could be crucified as a common criminal. It is as scandalous as the idea that a birth without acknowledged paternity could inaugurate the life that made known to us the love and grace of God. It also suggests that heterosexual people might be deeply indebted to homosexual people for many spiritual gifts that arise out of the very being of their unique life experience. Indeed, I have been the recipient of just that kind of gift from the gay and lesbian people who have shared with me their journeys with God through Christ.[200]

Here is the crux of one problem with regard to the liberal stand on homosexuality and the associated struggle for truth. If we assume Paul was not gay, the orthodox analysis of his writings on homosexuality stands as articulated earlier in this Chapter. On the other hand, accepting for an instant, Spong's thesis, one must raise two issues. First, if Paul knew personally of gay desire, he would therefore have intimate understanding of the nature that we label today as "homosexual orientation." Why would the Holy Spirit give him such conviction against homosexual acts and thoughts, if homosexuality was to be understood as a gift from God. Given a premise that Paul was gay, the argument that his writings on sexuality and immorality need re-interpretation because he did not have sufficient knowledge of the subject matter seems incredibly unwise. Second, he refers to his thorn as "a messenger of Satan":

To keep me from becoming conceited because of these surpassingly great revelations, there was given me a thorn in my flesh, a messenger of Satan, to torment me. Three times I pleaded with the Lord to take it away from me. But he said to me, 'My grace is sufficient for you, for my power is made perfect in weakness' (2 Corinthians 12:7-9).

In 1 Corinthians 5:5, Paul writes of handing a sexually immoral man over to Satan, so that his "sinful nature may be destroyed and his spirit saved on the day of the Lord." To expel him was to put him out in the devil's territory, so that being officially ostracized from the church would cause such anguish that he would repent and forsake his wicked ways. Another view is that Satan is allowed to bring physical affliction on the man, which would bring him to repentance. In this latter context, if homosexual orientation is to be seen as God's will, it needs to be seen as sinful behavior, for which repentance can bring the power and saving grace of Jesus Christ. Paul sees Christ as the source of power over this "thorn;" this "messenger of Satan."

To the orthodox Christian, Spong has insulted the third person of the Trinity, by claiming the Holy Spirit was ignorant of the human homosexual condition. Joseph Gudel, writing in the *Christian Research Journal*, underscores this point:

It is ludicrous to believe that the Creator of the universe, in guiding the biblical authors, was ignorant concerning the things we know about homosexuality through modern biology, psychology, sociology, and so forth. To deny scriptural statements about homosexuality on these grounds is to completely deny God's superintendence in the authorship of Scripture.[201]

A Lutheran pastor who had attended one of Spong's lectures wrote to him:

Are you suggesting that evil is not real? That it does not have an existence in and of itself? You do not seem to me to take the reality of evil seriously enough. The old story that you seem eager to reject, said that evil was so real and so deep that only God could root it out. That story went on to say that even for God it was costly, demanding the death of the divine son. You may well dismiss that story as mythological theistic thinking, but you also appear to have dismissed the reality of human evil. I do not believe that human life can be defined adequately until human evil is faced.[202]

Spong acknowledges that "the biggest weakness in liberal theological thought is that it minimizes the human capacity for evil."[203] However, he explains his views drawing on the Darwinian foundations of his faith. Humankind is a "work-in-progress" and until the process is finished evil will abound. He writes:

I start with the recognition that the cruelest things we human beings do to each other are direct byproducts of our struggle to survive the evolutionary process, and these actions are what drive us toward the distorted understanding that winning is the road to fulfillment.[204]

Characterizing the wrong committed upon homosexuals, Spong writes:

The fear in the noncomprehending early days of human history, then, was that if homosexuality were ever culturally accepted, it might prove attractive to a large number of people, threatening marriage, weakening society, and thus diminishing the potential for the tribe's survival.[205]

After using his "work-in-progress" model in application to Nazi persecution of Jews, Southern lynch mobs and riots at sports matches, Spong concedes he has no answers for the evil of AIDS:

There is yet another form of destructive behavior that I have experienced that I am not able to explain by reference to the human urge for survival. I recall being the guest speaker at the Meteropolitan Community Church's Cathedral of Hope in Dallas, Texas, a mostly gay and lesbian congregation. There I listened to their male choral group, 'The Positive Singers,' perform memorably and masterfully. The name of this group comes from the fact that every one of its members is HIV-positive, victimized by a potent virus that has terrorized the homosexual community. From where comes this evil? It surely cannot be located in our human incompleteness. Everything I know about both science and medicine tells me that these young gay adults did not choose their sexual orientation, and yet because they dared to practice their being in what was for them a natural way, they now live under a cloud that may ultimately be a death sentence. What sense does life make when what is a natural drive for people toward fulfillment or wholeness becomes the avenue of death for some?[206]

These are the experiences, the realities that make evil real and yet do not fit easily into my definition, which locates evil primarily in the incompleteness of humanity….How do we understand these things that seem to attack even our survival? [207]

Here Spong has neither faced the "scientific" ecology of the gay lifestyle, nor the "Scriptural" consequences of breaking the Leviticus Codes. In concluding his thinking on evil, Spong decided he had no final answers:

Perhaps there will someday be a completely adequate explanation for evil, but we have not found it.[208]

In closing this section on Rev. Spong's pro-gay theology, the following summarizes his boundariless faith:

Those who once called themselves Catholic and Protestant, orthodox and heretic, liberal and evangelical, Jew and Muslim, Buddhist and Hindu, will all find a place in the ecclesia of the future….In the ecclesia of tomorrow we will also find a way to take note of other special moments in life that have not in the past been thought of in the same breath as liturgy. I think of the decision, difficult as it surely is, to abort a fetus or to terminate a life on artificial support systems. I believe that both of these human decisions, when made responsibly, should be the subject of a liturgical act. So should the many other moments in life that cry out for a liturgical rite to wrap them into the meaning of worship. These would include such things as…divorce…loss of employment…retirement…[209]

Spong asks himself a rhetorical question and then answers:

So why does it matter that we reformulate the tenets of traditional Christianity or attempt to redefine God in non-theistic terms? What is the answer to the 'So what?' question from my critical listener?

We reimage God to keep the world from enduring the pain of a continuing reliance on a theistic deity….That same theistic God is quoted by people who want to impose their definitions of homosexuality or their values in the right-to-life movement on everyone else. So it matters how one thinks of God.[210]

In 1999, the New York chapter of a humanist organization presented Reverend Doctor John Shelby Spong with their "Humanist of the Year" award.[211]

Replacing Leviticus Code with the Condom Code

Thou shalt not lie with man, as with woman: it is an abomination (Leviticus 18:22). If a man lies with a man as one lies with a woman, both of them have done what is detestable. They must be put to death; their blood will be on their own heads (20:13).

The homosexual practices cited in Romans 1:24-27 were believed to result from idolatry and are associated with some very serious offenses as noted in Romans 1. Taken in this larger context, it should be obvious that such acts are significantly different than loving, responsible lesbian and gay relationships seen today.[212]

Troy Perry, Metropolitan Community Church founder

Rev. William R. Johnson contends that many lesbian and gay Christians are today engaged in the process of growing toward a new understanding of themselves as spiritual persons. He writes:

For most of us, the Acquired Immune Deficiency Syndrome (AIDS) pandemic has presented challenges to our spiritual selves that have demanded deeper explorations of that part of our being just so we could endure what we needed to endure. In many ways, we have been blessed by this unwelcomed, day-to-day encounter with the sacredness of life and the realities of suffering and death. Of necessity, many of us have opened ourselves to touching one another center-to-center, soul to soul.[213]

Johnson criticizes the tardiness of traditional Christian response to AIDS, giving his own summary of GBLTQ response to the pandemic. Notwithstanding, that his portrayal is at complete variance to the testimony of activists like Kramer and Kraus, and other authors such as Rotello and Shiltz, he writes:

Lesbians and gay men were the first wave of care-givers, educators, and advocates in this global pandemic. Not only did we do it, we did it well, bringing solace and quality care to many who had been abandoned by the church. In doing so, lesbians and gay men unintentionally shamed the church. We found, among one another, a true community of nonjudgmental, loving people for whom compassion had become a way of life. Ironically, for many the HIV/AIDS pandemic illuminates spiritual concerns that have always been part of lesbian and gay lives – though often unacknowledged personally or in the community. Gay and lesbian people who left the church took their spirits with them. Their spiritual lives did not end. Indeed, for some, spirituality became more vital than ever once deinstitutionalized.[214]

Johnson continues his apology of gay theology:

The sex-for-procreation rigidity of the Judeo-Christian tradition has caused many human beings to fragmentize sexuality from a holistic understanding of personhood....For those of us who are lesbian and gay, this means affirming our physical, emotional, psychological, social, spiritual, and erotic responsiveness to persons of our own gender as integral to our personhood. The quest for integrity is the ongoing process of integrating the components of <u>self</u> into a congruent, meaningful whole. Affirming our same-gender orientation, and its expression in social and erotic relationships, rather than accepting negative cultural or ecclesiastical definitions of our identity, is essential to the process of integration. As human sexuals we have a God-given right to responsibly express, not deny or repress our natural sexuality.[215] *[my underline]*

His premise, "As human sexuals we have a God-given right to responsibly express, not deny or repress our natural sexuality" lies at the heart of this section. We have covered pretty well all the key guidance found in Scripture. So let us approach the issue from another angle and challenge Johnson and like-minded theologians to justify "responsible self-expression."

This is really another way of asking the question first posed in Chapter 1. What is the sustainable philosophy for GBLTQ culture? Surely gay and pro-gay Christians have to articulate what responsible love looks like, and Christ deserves better than to preach a "God-ordained lifestyle" that only works with consistent use of prophylactics, drugs and finely articulated safe sex guidance. To the orthodox Christian and a large portion of secular heterosexuals, it is just not credible to claim rights to a professed "natural sexuality" that is only sustainable when the vast majority live in fear of death, require continuous "Wellness" indoctrination and a condom. If you are going to throw out the Leviticus Code, then what is a responsible replacement sexuality?

Betty Berzon, Ph.D., author of *Positively Gay: New Approaches to Gay and Lesbian Life* writes:

One of the greatest gifts that gay and lesbian culture has given to mainstream society is the ability to talk about sex, sexuality, sexual desire, and sexual activity openly and with respect. It is not a deep, dark (and often dirty) secret, but a wonderful part of relating in the most human and spiritual way possible to one another. Should you 'go-all-the-way on the first date?' (As my high school teachers would have put it.) No reason not to if you know what you are doing and do it safely. Should you wait to get to know one another first? Of course, if that is what you feel you need to do to find the happiness and respect you need and deserve. The right and wrong way to act sexually can come to each of us through reflection, self-knowledge, experience, and good honest information about our sexual desires and health needs.[216]

The reality of gay and pro-gay theology is that nothing can be drawn from Scripture to guide "responsible GBLTQ self-expression." Johnson and Berzon address spirituality and sexuality respectively, without any association to the Creator's design and guidance. Everything is self-centered. What God is Johnson referring to? The last chapter in this book addresses this question substantially.

Eric Marcus, author of *The Male Couple's Guide: Finding a Man, Making a Home, Building a Life*, writes under the topic "Not Having Sex On The First Date":

Plenty of long-lasting relationships have started with sex before, during, and after the first date. Nonetheless there are two good practical reasons to avoid having sex on the first date: (1) it's often ultimately less complicated than having sex and (2) there are no health risks if all you do is hold hands.[217]

Marcus advises his readers on how to stay out of bed on the first and even second date:

Saying I wasn't going to bed on the first date was one thing. Figuring out how to do it was something else. It took me more years than I would like to admit to learn how to put on the brakes. I did know having sex with a man who turned out to be a disappointment left me far more miserable than discovering that I didn't like him before we became physically involved. But my need for affection and physical contact almost always overpowered the part of my brain that controls rational behavior, even when I suspected I was making a mistake. Since I found my behavior so difficult to control, I changed tactics.

I made a commitment to myself: 'I won't have sex on the first date, or the first week, or until...' But that wasn't enough, I discovered that the secret to following through with a rational decision in the face of irrational passion was to put something other than clothing between me and my date...Don't (1)Go to his home or your home. (2)Go anywhere you will be entirely alone. (3)Avoid: Using the same car.[218]

"The whole culture has to change," says Larry Kramer. "We have created a culture that in fact murdered us, killed us. What you can't help but think, if you've got any brains, is don't people ever learn anything?" Such remarks won him few fans at Sex Panic. "A culture doesn't kill people," reports Kendell Thomes, a law professor at Columbia University, "The virus kills people." Sex Panic founder Michael Warner, an English professor at Rutgers University, argues that promiscuous sex is the essence of gay liberation, and that any attempt to fight AIDS by changing the gay way of life is doomed: "it is an absurd fantasy to expect gay men to live without a sexual culture when we have almost nothing else that brings us together."[219] Promiscuity and safe sex can co-exist, Sex Panic's members argue.

Current debate over the "suicidal" health risks associated with the gay lifestyle occurs against the backdrop of evidence that homosexuals are returning to anal intercourse without condoms. In a survey of 205 gay men in Miami's South Beach, Dr. William W. Darrow, a public health professor at Florida International University, found that 45 per cent had unprotected anal sex in the past year. The study showed gonorrhea rates are up, too. Recently, the Centers for Disease Control and Prevention reported that from 1993 to 1996, a survey of clinics in 26 cities found gonorrhea among such men rose 74 per cent.[220]

What are pro-gay and gay Christians saying about promiscuity? What are they saying about the health risks of the GBLTQ lifestyle? Again we must rely on Kramer to get the non-politically correct answer:

The facts: A small and vocal gay group that calls itself Sex Panic has taken it upon itself to demand 'sexual freedom,' which its members define as allowing gay men to have sex when and where and how they want to. In other words, the group is an advocate of unsafe sex, if that is what is wanted, and of public sex, if that is what is wanted. It advocates unconditional, unlimited promiscuity. Once again [previously during AIDS outbreak] it has become a battle over civil rights rather than an issue of public health. Why is public sex a civil right? I do not want to see straight people copulating in the park or in public washrooms.

The facts: Not one AIDS organization or national gay or lesbian group has been willing to speak out and condemn or even criticize what Sex Panic is saying. Criti-

cism from lesbians, the other half of our movement, is desperately needed as well. Promiscuous gay men must hear the message, 'Enough already! Haven't you learned anything from the past 17 years?' Yet lesbian activists, who alongside gay men have fought against AIDS, crawl into shells rather than confront the idiocy of what Sex Panic is demanding. Without a strong vocal opposition, Sex Panic is on its way to convincing much of America that all gay men are back to pre-AIDS self-destructive behavior that will wind up costing the taxpayer a lot of extra money.

Allowing sex-centruism to remain the sole definition of homosexuality is now coming to be seen as the greatest act of self-destruction. There is a growing understanding that we created a culture that in effect murdered us, and that if we are to remain alive it's time to redefine homosexuality as something far greater than what we do with our genitals. But that redefinition will require nothing less than remaking our culture.[221]

Tim Vollmer, writing in the *New York Native*, said the problem with the current safe sex campaign is that it does not confront the task of restructuring the premise of gay male sexuality. Instead, it implies that all gay men can do is simply wait till the epidemic is over [i.e. a cure discovered] before resuming life as before. It is a holding pattern, a freezing of an obsolete culture at its least dysfunctional level. "The danger with such a policy, if it is allowed to be more than just a transitional phase," says Vollmer, "is that it preempts any innovation of the gay experience. It is a policy of confinement and restriction, concentrating on what gay men can't do, what homosexuality isn't."[222] He further argues:

No matter how valuable the safe sex campaign is, gay men need more nowadays than a list of don'ts. In terms of coping with an injured self-image, sexuality, and lifestyle, today's situation has an urgency that must at least be equal to anything that existed in the 1950s and 1960s...To avoid the twin dangers of sinking with an obsolete culture or shifting back to an oppressive one, gay men must respond with the same energy and creativity they exhibited in the early days of gay liberation.[223]

Here proponents of same-sex marriage might lobby society in the erroneous hope and claim for an outpouring of homosexual monogamy and thus reduced lifestyle health risks. This positive claim of same-sex marriage appears small in light of science. In *Sex & Germs*, Cindy Patton found that gay monogamy was not going to usher in needed salvation for the so-called "obsolete culture." She writes:

Two recent studies from San Francisco and Chicago, however, indicate that coupling [gay monogamy] does not necessarily produce more discussion or safer sexual practices. These studies asked gay men why they had not changed a range of sexual practices, most of which the respondents agreed would decrease the risk of AIDS. In the San Francisco study, men in monogamous couples, in primary relationships with some sexual activity outside the relationship, and with no primary relationship but multiple partners, nearly all agreed that they hadn't implemented desired changes because they perceived their partner(s) to be unwilling to make that change. The second and third most common reasons were 'I like it too much to stop' and 'It just seems like what is expected' – a more diffuse articulation of the notion that certain practices, or a constellation of practices, are what makes someone gay. The Chicago study had similar results.[224]

Weinberg reported in *Dual Attraction*, the following interpretations of the meaning of "safe" in safe sex by bisexuals in the San Francisco area:

I never use safe sex with female partners. I hate condoms. Two or three years ago I decided to trust my intuition maybe ask a few questions. I said 'damn it, what's going to happen will happen.' (M)

I go to the baths in Berkeley about once a month. It's still very active there. I see a lot of unsafe sex there – guys being fucked without rubbers. There's also a maze with glory holes and no cock sticking out has a rubber on it. (M)

I go over to the baths at Berkeley a lot. I have oral sex there, never anal sex. I've never seen anyone in the baths use condoms with oral sex...I went ahead because I'm extremely oral. If oral sex caused AIDS, I would have been infected by now, that's my conclusion. (M)[225]

We don't go to swing parties anymore. We don't go to bath houses, that kind of thing. We have a close circle of lovers, there's no more anonymous sex. We're just cautious all around. (F)[226]

Weinberg also studied the meaning of "Sex" in Safe Sex. He and his associates found that AIDS has forced the "deconstruction" of the word "sex." "What was a life-affirming activity, a source of personal and social validation, was stripped of its wider meanings and became, first and foremost, a physical act constituting a prime route for a deadly virus. To a remarkable degree the "sex" in "safe sex" was focused primarily on the exchange of various "bodily fluids" regardless of the who, where, when, emotionality, passion, intimacy, and the like that gives meaning to sexuality. Not that these were absent, but they were secondary and were only considered important insofar as they were relevant to the issue of contagion."[227] For many bisexuals, sex became equated with death:

The concept that sperm is a deadly weapon has debilitated our society. (M)

I always practice safe sex. But I am uncomfortable with someone who's listed negative. I feel like I have a deadly disease – leprosy – and they may catch it. But there's a stronger connection with those who have tested positive. (M)

You feel dangerous. But I have to keep it in perspective and hold on to my sexuality in the face of horror. I feel like giving it up at times though. (M)

It's definitely put a damper on being sexually free and open. I'm inundated with the whole AIDS issue, since I know so many gay men. It places a mood on sexuality such that it's not easy, clear, or fun to the same degree it used to be. (F)

AIDS has definitely ruined my sex life. Condoms take all the fun out of fellatio and really make a penis look and smell like a rubber stick. Dental dams [latex between one partner's organ and the other's mouth] completely block sensation, smell, and taste. I have a lot less sex, and what I have isn't worth squat. (F)

I hated condoms when I had to use them for birth control. I can't imagine anyone enjoying having to use them. Rubber dams are even worse. Cocks and clits are warm and moist and soft. Rubber gloves are cold and unyielding barriers to sensation. (F)[228]

Are these the articulations of a God-given "right to responsibly express one's natural sexuality?" Again what God? Where is this God in literature, in history, in reality?

Weinberg found, among the bisexuals, a general widespread lack of sexual satisfaction, a decreased sexual repertoire, and the fear that safe sex might not be all that safe no matter what the precautions taken:

I felt a sense of loss and mourning about just giving up sexual practices with men I enjoyed, even doing safe sex. Sucking with a rubber wasn't a turn-on. I was very much into oral sex. I had just started to enjoy receiving anal sex when AIDS came around. I felt frustrated; even engaging in safe sex I felt anxious. What if the rubber broke? If someone came on me and I had a cut? Got to be not worth it. (M)

In every article or book I've read that refers to why people don't use condoms. I have yet to read anyone who seems to know why. It's because ejaculation is part of this satisfaction for many people, men and women. (M)

Sex becomes more complicated with condoms. I think there's some spiritual meaning in exchanging bodily fluids. That's gone when I wear a condom. (M)

You have to think about sex a little more before you do it now. You have to buy things; you have to make sure you are supplied with rubber items. You can't just spontaneously slip your hand in, you have to go find a glove. You have to think about where your supplies are. You have to be prepared. (F) [229]

Studying sexual etiquette, Weinberg found, "safe sex for bisexuals meant a dialogue with partners in which past experiences, current partners, likes and dislikes, health status, and so on were discussed before sex occurred. Again this often distracted from the experience of sex since clear rules of etiquette did not exist, and asking too many questions could call into question a partner's integrity. He records:

I feel like every woman I go out with I have to explain my past and explain a lot about how AIDS is transmitted. I don't think it's changed who I've had a relationship with but it's slowed up the sexualization of a relationship (F)[230]

He has AIDS, a full-blown case. I feel confident that we are performing the safest sex we can with the most pleasure and satisfaction. Most often I masturbate myself while he holds me. If he has the strength, we have intercourse and that of course includes condoms, using a sponge and lubricant with nonoxynol.[231]

I've organized jack and jill-off parties. The rules are no fucking and we provide latex gloves, rubbers – all under safe sex guidelines. People sign a statement that they will follow these. They don't always, though. I've got depressed offering these parties. (F)[232]

It seems clear from these testimonies that desire for peak pleasure and passion causes most to toss technological-behavioral prudence away in the face of reaching the maximum orgasm. To the orthodox Christian the divine boundaries for safe sex are clear – only in lifelong monogamous heterosexual marriage and even then, never to replace God as the central organizing principle of life. Pro-gay and gay Christians may continue to argue for freedom of individual sexual expression based on mutuality of desire and relationship; however, the failure of the Condom Code and other safe sex practices daily serve as reminder that something is wrong with the ecology of free love, non-monogamous sex, whether heterosexual or homosexual. Moreover, the impact of AIDS goes well beyond the tragedy of the individual. There are family, relatives and friends impacted by these deaths, not to mention the totally unrelated individuals who become infected by contaminated blood products, and the cost of AIDS treatment on the health system. What of AIDS in Africa?

As the basis of a credible and sustainable gay ecology, Gabriel Rotello contends the Condom Code is an abject failure. He refers in evidence to what is called "The Tragedy of the Commons." In the journal *Science* in 1968, Garret Hardin sketched out a dilemma concerning primacy of the individual over the public good; the idea that some "invisible hand" will always direct people to do what is best for the common good. He calls this dilemma the "Tragedy of the Commons." Hardin describes a town commons in New England. All the villagers have a legal right to graze their cattle on the commons and this arrangement benefits everybody equally. However, each time a new cow is added to the commons, it places stress on the environment. Only a finite number of cows can graze annually for a sustainable relationship. The "tragedy" lies in the fact that it is in each individual farmer's interest to add one more cow, since each farmer receives full benefit of that cow, while loss in grazing capacity is shared equally by everyone. In Hardin's equation, the "positive utility" of adding another cow equals roughly one for each farmer, but the "negative utility" is spread equally among everyone, and is therefore far less than one for any individual farmer. So the sensible course is for each farmer to add another cow. Everyone does, and the commons is destroyed.[233]

The relevance of this principle to AIDS and gay men was first pointed out by Martina Morris and Laura Dean in their famous paper on the effects of behaviour change on the spread of HIV. They find that if the average gay man in New York reduced his sexual contact rate to one "unsafe contact" per year, the level of HIV in that population would probably drop to less than 5 per cent in thirty-five years. But if the average rose to two unsafe contacts per year, HIV prevalence would rise to 60 per cent. "The implications of temporary returns to unsafe sex practices are not simply an increase in individual risk," they write, "but also the persistence of HIV transmission at epidemic levels in the [gay] population." This result is a classic example of the "Tragedy of the Commons," where the disjunction between individual and population level effects leads to the potential for worse case outcomes. Says Rotello:

Here the increment in individual risk from a slight increase in contact rate is negligible, assuming the individual acts alone. If all individuals make this choice, however, the aggregate impact is non-negligible, and the result is a phase shift in the population dynamics of the disease, dramatically increasing everyone's risk.[234]

According to Rotello, the problem is rooted in the difference between individual and aggregate risk. What each man gains by having occasional risky sex is, from his perspective, potentially much greater than what he loses, especially if his activity is not really very risky. "I can have plenty of sexual partners and do so perfectly safely," someone will typically say. "I always have safe sex, or at least almost always. Why should I change?" From his perspective he shouldn't. That's the "tragedy" part of the Tragedy of the Commons. Each person sees no need to change a system where his individual choices are indeed logical and beneficial for him. But all those "logical" choices add up and tip the entire system into disaster.[235] Writes Rotello:

Many people cannot fathom what we mean by 'commons' when we speak of gay men and AIDS. Most people think of sex as a private affair, and in the gay movement the concept of sexual privacy is elevated to almost a sacred principle, since much of the gay movement is based on the idea that sex is and ought to be nobody's business but your own. But biology is under no obligation to respect ideology, and the gay commons is as biologically real as the commons in an old colonial village. In a biological sense, every gay man who has 'private' sex joins together in a visceral, biological stream that flows through our blood and our bodily fluids both in time, connecting us to the private sexual acts of gay men years ago, and in space, linking us to the sexual acts of those all around us. By becoming sexually active, each of us influences the fate of our brothers, and is influenced by them as well. The question is not whether there is a gay commons; the question is whether that commons will remain polluted with HIV in such a way that it will continue to pose extreme danger even to those who make only modest contact with it, including gay youth who are just becoming sexually active.[236]

He continues:

HIV is without question the most mutable virus yet encountered, and there remains a very real danger that it will somehow manage to elude even the most potent drug combinations and emerge in drug-resistant forms. If it does, that would obviously be tragic for the unlucky individuals in whom it occurs. But if gay men mistakenly believe that the epidemic is waning and return to the habits of the past, rapidly transmitting new, drug-resistant strains of HIV across newly constituted viral highways, the potential for tragedy is almost unthinkable. It is all together possible that over the next several years gay men's failure to comprehend and modify our sexual ecology could lead to a Third Wave of the epidemic, this time with drug-resistant strains of HIV.[237]

The notion that multipartnerism does not matter, because the Condom Code is a workable version of safe sex is myth:

In fact, the Condom Code does not seem ever to have been very effective in containing the epidemic. The drop in new infections in the mid-eighties, for example, probably occurred because most of the susceptible gay men were already infected. Now that a new generation of susceptible young men have entered the gay world, they are getting infected at rates that indicate that about half will eventually get AIDS, which is about the same ratio as the older generation. The fact is that many people do not seem able to use condoms consistently enough to stem the epidemic. Condoms are very important in the battle against AIDS, but total reliance on the Condom Code blinds us to the fact that condoms are just one narrow possible arsenal of responses to AIDS. The Condom Code in the gay world is, in many ways, as much a political as a medical construction. Its dual purpose has been to prevent HIV transmission while preserving the 'sex positivity' of gay male culture, thereby proving that the gay sexual revolution of the seventies can continue during a fatal epidemic of a sexually transmitted disease. But it provides virtually no room for error, and is in many respects anti-ecological, a classic 'technological fix,' because it has never addressed the larger factors in the gay environment that helped spread HIV.[238]

Michelangelo Signorile, author of *Queer in America, and Outing Yourself: How to Come Out as Lesbian or Gay to Your Family, Friends and Coworkers;* and *Life Outside – The Signorile Report on Gay Men: Sex, Drugs, Muscles, and Passages of Life,* gives a personal testimony, in the latter book, on failing to live by the Condom Code:

Last year I spent a couple of grueling weeks on assignment in Hawaii. One night in a Waikiki gay bar I met your classic gay hunk: tall and masculine, with a buzzed haircut, razor-sharp cheekbones, a body of granite, and a Texas drawl. I'll make you see God tonight, he promised, trying to coax me to go home with him. It didn't take much for me to realize I needed a religious experience; we went to his place. As usual, one thing quickly led to another. But not as usual, he didn't put on a condom before we had anal sex, and I didn't demand he use one...I'd had a couple of Absolut Citrons. And I had made a quick decision – inside of ten seconds – based on heat-of-the-moment rationalizations that at some distance seem absurd: 1) Since he did not put on a condom, he must be negative; 2) He is a Navy petty officer and therefore is a responsible 'good' boy; 3) Since he is in the military he must be tested every six months and would be discharged if positive; 4) He's absolutely perfect – a gay male ideal – and I don't want to do anything to make him blow off the whole night; 5) I'm sure it'll be okay as long as he doesn't come; 6) This is Hawaii, and the AIDS problem can't be like it is in New York; 7) I'll do it this one time.[239]

Writes Rotello:

The very behaviors that gay activists had spent years promoting seemed to have contained the seeds of disaster. But since promiscuity and anal sex were perceived by many (though certainly not all) gay men to be central to liberation...The question then became, if anal sex and promiscuity equal liberation, and AIDS is spreading due to anal sex and promiscuity, how can gay men control the spread of AIDS without sacrificing liberation?...These two challenges created a dual imperative that has characterized gay AIDS prevention to this day: to prevent the spread of HIV, but only in a way that defends gay men against attacks from the right and preserves the multipartnerist ethic of the gay sexual revolution. In what was undoubtedly one of the tallest orders a prevention strategy ever had to fill, safer sex was to be a political and social as much as a medical or ecological construction.[240]

In gay safe sex guidance, once it was demonstrated that HIV could indeed be blocked with latex condoms, the advice to reduce partners was slowly abandoned and the advice to use condoms became the central tenet of the new gay sexual ecology. Indeed, so central did condom use become that David L. Chambers, in an insightful article in the *Harvard Civil Rights Civil Liberties Law Review*, dubbed the entire safer sex regime the "Code of the Condom." According to the code, risk lies almost exclusively in the exchange of fluids during anal sex, and therefore the "use of a condom is a biological [God-given!] necessity."[241] [my insert]

Another approach could be to urge men to refrain from anal sex altogether, in favor of things like oral sex and noninsertive activities such as masturbation. Writes Chambers, "Such a policy was followed in Holland until 1991. Men were encouraged to give up anal sex completely, and many apparently did."[242] Nonetheless, this approach was never seriously entertained by gay AIDS groups in the United States. Anal sex had come to be seen as an essential – possibly the essential – expression of homosexual intimacy by the 1980s. Writes Rotello:

Perhaps the most famous articulation of this view appeared in a 1985 New York Native interview with Joseph Sonnabend. 'The rectum,' Sonnabend said, 'is a sexual organ, and it deserves the respect a penis gets and a vagina gets. Anal intercourse had been the central activity for gay men and for some women for all of history.... We have to recognize what is hazardous, but at the same time, we shouldn't undermine an act that's important to celebrate.' Michael Callen was openly scornful of any attempt to discourage gay men from practicing anal sex. In his 1989 article: 'In defense of Anal Sex' in the PWA Coalition Newsline, Callen listed three basic reasons. First he considered such a message an equivocation. If, Callen wrote, the premise is that condoms aren't fully safe, then the message should be that everyone should 'stop having anal sex entirely.' This seems a rather muddled objection, since the message Callen was objecting to was precisely that: to stop having anal sex entirely. His second objection was that this avoids more difficult and complex messages, such as advising men to perform coitus interruptus, demanding better condoms from manufacturers, educating gay men about proper condom use, and demanding a 'national AIDS education campaign which speaks bluntly in non-clinical language that people can understand.' His third (and, I suspect, core) objection was that any message advising abandonment of anal sex was homophobic, since similar messages about giving up vaginal sex were not being directed toward heterosexuals.[243]

Instead, the code of the condom became virtually the entire message of prevention. "Condom distribution" became a rallying cry in gay bars, "Condom availability" a major goal of public education programs. The condom became a symbol of safety, prevention's magic bullet. All this was carried out, however, in knowledge of the fact that the Condom Code contained certain inherent risks:

Condom failure rates of approximately 10 per cent have only been a fact of life for heterosexuals attempting to use them to prevent pregnancy.[244]

A survey published in the American Journal of Public Health, for example, reported failures of 4.7 per cent to 8 per cent. Factors that led to failure included condoms being 'too small or too thin, the use of oil as opposed to water-based lubricants, breakage due to fingernails or jewelry, inexperience in condom use, physical stress of condoms inherent to anal intercourse, and the use of condoms not designed for anal intercourse.' In addition to mechanical failure condoms often fail to provide protection because people fail to use them consistently, which is hardly surprising given the lack of rational thinking that often precedes sex.[245]

An August 1992 update in MMWR reported that among serodiscordant heterosexual couples, the rate of HIV transmission was 9.7 per cent among those who used condoms 'inconsistently' and 1.1 per cent among those who used them "consistently". A 1990 study in the Journal of AIDS estimated that for heterosexual serodiscordant couples, the overall failure rates for HIV 'may approach those for pregnancy,' which the study cited as 10 per cent.[246]

Observes Rotello:

Anything that might undermine confidence in condoms was felt to undermine confidence in safer sex itself. It was hard enough to get gay men to use condoms in the first place, hard enough to convince governments to promote them, hard enough to get schools to make them available to sexually active teens. If in addition it were admitted that condoms failed on a low but fairly regular basis, the job of condom promotion might become impossible....Prevention activists were thus forced into a defensive posture, and as such were very reluctant to give any ground at all on the issue of condom effectiveness.[247]

Frank Browning summarized his view of the safe sex inconsistencies. At first, safe sex seemed simple, like following a cookbook: (1) do not exchange bodily fluids; (2) reduce the number of sexual partners; (3) avoid anal intercourse (or, at least, use a condom); and (4) do not engage in fisting (anal penetration by the fist and, sometimes forearm as well) or rimming (oral-anal contact). If gay men were simply to adjust their sex lives to conform to these simple rules, they could easily protect themselves from HIV infection. "Nearly everyone bought the program – at least for a while," says Browning, "some however, found the rules bizarre. Consider Rule 2: Reduce the number of sexual partners. Why? Because epidemiologists found high correlation's between the number of sexual contacts and HIV. However, if the monogamous man's partner is already infected, than probability analysis provides little protection. In following Rule 2, gay men feel they are often given subliminal permission – if not outright permission – to forget Rule 1. Indeed, by 1990, researchers had discovered through behavioral studies that unattached gay men were significantly less likely to expose themselves to HIV through risky sex than were men in serial monogamous relationships. Apparently, then, the reduction in the number of sexual mates has nothing to do with the prevention of viral transmission. So what is going on?... Rule 3: Avoid anal intercourse. But if condoms are effective, why avoid anal sex?"[248]

Stranger still is the rule against fisting. By 1984, it was clear that AIDS was the result of some microbe – HIV, and possibly other agents as well – could be transmitted via the blood or semen. Yet what, it was asked, could possibly be tranmitted from the fist to the rectum so long as the fist was clean or, at least, gloved in rubber? Researchers answered that inappropriate objects inserted into the rectum could cause abrasions or fissures through which HIV could later gain entry. But by the same logic, a mishap during any anal sex could also result in cuts and abrasions that, if the area was later exposed to blood or semen, could lead to HIV infection. Nonetheless, these scientists asserted, such practices are dangerous, dangerous because the rectum was not designed by nature to be penetrated by objects.[249]

When looking at the long list of diseases that swept the gay male world in the years leading up to AIDS, one sees that quite a few were primarily spread by oral-anal sex and many others were spread just as readily orally as anally. The list includes all forms of hepatitis, most forms of oral and genital herpes, oral gonorrhea, cytomegalovirus, Epstein-Barr virus, and all of the major intestinal parasites. The common wisdom then and now has been that these diseases are insignificant, mild and easy to cure, and they didn't have much to do with AIDS. Says Rotello, "the common wisdom is largely wrong. Herpes remains incurable in all its forms, as do Epstein-Barr virus and CMV. Gonorrhea has mutated into deadly and incurable antibiotic-resistant strains."[250] Gastrointestinal parasites are cured only with great difficulty, and the large doses of drugs needed to cure them place a major strain on the immune system. Clearly the practice of anal sex with many partners was not the only problem, although it was the first to produce such a catastrophic result. Yet the Condom Code focused almost exclusively on anal sex, preferring to ignore this wider web of ecological and behavioral cause and effect. Receptive oral sex while significantly less risky than receptive anal sex, nonetheless carries a risk of HIV infection, but this, too, was largely glossed over by the Condom Code. Oral sex has been a contentious subject in AIDS prevention from the start, for good reason. Many studies indicate that oral sex is the most popular sexual practice among gay men. Most studies also indicate that people find condoms extremely intrusive during oral sex, quite literally ruining the experience for many. As a result, prevention workers are understandably loath to advise using condoms.[251]

Epidemiologists who have studied the issue concur that the risk of infection during receptive oral sex is probably from one fifth to one tenth of the risk during receptive anal sex, perhaps even less. The reason even this degree if risk is not seen more often in studies, they argue, is that whenever a newly infected man indicated that he has had any anal sex, the infection is automatically assigned to that practice.

The tendency of anal sex to "mask" the risk of oral sex has had a psychological effect on the gay community as well, reinforcing the popular conception that oral risk is minuscule. Says Rotello:

Most AIDS groups and safer sex brochures traditionally have left it up to individual choice: You might want to use a condom during oral sex, but many people choose not to. It's up to you. More recently. Some have begun promoting unprotected oral sex, sometimes even to ejaculation, as a form of 'harm reduction.' One slogan: 'Oral Sex is Safer Sex.'[252]

Another area of controversy in the "Condom Code" is testing. Widely available in 1985, most gay AIDS groups advised gay men to avoid the test. Lack of effective therapies, they argued, meant that knowledge of HIV infection could not lead to useful therapies but would almost certainly lead to despair. Moreover, in the opinion of most AIDS groups the Condom Code fulfills any obligation an HIV-positive person might have to inform his or her partner. GMHC's pamphlet "Safer Sex for HIV Positives" was typical:

If you follow (the guideline to use condoms), you don't need to worry about whether your partners know that you're positive. You've already protected them from infection and yourself from reinfection....Just use your judgment about who to tell – there's still discrimination out there. The risk of discrimination to the infected person is as serious, or even more serious, than the risk of infecting one's partners. Therefore the right to remain silent and protect oneself from possible discrimination trumps the obligation to disclose and allow one's partners to make more informed decisions about the level of risk they are willing to take.[253]

Rotello describes the effect of testing:

Now many men knew that they were HIV-positive and a great gulf opened up in the gay male world between HIV positives and HIV negatives. Many who were positive saw little incentive to practice safer sex for their own protection. True, health experts warned of the possibility of reinfection with different strains of HIV, but many men considered that possibility less than fully proved. Experts also warned about the danger of other opportunistic infections, but many positive men were not particularly impressed with admonitions that they ought to forgo unprotected anal sex out of fear of contracting infections they might just as easily get from oral sex or, for that matter, kissing.

Given that, it might have made sense to amend the Condom Code, adding an absolute obligation to get tested and know your serostatus, and adding, for those who find out they are HIV positive, an absolute obligation to protect others from infection, even if those others are momentarily willing to take a risk. No such amendment, however was made. HIV-positive men continued to be told to practice safer sex for their own benefit, not out of any altruistic obligation to protect others. This had the unfortunate effect of implying to many HIV positive men that they were off the ethical hook when engaging in unsafe sex, particularly with anonymous partners. The Condom Code's ethic of self-defense allowed them to reason justly that if they found a partner who was willing to engage in risky sex, that partner must be doing so out of informed choice. And if that partner became infected, it was his own fault. A catch-22 thus arose in many sexual situations. An HIV-positive person could assume that if his partner was willing to engage in risky activities, that partner must also be positive.[254]

Once more, are these the articulations of a God-given natural sexuality? Are these responsible expressions of homosexuality? Where is gay-theology on these matters, if not silent? What does Peter Fink have to say about his 1976 "Pastoral Hypothesis," now that the experiment is decades long? His original hypothesis stated:

If homosexual love is sinful this will show itself as destructive of the human and disruptive of man's relationship with God.[255]

It is sometimes said that the adoption of the Condom Code was the "least transformative" change that gay men could have made in the face of the epidemic. "Harm reduction has been described as a 'philosophy' wherein the professional health care provider sets aside all judgments in order to meet clients at their own level regarding a problem or crisis." If an IV drug user comes to health workers and asks for help in avoiding HIV infection, health workers should not insist that the user give up injecting drugs in order to receive help. Instead, they should provide the user with clean needles and information to help avoid infection. Help in quitting drugs may also be provided but only if asked for. The reasoning is that many IV drug users don't want to quit using drugs; they just want to avoid HIV. So if health workers demand that they quit using drugs in order to get help, many users will be driven away from HIV prevention programs and needlessly become infected. Concludes Rotello:

In a sense, the almost exclusive focus on the Condom Code represents an effort by gay AIDS organizations to apply harm reduction to the gay community as a whole.....together with moralists and homophobes and their advice. This nontransformative approach is reinforced by the widespread belief that gay men cannot change their sexual culture even if they want to. Many activists openly express what the late journalist Randy Shilts called the "sex fiend" argument; that many gay men are insatiable satyrs who would respond to admonitions to change their basic patterns of behavior by hiding and perhaps even increasing that behavior rather than actually attempting to change it.[256]

This reasoning is also buttressed by the dual ideological imperative to fight AIDS but only in ways that support what is sometimes called "sex positive" gay male culture. Gay author Frank Browning relates that some of his straight friends were incredulous at the behavior of gay AIDS activists and prevention workers at the Fifth International AIDS Conference in Montreal:

For five days the discos were packed with gay doctors, nurses, activists, and researchers shamelessly cruising each other. A nearby bathhouse was doing land-office business. A JO (jack-off) club posted promotional fliers in the conference exhibit hall...Most of my straight friends have told me that they cannot fathom how an AIDS conference can also be a sex carnival. My standard flip response has frequently been 'But what else could it be?' The lust of men for other men has not evaporated just because funerals and memorial services have become nearly as ordinary as an evening at the theater. We could not relinquish passion to death.[257]

Michael Lynch wrote in the gay Canadian publication *Body Politic* during the heyday of the partner reduction message in the early 1980s. "Gays are once again allowing the medical profession to define, restrict, pathologize us." Gay liberation was founded, he said, on a "sexual brotherhood of promiscuity" and any abandonment of the promiscuity would amount to a "communal betrayal of gargantuan proportions." The Condom Code eliminated such concerns. By declaring that condoms fulfilled all obligations to prevention, the culture of multipartnerism could be justified and celebrated anew.[258]

AIDS activists also promoted the "degaying" of AIDS. At the time activists believed that the terrible experience of AIDS in the Third World was a harbinger of what was to come in developed countries, and that HIV's widespread dissemination among heterosexuals in Africa and Asia, was simply a result of those continents' "head start." In this view, heterosexuals around the world are pretty much all alike, so that what happens among heterosexuals in Uganda is bound to happen to their counterparts in Utah given enough time. Says Rotello: "When author Fumento challenged these ideas in his book *The Myth of Heterosexual AIDS* in 1989, he was savaged virtually everywhere." The widespread acceptance of degaying had a profound impact on gay men's vision of their own sexual ecology. If AIDS was not a "gay disease" why should gay men examine the ecological reasons their community was so devastated? Clearly it was just an accident of history, a fluke, a momentary incursion of an otherwise universal pandemic. As the Condom Code appeared to solve the problem of transmission, as the idea that AIDS would soon be striking millions of heterosexuals sank in, the obvious ecological implications of the epidemic for gay men could now be not only ignored but indignantly denied.[259]

In response to the Weiner and Starr survey 78 per cent say they are worried about AIDS in general, 36 per cent are not personally worried about contracting AIDS, 90 per cent are not worried at all about AIDS in their current relationships.[260] Fifty-two per cent said they now have the same number of sex partners while 44 per cent said fewer. Only 35 per cent said they have more dates before engaging in sex. Thirty per cent said they are using condoms more than before. As far as avoiding a relationship because of fear of AIDS, 74 per cent said they have not. Half said they rarely or never ask about sexually transmitted diseases and the other half said they do ask some questions. Some 70 per cent claimed they were never asked.[261]

Weiner and Starr observe, "In light of these problems it seems to us that attitudes and behavior are clearly separate and often different from espoused beliefs and knowledge. For example, that many more people use condoms and that, as in our survey, they use them more than previously does not mean that those who use them do so all the time." They ask, "If not, what does that say about concern?" Their study showed that over 90 per cent of those queried said they had sexual relations in the last year without using a condom – some frequently, others rarely or occasionally. [262]

If mankind accepts that multipartnered sex is okay and anal intercourse is a God-blessed sexual act, where would Queer Christians claim the boundaries now lie for operating within God's design? Is sin now solely a matter of volume – a few too many partners, a few too many penetrations, a few too much experimentation, a few too many public locations, a few too many STDs? What can gay and pro-gay Christians draw upon in Scripture to countenance GBLTQ sexual behaviors?

Frank Browning, illuminates the illogic of the Condom Code in addressing the truth exposed by the North American AIDS pandemic:

There are stories, true stories, from the West Side docks of Manhattan, from the trails of Griffith Park in Los Angels, from the warehouse catacombs along Folsom Street in San Francisco, of men whose journey's into sadomasochism led to suffocation, mutilation, dismemberment. Before the AIDS epidemic, these were dark tales at the periphery of the great gay adventure; the stuff of gossip...The arrival of AIDS changed all that. Mystified by a disease that seemed only to touch gay men, researchers began in earnest to explore the behavioral particulars of homosexual desire. They were regaled with tales of the kinkiest and most bizarre uses of the body, of violence and torture and abuse. They were stunned by the matter-of-fact accounts of men whose nipples were attached to chains and stretched, whose testicles were twisted in leather thongs, whose mouths were gorged on the penis of one unknown man while another would plunge his fist and forearm so deeply into their bowels that he could feel on his fingers the contractions of the heart.

Usually, when the researchers would repeat such stories, they would maintain a cool, professional detachment. Only in the glance of an eye, the slightly raised brow, would they offer any normative comment; yet the comment, however politely passed, was always present: The homosexuals have gone too far. Though the scientists were too considerate, too worldly, to charge homosexuality outright as a violation of nature, they offered a variant: If you press the body beyond its limit as an organism, you will violate the rules of self-preservation. It is within that 'bionormative' context that 'safe sex' – as a slogan, as an approved list of behaviors – was born.[263]

What is the truth? Where are the Queer Christian boundaries? What is the GBLTQ "God-given right to responsibly express their sexuality?" As a last pitch to those gay and pro-gay Christians, who would persist in challenging and ignoring the authority and authenticity of the Leviticus Codes, this section and chapter ends with a quote from Catherine M. Wallace's book, *Accounting For Fidelity: How Intimacy and Commitment Enrich Our Lives*. She relates a story involving her young sons:

'Does Daddy use condoms?'

I stopped grinding coffee beans and looked across the dark, November-morning kitchen at my eight-year-old son, who had set aside his raison toast with peanut butter...

'Mark [fifth-grade] says – Mark says the teacher says if you don't use condoms then you could both get sick and die. So we want to know. Does he? Every time?'[264]

CHAPTER SIX

THE PARADOX OF HOMOSEXUAL REORIENTATION

Many former homosexuals tell us that there is only one genuine reason that they have been successful: they have abandoned homosexuality in obedience to God's Word. They see changing their homosexuality as a side effect of an even bigger goal: being conformed to the image of Jesus Christ. One former homosexual said, 'My prayer since the day I entered ex-gay ministry has been the same: 'Lord, make me into the man of God that you created me to be.' This man, now married for fifteen years, did not come into counseling with the primary goal of becoming straight. He wanted to experience life in all its richness, as Jesus promised in Scriptures: 'I have come that you might have life, and have it to the full' (John 10:10).[1]

Bob Davies with Lela Gilbert, 'Portraits of Freedom'

I worked with Jay for over a year. In that time I witnessed a miracle. He ended all homosexual behavior. But even more, he had experienced tremendous inner healing and renewal. He had grown in his self-esteem and self-image. Most amazingly, his heterosexuality had stirred in him. He became interested in women. 'Lord,' I hesitantly prayed, 'You are wonderful. How glorious are Your ways. Now, Lord, I have a little request; would You just send me one more person to see if You and I can do it again?' That was ten years ago. Almost 100 clients later I have seen the Lord continue to perform the miracle of transformed lives. That's what this book is about.[2]

Dr. William Consiglio, 'Homosexual No More'

The Divided Kingdom

Every kingdom divided against itself will be ruined, and every city or household divided against itself will not stand (Matthew 12:25).

Christ can not be both liberating oppressed gays and lesbians into a "blessed" GBLTQ lifestyle – sanctifying gay ordination, consecrating gay marriage, approving of non-marital sex before, during and after union, codifying oral and anal sex as divine design, and permitting experimental sex to find God's sexual calling for each of His children; while He is also clearly delivering gays and lesbians from their "sexual abomination" in His eyes. Logic, whether secular or Scriptural based, tells us that one group of Christians is blind to the truth. Pro-gay and gay Christians can no longer deny the "scientific" facts and "spiritual" testimonial realities of reorientation. Bailey's invert theory and the gay gene theory, used to disregard orthodox Christian theology, have been discredited. Moreover, in an open, democratic and pluralistic society, the publicizing of reorientation can not be labeled a hate crime or homophobic.

Exodus International, typical of many ex-gay ministries, began as a sovereign move of God. In the early to mid-1970s, Christian ministries to men and women struggling with unwanted homosexual feelings sprang up spontaneously all over North America and overseas. In 1967, Roberta Laurila had a spiritual vision that one day there would be a worldwide network of ministries to help homosexuals come out of that lifestyle. She sensed God speaking to her: "If you'll leave your situation, I'll use you mightily." Roberta was living with her lover, but three weeks later she left. She began praying daily for God to raise up counselors throughout the world. Nine years later, Exodus began.

The general consensus among Exodus leaders is that temptation is not sin (Hebrews 4:15), but the homosexual orientation is an expression of humanity's sinfulness – and cannot comfortably co-exist within the context of a total commitment to Jesus Christ. In 1987, Alan Medinger described the calling:

'We are in a spiritual battle of staggering proportions,' he told over 200 delegates from 45 different Exodus ministries. 'Until now, widespread church support for redemptive ministry to homosexuals has been lacking, but AIDS is changing that. Voices in the church previously speaking out in defence of the homosexual lifestyle are now strangely silent.' During the early 1980s, Exodus ministries had noticed a growing disinterest in the church over the issue of homosexuality. Multiple books on the subject had poured off the evangelical presses in the late '70s, then there was silence. During that same time period, the theology of homosexual behavior had been fervently debated in mainline denominations, then most of the committees had turned their attention to other 'urgent' issues of the day. Then came AIDS. Suddenly, the topic of homosexuality was of crucial concern again. Pastors around the nation were shocked to discover that members of their church had been infected with the AIDS virus, mostly through homosexual activities. The problem of homosexuality – even in conservative churches – could no longer be ignored.[3]

So the AIDS issue created a new wave of interest in ex-gay ministry. According to Bob Davies, attendance at the annual Exodus conference climbed to 200, then 300; by 1989, over 400 delegates were present. In response the gay Christian movement did not take long to develop its own hostile offensive. Fundamental to its identity were two beliefs. First, homosexuality is not unbiblical and therefore, the movement could claim legitimacy. Second, homosexuals can't change, even if they want to. The necessity for the second belief was less obvious, but crucial. An unwavering belief among orthodox Christians is that homosexuals, like all sinners, need to repent. Having repented of their sin, Christ will enable them by His grace to lead Godly lives without indulging in homosexual practices. It was – and is – vital to the GBLTQ Christian movement's success that it convince everyone, especially its critics, that homosexuality simply cannot be repented of, any more than skin color or gender can be abandoned.[4]

Exodus International, a coalition of ministries dedicated to helping people overcome homosexuality, had for almost two decades been proclaiming a message in direct opposition to the gay Christian movement: that homosexuality was a sin, and that Christ could free the homosexual. No message could be more intolerable to the gay Christian movement, and in the mid-1980s they determined it had to be silenced. In 1989 Reverend Sylvia Pennington, whose career was devoted to assuring gay Christians that their behavior was acceptable to God, released her scorching analysis of the "ex-gay movement" titled *Ex-Gays? "There Are None!"* By compiling stories of women and men who had tried to change from homosexuals to heterosexuals (through Exodus and similar ministries), Pennington argued that anyone attempting to "go straight" was doomed to failure. Her book, the first published broadside against Exodus ministries, threw down the gauntlet from the gay Christian movement to any Christians who claimed to have overcome homosexuality. Debates between "Christian gays" and "ex-gays" were soon commonplace on talk shows and in print.[5] The paradox for pro-gay and gay Christians is captured in this letter:

Dear Sirs:

I understand that you are considering the ordination of professing homosexuals. Please would you consider my testimony before deciding.

I grew up in the United Presbyterian Church. It was there that I came to know and to love the Lord Jesus Christ. At age 12 I asked God to fill me with His Holy Spirit. I am sure that He did. Still, while in college I was drawn into relationship with another woman. I felt great about it at first; my sexual desires were being met, and I was still very much into filling the desires of the flesh.

It was six years before the Holy Spirit began convicting me, slowly, gently at first, then more and more powerfully until I could live with myself no longer. I went to my minister and confessed the whole thing....The Lord gave me a Scripture at the time. It was Revelation 21:5, 'Behold I make all things new.' He continues to renew our lives daily, and therefore I recognize in this other person a 'new creature in Christ Jesus.' Praise God! I cannot thank Him enough for lifting me out of the mire and setting me once again on solid ground.

Homosexuality is a dead end. While I was so busy gratifying the desires of my flesh it was impossible for God to give me the desires of my heart. Now He is free to do so. I have dated several young men in the past year, and have enjoyed each date. There has been fellowship and sharing about the Lord Jesus Christ. In addition I have a joy I could not experience before. I can once again look forward to getting married.

God wants the best for us. Let's not settle for second best. God bless you in your decision.

Sincerely in Christ[6]

Is Conversion Therapy Ethical?

Judging their own value system to be "so superior" to any paradigm that entertains sexual reorientation, Erinn Tozer and Mary McClanahan go so far as to deny the legitimacy of even the client's desire for change:

The General Principle of Social Responsibility states, 'Psychologists are concerned about and work to mitigate the causes of human suffering' (APA, 1992, Principle F, p. 1600). Proponents of conversion therapy argue that the refusal to provide a service that a client voluntarily requests is tantamount to refusing to mitigate suffering. They further state that it serves a 'prohomosexual' ideology (Gadpaille, 1981). Cautela and Kearney (1986) state, from both an ethical and a practical point of view it is our contention that the decision of whether or not to change an individual's sexual orientation must be made by the client rather than by society at large or subgroups of that culture.

However, several scholars have pointed out that someone who would voluntarily wish to change his or her sexual orientation is a misnomer (Davison, 1976; Halleck, 1976; Murphy, 1992; Silverstein, 1977). An individual's desire to change is a reflection of an oppressive and prejudicial society wherein lesbian, gay, and bisexual persons are considered deviant and inferior. Therefore, this request is not truly voluntary. If psychologists are complying with the Principle of Social Responsibility, they will recognize that the cause of human suffering, in this case, is the sociopolitical context wherein the gay population exists.[7]

Imagine yourself trapped, expending the prime of your life in bondage to cubical-style anonymous gay sex (with HIV positive callers), wanting personal deliverance, but finding that none in the GBLTQ community or the gay and pro-gay Christian communities offers a shred of hope. What are we to think of a community that proclaims "experiment as you wish," "join if you want," and then refuses to help you exit? How can a homosexual receive secular help or accept the grace of Jesus Christ, if he or she cannot find professional psychological counsel or Godly Christian deliverance ministry? The tremendous cognitive dissonance caused by the deliverance of even a few from the GBLTQ lifestyle, forces those remaining to actively pursue closing all avenues of escape and to deny all evidence of such freedom.

To GBLTQ activists reorientation therapies reinforce the social doctrine that homosexuality is deviant. In 1975, the APA issued a statement that urged "all mental health professionals to take the lead on removing the stigma of mental illness that has long been associated with homosexual orientations."[8] Says Tozer:

If psychologists are to abide by this statement and the Ethical Principle of Social Responsibility, they would not implicitly agree that being gay or lesbian is deviant by acquiescing to their clients' wishes to rid themselves of this 'condition.' Psychologists would instead focus their energies toward changing the sociopolitical context by being proactive allies to the gay community.[9]

Tozer and McClanahan describe the "affirmative" therapist as one who celebrates and advocates the validity of lesbian, gay, and bisexual persons and their relationships. They write:

Such a therapist goes beyond a neutral or null environment to counteract the lifelong messages of homophobia and heterosexism that lesbian, gay, and bisexual individuals have experienced and often internalized....The challenge is not to find adequate resources but, rather, to explore the client's biases as actively and honestly as possible when the client tells us, 'I think I'm gay, but I really don't want to be. Can you help?'[10]

What they and most gay and pro-gay Christians advocate is talking the client out of his or her wish. Tozer explains:

'What about the client who insists, even after this discussion, that she or he wants to be heterosexual? Is it ethical to exhort someone to embrace an identity that feels untenable?' No; yet, it is equally inappropriate to suggest to someone that feelings of same-sex attraction can be redirected into heterosexual attraction, given the absence of compelling evidence to support that reorientation.[11]

Finally, an affirmative therapist can encourage a client to focus less on the label of lesbian, gay, or bisexual than on her or his unique experience. This can help the person take the time to consider his or her needs and feelings without the perceived rush to have the 'right' identity. If the therapist continues to refuse to provide conversion therapy, and the client continues to insist that he or she desires reorientation, the possibility of termination emerges. Certainly, this should not be a hasty decision; indeed, rich material can evolve from these opposing agendas. The therapist can reiterate that she or he is not attempting to recruit the client to a lesbian, gay, or bisexual orientation; at the same time, she or he is not willing to collude with the message that such an orientation is bad, immoral, invalid, or unhealthy.

If the client remains steadfast in her or his desire to reorient to heterosexuality, however, termination becomes a very real possibility. We submit that in such cases, no action (barring risk of client self-harm, of course) is better than the wrong action. The therapist can provide the client with a bibliography of resources that factually refute the prevailing myths and misconceptions and that offer positive images of lesbian, gay, and bisexual persons. The therapist also can emphasize that she or he will be available for future nonconversion work if the client wishes to resume therapy. If the client wishes to terminate rather than proceed with nonconversion therapy; however, we believe that it is more ethical to let a client continue to struggle honestly with her or his identity than to collude, even peripherally, with a practice that is discriminatory, oppressive, and ultimately ineffective in its own stated ends.[12] *[my underline]*

This type of argument against ex-gay ministries was articulated by Father John McNeil, in 1976. Wishing to stop the treatment of homosexuals, he writes:

The relation between a willingness to change and success in therapy has led some clinicians to advocate what from a Christian point of view is a morally reprehensible procedure. Bergler, for example, speaks of 'mobilizing any latent feelings of guilt.'[13] *What he seems to be advocating is a deliberate effort to increase the guilt feelings and self-hatred of the patient. Beiber, who goes along with this type of practice, reports only twenty-seven per cent of his patients were cured under optimum conditions.*[14] *One wonders what happened to the other seventy-three per cent who left therapy unconverted but burdened with false guilt and shame concerning their incurable condition. To continue to hold out the false hope of a 'cure,' in light of almost total failure to truly effect a cure, is morally reprehensible; for nothing can be more destructive psychologically than to hold out a false hope to an already disturbed person. Connected with the issue of false hope is the danger of false guilt in the case where analysis fails to change sexual orientation.*[15]

Donald L. Faris, author of *The Homosexual Challenge – A Christian Response to an Age of Sexual Politics* writes:

Can homosexuality be changed? If a prevention was discovered for AIDS which had a 30-60 per cent success rate, what would happen? Would this remedy be hidden? Would it be denied? Would it be attacked because it was not 100 per cent effective? Surprisingly, something like this is actually happening. If an individual is not already infected with AIDS, ceasing to live the 'gay' lifestyle is the surest way to avoid contracting the deadly disease. But, far from being proposed as an option, changing one's orientation is the target of negative publicity among gay rights activists. The defenders of homosexual practice deny that homosexual orientation can be changed, despite the fact that there are scores of cases of successful reorientation. They also suggest that practicing homosexuals can speak more objectively about homosexuality than non-homosexuals or celibate or ex-homosexuals, and therefore nobody should listen to people who say that they have changed their orientation, or that, if they have not changed their orientation, they are comfortable as celibates. This is a little like suggesting that only practicing alcoholics can be objective about alcoholism. Naturally, as far as the homosexual rights activists are concerned, their cause is weakened when people decide to abandon the 'gay' lifestyle, even if it is for the purpose of saving their lives or mental health.[16]

Writes Faris, it is interesting to note the response of authors such as John Spong and Virginia Mollenkott, who espouse a "pro-homosexual ideology," to insights into the causes of homosexual inclination. Both simply assert, without a shred of evidence, that homosexual orientation cannot be changed. Mollenkott uses the argument that many famous men and women were homosexuals. She seems to be arguing, "Look at these famous people [Oscar Wilde]; if they were homosexual, it must be normal and healthy." Alas, even longer lists could be prepared of "famous people" who were alcoholics, pedophiles or manic-depressives. Fame has never been a guarantee of mental health, or even a very good argument for it.[17]

What cognitive dissonance is this? Referring back to the man-boy "boundary" of age 13 for gay sex (psychiatric manual: DSM-IV), one wonders what political agenda develops a construct which essentially states: "Psychiatry should give up treating homosexuals who want to change their orientation from partners thirteen and older (12 in Holland!) because there is only a 27 per cent improvement rate and the process breeds guilt; but [I assume] says continue to reform homosexual pedophiles who desire to stop seeking sex with those who are twelve years, eleven months, and younger. Perhaps, those who think in line with Tozer, McClanahan and McNeil would otherwise lock-up all pedophiles, as hopelessly inverted in their perverse ways and throw away the key. The anti-reorientation thinking is based on two patently false assumptions. First, is the notion of Bailey's invert – that people are either exclusively a hetero – or homosexual (a 6 or 0 on Kinsey's continuum), but never muddled in between. And second, as previously explained, is the notion that there is a psychologically and morally significant difference between sex with a 13 year-old (pedophilia) and sex with a 14 year-old (man-man sex). Moreover, it seems logical if experimentation can lead one into homosexuality (Oscar Wilde Effect), experimentation with reorientation should equally offer promise of freedom to those seeking escape.

Staying on the man-boy theme a little further, one must ask: When society continues to try and reform the pedophile, what should we do about the "false guilt" among the unsuccessful? Does the GBLTQ care? The reorientation success rate for pedophiles is even less than for man-man homosexuality. Is this grounds to stop their treatment? What social theory simultaneously asks 97 per cent of the population to restructure and re-culture (see Chapters 7 and 8) to accept and normalize the behaviour of the other 3 per cent – the so-called "GBLTQ minority," and also demands that treatment of men and women who wish freedom from this "minority" must stop? This is manic political hypocrisy at best. Why are gays and lesbians so insecure about anyone wishing to leave the fold? "Individual determinism" is okay for GBLTQ-identifying homosexuals in the face of the overwhelming heterosexual majority, but the GBLTQ community cannot afford such self-determinism among those wanting out. The idea, that the actual and perceived hope of exodus from homosexuality is somehow guilt-tripping those who remain makes mockery of free choice, pluralism and dare I say "individual rights."

More important, what Christian would tell another contrite heart, there is no hope – You can "come out" only in one direction or label yourself bisexual, but never again heterosexual? The magnitude of the recovery challenge is no reason to lose hope. Shall a declared pedophile, transvestite, addicted smoker, chronic alcoholic, or manic depressive give himself up to his condition, just because the recovery rate is not 100 per cent? What about the bisexual who wishes to restore a monogamous marriage? Who has the right to say "no you can't be helped?"

APA Fight Over Reorientation

Fortunately, alternatives do exist and the APA has not totally ruled them out. The most recent professional stance on the treatment of lesbian, gay, and bisexual clients was presented at the 105th annual convention of the APA in 1997. After years of contentious debate, the APA Council of Representatives passed a resolution regarding therapeutic responses to sexual orientation. The council recognized that prejudice and ignorance can prompt some lesbian, gay, bisexual, and questioning persons to pursue conversion treatment. The council also acknowledged the belief among some mental health providers that homosexuality is a mental disorder that can be "cured," despite considerable debate regarding the efficacy and ethicality of such treatments. In light of such observations, the resolution stated that the APA supports the dissemination of accurate information about sexual orientation, and mental health, and appropriate interventions in order to counteract bias that is based in ignorance or unfounded beliefs about sexual orientation. However, this resolution allows for conversion therapy and resulted from the obstinacy of psychiatrists who lobbied hard for reorientation and threatened to revisit the entire issue of mental disorder if the wording was otherwise. Dr. Mark Yarhouse of Regent University summarized a representative view in *Psychotherapy and American Journal of Family Therapy*:

Psychologists have an ethical responsibility to allow individuals to pursue treatment aimed at curbing experiences of same-sex attraction...not only because it affirms the client's right to dignity, autonomy and agency...but also because it demonstrates regard for diversity.[18]

The war over reorientation still rages. In May 2000, some 40 Exodus leaders demonstrated at the APA Convention in Chicago. They were joined by representatives from other parallel organizations which promote freedom from homosexuality through faith-centered counseling and "reparative therapy." The demonstration centered on the message that "reparative therapy" should be a viable treatment option for anyone wanting it. The APA and other secular groups had issued statements in the past two years condemning such therapy. Indeed, the APA had scheduled a debate between professional therapists supporting and condemning reparative therapy, but the debate was cancelled when the two pro-gay panelists withdrew. The debate was to have been moderated by Dr. Robert Spitzer, a psychiatrist who was instrumental in the 1973 decision to remove homosexuality from the Diagnostic and Statistical Manual of Mental Disorders. Dr. Spitzer witnessed an ex-gay demonstration at the 1999 APA convention and subsequently began interviewing dozens of men and women who claimed to have successfully left homosexuality; many of them are now married with children. Spitzer now believes that change in sexual orientation is possible for some people, and that reparative therapy should be an ethical option for those who desire it.

The May 2000 demonstrators carried signs such as: "Keep reparative therapy ethical," "I love my ex-gay husband," "I've changed – it's possible!" and "It's my right to change." Others spoke, "Thousands of men and women have found indescribable joy in overcoming unwanted homosexuality." And countless true stories from ex-gays confirm what counselors see every day: hope for change is possible for those struggling with same-sex desires. Yet, a small minority of psychological activists still claims that the ex-gay joy is not real. In response to Exodus, gay-rights activists told the media that they would be present to stage a counter-demonstration, but not one has occurred.

One is reminded of cognitive dissonance theory. Given a decision to label oneself G,B,L,T or Q, "dissonance" is likely to be aroused. In response people alter aspects of the decision alternatives to reduce dissonance, which leads to viewing the chosen alternative as more desirable (in this case "fixed") and other alternative – heterosexuality – as less desirable (in this case closed). This effect is called the spreading of alternatives and the theoretical paradigm is termed the free-choice paradigm. The theory also helps explain bi-phobia among the GBLTQ.

Scientific Facts on Conversion Success

What therefore, does science have to say about reorientation results? In 1997, NARTH surveyed 882 individuals who had experienced some degree of sexual-orientation change. Before counseling or therapy, 68 per cent of the respondents perceived themselves as exclusively or almost entirely homosexual. After treatment, only 13 per cent perceived themselves as exclusively or almost entirely homosexual. The respondents were overwhelmingly in agreement that conversion therapy had helped them cope with and reduce their homosexual attractions. Many perceived their homosexual behaviors as an addiction. A large majority said their religious and spiritual beliefs played a crucial, supportive role in overcoming their homosexuality. Areas of functioning in which the respondents report significant improvement: self-acceptance and self-understanding; sense of personal power and assertiveness; sense of clarity and security in gender identity; diminishment of loneliness and depression; improvement in emotional stability, self-esteem and maturity; better ability to resolve interpersonal conflicts; diminishment of homosexual thoughts, feelings and behaviors.[19]

Typical comments by respondents to the NARTH survey are as follows:

I wasted 14 years in therapy with therapists who had a 'you're gay, get used to it' mentality – which I find incredibly unethical.

My desire to develop my masculinity was never realized. Since treatment, it has developed in its own way, resulting in tremendous personal transformation – an enormous increase in personal worth, self-esteem, and the ability to take action.

I am delighted to have found reparative therapy – it feels healthy, and I feel honest for the first time in my life.

I was deceived for a number of years into believing that there was nothing I could do to change my sexual orientation...I tried counseling, but was simply told to stop fighting the homosexual feelings and accept who I was. I became trapped in the compulsion of cruising, going to the gay bars, and getting involved in a number of empty relationships...The greatest freedom came when I discovered that I could move away from the addiction of homosexual behavior, and began to see myself differently.

Armed with knowledge, hope and direction, change can be deliberate and planned. This is true for everyone and for any difficulty, not just homosexuality.

'Just The Facts' acknowledges that 'sexual orientation develops across a person's

lifetime' This being true, it is clear that competent professional counseling will have an effect on that evolving process.[20]

In 1993, the Hawaii Supreme Court decided that it might be unconstitutional to deny marriage licenses to homosexuals. For Associate Judge James Burns, the whole matter hung on whether or not homosexuality was "biologically fated."[21] The theory being, if it is unconstitutional to discriminate on the basis of gender, and gender is biologically fated, then why shouldn't it be unconstitutional to discriminate on the basis of sexual orientation, if homosexuality is biologically fated? In which case, civil marriage between homosexuals would qualify for constitutional protections. Here Neil and Briar Whitehead, authors of *My Genes Made Me Do It,* argue against such thinking:

We see it in homosexual people themselves, most of whom want to change their orientation at some stage. More than a third of gays now believe they were born that way – a 400 per cent increase in 50 years. They absorb the information that their sexuality is generic, inborn, ingrained, resistant to change, and their despair and anger fuels the fight for equal freedoms, which can only be ultimately disillusioning because it is based on a powerful untruth.[22]

According to Dr. Whitehead there is a very basic truth underlying the gene-myth:

There is nothing fixed or final about the homosexual orientation and its natural expression, homosexual behavior. No one has to stay homosexual or lesbian, in orientation or behavior, if he or she doesn't want to and informed support is available. No politician, church leader, church member, judge, counselor, homosexual person, or friend or family of a homosexual person, needs to feel forced into a position on homosexuality based on the apparent immutability of the homosexual orientation. Homosexuality is not inborn, not genetically dictated, not immutable.[23]

Sexual addiction is not an instinct, but can become something very close. If pleasurable sensations accompany certain fantasies and behaviors, which in turn relieve emotional pain and physical and mental stress, then a potentially addictive cycle begins. Kinsey argued that only a few positive or negative sexual experiences at the start could set one's life course. Initial experimental pleasures may start out innocently, indeed, without the context of stress and powerful fantasy, however, reinforcement increases the draw until it seems impossible to control. Again this could be called the "Oscar Wilde Effect." Must addictive behavior become an uncontrollable compulsion? As so many gay activists claim, is there no chance of deliverance from the bathhouse, the bushes, the washrooms, and from the risk of AIDS?

Writes Whitehead:

We can learn to bring our instincts under control, or we can allow our instincts to control us. Instincts develop because they are fed. No behavior takes us over without years of encouragement. If we have spent all our lives cultivating a certain behavior by thousands of repeated actions and responses, then it will eventually seem like a powerful urge – so powerful that it seems irresistible, or even geneti-

cally programmed. But nothing is unchangeable. If we lose our fear of death with training, and even enjoy the risks, if fathers can become 'mothers,' then sexual reflexes can also be trained. It may take a few years to reverse the training we have given them, but it can be done.[24]

The fact that exclusively heterosexual women can, in mid-life, develop lesbian feelings and behavior suggests reorientation should also be true. It is a well known clinical feature of lesbianism. It often occurs during marriage or after marriage break-up, with no clinically observable hint of prior existence – not even lesbian fantasy. Nichols[25] found among married bisexual women that many appeared to make dramatic swings in Kinsey ratings of both behavior and fantasy over the course of the marriage in ways that "cast doubt upon the widely held belief in the inflexibility of sexual orientation and attraction over time." Dixon surveyed fifty women who became bisexual after the age of thirty. They were exclusively heterosexual before, having had no earlier significant sexual fantasy about females, and quite heterosexually satisfied. They continued to enjoy promiscuous sexual relationships with both sexes.[26]

One must ponder the conviction among reorientation adherents that if considerable swings in sexual orientation can happen without therapeutic intervention, it makes sense that even more substantial changes can be achieved with motivated individuals who seek therapeutic and spiritual change to their lives. Here are some clinical facts[27]:

Dr. Reuben Fine, Director of the New York Centre for Psychoanalytic Training, remarked: 'If patients are motivated to change, a considerable percentage of overt homosexuals (become) heterosexuals.'

Dr. Bernard Berkowitz and Mildred Newman: 'We've found that a homosexual who really wants to change has a very good chance of doing so.'

Dr. Edmund Bergler concludes after analysis and consultations with 600 homosexuals over thirty years: 'Homosexuality has an excellent prognosis in psychiatric-psychoanalytic treatment of one to two years duration...provided the patient really wishes to change. Cure denotes not bi-sexuality, but real and unfaked heterosexuality.'

After twenty years of comparative study of homosexuals and heterosexuals, Dr. Irving Bieber wrote: 'Reversal [homosexual to heterosexual] estimates now range from 30 per cent to an optimistic 50 per cent.'

Dr. Charles Socarides said: 'There is...sufficient evidence that in the majority of cases homosexuality can be successfully treated by psychoanalysis.'

Scientists Masters and Johnson, after work with sixty-seven homosexuals and fourteen lesbians who requested reversion therapy, reported a success rate of 71.6 per cent after a follow-up of six years.

Psychologist Dr. Gerard van den Aardweg, after twenty years research into treatment of homosexuality, stated: 'Two thirds reached a stage where homosexual feelings were occasional impulses at most, or completely absent.'

Psychiatrist Dr. William Wilson claimed a 55 per cent success rate in treating homosexuals who were professing Christians.

According to Dr. Robert Kronemeyer, a clinical psychologist: 'About 80 per cent of homosexual men and women in syntonic therapy have been able to free themselves, and achieve a healthy and satisfying heterosexual adjustment.'

Dr. Robert L. Spitzer, a psychiatry professor at Columbia University, recently studied some 200 people, 143 of them men, who had claimed they had changed their orientation from gay to heterosexual. The average age of those interviewed was 43. Most had started efforts to change more than a decade before the interview. Many strategies were used to change their orientation. About half said the most helpful step was work with a mental health professional, most commonly a psychologist. About a third cited a support group, and fewer mentioned such aids as books and mentoring by a heterosexual. Spitzer concluded that 66 per cent of the men and 44 per cent of the women had arrived at what he called good sexual functioning. That term was defined as being in a sustained, loving heterosexual relationship within the past year, getting enough satisfaction from the emotional relationship with their partner to rate it at least seven on a ten-point scale, having satisfying heterosexual sex at least monthly and never or rarely thinking of somebody of the same-sex during heterosexual sex. In addition, 89 per cent of men and 95 per cent of women said they were bothered only slightly, or not at all, by unwanted homosexual feelings. Only 11 per cent of men and 37 per cent of women reported a complete absence of homosexual indicators.[28]

The Right to Choose

By definition, homophobia is "fear or hatred of homosexuals." Ex-gay ministries and many orthodox Christians neither fear nor hate homosexual people. All Christians can acknowledge that each person has been given the freedom (not license) to live out their sexual lives according to their wishes. Equally, Christians should respect that some gay and lesbian people do not want to be lesbian or gay. There are also a lot of people who are attracted to their own sex but who would never consider themselves gay or lesbian. Reorientation ministries are here for all those people; to offer support in their journey toward becoming the people they want to be.

Critics of ex-gay ministries say such attitudes contribute to homophobia. According to web site *FreeToBeMe.com:*

It's important to note that those critics are often pro-gay individuals who've never been gay or lesbian themselves or gay persons who have not experienced or desired sexual reorientation. Those who have found help and experienced change report that the life they lived as gay people was miserable for them, especially after the initial relief of coming out had passed. And we tend to put more weight on what they say as, after all, they have seen both sides.[29]

FreeToBeMe says that change happens through process. Sometimes people think that if they pray enough or wish hard enough, their homosexuality will just disappear. This is an unrealistic expectation. Changes in the area of sexual orientation happen as a result of a process which usually involves some hard personal work. Imagine wanting a vegetable garden. You could pray for years that vegetables would grow in your backyard. When nothing happens, you might even decide to be angry at some unseen being for not hearing your prayers. However, the reality is that we must prepare the soil, plant the seeds, water and weed, and do other work. This gives the best chance that there will be an abundance of vegetables to harvest.

In the same way, individuals who want to experience changes in their sexuality must do a lot of work as part of the process. They need to prepare the space in their lives for the growth desired. How long the process of change from homosexuality to heterosexuality takes depends on a number of factors. *FreeToBeMe* and other reorientation agencies contend that some of these factors include:

The root issues that are involved:

The more difficult or complex the underlying factors involved in a person's same-gender attraction, the longer the process of change may take. For example, the process may take longer for a person who has experienced severe sexual abuse in childhood than for someone who has experienced mild sexual abuse. For one man, most of the sexual abuse that happened in his childhood was worked through fairly quickly. One particular abuse incident, however, took four years to work through because of the degree of shame and destruction of personhood involved.

How much support a person has:

The more helpful things a person puts in place, the better progress he or she can expect to make. For example, a woman who only attends a support group will most likely make slower progress than another woman who is also in individual counseling, involved in her community, and has friends with whom she can share what is happening in her life.

One's ability and willingness to face difficult personal issues:

As the process of change involves facing difficult personal issues and the pain related to these issues, a person's ability and willingness to face these things will affect their rate of progress. Related to willingness is the question of whether a person truly wants change. Some individuals say they want to change, but are not prepared to take serious steps to accomplish this. A person who thinks, for example, that entertaining a little fantasy now and then is ok, should not be surprised when change doesn't proceed the way they hope.

FreeToBeMe claims it is not unusual for the process of change to take 5-10 years. This is no reason to despair. They are not talking about 5-10 years of going through hell! Many people change their identity much sooner than this. Significant relief from the intensity of homosexual feelings can also come much sooner.

Reasons GBLTQ Want to Change

Peoplecanchange.com offers a clear explanation of why homosexuals want to change their orientation. Many are just plain miserable gay:

In so many ways, 'gay' just didn't work for us. It was so easy to become sex-obsessed in the pornography- and lust-saturated culture of homosexuality. It was so difficult to feel connected to God or some kind of higher purpose in a life where the mantra seemed to be, 'If it feels good…nothing else matters.' We were living in dissonance with the values, beliefs and goals we'd held for a lifetime. We pined for love and acceptance from men, but it seemed that so many gays so idolized youth and physical perfection that we often felt more rejection from gays, not less. Still, we kept searching, partly because we didn't know where else to look and partly because we did find moments of pleasure and moments of real connection with good, decent and kind homosexual men. Those were the moments that kept drawing us back to homosexuality, hoping and believing that maybe the next boyfriend, the next encounter, would finally make us feel whole. But for most of us, the hole inside of us that yearned for male affirmation and acceptance just got bigger the more that we pursued healing in homosexuality. Several of us were plagued by thoughts of suicide. Some of us became sex addicts, no longer able to control our obsessive search for sex. Our lives became filled with darkness.[30]

Paul [not the Christian apostle] writes:

For 12 years, I lived life as an openly gay man. I had a partner of three years who I dearly cared for, a family of wonderful loving friends scattered around the world, a house, a new job, and the prospects of a beautiful life. There was just one question that periodically raised its ugly head: Why was I so insufferably miserable?

'I was amazed. I had everything that I ever wanted. Yet, I also felt an incredible black hole inside that seemed to be sucking the life out of me. How could this be? I kept trying desperately to fill it. I read a lot of philosophy, I thought a lot about existence and life, and tried various ways to reach a peace. Nothing worked, not one damn thing. The pain just continued to increase, steadily and persistently. All I wanted to do was cease to exist, to end the suffering.'

In short, we wanted to be men, and we simply defined 'real men' as straight men. As much as we tried to convince ourselves that homosexual men were just as masculine as straight men, that there was nothing emasculating about having sex with a man or pursuing the gay interests, we felt inside ourselves that that just wasn't true.

We felt called by God out of homosexuality into what for us was a far better life. At different times and in different ways, almost all of us turned to God in our turmoil, and felt this simple truth deep in our hearts: Homosexuality was wrong for us, and God would lead us out of the pain if we turned to him.

This became a powerful motivator in our lives. Coupled with the fact that for the majority of us, being gay just didn't work, a spiritual hope of eventual peace offered a tiny, flickering light at the end of a tunnel. We walked toward it.[31]

Paul contrasts his experience with a former male lover to his experience with his fiancé:

I recognize now, although I couldn't see it when I was living homosexually, that my homosexual relationships always had a huge piece missing. I didn't feel whole or complete with men. I was always lacking, wanting something more from them than they could give me. With my fiancé now, the best way to describe how I feel about our relationship is that we 'fit.' Physically, emotionally, spiritually, she fits. She complements the areas where I'm lacking, and I complement her, like a lock and key. And as I grow to love her more, my desire for her physically just keeps increasing. It's easy to see myself as both a companion and lover to her for the rest of my life.

That's completely different from my former relationship with my boyfriend Jim. As I grew to love him more, I grew to desire him (sexually) less. I now know why: I started to love him normally, as a brother, instead of as a lover. I had a tremendous, growing love for him. I adored him. I still do. He's one of the most loving, caring, humble men I have ever met. But our relationship was changing to one where we were companions, not lovers. And that is absolutely consistent with what I saw in other relationships. After awhile, they would become great friends but stop having sex with each other. They would start to go outside the relationship for sex. In 12 years in the gay world, I never met a gay couple that was entirely monogamous. One in the couple has always gone outside the relationship for sex, if not both. Always.[32]

For some the "Gay Pride" or "Gay Affirmation" wore off:

...it seemed for a time that the answer we were looking for was to accept and embrace our supposedly innate gay identity, 'come out of the closet' as a homosexual and claim 'gay pride.' In fact, those of us who did so found it to be an exhilarating, freeing experience – temporarily. No longer were we crippled by vacillation. No longer were we hiding in shame. No longer would we beat ourselves up with self-criticism and so-called 'homophobia.' At last we were 'out and proud.'

But no matter how right it was to free ourselves from shame, self-ridicule and self-hate, and no matter how much relief we found in finally getting off the fence and making a decision – any decision – homosexuality still felt wrong for us. Some of us denied this for a long time but we could ultimately lie to ourselves no longer. For us, it just felt wrong. Attempting to resolve our homosexual struggles by killing our conscience felt like it was killing our souls instead.

Almost universally, we felt alienated from God and our spiritual lives. We were out of integrity with our deeply held values and beliefs that had always anchored our lives. We felt more alienated than ever from the masculine world of straight men.

Sadly, most of us also found far less healing, acceptance and unconditional love among gay men than we had imagined we would. A common experience among us was that we experienced the gay world as a place that was fraught with promiscuity, lust, obsession with youth and physical appearance, addiction to sex, alcohol and lust. We found judgment, pettiness, spiritual darkness and brokenness. Although we experienced small pieces of healing there at times, for the most part, it only deepened the emotional and spiritual emptiness inside.[33]

There is No Gay Gene

Homosexuals Anonymous, a Christian fellowship for men and women asks, "Have genes or hormones made you homosexual?" Some have tried to maintain that, but there is little evidence to support such views. Their web site records many scientific testimonies. Dr. William Byne and Dr. Bruce Parsons of the Department of Psychiatry of the Columbia University College of Physicians and Surgeons state:

Recent studies postulate biologic factors as the primary basis for sexual orientation. However, there is no evidence at present to substantiate a biologic theory ... Critical review shows the evidence favoring a biologic theory to be lacking.[34]

After reviewing the scientific studies on genetics and homosexuality, Masters and Johnson concluded: "The genetic theory of homosexuality has been generally discarded today."[35]

Dr. C.A. Tripp summarizes the scientific experience regarding hormones and homosexuality as follows: "A number of clinicians have seen fit over the years to run their own experiments by administering testosterone to both effeminate and ordinary homosexuals. The results have been consistent:

When there were any behavioral changes at all, the subjects became more like themselves than ever. Their sex drives were usually increased and sometimes their effeminate mannerisms as well (when they had any), but there were never any directional changes in their sexual interests. From these experiments...it has become abundantly clear that the sex hormones play a considerable role in powering human sexuality, but they do not control the direction of it.[36]

More recently some have argued that the problem lies in our prenatal hormones. They suggest that stress during pregnancy may alter the production of sex hormones in the mother at a crucial time, changing the level of hormones reaching the brain of the fetus, thus affecting sexual orientation. Here too, however, the available evidence is against the theory. Thus, researchers have found that "...in the majority of intersex patients with known hormone abnormalities, the sexual orientation follows the sex of the rearing. Consequently, we have to assume that prenatal hormone conditions by themselves do not rigidly determine sexual orientation."[37]

Dr. Judd Marmor reported on the work of Richard Green. He writes:

...in a long series of studies on boys who showed effeminate behavior in childhood has demonstrated that although over half of these boys do become homosexual, a substantial minority of them do not. This indicates that gender-discordant children are not born homosexual, but rather are born with certain behavioral tendencies that, given contributory environmental factors, can predispose them towards homosexual behavior. Thus, a little boy whose behavior is effeminate, who does not like competitive athletics, and who prefers music and art, may be disappointing to a macho father, who tends to reject the boy and distance himself from him. The mother may respond by overprotecting her son. Such reactions disturb the boy's capacity to identify positively with his father and cause him to over identify with his mother. He may then ultimately develop homosexual erotic responses, which are reinforced by later experiences.[38]

Dr. John Money says:

With respect to orientation as homosexual or bisexual, there is no human evidence that prenatal hormonalization alone, independently of postnatal history, inexorably preordains either orientation. Rather, neonatal antecedents may facilitate a homosexual or bisexual orientation, provided the postnatal determinants in the social and communicational history are also facilitative."[39] *Dr. Earl D. Wilson writes, 'The disputed evidence for physical causes of male homosexuality is even weaker when it comes to lesbianism.'*[40]

Facts like these led John DeCecco, editor of the *Journal of Homosexuality* and professor of psychology at San Francisco State University to say:

The idea that people are born into one type of sexual behavior is foolish.' ... The move towards 'biologizing' homosexuality, he says, isn't the result of a scientific consensus, but a political consensus by those eager to label people gay or straight. Homosexuality, he says, is a 'behavior, not a condition,' and something that some people can and do change, just like they sometimes change tastes and other personality traits.[41]

According to *Homosexuals Anonymous*, some will find these truths deeply disturbing. They rob homosexuals of some favorite excuses. "We can no longer cry, 'I can't help myself. I was born this way.' These truths mean we have to take responsibility for our lives and our actions."[42] In doing this, however, these truths give homosexuals the key to freedom. They show GBLTQ that they are not prisoners to cruel fate or faulty genes or hormones. There is hope for us! As Masters and Johnson put it:

When dealing with problems of sexual preference, it is vital that all health-care professionals bear in mind that the homosexual man or woman is basically a man or woman by genetic determination and is homosexually oriented by learned preference.[43]

As Dr. Robert Kronemeyer has said:

From my 25 years' experience as a clinical psychologist, I firmly believe that homosexuality is a learned response to early painful experiences and that it can be unlearned. For those homosexuals who are unhappy with their life and find effective therapy, it is 'curable'.[44]

Joan Laird contends:

There is no strong evidence to date to conclude that lesbians are biologically sexed or gendered any differently than heterosexual women, and no strong evidence to suggest that lesbianism is rightly understood as gender inversion or perversion.[45]

Women who transition to lesbianism later in life are particularly problematic for an innate homosexual premise:

One of the problems with research in this area, which may be used to support the hypothesis that gayness or lesbianism is biological, is that it is often late adolescents or adults who are explaining their sexual orientation from a retrospective position. Kitzinger and Wilkinson point out that 'this focus on adolescence is a consequence of an essentialism that assumes a dormant, true lesbian self waiting to be discovered or revealed at puberty or shortly thereafter.' It does little to explain the experiences of women who may change their self-identity from heterosexual to lesbian in early, mid-, or even late adulthood. From their research with women who made transitions from heterosexuality to lesbianism, they concluded that 'adult women who make such transitions are no more driven by biology or subconscious urges than they are when, for instance, they change jobs; such choices could be viewed as influenced by a mixture of personal re-evaluation, practical necessity, political values, chance, and opportunity.'[46]

In 1989, the Centers for Disease Control (currently the Centers for Disease Control and Prevention, or CDC) funded the AIDS Prevention Project of the Seattle-King County Department of Public Health to develop, implement, and evaluate interventions targeting non-gay identifying men who have sex with men (NGI-MSM). Drawing upon personal or professional knowledge and experience, the project staff defined the risk population as homosexually active men who did not read the local gay press, did not participate in local gay events (such as parades or dances), and generally did not frequent publicly gay establishments (such as bars). However, based on interviews of 79 NGI-MSM at bathhouses and a movie-sex shop complex, secretive attitudes, risky behaviors, and denial of risk was evident among these men.[47] Project staff also surveyed individuals who have contact with NGI-MSM but are not themselves NGI-MSM: employees and managers of adult erotica businesses (bookstores, video arcades, X-rated theaters), public park groundskeepers, public and private transportation workers (rest-stop maintenance personnel, taxicab drivers), bartenders, vice officers, male escorts (prostitutes), counselors and therapists, and gay and bisexual support group participants. These interviews clarified points of access to NGI-MSM. The six priority groups were then defined as follows:

Hustlers, or men who have sex with men primarily for economic reasons, including adolescents living on the streets, low-income men, and non-gay-identified professional prostitutes or escorts.

Closeted (highly secretive) or coming-out men, including NGI-MSM who generally are not heterosexually active, but have some compelling reason not to identify as homosexual. Some men are closeted by choice (to maintain heterosexual privilege within the general population) and others by circumstance (men in the military or clergy). This sector also includes men who are in the process of coming to terms with their sexual orientation.

New Age men or experimenters, including NGI-MSM who reject conventional notions of sexual roles and feel free to participate in or experiment with a variety of sexual activities.

Incarcerated or formerly incarcerated, including men in and out of jail or prison who may experience same-sex behavior while incarcerated and who continue to practice this behavior after release from jail or prison.

People of color or cultural groups, including NGI-MSM from other sectors who are distinguished by cultural factors that allow or encourage same-sex behavior among heterosexuals or that restrict the ability of a member of a particular culture to identify himself as gay or bisexual if he is involved in same-sex activity.

Heterosexually identified bisexual men, including married men who have occasional same-sex encounters, men who have sex with men in all-male institutions (such as dormitories), and sexually active men who don't necessarily discriminate on the basis of gender. This sector is a 'catch-all' for the majority of NGI-MSM.[48]

Chistopher Hewitt, using both national surveys and surveys of self-identified gay men in the United States, analyzed the numbers, age distribution, life expectancy, and marital status of men who have sex with men. He concluded that five types of behavior can be distinguished: open preferential, repressed preferential, bisexual, experimental, and situational. These five categories have different patterns of sexual behavior, and the numbers in each category are influenced by changing social conditions, in particular the growth of gay neighborhoods, and public tolerance.[49]

Another study that looked at dimensions of sexual experience, as measured on Kinsey's Homosexual-Heterosexual Continuum, found significant variety. Male respondents were less apt to consider themselves exclusively homosexual in their feelings. Some 42 per cent of White and more than half of the Black homosexual males gave themselves a rating of 5 or less (i.e., not exclusively homosexual) on the scale. A minority of the White homosexual females (47 per cent) and barely a majority of Black homosexual females rated themselves exclusively homosexual in both their sexual behaviors and feelings. Some 75 per cent of the White homosexual females considered themselves more homosexual in their behaviors than their feelings; 55 per cent of White and 41 per cent of Black homosexual females said they had had sex dreams involving sexual activity with males.[50]

These studies concluded a variety of categories for homosexuality and confirmed that many could not be considered exclusively homosexual. Dr. Dean Hammer says: "We have not found the gene – which we don't think exists – for sexual orientation."[51] Says Neil Whitehead:

Hamer knows that any attempt to argue the existence of a 'homosexual gene,' a single, apparently autocratic, gene governing homosexuality, is nonsense, genetically. There is no single gene governing sexual preference or any other preference. There is no gene for smoking, dancing, or making sarcastic remarks.[52]

We know that many more than 100 genes are involved in IQ in humans because at least 100 separate gene defects are already known to individually lower IQ. If when many genes are involved, changes in behavior take place very slowly, over very many generations, how can homosexuality suddenly appear as it does in a family? The only possible way would be for many recessive "homosexual" genes to switch on spontaneously and simultaneously very early in the life of the fetus, and all the "heterosexual" genes to completely switch off. This is extremely unlikely. If many genes were involved the typical genetic pattern would be a gradual change in the family toward homosexuality – a few per cent each generation over the course perhaps thirty generations. Similarly, homosexuality would only slowly disappear in the descendants (if any) of a homosexual person. Contends Whitehead, any other proposed mechanism is highly speculative. Behaviors which do change slowly over the generations in a family or society are much more likely to be genetically influenced or determined, but homosexuality changes too swiftly to be genetically controlled or influenced by many genes.[53]

Although acknowledging that it is highly unlikely the GBLTQ community would accept the notion of non-heterosexual orientation resulting from genetic mutation, Whitehead studied the hypothesis. He concluded, from a biological point of view, that homosexuality does not appear to be caused by mutation. He explains why:

Just as many 'homosexual' genes would suddenly have to switch on and off if the sudden appearance and disappearance of homosexuality in families is to be accounted for, so, many genes would suddenly have to mutate if we want to argue that homosexuality is caused by mutation. The chances that even ten genes might spontaneously change from 'heterosexual' to 'homosexual' by mutation is much less than one in a thousand, and geneticists would find it inconceivable that hundreds of genes could do so.[54]

There is another difficulty with the mutation theory. Most conditions caused by mutations affect only a very small proportion of the general population: about 0.025 per cent of the population or less, in each case. Altogether, conditions caused by genetic mutation are found in about only 1 per cent of the total population. Homosexuality, with its total incidence (2.2 per cent), does not fit plausibly into the category of genetic diseases because the incidence is too high.[55]

Whitehead asks, "How could genetic homosexuality maintain itself in a population?" In reply he concludes "genetically enforced homosexuality (exclusively same-sex sex) would die out of the population in several generations." A gene is retained in the gene pool when an average of at least one child is born to every adult having that gene (one child per person). As unlikely as it sounds, surveys show that of persons classifying themselves as exclusively homosexual, one in five has a child. Moreover, according to surveys, bisexuals, have an average of 1.25 children each. On its own, that's enough to replace the adult gene or genes, but the average total number of children produced by bisexuals and exclusive homosexuals still comes to less than one per person – 0.9.[56]

No mainstream geneticist is happy with the idea that genes dictate behavior, particularly homosexual behavior. Geneticists G.S. Omenn and A.G. Motulksy said, when they talked about the difficulties of predicting behavior from gene structure:

The hopelessness of understanding behavior from simple analytical approaches can be compared to the hopelessness of seeking linguistic insights by a chemical analysis of a book.[57]

About 1 per cent of the adult male population is exclusively homosexual, and about 0.5 per cent of the adult female population is exclusively lesbian at any given time – a grand mean of 0.7 per cent of the total adult population. Around 2.2 per cent of the total adult population is GBLTQ.[58] The surveys of bisexual incidence come up with an interesting statistic. Of all homosexually active males, about 55 per cent are married (which is the average of a range of surveys finding between 25 per cent and 80 per cent). About 45 per cent of lesbians have been married.[59]

Those who accept that homosexuality may not be genetically determined, may then argue that the behavior is so long-term, so strong, and so resistant to change that it should be called an instinct or reflex. We have an instinctive blinking reflex when something comes near our eyes. Even male ejaculation is a reflex. It can be tricked by artificial stimulation – even triggered by electric shock.[60] Here Whitehead draws upon the instincts of survival and mothering to argue that instinctive responses are not always rigid and can be changed. He writes:

Young children have an instinctive fear of heights. In some experiments several decades ago, researchers placed a strong sheet glass over a deep recess created in a level surface and let babies crawl along the sheet glass. All the babies paused in fear at the apparent edge and retreated. This natural fear of falling is not absent in potential mountain climbers as babies, but the instinctive fear is abated through progressive training and experience. The mothering instinct leads timid ewes and tiny birds to charge humans and dogs if their babies are threatened. Mothers are equipped to conceive, carry, and suckle their young. They appear to be natural nurturers. Fathers on the other hand don't appear to have the same instinct to nur-

ture. Surveys usually show that they spend only about one third of the time with their children that mothers do. However, are human males biologically programmed or instinctively geared to be poor nurturers? Where do the good househusbands and domestic fathers come from? Indeed, if such discrepant nurturing instincts can be reprogrammed in both females and males, is there not equal likelihood that such is true of a so-called 'homosexual instinct?'[61]

Whitehead cites some revealing experiments:

In an unusual experiment, scientist Jay Rosenblatt took several-day-old rats and put them in with virgin females. The females showed no mothering instincts and of course could not nurse the pups, so the pups tended to languish. Rosenblatt replaced the pups each day, and by the sixth day there was an enormous change in the behavior of the virginal females. They began to look after the pups, licking them, retrieving them, and even more astonishingly, lying down as though trying to nurse them. Even though they were not primed by hormonal changes of pregnancy, the presence of the pups alone was sufficient to trigger the maternal behavior.

Rosenblatt tried exactly the same thing with adult male rats. After six days, the males started behaving just like the virgin females: licking the pups, retrieving them when they strayed, and even lying down as trying to nurse them! In other words, maternal 'instincts' were evoked by the presence of the pups in male rats, sometimes known to eat their infant offspring.[62]

The modern woman who insists that men are quite capable of mothering and nurturing children appears to have science on her side; fathers are certainly able to increase the quality time they already spend with their children. "House-husbands" have brought up very young children with the aid of glass bottles, powdered milk and rubber teats. There are even cases where older men with hormonal treatment have breast-fed babies.[63] Nor is nurturing behavior an over-riding instinct in human females. Some human mothers abandon their babies at birth. Hundreds of thousands of babies are aborted each year. Some women are poor mothers; some men are successful replacements. Says Whitehead, "It seems the mothering instinct can be developed or neglected in a woman, and evoked in a man."

Focusing on our sexuality, some 90 per cent of mankind have a powerful instinct to reproduce. The remaining 10 per cent for various reasons have no urge to personally contribute to perpetuating our species. Anhedonia is an often temporary state of being turned off from all pleasures, not just sexual ones. In a 1970 study, some 10 per cent of adults saw no prospect of sexual enjoyment with either sex.[64] For many pro-creation is not an overriding drive. [On the other hand, in Chapter 8 we will address the phenomenon of women changing their mind and deciding late in life that they really do want children.] Homosexuality cannot reproduce, so homosexuality cannot be considered an instinct to perpetuate the species. Says Whitehead, "If it could be called an instinct, it is no less malleable than any other of the powerful instincts that man experiences, which, we have seen, are subject to a huge degree to man's will and other environmental influences."[65] In sum my daughter's belief (based on Scripture and expressed in the guest speaker evaluation at the start of this book) is right – there is no gay gene. Gay theology can neither biblically nor scientifically claim the existence of a gene for homosexual behavior.

Psychology of Homosexuality

If the homosexual orientation is not "originally" and "predominately" rooted in something physical, biological or genetic, what other factors differentiate the development of homosexuals from heterosexuals? A number of clues have been discovered.

In 1952, Dr. Irving Bieber began directing a research team in a nine year project studying male homosexuality. In all, 77 analysts, each a member of the Society of Medical Psychoanalysts, provided information on two patient samples consisting of 106 male homosexuals and a comparison group of 100 male heterosexuals. The result was "the most authoritative study of its kind."[66] "No one has ever gathered so much finely discriminating detail on so many homosexuals, treated in depth by so many different doctors, and put through so many evaluations."[67] Dr. Bieber writes:

We have come to the conclusion that a constructive, supportive, warmly-related father precludes the possibility of a homosexual son....[68]

Another psychiatrist, after many years of study and practice treating male homosexuals, noted, "Homosexuals consistently describe their fathers as a weak, shadowy and distant figure, or an angry, cold or brutalizing one."[69] Dr. Elizabeth Moberly received her Ph.D. in psychology from Oxford University for her study of homosexuality. She found "that the homosexual – whether man or woman – has suffered from some deficit in the relationship with the parent of the same-sex; or 'homosexual,' relationships."[70] Sharon Wegscheider, a certified alcoholism specialist, a family therapist, a member of Virginia Satir's AVANTA network, and president of ONSITE, provides an illustration of how this can happen when she describes the patterns which appear in the family of a chemically dependent person. She describes one of the characters in this family as the "Lost Child":

He becomes a loner, looking after his needs himself and staying out of everyone's way....[71] *'Since he has never experienced warm human closeness, he is not prepared to make friends and engage in the social give and take of day-to-day school contacts. Yet in the midst of the crowd, withdrawing into himself leaves him feeling lonely, different, inept.'*[72]

Each human being learns what it means to be a man or a woman from the adults in his or her childhood family. The same-sex parent provides a lasting model of what he is to be, and the other parent an object for his first important relationship with a person of the opposite sex. These are powerful teachings if they occur. The Lost Child, however, has never felt close to either of his parents; he has been too insulated from them to experience this kind of learning. Consequently, he reaches puberty with no clear sense of his own sexual identity or how to relate in a healthy way to those of the opposite sex. As adolescent sexuality increasingly colors all aspects of the daily world he occupies, he is engulfed by yet another kind of confusion. True to his pattern, he withdraws. He rarely dates and in his loneliness suffers growing doubts about his own sexual normalcy."[73] Thus Ms. Wegscheider lists among the common characteristics of the Lost Child, problems with sexual identity and confusion about sex roles and sometimes about sexual preference:

Alcoholism and drug addiction are only two of many family experiences which can lead to confusion in sexual identity and sexual preference. Many things less severe than chemical dependency can result in a deficit in our relationship with our same-sex parent. A sensitive child can be easily hurt. My father was a fine man who had no problem with alcohol or drugs. He did, however, want me, his first born, to be exactly like he was: strong, tough, a fighter, and a doctor. These were things God had not equipped me to be. I felt that I was not what my father wanted, and that he did not love me. So I put up a wall between us and missed the love I needed to develop a healthy gender identity. Had you asked about our relationship, I would have told you, 'It's fine.' But, if I was being complete, I would have added the revealing words, 'but we're not close.'[74]

Dr. Moberly suggests other situations which may cause difficulty:

The illness of the child, especially when this involves hospitalization, i.e., a large measure of separation from parental care.

The illness of a parent. Even when this does not involve hospitalization, it may mark a period of inability to care for the young child, which may in turn affect the child's capacity for attaching to the parent.

The birth of a sibling, especially when this involves the mother's absence due to hospitalization, or a conspicuous lessening in the amount of care she gives to the child she has already.

The temporary, prolonged, or permanent absence of a parent.

The separation or divorce of the parents.

The death of a parent.

Adoption, fostering or living in an orphanage.

Being brought up in a succession of nurses, governesses, etc., i.e., a constantly changing succession of 'parental' figures.[75]

Alfred Kinsey's circumstance supports this contention, however, to illustrate Moberly's observations on the psychology of homosexuality, we need only look at the two principal lovers in Oscar Wilde's life. First, when Oscar was fifteen, the boy who is recognized to have led Wilde into gay sex was born, in Canada, under the name Robbie Ross. Robbie's father, John Ross, had become Solicitor-General of

Upper Canada, at the age of thirty-three, in 1851. His father's early death in 1871 greatly impacted Robbie. The tragedy left Elizabeth Ross not only as a young widow, but a single mother with five small children, Robbie being the youngest aged two. Money from her father's estate left her comparatively wealthy and with the means to move back to England that year. Montgomery Hyde writes:

When it soon became clear that little Bobby was a rather small and frail child, Elizabeth's protectiveness became all the more pronounced. This infuriated his sisters, Mary and Lizzie, who began to see him as a mummy's boy. Interestingly, though, his two brothers, Jack and Aleck – ten and nine years older than him respectively – both displayed a rather paternal attitude towards him. [76]

Back in England, Elizabeth had plans for her own life, which included travel on the Continent, as well as finding a place in London society. She soon dispatched Robbie to a prep school within easy distance of London: Sandroyd, at Cobham in Surrey. Sandroyd was designed to prepare young boys for future study at major public schools such as Eton or in some cases the Royal Navy. Later Robbie would stay at the Wilde residence. Writes Hyde:

His small size and rather weak constitution ill-suited him for sports. He rarely mentioned his schooldays in later life, or if he did, his comments were not recorded. It is highly likely, though, that with his looks he would have attracted quite a lot of amorous attention from older boys, or indeed, some of the masters. While any such experience, physically consummated or not, need not necessarily affect the sexual development of an individual, something certainly happened somewhere, either at school or on his travels abroad, to make him not just enthusiastically but contentedly homosexual by his late teens.[77]

Second, is Wilde's lover Bosie Douglas. John Sholto Douglas (Bosie's father) was the ninth Marquis of Queensbury. Hyde describes John Douglas as an eccentric Scottish nobleman; he may have been mentally unbalanced. His principal preoccupations were sport and atheism, and he knew much more about his horses and dogs than about the human members of his family. Apart from his ill-fated quarrel with Wilde, he is chiefly remembered as the author of the rules, which govern amateur boxing. But his profession of atheism had already won for him a contemporary notoriety. As a representative peer of Scotland he refused to take the oath in the House of Lords on the ground that this necessary preliminary was mere "Christian tomfoolery." In his private life he bullied his wife, who subsequently divorced him, on 22 January 1887, on the grounds of his adultery with Mabel Gilroy. He neglected his children, preferring instead the society of his mistresses and his sporting cronies. He was arrogant, vain, conceited, and ill-tempered.[78] It is one of the great ironies of history that the undoing of the aesthetic Oscar Wilde was by an obsessed gay son and his devout atheist father, and not as commonly assumed by the homophobic Christian right or a puritanical society.

In correspondence to his son "Queensbury" registered his complaint over his son's "intimacy with this man Wilde." Bosie's only response to this letter was to send him a telegram, which read simply: "What a funny little man you are! Alfred Douglas." Queensberry replied:

If I catch you again with that man I will make a public scandal in a way you little dream of; it is already a suppressed one. I prefer an open one, and at any rate I shall not be blamed for allowing such things to go on.[79]

Queensbury told Douglas that all future cards would go in the fire unread. He then repeated the threat of a thrashing. "You reptile," concluded this paternal epistle, "You are no son of mine, and I never thought you were."[80] Wilde met Bosie in 1892; Wilde was 38 and Douglas 22. Leaving aside briefly the issue of homosexuality, ask yourself as a parent or potential parent: Where you would stand, if your 22 year old daughter started a sexual relationship with a married man, sixteen years her senior, with two children and a wife? Again what would a genuine Christian pastor advise?

Perhaps this would come as little surprise to psychologists thinking like Moberly, but two years after the death of Constance Wilde, and after his own father's death, Bosie arose (to quote Marjorie Garber) from his homosexual "blindness" to contract a runaway marriage with a poetess Olive Custance, an heiress, who soon found that even her substantial fortune was insufficient to keep him in the style to which he was accustomed.[81]

While the experiences, listed by Dr. Moberly, do not always result in homosexual feelings, they can, in a sensitive child, cause a hurt which leads to such problems. To develop in a healthy way, a child needs love from its parent (or a consistent parent substitute) of the same-sex. She writes:

Needs for love from, dependency on, and identification with, the parent of the same-sex are met through the child's attachment to the parent. If, however, the attachment is disrupted, the needs that are normally met through the medium of such an attachment remain unmet.[82]

If these needs go unmet over a period of time, the child develops mixed and contradictory feelings towards its same-sex parent and tries, through a process of detachment, to survive without the love he or she deeply needs. The emotionally hurt youngster says of the same-sex parent, "I don't want to be like you." These feelings are transferred to all members of the same-sex so that the person experiences, at the same time, a deep desire for intimacy with persons of the same-sex and a strong desire to flee such intimacy. When puberty comes, these feelings get confused with erotic intimacy and a homosexual struggle begins.

Homosexual behavior is a mistaken attempt to meet a real need for non-sexual, same-sex, parent-child love. This need has been falsely understood as sexual, but homosexual behavior actually lessens the possibility of getting the real need met, because it involves guilt, deepens feelings of inferiority, and increases the ambivalence experienced in the same-sex relating. As Dr. Earl D. Wilson has noted, "The anonymous sex which many homosexuals experience seems only to strengthen the reparative urge and leave the person more desperate."[83] All this reduces a person's ability to have those healthy relationships with members of the same-sex, which are vital to coming to freedom from homosexuality.

As Dr. Moberly puts it:

Homosexuality is the kind of problem that needs to be solved through relationships. The solution of same-sex deficits is to be sought through the medium of... non-sexual relationships with members of the same-sex. It is the provision of good same-sex relationships that helps meet unmet same-sex needs, heals defects in the relational capacity, and in this way forwards the healing process.[84]

Here a good same-sex counselor may also be needed to help work through deep-seated hurts from the past.

According to Whitehead, "Homosexuality fits much more naturally into that group of human behaviors which are psychological in nature." Moreover, he says incidence studies argue for a high environmental influence in homosexuality:

A large Chicago study asked where people had been brought up during ages fourteen to sixteen years and whether they had any male homosexual partners during the last year. The percentages differed for different degrees of urbanization; 1.2 per cent of the males surveyed who had been raised in rural areas reported having homosexual partners during the last year; 2.5 per cent who had been raised in medium-sized towns reported having homosexual partners, and 4.4 per cent who had been raised in large cities reported being active homosexuals. For women, the percentages were 0.7 per cent, 1.3 per cent and 1.6 per cent, respectively. In other words where you are brought up is quite an important factor in whether you end up having homosexual partners.[85]

Whitehead noted that if homosexuality was genetically influenced, and for the sake of argument the rural rate of 1.2 per cent was used as the base, then in the cities, the balance (3.2 per cent) would be exclusively due to social factors. This means for males, that the environmental factor (3.2 per cent) is far more important than the alleged genetic factor (1.2 per cent).[86]

Whitehead also looked at the diversity of homosexual expression and culture and concluded again, there was little evidence of a genetic foundation. In 1994, an Italian-American geneticist, Cavalli-Sforza, published a huge genetic atlas, the outcome of a monumental study of the genetic characteristics of different ethnic groups. His conclusion was that, in spite of superficial differences (e.g. skin color), the different races are essentially the same genetically. In fact, something between 99.7 per cent and 99.9 per cent of the genes in any two unrelated people are the same.[87] If all ethnic groups share similar genes two assumptions can be drawn about genetically determined behavior: it will be predictable, specific in nature and similar all over the globe; and it will be present at roughly the same incidence in all cultures. If we look at homosexuality, we find none of the characteristics of genetic properties:

There is a huge variety of homosexual practices between cultures and even within them.

The incidence of homosexuality has varied considerably in different cultures. In some cultures, it has been unknown; in others, it has been obligatory for all males.

There have been, and are, rapid changes in homosexual behavior – even over a lifetime. Not only that, but entire types of homosexuality have disappeared over the course of just a few centuries.

In fact, anthropologists have found such huge variants in heterosexual and homosexual practice from culture to culture...that they mostly want to say that all sexual behavior is learned.[88]

A study by Yale University surveyed 190 different cultures, discovering that there was a wide range of heterosexual activity. There was no breast stimulation in six cultures; no kissing in nine; in two others, sexual excitement was correlated with scratching or biting; in one, urination was part of foreplay; in another, guest sex was practiced (i.e., it was good hospitality to offer your wife to a visitor). Among the Lepchas, all young girls were sexually experienced by eleven or twelve, and even as young as eight. Bestiality occurred only erratically in cultures; in some it was unknown; in others, it was tolerated. A survey by Paul Gebhard of the Kinsey Institute noted that fetishism, voyeurism, exhibitionism, and well-developed sadomasochism were very rare or absent, appearing only in more "advanced" societies.[89] The exponential rise in gay sexual liaisons – 20, 50, 200, 500, 1000, witnessed in Chapter 1, was not the result of genetics but the outcome of highly commercialized sex and gay liberation culture. We must ask ourselves, what portion of this past forty years of GBLTQ history was constituted from individual choice?

According to Whitehead heterosexuality requires a conducive nurturing environment to develop properly. In the 1950s, the World Health Organization asked British psychoanalyst John Bowley to research the mental health of homeless children. His response was a monumental book, *Attachment and Loss*. Bowley found that extreme emotional deprivation in early childhood produced children with very cold personalities who were unable to form lasting relationships. They also craved affection.[90] Psychologists differ over the details of the process, but all concede the importance of attachment to the parent of the same-sex (or a surrogate), the start of a dependent relationship, and imitation and modeling of that parent for formation of a sense of gender identity. A "bad" father who creates conflict is worse for the boy's masculinity than no father at all.[91]

Whitehead described the separate gender identities of very young children (3-4 years). By the age of eight, roughly 85 per cent of both sexes believe their own sex is best. Boys or girls who cross the line are mercilessly teased. Says Whitehead, "'No-girls-allowed' activities are common to boys, in the attempt, some psychologists believe, by the boy to consolidate his gender identity following the shift in identification to his father." R.A. Latorre wrote that sexual orientation "soaks in from the outside." A similar process happens for girls. The peer group has a similar role to that of the same-sex parent. Mixing mainly with their own sex strengthens a child's sense of being male or female, and the differences deepen.[92] This importance of parental and peer influences on later sexual behavior is revealed in the following scientific research:

Kendrick and colleagues at the Babraham Institute in Cambridge allowed ten ewes to raise goats from birth and ten nanny goats to raise lambs from birth. The fostered kids and lambs grew up in mixed flocks of sheep and goats but the kids fraternized mainly with lambs and adopted their play and grooming habits, and lambs fraternized mainly with kids. Once mature they ignored their own species and tried to mate 90 per cent of the time with the foster mother species. They kept this up every day during the observation period of three years, and even after years of mixing with their own species, the males did not revert (but females did).[93]

Concludes Whitehead, "If the sexuality of these lower animals was so influenced by learning, human sexuality will be more so." Psychological literature on homosexuality clearly reveals breakdowns in learning processes critical to the development of heterosexuality. Rather than bonding and identifying with same-sex parents, imitating and role-modeling, numerous studies of homosexuals show early breaches, negative relationships, and resistance to identification and modeling. One comprehensive study of homosexuality found 84 per cent of homosexual men said their fathers were indifferent and uninvolved compared with 10 per cent of heterosexual men, and that only 10 per cent of homosexual men identified with their fathers in childhood, compared with two-thirds of heterosexual men. M. T. Sagir and E. Robins found only 23 per cent of lesbians reported positive relationships with their mothers and identification with them, compared with 85 per cent of heterosexual women.[94]

In a review of literature, van den Aardweg says poor relationships with peer groups are even more common in the backgrounds of male homosexuals than poor relationships with fathers.[95] Bell et al. comment that children with reduced same-sex parent identification are more likely to develop "gender non-conformity" ("sissiness" in boys and "tomboyism" in girls; the sense of feeling "different" from their peers).[96] Nicolosi remarks that "the masculine qualities conveyed in healthy father-son relationships are confidence and independence, assertiveness and a sense of personal power." Without these attributes, he will not fit well into childhood male peer groups. Male homosexual clients characteristically say they were "weak, unmasculine, unacceptable." That's when the name-calling starts – "sissy," "girl." Saghir and Robins found that 67 per cent of homosexuals were called sissy or effeminate by others, (compared with three per cent of heterosexual men), and that 79 per cent of these men in childhood and early adolescence had no male friends, played mostly with girls, and rarely or never played sports.[97] A similar pattern is seen in lesbianism. Young girls resistant to mother identification and modeling do not fit well into female peer groups. Saghir and Robins' found 70 per cent of homosexual women were "tomboys" as children, compared with 16 per cent of heterosexual women. Sixty three per cent wished they were boys or men, compared with seven per cent of heterosexual women. The attitude persists into adulthood:

One of the two findings that differentiated lesbian women from heterosexual women was the feeling in lesbian women that they were less feminin and more masculine. 'They express disinterest in feminine accessories and fashion, prefer 'sporty' and tailored clothes, and shun make-up and hairdos. They see their social and domestic roles as being incompatible with those of other women. They behave more competi-

tively and are oriented toward career and accomplishments with little interest in raising children or in domestic pursuits.'[98]

Several major studies have highlighted more childhood and adolescent homosexual activity in pre-homosexuals and adolescents. Van Wyk and Geist, looking at a sample of 7669 white male and female Americans, say both lesbians and homosexuals were more likely to have had intense pre-pubertal sexual contact with boys or men. They draw a link between sexual abuse and later lesbianism, but they also say that most lesbians learned to masturbate by being masturbated by a female. Young girls retreating from distressing male sexual contact experienced release in female sexual contact. According to Whitehead, male homosexuals were more likely than heterosexual men to have been masturbated by other men or boys, they comment, and "once arousal to the particular type of stimulus occurs, it tends quite rapidly to form a pattern."[99]

Ex-gay support groups report that between 50 per cent and 60 per cent of homosexual men coming for help have been abused sexually. Finkelhor found young men sexually abused by older males were about four times more likely to engage in homosexual activity as adults. Nichols reported male sexual abuse of lesbians is twice as high as in heterosexual women. Gundlach and Reiss report a similar figure. Ex-gay groups report high levels of male sexual abuse (up to 85 per cent) in female homosexuals who come for help. Peter and Cantrell found more than two thirds of lesbians reported being forced into sexual experiences with males after the age of twelve, compared with only 28 per cent of heterosexuals.[100]

Ex-gay groups suggest that poor father and peer group relations lead boys to seek companionship. Adolescent sexual intimacy with another man leads to later association of sex with male interest, affection and acceptance:

One former homosexual, Michael Saia, says homosexual men are not looking for sex when they have their first sexual encounter. He says they are looking for acceptance, understanding, companionship, strength, security, and a sense of completeness. Sex becomes the way to get it. 'I was starved of affection,' said Bob. 'I didn't like the sex at first, I just wanted someone to really love me. I told myself, OK, if this is what I have to do to get the touch, I'll do it. Then it got to where I liked it.' [101]

Moberly, sees sexual abuse as a secondary contributor to homosexuality. She posits the main cause as early "defensive detachment" from the parent of the same-sex that interferes critically with the identification process that produces a sense of gender in children.[102] Says Whitehead, difficulties in attachment and identification lead to feelings of alienation in same-sex peer groups and from then on homosexual development follows a fairly predictable course:

A deep need for same-sex affection, affirmation, acceptance, and a sense of gender identity; masturbation and/or fantasy around a certain admired same-sex figure; a sexual encounter; the beginning of habitual responses; self-identification as homosexual; 'coming out;' finding partners; the homosexual lifestyle; civil rights. Most people with homo-emotional needs and homosexual responses, however, do not 'come out' to friends and family or live a visibly homosexual or activist lifestyle. In one of the largest studies of a homosexual population, Bell, et al., said homosexuality could not be traced back to 'a single psychological or social root.' However, they gave the highest values to a constellation of factors: negative relationship with the parent of the same-sex, 'childhood gender non-conformity,' and adolescent homosexual arousal and activity.[103]

Barriers to Change

Who Succeeds at Change in Therapy? David Matheson, reparative therapist in Los Angeles, writes: "In the years I've been working as a reparative therapist, I've noticed some common tendencies among men who are successful in diminishing homosexuality as well as some commonalties among those who are unsuccessful."[104] In general, success in this (or any) therapy process can be attributed to a single, simple principle: People spontaneously change for the better when they let go of their resistance to change. In other words, to change is natural if we can just get out of the way and let it happen. Of course, the problem with this is that men dealing with homosexuality typically have so much in the way that unblocking the natural change process can be like removing the Hoover Dam. There are tendencies that can all be seen in the context of resistance. That is, there are barriers that people unconsciously erect in their lives to prevent change. Often, these barriers are unintentional and occasionally they may even be unavoidable. The stronger and more ingrained the pattern of resistance is – and the less aware the person is that the pattern is actually resistance – the less success the person will have in changing. Understanding the reasons for the resistance is not really that important.[105]

Resistance may come from reticence to give up physical pleasure, discomfort with painful emotions that have to be faced, or simply fear of change. But regardless of what is causing the resistance, the resistance must be overcome or progress will be hampered. These resistant tendencies can be divided, according to Matheson, into four different areas: life situation, unwillingness to invest, unwillingness to risk, and living as a victim. He first listed the tendencies common among unsuccessful clients, then contrasted them with the approach taken by successful clients:

Life Situation

Extreme stress or commitments due to work, family, school, or church demands. Successful clients prioritize and eliminate from their schedule things that get in the way of what is most important.

A chaotic life that doesn't allow for a regular, ongoing therapy process. The chaos may be due to factors such as finances, work schedule, transportation problems, illness of self or family members, etc. Successful clients find ways to surmount or minimize chaos that occurs in their lives in order to allow the therapeutic process to continue.

Unwillingness to Invest

Not taking the problem seriously, as expressed in statements like, 'I don't need therapy,' 'I don't need a group,' or 'It's too expensive.' Successful clients recognize the seriousness of their situation and willingly do whatever is necessary to bring about change.

Ambivalence about committing to change, as expressed in statements like, 'I want to change, but right now I need this boyfriend.' Successful clients are willing to let go of whatever leads them away from their goal. That willingness may not be there all at once, but successful clients continue to push themselves toward it

False dependency on faith and spirituality without doing the psychological and emotional work necessary to bring about change. At its roots, homosexuality is NOT a spiritual problem. Spiritual problems develop when homosexual behavior is engaged in. But to begin with, same-sex attraction is a developmental arrest that is psychological in nature. Spirituality alone will not change homosexuality! This is why we so often hear the complaint, 'I prayed for years and the Lord never took this problem away.' Successful clients wisely ask for God's help with SPECIFIC needs, praying for opportunities that are needed, and allowing the Spirit to comfort and sustain them. Yet they never shift the burden of responsibility onto the Lord.

Unwillingness to Risk

Sacrificing authenticity for comfort, as expressed in statements like, 'I can't do this, it's too uncomfortable.' Unsuccessful clients get overwhelmed by their own emotions and withdraw from therapy. Successful clients willingly face their fears both internally (hurtful emotions) and externally (frightening relationships and situations). This is one of the main factors separating successful from unsuccessful clients.

Feeling such shame over your struggles that you refuse to be open with others about what you are going through. This is often expressed in statements like, 'I can't tell anyone about me,' or 'I have to work through this alone so that no one ever finds out.' Successful clients open themselves to other people and ask for help.

A rigid approach to life, which prevents you from going beyond previous limitations, seeing new perspectives, doing new things, exploring new ways of thinking and living, and doing things you've never done before. Successful clients are open to the possibility of change in every aspect of their lives.

Living as a Victim

Passivity, as manifested in statements like, 'I don't know what to do,' or 'I just don't think I can change.' This is also manifested as a tendency to NOT seek out help, or to be very narrow in the therapeutic activities you pursue. Perhaps you go to group meetings occasionally, but you essentially keep yourself ignorant of other opportunities. Successful clients take the responsibility for their change process and seek out every source of information and help available, such as individual and group therapy, straight male friendships, New Warriors participation, activity in a church, etc.

Being a 'Help-Rejecting Complainer'

These are individuals who are constantly complaining about the problems they face, and yet when help is offered they immediately come up with reasons why each suggestion won't work for them. Or they may half-heartedly try the suggestion just long enough to prove its ineffectiveness. Successful clients are willing to go outside the comfort of their complaints and actually try to solve their problems.[106]

Reorientation Process

For many people, change happens when they effectively do two things. First, one needs to deal with the root issues of homosexual attractions. These are the negative and damaging events and dynamics of childhood, such as sexual abuse, rejection, deficits in our relationship with our parents, shaming, etc. The past often continues to affect today. While what happened cannot be changed, how it affects us today and how we understand what happened can change. Second, as the root issues are being resolved, unhealthy patterns of living need to be undone and replaced with new thinking and new behaviors. If for years we have lived in certain ways, which were influenced by the hurt and pain of childhood, those ways will have become habits or patterns, automatic ways of doing things and of responding. Often, these patterns will have been reinforced by fantasy and masturbation. If they are unhealthy habits, they need to be unlearned and new ways of living and responding need to take their place.

Peoplecanchange.com describes the process of change as follows:

Change happens in the three areas of behavior, fantasy, and attraction. The goal for a person who wants to change their sexual orientation is to experience a decrease in homosexual behavior, fantasy and attraction, and a corresponding increase in heterosexual attraction.

As change is a process, it is important to realize that change in one area may happen sooner than change in another area. While we can make choices about what we do and what we think about, we have less control over feelings and attractions. For example, J. chose not to be sexually active any more, and thus his homosexual behavior ceased, even though he still was attracted only to men and had fantasies about them. Subsequently, as he started working through various issues, he began to notice some attraction to women, even though his attraction to men had not yet changed. Much later, he began to find men less attractive than before. Do not be discouraged when one area starts to change and another does not – this is normal.

Things get worse before they get better. This is a reality that many of us have experienced on our journey out of homosexuality, and it is important for a person starting on the journey to be aware of it. As we begin to work through difficult issues from the past, there is often much pain to face. Things may seem worse simply because we are starting to face past issues which before we ignored or denied. If we are used to dealing with our pain by drowning it with alcohol, sex or other addictions, we can expect the temptation to drown the pain to be stronger than before we started to face it. As well, this journey of change involves talking about sexual issues, which can be arousing in and of itself. This is normal. Over time, discussion of sex will become more matter of fact. When things first get worse instead of better, do not despair or give up. Continue to work through your issues and find freedom and resolution. Put extra support in place – let a close friend know what you are feeling, attend a support group, talk with someone who's been there.

Sometimes it will seem like nothing is happening. In the process of change, there will be times when nothing is happening. This may be because we need a break after doing some hard personal work. This may be because there is something blocking further progress. If you feel that you are on a plateau and that you may be 'stuck' at this place in the process, talk to someone about it. Often another person can be instrumental in helping us identify what is preventing further change and what can be done to overcome that block.

There are some important resources that will help in the process of change. First, close friends whom you trust and who accept you as you are, and with whom you can talk about difficult personal issues related to your same-gender attraction. You cannot do this alone. In particular, straight same-sex friends can help you to understand that you are accepted as a man or as a woman by those who have no sexual interest in you. Second, accountability mentors can help keep you true to your goals. For example, if you have resolved that you do not want to buy any pornography but still find it a temptation to do so, this person can ask you regularly whether you have bought any, encourage you to stick with your resolve and, when you do give in to temptation, help you examine why you did. Third, well-run support groups are a safe place for sharing honestly and openly, learning more about homosexuality and meeting with others who share your goal of overcoming homosexuality. There is much to learn from others who are on a similar journey to yours. Fourth, individual counseling can be very helpful in working through some of the more difficult issues. Whereas support groups provide more general information and support, counseling is an opportunity to focus on your particular situation in detail with someone who is equipped to do so. Choose a counselor carefully, finding out their perspective on change and homosexuality and what kind of experience they have working in this area. Do not be intimidated by counselors who attempt to discourage you or influence your journey to a path other than the one you choose. There are many good therapists who will support and affirm your journey. Keep looking until you find one. Fifth, educate yourself with the many resources available. There are good books, articles, and newsletters which you can read, web sites to browse, and conferences to attend. While information does not by itself produce change, it can give greater understanding and insight. *Peoplecanchange* recommend talking to those who have left homosexuality and reading their stories.[107]

Peoplecanchange place great importance on "turning our lives and will over to God":

We have found that the path out of unwanted homosexuality is a profoundly spiritual one. Some of us experienced this as a significant religious conversion or spiritual enlightenment where we felt God's deep love for us and guidance for our lives. Others experienced it as the spiritual peace that comes from emotional healing, from loving and forgiving ourselves and others, from breaking down walls that have long prevented us from accepting the love of others, and from learning to really trust God, sometimes for the first time in our lives. This peace, joy and connection to God grew as we began to heal emotionally, build brotherly relationships with other men, surrender all forms of lust, and embrace a new identity as a heterosexual man.[108]

Ex-gays explain some of the changes likely needed in order to heal:

We opened our hearts to a newfound willingness to do whatever it might take to make our lives right with God...and whatever he might guide us to do.

We started to accept and trust the many witnesses of others who had experienced change for themselves. As we did, we found new hope that change was indeed possible, rewarding and worth the effort.

We stopped trying to change through our own will power, without God's intervention – or, at the other extreme, stopped begging God to do all the work of changing us, without our having to do anything different or learn anything about ourselves in the process. Instead, we began working a spiritual program that many of us found can be summarized in the Twelve Steps of Alcoholics Anonymous, Sexaholics Anonymous and other Twelve Step programs (although each of us went about these kinds of spiritual steps in somewhat different ways and through different faiths): 'We admitted that we were powerless over our addiction – that our lives had become unmanageable. Came to believe that a Power greater than ourselves could restore us to sanity.' (Steps One and Two) 'Made a decision to turn our will and our lives over to the care of God as we understood Him' (Step Three), and 'Made a searching and fearless moral inventory of ourselves. Admitted to God, to ourselves, and to another human being the exact nature of our wrongs. Were entirely ready to have God remove all these defects of character. Humbly we asked Him to remove our shortcomings.' (Steps Four, Five, Six and Seven) 'Sought through prayer and meditation to improve our conscious contact with God as we understood Him, praying only for knowledge of His will for us and the power to carry that out' (Step Eleven).

Most of us joined a faith community of some kind to enjoy spiritual fellowship and mentoring in our continuing efforts to yield our will and our hearts to God. To strengthen us, we used individual and group prayer, meditation and study and pondering of 'wisdom literature' that we held as scripture. Humbly reaching out to God for help was usually an early, vital and ongoing part of our healing. It was not the end. Most of us still had much work to do to overcome our self-destructive behaviors and our estrangement from other men and from our own masculinity, as well as other emotional issues that had caused our homosexual desires. Change was not as simple as 'praying it away,' no matter how much faith we had, as long as we re-

mained trapped in fear, distrust, isolation and hurt, unwilling to do the painful work of healing our inner lives and our relationships with others. But a renewed spiritual life became the fuel that powered our journey and showed us the way – a journey to a new identity, a new way of being, and a new life.[109]

Most ex-gays broke off ties to their homosexual pasts. They discontinued homosexual relationships and habits, threw away destructive books, magazines, videos and other materials, and took themselves out of tempting environments. They made every effort to stop feeding the lust with new images and fantasies. Some mapped out their lust cycles on paper to help recognize events, feelings and stresses that often triggered lust and longing for male comfort. They shared this 'map' with mentors and identified practical steps to break the cycle. Rather than trying to STOP destructive behaviors and thought patterns, they sought to proactively REPLACE them with new, healthier ones: rather than fighting lust, we learned to surrender it to a Higher Power, asking God to do for us what we could not do for ourselves.

We sought to replace sexual feelings for men with healthy brotherly love for them and a more godly view of ourselves as men.

When tempted, we learned to pick up the phone and call a mentor, admit our struggles, and connect with the reality of brotherly love in place of the fantasy of homosexual lust. Over time, many of us found that this authentic connection became more satisfying than lust. We practiced other new ways to respond to our lust triggers, such as physical exercise (especially with male friends), meaningful emotional connection with men, therapeutic massage, prayer and more.[110]

Ex-gays came to recognize and respect their legitimate needs for physical and emotional bonding with other men and began to work proactively to fulfill these underlying needs rather than resist them. They developed a deliberate, proactive program to ensure this hunger for male connection was "fed" regularly with healthy "food," instead of suppressing it until so starved for male affection and affirmation that they would do anything to feed it. They determined to keep getting back on our feet no matter how many times they "fell," convinced by faith and the experiences of others that as long as they never gave up, eventually they would break free of the cycle of lust.

This process is definitely not about will power, although will power can help one escape from individual temptations. According to *Peoplecanchange:*

Real healing from lust comes not from willpower but from 'heart power' – the power of the heart, rather than the mind, to effect powerful change. This change of heart results when we foster healthy desires, come out of secrecy and become completely honest about our thoughts and actions with trusted mentors, feed our souls with the unconditional love of God and brotherly love of others, and consistently work to surrender our will to God's.[111]

So what could be so wrong with such healing reparative therapy, if it is what an individual wants? That it is politically incorrect in today's society and the source of considerable ire for the GBLTQ and pro-gay heterosexual supporters only reveals the hypocrisy of identity politics.

Role of the Church

What counsel then should Christians give active homosexual believers? First of all, we should advise practicing homosexuals that we have no desire for them to leave the church, but urge them to remain, reconsider, and search their consciences in order to move toward repentance and counseling with those who will not encourage them in sin. But if they insist on affirming their practice publicly and promoting a sub-Christian lifestyle, they should, out of love for God's church and His people, transfer to another denomination which endorses their way of life, such as the Unitarian Church, United Church of Canada or the Metropolitan Community Churches, sparing the major denominations an explosive controversy. At present it seems that the church's left wing often specializes in calling for repentance from social sins, while its right wing specializes in attacking individual sin. The church cannot make progress in a mission when its left foot is persistently tripping over its right. The time is ripe for a kind of evangelism, which will identify and call for the abandonment of sin in all these areas, and will also clearly present the fact that repentance is not complete without accompanying faith in Jesus Christ.[112]

What is the church's responsibility with respect to the civil rights of the gay community at large? We have already stated that the Christian Church is under no obligation from God to force its own mores, derived from Biblical revelation, upon the non-Christian society, which surrounds it. This kind of enforcement may in fact short-circuit the Gospel witness, since it results in paradoxical situations in which Christians are in effect persecuting non-Christians, which has happened too many times before in the Church's history. Christians should commend the Gospel to gay persons by standing behind their legitimate concerns for freedom in our society. In the Old Testament, homosexual practice was condemned by Law in order to prevent its destructive social consequences, but under the New Covenant, equipped with the salt of the Gospel and the power of the Holy Spirit, we may use overtures of love instead of legal restraints in meeting this problem. But the civil rights of Christians and others who find active homosexuality abhorrent must also be preserved. These must not be forced by law to employ publicly self-affirmed gays in church-related works or in schools (even at the college level in the case of Christian colleges). Gay people will see that the church is not promoting a vendetta against them but is simply preserving its own civil rights. Most importantly, the gay community will not be misled into thinking that the church has affirmed God's blessing on the active gay lifestyle, an act which would be interpreted as charitable tolerance but which would actually be an expression of supreme hatred, encouraging people to continue practicing a lifestyle which God has very clearly ruled out of His Kingdom.[113] [The role of the Church toward same-sex marriage will be developed further in Chapters 7 and 8, and concluded in Chapter 9.]

Gay Christians often maintain that personal prayer has not changed their condition or helped them to control it. But how many have rooted themselves in a close community of believers and requested corporate prayer for liberation? Truly welcoming homosexuals (alcoholics, workaholics, adulterers and the hurting…) into the church means offering them help. Many years ago the Methodist evangelist William Gowland wrote:

It might be more sinful to pass a pious resolution about prostitution and then retreat from the costly task of seeking to bring the prostitute to God, than to be a prostitute.[114]

In many ways this wisdom parallels the church's relationship to the GBLTQ community. In staking out Christian "boundaries," we run counter to the GBLTQ lifestyle. Here, we must offer a loving, supportive and patient outreach. While upholding Scriptural truth, we dare not forget what our own condition was before Christ. Nor should we overlook His daily grace undergirding our ongoing deliverance. Condescending piety only hinders any opportunity for a reorientation ministry. This matter of proclaiming God's grace and keeping a humble attitude towards practicing homosexuals is critical to understanding and properly proclaiming the Christian worldview. And here ends the examination of gay and pro-gay theology and reorientation science from an orthodox Christian worldview.

In the next part the practicality of the competing worldviews is examined across the full spectrum of life stages. There are *individual* and *societal* consequences associated with either paradigm, which an informed reader should consider. The competitive dynamics are mostly characterized as "zero-sum" – a gain in membership or acceptance of one paradigm axiomatically reduces the impact of the other. In Chapter 8, secular heterosexual, Christian, and gay marriage models will be examined. The societal advantages and disadvantages of the GBLTQ demand for "sameness" in marriage are developed. The lesbian and single heterosexual female demand for cloned children will also be studied.

PART FOUR

THE PRACTICALITY OF COMPETING WORLDVIEWS

Why the future of the family and the gay movement are linked:

In the 1980s, two powerful metaperspectives converged to begin a reshaping of the field of family theory and practice. The first was post-modernism, particularly social constructionist thought, which challenged essentialist notions about families and family processes as well as prevailing systemic metaphors. The second was the feminist critique, which brought not only an intense examination of existing family theories for their failure to address gender as a powerful organizing variable in family life but a revisioning of theory in a way that made gender awareness critical to family therapy practice....in the last decade, feminist writers... have questioned Western cultural assumptions about gender and sex and the intersections between them, as well as heterocentric assumptions about the concept of 'family' itself...others have recognized that anatomical sex, sexuality, and gender are mutually constructed in varying cultural contexts. Many have pointed out how traditional heterosexual family organization is usually implied and privileged in our theories and models, while same-sex couples and other family forms are excluded. Recent feminist theorizing has also called to question the privileging of gender as an irreducible or even primary variable in the organization of all family life.[1]

'Gender in lesbian relationships: Cultural, feminist, and constructionist reflections' Journal of Marital and Family Therapy, Oct 2000

...we see quite clearly that bearing and raising a child is an ordeal. The individuals whom we have painstakingly inducted into child-free society and established there, with a lifestyle centered entirely upon achievement and self-gratification, have now to disrupt that pattern. The [parental] sacrifice is enormous, and they expect no reward or recompense. If the management of childbearing in our society had actually been intended to maximize stress, it could hardly have succeeded better. The child-bearers embark on their struggle alone; the rest of us wash our hands of them.[2]

Germaine Greer, 'Sex and Destiny: The Politics of Human Fertility'

CHAPTER SEVEN

BABIES, CHILDREN, ADOLESCENTS AND PARENTING

In 1972, Pierre-Claude Nappey asked what the design and purpose of homosexuality was in nature:

However much we may relativize the notion of a sexual norm and however much we may personalize the ethical exigency on which it is based, we are still not shedding any light on the reputedly obscure question of why homosexuality exists...The question is not whether a certain type of behavior is excusable owing to the particular circumstances of the individual concerned, but whether it is an integral part of the much vaster behavioral pattern of the collectivity and whether it contributes in some way to the proper functioning.

Homosexuality must be seen ...as corresponding to a definite finality. My own feeling is that not only is it possible for homosexuality to be of equal value with heterosexuality in individual cases, but that it has overall significance and a special role to play in the general economy of human relations, a role that is probably irreplaceable.[1]

A goal of this and the next chapter is to continue to study the impact of homosexuality on society. In as much as North American society has arrived at a "definite" crossroads, Nappey is right that no more urgent task faces humankind than the difficult challenge of determining this "finality." In 1976, John McNeil wrote in regard to Nappey's question of the purpose of homosexuality:

For on its discovery depends both the ability of the homosexual to accept himself or herself with true self-love and understanding and the ability of the heterosexual society to accept a homosexual minority, not just as objects of pity and tolerance at best, but as their equals capable of collaborating in the mutual task of building a more humane society.[2]

We now have some 40 years of evidence upon which to study the purpose and impact of GBLTQ liberation. In considering societal issues like raising babies, children and adolescents, parenting, coupling and marriage, it will be valuable to keep in mind the per cent of society demanding the "reinventing" of our institutions and the numbers in the GBLTQ community who have any personal experience upon which to base their restructuring philosophies and ideologies. The 2001 Canadian Census reports:

Same-sex partnerships account for 0.5 per cent of all couples. While males account for 55 per cent of same-sex couples, only three per cent of them have children. Fifteen per cent of same-sex female couples have kids.[3]

Converted into more tangible figures, these census percentages mean that in a crowd of 100,000 male parents, 9 are gay. In a crowd of 100,000 female parents, 34 are lesbian.

The Unorthodox Family

Marriage no longer serves women very well...There isn't any way, in modern, secular society, to reconnect marriage and maternity. We'd have to bring back the whole 19th Century: restore the cult of virginity and the double standard [women virtuous, men promiscuous], ban birth control, restrict divorce, kick women out of decent jobs, force unwed pregnant women to put their babies up for adoption on pain of social death, make out-of-wedlock children legal nonpersons. These days if women can support themselves, they don't need to marry for what was politely called security but was, to put it bluntly, money. If single women can have sex in their homes, the respect of friends and interesting work, they don't need to tell themselves that any marriage is better than none. Why not have a child on one's own? Children are a joy; many men are not.

Katha Pollitt, feminist

Pollitt's conclusion proposes the demystification of marriage as the inevitable middle-class ideal. ('Instead of trying to make women – and men – adapt to an outworn institution, we should adapt our institutions to the lives people actually lead' by offering single mothers the options of parenting leave, day care, flexible schedules, and pediatricians with evening hours.) Marriage used to be a prelude to childbearing, now the child often comes either before or instead of the marriage.[4]

Marjorie Garber, 'ViceVersa: Bisexuality and the Eroticism of Everyday Life'

According to Alice Rossi, author of *The Family*, a very diverse set of groups now share the common view that the "traditional nuclear family" and monogamous marriage are oppressive, sexist, "bourgeois," and sick. Supporters of sexual liberation, self-actualization, socialism, humanism, gay liberation, existentialism, and certain segments of feminism have joined hands in this general denunciation, although rarely defining what they mean.[5] Using Katha Pollitt's manifesto as the stereotype, their traditional family refers to a legal marriage between a man and a woman who share a household with their legitimate offspring, with the male as the breadwinner and the female as a homemaker. Rossi notes that the alternative "variant" or "experimental" families and marriages would then include a wide array of forms, from cohabitant heterosexual couples, multilateral marriages, single-parent households, dual-career couple with or without children to families traditional in everything except consensual participation in co-marital, swinging, or swapping sexual relationships outside the marriage. This is a wide assortment indeed, and interestingly the "traditional" category has been counted at something less than a third of the actual families in the United States simply by regarding the criterion of an employed wife as being sufficient to classify a family as a variant form. By doing this, of course, the researcher also artificially exaggerates the degree to which genuinely variant marriage and family forms are prevalent in our society.[6]

But there is a further interesting characteristic of feminist literature. Although the titles of publications on alternate-family forms almost always refer to "families," in fact the works themselves focus almost exclusively on the adult relationship between men and women in and out of or in addition to marriage. They rarely concern themselves with children, parenting or parent-child relations. For example, Rossi did a study of a special issue of *The Family Coordinator* magazine, which consisted of fifteen articles published under the title "Variant Marriage Styles and Family Forms."[7] A simple content analysis, revealed that marriage and the male-female relationship are receiving the central attention in this new genre of family sociology, not family systems or the birth and rearing of children. A decade later, Sylvia Ann Hewlett writes of this anti-parenting bias as a global radical feminist phenomenon:

The MLD [Italian Women's Liberation Movement] has been particularly concerned with issues of sexual and personal freedom – divorce, abortion, and nonsexist education. These radical feminists have sometimes worked against, or shown no interest in, legislation that promised to improve the material conditions of women's lives. As Daniela Columbo said in an interview, 'the feminist movement has been more interested in abortion and sexuality than in work on family issues.' To take an example, feminists failed to support the Family Charter because they didn't like the language of the legislation and because it was not central to their own, highly personal, agenda. Yet,…'the Family Charter has produced more security for more women than any other piece of legislation in recent Italian history.' No wonder the women in the political parties and in the church find it hard to identify with the radical feminists.[8]

Rossi reasoned that the implicit premise in much of this literature is the right of the individual to an expanded freedom in the pursuit of private sexual pleasure: "I want what I want when I want it." Feminists variously refer to monogamous marriage as "sexual monopoly," a "form of emotional and sexual malnutrition," and a "condition of sexual deprivation." Variant families are entered into not with an expectation of permanence, as traditional nuclear families are, but with "the expectation that relationships will continue only so long as they serve the mutual benefit of the members." The feminist goal is "total freedom of choice in sex partners throughout one's life."[9]

There are several problems posed by these views of family relations that are often revealed in the actual experiences of men and women who are currently experimenting with new forms of marriage and family relations. The sexual liberationist clearly rejects the "patriarchal family" primarily because of the "double standard." But what is not clear is whether the new single standard will be modeled after what had been the male pattern, the female pattern or some amalgam of the two. Is the feminist vision a movement toward virtuosity or promiscuity? Rossi argues that a close reading of the literature on contemporary sexual practices and on the attitudes of the young suggests the model is a promiscuous male pattern: early initiation, sexual diversity, physical play through casual sex. In studies of adolescent attitudes toward sexuality, it has been found that adolescents are coming to regard sex as a "good way to get acquainted," a means to *develop* rather than to *express* couple intimacy. At the same time, extremely large gender differences still exist among the holders of such attitudes, with men two to three times more apt than women their own age to endorse the more casual attitude to sexuality. The literature on co-marital sex shows that, in three out of four cases, it is the husband who initiates the seeking of other sex partners, participation tends to last about six months, the wives tend to be homemakers with neither jobs nor community involvement, and the couples are very careful to keep their sexual activities a secret from their children. Sexual liberation then, seems to mean that increasing numbers of women are now following male initiatives in a more elaborate, multipartner sexual script.[10]

If Rossi is correct, and there is little conflicting evidence, it appears that the feminist movement brought about a self-inflicted *oppression*. First, the movement has done immeasurable damage to those marriages where both parties are happy; indeed, families in which the husband remains monogamous (no double standard); and couples are mutually supportive (financially and with regard to child care); even in love! Second, the liberation movement launched its female converts into the untenable pursuit of full equality on the battlefields of promiscuous sex and career employment. The personal histories of Mary Wollstonecraft, Emma Goldman, and Margaret Sanger stand as clear testimony to the despair of trying to imitate men in the quest for unfettered sex and the challenge of maintaining a *feminine* private persona and a public *business* character. But the double standard also fails those men who chase its myth. Are men who pursue promiscuous lifestyles really getting away with it or do they gradually become incapable of showing real love and intimacy? Are the promiscuous lifestyles of Henry Morgentaler and Alfred Kinsey models to be taken up in the name of feminist equality? Regarding public employment, mostly women who have remained childless have been the unqualified victors. Few will argue that there are careers which women cannot do as well as men. There is no question about this. Yet the now evident tragedy for those who chose career over marriage and motherhood and in the end wanted "to have it all," is that biology follows no ideology and is blind to all social maneuvering.

In April, 2002, *Time* carried a cover story on "Babies vs Career." Pamela Madsen, executive director of the American Infertility Association explained now women were told for years they could wait until forty or later to have babies. But the message is now clear and devastating:

Those women who are at the top of their game could have had it all, children and career, if they wanted it. The problem was, nobody told them the truth about their bodies.[11]

And the truth is that even the very best fertility experts have found that the biological clock cannot be adjusted. Says Sylvia Hewlett:

Women who also hope to have kids are heading down a bad piece of road if they think they can spend a decade establishing their careers and wait until 35 or beyond to establish their families.[12]

Furthermore, in *Creating a Life, Professional Women and the Quest for Children,* Hewlett describes accomplished career women desperate to get hitched. Some "with loudly ticking biological clocks" are willing to pay $9,600 for a six month, 276-hour course intended to lead a woman directly to the altar.[13]

But the sagacious Hewlett had identified this issue in the mid 80s, when she wrote:

The feminists of the modern women's movement made one gigantic mistake. They assumed that modern women wanted nothing to do with children. As a result they have consistently failed to incorporate the bearing and rearing of children into their vision of liberated life. This mistake has had serious repercussions.[14]

Beyond the baby crisis, the failure of the Equal Rights Amendment (discussed in Chapter 2) came as a result of the majority viewing among other things the legislation as an adverse erosion of motherhood. In 1986, Hewlett cited the growth in artificial insemination as an indicator of the desire of women to procreate. She quoted an estimated 1.5 million Americans would be created this way by the year 2000. A greater social shock; however, is that two-thirds of the women undergoing artificial insemination are single.[15]

Another concern arising from the variant family ideology is the need for a widening of the circle of sexual partners that is implicit in the notion of expanded freedom of private sexual pleasure. As Rossi theorizes any marital relationship that includes two busy people with busy lives will be frequently out of phase in sexual desire for each other. She points out, if by practicality little sex is taking place at home, under the new ideological "cult of mutual desire," there necessarily must be either a considerable decline in the frequency of sex or access to more than one partner. She notes:

It is but a short step to the view that spouse swapping or co-marital sex, is precisely what contemporary marriages need to remain intact, healthy, and self-actualizing for both partners.[16]

For a married woman not to enjoy sex with men other than her husband, or in some quarters, not to be bisexual is to be out of step with the times – an old-fashioned spouse or a poor feminist. The message seems to be that to be faithful, possessive, exclusively heterosexual and able to postpone gratification are signs of immaturity and oppression. The ideology claims that:

...conquest of sexual jealousy...could be the greatest advance in human relations since the advent of common law or the initiation of democratic processes. The increased frequency and incidence of swinging and swapping...could then be viewed...as [presaging] a new era in sexual and interpersonal relationships.[17]

No doubt Goldman and Sanger would applaud.

The notion of self-centered parenting – only when convenient – deep-seated in the unorthodox family ideology is further cause for concern. What is the impact of sexual liberation here? Can women or men be parents only when they want to be or only when their children want to be parented? For anyone who knows about the developmental needs of children or the importance of the parents' emotional attachment to them, the answer would be "no." But as Rossi points out, this is not the case in the new family sociology. The following quotation advocating communal families illustrates explicitly what is implicit in much of this literature:

By always having some children in our unit, we will be able to assume parental roles when and for as long as we want...Our children will have an advantage [in that] from the adults they can select their own parents, brothers, sisters, friends...Our social ties will not be forced nor strained by the mandates of kinship and marital obligation.[18]

Here the image is clear; in the post-nuclear family era, the adult can turn parenthood on and off and exchange children as well as sexual partners.

In additional studies there are ample hints of difficulties and strains arising when such an ideology is put into practice. In Kanter's studies of urban middle-class communes, she points to a tendency to view children as miniature adults, free to establish relationships with adults other than their parents in the communal household. But since notions of discipline and tolerance of children vary among adults, Kanter reports a considerable amount of confusion among the four-to-twelve year old children she interviewed, as a consequence of what she calls the "Cinderella Effect" (rapid demands or corrections by a number of unrelated adults to the same child at the same time). There is also evidence that the sharing of children creates emotional difficulties for many parents, particularly the mothers of children, until eventually parents tend to reserve for themselves the right to protect and punish their children. The researchers note that very rarely did a mother allow a male communal member to invoke sanctions with her children, and even when he did, it was clear that he was acting for the mother through some form of delegated authority.[19]

Despite the ideology, another study notes that infants and knee babies are almost universally in charge of their mothers, and whatever sharing takes place of children from two to four is largely confined to the group of mothers with young children; only children over five are supervised by other adults, and then with the difficulties noted earlier.[20] The failure of communal family ideology is well illustrated in Rothchild and Wolf's book on children of counterculture parents.[21] The report provides an overall portrait of children almost uniformly neglected, deprived, and tormented; many are uneducated, disorganized, and disturbed; a pervasive boredom and lack of joy and serious problems of mal- or undernourishment were prevalent. It comes as a shock after viewing such a dysfunctional environment for raising children to find the authors concluded that the communes are a success in childrearing because they have done away with materialism and competitiveness. Says Rossi, "In reality, the counterculture parents are obviously trying to rear children without having to be bothered by them."[22]

Rossi further concludes that just as in the sexual script, the parenting script in the new family sociology seems to be modeled on what has been a male pattern of relating to children, in which men turn their fathering on and off to suit themselves or their appointments for business or sexual pleasure. The role models in both the mating and parenting scripts in the new perspectives on the family are just as heavily masculine in character as the older schools of thought about the modern family, if not in a generic sense, then in the sense that parenting is viewed from a distance, as an appendage to, or consequence of mating, rather than the focus of family systems and individual lives. Rossi ends, "It is not clear what the gains will be for either women or children in this version of human liberation."[23] Hewlett supports Rossi's conclusion that in practice the equality of modern feminism has meant the adoption of a "male model." Here Hewlett is speaking of the many women of single-minded career focus, and the resultant "epidemic of childlessness" among professional women. She found that 42 per cent of high-achieving women in corporate America were still childless after age forty. For women earning over $100,000 the figure rose to 49 per cent.[24] Dr. David Adamson, a leading fertility specialist at Stanford University says, "They've been making a lot of money, but it won't buy back the time."[25]

Regrettably in this war of "family-organizing ideologies" half victories, like many compromises, seldom pleases either side. The root causes of the disharmony are seldom resolved and both sides feel betrayed or at best remain inconsolable. Arlie Hochschild, in *The Second Shift: Working Parents and the Revolution at Home*, refers to the "Stalled Revolution."[26] Here she sees the "exodus" [note the liberation terminology] of women into the economy as not accompanied "by a cultural understanding of marriage" that would make the transition smooth. There is no mention of a cultural understanding of "parenting." Rather she says:

A society which did not suffer from this stall would be a society humanely adapted to the fact that most women work outside the home.[27]

Again the vision is one of changing society to suit the individual at work, and at the same time, lowering the importance of the parenting role in society. Demonstrating a whimsical understanding of workplace dynamics in a competitive global economy, Hochschild advocates that the workplace should allow parents to work part time; to share jobs; to work flexible hours; and to take parental leaves to give birth, tend to a sick child, or care for a well one. She refers to Delores Hayden's *Redesigning the American Dream*, suggesting that the New Society would include affordable housing closer to places of work, and community-based meal and laundry services."[28]

Why has the feminist movement misjudged the significance of motherhood, fatherhood and therefore parenting? In the nineteenth century feminists held motherhood in great esteem. Elizabeth Cady Stanton stated in an address to the National Woman Suffrage Association in 1885:

Surely maternity is an added power and development of some of the most tender sentiments of the human heart and not a limitation.[29]

Hewlett observes that all five women who organized the Seneca Falls Convention on women's rights in 1848, were married and had children. Stanton later wrote of this group that they "were neither sour old maids, childless women nor divorced wives."[30] Susan B. Anthony loved babies. In a September 1857 letter to Stanton she wrote that reproduction was:

...the highest and holiest function of the physical organism...to be a mother, to be a father, is the best and highest wish of any human being.[31]

In contrast to the "First Wave" feminists, the Second Wave was openly hostile to both mothers and children. As explained in Chapter 2, Betty Friedan, author of *Feminine Mystique*, the notable exception, was as a result dethroned from National Organization For Women (NOW) in 1970. Second Wave feminists identified the family and the biological function of motherhood as the central institutions of male power serving to enslave women in the interests of men. Radical feminists even envisaged a utopia where childbirth through science could be removed from the domain of women's bodies.[32] Hewlett concludes:

Rather than help women cope with their double burden – in the home and in the workplace – modern feminists have encouraged women to avoid both marriage and children.[33]

Danielle Crittenden, author of *What Our Mothers Didn't Tell Us: Why Happiness Eludes the Modern Woman* (1999) writes in response to the feminist antimale ethos:

But the unfortunate discovery of my generation is that economic equality brings us no closer to 'flourishing love' than the old sexual division of labor. Actually, as the divorce rate indicates, we have drifted rather further away. And this is because successful marriage has less to do with reaching equity with our husbands than it does in understanding, and accepting, the different compromises and sacrifices men and women make over the long course of marriage – compromises and sacrifices that arise out of sexual differences, and thus our different reasons for getting married in the first place. To this degree, feminists like Simone de Beauvoir were correct: Traditional marriage did rest upon a bargain that presumed sexual disparity. But we have discovered, in having attained such egalitarian marriages as anything de Beauvoir could have hoped for, is that this sexual disparity is not political in nature – arising from a 'patriarchal society' determined to prevent women's equal participation in the workforce. It arises from the different roles we naturally assume when we become mothers and fathers.[34]

Crittenden contends it is hard to appreciate marriage and family dynamics if you are neither married nor have children, which may explain why so many of the proponents of radically egalitarian marriage have been childless and unmarried: Virginia Woolf (married, no children); Simone de Beauvoir (childless, never married); Emma Goldman (many marriages, childless); Margaret Sanger (many marriages, children abandoned); Henry Morgentaler (many marriages, children scattered); Gloria Steinem and Susan Faludi (at the time of publishing their books on women, childless and unmarried).

Symptoms of Crisis

Several years ago, when my third child was 17, he and I had a typical parent-teenager clash...this time about drugs. He stormed downstairs to his room and slammed the door, leaving me standing in the middle of the room feeling wretched and powerless. Even having already reared two adolescents, I had no more idea how to get the present one to do what he should...I couldn't imagine, standing there that night, how I was going to live through two more adolescents. Suddenly I began to feel very angry...I realized that I was furious at the anguish I had suffered so long as a mother and the misery that seemed still to stretch so endlessly before me...Then, thinking of my tyrant son sulking down in his room, and feeling an unaccustomed invulnerability, a new firmness at the center, I thought, 'That kid can go to hell in a handbasket!'...He's just going to have to decide for himself whether he's going to self-destruct or not, and I'm going to have to be happy no matter what he decides. I felt as if I had been holding his heel as he hung upside down over the abyss. One cannot live one's own life while holding someone else's heel. I decided I needed to love myself first and be true to myself, do what's best for me, assuming that whatever is best for me is best for everyone around...Without knowing exactly what I was doing, but for the sake of survival, I detached myself from my children then as sources of well-being for me...[35]

Sonia Johnson, Wildfire: Igniting the She/volution

Whether as forthrightly as Sonia Johnson records or in subtle decisions over time, more and more parents have turned away from parenting responsibilities as traditionally provided. Striking in Johnson's monologue is the absence of the father or any male influence over her boy. Indeed, whether she is divorced or not, her story contradicts the radical feminist notion that single parenthood is just another "variety" of family system equal in effectiveness with the traditional model. The dilemma of the problem child raises vexing challenges for advocates of single or same-sex parenting. When children are angels, any model seems to work; however, the likelihood of having a difficult child remains high in families of more than one child, not even to mention the variant family difficulties caused by everyday life, such as poverty, job stress and alcoholism.

Just how many single parents and one guardian children are there? In 1996, 14.5 per cent of Canada's families were single parent variety, making it the third largest family type, reflecting a growth of 33 per cent since 1981. Over 83 per cent of these are headed by women. Over 1.8 million or 20 per cent, of Canada's children live in single parent families. According to John Conway, author of *Canadian Family in Crisis*, one in two Canadian children will live part of their lives in a single parent family.[36] In the 1960s, 63 per cent of single parent families resulted from the death of a spouse, 32 per cent from divorce and 2 per cent from never wed mothers. By 1996, 20 per cent of such families resulted from death, 54 per cent from divorce, while 25 per cent were headed by single never married mothers.[37] This trend started in the 1970s and has risen until some 87 per cent of unmarried mothers keep their babies. Conway observes that the increase is supplemented by a rise in the number of older single mothers, often professionals, aged 30 to 39, seeking to become mothers without being wives, and sometimes doing so through artificial insemination.[38] Some 17 per cent of single parent families are headed by a male.[39]

Female single parent families are the most challenged economically. In 1996, 54 per cent of them were below the official poverty line.[40] However, 87 per cent of single mothers with two children are below the poverty line. Among teenagers, Hewlett reports, the statistics are appalling. Although births among American teenage girls declined from 1960 through 1986, the proportion of unmarried teenagers who had children had risen sharply. By 1986 there were close to half a million births to unwed teenagers every year. In 1960, 15 per cent of teenage girls who gave birth were unmarried; by 1986 this figure had reached 61 per cent. She notes teenage unwed motherhood is rising among Whites but it is still much more common in the Black community. One out of every three black mothers is an unwed teenager, and a third of these go on to have a second child while still in their teens. Hewlett writes:

Marriage has become an almost forgotten institution among black teens. In whole sections of the Black community, children are being raised almost exclusively by very young mothers without male role models.[41]

Hewlett, further cites the case of Becky Kraus, exposing the futility of throwing money at the single mothering problem:

...her problems cannot be solved by the simple application of larger doses of money. Better social supports would help at the margin – an after-school program, for example, would reduce the emotional toll of being a latchkey kid – but in the main, Becky's enormous load of pain, her poor performance at school, her inability to make sense of the future are all wrapped up in her parents' divorce, her absentee father and stressed-out mother. She feels that both her parents missed out on her childhood, leaving her exposed and rudderless, coping more or less badly with the difficult business of growing up...[42]

Of total marriages among the 15 to 19 year age group, common-law unions accounted for 75 per cent of the total.[43] Transitional families represent families in which the wife works until the birth of a child, stays home for a portion of the child's younger years, and then returns to work. Conway states this model is the family of choice for many Canadians, an effort to combine for both women and the family the benefits of work outside the home with the benefits and fulfillment to be found, for mother and child, in a period of full-time parenting. In 1981, 52 per cent of all married women with children stayed home. By 1999, this had fallen to 30 per cent. When the economy improved after 1986, the employment participation rate of women in this category dropped suggesting that many of them were reluctantly in the workforce out of economic necessity.[44]

The blended family also called the reconstituted, melded or remarriage family, is increasingly common. In 1967 only 12 per cent of all marriages were remarriages, while by 1997 over 25 per cent were remarriages.[45] Conway contends that the rise in the divorce rate in Canada combined with remarriages, some for the third and fourth time, along with a rising common-law rate suggests the majority of families are based on remarriage. For those prophesying the end of heterosexual marriage, accelerating divorce rates have not heralded the death of the family; rather high rates of divorce and remarriage have resulted in reorganization into blended families. Clubb Neuman, in *Love in the Blended Family*, reports that the biggest problem faced by a blended family is "inherited leftovers," particularly ongoing emotional relationships.[46]

More families are having no children, and those that do are having fewer. In 1996, 35 per cent of families were childless, up from 29 per cent in 1961. Each Canadian woman will, on average, have 1.6 children, down from about four in 1960. The number of childless, never-married women aged 35 to 39 has almost doubled over the past 30 years to 13 per cent, while almost tripling among those aged 25 to 29 (14 to 38 per cent). For the first time in history, the fertility rate of women aged 30 to 34 has surpassed that of women aged 20 to 24, as women who postponed having children are having them and as fertility (number of females) among the formerly most fertile group of women continues to drop "dramatically."[47] In 1961, 40 per cent of the population was under the age of 18, by 1995 that figure had fallen to 24 per cent. According to Conway, if current trends continue Canada's population will peak in 2011 and begin an absolute decline. As demographer Karol Krotki put it:

There is no doubt that our society is dying out in a statistical sense – what we need is another baby boom.[48]

Notwithstanding the central role of parenting in the successful continuation of society, contemporary attitudes towards children and child rearing are at a new depth. Children are seen as either "financial liabilities" or "emotional assets" when a more accurate perspective is both. Under the title, *The Cost of Starting Families First*, James Poniewozik tallies the liabilities:

Babies cost you dearly...parenthood is a series of transactions, investments and calculations of risk vs. reward. Your children will cost you thousands of dollars, sure, but also chunks of your youth, middle and old age, physical stamina and, at least for many women, career opportunities...Of course this is true at any age. But to extend the financial metaphor, deciding to have her family while she's in her 20s changes a woman's investment horizon.[49]

John Conway agrees that "children bring no economic rewards to the family," yet he sees people continuing to have children for the "emotional gratification" they bring, regardless of family circumstance and age of parent. More and more kids are lining up at food banks and school meal programs.[50] The number of Canadian kids aged six to twelve who were either unsupervised "latchkey" kids or received care from an older sibling was 400,000 by 1996. In America, the U.S. Census estimated that 2.1 million children under 13 were left unsupervised before and after school. Others put the figure at five to seven million.[51] Even less encouraging has been the rate of suicide among teenagers. For those ages fifteen to nineteen the rate tripled between 1960 and 1986, going from 3.6 to 10.2 deaths per year per 100,000 persons in that age range. In 1986, 10 per cent of teenage boys and 18 per cent of teenage girls attempted suicide.[52]

A wealth of less dramatic evidence indicates that the emotional well-being of children and adolescents has deteriorated over the past three decades. According to a 1990 American Medical Association report, today's youngsters "are having trouble coping with stresses in their lives and more have serious psychological problems" than a generation ago.[53] Elementary-school teachers identified twice as many needy children in 1986 as in 1970. And more teens seek psychiatric help than ever before. Since 1971 the number of adolescents admitted to private psychiatric hospitals has increased fifteen fold, a particularly striking statistic given that the teen population has shrunk over the last twenty years.[54] Experts in the field point out that these disturbing trends are not due to a national epidemic of crazed kids; rather, family turmoil – provoked by divorce, disappearing fathers, mothers at work, and lengthening work weeks – has left many parents too overwhelmed to set limits or impose controls on children. For example, the pressures on newly divorced mothers are often so severe that "parenting breaks down and becomes inconsistent and erratically punitive." The children retaliate, venting their pain and frustration on the only available parent. One divorced woman said that the constant harassment felt "like being bitten to death by ducks."[55]

In harried dual-worker or single-parent families, even time-honored traditions such as eating family dinners or taking summer vacations are being squeezed. Over the last decade the length of the average family vacation has declined 14 per cent, and the number of families that eat their evening meals together has dropped 10 per cent.[56] Massachusetts Mutual Insurance Company surveyed parents and found nearly half were concerned about having too little time for their families. The majority believed that "parents having less time to spend with their families" is the single most important reason for the decline of the family in American Society.[57]

Dismissing the litany of evidence and comments countering liberationist ideology, Susan Faludi labels all as myth and anti-feminist backlash:

This bulletin of despair is posted everywhere – at the newsstand, on the TV set, at the movies, in advertisements and doctor's offices and academic journals. Professional women are suffering 'burnout' and succumbing to an 'infertility epidemic.' Single women are grieving from a man shortage. The New York Times reports: Childless women are 'depressed and confused' and their ranks are swelling. Newsweek says: Unwed women are 'hysterical' and crumbling under a 'profound crisis of confidence.' The health and advice manuals inform: High powered career women are stricken with unprecedented outbreaks of 'stress-induced disorders,' hair loss, bad nerves, alcoholism, and even heart attacks. The psychology books advise: Independent women's loneliness represents 'a major health problem today.' Even Betty Friedan has been spreading the word: she warns that women now suffer from a new identity crisis and 'new problems that have no name.'[58]

Faludi goes on to explain:

...prevailing wisdom has supported one and only one, answer to the riddle: it must be all that equality that is causing all that pain....They grabbed at the golden ring of independence, only to miss the one ring that matters. They have gained control of their fertility, only to destroy it. They have pursued their own professional dreams –

and lost out on the greatest female adventure. The women's movement, as we are told time and again, has proved women's own worst enemy.[59]

Mona Charen, a young law student, writes in the *National Review*, in an article titled, "The Feminist Mistake":

In dispensing its spoils, women's liberation has given my generation high incomes, our own cigarettes, the option of single parenthood, rape crisis centers, personal lines of credit, free love, and female gynecologists. In return it has robbed us of one thing upon which the happiness of most women rests – men.[60]

Faludi's book, *Backlash* highlights the polarity of evidence and the need for informed choice. Either the "backlash" is fueled by (from Faludi's perspective) heterosexual-based homophobia and misogyny or the opposite is true – the feminist movement is persisting in its own heterophobia and pro-homosexual agenda. The stakes are enormous for individuals and society at large. Faludi claims the afflictions ascribed to feminism are all false. From "the man shortage" to "the infertility epidemic" to "female burnout" to "toxic day care," she blames the media and advertising who create "an endless feedback loop that perpetuates and exaggerates its own false images of womanhood."[61] Returning to the source of the matter Faludi restates her feminist agenda:

It asks that women not be forced to 'choose' between public justice and private happiness. It asks that women be free to define themselves – instead of having their identity defined for them, time and again, by their culture and their men.[62]

In my (myopic-Christian) view, this agenda is a declaration that women not be forced to choose between career, family, and after marriage, one lifelong monogamous spousal sexual relationship. Moreover, this agenda says that women should not be forced to express their sexual identity as exclusively heterosexual, even if already in marriage with a man. Here the earlier conclusions of Alice Rossi and Sylvia Hewlett ring true – "I want what I want when I want it" and "the feminist movement is more interested in abortion and sexuality than in working on family and marriage issues." How different this version of feminism is to that envisaged in 1966, when Betty Freidan started NOW declaring "men should be part of it." Then the Organization's commitment was:

...to take action to bring women into full participation in the mainstream of American society now, exercising all privileges and responsibilities thereof, in truly equal partnership with men.[63]

Clearly, from the historical facts presented in Chapter 2, Freidan's feminism assumed a heterosexual worldview and here we see Faludi's does not. Indeed, rallying against the omnipotent vices of patriarchy and heterosexism, Faludi raises again sexual harassment statistics and declares that men are getting less considerate. Women are feeling less safe on streets. Less women are in politics. Divorce settlements are favoring men. And domestic-violence shelter usage is up 100 per cent. She sums up her feminist paradigm:

Eternal oppression – fear and loathing of feminism arise as a backlash to 'women's progress,' caused not simply by a bedrock of misogyny but by the specific efforts of contemporary women to improve their status...[64]

Who are you to believe? What is the truth? The benefit of addressing such questions in the year 2004, is that a wealth of data exists upon which to credibly assess the "status" of women's progress under Faludi-style feminism. Equally important, after four decades of social experimentation, the status of the family and its constituent members can be assessed. We need to continue the study of the family crisis by refreshing our understanding of the impact of increased divorce.

Collateral Damage From Divorce

Pro-family groups in the United States have united in a campaign to close down a web site allowing couples to divorce online. The Seattle-based site offers people in California, Washington, Florida and New York the option of dissolving their marriages online for $249 US.[65]

My world is an upper-middle-class place with few hardships of any real kind but for the almost complete lack of familial stability. Last January, my father's wife (three years older than I) gave birth to my first sister (correction: first blood-related sister). Last summer, my mother phoned me to say that she and Howard had gone to Nevada to get married (his second, her third, after seven years of living together)...In the same month (my boyfriend's) mom separated from her husband (his third marriage) of two years and asked [him] to 'hide' her $8,000 engagement ring lest it be deemed community property...We are the kids of transient parents, all grown up, who run from making an emotional commitment to our girlfriends and boyfriends at all costs. To be sure, we will run in the same direction when we are parents: away from our children. It's indicative of our age that we know more parents who mail monthly child-support checks than we do those who make a point of having Sunday dinner with their kids.[66]

Cynthia Rutherford,
Student Harvard Business School

All mom did for days was cry. Even for weeks, if I just asked what had happened, why they did it, she'd just burst into tears and run into her bedroom.[67]

In *Divorced Kids: A Candid and Compassionate Look at Their Needs*, Warner Troyer describes the experiences and perceptions of the hundreds of divorced kids he interviewed. He calls their comments a sociological short-hand for the experiences of such children in general. At the time of her interview Candy was five. She was not keen on being asked to explain how she came by her views, but they are clear, forthright, fixed. This passage came to Troyer in a "cohesive chunk," unedited and unequivocal:

Mommies and Daddies should stay together. They always should. They shouldn't never break up. Not never. I don't know why, but I know. They shouldn't. And I don't want to have kids when I'm big. Cause. Not never.[68]

Alice was fifteen at the time of her interview and a few years after her parents separated:

They were having another one of their arguments one night, after supper. Then, before I realized, dad had just left. I thought he had just gone for a drive, but he didn't come home. The next day Mom sent his clothes somewhere in a taxi. I was so pale; then I started to cry and I just couldn't stop. The sobs just kept coming. It was a kind of emotional breakdown. No matter how much comforting I got it couldn't warm me – I was so cold.[69]

Troyer's main theme: "Society…still pays lip-service to a notion that divorce is aberrant."[70] All participants in divorce, including the children, pay a social price for their condition. The divorce rate has risen steadily through the century and between 1970 and 1980, it actually doubled. Experts estimate that 49 per cent of all men and women who marry today are likely to divorce sometime before they die. According to Lenore Weitzman's *The Divorce Revolution,* in the first year after divorce women experience a 73 per cent loss in standard of living, whereas men experience a 42 per cent gain.[71] Despite increasingly tough child support enforcement laws, by the 90s only 51 per cent of mothers who were entitled to child support received the full amount, 25 per cent received partial payment, and 23 per cent received nothing at all. Nationwide (US), 4.6 billion dollars is owed by fathers to the children of divorce.[72] According to Frank Furstenberg and Kathleen Mullan Harris:

…men regard marriage as a package deal…they cannot separate their relations with their children from their relations to their former spouse. When that relationship ends the paternal bond usually withers.[73]

Most divorced fathers have distressingly little emotional contact with their children as well. According to the National Children's Survey conducted in 1976 and 1981 and analyzed by sociologist Frank Furstenberg, 23 per cent of all divorced fathers had no contact with their children during the past five years. Another 20 per cent had no contact with their children in the past year. Only 26 per cent had seen their children for a total of three weeks in the last year.[74] One quarter of all children are growing up with little of no contact with their fathers. In 1970, 12 per cent of children lived with their mothers alone; by 1988 this figure had reached 24 per cent. Of the 15 million children without fathers, some 10 million are the product of marital separation and divorce and close to 5 million are the product of out-of-wedlock births.[75]

For most children the partial or complete loss of a father produces long-lasting feelings of betrayal, rejection, rage, guilt, and pain. Judith Walerstein shows how children yearn for their fathers in the years after divorce, and how this longing is infused with new intensity at adolescence. For girls the peak years are early adolescence, twelve to fifteen; for boys the need for a father crests somewhat later, at ages sixteen to eighteen.[76] Troyer cites "shock" as a common denominator. Only among a very few of the kids of divorce was separation expected. He describes these kids facing divorce – "its pain was met by this handful with the relief felt after the extraction of a sore tooth."[77] But for the overwhelming majority, Troyer says "a numbness" occurred, which "soon triggered anger at being "overlooked" by preoccupied parents:

It was as if we just went with the house. We were part of the furniture.

I don't know why we couldn't have gone, all of us, to talk to some professional, some advisor, to see which of them really wanted us, and what we wanted.

I felt like a piece of baggage and they just decided where was the best place to store me. Nobody cares what kids need.[78]

In twenty-five years of journalism Troyer encountered only one adult response that compares with the pain evidenced by youngsters of divorce. It came from a widow of a man who had died of a heart attack, after ten years of having kept his heart condition secret from her:

That son-of-a-bitch, she ground out through a spate of tears. He knew for years. Why in hell couldn't he have told me? Maybe I could have helped. At least I might have been better prepared. I'll never forgive the bastard.[79]

Troyer contrasts the typical parent's cognitive spin on divorce – "Children are so adaptable; they have really adjusted beautifully," with reality. Yes they are certainly adaptable, "that's the rub." Says Troyer:

In circumstances of marital break-up children are the fastest learners imaginable. But, like the once-burned cat, the children are now forever twice-shy. Trust fades. Their quickly absorbed lesson is the rule of 'expect too little.'[80]

Their gut reaction may range from bitterness to resignation, from rage to apathy or patronizing patience. Wishes are rarely granted; tooth fairies almost never find the right street address; and Dad will likely fail again. Troyer recalls his own personal experiences with the coping schemes of his children of divorce:

The most personally depressing words I've heard from one of my own children, after two failed marriages, were those of my six-year-old son, Peter. I had let him down in what, in adult terms, was a minor matter…Peter responded with more self-control, more grace and more gravity than should be possible in any child of six: 'That's OK, Dad,' he said. 'It doesn't matter.' But it did…That evening I began recalling a whole series of those softly spoken absolutions from my youngest son. They filled me with remorse and, more vitally, with alarm. I didn't want my child to expect too little of life.[81]

In the time between her third and fourth birthdays my youngest daughter, Anne, avoided the traps of apathy or resignation. When, after an extended radio taping, a crush of traffic and a failure to budget my time adequately, I arrived, an hour late, to collect her with Peter for the weekend, she was loving but direct, and indignant: 'Where were you, Dad? Why were you late today?' Peter, leaning against a banister beside his younger sister while he pulled on his snow boots, interrupted the beginning of my explanation. His words tumbled over one another, rushing to stem the explanation that might only lead to renewed hope: 'It's OK, Dad. Anne, it's OK. It doesn't matter. You don't have to explain, Dad. It's all right. We understand, don't we, Anne? It's all right. We had lots to do, didn't we, Anne?' It was three days before I learned from the au pair girl that both children had waited outside, on a raw day, for forty minutes before returning to their TV program and their waiting-for-Daddy-who-is-late-again.[82]

There are success stories: examples of children who make healthy adjustments and cases where divorce is better for children than a severely troubled marriage. But the scholarly evidence increasingly confirms that divorce and father absence leads to serious emotional damage. Divorce seems to be an important factor in teen suicide. A study of 752 families by researchers at the New York Psychiatric Institute found that youngsters who attempted suicide differed little from those who didn't in terms of age, income, race, and religion, but were much more likely "to live in non-intact family settings" and to have minimal contact with the father.[83] A 1989 survey of teenagers discharged from psychiatric hospitals found that fully 84 per cent were living in disrupted families when they were admitted.[84] Indeed, the research shows that in nations as diverse as Finland and South Africa, anywhere from 50 to 80 per cent of psychiatric patients come from broken homes.[85]

According to a 1988 UCLA study, although "mothers are more active than fathers in helping youngsters with personal problems…with regard to youthful drug use, father's involvement is more important." Among homes with strict fathers, only 18 per cent of children used alcohol or drugs. In contrast, among single-mother homes, 35 per cent of children used drugs frequently.[86]

But a child doesn't have to end up in a psychiatric hospital, or strung out on drugs to suffer the emotional fallout of divorce. Some of the psychic consequences are much more subtle. Wallerstein talks about the "sleeper" effects of marital disruption, problems of commitment and attachment that may surface many years after parental divorce. According to Wallerstein, when it comes to forming relationships in adult life, "it helps enormously to have imprinted on one's emotional circuitry the patterning of a successful, enduring relationship between a man and a woman."[87] This is precisely what most children of divorce lack. Troyer details two examples of this phenomenon:

It's best not to – plan too much – about the future or what you will be doing. Like, Dad always wants – to go on a camping trip – every summer – with me. We did – once; before they were separated I mean. But he really works hard – to support everybody – and everything – so up until now we haven't actually gone – camping. Something has always come up – every summer; well, it's only been three summers since the divorce. So anyhow, it's not fair – is it? To depend on them too much. No fair to them – if you understand – to make them – feel there is pressure about this stuff – because they may not think – that you understand when they can't make it.[88]

My sister Lois doesn't talk about it, at all. She just won't talk about it, at all. She just won't....She heard about it by mail, in a letter from Mom, about three weeks after it happened; she was away at college, near Boston. I guess that's a pretty hard way to find out. And, see, she was the oldest, she was the closest to Dad, and he didn't even call her or write to her to tell her what was happening, what had happened.... And then she's broken up with her boy-friend. He has called here and she just won't talk to him; she just stays in her room most of the time and won't talk or anything, just cries a lot; and now she's talking as if she might quit college, too – not go back this fall; and that's crazy. But you can't tell her, cause she won't talk. She's just belligerent about it.[89]

The evidence that marital disruption and father absence contribute to educational under performance is clear. Two-parent families seem to make for better students than do one-parent families. To cite a report by the National Association of Elementary School Principals:

One-parent children, on the whole, show lower achievement in school than their two-parent peers. Among all two-parent children 30 per cent were ranked as high achievers, compared to 17 per cent of one-parent children. At the other end of the scale the situation is reversed. 23 per cent of two-parent children were low achievers – while fully 38 per cent of the one-parent children fell into this category.[90]

In divorce the proverbial "sins of the fathers" appear to invariably "descend to the sons." All of the adults that Troyer interviewed felt that divorce in their childhoods had altered or atrophied their prospects for a full and happy marital relationship. Many said they had determined in their youth that they would have no children of their own – had even made that a condition of marriage in later years. Even at forty or fifty years of age and beyond, these former "divorced kids" were fearful of commitment, uncertain as to their ability to maintain enduring relationships. Some, divorced themselves, specifically blamed their parents for their marital failures. They had "rushed into marriage to find the emotional security they missed at home" or they had "been conditioned to believe there was no permanence in marriage." Not one adult in Troyer's sample, at any age, regarded the separation of their parents as irrelevant to their own well-being. Most described the event as the most traumatic of their lives.[91]

Eleanor B. Alter, a prominent divorce lawyer in New York, said that she counsels mothers and fathers to cut back their hours if they want to win custody after divorce because judges must choose between two alternatives, and the parent who works fewer hours often looks like the better choice. Says Alter:

Often its one investment banker against the other. It's not just that women cut back on their careers. I've told men to cut back, too. Maybe this wife is awful but she's at home.[92]

Pathetically, (at 150-300 dollars an hour) lawyers tot up each breakfast prepared and each dinner missed, compare how often Mommy took the child to the doctor with the times Daddy visited kindergarten and judges are too often reduced to travesties like counting hours of daylight that mothers are there.[93] Little wonder for adults of divorce, memories of the separation were as sharp, clear and painful as, in Troyer's words, "yesterday's visit to the dentist."[94]

Why Do You Work?

It is important here to introduce the Christian paradigm regarding work in order to contrast the impact of the competing worldviews on the family, indeed on marriage. Our society has developed the mindset which holds out the promise that work will give us wealth, prestige, esteem, purpose, values, standards, success and happiness. The notion further claims that the harder you work, the more you will receive, and the greater will be the consumption benefits. This materialistic ethic has combined with a growth in individualism – the self-centered ethos described earlier by Sonia Johnson, as she "detached" herself from her responsibilities as a mother to her children. The level of acceptance of materialism and individualism in society has led to the dominant trend of two spouses working (in theory to benefit the "family"). In her book *A Mother's Place: Taking the Debate about Working Mother's beyond Guilt and Blame*, Susan Chira articulates her new vision of *liberated* motherhood:

Reimaging motherhood requires understanding that working does not destroy the joyous sense of connection to a child or diminish the all-important influence of the family on a child's life. It means enduring children's resentment of work while explaining that work has value. And it means embracing a new psychological ideal of motherhood, one that abandons the pursuit of perfection and the reverence for sacrifice....Is it really the end of the world if a mother is not at home when a child returns from school? How about doing what my friend does; programming the phone so that her young son can push a button; get her office; tell her he's home; chat a little about his day...Much as I hope that my children can see my love of work as a legacy that they may one day share in whatever path they choose, I also must accept that there are times when they see my work as a burden and a competitor....If children do chafe at times because of jobs, they must understand why mothers work. Many mothers...can say that without work, there is no food on the table. There is another equally valid explanation – that work is important to the mother, that helping support her family makes her proud, that the work itself makes her happy, maybe even that it contributes something to other people or the world at large. Work has an intrinsic value, one that mothers can convey to their children.[95]

The "work-oriented" philosophy, undergirding Chira's vision of motherhood is seen by many as innately visionary, critical to achieving gender equality, and beneficial to society. However, her supposition needs to be questioned and it should be no surprise that it is not grounded in sound Christian values. The issue is not who works, as much as why they (the parenting couple) choose work over other responsibilities, particularly parenting. The Christian Business Men's Committee[96] counters careerism, workaholism and preferential allegiance to work over family, with four Christian principles that will provide a basis for discussion of the trade-off of career and parenting. To these I have added a fifth principle specifically addressing divorce.

Principle #1 – *We Do Not Work to Earn a Living*. Jesus said, "Do not store up for yourselves treasures on earth, where moth and rust destroy, and where thieves break in and steal. But store up for yourselves treasures in heaven…For where your treasure is your heart will be also' (Matthew 6:19-21). In the same chapter, Jesus declared, "No one can serve two masters. Either you will hate the one and love the other…You cannot serve both God and money" (6:24). For Christians, the source of all benefits is God, "seek first the kingdom and his righteousness and all these things will be given to you"(6:33). Those who do not understand or accept this precept are too frequently driven by the contrasting belief that providing for one's needs in the final analysis is an individual responsibility. Ask many Christians why they chase the dollar in the marketplace, if they are honest with themselves, they would say, "because I am afraid that if I allowed Jesus to determine my standard of living, He would establish it lower than where I want it to be. So I chase money in violation of His guidance in Matthew 6, and when I succeed, I give Him the credit."[97] Furthermore, what are the costs to other relationships of private self-ambition? In a market place operating a on survival of the fittest rationale, the attitude towards others at work and home becomes manipulative and exploitative. As ambition grows relationships that enhance your career prosper and others atrophy. What if the obstacle to success is an exhausted wife, a friend at work, a newborn, a spouse's health problem, or a spouse's transfer? In business winning usually equals survival, but in Christ's Kingdom, such Darwinian and Kensian dynamics are turned upside down. Tired of the disciples bickering amongst themselves, Jesus asked them, "What were you arguing about on the road?" But they kept quiet because they had been quibbling about who was the greatest. Sitting everyone down, Jesus said: "If anyone wants to be first, he must be the very last, and the servant of all" (Mark 9:33-35).

Principle #2 – *There is no cause-effect relationship between how hard you work and how much you make*. The idea that a given amount of work produces a given result does not take providence (and business politics) into consideration.[98] Some people are born into wealth, some into poverty. Some experience drought, stock collapse, accidents, layoffs, poor health. Some are born with talents, others are less gifted. This principle does not imply that people are not to work hard but rather we are to work hard for God, "Whatsoever ye do, do it heartily as unto the Lord and not unto men" (Colossians 3:23). The mechanic working all his life for extra college money for his children has given no less effort, in God's eyes, than the Harvard grad who finally succeeds at becoming a CEO.

Consider these areas of your life: self, children, work, spirituality, spouse, friends, and relatives. How do you prioritize these competing relationship goals? Which are critical to maintain? Which are less important? How do you set goals in each area and how do you plan to achieve the targets? How much time and effort do you spend on each? The belief that there is a cause-effect relationship to how hard you work and how much you make affects family planning. In a "work or money-oriented" planning approach you set out what promotion is to be achieved or how much is to be made in the year and then you order the priorities according to career or income objectives. What happens with this approach is that the market place will dictate the level of commitment to all the other areas of life. When career aims or financial goals are not reached, instead of looking to God for guidance and provision, the work or money-oriented person simply begins to work harder. Family priorities and time with the Lord give way to the pressing need to meet financial goals. The worst stereotype of this phenomenon is the careerist who is never satisfied. There is always a bigger house, a more expensive car, a more challenging assignment and a higher rung on the corporate ladder. These people are driven and usually leave a trail of broken marriages and discarded parental responsibilities.

The *Meridiam Websters Collegiate Dictionary* defines careerism as "the policy or practice of advancing one's career often at the cost of one's integrity." Other sources describe careerism as self-serving; a shift from an attitude of self-sacrifice and moral commitment to one of materialism; the desire to be, rather than the desire to do; the pursuit of promotion without a clear sense of what to do once it is attained; preoccupation with career advancement that replaces concern for basic duties; and placing self-interests above the interests of the organization to accelerate personal advancement.

The relationship between careerism and family-orientation is a zero-sum game – when careerism burgeons, interest in and support of family suffer (constrained by time and thought the person is captured by his career). Blinded by ambition the careerist invariably does harm to relationships viewed unimportant from the perspective of career. Like a balloonist trying to set a new altitude record, the careerist will toss overboard everything in the pursuit.

Competitiveness and ambition can be valuable attributes when properly channeled. They become destructive forces only when they detract from the family's welfare. Problematic for the work-oriented double income family is that to the extent an ambitious individual indulges in careerism, he tends to encourage careerism in his spouse. The result can be a self-perpetuating situation where couples compete against each other.

Published in *The Radical,* under the title "Careerism is Unhealthy," Chris Lindsay writes:

One of the most popular idols in Canada today is obsessive devotion to a career...many men and women today fanatically worship their careers. They are workaholics willing to work 60 hours a week or even longer to climb the corporate ladder...People who are extreme in pursuing their career often sacrifice time with their family and friends, get minimal exercise, and have no personal creative interests outside of working. They live unbalanced lives and eventually the consequences catch up with them. They live in loneliness, get sick from stress and fatigue, and if they lose their jobs they have no other identity. Careerism is an idol that is trapping many white collar workers into a prison of work. Unfortunately there are no laws that protect salaried workers from the pressure to work excessively long days. Un-

less people stand up and say no to their employers (and reject the idol of careerism) they can be pressured into working 50, 60, or even 70 hours each week.[99]

In *Woman on a Seesaw: The Ups and Downs of Making It*, Hilary Cosell describes her single-minded focus on career, which barely made time for a husband and precluded children:

There I was, coming home from ten or twelve or sometimes more hours at work, pretty much shot for the day, and I'd do this simply marvelous imitation of all the successful fathers I remembered from childhood. All the men I swore I'd never grow up and marry, let alone like...The men who would come home from the office, utterly useless for anything beyond the most mundane and desultory conversation. And there I'd be, swilling a vodka on the rocks or two, shoving a Stouffer's into my mouth and staggering off to take a bath, watch 'Hill Street Blues' and fade away with Ted Koppel. To get up and do it all again.[100]

According to Scripture, career planning (for the married) always has family as a priority. Even seemingly "called" ministers have become worthless in service to the Lord, by neglect of their spouse and family. Selection of leadership and management in our churches is based on one's performance as husband, wife and parent:

Now the overseer must be beyond reproach, the husband of but one wife...He must manage his own family well and see that his children obey him with proper respect. (If anyone does not know how to manage his own family, how can he take care of God's church?) (1 Timothy 3:2-5).

Family-oriented spouses and parents need to ask tough career questions. Should I take that great out-of-town job, even though it means I will be home less? Should I take the easier job in the less competitive business culture, instead of the higher paying and more demanding job with less-than-friendly co-workers? How rewarding is a happy and stable family, if I am stuck in a dead-end job? What is this pace doing to my long-term health? What is the probability of completing my other life goals if I continue on this course at this pace? Will it relieve the stress if I change my job to build a stronger relationship with a troubled son or daughter? Suppose that the ultimate standard of our work were to be, not advancement and profitability, but the welfare and durability of our human relationships.

Principle #3 – *Significance is Not Found in the Kind of Work You Do*. Significance and sense of personal worth is found in a person's relationship with God. Jeremiah 9:23-24 reads, "Let not the wise man boast of his strength or the rich man boast of his riches..." If one looks to his vocation as the source of his fulfillment and receives negative feedback from those with whom he works, he develops a low self-image. Conversely, the greater the recognition of man the greater the sense of worth. When a person's significance is a derivative of her vocation and she loses her vocation, she loses her reason for living. Men and women who choose not to make parenting a proper priority in their lives, are fooled by the myth that the career gives them importance and over an entire life span satisfaction. Significance is not to be found in the kind of work one does, nor the gifts one has, but in being part of the family of God.[101]

Principle #4 – *There is No Intrinsic Value in the Product of Your Work.* Things we produce may have utilitarian value, but what is more important is the value of our activities in God's eyes. 2 Peter 3:10-12 reads:

The day of the Lord will come like a thief…the elements will be destroyed by fire, and the earth and everything in it will be laid bare. Since everything will be destroyed in this way, what kind of people ought you to be? You ought to live holy and godly lives as you look forward to the day of God.

It is not the fruit of the labor that produces significance but the focus of that labor, which must be God's service. For example, a missionary for the gospel is likely engaged in "secular" work if the focus of his life is someday becoming president of the mission. Likewise, if a garbage collector does his work always looking for opportunities to serve the Lord, his work will have God's blessing as a ministry.

Again there is no better purpose to one's labor in God's eyes than to establish and maintain a loving marriage and nurturing family. Consider two double income situations. The actual nature of the work in these examples is not important, it is the purpose behind the work and the attitude of the worker to her family that are of interest. From a Christian perspective the first has obvious intrinsic value and an apparent blessing. The second has no focus other than self and results in the person's family being taken away. Reina Sanchez has raised seven children while working long hours in a New York City garment factory. She and her husband came to America from the Dominican Republic, and she boasts proudly that four of her children are students (three of them in college) and three are married. She must leave home well before her children do to arrive at her sewing machine by 7 a.m. For her the precious hours are after she leaves the factory at 4 p.m. and arrives home to talk to her children about their days. Her husband is also home at night with the family.[102] There is no evidence of family crisis or marital dysfunction. The priority for the Sanchez' is their family. Reina does not define her work as a career, rather in her words:

I work because I have to, but I dedicate all my spare time to the children to raise them properly. I speak with all the children about what they've done. I answer their questions honestly, no matter how embarrassing the questions are. You have to make them see that you trust them and they can trust you, too.[103]

The point is the Sanchez priorities and focus are on family and they have been blessed. On the other hand, Marcia Clark, prosecution lawyer in the O.J. Simpson trial, had filed for divorce from her husband of fourteen years on June 9, 1994, three days before Nicole Simpson and Ronald Goldman were killed. In December, she filed for an increase in child support, arguing that the long hours and intense publicity of the trial had forced her to spend more money on baby-sitters, personal grooming, and new clothes (five new suits for $1,500). She told the courts she had been working six- or seven-day weeks for sixteen hours a day (112 hours per week). As a result, she needed baby-sitters to pick up her children from school, spend time with them at night, and cover for her on weekends when she worked. Gordon Clark's court papers show a man devastated and bitter at his wife's insistence on divorce. He accused his wife of infidelity, deceit, and neglect of their children. He said that his former wife worked an intense schedule at least half a year, whenever she was in trial:

While I commend the petitioner's brilliance, her legal ability and her tremendous competence as an attorney, I do not want our children to continue to suffer because she is never home, and never has any time to spend with them.[104]

Gordon charged that his ex-wife saw her two sons, then three and five years old, at most one hour a day. Susan Chira, said of the custody case:

Many women could not justify an argument that Marcia Clark should be the primary caretaker of her children when she had to work...sixteen hours a day, and Gordon Clark, a computer engineer, arrived home every night by 6:15 p.m. More telling, though was the criticism she received for failing to trim her sails to accommodate her children. Clark had tried a supervisory job with better hours and the same pay, but she didn't like it. Her ambition smacked to many of hubris.[105]

It is not the amount of fruit, which an individual produces that pleases God, but the degree to which he/she is faithful to the opportunities God assigns. Parenting is incredibly high on God's priority list along with sustaining a lifelong monogamous marriage. He hates divorce.

Principle #5 – *God Loves Family and Hates Divorce.* Here Christian churches have failed miserably to explain and uphold the belief that it is God's will that the first marriage survives for eternity, and indeed flourishes:

You cover the altar of the Lord with tears [shed by your unoffending wives, divorced by you that you might take heathen wives], and with your own weeping and crying out because the Lord does not regard your offering any more or accept it with favor at your hand. Yet you ask, Why does He reject it? Because the Lord was witness [to the covenant made at your marriage] between you and the wife of your youth, against whom you have dealt treacherously and to whom you were faithless. Yet she is your companion and the wife of your covenant [made by your marriage vows]. And did not God make [you and your wife] one [flesh]? Did not One make you and preserve your spirit alive? And why did God make you two one? Because He sought a godly offspring [from your union]. Therefore take heed to yourselves, and let no one deal treacherously and be faithless to the wife of his youth[106] *(Malachi 2:13-15).*

The Apostle Mark records:

Some Pharisees came and tested him by asking, "Is it lawful for a man to divorce his wife? 'What did Moses command you?' he replied. They said, 'Moses permitted a man to write a certificate of divorce and send her away.' 'It was because your hearts were hard that Moses wrote you this law,' Jesus replied. 'But at the beginning of creation God 'made them male and female.' For this reason a man will leave his father and mother and be united to his wife, and the two will become one flesh. So they are no longer two, but one. Therefore what God has joined together, let man not separate.'

When they were in the house again, the disciples asked Jesus about this. He answered, 'Anyone who divorces his wife and marries another woman commits adultery against her. And if she divorces her husband and marries another man, she commits adultery' (Mark 10:2-12).

Frankly, there are no career goals, no business opportunities, no inter-spousal rivalries, no time shortages, no exhaustion, no bankruptcies significant enough to justify divorce. A useful metaphor in summation of these principles is illustrated by a family-oriented circus juggler:

She has one ball for each of self, spouse, children, God, and work. Tossing them and balancing each with great care, an onlooker asks, 'Have you ever had to drop one? If so which?' She replied without hesitation, 'Oh yes a number of times over my career. Once things get too busy one of the balls has to go. For me the choice is easy. I have always dropped the work ball. You see its rubber, but all the others are crystal glass.'

Anti-Parenting Culture

There is one more cardinal point in Engels' theory of sexual revolution, bound to provoke more controversy than all others: 'with the transformation of the means of production into collective property, the monogamous family will cease to be the economic unit of society. The care and education of children becomes a public matter.'...There is something logical and even inevitable in this recommendation, for so long as every female, simply by virtue of her anatomy, is obliged, even forced, to be the sole or primary caretaker of childhood, she is prevented from being a free being. The care of children, even from the period when their cognitive powers first emerge, is infinitely better left to the best trained practitioners of both sexes...rather than to harried and all too frequently unhappy persons with little time nor taste for the work of educating minds, however young or beloved. The radical outcome of Engels' analysis is that the family, as that term is presently understood, must go.[107]

Kate Millett

The above anti-parenting rhetoric from the "High Priestess" of the feminist movement, a self-declared lesbian, is clear. Sylvia Ann Hewlett says:

Some feminists rage at babies; others trivialize, or denigrate them. Very few have attempted to integrate them into the fabric of a full and equal life...One might say that motherhood is the problem that modern feminists cannot face.[108]

The book titled *Lesbian Nation*, philosophically captures the Second Wave of feminism by revealing the movement's relationship to marriage, parenting and family. In the book Jill Johnston declares heterosexuality the female form of treason.[109] Germaine Greer's *The Female Eunuch* explains the impotence of the female.[110] Kate Millett's *Sexual Politics* made natural relations among the sexes a power struggle.[111] Kathrin Perutz's *Marriage is Hell*, attacks the institution.[112] Ellen Peck's *The Baby Trap* argues that babies are incompatible with liberation.[113] The prolific Gloria Steinem, wrote on issues as diverse as the crime of genital mutilation and praise for women's bodies, but according to Hewlett, not much "is devoted to motherhood, family, or children."[114] Hewlett writes:

To be liberated came to mean wiping out all special female characteristics, leaving behind an androgynous shell of abstract personhood. Stripped of their men and their children, these unfettered women could clone the male competitive model and fulfill their destiny in the business community.[115]

A further step towards debunking feminist anti-parenting ideology can be taken by viewing the web site: Flag.blackened.net. Under the title "What methods of child rearing do anarchists advocate?" is written:

If one accepts the thesis that the authoritarian family is the breeding ground for both individual psychological problems and political reaction, it follows that anarchists should try to develop ways of raising children that will not psychologically cripple them but instead enable them to accept freedom and responsibility while developing natural self-regulation. We will refer to children raised in such a way as 'free children.'

...under the influence of a compulsive, pleasure-denying morality, children are taught to inhibit the spontaneous flow of life-energy in the body. Similarly, they are taught to disregard most bodily sensations. Due to Oedipal conflicts in the patriarchal family, parents usually take the most severely repressive disciplinary measures against sexual expressions of life-energy in children. Thus, all erotic feelings, including the erotically-tinged 'streaming' sensations, come to be regarded as 'bad,' 'animalistic,' etc., and so their perception begins to arouse anxiety...the person is eventually left with a feeling of inner emptiness or 'deadness' and — not surprisingly — a lack of joy in life.

... crimes in our society would be greatly reduced if libertarian child rearing practices were widely followed.... In other words, the solution to the so-called crime problem is not more police, more laws, or a return to the disciplinarianism of 'traditional family values,' as conservatives claim, but depends mainly on getting rid of such values.

In as much as they are describing controlling and hypocritical families like that of Alfred Seguine Kinsey (Senior), it is hard to not empathize with them on the toxic environment they critique. However, the notion of a pro-sex, no-rules, boundary-free parenting model seems incredible. By anarchist philosophy, religious, patriarchal, moralistic, traditional, disciplinarian or conservative families all fall under the negative term "authoritarian." Not surprising Emma Goldman's thinking is manifest in the analysis. Anarchists wish to win children away from parental, conservative cultural and religious influences. All orthodox institutions are fair targets:

There are other problems as well with the moralism taught by organized religions. One danger is making the child a hater. 'If a child is taught that certain things are sinful, his love of life must be changed to hate....it is a short step to the idea that certain classes or races of people are more 'sinful' than others, leading to prejudice, discrimination, and persecution of minorities....

Abortion advocate and feminist Diane Alstad embellishes anarchist ideology in her differentiation of feminist family values from traditional family values. She says:

One of the main differences is that the old family values and roles are authoritarian and patriarchal. The big traditional authoritarian values are duty, obedience, loyalty, and respect for authority, inside and outside the family. Much of this is fear- and guilt-based. Duty means doing the authoritarian rules and roles. Their ideal is to break a child's will to inculcate dependency and obedience, which meant obeying male authorities and being God-fearing, literally....Parents use guilt, fear and punishment for control, as does religion.[116]

On the other hand, Alstad describes feminist and liberal family values:

[They] have no fixed sex roles. Duty is self-defined rather than culture-defined, related to how one wants to live and operate in the world. Loyalty is chosen and deserved based on how you and others are treated....Ideally parents would avoid resorting to guilt and fear for control. They would foster a child's independence as soon as possible by linking freedom with acting responsibly. The ideal is to raise children to be self-respecting, self-confident, self-trusting, competent people who can succeed and help make the world a better place.[117]

Alstad's view is not novel, not even experimental; it's counter-evidence and anarchist-based. Science already shows that parent-child relations can easily spiral in the negative direction if parents fail to become consistent and evident authority figures. A recent report for Health Canada found that teenagers are punching, kicking, threatening to kill and otherwise abusing their parents in increasing numbers "partly because permissive mothers and fathers are not keeping a tight enough rein on their children." According to Barbara Cottrell, a Halifax-based researcher:

Terrified parents should stop treating their offspring as friends and equals and begin to act as the loving authority figures they are supposed to be.[118]

The report said that boys and girls can be abusive toward their parents, but mothers are more likely to be the victims, perhaps because they are seen as more vulnerable. Writes Cottrell:

Children sometimes lash out at their parents because they have never faced clear rules and guidelines for their behavior…The lack of control can leave the teenager fearful, prompting them to misbehave.

Parents of the baby-boom generation often feel they should treat their children as friends, not as dependents who need their authority and guidance. [119]

Contrary to anarchist dogma, the report recommends that parents set clear limits for their children and enforce them resolutely. This advice of course presupposes "two" parents (acting as a tag-team in the home arena); two spouses who are supportive of each other would help; and parents interested in a genuine relationship with their children are essential. These are not assumed in the feminist variant family model. Underpining radical feminist thought, is the belief that relationships should exist in the absence of rules, boundaries and thus consequences. Adherents seek some free sex, gender-free, and otherwise unencumbered state.

To thrive, says anarchist ideology, humankind needs to break existing rules, thwart constraining institutions and end current ways of thinking. Such thinking is the converse of Biblical intent. Scripture teaches us to "honor your father and your mother" (Exodus 20:12). Today's youth live in a culture that encourages them to question authority rather than to honor it. Some of this suspicion is justified because of the suspect nature of many parents (i.e. Kinsey's father), governments, and religious institutions. However, Martin De Haan writes:

The Bible treats parental honor as a timeless cross-cultural principle. If we do not learn to respect the authority of our parents (even before learning to evaluate it critically), we are not likely to learn the difference between good and bad authority in other areas of our life. If we grow up despising our parents, we are likely to rebel not only against them but against all authority – including God Himself.[120]

In *The Shelter of Each Other: Rebuilding Families*, Mary Phipher observes anarchist doctrine in "America's belief in independence" which "leads us to value rebellion in our children." She writes:

There is a belief that to grow up people must reject their parents. We are a culture that portrays parents as baggage, impossible to ignore but generally a pain in the neck. Teenagers hear that families are a hindrance to individual growth and development, and sadly, teens who love their parents are made to feel odd. This sets up teenagers for trouble. Just when adolescents desperately need their parents' guidance and support, they are culturally conditioned to break away. They must tackle difficult questions about sex, drugs, peers and chemicals on their own. Rebels do not ask for advice and help.[121]

A good example of this anarchist doctrine in action is the following extract from the Planned Parenthood, PFLAG and CBCA pamphlet titled "Be Yourself":

The teen years are a time of figuring out what works for you and crushes and experimentation are often part of that. Over time, you'll find that you're drawn mostly to men or to women – or to both – and you'll know then….<u>Telling friends and family</u>

AT THIS POINT is premature. This is not to suggest being gay, lesbian or bisexual is something to be ashamed of and to hide (it isn't) but our society doesn't really understand homosexuality and, right now, you probably don't need the hassle of dealing with any negative stuff that telling might bring. [my underline]

Furthermore, the culture of rebellion makes the whole idea of commitment confusing. Add in the ideology of androgynous equal gender and the result is chaos. As witnessed in Margaret Sanger's and Henry Morgentaler's free sex lifestyle, it becomes unclear whether fidelity, loyalty and even duty to another is healthy or unhealthy, good or bad. The result has a dangerous impact on family. Like Rossi and Hewlett, Germaine Greer sees feminism as the masculinization of women, with mostly negative anti-parenting consequences:

The closer women draw in social and economic status to the male level the more disruptive childbirth becomes. In order to compete with men Western woman has joined the masculine hierarchy and cultivated a masculine sense of self. The acknowledgment of her pregnancy means that she must step down from all that and enter the psychological equivalent of the birth hut; what happens to her there can have convulsive effects upon what she has come to think of as unalterable, her personality. In exchange for her settled self-image she has a body which inexorably goes about its own business, including biochemical changes in the brain. The period following the birth of a child has been called a fourth trimester. Mother and child remain attached as it were by an invisible umbilical cord. A mother is no longer self-sufficient but at the mercy of the child's indomitable love and egotism....From henceforth her attention will be divided. If she returns to work and brings baby to the office, the divided nature of her attention is obvious. She may encounter support as she breast feeds in the boardroom but she will also encounter ridicule. If she stays at home for her two years paid leave (supposing she has such an unusual privilege) and returns to work without loss of seniority, she is not the same worker who left to bear a child. Asking her to continue as if nothing had happened is absurd. Contemplated through the eyes of the ostracized dyad mother-and-child, the work of business may well seem cruel and silly, and a key to the executive washroom a poor reward. Meanwhile the child's development is taken over by professionals: the mother begins her long struggle with guilt. [122]

In contrast to North American culture, Greer reflects on womanhood in the developing nations. There women who wear cortes, huipiles, saris, jellabas, salwar kammeez, or other ample garments, can swell and diminish inside them without embarrassment or discomfort. Because mothers are younger the changes of pregnancy are less likely to leave permanent unsightly signs like stretchmarks. Such mothers are more likely to see pregnancy as the culmination of their development than as the ruination of a mature body. Says Greer:

There are those who will compliment the young mother-to-be on having reached the pinnacle of female beauty.[123]

According to Greer, it is largely as an unconscious reaction to this diminution of women's role that women are now exerting such pressure to be allowed into the competitive male hierarchy.[124]

In Greer's view, motherhood is virtually meaningless in our society. Moreover, the West has no grounds for supposing that the fact that women are still defined by their mothering function in other societies is simply an index of their oppression. She writes:

We have at least to consider the possibility that a successful matriarch might well pity Western feminists for having been duped into futile competition with men in exchange for the companionship and love of children and other women.[125]

Susan Greenberg, offers another reason for the negative image of motherhood and its indicator – the falling birthrate. She writes:

Today's exhausted, overworked parents may be reluctant to admit: it's [low fecundity] easier. And cheaper. [126]

French sociologist Jean-Claude Kaufman attributes the rise in one-child families to "the growth of individualism." What might be labeled the "Sonia Johnson Effect" – dropping responsibility for child rearing, in favor of self-interest. Says Kaufman, the lone child increasingly results from a compromise between the parents hopes for themselves and the dream of family. A one-child family is not an ideal but a way of resolving a contradiction. Writes Kaufman:

With one child, it's more feasible, fiscally as well as emotionally, to take the family to a four-star restaurant or on safari to Tanzania. It's much more manageable to live in a cramped, big-city apartment with one kid than with two or three. And when it comes to education, there's no comparison.[127]

However, Greenberg sees a dark side to this demographic trend. The decline in population growth is almost exclusively a developed nations' phenomenon. By 2050, nine of ten people will live in a developing country.[128] Says Dr. Edward Shorter, chairman, History of Medicine in the Faculty of Medicine at University of Toronto:

The declining birthrate reflects nothing less than a fundamental shift in the meaning of child-bearing. Having children used to be a way of building the family, of adding building blocks to society. But now it's seen primarily as a means to self-fulfillment, and for many women, once they've had one child, they're fulfilled. In a few years, though, they may find out raising a singleton is not as happy as raising more than one. [129]

In the United States, the trends have recently turned around. According to a March 2002 announcement by National Center for Health Statistics, American women are having more children than at any other time in the past three decades. Of this reversal Journalist Anne Kingston writes:

The rise in the U.S. fertility rate has been attributed to a confluence of social, eco-

nomic and technological factors, including fertility treatments that enable even 50-year-old women to conceive a child – or two or three.[130]

The anti-parenting ideology of feminists also manifests itself in spousal dynamics. Daphne Patai, author of *Heterophobia: Sexual Harassment and the Future of Feminism* (first introduced in Chapter 2), contends that from its earliest days, feminism was divided into factions: one embracing heterosexuality and the other "pure womanhood" – lesbianism. According to Patai, heterosexual women were judged to be outside the fold of the "good feminist fight":

This feminist intolerance and self-righteousness contributed to a situation in which heterosexual women are made to feel that they are not 'real' feminists. Aware of being 'compromised' by their attachments to men, such women have often acted apologetic towards their lesbian feminist colleagues and friends. This, in turn, has been a major contributing factor to the failure to challenge the extreme anti-male rhetoric produced by some feminists.[131]

It was this holier-than-thou intolerance, witnessed when Radicalesbians outed Kate Millett, which precipitated the resignation of Betty Friedan from NOW, and the inevitable public demise of Millett as High Priestess of the women's movement. Decades later the family is still reeling from radical feminist shocks, which from the perspective of children within a family, must be seen as attempting to drive a wedge between male and female, husband and wife, parent and child. A key to building this wedge was dismantling the legal protections once afforded to women who made "monetary" sacrifices for the family. Now when a marriage breaks up, as almost half do, a wife is seldom entitled to alimony, no matter how much less she earns than her husband. Danielle Crittenden writes:

In the 1970s, feminists campaigned against alimony on the explicit grounds that its elimination would flush women out of the home and into the workforce where they belonged. The revocation of the old promise that marriage meant 'assured support as long as they live,' wrote feminist sociologist Jesse Bernard in her book, The Future of Marriage, 'may be one of the best things that could happen to women. It would demand that even in their early years they think in terms of lifelong work histories; it would demand the achievement of autonomy. They would learn that marriage was not the be-all and end-all of their existence.' But when women are forced to think in terms of lifelong work histories, there is a cost to be paid, and it is paid by them and their children.[132]

One can only ponder in bewilderment the logic in the feminist rationale of "commitment" in their variant family. NOW president Karen DeCrow writes:

No man should allow himself to support his wife – no matter how much she favors the idea, no matter how many centuries this domestic pattern has existed, no matter how logical the economies of the arrangement may appear, no matter how good it makes him feel.[133]

Simultaneously the message has also been sent to women "don't depend on a man to take care of you." So now there are women who postponed marriage and childbirth to pursue their careers only to find themselves at thirty-five still single with their biological clocks winding down and no husband in sight. There are unwed mothers who now depend on the state to provide what the father's of their children won't – a place to live and an income to support their kids. Newlyweds start out under the statistical probability that half of their marriages will collapse into a "no fault" divorce. If the feminist logic behind the variant family is not flawed enough, the theory for familial sexual relations is worse. On top of a confused understanding of internal and external divisions of labor, the family is to bear the burden of free sex relations (homosexual, heterosexual or both) in the name of liberation. Daughters in these families, who believed they could lead vigorous sexual lives while at high school, end up in an abortion clinic (without their parent's knowledge) or attending school pregnant. Sons are indoctrinated to believe commitment in sexual relations ended with comprehensive technological and legal provisions to eradicate procreation. What is unfolding here is a familiar and depressing story of political and ideological mania overruling commonsense and misguiding its adherents.

Rooted in this ethos of irresponsibility and anti-dependence is a resistance to what can only be called "growing up." Crittenden writes:

The quest for autonomy – the need 'to be oneself' or, as [feminist Elizabeth] Wurtzel declares, the intention 'to answer only to myself' – is in fact not a brave or noble one; nor is it an indication of strong character. Too often, autonomy is merely the excuse of someone who is so fearful, so weak, that he or she can't bear to take on any of the responsibilities that used to be shouldered by much younger more robust and mature souls.[134]

Crittenden is struck by the number of single contemporaries – men and women in their early to mid-thirties – who speak of themselves as if they are still twenty years old:

Yet at the suggestion of marriage – or of buying a house or having a baby – these modern thirtysomethings will claim, 'But I'm so young!'...In the relationships they do have – even 'serious' ones – they will take pains to avoid the appearance of anything that smacks of permanent commitment. Although prepared to share apartments, cars, weekends, and body fluids, they reserve the right to cancel the relationship at any moment.[135]

Here Hewlett's observance agrees with Crittenden. She writes:

In the late 1960s Americans began their modern quest for personal growth and self-realization. Psychic self-improvement became chic, and books with titles such as Looking Out For Number One, Pulling Your Own Strings, and How To Be Your Own Best Friend sold like hot cakes. According to sociologist Robert Bellah, starting around 1965 a new 'therapeutic mentality' took root in our culture. The therapeutic mentality focuses on the self, rather than on a set of external obligations. It encour-

ages an individual to find and assert his or her true self, and to define this as the only source of genuine relationships to other people. External obligations, whether to parents, children, or religion, are to be severely limited because they interfere with a person's capacity for self-love and relatedness. In its purest form, the therapeutic mentality denies all forms of duty or commitment in relationships, replacing these values with the ideal of full, open, honest communication among self-actualized individuals. Like the classic obligation of the client to therapist, the only requirement for the therapeutically liberated lover or spouse is to share feelings fully with his or her partner.[136]

Christopher Lasch believes that in the late-twentieth-century America, therapy had replaced religion in providing the core values in adult lives. As he puts it:

...even when therapists speak of the need for 'meaning' and 'love,' they define love and meaning simply as the fulfillment of the patient's emotional requirements. It hardly occurs to them to encourage the subject to subordinate his needs and interests to those of others, to someone or some cause or tradition outside himself. [137]

In Lasch's bitter words, mental health has come to mean "the overthrow of inhibitions and the immediate gratification of every impulse." He quotes Woody Allen in the movie *Sleeper*: "I believe in sex and death."[138]

Clearly one has a choice between two competing truths. In opposition to views similar to Greer, Crittenden, Rossi and Hewlett are those that slander the importance of motherhood and the family. In *Woman's Estate*, feminist Juliet Mitchell describes women with families as inclined to:

...small-mindedness, petty jealousy, irrational emotionality and random violence, dependency, competitive selfishness and possessiveness, passivity, a lack of vision and conservatism.[139]

And if, according to these feminists, the women in our families are despicable, by corollary so must be our families and our marriages.

Failing in the rhetorical war to separate women from their heterosexual partners, the feminist movement more recently revised their strategy and refocused more energy on impacting straight women. The new slogan, "Managed properly, women could have it all." The magic in this revised familial, business, sexual, and social mathematics gave rise to the "super mom" and the "domestic" foreign-national home care provider and daycare worker. In the feminist re-image, according to Arlie Hochschild:

The supermom is almost always white and at least middle class. In reality, of course, daycare workers, baby-sitters, au pairs, maids, and housekeepers are often part of two-job couples as well. This growing army of women are taking over the parts of a 'mother's work' that employed women relinquish.[140]

Hochschild notes that daycare workers often make their work a life vocation. At $10,000 or less annual salary these women have no hope of hiring others to clean their homes and supervise their kids. Yet the upper and middle-class working mother is held out as a role model to these women as much as to others.

Motorola CEO Micheline Bouchard, represents a success story for this new feminist model. Recognizing that competence alone was not going to get her to the top she recalls:

I discovered it was not that easy to get into the first level of management. It took me 10 years to get promoted. It took my (male) colleagues six or seven. I was angry, even aggressive. I just would not accept that kind of attitude. Then I realized my competence alone was not going to bring me to the top. I had to build a network of supporters.[141]

Unlike most working women who agonize over the endless juggling of home and office duties, Bouchard decided early on that her career would come first. She turned the care of her son and daughter over to a nanny. Says Bouchard:

I made a conscious decision to focus on my career. I had a nanny. I was lucky to have someone who would love and take care of my children.

One time, the nanny said, 'Don't feel guilty about not being with your kids. You can have peace of mind. I love your children and will take care of them, but they know you're the mom.'

After that Bouchard was able to act more naturally around her kids and put her guilt aside. She says,

We are a very close-knit family. The kids are still at home. We can talk for hours. My daughter can call with problems that may seem significant or insignificant. They can speak with me any time and have access to me even if I can't be there.[142]

She lives in Toronto during the week and commutes to south-shore Montreal on the weekends to be with the children and her husband, Jean-Claude, who is vice-president of sales and marketing for a Montreal high-tech firm. "I have to allocate time so I can have spare time," she jokes. "We're sailors." She and Jean-Claude dream of spending their retirement years sailing around the world, they would like to have a "65-footer."

Further evidence of class hypocrisy in the feminist movement is the anti-parenting policies refuting the need for liberal parental leave. Hewlett cites the ridicule she received from a feminist for advocating more social programs for mothers. She says:

Many of my feminist colleagues did not have children and were less than enthusiastic about families. Indeed, one of them accused me of trying to get a 'free ride' when I spoke out at a meeting for a college maternity policy. Didn't I understand that if women wanted equality with men, they could not ask for special privileges? She and her (childless) colleagues were passionate in their insistence that liberated women should strive to replicate the career patterns of men.[143]

Hewlett asks: "Does NOW realize that women are not men?"[144] She observes:

The hard-edged personality traits cultivated by many successful professionals – control, decisiveness, aggression, efficiency – can be directly at odds with the passive, patient, selfless elements of good nurturing. [145]

Catherine M. Wallace joins Hewlett, Rossi, Greer and Crittenden in voicing her concern for the collision of career-dominant feminism with good parenting:

...I worry about what this incessant, high-volume indoctrination [careerism] will reap when our children discover, perhaps decades from now, that having children and caring faithfully for children even in one's thirties will interfere with maximizing income and professional advancement. And I worry that our children hear these messages as explanations of why they do not have more of our time and attention. Are we teaching them that children as such are onerous burdens who interfere with parent's careers?...That they matter less to us than money?...Cost-benefit sex ed programs are not secular at all: They teach the worship of careers or money above all others gods.[146]

The anti-parenting study ends where it started, with another feminist who refuses to concede the legitimacy of motherhood and the need for children to receive a major part of their nurturing from the mother. Susan Chira discounts a strategy model put forth by women like Barbara Whitehead and Sylvia Ann Hewlett which advocates a fifty-fifty balance of family tasks, over the lifetime of the marriage, rather than in a given day or meal hour event. For Chira, the problem with this scenario is that such decisions often have lifelong ramifications, as Rhona Mahony pointed out in her book, *Kidding Ourselves*:

If the man [husband or father to most] is earning more money, his job is more important to the household economy and usually stays that way because he usually continues to advance while interruptions to a woman's career mean she will lag behind him in earning power. That means that the woman must often continue to make career sacrifices, even when it is supposedly her turn to race ahead, because the man's job contributes so much more to the household. The person who earns less often has less bargaining power, too.[147]

The meaning behind the term "bargaining power" has important implications in a lifelong commitment in marriage and in parenthood, but Christians can not adhere to such a competition-based paradigm as a central philosophy in their families. God has detailed that "the first shall be last and the last shall be first." To win in this paradigm requires humility and service. Love has a chance to spring from such guidance but not from feminist ideology. Michael Porter articulates bargaining power as a competitive essence in beating your opponent in the marketplace – economic Darwinism. A marriage is not a business. Parenting has nothing in common with the marketplace. Scripture records in marriage we are to:

Submit to one another out of reverence for Christ (Ephesians 5:15-21).

Family Risk Factors

Genetics, environment and providence play out in each family, insuring no two families are alike. A few family differentiators include: size, economic status, age of parents and children, mix of sexes, blend of biological origins, extent of sibling rivalry, health status, innate intelligence, hyperactivity, temperament, coping power, etc. What factors bring about family difficulty or promote relationship success is a complicated subject. Psychologist, Dr. Mary Pipher, says honest parents don't always raise honest kids and abusive parents sometimes have wonderful children. She has known very unhappy children to have come from "sensitive, child-focused" parents. Kids who are ignored sometimes become beautiful independent happy adults.[148] Nonetheless, most of us understand that mental, physical or sexual abuse is toxic for children. We're all familiar to some degree with the legacy of each. But recently it has become evident that more minor inadequacies in parenting produce long-term damage of a similar kind. According to Shelley Taylor, author of *The Tending Instinct: How Nurturing Is Essential for Who We Are and How We Live*, a "risky family" is one in which children don't get the warmth and nuturance that help them form the biological and emotional repertoire that early tending usually creates. When children are left to fend for themselves, and when children just don't get a lot of physical affection and warmth, they are at risk for emotional disorders such as depression or anxiety, and for health problems as well.[149]

According to Howard Bloom, a host of studies have shown that "babies can be given food, shelter, warmth, and hygiene, but if they are not held and stroked, they have an abnormal tendency to die." [150] Bloom cites a survey of seven thousand inhabitants of Alameda County, California, which showed that "isolation and lack of social and community ties" opened the door to illness and early demise. An even broader investigation by James J. Lynch of actuarial and statistical data on victims of cardiovascular disease indicated that an astonishing percentage of those killed by heart problems each year have an underlying difficulty that seems to trigger their sickness. This can be characterized as a "lack of warmth and meaningful relationships with others."[151]

In considering the impact on society of the new "variant families" we need to be aware of the elements of what Taylor calls the "risky family." We need to recognize the emotional consequences of these risky families, because as Taylor says, "it 'makes sense' that cold or hostile parents might produce a depressed or angry child."[152] Indeed, her study verifies the evidence presented by Howard Bloom that these families spawn chronic disease. Taylor writes:

We suspected that harsh or chaotic families would produce some damage in children, but we were completely unprepared for the sheer range of adverse outcomes these risky families seemed to foster. Vincent Felitti and his team studied 13,500 cases to correlate harsh, neglectful, conflict ridden family environments with medical health as an adult. Questions asked how often they were insulted, sworn at, put down, or physically hit or kicked to the point of injury, whether they had been sexually abused, and whether one or more in the family was a problem drinker or drug abuser. More than half of the study reported at least one condition. Those who had grown up in families marked by turmoil or neglect developed more health problems as adults. They were more likely to have had a bout of depression or to have tried suicide and they had more problems with drugs, alcohol, and sexually transmitted diseases. Significantly, they also had higher likelihood of heart disease, diabetes, stroke, chronic bronchitis, hepatitis, and cancer.[153]

Taylor observes that children from risky families often turn into adolescents who are risk-prone. They smoke, do drugs, and have sex early; often they do all of these things. Indeed, what is notable about adolescents is how these behaviors cluster. No great surprise there, you may think – bad peers, bad behaviors. But the peers didn't come first. "You pick your friends and they pick you." According to Taylor, offspring from risky families who reach adolescence with poor social and emotional skills and a moderate dose of peer rejection gravitate toward similar friends.[154] But why all these problem behaviors? Taylor takes this question and turns it on its head. Instead of asking why some adolescents smoke, drink, sleep around, and do drugs, she asks why many adolescents do not. After all, each of these behaviors – drinking alcohol, smoking, doing drugs, and having sex – provides its share of pleasures. So why don't "good kids" indulge themselves?

Adolescents who grow up in warm, nuturant families and elude these temptations typically have two answers to this question, writes Taylor:

First, they are worried about the consequences of their behavior – the risk of disease from unprotected sex and the fear of arrest if they possess illegal drugs, for example. They know they have a lot to lose from drugs, alcohol, smoking, and promiscuous sex, and they don't especially want to risk it.

Second, adolescents from nurturant families don't want their parents to find out. Despite their increasing freedom, they know that their parents still have a pretty good idea of what they do, and they don't want the discomfort and awkwardness of disappointing them. Adolescents from risky families often have parents who don't monitor their activities as well to begin with, and so the likelihood of their getting caught is decreased. To some degree, these adolescents also care less about getting caught. Their parents' love, affection, and esteem are not things they have much of already, and so they lack the motivation to preserve them. As Bob Dylan wrote, 'When you got nothing, you got nothing to lose.'[155]

In a landmark study Chicago sociologist James S. Coleman has shown that family background matters far more in determining student achievement than any attributes of the formal education system. Across a wide range of subjects in literature, science, and reading, "the total effect of home background is considerably greater than the total effect of school variables." Overall, Coleman estimates the home to be almost twice as powerful as the school in determining student achievement at age fourteen.[156]

Commenting on the discreet biological implications of risky families, Taylor notes that children who grow up in harsh families may have disrupted patterns of serotonin activity, which can lead to irritable depression and other mood problems. Dopamine, a neurotransmitter associated with positive mood, may also be in shorter supply in offspring raised in risky families. Most evidence is from animal studies only, but it is suggestive. Animals who are deprived of nuturant mothering early in life have permanent alterations in their dopamine and serotonin activity. Since using alcohol and drugs and even having sex can raise levels of these circulating neurotransmitters, at least temporarily, the adolescents who use them often find their moods improve. By comparison, when adolescents from supportive families say they don't do drugs, smoke cigarettes, or drink alcohol because these substances don't feel good to them, they mean it. They may not experience the same rewarding high that adolescents from risky families get from substance abuse.[157]

How do these combined problems in childhood and adolescence lead to the increased risk for disease in adulthood? These outcomes occur because of the long-term effects of grinding, chronic, unalleviated stress on the systems of the body. They come from the accelerated aging that poor tending fosters. In essence, these biological systems just wear out.[158]

When social bonds are strong they provide benefits similar to those that early tending from parents so clearly confers. These processes begin as early as the womb. At the moment of conception, the fetus develops a social life. For all practical purposes, the mother's social environment is the fetus's social environment. It is muffled and diluted to be sure, but the developing offspring is present and affected by everything the mother does and all that happens to her. When the mother goes to work, so does the fetus. When she listens to music, has a meal, or fights with her husband, the developing infant is there. But whether the mother and infant have support from others during this important time matters greatly to how the baby develops.[159]

When a mother is under stress from poverty, abuse, or fear of unemployment, for example, her body activates a hormone called corticotropin-releasing factor (CRF). Says Taylor:

CRF is necessary for proper development of the baby, but at high levels, it can be harmful. If such hormones are constantly bombarding the vulnerable hippocampus of the developing infant, they can affect the baby in ways that will influence his concentration, ability to learn, and even his temperament.[160]

Some startling evidence for this comes from Israel's seven-day war. Mobilization of all men of fighting age left many young, pregnant women not only under intense wartime stress, but without the support of their husbands. What was the effect on their children? Writes Taylor:

For the most part, their offspring were normal, but compared with boys born before the war, the boys born during the war were more difficult and harder to console. They were also more withdrawn, irritable, and hyperactive. They walked and talked a little later and took longer to be toilet trained. As they grew older, some more subtle and disturbing difficulties emerged. Compared to their peers, the war boys were more aggressive and antisocial. The stress hormones, so evident in their mothers and unrelieved because of the absence of social support from their fathers, took a modest but permanent toll.[161]

Both Taylor and Bloom have raised the importance of nurturing relationships as a unique and self-evident component of our health; initially even eclipsing our need of food, shelter and other material goods. All right, so how can a family have great relationships? What family models promote nurturing relationships among all members of the family? Like Taylor's approach to the issue of the causes of poor behavior, more can be learned by turning these relationship questions around – asking what prevents good relationships? From this perspective we need to view the orthodox, feminist and GBLTQ family models considering two factors: time deficit and relationship boundary development.

In her book *A Mother's Place*, Susan Chira, reveals the complexity of family dynamics and relationships from the mother's perspective:

Yet for the first time in my working life, I felt my job cut me off from my family. My days were longer, and the work felt relentless. As a reporter, I had frantic days and slow ones…As an editor, the pace never slackened; it only ricocheted from busy to crazy and back to busy again. In the first weeks of my new job, as I struggled to learn unfamiliar skills and absorb a different way of working, I was exhausted, distracted, and, much of the time, sad. It was harder than usual to shed work like a skin and embrace the joyful chaos of home. I arrived home and my children rushed to greet me, but I felt desolate at how much time I had missed with them. My husband took on several tasks I had once assumed: calling the pediatrician, investigating and setting up after-school classes for the children, talking to our baby-sitter. Rather than feeling relief that he was lessening my burdens, I was oddly bereft, as if performing those jobs had helped me feel close to the children.

Worst of all, I was hit by waves of unusual jealousy and self-doubt. Every time my son stretched out his arms to his father, I worried he had learned to turn to him instead of me. Eager for intimacy with my daughter, I found myself pressing her too intently for news about her day. I noticed how I clung more tightly to my son when I put him to bed, how I stayed with him longer than necessary because I needed to smell his skin and nuzzle his hair. One weekend morning, when I was too exhausted even to play with the children, I struggled to hold back tears, lashing myself with the same accusations that enraged me when others leveled them at working mothers.[162]

The Time Deficit:

Most parents want to spend more time with their children. Writes Chira: "Of all the costs of working, the most profoundly mourned and anguished over is the lack of family time." And this is proven consistently as parents confess their guilt in polls and interviews. Many parents believe they must put in long hours to save their jobs. With service jobs one of the fastest-growing sectors, more people must work at nights and on weekends, and about one-sixth of American parents of children under age six work split shifts, which can offer each parent time with children but less time together as a family.[163] Arlie Hochschild describes double-income households as a manic assembly line, where children run through their paces at the caprice of adults who do not even have the time for a game of catch or to read their child's poem.[164] William Mattox, of the Family Research Council, struck a typical chord in saying: "Couples who work a combined 80-hour week find themselves too pooped to parent."[165] Chira concludes, "It's time to quit pretending the two-career model is good for children."[166]

Over the last four decades there has been a sharp decline in the amount of time parents spend caring for their children. According to economist Victor Fuchs, children have lost ten to twelve hours of parental time per week since 1960.[167] Parental time has been squeezed by the rapid shift of mothers into the labor force; by escalating divorce rates and the abandonment of children by their fathers; and by an increase in the number of hours required on the job. Today the average worker puts in six hours more on the job per week than in 1973.[168] A prime cause of this decrease in parental time is the enormous shift of women into the paid labor force. In 1960, 30 per cent of mothers worked; by 1988, 66 per cent of all mothers were in paid labor force. This dramatic increase has eaten into the amount of time mothers are able to devote to their children.[169]

University of Maryland sociologist John Robinson has shown that the more hours mothers are employed, the fewer hours they can give to "primary-care activities" such as playing with and talking to children; dressing, feeding, and chauffeuring children; and helping with homework. According to Robinson, employed mothers spend an average of six hours each week in primary child-care activities – just under half the average time logged by non-employed mothers and roughly twice that of fathers (employed or non-employed). Using his ratios, the double-income parents spend nine hours a week with their children and single income parents spend fifteen hours or 40 per cent more time. Extrapolated over 13 years to adolescence, the single income child will receive 4,056 additional hours of parental tending; by age 18 another 1500 hours.

The data shows that the amount of "total contact time" – defined as time parents spend with children while doing things – has dropped 40 per cent during the last quarter-century.[170] This drop is significant, says Hewlett, because many of the things parents do with children, whether it's visiting Grandma or shopping for groceries, play an important role in building strong parent-child relationships and in giving families a shared identity. Studies that focus on "all-out, undisturbed, down-on-the-floor-with-the-blocks time," fail to provide an accurate gauge of parent-child interaction precisely because they do not recognize the importance of just being together.[171]

The term *Second Shift*, coined by Arlie Hochschild in her book by that name, is loaded with relationship significance. The second shift takes on particular meaning within a paradigm she calls the "stalled revolution." The "Second Wave" revolution brought women into the workplace in double the numbers of the 1950s. Some of these women, previously fully engaged at home, or whose mother had previously devoted an entire life to their nurturing, soon found that the need for domestic duties had not disappeared, but beckoned relentlessly. Hence the second shift in the home had to be "filled." Feminist liberation ideology made no attempt to tally family domestic duties into their calculations. To the contrary, in their eyes it was through these very duties that women's oppression was manifested. Their minimization strategy saw more state intervention as the panacea – more contraception education, more support for single mothers, more abortion clinics, funded abortions, and universal daycare. Unfortunately for the liberation movement, the death of the Equal Rights Amendment (ERA) and the continued reticence of government to fund a national daycare system has left all women in an uncomfortable compromise position. (See Chapter 2, Third Wave Feminists, for current revolution goals, which still include an ERA). Reluctantly and later came a feminist demand for men to take on more of the second shift duties.

Addressing the fact that there is no more time in the day than when wives stayed at home, Hochschild created the paradigm of "a speed-up in work and family life." She says it is mainly women who absorb this "speed-up." In her study twenty per cent of men shared housework equally. Seventy per cent of men did more than a third and less than half the work, and 10 per cent did less than a third of the duties.[172] For comparison Danielle Crittenden cites polls by the Gallup Company revealing that 85 per cent of married people today say the husband helps with the housework, 73 per cent say he helps with cooking, and 57 per cent say he helps with the dishes.[173] Compared with the feminist patriarchal analysis of the 60s, 70s and 80s, which claimed the vast majority of husbands did next to nothing at home, these figures are an important start toward the feminist ideal. Here for historic truth, Crittenden points out that a survey in 1949 found that 62 per cent of husbands helped with the housework, 40 per cent with the cooking, and 31 per cent with the dishes.[174] The first thing to go in war is the truth!

Notwithstanding these conflicting data, Hochschild explains that one reason women feel more strained than men is that they often do things in parallel while men do activities in series. Women juggle job, children and housework; apparently men juggle job and children. Women "mother" the house and men "mother" the children. "Women spend more time on maintenance, feeding and bathing children, enjoyable to be sure, but often less leisurely or 'special' than going to the zoo."[175]

The use of "shift" in place of "homemaking" carries more significance. Hochschild explains that the term came from a woman, who borrowed it from industrial life. Although the woman didn't want her family life reduced to a job, as she put it, "You're on duty at work. You come home, and you are on duty. Then you go back to work and you're on duty."[176] Hochschild says:

In the era of a stalled revolution, one way to reverse this devaluation is for men to share in that devalued work, and thereby help to revalue it.[177]

For double income couples and families this advice brings the best promise of a positive win-win outcome. Many working mothers are already doing all they can at home. She forcefully argues two issues: "Now it's time for men to make the move. In an age of divorce, marriage itself can be at stake," and "if women want men involved at home, they will have to share the power and the respect for the work it takes."[178] Here perception is as important as reality.

Given practical time constraints and their consequences upon family dynamics and relationships, the notion that a freer sex ethos, as espoused by Emma Goldman, Margaret Sanger and Kate Millett, might bring improvement to the family domestic situation lacks credibility. Similarly, the idea that some GBLTQ family variant, with additional sexual relationships to integrate and manage, can somehow be equal to or better than a monogamous orthodox family model, seems flawed. If these extra marital affairs are open, the marriage and thus family intimacy is weakened. If the extra-marital affairs are secret, the impact is worse. Dr. Barry Lubetkin, president,

American Board of Behavioral Psychology, reminds us of the difficulties and the toll of conducting sustained extra-marital affairs:

First let me say that I believe it always has costs – emotional costs. It doesn't come free. Human beings are not built to be that deceptive for that long a period of time. I think it is an exhausting effort to keep that information away from a spouse….I think that people who are planning for a long-term affair need to be prepared for long-term consequences – depression, anxieties, what have you.[179]

Not surprising, Lubetkin concludes that "serial monogamous relationships disrupt families."[180]

Boundaries:.

Mary Pipher observes that nonstop data blurs the boundaries that hold our lives in place. Boundaries are obscure between places and times, between sexual and violent material, between funny and sad, trivial and important, news and entertainment and fact and fiction. Public and private behaviors are indistinct and the boundaries between childhood and adult disappear. Time as a boundary is a major threat to the family. Shops used to be closed on Sundays and after six at night. Town whistles signaled when to rise, eat and go home for lunch and dinner. Everyone's life had more or less the same structure. Now television operates non stop, along with many convenience and grocery stores, automatic tellers and busses.[181] The culture we live in seems bent on irradicating boundaries – points at which we say no; lines beyond which we recognize danger; volumes of consumption beyond which marginal utility is negative; conditions under which two sides of a relationship flourish or beyond which they atrophy.

Psychologists Henry Cloud and John Townsend (introduced in Chapter 1) observe that external boundaries help define relationships with others and internal boundaries regulate our soul and set personal responsibilities for ourselves. Together they define "what is me and what is not me."[182] They write:

We've all been around middle-aged people who have the boundaries of an eighteen-month-old. They have tantrums or sulk when others set limits on them, or they simply fold and comply with others to keep the peace. Remember that these adult people started off as little people. They learned long, long ago to either fear or hate boundaries.[183]

Developing boundaries in young children is that proverbial ounce of prevention. According to Cloud and Townsend, if we teach responsibility, limit setting, and delay of gratification early on, the smoother our children's later years of life will be.[184] And the simpler our parenting. Refuting anarchist child-rearing ideology, they contend that boundaries play a primary role in self-fulfillment and avoiding the burnout of child, parent or spouse. Their advice:

Our limits create a spiritual and emotional space, a separateness, between ourselves and others. This allows our needs to be heard and understood. Without a solid sense of boundaries, it becomes difficult to filter out our needs from those of others. There is too much static in the relationship.[185]

The purpose in raising the boundaries issue again is not just because their establishment and maintenance are important (which was shown in Chapter 1), but rather the fact that nurturing boundary development is not possible without the investment of time and energy. In a metaphor where the family is considered a market economy, then "time" would be the "currency" of exchange. Without investing time into spousal and parental relationships there can be little relationship and even less boundary definition. Stephen Covey developed the illuminating paradigm of the "emotional bank account." In personal relationships, acts of commitment, dependability, integrity, unselfishness, honesty, fairness, and respect become emotional deposits and failed commitments, broken promises, disrespect, abuse and other unloving actions are seen as withdrawals. As Troyer described earlier, the divorced dad who missed one pick-up timing by an hour would not have been in trouble, had there been other "deposits" that a child could draw upon. What of the child who receives only withdrawals? Is suicide not an action of declaring acute bankruptcy? Likewise, having your child get up at 0530 hours to ensure one hour of quality time per day will not achieve what Cloud and Townsend are advocating in boundary development or what Taylor and Bloom are warning to avoid risky child-rearing.

As Pipher shows, the threats to healthy boundary development and maintenance come from many and varied areas. In knocking down taboos, boundaries, and institutions, in order to create space for themselves, the GBLTQ liberation movement has resisted defining itself other than in terms of "inclusive," "positive," "open," "free," "pro-choice," and "minority." But none of these terms are of utility in resolving boundaries disputes or clarifying relations between husband and wife, parent and child, homosexual and heterosexual. A movement predicated on never using the "no" word on moral grounds or even in practical behavior is seamless and dangerous to others. The ideology has little to offer the family unit and purports mostly increased risk factors, such as less parenting time, less parenting priority, and less male and female (two-sex) parenting.

Cloud and Townsend conclude, "The basic problem in human relationship is that of freedom."[186] In reality freedom (also the sense of freedom) requires a context of constraint for its manifestation. For example, unconstrained by family relationships and other responsibilities, the careerist often becomes a driven, single identity man or women, isolated and heading for burnout, vulnerable to corporate whims. Unconstrained by moral or marriage bounds, the free sex adherent often lives in slavery to pleasure. No matter how many orgasms are reached, or partners had, the desire only deepens, and the inability to say no to one's urgings drives one deeper into despair and hopelessness.[187] The free sex activists must be challenged with questions like: When is it too early to engage in a sexual relationship and why? How many sexual partners are too many and why? Are there any sexual acts which are wrong and why? Are not "free sex" and "marriage" mutually exclusive ideas? Why would a movement bent on destroying boundaries wish to be granted marriage status?

Facing a feminist and GBLTQ tidal wave (of experimental, variant, liberating, and sex-dominant cultural notions), which batters unceasingly at the heterosexual family's foundation, are the real "cornerstones of civilization" – a happy affirmed tending mother, beside whom is a loving supportive husband, and behind them, their children. This is not a mother who has no life beyond the home, but one who lives in a society that recognizes that families go through cycles where tending must be the priority. Successful families, and by macro-logic, successful societies, need to uphold family-oriented priorities and policies. Here the longstanding legislated definition of marriage – the unique institution for heterosexual pairing and child rearing – acts as a boundary marker for societal protection. Like a harbor breakwater, the traditional definition dissipates the impact from the battering of anti-marriage and anti-parenting influences on this last heterosexual and procreative space. The societal turbulence negatively impacting some 97 per cent of society, resulting from the redefinition of marriage for a very few "committed GBLTQ monogamists" (perhaps much less than 1 per cent of society) dwarfs the potential benefits.

Here government must establish the appropriate constitutional balance between "individual rights-based preferences" and "communal and democratic societal preferences." In Chapter 8, marriage models will be examined including the "paradoxical" idea of homosexual marriage. Some argue that giving GBLTQ equal marriage rights with heterosexuals will have little or no negative impact on the heterosexual family. The entirety of this book begs to differ. In the last chapter is a list of philosophical questions which society, as a whole, needs to ask. These are issues of democracy and the direction of society – do we want more of something, less of another within our nation. Those who contend that the majority should be silenced by the Charter of *Individual* Rights and Freedoms guaranteeing self-determination of sexual orientation must explain how such an "individual" rights-based premise applied to gays and lesbians should not also be used by people with a bisexual, polygamist or a man-boy orientation. Redefining marriage opens a Pandora's Box of family risk factors, which really need to be contained, and indeed, diminished. No doubt somewhere in Canada or the United States there is a "loving and committed" bisexual trio wishing societal affirmation and to be united in legal matrimony.

Teen Sexual Liberation

The anarchist web site (http://flag.blackened.net)[188] under the title: "What is the anarchist position on teenage sexual liberation?" reads:

One of the biggest problems of adolescence is sexual suppression by parents and society in general. The teenage years are the time when sexual energy is at its height. Why, then, the absurd demand that teenagers 'wait until marriage,' or at least until leaving home, before becoming sexually active? …Sexual freedom is the most basic and powerful kind, and every conservative or reactionary instinctively shudders at the thought of the 'social chaos' it would unleash – that is, the rebellious, authority-defying type of character it would nourish. This is why 'family values,' and 'religion' (i.e. discipline and compulsive sexual morality) are the mainstays of the conservative/reactionary agenda. Thus it is crucially important for anarchists to address every aspect of sexual suppression in society. And this means affirming the right of adolescents to an unrestricted sex life….anarchist proposals for teenage liberation are based on the premise that unrestricted sexuality in early childhood is the necessary condition for a healthy sexual freedom in adolescence.

Applying these insights to our own society, it is clear that teenagers should not only have ample access to a private room where they can be undisturbed with their sexual partners, but that parents should actively encourage such behavior for the sake of their child's health and happiness (while, of course, encouraging the knowledge and use of contraceptives and safe sex in general as well as respect for the other person involved in the relationship)....

For many parents the notion of teenage sexual liberty, as espoused by the authors of the above, is truly their worst nightmare. Yet public schools often allow social agencies, most of which are not as forthright as the authors at *Flag.blackened.net*, into our schools essentially proselytizing the students into free sex or positive sex philosophies.

Glorianne M. Leck contends that public schools should affirm the value of sexual diversity:

It is the political goal of generating democratic values that remains and must be seen as the primary function of public schooling in a democratic state...[therefore] the job of school personnel is to facilitate social interaction and to provide each child with a full opportunity for success within a compulsory public school setting. That means it is not appropriate to ask someone to hide – or deliberately try to make invisible – the sexual diversities represented within and among the students in our schools. It is rather to allow sexual, racial, religious and other identities to be disclosed and/or developed in a safe, considerate, and healthy manner without violent imposition on or interference from others who would try to consider their own identity issues and/or ideological biases. That means to me that gender; sexual orientations; affections; preferences; age privileges; and racial, religious, and political, and/or personal power are matters to be understood and negotiated under protection of as well as scrutiny of the public eye.[189]

Most will agree that teaching respect for homosexually oriented individuals is appropriate and right. Abuse in all its forms is wrong. However, demanding affirmation of homosexual behavior and/or positive sex behavior goes beyond the ethic of tolerance, and in fact becomes intolerance when it violates the value systems of many. Applying Leck's vision of educational responsibilities does not require the student's acceptance or "conversion" to some notion of pluralistic inclusivity. Respect of one another's different religious beliefs does not require, for example, that the Muslim accept Christianity, Witchcraft or any other belief system as equal. It is not the domain of schools to teach its students what sexuality to value. Racial and ethnic prejudice discriminates against an unchangeable and morally neutral aspect of another person's nature. However, disapproval of some types of sexual behavior is not the same as being "prejudiced," "bigoted," or "hateful" toward people because of their race. When gay author Larry Kramer, wrote *Faggots* (1978), warning gay men of their lifestyle that "spares no one and nothing," he was not "prejudiced." When he and gay AIDS activist Bill Kraus expressed disapproval of homosexual behavior during the 80s AIDS crisis, they were not "bigoted." When Gabriel Rotello wrote in *Sexual Ecology: AIDS and the Destiny of Gay Men*, that gay sexual practices brought on the AIDS pandemic in North America, he was not "hateful." When a parent writes a book like this one, to defend his daughter's religious beliefs, it is not anymore "homophobic" than the actions of Kramer, Kraus and Rotello; all who wished for less denial and greater acceptance of the truth.

In the spirit of Leck, one would hope that a presentation on homosexuality would be balanced and informative. When Mary (my daughter) came home from the presentation on homosexuality at her school, she brought with her a pamphlet by Calgary Birth Control Association (CBCA) titled, *What Everyone Should Know About Lesbian, Gay, Bisexual, Two-Spirited & Transgendered Youth*. Portions of the pamphlet are as follows (some lines have already been quoted):

Have Courage Oppose Homophobia

At CBCA we believe that sexuality is a <u>*natural and healthy*</u> *part of life which should be valued and respected. In our work towards equality, we acknowledge discrimination and promote the right to* <u>*positive sexual health*</u> *for all people.*

Our sexuality develops over time. Don't worry if you aren't sure. <u>*The teen years are a time of figuring out what works for you, and crushes and experimentation are often part of that*</u>*. Over time, you'll find that you're drawn mostly to men or to women – or both – and you'll know then.* <u>*You don't have to label yourself today*</u>*.*

<u>*It takes real courage to explore your feelings and to acknowledge*</u> *– even to yourself –* <u>*your sexual orientation.*</u> *The first step toward self-acceptance is to be honest with yourself. Few things are more satisfying than being your whole self.*

Although it's great to be able to share all of who you are, only you can decide when (and to whom) you're ready to come out. <u>*Choose carefully – not everyone will be supportive.*</u> <u>*Making contact with other gay, lesbian, bisexual, transgendered and two-spirited youth can be an important source of support*</u>*.*

Being lesbian, gay, bisexual, two-spirited or transgendered is a <u>*totally normal and healthy expression of self. At least 10% of any community – at any given time in history – is gay, lesbian or bisexual. That means that in [your city] at least one in every ten youths is gay, lesbian or bisexual*</u>*.*

One of the hardest things for gays, lesbians, bisexuals, two-spirited and transgendered people <u>*to deal with is other people's homophobia. Sometimes people can be mean*</u>*.*

Although it still exerts its <u>*ugly power, homophobia*</u> *is old. All over the world, people are beginning to see that* <u>*hatred and fear of people*</u> *who are different to themselves are destructive to us all. If this news has not reached your city, town, high school, peer group, it will.* <u>*People all over the world are speaking out against hatred and discrimination. It's the only right thing.*</u>

Furthermore, this pamphlet is a testimony to the strategy that the ends justify the means. I didn't like the pamphlet three years ago and I still don't. The underlined segments in my view represent errors of omission and commission, and the use of the term homophobia in the pamphlet is a manipulative construct to put the reader on the defensive. Furthermore the pamphlet violates the notion of any sensitivity to the majority of it's readers. Handing such a pamphlet to any typical class of 45 students, in either Canada or the United States, would surely place the text in the hands of dozens of Christians, not to mention Muslim, Jewish, and other students of theistic faith. What are they to think? And do the authors care? The answers are "it doesn't matter, change your faith," and "no we do not care." Here Leck's educational vision of "generating democratic values," appears to miss the goal of an honest and fair dialogue on the issues. Mary's Public School had not ensured that the subject of homosexuality was "understood and negotiated under protection of as well as scrutiny of the public eye."

Two years after the guest speaker incident with my oldest daughter, I was in the student counseling office at the same High School, with my youngest daughter. On the wall in the waiting area was a poster advertising a web site for students wishing to connect with Gay and Lesbian Community Services Association (GLCSA). At home I visited the main web site www.glcsa.org. Within seconds a drop-down response window said the following, asking for my vote:

Cut vs. Uncut. Please sing-a-long... 'Penis in the morning, penis in the evening, and penis at suppertime. When you crave for penis, tell me what's your favorite kind?' Crash Helmet (CUT); Turtle Neck (UNCUT); It doesn't really matter.

I don't believe schools adequately review such web sites and if they do, the links are often the source of other problem areas. Much of the text at this web site was full of errors of omission and commission. At *(http:// www.glcsa.org/ok/sex.htm),* under the topic "Homosexuals Choose to be Gay, Lesbian, or Bisexual," the authors refute the idea that GBLTQ have any choice in expressing their sexuality:

This myth does not consider the biological nature of all people's sexual orientation....homosexual, bisexual, and heterosexual orientations are an example of the biological diversity of human beings, a diversity with a genetic basis. ...Now knowing the above information, it may not make much sense to suggest that homosexuality is a choice. The lived experiences of homosexuals also suggest that homosexuality is not a choice. Many homosexuals have an awareness that they are different than other people of their own gender or even that they are oriented toward members of their own gender at a very early age.

This position rejects a ton of contradictory scientific evidence, loses credibility with bisexuality and ignores Kinsey's own Continuum Model. The notion of just polar extremes (Kinsey 6 or 0) – 100 per cent homosexual or heterosexual, or a Kinsey 3 in the middle ignores the results of numerous studies and testimonies. We have already studied the facts of reorientation.

CBCA and the authors of this web site make no attempt to comment on the risks of "experimentation" and its impact on orientation. If, as male swinger's claim, they can indoctrinate a heterosexual wife into wanting bisexual behavior in a few parties, what can happen to an experimenting 12-year-old? According to *FreeToBeMe*, having sex with another person of the same-sex will not tell you whether you are gay or lesbian. What it will tell you is that your body is designed to respond to physical and sexual touch, and that sex can be enjoyable and pleasurable. And that by itself won't tell you whether you are gay or lesbian. As well, if you do not want to be gay or same-sex attracted in your adult life, it would be best not to experiment sexually. Such experimentation builds a connection in your mind between (sexual) pleasure and being with someone of the same-sex. This makes change a bit harder than for someone who is attracted to the same-sex but has never acted on it. Experimentation may also reduce the possibility that you will experience your sexuality becoming more and more heterosexual in orientation by itself as you grow up.[190]

Drawing again from the GLCSA web site (www.glcsa.org/ok/recruit.htm), the authors under the title "Homosexuals Were Recruited to be Homosexuals," say "It is not possible to recruit." Here is the "gay gene" hypothesis in a different form. The web site states:

Regardless of how long it takes a homosexual person to find the courage, or feel safe enough, to admit his or her own feelings, people must keep in mind that it is likely the sexual orientation of all people has a biological and genetic basis. Consequently, it would be impossible to recruit heterosexuals to be homosexuals given that heterosexuals are genetically and biologically structured to always be heterosexuals.

They continue with another error of commission referring to Kinsey's report (1948) claiming he found in his samples "that approximately 13 per cent of men and 8 per cent of women had more homosexual experiences than heterosexual experiences." Actually Kinsey claimed 13 per cent had had at least one homosexual contact that resulted in an orgasm.[191] They admit that other surveys have shown fewer proportions of homosexuality within their samples, as low as 4 per cent of men and 1 per cent of women, but go on to say a Calgary survey found 11.1 per cent of its sample to identify themselves as homosexual or bisexual.

The web site reiterates, "Gay, lesbian, and bisexual people and their organizations do not recruit others." Rather the site states:

Some gay and lesbian people have encouraged the existence of positive role models and safe places so that homosexuals have an opportunity to be 'true to themselves.'

How is one to view "role model" and "opportunity to be true to themselves" against the Ancient Greek "pederasty family structure" now advocated by homosexuals Marshall Kirk and Hunter Madsen (see "A Scriptural Boundary for Man-Boy Sex?" Chapter 5). Moreover, Alfred Kinsey would argue against their notion of being "true" to an innate self, which is waiting to be discovered. Biographer, James H. Jones, writes:

In essence, Kinsey argued that sexual identity was largely the result of how people, responded to their early sexual experiences. 'After one has a pleasurable first expe-

rience, of either sort,' he explained, 'he looks forward to a repetition of the experience with such anticipation that he may be aroused by the sight or mere thought of another person with whom he can make contact.' Reminding the young man of his own history, Kinsey argued that 'unsatisfactory experience, of either sort, will (as in your early contact with the heterosexual) build up a prejudice against any repetition of that experience.' Therefore, it seemed clear that sexual identity followed the pleasure principle. 'Whether one builds a heterosexual pattern or a homosexual pattern depends, therefore, very largely upon the satisfactory or unsatisfactory nature of his first experiences,' Kinsey declared.[192]

As explained in Chapter 5, "Consequences of Sexual Experimentation," Kinsey felt labels such as homosexual and heterosexual did not make sense. People engaged in homosexual acts; they were not homosexuals. Therefore the only proper use for the word was as an adjective, not as a noun. Pressing his point, he declared:

It would encourage clearer thinking on these matters if persons were not characterized as heterosexual or homosexual, but as individuals who have had certain amounts of heterosexual experience and certain amounts of homosexual experience.[193]

Returning to GLCSA's claim "It is not possible to recruit," one finds two clicks into this GLCSA web site (advertised at my daughter's High-School counseling office) ads for available GBLTQ members of Gaycanada. For example (modified):

> *London Lloyd, Divorced, 6'0, 180, Mixed color hair, Blue eyes*
> *Gender: Male Age: 45 My personality can be:*
> *Extroverted/Social, Intellectual, Loving/Caring, Romantic*
> *I identify my sexuality as: Gay*
> *My Body Type is: Chubby*
> *My overall Mannerisms tend to be: Masculine*
> *The degree of "Outness": To some people*

The National Association for Research and Therapy of Homosexuality (NARTH) advise that "the teen years aren't the best time to 'come out'?" They say confusion about sexual orientation is fairly common during adolescence, and it is risky to label teenagers "gay," "lesbian" or "bisexual," before they have the wisdom of adulthood and the opportunity to make a fully informed choice.[194] Life decisions requiring wise and mature judgment are best reserved for adulthood, at a time when they will be based on more than feelings. Says Dr. George Rekers, professor of neuropsychiatry and a specialist in psychosexual disorders at the University of South Carolina School of Medicine:

No service is done to our children by offering them lifestyle options before they are properly...able to...make informed choices about them. Counseling of a sexually questioning teen need not encourage such self-labeling. Initially, it is sufficient to acknowledge the student's experience of same-sex attraction; later, how to proceed in counseling should be determined by the student and his parents, after all the options are realistically offered.[195]

Ask yourself at what age would you wish public schools to unilaterally counsel children (individually) on sexual orientation questions and not defer to or involve the parents? At what age would you like the school to refer your son or daughter to the GLCSA web site without your permission?

This is where sex liberation ideology and GBLTQ activism seriously undermine supporting parents and therefore the traditional family. The potential GBLTQ adolescent is usually not sure of his or her identity. What voice should they follow? What does a welcome into the GBLTQ community entail? Is it appropriate for GBLTQ, positive sex and otherwise free sex advocates to counsel and mentor a minor without parental knowledge? NARTH offers more justification to delay decisions about sexual identity?:

When schools label some teenagers gay, there is a serious risk of mislabeling a portion of sexually confused students. A 1992 study of 34,707 Minnesota teenagers published in Pediatrics reported that 25.9 per cent of 12-year-olds are uncertain if they are heterosexual or homosexual. However, by adulthood, only about 2-3 per cent of adults will self-identify as homosexual. This means that almost 24 per cent of these 'sexually questioning' teens could erroneously be identified as homosexual if they are affirmed as gay by a school counselor or an on-campus gay club.[196]

Another study showed that early self-labeling as homosexual or bisexual is one of the top three risk factors for homosexual teen suicide attempts. The risk of suicide decreases by 80 per cent for each year that a young person delays homosexual or bisexual self-labeling.[197]

The author of a recent book, *Beyond Gay*, talks about his youthful struggle with homosexuality. He says he was fortunate not to have been influenced by gay on-campus clubs or counseling programs before he had a chance to meet the "wise and loving friends" who would later give him a broader perspective. "For this," he says, "I am deeply grateful."[198] Many factors can lead a "questioning" youngster into homosexual behavior – including curiosity, a feeling of not fitting in, the experience of earlier molestation, and a desire for attention and a sense of belonging. In particular, gender-nonconforming boys tend to idealize their male peers due to a sense of masculine inferiority. The teen years serve as a transitional phase when affectional, emotional and identification needs can easily be eroticized.[199]

The last area to look at under the title "Teen Sexual Liberation" is the literature that is circulated to our schools. The well-known and respected national organization "Parents and Friends of Lesbians and Gays" (P-FLAG) serves as a support group for parents seeking guidance for their homosexual children. P-FLAG is recommended as a resource group by the U.S. Department of Education and U.S. Department of Justice in its manual, "Preventing Youth Hate Crime." The many schools, community agencies, and even nationally syndicated newspaper columnists refer families to it. P-FLAG has affiliates in Canada (CBCA for example) and in all 50 states, with about 70,000 families among its membership.

However, a look at some of P-FLAG's literature and recommended books reveals the stereo-typical positive sex ethos. First-person stories aimed at teens tell in pornographic detail of the delight of a young girl's sexual seduction by her lesbian teacher; of gay relationships between teenage boys and much older men; and of the precise how-to's of masturbation. Teenagers are specifically encouraged to use only their feelings as a guide to sexual behavior; to be their own judge of what is right and wrong; and to "have fun" experimenting. If a sexual behavior feels good, the ethos says, it will tell them "who they are." Teenagers are encouraged to see religious traditionalists as mean-spirited and hypocritical, while at the same time, to see gay consciousness as "sacred." Says NARTH, "Were similar books recommended by parenting groups for 'straight' teenagers, they would be considered violations of community standards of decency."[200]

Some of the recommended books are relatively "tame" on the surface, justifying teenaged homosexual experimentation with the usual "This is me. This is who I am." Others go much further – glorifying sex with animals, witchcraft, feminist goddess worship, worship of sexual pleasure as a form of religion, promiscuity with hundreds of partners, bisexual orgies, and voyeurism. Ironically, one of their booklets, "*Beyond the Bible: Parents, Families and Friends Talk about Religion and Homosexuality*," has a section entitled, "Caution: Hate Groups." Listed organizations include Promise Keepers, Focus on the Family, Concerned Women of America, and Family Research Council.[201]

That pamphlet recommends that religious seekers read *Gay Soul: Finding the Heart of Gay Spirit and Nature*, a book which labels gay sex "sacred." In it, first-person stories are told of gay men delightedly flouting their vow of celibacy in seminaries; of a man reporting that he had a peak orgasmic experience during sex with God; and of sadomasochic torture being enjoyed by a psychotherapist as a mystical experience. Another writer in the anthology labeled as "sacred" the experience of incest between fathers and brothers. But the most damaging P-FLAG pamphlet is "*Be Yourself: Questions and Answers for Gay, Lesbian and Bisexual Youth*," which includes a recommended reading list specifically aimed at teenage readers. From the pamphlet's recommended book *Young, Gay and Proud!* by Don Romesburg, ed., AlyCat Books, 1995[202] – one of the "tamer" publications came the following.

In the chapter, "Getting Started":

There are all sorts of stupid rules, like that...guys shouldn't wear dresses. Girls aren't supposed to shave their heads. People might say that certain kinds of sex are dirty...we all know about all these 'rules'...Many of them are more than just foolish--they can be destructive...No one has the right to make anyone else feel bad about their sexuality or their sexual choices...There is no right or wrong way boys or girls should act, and sex by itself never hurt anyone. The only rules we need are simple: do what feels right to you, and take care not to hurt anyone else. That way, maybe we can all be comfortable with being the best thing of all – ourselves.

From the chapter for teenage girls, "Doing It: Lesbians":

In lesbian loving, there are no rules, and we don't want any...Being a lesbian means exploring.' (The author proceeds to suggest that her teenage reader masturbate, graphically describing how best to do so, and suggesting techniques for mutual masturbation with a girlfriend.)

No one can tell you what is right for you, but you...Sex with someone you choose, at a time and place of your choosing, can be exciting and fun...you're the only one that can know what you're ready for, and when.

The booklet *Be Yourself: Questions and Answers for Gay, Lesbian, Two-spirited and Bisexual Alberta Youth* was a literature reference on the pamphlet Mary brought home. This booklet is the result of a partnership of Planned Parenthood Alberta, PFLAG Calgary and International, and the Alberta Gay, Lesbian, Bisexual, Two-spirited Youth Outreach Project. Under the title "Will I Be Accepted?" the authors write:

Women weren't legally considered to be persons and therefore could not vote, hold or inherit property in Canada until 1929 when five Alberta women (The famous Five) fought for legal recognition as persons. It takes time to overcome prejudice and change attitudes. If you're gay, lesbian or bisexual, you're going to run into prejudice. Our society has a 'heterosexual assumption.' We're taught – by our families, our schools, our religions and the media – to assume that everyone is straight and we're often influenced to discriminate against those who aren't. That 'assumption' has begun to change only recently.

In symbolism this PFLAG/CBCA booklet and the previous referenced literature are representative of the philosophies embodied in what I am calling the "Pivot of Civilization" paradigm. A view that says among many things that families, marriage, religion, educational institutions and much of society must either be overhauled or neutralized. This last passage in particular is saying that Christianity and most other faith-based religions are wrong. On the battlefield of intolerance both sides are now eye to eye, face to face. Crying prejudice while concurrently trying to force one's values and behavior on everyone is doubly intolerant, in both thought and deed. The problem for feminists, GBLTQ activists and others in the Pivot of Civilization camp, is that tolerance should implicitly mean not criticizing the religious values of others. However, in the "postmodern era" where the secularist assumption is that theistic faith is dead, this taboo has been lifted and Christianity in particular has been ripe for attack. Highlighting the hypocrisy, Diana Alstad, co-author of the paper *Abortion and the Morality Wars: Taking the Moral Offensive* says:

...tolerance should be redefined so that people can criticize any beliefs, including religions, and show why certain ideas are wrong or harmful. This isn't forcing values or behavior on anyone. It's using the democratic marketplace of ideas as it is meant to be used – to win people's minds through reasonableness, argument and debate.[203]

Here both sides can agree with her:

Tolerating the intolerant is no longer tolerable. Tolerating those who consider themselves at war with us puts us in an untenable, dangerous, one-down position. I'm not favoring another form of intolerance; I'm redefining tolerance. I accept peo-

ple's right to be intolerant, but I have the right to fight against it and verbally challenge it.[204]

Abstinence

It is time to move beyond the view that sexuality is a natural force that needs liberation from a repressive society. School curriculum implies abstinence is an option, but the teaching of how to remain chaste or abstinent and why it is so important is missing. It is critical that abstinence be presented as the healthiest and only sensible choice. Curriculum teaches students to say no to drugs and alcohol but emphasis in sexual decision-making implies that most students are or will be sexually active – and it is their right to do so.

Before getting into the matter of abstinence and pre-marital sex, the following questions are offered to chart your current views on the issue. Anarchists, sex positive agencies like CBCA and Planned Parenthood, and pro-gay activists argue that with mutual consent, sex is morally alright under most circumstances. When the two parties concerned have consented voluntarily on the basis of adequate information, and the sexual interaction is not profitable for one at the expense of the other, or the benefit is disproportionately meager, then sex is permissible. Given that you have an unmarried son or daughter, at what age would you be happy to know he or she is sexually active with an opposite sex partner on a monthly or more frequent basis? (circle your choice)

Son or daughter with a partner of the same age?

9 – 10 – 11 – 12 – 13 – 14 – 15 – 16 – 17 – 18 – 19 – 20 – 21 – 22 – 23 – 24 – 25 – Never

Son or daughter with a partner three years older?

9 – 10 – 11 – 12 – 13 – 14 – 15 – 16 – 17 – 18 – 19 – 20 – 21 – 22 – 23 – 24 – 25 – Never

Son or daughter with a partner ten years older?

9 – 10 – 11 – 12 – 13 – 14 – 15 – 16 – 17 – 18 – 19 – 20 – 21 – 22 – 23 – 24 – 25 – Never

Given that you have an unmarried son or daughter, at what age would you be happy to know he or she is sexually active with a same-sex partner on a monthly or more frequent basis? (circle your choice)

Son or daughter with a partner of the same age?

9 – 10 – 11 – 12 – 13 – 14 – 15 – 16 – 17 – 18 – 19 – 20 – 21 – 22 – 23 – 24 – 25 – Never

Son or daughter with a partner three years older?

9 – 10 – 11 – 12 – 13 – 14 – 15 – 16 – 17 – 18 – 19 – 20 – 21 – 22 – 23 – 24 – 25 – Never

Son or daughter with a partner ten years older?

9 – 10 – 11 – 12 – 13 – 14 – 15 – 16 – 17 – 18 – 19 – 20 – 21 – 22 – 23 – 24 –25 – Never

If your children were perfectly versed in sex knowledge (www.positive.org) and "safe sex practices," as Gabriel Rotello critiques them, would your choices change? Chances are, if your views remain unchanged by level of safe sex knowledge and by the age of the child's sexual partner, you see the issue as a moral matter and not a simple risk/benefit analysis.

Few would argue that empowering our children to make an informed decision on when to start a sexual relationship has merit. The United States, for example, has one of the highest teenage pregnancy, abortion and childbirth rates in the West. Each year, one million girls under the age of 20 (1 in 10) become pregnant and 43 per cent of all adolescent girls will have been pregnant at least once by the time they turn 20. And for those who keep their babies, numerous studies have shown that parenthood is likely to lead into poverty.[205] According to a National Survey of Family Growth (NSFG) study, from which these data are taken, pregnancy, abortion, and birth rates were in fact substantially higher after adjustment for sexual experience and sexual activity. In essence the real risk of pregnancy for sexually active teens was more than 1 in 5 in 1995.[206]

The NSFG data suggest that the decline in teen pregnancy rates since 1991 is attributable to a decrease in the proportion of teen women who are sexually experienced and sexually active. Similarly, data from the National Survey of Adolescent Males indicates that the prevalence of sexual experience among never-married males aged 15 to 19 years was lower in 1995 (55 per cent) than in 1988 (60 per cent). Improvement in contraceptive use at first intercourse also may have played a role in decreasing the risk of unintended pregnancy for some teens. NSFG data show that from 1988 to 1995, contraceptive use at first intercourse increased from 65 per cent to 76 per cent. However, NSFG data on current methods of choice – defined as the methods used during the previous month – showed no change from 1988 to 1995. In both years, 18 per cent of sexually active teens aged 15 to 19 years (7 per cent of all teens) were not current contraceptive users.[207]

While the above data is encouraging as a trend, there is a large jump in sexual activity among teens under 16. Some 40 per cent of 15-year-olds report being sexually active, according to the Centers for Disease Control and Prevention, compared with just 10 per cent of 15-year-olds in 1970. These and even younger children have the highest odds of contracting a sexually transmitted disease, and if pregnant, are the most likely to drop out of school. Of these girls, nearly 1 in 3 gives birth to a second child within two years.[208]

These statistics usually invoke one of two responses from parents and educators. One opinion calls for more emphasis on abstinence, the other asks for more effective education to increase contraceptive savvy. Proponents of abstinence seek credit for the overall heartening trend as abstinence initiatives continue to bear fruit. In 1998, 700,000 young people (up from 450,000 in 1997) signed cards pledging abstinence until marriage as part of the *True Love Waits* movement. And a *New York Times/CBS News* poll showed that nearly half of all teens now say sex before marriage is "always wrong."[209] Some argue the drop in pregnancy rates as evidence that the sexual counter-revolution is gaining ground. This notion is supported by a March 1997 study, which found that 95 per cent of people surveyed believe teens should be completely abstinent.[210] Going over parents and politicians, *Newsweek* surveyed what kids thought:

Rejecting the get-down-make-love ethos of their parents' generation, this wave of young adults represents a new counterculture, one clearly at odds with mainstream media and their routine use of sex to boost ratings and peddle product….It's clear that religion plays a critical role in this extraordinarily private decision. But there are other factors as well: caring parents, a sense of their own unreadiness, the desire to gain some semblance of control over their own destinies.

Newsweek also reports from a Centers for Disease Control study, that the number of high-school students who say they've never had sexual intercourse rose by almost 10 per cent between 1991 and 2001.[211]

Advocates of sex education claim the improvements are the result of more effective contraception practice. Condom use among young women has risen sharply, from 18 per cent in the 1970s to 36 per cent in the 1980s to 54 per cent in 1995. In 1995, 91 per cent of women said they had been taught safe-sex methods of preventing AIDS transmission. Both sides can claim some solace in the trends, still it seems equally reasonable to assume that the AIDS virus, which caused considerable shift in gay sex practices (volume and type) has also contributed to the "safer" trend of less sex among our youth.

If condom use is up while sexual activity is down (both beneficial inclinations), is there common ground for teaching both abstinence and "safe sex?" Joyce Elders in the early 90s, favored the middle road. She told *U.S. News* that she supports newer hybrid programs that "stress abstinence," particularly for the youngest teens, but believes it is unrealistic to demand abstinence only. She wants to "give kids the tools" to resist peer and societal pressures to have sex and aims to induce a new sense of social values in the young. Says Elders:

We need to have our kids understand that sex is good but it has to be appropriate. Teens should be taught to make sound decisions about sex if they choose to have it including informed choices about birth control.

But, responds Family Research Council Director Gary Bauer, that approach sends a mixed message, akin to saying "it's illegal to shoplift, but if you do it, here are some tips on how to avoid getting caught."[212]

The difficulty in the sex education issue is: (1) how to impart necessary knowledge of healthy sex practice without promoting the idea that teens should be "promiscuous" or "sexually active," and (2) how to empower teenagers and kids to say no. Exacerbated by a politically charged atmosphere for policy and curriculum development, most schools (like my daughter's) continue to give facts through their own staff or outside agencies in the absence of a philosophy of what to do with the information. And this particularly places a policy of voluntary restraint (abstinence) at a disadvantage, since the whole concept can only be properly developed through instruction in values. I have shown that agencies like Planned Parenthood, NOW,

GBLTQ activists, Parents, Families and Friends of Lesbians and Gays (PFLAG) and CBCA, all advocate the "sex positive" ethos. To the extent that they have influence on school boards and as instructors they promote a philosophy of "early experimentation" and that teens should be engaging in sex.[213] Moreover, in doing so, these agencies tacitly say it is all right to disobey your parents on the issue. On the other hand, a strategy that teaches solely abstinence would reinforce the values of a major portion of any student body, but fail miserably to give the other significant portion of students protective knowledge they need. A value-oriented approach needs to counter the "sex-positive" ethos while still allowing the cold facts of risky-sex hazard reduction. The assumption behind such an approach is that a properly informed teenager will most often make a sound decision. Thus a more comprehensive goal should be their enlightenment on a number of important issues left out of most sex education curriculum.

Chris, a 16-year-old from Longmont, Colorado, comments on an "enlightened" sex-ed package:

We watched their slide show in eigth grade and it just has pictures of all these STDs. It's one of the grossest things you have ever seen. I didn't want to touch a girl, like, forever.[214]

Harie Hughes tosses a pair of black fuzzy dice across the classroom floor. "Sex before marriage is like gambling," she tells students in her federally funded abstinence workshop, titled "Passion and Principles." Each number on the dice represents a risk – pregnancy, a sexually transmitted disease, a broken heart. Her presentation similar to the one Chris saw has screen fills of grotesque images – a uterus swollen by pelvic inflammatory disease, a penis oozing pus from gonorrhea. "Eeeeeeew," the students groan. Afterward, many seemed persuaded. "That totally changed my view on pretty much everything," says freshman Laura Hurst, 14. "Ohmigod."

Pat Wingret has established a short list of "basic truths about Teen sex":

(1) adolescents, especially girls, are more vulnerable to STDs than older people and the earlier teens initiate sex, the more likely they are to get infected; (2) kids are less likely to use a condom properly; (3) the fastest spreading STD is human papillomavirus (HPV) which can cause cervical cancer; (4) some STDs are not curable; (5) teens who use both birth control and a condom can still get infected; (6) alternative behaviors, such as oral sex, are not safer, as many teens believe, Virtually all STDs that can be transmitted through intercourse can also be spread orally; and (7) some STDs (genital herpes, syphilis, HPV) can cause lesions that may not be covered by a condom. Skin-to-skin contact with a lesion can spread the disease even if someone is wearing a condom.

Amanda also saw the full picture type of presentation. Could these gruesome images put them off sex for life? Chris and Amanda say "no." "They're sure that whoever they marry will be disease-free."[215]

The second difficulty in sex education deals with choice and the concept of mutual consent. How can a teen say no to a friend? The sex positive notion "Just remember, sex is only fun if everyone agrees on what they're going to do" or "if it is between consenting persons, why not," amounts to deception. In reality sex among youth doesn't happen in a tranquil levelheaded environment. Mate and peer pressures are tremendous. In setting the boundaries for sexual abuse, debate often centers on the notion of consent. First, what happens when a child or teenager does not resist but at a later date – as an adult for example – comes to feel coerced and harmed? In addition, the concept of consent implies that children and teenagers can give free consent. In our society teen pressure; and in incest cases, parental pressure from the father, can persuade their daughters to "consent" to sexual activities which the daughters later regret. Currently, the age of consent varies greatly. In Canada the age is 14 for both heterosexual or homosexual. In Pennsylvania, the age of consent is 14 except for same-sex sexual relations where it is 18.[216] In the Netherlands, as part of the political resolution of homosexual marriage rights, the State agreed to recognize homosexual marriage with the right of adoption, however, it excludes the right to alternative insemination for lesbian couples and the age of consent for homosexual sex was set at 12. Specifically, in the Netherlands sex between an adult and a young person at ages of 12 to 16 is allowed, as long as the young person consents. Sexual misconduct may only be prosecuted by complaint from the young person or the young person's parents.[217]

This boundary line is particularly sad even from our liberal North American perspective. As noted earlier, the American Psychiatric Association still draws the line for pedophilia at age 13. One cannot help but wonder why the Netherlands did not settle for age 11 or 10; and what was the original negotiating position of the GBLTQ community in that country? Such negotiations have no legitimacy from a Christian perspective, but even most secularists should sit up and take note. In as much as there is a difference between the heterosexual and homosexual ages of consent (Pennsylvania) there are likely grounds for discrimination. Yet for those wishing the age to be raised the GBLTQ age discrimination issue has less potency – the goal should be to raise the bar to the more mature age, rather than lower the standard to the earliest age. The dire "relativism" of the consent issue is illustrated in the threat posed by the European Economic Union to this hard won age of 12, in the Netherlands. A proposal has been approved by the European Parliament that would criminalize forced sex with minors. According to a gay spokesperson, the problem with the proposal is that it counts "seducing" as one of the forbidden methods of force – and since few unforced sexual liaisons take place without seduction, it basically criminalizes the majority of sex acts that involve someone under the age of 18.

The National Society for the Prevention of Cruelty to Children (NSPCC) completed a study entitled Child Maltreatment in the United Kingdom, based on interviews of 2,689 people aged between 18 and 24. According to the NSPCC's own summary, far more of the respondents had experienced unwanted sexual behavior with non-relatives than with family members. Nearly all occurred with people known to the child, the vast majority with "boyfriends" and "girlfriends." Up to 75 per cent of those reporting sexual acts against their wishes were female. [218] According to Statistics Canada more than half of young teen mothers are made pregnant by men in their 20s or older. The study examined the 72,000 teen pregnancies in Canada in 1992, 1993, and 1994. It found that 54 per cent of the babies born to mothers 17 or younger had fathers who were 20 or older at the time of birth. Sixty-three per cent of the fathers were at least three years older than the mothers. One quarter of the fathers were six years older or more. The numbers are particularly dramatic for the 771 babies born to girls aged 12, 13, and 14 during the three-year span. More than half – 51.2 per cent – of the fathers were legally adults and 25 per cent were 20 years or older.[219] Perhaps it is time we stopped the sex positive illusion that teens are having experimental sex with peers of equal sexual maturity. The statistics show that this is not a mutual *learning* phenomenon.

That women may actually be the losers in the liberation revolution is an idea just dawning on this generation of young women, who feel as sexually free as it is possible to feel and yet are so often powerless to experience anything more with the opposite sex than unsatisfying, loveless flings. Danielle Crittenden says, boys – even nice boys – rarely ask girls out anymore, to a movie or for coffee. Instead, young people go to big parties or out with each other in large packs, drink, pair off, and, if the mood suits, have sex. A female undergraduate at Georgetown University wrote in a campus publication about the sexual anarchy of college social life:

All men want to do is hook up – and most of them don't bother to call in the morning…these random hook-ups haven't added one iota of power to the average women…To be sure, there are lots of girls who aren't bothered by the casual overnight scene…But in the real world, the more casual that women allow their physical relationships with men to become, the less respect they earn. Men don't date because they don't have to.[220]

A young graduate of Princeton said:

It was gross, I had a boy friend between my freshman and senior year, thank God, which saved me from having to participate in the dating scene. Even for formal dances, boys wouldn't bother to ask girls to go with them, and some girls would get desperate the few nights before the dance, not wanting to just 'show up' or arrive in a group, so they'd call and ask out the boys themselves. It was brutal.[221]

Overlooking the "eye-popping" level of promiscuity recorded in a 1997 *New York* magazine cover story on sex at private schools, Crittenden was struck by the boy's old fashioned reactions to the girls who slept with them. She writes, even among these decadent, cynical teenagers, a surprisingly familiar morality play was taking place. While female students boasted like boys of their sexual experiences, they were aware that their reputations had been badly damaged and that the boys had lost respect for them. "Everybody knows who everybody's had sex with, and everything is reputation," acknowledges a female student from Columbia Prep. The boys learned quickly which girls were experts at giving sexual pleasure – "the queen of buffs" – and who slept with everyone – the "hos," "trocks," and "hoochies." The girls who continue to cling to their lovers offered sad and self-deluded excuses:

We're not just there [having sex in gangs]. We have a role….They get really territorial about us….They would be nothing without us.[222]

Crittenden concludes:

In order to keep the boy's attention, the girls were reduced to being grateful caregivers – the women the men always come back to in the end, who fetch them drinks, who are there for them when they strike out at bars, who nurse them when they're sick and even tidy up after them. This the deal of which liberationists should be proud.[223]

"Who do you think babies and holds their head over the toilet?" a girl named Alex told the *New York* reporter. "At the end of the night," said another girl, "if they've trashed somebody's house, the girls are like, 'We're sorry,' 'Thank you very much,' and 'we help clean up.'" But that wasn't exactly how the boys saw it. "I treat 'em how I meet 'em," said a male student callously. "If you meet 'em and the girl's …[performing oral sex] in the bathroom, then they're gonna get treated like that." The girls who sleep around "are not girlfriend material." Explained one, "You're not going to go out with a girl who's a shookie [slut]." Yet as one of the girls put it, in order to win the boy's attention and acceptance, "She has to be down and dirty. They have to see you not be a priss – be like a man basically."[224]

Writes Crittenden:

And there, in a sentence, is the catch-22 of sexual liberation – not just for the elite students of Manhattan private schools, but for all of us. The goal was for women to be as free as men to express their sexual desires, and as frequently, without consequence. But the truth is, of course, that there are consequences – and very predictable one's, of our grandmothers' I-told-you-so variety. There's a crude Yiddish expression that sums up the ancient sexual bargain between men and women: 'No chuppy, no schtuppy.' It means, literally, 'No marriage, no sex.' There's that other cliché, 'Why buy the cow when she's giving away the milk for free?' We may smirk at its primness, but as women – even liberated, sexually uninhibited women – we still know exactly what it means.[225]

Again, like Mary Wollstonecraft's vain pursuit of her lover Imlay or Emma Goldman's personal torture with Reitman's *insensitive* promiscuity, there is a double edged cut to *free sex*. The paradox is that all women who choose to compete in the market are bound by its amoral dynamics which say the best deal (high pleasure, low commitment) sells first; and in a free market, it says consumption of one woman does not limit consumption of another, and another, and another. After all they're free. The sexual revolution, from a male point of view, could be summed up as, "You mean I get to do whatever I want – and then leave? Great!" Crittenden says:

If men feel that they can flit from woman to woman, they will. They will enjoy our availability and exploit it to their advantage. But if women as a group cease to be readily available – if they begin to demand commitment (and real commitment, as in marriage) in exchange for sex – market conditions will shift in favor of women.[226]

Two phenomena need to be factored into the further analysis of abstinence. First, in the 1950s, less than 25 per cent of Americans thought premarital sex was acceptable; by the 1970s, the figure was 75 per cent. Second, between 1960 and 1980, the marriage rate dropped by about 25 per cent; the average age of marriage for both men and women rose steadily; and the number of divorced men and women jumped by 200 per cent. In 1972, the average age of marriage was 20; in 1996 the average was 24. Thus the impact of the sexual liberation and feminist movements has been the extension of singlehood by some half decade, along with delaying the reproductive window with it. All told, according to a study by *Adweek* magazine, single people as a percentage of the total American adult population rose from 28 per cent in 1970 to 41 per cent in 1993, when the sexual revolution was in full swing.[227]

Scott Stossel writes:

From the Kinsey reports onward, this constant tension between permissiveness and restraint, between old cultural authorities and new ones, led to a growing moral bewilderment. What was right? Nobody knew anymore. The sexual revolution and its aftermath caused this tension to intensify. A 1977 Time poll found that 61 per cent of Americans believed it was harder and harder to tell sexual right from wrong than in the past. And the most striking feature of the 1993 Janus Report on Sexual Behavior was the increase in uncertainty between its two polling periods....Perhaps the most confusing thing was that 'science,' deployed by Kinsey to establish what Lionel Trilling called a 'democratic pluralism of sexuality,' was now, in the age of herpes and AIDS, fused to moral arguments for monogamy and restraint. The Age of Aquarius turned into the Age of Confusion.[228]

Given these facts, the positive sex lobby should concede the legitimacy of abstinence for solely health purposes, if moral persuasion has no lever. It appears in the post-AIDS era, that the positive sex ethos is no longer the herald of the future. Stossel says, swept away by AIDS and a revival of sturdy family values, the sex revolution is dead. Some findings from the National Health and Social Life Survey of 3,432 subjects include: 94 per cent of Americans were faithful to their spouses (up from around 60 per cent in the latest Kinsey survey); only 33 per cent of Americans had sex twice or more per week; and the median number of lifetime sex partners for women was two, for men six. One of its more telling findings was that married people had the most sex, single people the next most, and divorced people the least. "The more partners you have," the report's authors wrote, "the more time you are going to spend finding and wooing them – time that a married couple could be having sex."[229] In other words, if you like sex it doesn't pay to be a swinging single. Instead, get married and stay married. Our findings, the authors wrote:

...often directly contradict what has become the conventional wisdom about sex. They are counterrevolutionary findings, showing a country...that, on the whole, is much less sexually active than we have come to believe.[230]

So why are public schools hosting advocates of free sex or positive sex ideologies? Often the decision-makers are well meaning but poorly informed or blinded by politics. Many teachers unions are politically pro-GBLTQ. However, school presentations can acknowledge the worth of abstinence in meaningful ways without sliding into a controversy of teaching "ethical, moral and religious values." An honest portrayal of the practicalities of juvenile sex should be enough. Most kids are like Amanda and Chris – capable of forming an opinion given the true facts:

The emotional benefits are not the only reason to save sex for marriage. The Medical Institute on Sexual Health reports the following findings on sexually transmitted diseases: '15.3 million Americans are newly infected with an STD each year, including 3 million teens.' 'Adolescents and young adults (15-24) are the age groups at the greatest risk for acquiring an STD. Approximately two-thirds of all people who acquire STDs are under 25.' 'Twenty-five per cent of all newly reported HIV infections are found in people under age 22. Fifty per cent of all newly reported HIV infections are found in people under age 25. HIV has already taken the lives of more than 375,000 Americans. By the way of comparison, America lost approximately 400,000 people in World War II.' 'The risk of pelvic inflammatory disease (PID) is as much as 10 times greater for 15-year-old females than for 24-year-old females. PID can cause sterility.' 'Human papilloma virus (HPV) is an STD that causes genital warts. It also is the cause of more than 90 per cent of all cervical cancer. Cervical cancer takes the lives of about 5,000 American women yearly, and condoms provide almost no protection against HPV. It is estimated 5.5 million new infections occur each year with at least 20 million people currently infected.'[231]

In a politically correct atmosphere few adults talk to students of the benefits of marriage for sexual fulfillment. Bridget Maher concludes:

We live a culture that is saturated with sex. Television, movies, advertisements and magazines constantly bombard us with messages that it's okay to have sex with anyone. Because our minds are continually being filled with these messages, it's easy to think that sex in marriage is not worth waiting for, but social science and information on STDs tell us otherwise.[232]

The largest study ever done on sexuality found that married people have the best sex:

Of all sexually active people, faithfully married couples experience the most physical pleasure and emotional satisfaction with their sex lives.[233]

Faithfully married people have the best reported feelings about sex; they feel 'satisfied,' 'loved,' 'thrilled,' 'wanted,' and 'taken care of.' They are also the least likely to feel 'sad,' 'anxious or worried,' 'scared or afraid,' or 'guilty' about sex.[234]

When you use something the way it was meant to be used, it works great. Sex within marriage is not only the best protection against sexually transmitted diseases; it is also the way to have a truly fulfilling sex life. School educators must recognize that promoting early and pre-marital sex is injuring, if not killing many youth. Promiscuity (free sex) is not free. Martha Ainesworth, an AIDS expert with the World Bank says "reaching young people is not easy as we know and it is difficult to change a teenager's behavior." [235] Richard Marlink, director of the Harvard AIDS Institute says, "the prevention efforts for young people doesn't work." Apparently half of the new infections are reported among the younger than 25 year olds. Approximately a dozen Canadians become infected with HIV every day. The median age of infection among homosexuals dropped from over 30 to less than 25.

Among drug users, prisoners, aboriginals and prostitutes the infection rates are rising as well. Donald Sutherland of the Laboratory Centre for Decease Control states that the epidemic is not going away. The federal government is currently spending $42.2 million a year to fight this disease. Non-government organizations close to high-risk groups receive the prevention money, which is used for workshops on homophobia and distribution of free condoms.[236] And many wonder why AIDS prevention is not working!

Dennis Bueckert of *The Canadian Press* also points out that a campaign to promote safe sex among young people and prevent the spread of AIDS is not working anywhere. Two decades after the appearance of the HIV virus the latest statistics show that the "safe sex" message is not working. Although the death rates have fallen because of improvement in treatments, new infections are rising particularly among young homosexual men.[237] True there are new multi-drug cocktails that greatly extend the life of the average AIDS patient; however, they have serious side effects and are very costly (approximately $28,000 per patient per year).

Another approach seen as outdated by free sex activists is to empower youth to say no. Dr. Marion Howard in the late 1980s made a discovery while she was surveying teens who received birth control information at her Atlanta clinic. She says:

Her clients wanted birth control, but 84 per cent wanted to know how to say no to someone pressuring them for sex – and to say no without hurting their feelings.[238]

As a result, Howard developed a curriculum called "Postponing Sexual Involvement (PSI)." Discarding the old-fashioned approach – a gym teacher with a pointer and a reproductive-system poster giving rote lectures on sexual plumbing – Howard opted for a peer system that relies on teens as teachers. In PSI, older teens – especially school leaders and athletes – are chosen as believable messengers for the spiel: "I can postpone sex and still be cool." And teen leaders must also embrace abstinence themselves. "I'm happy because of my beliefs," says Monique Chattah, a Cincinnati peer leader. "I have a better self-image."[239]

The heart of PSI is role-playing. In a typical PSI class students played out a classic confrontation: Boy takes girl on an expensive date and then insists on sex. The girls practiced handling the pressure, then the exercise was reversed, with the girl as the aggressor. This led to an open discussion of respect, values and even the way sex is glamorized in the media to sell products.[240] The early signs are that PSI is filling an important need. National studies show that only 17 per cent of girls say they planned their first sexual intercourse – meaning most apparently have sex because they don't know how to thwart advances, says Christopher Kraus, the coordinator of Cincinnati's PSI program.[241]

A 1991 survey of Atlanta students found that those who had gone through PSI training were five times less likely than other teens to have started having sex by the end of eighth grade. When exercising "free choice" is everyone's declared goal, what is wrong with giving teenagers the understanding and empowerment to say "no," if that is their wish?

Abortion

For you created my innermost being; you knit me together in my mother's womb. I praise you because I am fearfully and wonderfully made; your works are wonderful...My frame was not hidden from you when I was made in the secret place. When I was woven together in the depths of the earth, your eyes saw my unformed body. All the days ordained for me were written in your book before one of them came to be.

Psalm 139: 13-16

If we should but control our lusts at the start and if we would not kill off the human race born and developing according to the divine plan, then our whole lives would be lived according to nature. [242]

Clement of Alexandria (c.A.D. 150-220)

Abortion is a secular wrong not just a religious wrong. One of the broad principles, is you don't kill innocent life. The notion that the fetus constitutes human life that is indistinguishable morally from born life is so basic, the issue was originally religious.[243] Two feminist foremothers were adamantly opposed to abortion. One needs only to turn to *The Revolution*, Susan B. Anthony and Elizabeth Cady Stanton's publication, to discover this fact. In this 1869 publication, Anthony termed abortion "child murder," and Stanton classified abortion as "infanticide." When addressing a woman's responsibility in having an abortion, Anthony said:

Guilty? Yes. No matter what the motive, love of ease, or a desire to save from suffering the unborn innocent, the woman is awfully guilty who commits the deed. It will burden her conscience in life, it will burden her soul in death; but oh, thrice guilty is he who drove her to the desperation, which impelled her to the crime!

As early as 1772, Mary Wollstonecraft discouraged women who wished to 'discharge the first duty of a mother; and either destroy the embryo in the womb, or cast it off when born.'[244]

According to Feminists For Life of America (FFLA), the term "pro-life" refers to the position that human life is intrinsically valuable; in other words, human life ought to "count" in society, regardless of whether it is useful, convenient, or pleasant. The FFLA, combined with the National Coalition for Life, total some 1.3 million women organized in the United States to convince other women "to refuse to choose." For these women, most Christians, and many others of religious and secular beliefs, the act of abortion stands as a grievous defilement of womanhood and debasement of the value of pregnancy. Like- minded people contend the act of abortion does not improve the self-esteem of women nor improve the lot for women as a whole.

The controversy over abortion is hardly a contemporary phenomenon. Some 2500 years ago the Hippocratic Oath struck an anti-abortion cord:

I will give no deadly medicine to anyone if asked, nor suggest any such advice;

likewise, I will not give a pessary to a woman to induce abortion. I will live my life and practice my art with purity and holiness.

Before the 1973 Supreme Court decision which legalized abortion (*Roe vs Wade*), the yearly average number of abortions was 235,000. Between 1973-1996 the yearly average was 1,570,500. The number of surgical abortions in 1996 was 1,370,000, which was down from the 1990 figure of 1,610,000. The annual revenue from abortion is about $500 million per year and the sale of unborn children's parts could push that figure into the billions.[245] The following table details abortion statistics for the United States in 1996, along with biological descriptions of the human lives at time of operation.[246]

Age of Fetus (Weeks)	Description	(%) Of All Women Who Have Abortions	Number of Aborted Babies
1-6	Week 4 - Girl/Boy is 1/4 inch long, 10,000 times larger than Week 1. Blood flowing in veins is different than mothers. Muscles are developing, arms and leg buds visible. Distinct head with outline of brain and eye vesicles. Week 5 - Forehead, eyes, nostrils and mouth evident. Week 6 - Ears, hand and feet visible. Brainwaves can be recorded. Muscles start working together.	16	219,200
7-8	Fingers and toes defined. Finger prints permanently engraved on skin. All organs present, complete and functioning (except lungs).	38	520,600
9-10	Body is sensitive to touch. Sucks thumb, swallows, squints, frowns. Can clench fist.	23	315,100
11-12	Finger nails and toenails exist. Working taste buds. Facial expressions clear, including smile.	11	150,700
13-15	Sex of baby is identifiable.	7	95,900
16-20	Heart pumping 6 gallons of blood every day. Baby turns around, exercising muscles. Rapid eye movement can be recorded while the baby sleeps, indicating dreaming. Now weighs about one pound and is near one foot long. If born at 5 months has 35-50 % chance of survival with dedicated medical support..	4	54,800
21+	Can open and close eyes and recognize mom's voice. Weeks 21-28 - baby fat fills out skin. Birth at Week 24 - 34 % survival. Birth Week 28 - 90 % chance of survival. Week 36 - ready to be born.	1	13,700
Total		100	1,370,000

Under the title "In Hebrew 'Uterus' Means 'Compassion,'" Janet Podell writes:

...history has given us a compelling reason to pay attention to Judaism's warnings against the unnecessary destruction of life. God calls on us to turn away from all forms of idolatry. The idols of our day are not statues, but ideologies. Instead of the Creator, people worship social and political causes such as radical feminism, which

elevates women to quasi-goddesses while insisting that unwanted children are worthless nonentities who can be disposed of at will. How strongly this reminds me, as a Jew, of the Nazi ideology that declared the Aryans quasi-gods while encouraging the extermination of unwanted people as vermin. On my wall is a quote from a German pastor who protested against the Nazi killing of mental patients. He wrote to Hitler, 'Who if not the helpless should the law protect?' It is the same question we should be asking ourselves today.[247]

Dr. Pamela E. Smith, M.D., President of the American Association of Pro-Life Obstetricians and Gynecologists says:

The Hippocratic oath was never a law, but a guiding principle for conduct. It was held to for centuries, but now that we have lawyers deciding what the ethical standards of our nation should be, the AMA [American Medical Association] has decided that whatever is legal is moral. The Hippocratic oath is no longer considered relevant to our society because the law allows us to do things the oath does not.[248]

The perspective of those who see human life commencing at conception is aided by a simple hypothetical legal example put forth by journalist Cynthia Gorney:

What do you say to people who support abortion on demand who ask you, 'Where are these people [pro-lifers] coming from?'

What I say is this: 'The Supreme Court has just decided that states have to make it legal for women who are in a terrible situation to dispose of their three-year-olds in medical clinics. It's a grave and serious matter, but ultimately, the three-year-olds are the offspring of those women, and it must be up to the women and their doctors to decide when, and if, those three-year-olds get terminated.' That is how Roe v. Wade looks to right-to-life people. It's that horrifying.

'If that happened tomorrow, would you try to overturn it or stop other people from doing it?' That's the way I tend to explain it. There is often a stunned silence and they'll say, 'Really? It really looks like that?' And then they rethink a lot of things that they have thought about pro-life people. The thing that is hardest for pro-choice people to understand is that most pro-life people are in this because it is genuinely clear to them that once conception or fertilization takes place, you're talking about a human life that is as individual and as different as a born life; that this is the central motivation, not taking women back to the 1950s or overturning the advances of the last 20 years or making sure people don't have sex.[249]

Frederica Mathewes-Green, writes under the title "The Bitter Price of Choice":

A woman with an unplanned pregnancy faces more than 'inconvenience;' many adversities, financial and social, at school, at work, and at home confront her. Our mistake was in looking at these problems and deciding that the fault lay with the woman, that she should be the one to change. We focused on her swelling belly, not the discrimination that had made her so desperate. We advised her, 'Go have this operation and you will fit right in.'...It is a cruel joke to call this a woman's 'choice.' We may choose to sacrifice our life and career plans, or choose to undergo humiliating invasive surgery and sacrifice our offspring. How fortunate we are – we have a choice! Perhaps it's time to amend the slogan—'Abortion: a woman's right to capitulate.'... we're lying down on abortion tables 1,600,000 times a year to ensure the status quo. We've adapted to this surgical substitute, to the point that Justice Blackmun could write in his Webster dissent, 'Millions of women have ordered their lives around' abortion. That we have willingly ordered our lives around a denigrating surgical procedure – accepted it as the price we must pay to keep our life plans intact—is an ominous sign...More insidiously, abortion advocacy has been poisonous to some of the deeper values of feminism. For example, the need to discredit the fetus has led us to the use of terms that would be disastrous if applied to women. 'It's so small,' 'It's unwanted,' 'It might be disabled,' 'It might be abused.' Too often women are small, unwanted, disabled, or abused. Do we really want to say that these factors erase personhood?[250]

At the start in the 60s, prior to Dr. Henry Morgentaler, the goal was simply to end the death and injury to women submitting to illegal abortions. Sadly, in the era of "abortion on demand," those who see abortion as a surgical convenience and who will end any number of pregnancies without reservation, are unable to look at the gruesome handiwork they defend. Across the country, they shrink from photos of babies killed in abortions. Through political pressure the pro-abortionists compel television stations to refuse advertisements showing partial birth or other abortion artifacts. They will not even allow viewers to see what their policies have wrought. According to Benjamin Stein:

They are like the Germans who refused to think about whatever was happening at Dachau and then vomited when they saw and never wanted to see again. And for those who don't care to make the trip down that road, perhaps you can imagine the feelings of tens of millions of us who see clearly that abortion is a violent killing of the most innocent of humans.[251]

In 1999, Diana Alstad, co-author of the paper "Abortion and the Morality Wars: Taking the Moral Offensive," was interviewed by Karla Mantilla for *Off Our Backs*. Alstad gave her views regarding the justification of abortion and feminist family values. She said:

There are four main types of justifications for abortion - legal and social rights, health, family planning, and morality. The pro-choice movement mainly uses the first three types, especially rights. For most people morality is more basic, so whoever dominates the moral climate of opinion can undermine the other's rights, as well as access and availability. This is exactly what's been happening to us. The pro-choice movement has been on the moral defensive for twenty years, ever since the religious 'right' captured the moral high ground by making their 'pro-life' terminology morally condemning abortion predominant...[252]

The mutual exclusivity of the worldviews exemplified in Margaret Sanger's ideology and that of Christianity is clearly illustrated by Alstad:

I view the abortion fight as the front line in America of a much larger battle, the planetary battle that I call 'the morality wars.' This is a battle for people's minds over 'Who has the right to decide what's right?' and 'What gives them the right to do so?' It's between the forces of the old and the new, between authoritarianism and democracy. Essentially, it's fundamentalist, patriarchal belief systems versus modern, evolutionary, feminist, feedback-based creative approaches to living and solving our many global problems. Fundamentalists of various stripes are getting more and more violent worldwide. Now, increasingly, morality warfare has escalated to killing abortion providers. We must turn the tide. It's time for us to focus on morality and challenge the 'religious wrong's' moral monopoly.

We must never forget that abortion is the bottom line of birth control. Without it, women don't have control over their bodies, and therefore over their lives. Without it, the competitive playing field of money, power and independence is so skewed in men's favor that women really cannot have equal opportunity.... The abortion battle is really about power and keeping women down. The pro-life side is pro-force – forcing a prescribed behavior on others, forced motherhood as punishment for sex, forced submission to biology, using force to uphold the patriarchy. We should call this battle 'pro-freedom' or 'pro-choice vs. pro-force' to unmask what lies under their lofty verbiage.[253]

Those like Alstad, who contend that abortion empowers women have not weighed the consequences women now face from opportunistic uncommitted men – those who converted with alacrity to the ethos of free sex. According to Carol Stream, of the 1.5 million women who have abortions annually:

...about 2/3 say they cannot afford a child; and 1/2 say they do not want to be a single parent or are having problems with their husband or partner. About 14,000 women [in the US] *have abortions each year because they became pregnant after rape or incest.*[254]

Ms. Goldner's story is representative of some 50 per cent of women who reluctantly choose abortion:

Two years ago, when Miss Goldner discovered she was pregnant, she was happy: 'I felt ready. I was 34, and although I might not have chosen to have a child right then, I wanted the baby. I also thought my boyfriend and I were in a solid relationship, though we were going through a tense period.' Unfortunately, her boyfriend had different ideas. 'I hoped he would embrace me and our child. But he couldn't. All he said when I told him the news was, `You poor thing.' 'Miss Goldner still did not give up, reminding him shyly, 'We could get married.' Her boyfriend, as it happens, couldn't have disagreed more. 'I am pro-choice,' Miss Goldner continues, 'but the decision to end a pregnancy was not a choice I ever wanted to make.' She alludes to some nerve condition her then-boyfriend was suffering from, which he was vaguely *concerned might be passed on to their child. In any case, it soon emerges that this was not the real point of contention between them. Miss Goldner explains: 'I considered having the baby on my own; my boyfriend pleaded with me not to. In the end, I agreed with his viewpoint: My child should have a father. A good and loving father.'*[255]

Obviously, much of the pro-life effort is targeting the wrong sex. Wendy Shalit writes in her article "Whose Choice?":

We should start asking about all the dishonorable boyfriends behind these women's 'choices.' For the woman who seeks an abortion is not a woman lusting for baby-killing, nor is she typically a woman who delights in her opportunity to exercise this particular freedom. Instead, women like Diane Goldner have more often than not once said hopefully to their boyfriend, 'We could get married ...?' and have been told: not in a million years. 'You poor thing' indeed.[256]

Shari Plunkett, founder of First Resort chain of pregnancy-help centers, confirms the notion that a majority of women would not resort to abortion given a supportive circumstance. She says:

Sixty per cent of the women we work with who were seriously contemplating abortion decide to carry to term. Ultrasound plays a big part in this. Some women go into the procedure talking about having an abortion and come out saying, 'I'd better start thinking about names.' Over the 14 years I've been doing this, we've seen 15,000 to 20,000 women, and I've never seen one come back and say, 'I'm so angry that you helped me carry this baby to term.'"[257]

Anthony Clare, clinical professor of psychiatry at Trinity College Dublin, also claims that one of the greatest failures of 20th-century society has been the failure of men to participate more fully in parenthood. This, he said, was a key factor that has discouraged many women from continuing their pregnancies.[258] Frederica Mathewes-Green, in her book *Real Choices,* summarized the findings of a study of post abortion women conducted by National Women's Coalition for Life. Two key questions asked were, "Why did you decide to abort? What might have changed your mind?" Extensive questionnaires were sent to nearly 2,000 pregnancy-care centers, asking those who actually dealt with women facing crisis pregnancies about the problems their clients found so daunting. The response rate was over 10 per cent. Mathewes-Green also went to seven cities around the country to hear the stories of women who had had abortions. She writes:

In the beginning, I assumed that women felt driven to abort because of material needs – housing, medical care, job security, child care, that sort of thing. I was surprised that these problems were relatively minor factors in the decision-making process. Far more significant were problems with relationships – particularly with the father of the child and with the woman's parents. I discovered that in almost every case, a woman chooses abortion to accommodate the wishes of others who do not welcome her child. I recall that the women interviewed in Carol Gilligan's pro-abortion book Different Voices reported very similar reasons for aborting.[259]

So much for abortion being the "front line in the planetary battle over morality." So much for the "bottom-line in women's control over their bodies." So much for the bottom-line in women's control "over their lives." Remember the Calgary Birth Control Association is "a strong supporter of the feminist analysis of women's issues." So why are our public schools giving access to such agencies who would uphold Diana Alstad's dictum:

The abortion battle is really about power and keeping women down?

Really? FFLA president Rosemary Bottcher discredits this radical feminist untruth:

Isn't it ironic that pro-choice rhetoric emphasizes a woman's power, independence and autonomy in choice making, while the women actually making the choices talk most often about loneliness, betrayal and abandonment by those they love? [260]

According to Mathewes-Green:

The single most important factor in how a woman feels about an unplanned pregnancy is the attitude of the baby's father. If he says, 'I love you; I love our baby; I'll do anything to make this work,' she is far less likely to choose abortion than if he declares, 'I do not want this baby! You must have an abortion!' [261]

To improve women's lot, she proclaims:

We can affirm and value the male instinct to protect his family. We can respect the man who exhibits character, strength and fidelity by accepting responsibility for the well-being of his mate and his children.[262]*...Some feminists aren't going to like hearing talk about male and female instincts, or the need of women to be protected by men. Feminist theory sometimes fails to describe reality. Biology has its own logic. Women have a primal bond with their children; were it not so, the human race could not survive....Most women want to provide this care, but they need the assistance of their mates, because it is an arduous task. Male-bashing was a lot of fun, but it's gotten out of hand. Our expectations of men with respect to relationships and responsibilities has plummeted to zero.* [263]

The radical feminist notion of the merits and naturalness of free love is absolute fiction and must be exposed as such. Women cannot win or even achieve equality in a free love market. This story further illustrates the myth:

We had discussed our options before ever becoming sexually active. We knew that if <u>we became pregnant</u>, <u>we would have an abortion</u>. In the summer before my Sophomore year and his Senior year, we were practically living together. We spent the nights together, and were having sex 3-4 times a day. Always protected. Well.....

one afternoon in mid August, while we were having sex, he realized that the condom had broken. We both freaked out on each other and instantly knew that we were going to have a problem. The next few weeks he withdrew from me. He avoided me completely. I was sick with fear and anger. I felt like he was abandoning me. We started school, and I was pushed further and further away from him. We were two or three weeks in to the school year, and I was late...When it [EPT] showed positive, he was irate, and left me, alone. I sat at home crying and feeling my entire world crumble around me. I lay on the bedroom floor crying hysterically...[264] *[my underline]*

After her abortion (note the tragic switch in person from "we" to "I"):

That year I attempted to commit suicide a few times. I hated myself and would hit myself, scratch, cut and even poison myself. I was falling into a deep depression, and I realize, I never recovered from it. I would see babies, and wonder. I would look at the kids clothing section, and I would even talk to my baby's 'spirit,' asking for forgiveness. I am now 27. I'm single, and have not had a healthy, normal relationship, ever. I am very distrusting of men.... I have no one to discuss it with that has the ability to show emotional support. They do not provide you with the tools or knowledge to deal with your life post procedure. I need to take control of the situation and be able to forgive men (3/9/00).[265]

When asked, "What do you say to pro-lifers who can't fathom the mind of abortion advocates?" Diana Alstad replies:

A lot of pro-lifers don't see that for most pro-choice people there is something between life and nonlife, which sounds nonsensical to pro-life people. Everybody that I know who is pro-choice believes that there's something going on in the uterus that's 'potential life.' The in-between stage is mysterious to the pro-life person and totally clear to the pro-choice person.[266]

In response to the Unborn Victims of Violence Act 1999, the radical feminists showed in "clear" their hypocritical convictions for empowering women. The National Organization For Women fought against the Act, even though the goal of the legislation was to punish anyone who injures a fetus. In NOW's view any doctor can error and kill the fetus prior to delivery – it doesn't matter.[267] Can you imagine the cognitive dissonance driving the conviction that the unborn have no status?

This anti-preborn ethos was not a "First Wave" tenet and the idea was not always in the NOW manifesto. Pro-life feminists acknowledge that this "Second Wave" of feminism had anti-abortion activists at its start. Chicana activist Graciela Olivarez, a high school dropout who became the first woman graduate of Notre Dame Law School was a staunch pro-lifer. Along with Betty Friedan and 26 others, Olivarez was a charter member of NOW. When the national organization was founded in 1966 abortion advocacy was conspicuously absent from the charter. Not until a year later did NOW adopt a pro-abortion position, and then only after heated debate. But Olivarez, unlike the organization she helped to found, went on to continue her belief in the indivisibility of all human rights.[268] Her view on this "matter of life and death," she asserts, "shouldn't be brushed aside as a denominational hang-up." She called upon anyone who considered the unborn child "a mass of cells" to witness an abortion procedure, as she had done. She prophetically detailed the harms of making abortion more accessible:

Advocacy by women for legalized abortion on a national scale is so anti-women's liberation that it flies in the face of what some of us are trying to accomplish through the women's movement – namely, equality – equality means an equal sharing of responsibilities by and as men and women....What kind of future do we all have to look forward to if men are excused either morally or legally from their responsibility for participation in the creation of life...? To talk about the 'wanted' and the 'unwanted' child smacks too much of bigotry and prejudice. Many of us have experienced the sting of being 'unwanted' by certain segments of our society....I am not impressed or persuaded by those who express concern for the low-income woman who may find herself carrying an unplanned pregnancy and for the future of the unplanned child...because the fact remains that in this affluent nation of ours, pregnant cattle and horses receive better health care than pregnant poor women. The poor cry out for justice and we respond with legalized abortion.[269]

As Olivarez predicted over a quarter century ago, the increased availability of abortion has compounded rather than cured the complex evils of sexism, racism, and economic injustice. It is long past the time for taking her prophetic protest to heart. Arguing against Olivarez and other pro-lifers, are many women who have no intention of marrying a man nor giving birth to a child. Thus by choice they give up nothing in their quest for equality. They have succumbed to what has previously been referred to as the "masculinization" of their gender. Regrettably, what they have done to women who want an orthodox marriage and family is turn their world upside down.

What is ironic and unfortunate, is the fact that radical feminism plays into the "foul" hands of chauvinist men. This is the first tragedy of the liberation movement. The ample testimonies of the abrogation of male commitment in the event of pregnancy depict a new oppression by the violence of abortion. The ease with which men walk out of marriages damages women more than men. Also the advent of free sex has forced many women to reluctantly compete in an amoral sexual meat-market. The female, around age 15, starts to inhibit her body's natural biology through pharmaceuticals, technology and ultimately medical intervention, if needed, recognizing all along that as a sexually active person the margin of error in favor of unplanned pregnancy and STD is high. And we wonder why many women are depression prone.

The second tragedy, perhaps of greater impact on society, is the complete diminishment of the role of father and husband. Fidelity has been eclipsed by the darkness of promiscuity. Confusion reigns supreme in the role of parent and spouse. Projection of the feminist variant family model onto our culture has undermined the traditional model, particularly damaging the traditional families which were operating free of oppression, inequality and infidelity. In summary, positive aspects of society like traditional family values have been subverted, while negative ones like "anything goes," "free sex," "early experimental ethos," "multipartnerism" and "divorce-on-demand" philosophies have been elevated.

The third tragedy of the feminist movement is related to the new oppression of abortion violence upon women – the health risks and after effects of abortion. In a study of post-abortion patients only eight weeks after their abortion, researchers found that 44 per cent complained of nervous disorders, 36 per cent had experienced sleep disturbances, 31 per cent had regrets about their decision, and 11 per cent had been prescribed psychotropic medicine by their family doctor.[270] A five year retrospective study in two Canadian provinces found significantly greater use of medical and psychiatric services among post-abortion women. Most significant was the finding that 25 per cent of aborted women made visits to psychiatrists as compared to 3 per cent of the control group. At especially high risk are teenagers, separated or divorced women, and women with a history of more than one abortion.[271]

Some 19 per cent of post-abortion women suffer from diagnosable post-traumatic stress disorder (PTSD). Approximately half had many, but not all, symptoms of PTSD, and 20 to 40 per cent showed moderate to high levels of stress and avoidance behavior relative to their abortion experiences.[272] Thirty to fifty per cent of aborted women report experiencing sexual dysfunction, of both short and long duration, beginning immediately after their abortions. These problems may include one or more of the following: loss of pleasure from intercourse, increased pain, an aversion to sex and/or males in general, or the development of a promiscuous lifestyle.[273] Approximately 60 per cent of women who experience post-abortion *sequelae* report suicidal *ideation*, with 28 per cent actually attempting suicide, of which half attempted suicide two or more times. Suicide attempts appear to be especially prevalent among post-abortion teenagers.[274] Post-abortion stress is linked with increased cigarette smoking. Women who abort are twice as likely to become heavy smokers and suffer the corresponding health risks.[275] Post-abortion women are also more likely to continue smoking during subsequent wanted pregnancies with increased risk of neonatal death or congenital anomalies.[276]

Abortion is significantly linked with a two-fold increased risk of alcohol abuse among women.[277] Abortion followed by alcohol abuse is linked to violent behavior, divorce or separation, auto accidents, and job loss.[278] Many post-abortion women develop a greater difficulty forming lasting bonds, with a male partner. This may be due to abortion related reactions such as lowered self-esteem, greater distrust of males, sexual dysfunction, substance abuse, increased levels of depression, anxiety, and volatile anger. Women who have more than one abortion are more likely to require public assistance, in part because they are also more likely to become single parents.[279] Women who have one abortion are at increased risk of having additional abortions in the future. Women with a prior abortion experience are four times more likely to abort a current pregnancy than those with no prior abortion history.[280] Approximately 45 per cent of all abortions are repeat abortions.[281] Another survey of post-abortive women found that 60 per cent commented that the decision to abort made their lives worse and 94 per cent regretted the decision to abort.[282]

Pro-abortion feminists have also argued the notions that an abortion improves the quality of nurturing and opposition to abortion treats motherhood as a mechanical role and biological duty. Diana Alstad makes this feminist point:

Fundamentalists leave the nurture out of nature, omitting that it takes years of loving care to create a truly human being, not just biological conception or a fetus. The need for love and nurturing and what it means to not have them are conveniently absent from their morality. Yet how a child is taken care of directly affects its survival and what it will become. Proper nurturing can't be forced. Since the mother is the foundation of childcare, how can she not have the last word as to whether she wants to do it or can do it adequately? Only she can be the ultimate judge of whether she's up to it and what the personal moral choice is for her.[283]

Everything in this book asserts that orthodox Christianity and traditional family supporters have considerable knowledge of the concept of nurture. The whole argument for the traditional family model is its optimum environment for nurturing. The litany of feminist arguments against marriage and in contradiction of the role of heterosexual parenting disprove the notion that feminists are interested in the "quality" of our children's lives. The fact that many feminists are willing to argue that parenting without the father is an equivalent to the orthodox family model further negates this belief. Nonetheless, Alstad carries the "quality" idea further:

The moral discourse needs to be raised to a higher level that takes the context and total picture of what it takes to create a healthy child, a fulfilled mother, and a viable society into account. Abortion is usually moral if one looks at its repercussions on living people. It's good for women, children, men, families, and for society overall. Forcing a woman to have a child she doesn't want is bad for all concerned, the woman, children and society. It's the height of immorality, especially in a time of violence and overpopulation. One of the biggest sources of violence on the planet is unwanted children and children who weren't properly loved and cared for whether by their parents or society. A world is being created that's full of people without hope, often driven by hatred and envy, who don't care about their own lives, let alone others.[284]

Although this "people without hope" analysis is straight from the lips of Margaret Sanger (quoted in Chapter 3) we need to further examine the "quality" issue. Anthropologist Marvin Harris has explained infanticide as an adaptation human cultures use to optimize their density. J.B. Birdsell, an anthropologist claims, "the practices have the effect of homeostatically keeping the population size below the point at which diminishing returns from local habitat would come into play." Nice as it sounds, Adrian Forsyth says:

Evolution does not follow the same principles as resource management. Individuals may try to prevent other people from having children who would overburden the community's resources, but would they kill their own offspring for the common good? It can easily be seen that if abortive behavior in humans were genetic in origin, as it is in so many species, individuals who abort offspring for the good of the population would become scarcer in each generation than those who would selfishly reproduce at a high rate.[285]

According to Forsyth, abortion as population control does not make any biological sense for the individuals whose offspring are destroyed. Rarely, if ever, will individuals pursue strategies that benefit a diverse population of loosely linked individuals at great expense to the related family unit. On the other hand, infanticide parallels the Freudian idea of a death instinct. Yet these constructs make no adaptive sense; they would be virtually impossible to evolve and embed as instincts in the human machine.[286] Both views – population-level selection for altruistic abortion and a pathological instinct to kill one's offspring – can be rejected as explanations for abortion. Instead, drawing on Darwinian (secular) science, we must ask what the selective consequences are for an individual who does or does not employ abortion or infanticide.

For a female, who pays a high physiological price for each offspring reared, there is a conflict between the quantity and the quality of the offspring. At some point, an increase in childbearing will conflict with the task of caring for a child. The conflict between quality and quantity is well documented for our own species, especially in impoverished populations where resources are limited. UNICEF data show that a pregnancy improperly timed can lower the lifetime fitness of a woman. Pregnancies at either end of the reproductive life span, at too old or too young an age, are accompanied by substantially higher infant mortality. If the interval between births is shortened, infant mortality goes up. A birth spacing of a year or less, for instance, produces twice the infant mortality of a two-to-three-year spacing. And as the number of children per woman increases, infant mortality increases. A child in a family of five siblings is twice as likely to die as one in a family of two.[287]

Infanticide to regulate litter size and to lessen future investment costs is practiced widely in animals. The difficulty of producing enough milk for more than one infant is often cited as a reason for twin infanticide in hunter-gatherer cultures; when nomadism is involved, simply the problem of transport has been justification. Estimates of the infanticide rate for nomadic Australian Aborigines run at 20 to 40 per cent. Female infanticide seems to be an economic strategy employed because it affects the resources of the parents.[288] Writes Forsyth:

Abortion makes much adaptive sense for plants and animals faced with an unpredictable resource base and genetic pool. Yet for humans, it is a paradox. It makes less sense for low-fecundity organisms with plenty of scope for mate choice and resource choice. Perhaps that is why some societies are unforgiving of the strategy when it is employed for individual benefit. Abortion remains a large part of the human reproductive strategy, which testifies to the strength of individual self-interest.[289]

One must ask is any of this survival of the fittest theory a legitimate argument for abortion in North American society? With the birth rate below replacement in Canada and just recently back at replacement in the United States, the notion of sacrificing one child for the benefit of others is incredible. Margaret Sanger's and Diana Alstad's impression of womanhood buried under the burden of decades of unceasing birthing is equally unbelievable. North American aboriginal women were hardly birthing *factories* over the centuries. Before the advent of technological contraception and Western culture, the more *primitive* civilizations relied on lactation related to regular breast-feeding as a natural contraceptive, and the mores of abstinence, and planned birth spacing to assure optimum fecundity. Forsyth sees abortion, as a paradox that is difficult to accept because it says less is more. For regions where survival is at stake abortion and infanticide were used and still are used by some cultures and some women to *raise* their reproductive success, not reduce it. The logic behind the paradox of abortion for these people explains why a healthy twin was discarded, why the malformed were destroyed. Lives are valued according to the reproductive and genetic return they are expected to yield.[290] So what of our society? Have you heard of anyone throwing away one of her twins? Do we not celebrate triplets and quadruplets? Society goes out of its way to support such eventualities? We would be outraged by the idea of drowning three of the quintuplets so that the remaining twins could have a better quality of life. So is there a legitimate argument for "quality of life" abortions? Who wants to tell their "only-child," the extra's you have in life are because we aborted two earlier siblings or the diagnostic on your genetic makeup was much better than our first two attempts, which we aborted. So congratulations son (daughter)!

Consider whether Dmitry Ivanovitch Mendeleyev would have made the humanist-eugenicist "Quality of Life" screen. The principle cartographer of the chemical kingdom, Mendeleyev was born the youngest of fourteen impoverished children in Siberia. By his early thirties, the tall, stooped man had a stark resemblance to Rasputin. Nonetheless, Davies describes Mendeleyev's brilliance:

As a youth, Mendeleyev was obsessed with understanding the physical properties of the elements. By his early thirties… [he] was professor of inorganic chemistry at the University of St. Petersburg, determined to understand the atomic relationships among groups of elements….One night in February 1869, Mendeleyev had a dream in which he saw the alignment of the known elements in a single table.

In 1955, almost fifty years after his death, Mendeleyev received the ultimate honor for a chemist (arguably greater than the Nobel prize) when scientists artificially created the 101st element in the periodic table and named the short-lived radioactive isotope mendelevium. The Russian thus joined the select company of Albert Einstein, Alfred Nobel, and Enrico Fermi to have an element named after him.[291]

Brenda Drummond of Carlton Place, Ontario, was charged with attempted murder in 1996 after she unsuccessfully attempted to kill her unborn child by discharging a pellet gun into her vagina. A pellet lodged into the baby's head and two days later, emergency surgery was used to save the baby's life. Representing society, how would you proceed with the case? Should attempted murder apply? If Brenda's boyfriend or husband shot the baby five minutes after birth would he be a murderer? Does the location of the baby (inside or outside the mother) change your view?

In fact, the charge was dismissed after Drummond's lawyer succeeded in convincing Ontario Court judge Inger Hansen that the case was merely a failed abortion (which is not a crime in Canada) and that the baby (named Jonathan) had no legal protection at the time of the shooting since he had not yet been born. Drummond pleaded guilty on February 3, 1997 to failing to provide the necessaries of life to her child and received a suspended sentence and a 30 month probation, for not reporting the baby's injury.[292]

According to Christianity, no line other than conception can be drawn between life and personhood. There is no such thing as a morality-free stage called "pre-personhood," defined by pro-choice adherents and discussed in Chapter 3. Peter Kreeft argues:

...birth is only a change of place and relationship to the mother and to the surrounding world (air and food); how could these things create personhood? As for viability, it varies with accidental and external factors like available technology (incubators). What I am in the womb – a person or a non-person – cannot be determined by what machines exist outside the womb! But viability is determined by such things. Therefore personhood cannot be determined by viability.[293]

If the fetus is only a potential person, it must be an actual something in order to be a potential person. What is it? An ape? There are no "potential persons" any more than there are potential apes. All persons are actual, as all apes are actual. Actual apes are potential swimmers, and actual persons are potential philosophers. The being is *actual;* the functioning is *potential.* When pregnant, no woman has ever proudly announced, "She is going to have a fetus." Equally, when anxious to abort a pregnancy, no woman wants to announce, "She is going to kill her baby." The State solution – segment human life and value, legislate the worth of a human life by the inclination of the mother (and often the father), and deny the fetus rights in the human race. What is God to do with a compromised society, which pays doctors to do their best to save one fetus and in the same hospital pays other doctors for the systematic killing of another?

Recent data is showing that society is seeing more and more the immorality of abortion. The Alan Guttmacher Institute, a New York pro-choice think tank, reported in October 2000, that the overall abortion rate in the United States declined 11 per cent between 1994 and 2000, with a 39 per cent drop among adolescents age 15 to 17.[294] A Zogby International poll commissioned for the *Buffalo News* (New York) in December 2002 found that 32 per cent of Americans changed their opinions on abortion during the last decade, with 21 per cent becoming more negative – indicating twice as many changed to the negative view than those becoming pro-abortion. More than two thirds of those queried said they strongly would advise a pregnant woman not to get an abortion. Moreover, the strongest age group opposing abortion consisted of young people 18 to 20 years old. Says Steven Mosher, director of the Population Research Institute:

The abortion-survivors generation, those kids born since the Roe decision in 1973, are much more prolific than their elders. If you survey people at pro-life meetings, the average number of children is four. If you survey people at a National Abortion Rights League meeting, the average is probably about one half of a child...It means that the ranks of our opposition are going to be decimated by what we might call a form of self-imposed collective suicide.[295]

Ironically, we can end this chapter with the *pro-life* wisdom of the pivotal feminist, Gloria Steinem (whose father had walked out on the family). She writes of her mother's sustaining conviction that "little strangers arrive" with intrinsic value and mothers have a duty to care for them. Steinem writes:

In spite of a childhood marked by more discipline than love – and in spite of the difficulty she and all parents find in giving their children something they themselves did not experience – my mother did her best to make us feel unique and worthwhile. Over and over again, in every way she knew how, she told us that we didn't need to earn her love. We were loved and valued (and therefore were lovable and valuable) exactly as we were. What seemed to help her in this heroic effort to break with her own past was a childrearing theory she had absorbed from theosophy, a school of spiritual thought that blossomed in the early twentieth century and survives to this day in the writings of Krishnamuri, Annie Besant, Madame Blavatsky, and many others. 'Children don't belong to us,' she used to say, paraphrasing what she had learned from this blend of many world religions, especially Eastern ones. 'They are little strangers who arrive in our lives and give us the pleasure and duty of caring for them – but we don't own them. *We help them become who they are.'*[296]

Steinem and other pro-abortion activists must answer two spiritual questions. Who do these "little strangers" belong to? What on God's earth gives a pregnant mother the right to refuse the "pleasure and duty" of caring for them?

CHAPTER EIGHT

SINGLES, COUPLES, MARRIAGE AND ALTERNATIVE FAMILIES

Men and women are not evolved for one sex partner – Jane Goodall observed one female chimpanzee copulated with seven males 84 times in eight days.[1]

I always recognized that deep but vague yearnings propelled me to meet men. Sometimes I hoped my sexual adventuring would bring me love. In those years, sex was one of my prime recreational activities. Retrospectively and after years of therapy, I began to wonder whether my sexual drive was indeed the need that I sought to satisfy, and to question why it was that even really great sex rarely left me feeling like I had had enough?...Being sexual was a form of creative self-expression. The times I just wanted to play, having sex with a large number of men was simply the adult equivalent of the proverbial kid in the candy store, where if one was fun, two or three was even more fun. At other times it was an attempt to scratch an itch that had nothing to do with sexual desire and was about trying to squelch unpleasant feelings like loneliness, boredom, depression, or fill in a sense of internal emptiness...When needs that were more complex than 'feeling horny' were at play, propelling me to have, no quantity of sex left me feeling satisfied or good.[2]

Michael Shernoff, 'Gay Men's Sexualities: Reflections at the Dawn of the Millennium'

This kind of unrestrained self-indulgence proves terribly self-destructive in the end, as my baby boom generation rediscovered the hard way. 'Free love,' like its next of kin 'recreational drugs,' proves to be neither fun nor free in the end.[3]

Catherine M. Wallace, 'For Fidelity: How Intimacy and Commitment Enrich Our Lives'

In facing one's choice of worldviews, a decision must be made on the origins of mankind. In previous chapters we have established Christian theology on the origin of man and the judgment upon wanton animalistic sexual behavior. On the other hand, can we take any solace in our evolutionary primate heritage and the sexual freedom Jane Goodall implies in her observations of chimpanzees? Assuming for a moment that Darwin is right, we don't know why the copulations Goodall observed took place. Perhaps the female chimpanzee wanted to disguise the patriarchal relationship of a potential baby. Perhaps the female was bored, lonely, depressed or experimenting in a fit of creative self-expression. Maybe the activity constitutes male sexual abuse. Regardless, the above reflections of Michael Shernoff suggest human happiness in life has little to do with the volume of copulations, types of sex acts, and numbers of partners. What men and women long for is human relationship. This chapter addresses modalities for managing the paradox of free sex and human intimacy. Again the goal is to equip the reader to decide between two competing worldviews. One is either in one camp or the other, but never both.

Singles Life

Plenty of long-lasting relationships have started with sex before, during, or after the first date...Courtship is the period that starts after the first several dates, when you realize that you would like the relationship to continue, and can extend for weeks, months, even years, depending on how fast you move. Courtship can be as anxiety inducing as it is wonderful. Should I call him? Will he call me? What did he mean by what he said? Is he holding back because he doesn't want to see me anymore, or is he recovering from his last relationship? Should I ease off? Should I press ahead? What tactics should I use? What should I do?[4]

Eric Marcus, 'Together Forever: Gay and Lesbian Marriage'

It seems extraordinary, given all the risks of disease that Marcus could be advocating sex before and during courtship not to mention on a first date. Is courtship really only about a decision to continue a sexual relationship? In the animal kingdom courtship has to do with selection of a mate with which to form a parental bond. The eight-day frenzy between one female chimpanzee and seven males is not courtship under this definition.

According to Carolyn Koons and Michael J. Anthony, four of every ten adults are single. These mostly heterosexual singles fall into four categories: never married, divorced, separated and widowed. Of these single adults, more than 60 per cent have never been married, 25 per cent are divorced or separated, and 15 per cent widowed. In 1990, singles headed 42 per cent of all households. A single adult heads some 25 per cent of all households with children and a quarter of all adult men have never been married.[5]

The fact is singleness is even more pervasive in the gay culture and stable long-term relations are not the norm. Setting aside the ecological record established by Gabriel Rotello, one discovers that other gay lifestyle experts still see multipartnerism as the predominant characteristic of gay culture. In her book *Permanent Partners: Building Gay & Lesbian Relationships That Last*, Dr. Betty Berzon writes:

One reason we do not more often have an expectation of [permanence] in our relationships is that we do not have much visible evidence of long-term partnerships in our community. We know there have been people together for decades. But where are they?...Since one tends to socialize in an age group approximating one's own age, the gay or lesbian person in the first two, three or four decades of life is unlikely to socialize with couples in the fifth, sixth, seventh, or eighth decade of their lives. In a subculture that idealizes youth, being gay and gray does not exactly make one a hot ticket. Older gays and lesbians often regulate themselves to separate and unequal meeting places. Out of anxiety over our own aging, we denigrate their social gathering places as 'wrinkle palaces' or 'menopause mansions,' thereby reinforcing our isolation from them. Effectively we collaborate to hide older gay and lesbians from view, and in the process we are cheated of witnessing their longstanding partnerships.[6]

Berzon contrasts the gay "lifecycle" with the heterosexual norm:

How different it is in the non-gay world. We see grandma and grandpa enjoying their golden years together, and we are warmed by the sight. It is reassuring to know that people can love and trust and be supportive of one another over a lifetime. We feel good when we come in contact with the visible evidence of such a relationship. And where are our elders in the gay and lesbian world? Certainly not in so honored a role. Certainly not valued and celebrated by their own community. Actually hidden from sight for the most part, not treated with difference but too often with derision.[7]

Perhaps those gay seniors, who have survived the gauntlet of disease and have learned from certain experiences, chose to disassociate themselves from the relational and gratuitous instability of younger gay culture. Moreover, younger generations of gay singles are apparently resistant to any restrictions on their promiscuous gay sex life in the era of AIDS. Writing in *The Culture of Desire: Paradox and Perversity in Gay Lives Today*, Frank Browning says:

After the AIDS shock, initial sex for its own sake – raw, naked, wanton sex – made a comeback sometime around 1988 in the gay wards of New York and Los Angeles and San Francisco. For awhile, five years or so, the pull of AIDS had hung so heavy that sex talk seemed filtered through nostalgia. Therapists spoke about how many of their gay clients used up their fifty-minute sessions talking about sexual dysfunction. Newspapers and magazines, hetero and homo, devoted thousands of column inches to reports about how gays had 'grown up,' matured beyond sexual 'self-indulgence' through which they had 'acted out' during the bacchanalian seventies. Then to the surprise of the sage observers, along came Queer and a new sexual fierceness.[8]

By the spring of 1991, New York, L.A., and San Francisco had seen a proliferation of the revived sexual underground. Gay male 'invitation' clubs reappeared, a half dozen at least in each city. They weren't bathhouses with cubicles, cots, and doors, but open rooms in warehouses of depleted industrial zones, where in small hours of the morning, young men lined up with their buddies to probe, caress, and gnaw at one another's flesh in dimly lit tangles of animal abandon. It was the dawn of the sex resurrection.[9]

Contrary to the notion that sex is the "Pivot of Civilization," history bears a different witness. George Gilder writes of the perverse side of sex:

Sexual hungers spring not from the rational heights of the brain but from its glandular depths, not from the lofty cortex but from the unruly domain of the hypothalamus. A major goal of every civilization must be to bring these compulsions under control by the force of aspiration, worship and reason.[10]

Here the issue of strength of mind and spirit over body applies equally to gays and straights. Gilder describes what many secularists and evolutionists attribute to unfulfilled primate urgings:

Society has never succeeded in controlling the related male circus of heterosexual prostitution. Like the gay bathhouses, the dank and dingy, (or luxurious) massage parlors, the fetid half-hour hotel rooms, the menacing mince of the streetwalker, the glower of her pimp in the shadows all defy the illusion that men are remotely reasonable about sex.[11]

The sex business flourishes because men pursuing sex are often beyond sense or self-control. If you put up a sign offering flesh for sale and bath it in purple light, they come like moths. You can get men to spend their last fifty dollars to sit naked on a couch in a cold room and talk to a dull girl without clothes. You can get men to risk disease, robbery, and self-loathing sleeping with a streetwalker. You can get men to sit in the darkness and watch other people copulate with animals on a screen. Men with hardly the money to pay the rent and eat splurge on glossy magazines with bizarre pictures or squander their entire paychecks for a few minutes with a whore. In many ways the underworld of heterosexuality seems no more rational than the free-for-all of homosexual life. Yet otherwise sane and responsible men around the world lunge and flounder for the most sordid heterosexual offerings.[12]

According to Jesse Bernard, single men are far more prone to mental disorders than any other large group of Americans, with the possible exception of the divorced.[13] Single men between twenty-five and sixty-five are over 30 per cent more likely than married men or single women to be depressed; 30 per cent more likely to show "phobic tendencies" and "passivity;" and almost twice as likely to show "severe neurotic symptoms." They are almost three times as prone to nervous breakdowns. They can't sleep (three times more insomnia), and if they do sleep, they are three times more likely to have nightmares.[14]

Perhaps the most shocking data come from a study by Leo Srole and Associates, called "Mental Health in the Metropolis: the Midtown Manhattan Study." Srole's report found that married men and women do not greatly differ in their mental health: about one-fifth of both are impaired. In this survey, unlike some others, single women are slightly better off. But like all other available data, the report shows single men to be in the worst condition and deteriorating most rapidly with age. Between the ages of fifty and fifty-nine, an astonishing total of 46.1 per cent of all single men in the Manhattan survey suffered "mental health impairment."[15] Here is another major reason why Dr. Berzon observes few role models for gay youth.

Even in the realm of sex single men do less well than married men. Though single men are far more promiscuous, they also have less total sexual experience than married monogamous men (and women). In the younger age groups single men have only about one-fifth as much sexual activity as married men of the same age, and less than half as much sexual activity as single females. Single men also fail five times more often than married men in evoking orgasm.[16]

Heterosexual courtship advocate Amy Kass writes:

Beneath...the self-protecting cynicism are deep longings for friendship, for wholeness, for life that is serious and deep and for associations that are trustworthy. The young are mainly just scared, and no one has offered them hope or proper guidance.[17]

Husband, Leon Kass also decries the loss of traditional courtship among singles:

Today, there are no socially prescribed forms of conduct that help guide young men and women in the direction of matrimony...[they] lack a cultural script whose denouement is marriage. To be sure there are still exceptions to be found, say, in closed religious communities or among new immigrants...But for most of America's middle- and upper-class youth – the privileged, college-educated and graduated – there is no known explicit, or even tacit, social paths directed at marriage...for the great majority, the way to the altar is uncharted territory: It's every couple on its own...<u>without a compass</u>.[18] *[my underline]*

Simply put, the "courtship" concept is a reaction to the dating model that is thought by many to be unhealthy. Dating couples go through a series of short-term and often unsatisfying relationships over a period of five or ten years or longer. They are being taught to flit from one relationship to another like a honeybee buzzing from flower to flower. Why would they not be inclined later to bail out on a marriage partner when bored or frustrated? Dating also encourages sexual familiarity and experimentation. It isn't difficult to understand why an increasing number of parents feel this experimental model undermines commitment, exclusivity, and permanence in marriage.

In 1998, *The Chicago Tribune* magazine featured an article by Leon Kass entitled "Courtship's End: Men and Women Are Paying a High Price for Their Individualism." Pointing out the lack of preparation of today's youth for the phenomenon of marriage Kass writes:

Now the vast majority go to college, but very few go with the hope, or the wish, of finding a spouse. Many do not expect to find even a path to a career; they often require years of postgraduate 'time off' to figure out what to do with themselves. Sexually active – in truth, hyperactive – they flop about from one relationship to another; to the bewildered eye of this too-old but romantic observer, they manage to appear all at once casual and carefree and grim and humorless about getting along with the opposite sex...

The young men, nervous predators, act as if any woman is equally good: They are given not to falling in love with one, but to scoring in bed with many. In this sporting attitude, they are now matched by some female trophy hunters. But most young women strike me as sad, lonely and confused; hoping for something more, they are not enjoying their hard-won sexual liberation as much as liberation theory says they should.[19]

Today a single teenager or adult can "go through" several serious girl/boyfriends without her/his parents ever meeting one of them. Such loose, indeed promiscuous dating practices contribute little to the success of marriage. Doing anything without clear rules and boundaries is dangerous. Teenagers and college-age men and women need some idea about how to pursue and find the proper mate. The current lack of guidelines and support structure for this very important life decision results from many factors outside the teenager's control. These factors include poor role models in parenting, lack of parental wisdom, and poor relationships with parents; loss of authority and accountability in the culture and the church; physical distance from extended family and even from parents; loss of community; an emphasis on instant gratification; a media-driven and peer-driven culture; upheavals of careers and frequent relocating of families. All of these influences accentuate current dating practices by making the decisions of young adults into "private" decisions in which their families have no say.[20]

The courtship model, by contrast, seeks to postpone emotional and physical entanglements until they occur with the probable husband or wife. The family is very supportive in helping to choose that special individual for a serious courtship when the time is right. Until then, relationships between the sexes are limited to group situations in carefully controlled settings. Physical intimacy for the sake of titillation and experimentation is considered to be most inappropriate. It is the ultimate in "saving oneself" for the man or woman with whom a lifetime will be spent.[21]

William Cutrer, M.D. and Sandra Glahn comment on "How Far Is It OK to Go Before Marriage?":

What is not okay? Anything that stirs desire to sin. (That would include just about anything accompanied by moaning.) The standard is spelled out for us in 1 Thessalonians 4:3-8, which tells us not to defraud each other sexually. 'Defrauding' is intentionally creating or sustaining a desire that cannot rightfully and righteously be met.

Many have defined vaginal intercourse as the only premarital no-no. Thus, many unmarried Christian couples practice oral sex, anal sex, Cybersex, phone sex and 'outercourse' (where there is intentional prolonged contact without penetration). They engage in these practices rationalizing that they have adhered to God's standard. Yet God's standard draws the line at lustful thoughts, requiring moment-by-moment dependence on God's power and commitment to His Word.[22]

Letha Scanzoni writes:

It is unfortunate that many Christian young people so misunderstand the teachings of Scripture that they believe they can become 'promiscuous petters' with a variety of partners and yet feel they are 'preserving their virginity' for marriage. This misunderstanding no doubt results from the church's traditional insistence on chastity, while neglecting to help youth develop a Biblical understanding of what chastity is and why it is important. A standard of continence cannot make sense until one comes to the realization of the meaning of sex as God intended it and to a full understanding of what marriage is.[23]

Couples, who rationalize their behavior, find themselves caught up in a cycle of obtaining sexual satisfaction in illegitimate practices, followed by conviction, guilt and a hardening of heart against the guilt so that it becomes easier to lower the standard the next time. This is a dangerous pattern. It keeps them sliding down a slippery slope as they go further each time, continually pushing the limits. It also helps them link sexual pleasure with guilt, which can create difficulties for them later.[24] We have seen, in Chapter 7, how the free sex advocate would propose to avoid potential "hardening of the heart," by granting the young son or daughter a private room and familial space to experiment and hone his or her sexual yearnings with friends. Is this the direction you want your children and society to go?

Assuming your answer is no, then how do we teach going from 'Stop! Stop!' before marriage to the mentality that spouses must be sex gods and goddesses once married? To this question Cutrer and Ghaln write:

You can begin by changing 'Stop, stop' to 'Not yet, not yet.' The best lovemaking follows covenantal commitment between partners. A 1994 study, 'Sex in America,' generally considered the most accurate and complete study ever done, indicated that 'intimate, exclusive relationships between spouses or committed partners provide, by far, the greatest degree of sexual satisfaction.' Understand that God designed marriage to provide the right context for sex. Next, get rid of messages in your mind that say sex is bad. We should not teach that sex is bad. We should teach that it is sinful outside of marriage. Attraction and the desire for pleasure are normal, not evil.[25]

Solomon's Song of Songs gives us some direction here. Before the couple marries, we read of their passionate feelings. Yet we also read in passage 3:5:

I adjure you, 0 daughters of Jerusalem, by the gazelles or by the hinds of the field, That you will not arouse or awaken love until it pleases.

Feelings of physical passion are good. God put them there. But as was true three thousand years ago when God inspired Solomon with these words, you don't go to bed with your dating partner or your wife-to-be. God designed sex with boundaries. Four times in Solomon's book we read, "Don't arouse love until it pleases." The word "arouse" means a violent awakening. Both man and woman must take responsibility for stopping. It's neither "her job" nor "his job" to apply the brakes; they're both responsible for holding the line. Yet after the wedding, Solomon records that God tells them to "drink and imbibe deeply."

In courtship, it's expected that they will wait. But once married, it is expected that they will not wait. The poet seems to be indicating that this is the voice of God Himself. The silent observer, designer and blesser of their physical love, God pronounces His full approval on everything that has taken place, encouraging them to drink deeply of His gift. He created us and designed us as sexual creatures. He has revealed the "rules" for our benefit and in our best interest. Sin often is a consequence of indulging a natural, normal desire in the wrong way, place or time.[26]

Courtship may also come with a biological window for the never married. "By the time they hit thirty; still-single women are in a panic," says Pamela Paul, author of *The Starter Marriage and the Future of Matrimony.* In the *Atlantic Monthly* Barbara Dafoe Whitehead issues a bleak warning to the aging single female:

Men may be able to pursue their careers single-mindedly during their twenties and postpone marriage until their thirties without compromising their fertility or opportunities to find a suitable mate, but women cannot.[27]

It is not surprising that the most common time for females to enter into therapy is around their thirtieth birthday. Ilene Rosenzweig writes in *The New York Times:*

Sure it is more socially acceptable to stay single longer, but the assumption remains that women who do so are either obsessive 'career gals,' as my grandmother would say, or unable to throw an effective lasso.[28]

Twentysomethings are under a tremendous amount of pressure to get married – from their friends, their peer groups, and their families, even their colleagues. One by one, as friends, co-workers, and siblings begin to sport wedding bands, the pressure mounts. Friends get divided into two distinct groups: the Single Ones and the Married Pairs.[29]

In 2000, a *Youth Intelligence* poll revealed that 68 per cent of three thousand single and married young women said they'd rather not work if they could afford it. The *Wall Street Journal* concluded, "The New Economy has meant a return to the Old Family, with Dad as the sole breadwinner."[30] According to Pamela Paul:

The prefeminist wifely request was very simple: food and shelter. Now that women are their own breadwinners, the stakes have changed – and gotten much higher. Women still look for someone that represents stability, constancy, and trustworthiness, but they also require a great deal more....Barbara Ehrenreich calls the current ideal husband 'the perfect, all purpose Renaissance man.' He should be a co-provider and a reliable financial partner; a co-conversationalist and sparky dinner companion, fully briefed by CNN. In the event of children, we expect he will further develop into a skilled co-parent with a repertoire of bedtime stories and remedies for runny noses. He should be prepared to jump into sweats and serve as a sturdy fitness partner, plus handling home repair; a husband who can't locate a fuse box is about as useful as one of those little plastic tool kits from Toys 'R' Us. And since we are modern women, we have every right to think he will manage, in addition, to be a tireless and imaginative lover, supplying orgasms virtually on demand.[31]

Men are also looking for what Pamela Paul calls "tradition plus" – a new breed of female companion – independent and dependent at the same time. She writes:

They want a woman who can earn her keep, entertain herself, and stand on her own two feet under a variety of circumstances. She needs to be tolerant of his working hours, able to live her own life, and skilled at maintaining a balance between both partner's competing demands. However, when push comes to shove, women are still expected to encompass the traditional wifely virtues and perhaps make the necessary sacrifices 'when the time comes.' Most modern men want the perfect hybrid of traditional wife and modern women, a complicated creation that most women haven't figured out how to become.[32]

According to Stephanie Coontz, in the 1950s:

...very few people spent any extended period of time in a nonfamily setting: They moved from their parents' family into their own family, after just a brief experience with independent living, and they started having children soon after the marriage.[33]

By 1970 the median age for women getting married was 20.3 years of age; today it is 24.1 years. For men it was 23.3 in 1970; today it is 26.3.[34] The longer period of singleness has allowed for greater focus on careers by both sexes, however, this trend has slipped of late. In a 1999 poll, 55 per cent of Gen X women agreed that "having a career is not as rewarding as I thought it would be" – up from 41 per cent only a year before.[35] Says Paul:

If work doesn't work, these women need to find something else around which to build their identities, and their idea of what's important to them has become interwoven with the idea of marriage.[36]

In a 1999 poll, 43 per cent of Gen Xers said they "would like to see a return to more traditional standards in their sexual relationships;" 41 per cent wanted more traditional standards in social relationships overall. Katie Roiphe calls the current yearning "the dream of a more orderly world":

The progressive whirl of the past few decades, the lifting of one taboo after another, the speed of political change and the resulting freedoms, seem to have left us with a deep, almost perverse nostalgia for the most stifling, moralistic moment in history we can image. Only it doesn't seem stifling and moralistic anymore, it seems civilized.[37]

Sociologists have found that children who grow up in single-parent or step family situations have weaker kinship ties overall. They are less likely to rely or depend on their parents, and instead build a network of support among their peers. According to a *Newsweek* study of today's teens, this generation is strongly peer-driven and team-driven.[38] Such children become more easily influenced by a variety of outside parties – boyfriends and girlfriends, the media, and their friends. However, in today's fast-moving society, friends come and go, tribes form and break up, social lives are fluid. The genuine search for human intimacy in the face of this leads to an unusual eagerness to marry and start a family of one's own. Psychology professor Robert Ziller says:

People are rebelling against the idea of being uninvolved in family or community. Weddings are a way to reestablish bonds among individuals, their families, and their communities.[39]

Leon Kass and his wife, Amy, stalwartly teach traditional courtship rituals and morality:

Classical courtship begins by holding back sexual desire, and uses desire's energy to inspire conduct that will demonstrate devotion and gain devotion…Courtship enables a couple to develop habits of the heart. Dependability. Fidelity…those are the goods of courtship if it has marriage as its end.[40]

In a 1997 essay "The End of Courtship," Kass asks:

Is there perhaps some nascent young feminist out there who would like to make her name great and will seize the golden opportunity for advancing the truest interest of women (and men and children) by raising (again) the radical banner 'Not until you marry me?' And, while I'm dreaming, why not also, 'Not without my parents' blessings?'[41]

Offensive Against Marriage

Catherine M. Wallace, author of *For Fidelity: How Intimacy and Commitment Enrich Our Lives*, contends that American popular culture seeks to integrate sexual desire into its own dominant metaphor called the marketplace. She writes:

Implicitly or explicitly, we imagine something like a social market within which each person seeks to satisfy sexual drives and to remedy loneliness attendant upon modern American individualism. Appropriate sexual relationships, according to popular American culture, reveal the implicit presence of a good, clean contract. That is, both partners agree openly and fully to the terms and the duration of their relationship.[42]

Marketplace sexuality is profoundly hedonist in its emphasis on one's pleasure as the greatest good…sexual feelings and needs are 'managed' so as to 'optimize return.' Such [sexual] relationships are not for better or for worse but only for as long as the relationship is fulfilling or fun or self-enhancing. It's management hedonism: I exploit you, but not too much; you exploit me, but not too much. The bottom line, the spreadsheet, has to stay balanced, and it's that vision of quid-pro-quo balance that makes marketplace sexuality inherently exploitative.[43]

Continuing the marketplace metaphor, marriage is no longer just about falling in love. Thanks to capitalism, we can make money individually. Thanks to feminism more of the working age population is drawing a salary. Pamela Paul writes:

Americans bemoan the rise in prenuptial agreements because of the message it sends about divorce, but it also implies that people are really just after money when they marry. Men complain about 'high-maintenance women;' what they mean is, not every man can afford to marry them. We talk about marrying up, marrying down, and 'perfect mergers.'[44]

David Popenoe of the Marriage Project points out:

The nature of marriage has changed so much. It has become a kind of close friendship with a sexual relationship between a man and a women. That's a change. Before, it was a multifaceted institution. A partnership that was legally bound, typically a religious partnership, and a partnership between two families...in times past, men, by and large, had mostly male friends and women had mostly female friends. Today, we're together in an entirely different way. It's stripped down, mainly to the two of them. They're best friends, often isolated, alone, and this is something pretty new.[45]

Says Bethany, who divorced at age twenty-five: "I firmly believe that marriage should be for life. I don't think people take it very seriously anymore, and that's a terrible thing."[46] Today people jump into marriage without knowing which role they wish to play, or worse they radically change their mind after the wedding, to the spouse's surprise—what I want, when I want. Men can choose from a menu which includes: single man, homosexual, bisexual (wife primary or secondary relationship), live-in lover, sole bread-winner, shared dual income, househusband, married-for-now or married-for-life husband, and a single dad. The woman can be a single woman, a career woman, a housewife, a lesbian, a bisexual (husband primary or secondary relationship), a single mom by choice, a live-in lover, a married-for-now or a married-for-life wife.

The prevailing North American culture fosters a mind-set that encourages people to value selfishness above generosity, independence above community, self-satisfaction before compassion. Capitalism is all about freedom and individualism, not duty and community. Says Pamela Paul, "My dues. My wallet. My time." In 1996, Gen Xers responded with 69 per cent agreeing with the statement "I have to take whatever I can get in this world because no one is going to give me anything." Only 43 per cent of respondents in the 50s and 60s felt the same.[47] Growing up in the give-it-to-me era, we believe we can forge these bonds without ever making the kind of personal sacrifices or compromises that meaningful relationships require. Forming serious attachments is difficult when the bottom line is, how are my needs being served? "Is it worth it?" means "Is this worth it for me?"[48] Sociologist Larry Bumpass attributes the high divorce rate in part to this "increasing cultural emphasis on individualism."[49] Pamela Paul writes:

To succeed, some degree of autonomy is necessarily lost. But we're scared of letting go – heaven forbid – giving in. We've been taught by divorce and by other destabilizing aspects of our society that we can't depend on anyone but ourselves. And having become sexually active earlier than previous generations, today's twentysomethings typically go through several monogamous relationships and countless casual affairs before heading to the altar. We have been used, bruised, hurt, and bewildered by the opposite sex a lot more often than the maidenly women and bachelor men of yore. We mistrust others. In America's cult of the individual, we-ness doesn't necessarily feel natural or necessary. Autonomy is not always what we want; it's what we've gotten used to.[50]

In our self-centered culture, if marriage means limiting our choice we can simply eliminate the marriage. Kari Jenson Gold writes:

It may well be that marriage 'till death us do part' is simply a doomed enterprise. In a world so ruled by the jargon of therapy there is little room for a permanent relationship. In this ever-optimistic world there are no external absolutes, no original sin, only the relentless pursuit of 'health' and 'fulfillment.' If what we all aspire to is health rather than virtue, gratification rather than strength of character, how can we hope to find a foundation for a lasting commitment? If I have 'grown' and my mate hasn't kept up, or is even impeding my own 'growth,' what possible reason could I have for remaining faithful? The 'healthy' choice is clear: find someone better suited to my current needs. The notion that a man and a woman should be devoted to the other 'through sickness and health,' should place their good as a couple over the good of each individual, is then just silly.[51]

As Neil LaBute, director of such marriage-phobic movies as *Your Friends and Neighbors*, observed in a recent interview:

During my mother's era, you got one shot at marriage...You made your bed and that was that. Now we see a whole different mindset. You see Charlie Sheen in Us magazine, after a disastrous, or semidisasterous run of relationships and marriages, saying about his recent failed marriage: 'You buy a car, it breaks down, what are you going to do? Get rid of it.' That's a vast change in sensibility in relatively short span of forty years ago.[52]

In the anthology *Generations: A Century of Women Speak About Their Lives*, a ninety-two-year-old woman says:

Today a lot of marriages break up because people are not willing to recognize certain differences in their characters and make compromises...You can't have a relationship with a person for a life time and be a complete human being yourself without painful things happening. They have to be faced and handled. Today's human beings, I think they are too frivolous about this. Marriages fall apart too easily. It is very sad. It's preposterous.[53]

As the 1999 report "The State of Our Union" puts it:

Not so long ago, the marital relationship consisted of three elements: an economic bond of mutual dependency; a social bond supported by the extended family and larger community; and a spiritual bond upheld by religious doctrine, observance, and faith. Today many marriages have none of these elements.[54]

Instead, the 2001 report showed that 94 per cent of twentysomethings thought "when you marry you want your spouse to be your soul mate, first and foremost."[55] According to psychology professor Chuck Hill:

The high divorce rates, rather than implying that marriage is doomed, instead partly reflect the higher standards we have for marriage…Now people want their psychological needs to be met in marriage.[56]

Instead of looking toward a stable job, a home, a supportive community, intergenerational family, religious creed, or other traditional institutions to serve our needs, we turn to marriage.[57] We want marriage to make us feel intellectually stimulated, emotionally fulfilled, socially enhanced, financially free, and psychologically complete.

According to the National Marriage Project:

Increasingly, happiness in marriage is measured by each partner's sense of psychological well-being rather than the more traditional measures of getting ahead economically, boosting children up to a higher rung on the educational ladder than the parents, or following religious teachings on marriage. People tend to be puzzled or put off by the idea that marriage has purposes or benefits that extend beyond fulfilling individual adult needs for intimacy and satisfaction.[58]

Pamela Paul writes of those who call for traditional courtship:

The courtship contingent, ever ready, places the fault squarely with women. The charges generally run like this: women, and specifically feminists, set the ball rolling inexorably downhill by demanding economic and sexual freedom, both of which compromised femininity and negated the importance of masculinity.[59]

As Melinda Ledden Sidak of the conservative *Independent Women's Forum* explains:

Women, the traditional enforcers of sexual morality, abandoned their posts in the 1960s and 1970s under the onslaught of the sexual revolution. It has never been men who took the lead in enforcing the sexual code. Left to their own devices, men apparently are programmed to prefer sex with as many women as possible. It has been the special province of women to civilize men and to ensure a stable and secure economic and social position for themselves and their offspring by guarding fiercely the sanctity of marriage.

Due to woman's 'promiscuity,' man no longer has any reason to respect her or treat her well. Instead he succumbs to his basest instincts, sleeping with her and rejecting the consequences, refusing to marry or cheating on her when he does, and eventually divorcing her guiltlessly to seek out younger prey. Clearly, marriage cannot survive without premarital virginity, chaste womanhood, chivalrous maleness, a return to traditional gender roles within marriage, and public vilification of every alternative. In short, marriage cannot exist without every advance of the women's movement systematically reversed.[60]

If nothing else, the inclusion of GBLTQ union within heterosexual marriage symbolically says to society and more specifically our youth – "Nuts to traditional marriage." Then where is society heading? What is this so-called "feminist modern woman's" sexual profile? According to Dalma Heyn, author of *Marriage Shock: The Transformation of Women into Wives,* it looks like this:

The average young woman – working, assertive personally and professionally – is comfortable with independence, employment, autonomy, and multiple sexual relationships. She began having sex, according to the newest Kinsey Institute Report, between the (median) ages of sixteen and seventeen. If she marries at the age of twenty-seven, then, she will have been making love – with one man or several, simultaneously or serially, alone or cohabiting – for a decade. She is used to pleasure as to pleasing, and envisions having both in equal measure in an egalitarian marital relationship.[61]

Heyn wishes to see marriage reinvented for the needs of this "feminist modern woman." She writes:

Yet we send this sexually experienced modern woman to the altar the way we sent her virginal, voteless, and homebound great grandmother: with revelry and relief, and the vague, romantic prayer that if she has chosen Mr. Right right, she will, sure enough, live happily ever after. The odds are against it. But as a culture we continue to support, with our hopes, our silence, and our denial of crucial new realities, a relentlessly dewy-eyed picture of marriage.[62]

Heyn's model for a renewed marriage:

A new kind of marriage in which a wife's creativity, her spontaneity, her spirit – in the broadest sense, her sexuality – are all set free? [63]

Heyn hopes to smash some of the structural boundaries of the traditional marriage and create a transformed arrangement which lets "light" into every part of women's lives. She asks, "How can a woman be discontented when she's just taken on the very role (marriage) she's longed for most? What do women want?" Heyn cites a 1994 infidelity survey in *New Women* magazine, in which 83 per cent of the respondents said they believed that "wives submerge a vital part of themselves" when they marry.[64] According to Heyn it is sexual pleasure (which may include lesbian love) which is abandoned:

The women I spoke with, whether in their twenties or their sixties, began revising their previous, premarriage lives as soon as the ring was on their finger. No sooner were the wedding photos taken than they began to alter the picture of who they were before marriage, as if to shutter up a building before gutting it. Burning old love letters is a premarriage ritual that many women confessed to. Yet it was a ritual that felt neither destructive nor dangerous, but rather protective and loving: They believed they were welcoming marriage in by saying good-bye to the past. But their good-byes sounded suspiciously like 'good riddance.' This past – a modern woman's years of single, sexual, autonomous living – seems to need to be not just lovingly released but brusquely jettisoned at the altar. At marriage something extraordinary happens to a woman. She decides that a substantial chunk of her history is unwelcome and has to be cast off, as if it were a spent but still radioactive first-stage rocket that must not be allowed to accompany her into the perfect orbit of married life.[65]

She writes about Sarah, a twenty-nine-year-old social worker married less than a year. The new wife felt "stupid" when she talked about the turbulence of her former relationships:

Stupid? How? Stupid because it was all so fraught. Everything was so intense, so meaningful all the time. What was stupid about it, if it was meaningful? All those relationships feel now just like so much wasted time, so many wasted emotions spent on all those men who I don't remember anymore, Sarah says. And even if I could, and I liked them, I couldn't see them for dinner, even if I wanted to – right? Because you can't. And so a whole vibrant history of sex and intensity, joy and rage and agony gets bleached out and shrunken down to little more than a prologue to marriage, an opening act for the main attraction, a tryout for 'the real thing.' Or highlights – like Tami's or Sarah's Greatest Hits – summed up and recorded on a single disc.[66]

Says Heyn:

Protecting her husband from hurt and jealousy is a key motive for a women's self-revision, but she is protecting herself as well: from being revealed in some imagined unlovely light, as too experienced, too knowledgeable, too sexual, too problematic, too hungry or insatiable, too something.[67]

Heyn makes no claim that husbands may also choose to hide their past to avoid jealousy. (We know from Emma Goldman's letters that at least *one* woman has demonstrated vulnerability to jealousy, even when unmarried and a free love advocate.) Of women Heyn writes:

The healthy pleasure seeking that all the magazines urge on the independent young woman seems suddenly not so appealing in a wife. Many women hide from their husbands the better part of their sexual history, slashing the number and importance of the men they've been involved with, editing not only what they did and with whom, but entire chapters, whole human beings, right along with what they felt, as if the unexpurged version had the power to ruin their lives.[68]

Here one must ask if Heyn is suggesting, outside of marriage, and in a free sex culture, that lovers feel open to discuss, without inhibition, all their previous lovers with their current sexual partner. The implication that such secrecy is only in marriage lacks credibility. If such open conversations have taken place before marriage, they were likely to gain information about sexually transmitted diseases. There is ample evidence of unmarried lovers wishing to avoid parading their sexual histories for the sake of following "safe sex practices." What Heyn is really observing is the fact marriage elevates matters to a higher standard of trust and expectation. This trust factor plays out as fidelity. And there is something incredulous and naturally counter-fidelity in claiming a marvelous free sex past, enriched with numerous erotic lovers (where, when and however you wanted them), which somehow now will not continue.

Sadly, what becomes clear as Heyn develops *Marriage Shock* is the stereotypical radical feminist painting of the husband against a tired background of patriarchy. The story reads: in marriage a man feels no "shock;" he can and does commit adultery (have his "own pleasure") without consequence; he can and does pursue personal goals, i.e. career and golf, independent of impact on family (and social judgment); there is no difference in social status between a bachelor and a husband; and his goals for himself do not change in marriage. In this absurd marriage-equality diagnosis, Heyn chooses to accept this feminist view of the husband and then proscribes that the wife simply mirror her masculine counterpart, over turning centuries of contrary psychological and sociological theories. She even quotes this history from Dr. O. A. Wall, who wrote in his 1932 book *Sex and Sex Worship*:

Lust is seldom an element in a woman's character, and she is the preserver of chastity and morality...[if women were] as salacious as men, morality, chastity, and virtue would not exist and the world would be but one vast brothel.[69]

The formula for heterosexual marriage ills, particularly women's marriage-based depression – universal application of "The Single Standard," infidelity for all! To this Heyn writes:

For two centuries, women were supposed to be, by nature, above or without desire, able to enjoy sex at best only passively, 'vaginally,' and then only in marriage... After three hundred years of the Wife's reign, the verb 'to want' always implies a male subject. The Wife was constructed to be without desire, to have won, upon marriage, everything she could ever want, to be, perfectly satisfied and sexually dead to the world outside it.[70]

We're zookeepers, guarding and protecting our erotic, endangered, wild animals, making sure that nothing we do or say, read or think, know or feel threatens their security, and that, above all, nothing reveals our guilty yearning to burst out of this arrangement in which our pleasure, our desire, our power to stay or leave – our conduct – is always, always suspect. The terror is that if a wife does what she wishes..., everything else – society, the family, children – will go to hell; that only a wife's self-sacrifice assures reliable family bonds; her desire promises chaos and abandonment....

Here again we find the lesbian underpinnings to feminism, and associated with it, signs of manic cognitive dissonance. Imagine vaginal sex (the procreative sex-engine for all humankind, not to mention most of the animal kingdom) is now equated to "passive sex." Heyn continues:

Perhaps another framework, pleasurable and comfortable and roomy enough for both sexes, one that allows both of them their full sexuality, expression and transgression, goodness and badness, would be more lasting. Rather than forcing her back to the zoo, where men are incorrigible so somebody has to be good, why not create another framework, one that assumes the morality and sexuality of both husband and wife – so she'll want to stay?[71]

Can you imagine a marriage based on a new standard of sexual conduct, one that proclaims us all equally vulnerable, equally sexual, equally human? Can you envision an institution in which a wife's desires are acknowledged as real, as separate from her family's, and then openly discussed and acted upon? Can you imagine a time when seeing to wive's pleasure, our own separate pleasure, is crucial to the future of marriage? Come join the revolution. We're about to over throw the Wife.[72]

Remember Dalma Heyn, next time someone says that including lesbian union within traditional heterosexual marriage will have no impact on the institution. She is really advocating a lesbian version of the Roman and Greek homosexual era discussed in Chapter 4. This is a paradigm where same-sex pleasure is seen to offer the greatest eroticism. In this context, marriage for pro-creative purposes should be maintained as a secondary societal duty (at least until breakthroughs in genetic engineering make traditional birthing redundant and the need for heterosexual marriage optional). Heyn adds:

Words like honor and duty, forever and compromise; phrases like 'settling down' and 'taking responsibility' – our good conduct – have a way of adding such weight to what started out as an easy, fluid, breathing relationship that by the time family and children and values get thrown in, we begin to believe that pleasure is 'selfish.' Which is too bad.[73]

Let's replace that stern, rigid, either-or language we hear when we marry, the voice of the Witness, with the voice of our authentic selves, our fluid sensibility. Let us bring into the dialogue of our marriages the distinctive 'babel of eroticism, attachment, and empathy' – that powerful, flowing, oceanic delight that women take in their relationships and pour back into them...Such a female language, with its fluid, emotional tones and its extensive three-octave range – the capacity for fun and joy, the sheer unself-conscious expressiveness of it – cannot even be imagined. The full range of female pleasure is as unlikely to be celebrated inside the institution of marriage as Mardi Gras is in the military. A wife must rush out of doors, go AWOL, or she will be silenced.[74]

Here bold and boasting in prophesy is once again what I have labeled the "Pivot of Civilization" ideology. It says all life's power and happiness swings on the pivot of sexual pleasure. Moreover, it advises that the key to life's success is the ordering of everything around orgasm. Heyn puts Sanger's ideology this way:

Fun is sexy. It's life-affirming. It's subversive...What's more, it turns out that pleasure, rather than being something you can have for dessert once a month after loftier, worthier goals are met, seems instead to be the shortest route to these goals. Fun turns into trust; fun creates respect; fun produces spiritual bond; fun generates intimacy...How do children learn, after all? Through hours of play. What is good sex? Adult play.[75]

Leaving aside the lesbian rallying call (to be "our authentic selves") and their associated idol of the "infinite orgasm," the following quote from Germaine Greer's book *Sex and Destiny: The Politics of Human Fertility* is offered as a testimony on behalf of traditional "Husband and Wife" marriages, the Biblical marriage relationship and the error of calling vaginal sex "passive." Greer met this lady on a Sydney street the morning after she had participated in a debate on women's right to abortion in the Sydney Town Hall:

'You are very stupid. You think you are very clever, but you are really very stupid,' 'Very likely,' I replied, 'but why do you say so?' 'You stupid feminists,' she went on, 'don't you know what it is to have a good man's love.' (Well, I had heard that one before but she would brook no demurral.) 'My husband loves me. He doesn't make me take dangerous medicines or have gadgets put inside me. He takes care of me.'...she had two children and no abortions, nor had she ever been afraid that she might fall pregnant and never had been inorgasmic with her husband, who was a skilled and attentive lover still. She was Hungarian. My naïve dismissal of coitus interruptus on the Town Hall stage has never been repeated. Instead I have often asked men if they have ever performed coitus interruptus over extended periods, and whether they found it frustrating or difficult if they have. One respondent told me he had experienced great tenderness and a positive pleasure in taking the responsibility, which was the last thing I expected to hear. The clock can probably not be turned back, but it is truly ironic in these days of female emancipation that the young women in my college audiences in the United States do not feel that they could ask their lovers to do as much for them as that husband of that middle-aged Hungarian woman...[76]

Thankfully the informed have a choice in how we order our lives – "fidelity and intimacy" or "sexual infidelity and jealousy." Heyn and like-minded feminists ignore what I have coined the "Emma Goldman Phenomenon" – her excruciating jealousy and pain derived from trying to live a free sex ideology. Overlooking this major shortcoming of promiscuity, one still wonders how more sex, more variety and more partners can make communication within a marriage or family, between husband and wife or parents and children, any better. We have seen how bisexuals must order their relationships and regulate their daily and weekly lives. Don't speak of parenting here. What part do more external sexual relationships have in improving a floundering marriage?

Heyn even knows the correct answer to the question, however, blinded by feminist optics, she argues that men will never be faithful, so by corollary why should women:

Men rarely confuse the 'shoulds' of their role with their own needs, desires or character. So while men may appreciate the value of selflessness, no one expects them to be innately, biologically self-sacrificing, as if any other impulse were a violation of their very nature.[77]

Heyn cites Jessie Bernard's 1972 warning: "Marriage may be hazardous to women's health."[78] She cites marriage, not "genetics, PMS, birth-control pills, or even poverty" as the key source of hitched woman's depression. Heyn also cites noted depression expert Ellen McGrath, M.D., writing: "the clear correlation between marriage and women's depression remains 'psychology's dirty little secret.'"[79]

Where is the truth? What voices are shaping the thinking of the modern woman and wife? Sexual liberationists often declare that their true end is sexual freedom for both men and women. But nothing is finally free, least of all sex. Sex can be cheapened, but then, inevitably, it becomes extremely costly to society as a whole.[80] George Gilder calls feminism and sexual liberalism an ideology of personal hedonism based on fear of the future, the old sophomoric canard of "eat drink and be merry, for tomorrow we die"[81] (earlier quoted by Emma Goldman in her capitulation to Ben Reitman). But it is a kind of aimless copulation having little to do with the deeper currents of sexuality and love that carry a community into the future. Most heterosexual parents can empathize with Gilder's views:

I do not want to see my daughters grow to be like the feminist leaders now reportedly longing to have children as they approach their fifties. I do not want my wife to feel she is unequal to me if she earns less money than I do, or unequal to the careerist women I meet at work. I understand that sexual liberalism chiefly liberates men from their families, and I love my family more than I long to relive a bachelor freedom or marry a coed. I understand the desire of many lesbian women to want a form of radical feminism – so-called 'separationist ideology' from necessary connection with men and so-called 'patriarchal' heterosexual institutions.[82]

Martha Ruppert comments:

To some people, the idea of a family tree is nothing more than an exercise for genealogists. But in reality, for many families, the tree is rotting and breaking apart from neglect, infidelity, cohabitation without the marriage covenant, divorce, and out-of-wedlock births.[83]

In the September 1998, *Reader's Digest*, Mary Roach wrote of her thoughts just before marriage in her article "Much Ado About 'Mr. Right'":

I used to balk at the idea of lifelong fidelity. But what did I gain for my decade and a half of relative freedom? The heart leaping off a cliff and flying through the air. And shortly thereafter hitting the ground. Heart pulp. Guilt and regret. The knowledge that by refusing to commit myself fully to a relationship, I destroyed it.

Something else I failed to grasp is that all marriages are group marriages. I am marrying a man...his warm, welcoming parents; his sister; his cousins; their families. A whole clan of hearts and minds that wants me to sign on. What could be more wonderful?

My own family was small and cut off, a lone asteroid out of its orbit. Growing up I had no grandparents and never got to know my aunts and uncles. Marriage is a second chance to belong.

Would I belong if we simply lived together? Past experience says, not really. To share a house with someone but not marry sends a message – to him, to our families, to everyone. It says, I love this man, but I'm not sure he's it. That's a message I don't wish to send anymore.[84]

According to author Mark Lee:

Critics may attack marriage, not so much with facts as opinions. Some arguments are non-sequiturs; they do not follow logically. For, example, according to Time magazine, British biologist Alexander Comfort asserted: 'A husband or wife is expected to be mother, father, child, uncle and aunt; this is a greater burden than any one human being can possibly carry.' And what is his answer to these role problems? According to Time: 'Group sex is a way of sharing the burden,' and Alexander Comfort anticipates a future 'in which settled couples engage openly in a side range of sexual relations with friends.'[85]

What do sexual relationships with friends have to do with making mothers, fathers, aunts and uncles meet role needs in the family? Alexander Comfort argues unpersuasively:

Most people have been married more than once, and adultery is universally tolerated. Open marriage would simply legitimize what we already live.[86]

I wonder how Comfort would view the issue of same-sex marriage and its impact on heterosexual marriage? Where is the truth contends Mark Lee:

It is unbelievable that a sophisticated person would make statements like these when he knew, at the time of the statement, that two thirds to three-fourths of marrieds live with their original spouse. And adultery is still frowned upon, even though there may be no legal sanctions against it. Comfort, like others would diminish traditional life based on bizarre or minority conduct – conduct accented by the media. They make war on the American family. And they presume that their attacks have won the war.[87]

Cohabitation

In the 1970s, marriage often seemed either absent or irrelevant. Parent's didn't discuss matrimony with their children even if they stayed married; if they divorced, they avoided the topic entirely. The underlying sentiment against parents giving advice to their children about marriage seems to have been, Who am I to Talk? With rare exception, the people interviewed for this book said their parents gave them no lessons about marriage, no guidance, no warnings, no encouragement, no words of wisdom. Just silence...[88]

More than 40 per cent of today's marrying generation spent time growing up in a single-parent home by the time they were sixteen.[89]

Cohabitation is often called a "trial marriage" for those who cannot love unconditionally. Cohabitation is a variation on free sex experimentation. It is serial partner experimentation. Today's marrying generation believes that "testing things out" will lead to stronger marriages and weed out potential mistakes. In a 2001 survey of twentysomethings, 62 per cent agreed that "living together with someone before marriage is a good way to avoid an eventual divorce," and 43 per cent would only marry after living together.[90] However, granting a marriage license to a seemingly successful experimental (exploitive-based) relationship does not make that relationship either moral or mature. Catherine Wallace writes:

...having sex and living together inevitably blurs the boundaries between two people, with all the temptations to denial and to projection that such blurring invites.[91]

According to Marriage Project at Rutgers University, over half of first marriages today are preceded by cohabitation – compared with about 10 per cent in 1965.[92] Cohabitation has been steadily on the rise over the past four decades, increasing 864 per cent since 1960.[93]

Pamela Paul found that recent studies show that couples who live together beforehand have rockier marriages and a significantly higher divorce rate – some studies claim up to 48 per cent higher.[94] One report shows that first marriages beginning with cohabitation are almost twice as likely to end within ten years.[95] In *The Case for Marriage*, Maggie Gallagher and sociologist Linda Waite argue against cohabitation. According to Waite, live-in couples are less financially stable, less faithful, and less happy than their lawfully wedded counterparts. They have a higher rate of domestic violence than married couples, and when they do marry they divorce more often.[96]

The two individuals in a trial marriage often have very different conceptions of what cohabitation is and where they're heading. One person may see living together as a testing ground on the road to marriage, while her partner views it as a convenient form of serious dating: no need to commute to her home closet in the morning after yet another night at her boyfriend's apartment. A woman may be certain of her own desire to marry her live-in, while her unsuspecting mate thinks the situation is strictly on a trial basis. Or vice versa.[97] Cohabitation is predominantly seen as a means to an end – not an end in and of itself. As such, trial marriages are usually short-term arrangements. People either break up or, more likely (approximately 60 per cent) get married – typically within a year and a half.[98] Paul says love in a trial marriage is inherently conditional: "I'll love you for as long as this works out/makes me happy/fulfills me."[99]

Max, a thirty-one-year-old salesperson from Connecticut, regrets having lived with his girlfriend before getting married at twenty-six:

I think it was a bad idea. It took a lot of mystery out of everything. Once we got married, it felt nothing had changed. There was nothing of value that was different. We went on our honeymoon, we came back, and it was just the same thing.[100]

Another common observation is that children of divorce are more wary of marriage than their counterparts from intact families. Children of divorce typically cohabitate before marriage. Divorced parents often tell their children to "live together first" in an effort to prevent the same mistakes being made.[101]

Cynicism towards marriage is often a mask for an underlying fear of being let down, a fear that causes many couples to avoid marriage in the first place. Instead, they gravitate toward trial marriages, which are supposed to protect you from making a commitment that you can't or won't want to keep. The idea is that cohabitation will lessen the chances of divorce because instead of divorcing, you can simply part ways if the relationship falls apart. And this is probably true. But at the same time, by creating a short-term, casual mind-set and individualistic approach to relationships, trial marriages may end up encouraging divorce. Trial marriage breeds the mentality of letting go, moving out, moving on, and starting anew – making it psychologically easier to end long-term relationships. It becomes less difficult and more justifiable with each turn. If you've been able to break up the serious commitment of cohabitation, isn't it just one small step to breaking up a brief, unrewarding marriage? Getting used to having an out can become a self-fulfilling prophecy for a real marriage down the road.[102]

As William Doherty, director of the Marriage and Family Therapy Program notes:

I wonder what [cohabitation] teaches people about commitment and about working through problems. Fifteen years ago, I might have said, 'It's a good idea.' Five years ago, I would have said who cares?' But now, I'm hoping my own adult children do not cohabitate.[103]

Serial monogamy and cohabitation lead to a persistent sense of failure among its participants, who watch again and again as yet another relationship doesn't work out. We learn not to sacrifice, not to risk, not to get hurt. We erect barriers and defense mechanisms because we know that what we give will eventually be taken away. We hedge our bets, we hold back, and we refuse to commit. When we do commit, we do so on our own narrow, inconsistent terms. Trial marriages usually end because the relationship fails to make one party happy. There is no cause, ideal, or commitment – no "for the sake of our marriage" complication – outside the well-being of the two individuals involved, whereas in a marriage, the marriage itself acts as a third, overriding entity. [104]

The *National Longitudinal Survey of Children* tells us cohabitation negatively impacts children. In 1993-1994, 20.4 per cent of births were in common law unions, twice that of 10 years before. Results are clear that children born to married parents, not lived in common law, are 3 times less likely to experience family breakdown. Within 10 years 14 per cent of married with children break-up and 63 per cent of common law with children.[105] More than 3.9 million babies were born to common law couples in 1998, up 2 per cent from 1997. Meanwhile, the number of "unwed births" – 1,293,567 – reached a new high, which experts attribute to a surge in cohabitation. Data from the early 1990s indicate that 40 per cent of unwed births are to cohabiting parents.[106] Sociologist Barbara Dafoe Whitehead and David Popenoe reported in 1999 that cohabitation was replacing marriage "as the first living together union," especially among young adults. Their studies also show that cohabiting is less stable than marriage.[107]

The instability of marriages and cohabitations diminishes the role of fatherhood. Cornel West and Sylvia Hewlett in *The War Against Parents* write:

Escalating rates of divorce and out-of-wedlock birth mean that close to half of all fathers lose contact with their children, and this has left a deep emotional voice in the soul of men….this voice fosters profound feelings of worthlessness and can trigger anti-social behavior. Despite a large body of research on the fallout of fatherlessness on children, the expert community has paid little attention to how child absence affects fathers. Not surprisingly, the misery of the adult often mirrors the child.[108]

Heterosexual Matrimony

There is always someone else who would love me more, understand me better, make me feel more sexually alive. This is the best justification we have for monogamy – and fidelity…

You can be occasionally unfaithful, but you can't be occasionally monogamous. You can't be monogamous and unfaithful at the same time…

Monogamy and infidelity: the difference between making a promise and being promising.[109]

Adam Phillips, 'Monogamy'

According to Pamela Paul:

Marriage is no longer about creating a new unit through procreation; it's about creating a new unit ('the marriage' itself) while maintaining two individual ones – both of whom are somehow meant to become better, stronger, happier, and more worthy in the process. Not only is there no central goal to marriage, the multiple 'goals' of marriage are so diverse and demanding that one may as well say, 'What I want from marriage is a happy life.'[110]

She says, a number of young marrieds she interviewed were keen to escape their birth families and establish their own family structure. James, a multimedia designer from Washington State, explains his wife's desire to marry:

Her parents were both on their third marriages, and there was no security in her home growing up. She told me that was a big attraction for her, the fact that I was so stable and came from a stable home.[111]

According to Catherine Wallace, sexual intercourse ought to be the exclusive and embodied language of commitment between two people. Traditionally, that sort of commitment is called "matrimony." Individual relationships of this kind are called "marriages" for heterosexuals and "domestic partnerships" for homosexuals.[112] Although matrimonial intimacy is the paradigm of the intimacy that underlies all real community, the fact remains that marriages are different in degree from other relationships. Wallace argues that the full measure of intimacy is necessarily sexual because our bodies are ourselves. We must undress, both emotionally and physically, in order to satisfy our deepest needs for full intimacy. But that undressing entails an equally full measure of vulnerability. Thus complete intimacy cannot develop except within the security or confidence of a serious and permanent commitment to the relationship.[113] Here lies the difference between cubical sex with anonymous partners, first date sex with a relatively unknown partner, a Wednesday night regular adulterous rendezvous, multipartnered sexual arrangements; and sexual intimacy between monogamous lifelong marriage partners (what the Hungarian woman described to Germaine Greer!).

In the absence of full confidence in the reliability and seriousness of the commitment between partners, both common sense and psychic self-preservation will demand a guardedness, a holding back, a tentativeness that impedes the development of full intimacy. Says Wallace:

It explains a key difficulty in talking to our kids about sex: The young are, on the whole, blissfully but unconsciously certain of their own invulnerability. They do not realize as we do, how profoundly they can be hurt by a casual sexual affair or a sexual infidelity of a spouse.[114] *[unless witness to their own parents breakup over adultery]*

In the war of sex ideology, the reality of fidelity – particularly the faithful husband's fidelity, impacts the battle like a strong cloud of mustard gas drifting over the radical feminist front lines. Normally ardent and enthusiastic under the banner of resisting "oppression and patriarchy" these feminists have no defense against a committed, supporting, faithful and even romantic husband. Witnessed in the consistently phobic reception given REAL Women, radical feminists simply refuse to acknowledge happily married heterosexual women. From the monogamous heterosexual perspective, had the sexual liberation era not recruited so many to be unfaithful, undutiful and non-spouse-oriented, this battle would not have inflicted the casualties it has, the damage on children, nor lasted as long. In the war of sex ideology, the reality of heterosexual infidelity, acts like an unfortunate wind change, saving the feminists from extinction and giving their side renewed hope as they witness the toxic carnage to marriages and to heterosexual women in particular. Key here, is the strategic use of infidelity in achieving liberation goals. The pact of radical feminist, GBLTQ, sex positive and free love supporters, at the height of their successes in the 70s, all proclaimed marriage and fidelity dead.

But marriage is not dead. Its resilience is awesome. And the counter-battle is in motion. In battle parlance, the radical feminist ideologies failed to win enough converts to consolidate their gains. Their problem continues to be a failure to develop a sustainable and credible replacement philosophy. One should not be surprised; therefore, to see the movement change strategies midstream (and 180 degrees), falling back onto the historically winning tactic of fighting individual rights-based legal battles. Ironically, the key symbol now for radical feminists and GBLTQ is equal access to the institution of marriage.

The counter-feminist revolution can be described through ideas such as covenant marriages (new "undivorceable" unions offered in several states), marriage-training high school classes, and calls to repeal no-fault divorce laws and the so-called marriage penalty tax.[115] In a 1999 poll more Boomers (1946-1964) than Generation Xers (1965-1978) agreed with the statement: "People should live for themselves rather than their children."[116] In a 1995 poll, Gen Xers overwhelming favored family over career. Over half said they respect women who devote themselves wholeheartedly to their families (53 per cent) compared with only one third (33 per cent) who respect those who devote themselves to career.[117]

Pamela Paul cites a March 2000 poll, in which 86 per cent of Americans responded yes when asked, "If you got married today, would you expect to stay married for the rest of your life.?"[118] In its 1998 report, "Time to Repaint the Gen X Portrait," the Yankelovich research firm warns, "Expect the Gen Xers to place paramount importance on family togetherness."[119] For some 63 per cent of Gen xers, "the good life" means having two or more kids.[120] Over half claim that they get most or all of their satisfaction from home and family, rather than from away-from-home activities like work or friends.[121] Of those surveyed, 92 per cent believed that "it's critical for children today to have activities that anchor them to their families, like regular sit-down meals or weekly religious services." Eighty-five per cent believe "people should pass on to their children a sense of belonging to a particular religion or racial or national tradition," and 83 per cent felt that "even though men have changed a lot, women are still the main nurturers."[122]

Today's twentysomethings look down on the radical lifestyles of a rebellious yesteryear. Despite the commotion of the sexual revolution, nobody is rushing into open marriages. According to a 1998 *NBC/Wall Street Journal* poll, 90 per cent of Americans believe that extramarital affairs are "always wrong" or "almost always wrong," up from the 1970s and 1980s, and Gen X disapproves of adultery to the same extent that their parents and grandparents did.[123] In 1972, 10 per cent of eighteen-to-twenty-four-year-olds considered premarital sex wrong; by 1998, the number had more than doubled to 23 per cent.[124] Paul further claimed in a poll taken in 1977, when Boomers were in their twenties, 56 per cent desired a "return to traditional family life;" contrast that with the 74 per cent of Gen X respondents who agreed with the statement in 1999.[125]

In 1999, only 10 per cent of Americans described themselves as divorced "last year" – because though almost half get divorced at some point, many had since remarried. Divorced status is decidedly not a permanent one.[126]

At its most fundamental level, marriage was created for two twined purposes – permanent sexual companionship and the raising of children. However, today sex has become almost entirely divorced from the notion of marriage. Rare is the women who claims she's marrying in order to have intercourse. Even pregnancy doesn't lead to marriage. Today, only 23 per cent of women pregnant and single marry before giving birth.[127] So in what direction do you wish society to move? We do have a choice. The cultural destiny of Canadians and Americans is not pre-determined. Here we next look at what Christianity has said of the institution of marriage for more than two thousand years?

Christian Marriage

This section builds upon the evidence presented in Chapter 4, under "Christian Patriarchy." On the subject of fidelity, Catherine Wallace writes:

...fidelity does not produce happiness in the way that a factory produces widgets. It's not quid pro quo in that way, this for that, trade a little fidelity for a little happiness or a lot of fidelity for riotous delight morning after morning for happily ever after. Life is not that simple. Those who are faithful enjoy something that those who are not faithful do not enjoy, but fidelity is not a means to an end of joy in the way that a light switch is a means to turning on a light. [128]

Fidelity is more like the skill of the flutist. To arrive at the world class performance requires endless practice. It is a calling to be a particular kind of person with a particular kind of life. It was once called a 'discipline,' which is to say a defining or characteristic set of choices, virtues, and activities. And so with marriage. Sexual fidelity cannot guarantee marital happiness; just as practicing the flute cannot guarantee a booking at Carnegie Hall. On the other hand, no one gets such a booking who has not practiced with real devotion. For those trying to experience a genuinely happy marriage, the virtue of fidelity is a central discipline shaping their lives, not merely a good investment of energies.[129]

A younger adult – a teenager, perhaps – may learn to abstain for now from genital sexuality, but a full understanding of sexual fidelity takes decades. That full understanding arises not from abstract studies but from an embodied life. The only way to learn about integrity is to begin by not lying, as one begins to understand nonviolence by not hitting or begins to understand sexual fidelity by not having casual sex.[130]

In the "marketplace" marriage or Heyn's "open" marriage, a partnership that is not reasonably consistent in its gratifications becomes a net loss and ought therefore to be terminated or offset by outside sex. In these models, a marriage is like a business, which has a bottom line. Wallace writes:

Sexual fidelity might seem, from the outside, to demand deep and painful sacrifices; in fact it is not a sacrifice at all but rather a blessing, a movement away from zero-sum cost-benefit calculations and toward the compassionate depths of generative life and the grace of that authentic prosperity that is never afraid to share.[131]

The promiscuous are left wondering how they can put some meaning into their lives. As one college student complains:

It's one of the biggest problems of our generation, the fact that no one attaches meaning to anyone. People say they love whoever they want and have sex with whoever they want, but what it all comes down to is you end up in a void of meaninglessness.[132]

Pamela Paul writes:

Our longing for ideas and beliefs larger than ourselves has led to a surge in spirituality. In a 1998 poll of college freshmen, 90 per cent believe in God, three fourths believe in life after death, most attend religious services, and almost half believe that religion will be more important in the future.[133]

After reading a review of a book on cohabitation contracts, Ann Brown, was struck by the emphasis in all the sample contracts on the rights of the individual: rights to property, rights to children, rights to child support and rights to a career. She contends the same emphasis on rights may be apparent among interpreters of Apostle Paul's teaching on marriage. At one extreme are those who argue for a hierarchical model to establish the husband's right to rule and to emphasize the differences between the sexes. At the other are those who argue for an egalitarian model to give equal rights to husband and wife and to relativize the differences between the sexes. Says Brown:

Both models fall short of the biblical ideal as set out by Paul in Ephesians 5. He made no mention of rights, only of the obligations of husband and wife. His model marriage is one of self-giving in which each partner loves the other unconditionally. It is a picture of unity and diversity.[134]

Instead of emphasizing rights, Apostle Paul described the responsibilities of both partners. These are revolutionary by the standards of any culture. He began by telling husband and wife to 'submit to one another out of reverence for Christ' (Ephesians 5:21), then went on to set an extraordinary standard of self-giving for them both. It is a tragedy that Ephesians 5 has been understood as endorsing an oppressive model of marriage; it does just the opposite. The events described in Genesis 3 marked the beginning of hostilities between the sexes. Explains Brown:

The teaching of Ephesians 5, by putting the emphasis on self-giving, is designed to avoid the power struggle that was set in motion in Eden.[135]

Apostle Paul explained the husband's headship by giving two illustrations. Husbands are to love their wives 'just as Christ loved the church and gave himself up for her' (Ephesians5:25) and 'as their own bodies' (Ephesians 5:28). Headship is primarily defined in terms of self-giving. Headship is not tyranny. John Chrysystom explains:

Take then the same provident care for her, as Christ takes for the church. Yes, even if it shall be needful for you to give your life for her, yes, and to be cut into ten thousand pieces, yes, and to endure and undergo any suffering whatever, refuse it not. Though you should undergo all this, yet you will not, no, not even then, have done anything like Christ.

In his first letter to the church in Corinth, Paul compared the relationship between the sexes to the relationship between God and Christ. He wrote: 'Now I want you to realize that the head of every man is Christ and the head of the woman is man, and head of Christ is God' (1 Corinthians 11:3). The relationship between man and woman reflects the unity and diversity of the Trinity. This is a beautiful picture. The Father and Son are equal but the Father is head. It would never occur to us to think that because God is described as the head of Christ, Christ is exploited in this relationship. So we should not assume that man's being head of the woman means exploitation. 'Man's headship of the woman is no more incompatible with the equality of the sexes than the Father's headship of the Son is incompatible with the unity of the Godhead.'[136]

He was very careful to qualify his remarks on Genesis 2 by adding, 'In the Lord, however, woman is not independent of man, nor is man independent of woman. For as woman came from man, so also man is born of woman. But everything comes from God'(1 Corinthians 11:12). Man is not superior to, or closer to God, than woman.[137]

Therefore, does the husband exercise authority over the wife? What is the wife's role in decision-making? Does the husband's career come first? According to the Bible, should a woman never take initiative? What is the practical outworking of headship? It is obvious, for example, that the husband does not act as savior for his wife. The husband is to lead in self-sacrificial service. Brown writes:

If 'headship' means 'power' in any sense, then it is power to care not to crush, power to serve not to dominate, power to facilitate self-fulfillment, not to frustrate or destroy it. How could a husband who is trying to put this into practice contemplate making decisions with no reference to his wife? How could a Christian husband subject his wife to violence and brutal domination? The Bible holds out a warning that if men do not live considerately with their wives, and do not treat them with respect as the weaker vessel (presumably this means the more vulnerable physically), then their prayers will be hindered (1 Peter 3:7).[138]

Reciprocity is fundamental to Christian marriage. In Ephesians 5, Paul begins the command to the woman with "but," though this is not present in all translations. Ephesians 5:24 should read "But as the church is subject to Christ, so let wives be subject in everything to their husbands." The implication is that she, too, must behave responsibly. The word used for "submission" has military connotations; the wife is "to order" herself so that she and her husband function as one. The onus is on the wife to give herself voluntarily, not on the husband to make her submit.[139] The woman who is idealized in Proverbs 31:10-31 does not have a narrowly defined role; she demonstrates her competence in many different areas of life. It does not tell us how to organize the division of labor in a home, or which style of parenting to adopt, or whether dual career structures are advisable. Christian marriage should be a competition in self-giving not for rights.[140]

According to Pamela Paul:

The best marriages seem to be the ones in which responsibilities are shared because each partner cares enough about the other person not to want him to shoulder too much of the burden, not because that partner is so preoccupied with ending up carrying the bulk of the load herself. Rather than being obsessed with our own expected contributions and what our partner takes for granted, we could focus on what we can do best, and what our spouse appreciates our having done. Giving to each other often has nothing to do with rights or assumptions or control but has everything to do with caring...Every kind of giving needn't be considered a form of 'giving up.'[141]

Lisa Kruger, writer of the film *Committed,* says:

I know 'it's better to give than receive' is one of the oldest notions in the world. But I feel like we've relegated that idea to the furthest back burner. We're very intent on getting what we deserve, getting what's ours. I see the pendulum swinging the other way. Because this endless getting, getting, getting is an empty goal.[142]

Pamela Paul contends:

Marriage isn't meant to be tracked like some kind of running tab. Ideally in marriage one partner is meant to care equally, if not more, for his partner's well-being than for his own. And if this is true, it simply works better to assume that things will even out in the end than to bicker about petty imbalances along the way...Human beings were never meant to function on a purely individualistic basis; we are fundamentally social creatures. We not only desire the company of others – we need it, and we actually serve ourselves in the process of both needing other people and giving of ourselves.[143]

As most anthropologists see it, however, the reason for the social-familial goal is simple. The very essence of marriage, Bronislaw Malinowski writes, is not structure and intimacy; it is "parenthood and above all maternity."[144] The male role in marriage, as Margaret Mead maintained, "in every known human society, is to provide for women and children."[145] In order to marry, in fact, Malinowski says that almost every human society first requires the man "to prove his capacity to maintain the woman."[146]

With Malinowski's anthropological given, where better to go for a description of the current Christ-Centered Family model then 600 happily successful husbands and wives. Advocate of traditional Biblical family values, James C. Dobson, Ph.D. describes the model based on the survey:

The panel first suggests that newlyweds should establish and maintain a Christ-centered home. Everything rests on that foundation. If a young husband and wife are deeply committed to Jesus Christ, they enjoy enormous advantages over the family with no spiritual dimension.

A meaningful prayer life is essential in maintaining a Christ-centered home. Of course, some people use prayer the way they follow their horoscopes, attempting to manipulate an unidentified 'higher power' around them. It is impossible for me to overstate the need for prayer in the fabric of family life. Not simply as a shield against danger, of course. A personal relationship with Jesus Christ is the cornerstone of marriage, giving meaning and purpose to every dimension of living. Being able to bow in prayer as the day begins or ends gives expression to the frustrations and concerns that might not otherwise be ventilated.

On the other end of that prayer line is a loving heavenly Father who has promised to hear and answer our petitions. In this day of disintegrating families on every side, we dare not try to make it on our own.

What will you do when unexpected tornadoes blow through your home, or when the doldrums leave your sails sagging and silent? Will you pack it in and go home to Mama? Will you pout and cry and seek ways to strike back? Or will your commitment hold you steady?

These questions must be addressed now, before Satan has an opportunity to put his noose of discouragement around your neck. Set your jaw and clench your fists. Nothing short of death must ever be permitted to come between the two of you. Nothing![147]

God has expectations for marriage. When God said, "It is not good for man to be alone," and when He created Eve as an answer to that loneliness, He had very specific expectations for marriage:[148]

Marriage will enable us to serve someone else's needs. In 1 Corinthians 7:28-35, Paul explains that marriage comes with responsibilities. Husbands and wives must spend much time working hard to please one another.....

Marriage will change us for the better. Scripture doesn't tell us to make sure our life-partner loves, respects, and gives us all the affectional, financial, and physical satisfaction we long for. The Bible doesn't promise that God will make our mates into the kind of people we pray they will be. It does tell us, however, what kind of a heart God can enable us to have if we do our part in bringing out the best in our mate. Marriage by its very nature demands our own spiritual growth. For us to live with and love someone else, 'for better for worse, for richer for poorer, in sickness and in health,' requires that we learn to put his or her interests ahead of our own.

Marriage will place us under the mutual spirit of love. The Bible makes it clear that when a man and a woman join in marriage, they become one. And the controlling factor of their oneness is their mutual commitment to care for one another's well being for as long as they both live...With love comes the responsibility to do everything possible to bring out the best in a mate rather than the worst. Love will not let us indulge the immorality or support the destructive addictions of our partner. As our God shows us by His example, love is tough when circumstances call for it.

...Husband and wife are to love and be true to and cherish each other – exclusively![149] *There must be absolute faithfulness. Adultery is forbidden (Exodus 20:14). Paul listed adultery first in his list of sins of the flesh (Galatians 5:19). Here are*

some implications of absolute faithfulness: concentrate our love on our mate, avoid flirtations, flee from temptation, do not be disloyal in small matters, and control our fantasies.[150]

In *Preparing for Marriage*, David Boehi et al., describe Genesis 2:23 "This is now bone of my bones and flesh of my flesh; she shall be called Woman, for she was taken out of Man," as a cornerstone principle of marriage. Just like Adam, you must individually receive your mate as God's provision for your need for companionship. Receiving your mate demonstrates your faith in God's integrity. Adam's focus was on God's flawless character, not on Eve's performance. He knew God and knew that God could be trusted. Adam enthusiastically received Eve because He knew that she was from God. Adam's faith in God enabled him to receive Eve as God's perfect provision for him. Before your marriage you must receive your mate in the same way. If you decide your fiancé(e) is indeed God's provision, you need to accept your fiancé's strengths and weaknesses. Will you unconditionally accept good habits (that are known) and bad habits (that you haven't learned yet)? Will you look beyond physical attractiveness to the God who is the provider, who knows what He is doing? You must maintain this continual acceptance for life.[151]

Reaffirming Leon Kass' courtship concept, which includes parental input, Martha Ruppert, amplifies the nature of God's provision for a husband or wife:

I knew a sixteen-year-old girl who was being wooed by an older man. Of course her parents were alarmed. The girl thought the matter was settled when she announced that God had revealed to her that she was to marry the guy. In her mind, all she had to do was 'hear from God' and that was the end of the discussion. What if she had been eighteen or twenty or thirty-two? Would she automatically know God's will any better then?

Believing we have heard from God is an extremely subjective matter, one that is still too easily warped in emotional desires. If God is powerful and wise enough to speak to young people, He can reach the ears of their parents too. If young people truly know the will of God, they can trust Him to bring it to pass and have absolutely nothing to fear from the counsel of their parents.[152]

Ruppert concludes that the divorce rate among Christians reflects our misguided custom of allowing the most vulnerable members of the body of Christ, our young people, to make marriage choices alone. She writes:

It is true there are many, many things in our children's lives that we entrust to God's sovereignty. We just don't want that 'trust' to be the final act of desperation as the result of our abdication of responsibility. As Christians, it is time we stand against our culture and establish accountability within our families. If we do not seek to have meaningful input regarding the potential marital unions of our children, then we find ourselves muzzled and on the sidelines while our children are led around by their emotions. We will find ourselves watching helplessly while our children suffer through disappointment, despair, and even divorce as they struggle with miserable unions. So many regretful parents would give anything if they could have somehow warned their children against unwise marriages.[153]

Can a couple ever know enough at the start to conclude this is the lifelong marriage relationship? No. The act of marriage by design (and in practical reality) is an act of faith. For Christian believers, taking the marriage vows is an act of trust in God's provision (your spouse) and His ability to supply sufficient grace in the years ahead.

Ken Nair, in *Discovering The Mind of a Woman,* develops further the Christian paradigm of the spouse as God's provision. He starts with comments on the misguided notion that "the role of boss means that the husband can disregard his wife's needs while abundantly taking care of his own." He writes:

For, example, a 'Christian' farmer had two sons for whom he consistently purchased the latest tractors and field machinery. He drove a nice truck. But he refused to install plumbing in the house, making the wife carry water from a well several hundred feet from the house while he had the luxury-equipment.

...traditional thinking, which portrays the man as the boss in the home, is going to be undermined by scriptural teaching – but the genuine spiritual leadership of the man is going to be reinforced. Men will be asked to stop thinking of themselves as the boss, the king, the emperor, or possibly even the dictator. Instead, they will be asked to earn positions of leadership in the home by dying to self (putting self last, and others first, including the wife). This does not mean ignoring responsibilities as husbands – it means re-evaluating attitudes.[154]

Nair contends:

Contrary to popular notions, most wives do not want to occupy the throne in their marriages...she is designed by God to feel secure only when she sees that her husband is not the final authority in their marriage, that he is looking to God for direction and guidance. Only then can she be confident that her relationship with her husband will be based on scriptural principles and not her husband's personal preferences... If you are Christlike and convinced that she is more important than you are, your first concern when you walk in the house will not be that your needs are met. You will be concerned about your wife and children first.[155]

Nair points out that most of us "don't think of our wives as God-given, valuable assets, worthy to include in our problem-solving process."[156] Moreover, most husbands do not reflect Christ-likeness in their relationships with their wives. Nair writes:

If Christ did not seek to promote Himself or His interests, but found His importance in glorifying God, a man can practice not promoting himself or his interests by preferring his wife. She in turn will be his glory because he is obedient to God (1 Corinthians 11:7).[157]

If you accept the fact that you and others have spirits deserving attention, the next step is to stop resenting your wife and what she is saying and doing. Instead of seeing her as a problem, consider her as a mirror in the hand of God, revealing how sensitive and insensitive you are. Once you do that it is amazing how much she can help sensitize you to the needs of her spirit and to those of others' spirits.[158]

In closing this section on Christian marriage, I cite the bottom-line, by drawing once more upon Ken Nair's wisdom:

As you can see a woman determines for herself if a man has Christ-like character from a variety of life's experiences. But more than anything, a wife determines her husband's Christ-like character by his willingness to let her participate in his life. More often than not, that means that her husband is willing to be held answerable even to his wife as the Holy Spirit alerts her to his character flaws. Too many husbands, even in our enlightened generation, reveal the natural tendency to think of themselves as the boss or ruler of the marriage. This attitude is reinforced by the popular notion in Christian circles that a woman's only requirements in marriage are to be a silent, obedient, submissive wife….Implicit in this attitude is that wives are to be flawless – while husbands excuse their behavior by rationalizations, none of which will hold up when they appear before the great Judge of the universe. God is not deceived by spiritual rationalizations of inexcusable behavior in the home by self-styled Christian leaders.[159]

Paradox of GBLTQ Marriage

On one side of the divide are those who believe that granting gay and lesbian people the legal right to marry will somehow destroy family life, undermining the very foundation on which families are built. On the other side are those who, like me, believe that legal marriage for same-gender couples is a constitutional right and completely irrelevant to the success of the heterosexual marriage and family.[160]

Eric Marcus, 'Together Forever: Gay and Lesbian Marriage'

From a Christian perspective, society has been and may very well continue to be careless about its foundational philosophies and values; moral and cultural boundaries; and institutional provisions handed to our children and future generations. This is not just a comment on the direction of societal trends, but a critique of the "liberalization" process over the past forty years. Ironically, in staunch democracies like Canada, governments have permitted seemingly isolated, incremental and individual rights-based court decisions (private charter rights arguments) to be the change agent for society over the collective and public rights of the majority. At the time of acceptance of the Canadian Charter of Rights, the question was asked seven times, would this Charter affect the definition of marriage, and seven times the answer was no. Although Prime Minister Trudeau was a humanist, which no doubt played no small role in his thinking about the Charter, one wonders if then he had foreseen the same-sex marriage challenge. A valuable lesson from the past forty years is that the state cannot, as then Justice Minister Pierre Elliott Trudeau said in 1967, divorce itself from the privacy of the individual "bedrooms of the nation." Surely the inability of society (gay or straight) to clamp down on bathhouse sex in the face of the AIDS crisis heralds a need to reappraise the Western ideology of prioritizing individual rights over collective rights and private protections over public protections. Here we have to a large extent already studied the growth of "individualism" and the consequences it has had for marriage, family and society.

Perhaps Emma Goldman was right when she described the limitations of the "ambitionless" and "compact majority." She said:

The majority cannot reason, it has no judgment. Lacking utterly in originality and moral courage, the majority has always placed its destiny in the hands of others.

To let the courts decide a momentous and symbolic issue such as the nature of marriage would be most regrettable and would be playing into the hands of strategists grounded in Goldman's worldview. Political correctness, political expediency and generally being unaware (asleep at the proverbial legislative wheel), has allowed the GBLTQ community and radical (lesbian) feminist activists to attack the majority of society through an unremitting assault upon the heterosexual institution of marriage and its underlying values. Ironically, now recognizing their inability to kill marriage and traditional family values outright through direct assault, the strategy has changed to legalized sameness and the revised goal to reinvent marriage to include the ideology of the GBLTQ lifestyle. Do you really believe the toxic liberation ideologies evidenced over these pages will somehow be neutralized, contained or overcome by a "sameness" definition of marriage? It stands to reason that legislative acceptance of GBLTQ into the heterosexual institution marriage, brings with it tacit, if not formal (legal) acceptance of GBLTQ culture, values and behavior as fully equal and compatible with heterosexual marriage and family values. The premise of such equivalence runs against all evidence presented and is an unconscionable falsehood. It is the insistence that GBLTQ space must be included within heterosexual space, which most upsets same-sex marriage opponents, although "completely" monogamous unions within the GBLTQ culture could be beneficial.

As Marcus points out at the start of this section, society is literally at a crossroads. The marriage debate will force nations, such as Canada and the United States, to choose either to continue on a secular route, away from theism or to stop and reconsider God's place in the nation and the need for change. The problem with the magnitude of change precipitated by a "sameness" declaration is that it will move the society so far down the secular road that theism will be irretrievably out of state sight. For many the status of marriage has become a "barometer for measuring the culture's decline, the porousness of its moral fiber."[161] As noted previously, for others, marriage is seen as a zero-sum game – the idea that you simply cannot say that marriage is a good thing unless alternatives are simultaneously seen as bad. As most orthodox adherents see it, the government supports alternative lifestyles over traditional marriage. According to Maggie Gallagher:

Over the past thirty years, American family law has been rewritten to dilute both the rights and obligations of marriage, while at the same time placing other relationships, from adulterous liaisons to homosexual partnerships, on a legal par with marriage in some respects. To put it another way, by expanding the definition of marriage to the point of meaninglessness, courts are gradually redefining marriage out of existence.[162]

Thus the societal "crossroads" can be further explained in two ways. First, "It has become impossible to defend the rights of alternative lifestyles while still championing the virtues of traditional ones."[163] Here Orthodox Rabbi Reuven Bulka of Ottawa says, "nobody wants to look like they're denying anyone else equal rights – that's the mantra of today, equal rights." "Still with regards to the definition of marriage," says Bulka, "this is not an issue of equality, but a claim to sameness; and it's not the same." Marriage has always been "a sacred thing throughout the history of civilization," and religious traditionalists are "defending what they see as the sanctity of marital union." "If everything is marriage," says Bulka, "then nothing is marriage."[164] In the same article, Tom Langan, a member of the Interfaith Coalition on Marriage and Family (ICMF), an ad hoc advocacy group of Sikhs, Muslims, Catholics and Evangelical Christians comments:

Who would have thought a small group like the homosexuals could come within a hair's breadth of changing the definition of the most basic (human institution)?[165]

Emma Goldman for one!

Nan Hunter argues, "Legalizing lesbian and gay marriage would have enormous potential to destabilize the gendered definition of marriage."[166] In other words, the activists' turnaround in favor of marriage is seen for GBLTQ not as an end in and of itself so much as a means to further impel a general redefinition of masculinity and femininity.[167]

Second, since marriage is a public heterosexual institution involving the vast majority of males and females, it has taken on symbolic importance to those in the GBLTQ community wishing to see themselves barred from nothing. William N. Eskridge, author of *The Case for Same-Sex Marriage: From Sexual Liberty to Civilized Commitment* writes:

Marriage, in short, is the last legal bastion of compulsory heterosexuality (Adrienne Rich's term). It is the most blatant evidence that gay and lesbian citizens must sit in the back of the law bus, paying for a first-class ticket and receiving second-class service.[168]

Mr. Shane McCloskey and his partner of five years, Dave Shortt, are one of eight B.C. couples who went to court after they were denied marriage licenses. McCloskey says:

'It is disheartening'...'In our minds it was a pretty simple case. One of the main things that we were arguing was that by not being allowed to get married it was discrimination. The ironic part of the judgment is that the judge agreed with us, but said that it was justifiable. None of us think that discrimination is justifiable in any circumstance.'...'For Dave and I it is a question of equality,' Mr. McCloskey said. 'Just not being able to get married because we happen to be of the same sex is really

unfair. We have just as meaningful, loving and committed a relationship as any of our heterosexual family and friends.'[169]

But marriage already discriminates within the heterosexual "community." Marriage must be only to one opposite sex spouse. Polygamy is not allowed. Marriage can not be to a close relative, a son, a daughter, a father or a mother. Why were these boundaries established? To stabilize and protect heterosexual families.

Notwithstanding McCloskey's stated intentions, the supreme GBLTQ cultural goal is not to espouse basic virtues of loving and committed relationships such as premarital abstinence, marital monogamy, or lifelong fidelity. McCloskey and Shortt may be "sincere" in their objective, but they are blind to the implications for others and blind to the intentions of the majority of the GBLTQ community. They choose to see discrimination rather than conflict of lifestyle. They claim membership in the GBLTQ, with its related culture and ecology, but choose not to see that granting marriage to them as individuals means granting inclusion to all of their community. Other gays and lesbians seeking marriage are less politically correct. Brian Mossop and his lover, Ken Popert spent seven years in B.C. court battles and took their case to the Supreme Court of Canada. Yet they do not believe in the institution of marriage and family. Popert admits:

I am in a web of relationships, but there is no centre and no boundaries. It's not structured and institutionalized, the way the family is. Each person can feel at the centre of it – because in fact there is no center.[170]

And in a recent legal challenge in BC, homosexual lovers Cynthia Callahan and Judy Lightwater admitted they have no intention of living together once they are married.[171] Thus the current liberation goal can be defined as freedom from all societal prohibitions through civil protections for access into all areas of "heterosexual space."

In the McCloskey verdict, Judge Pitfield concluded that marital discrimination against same-sex couples is justified. He writes:

The objective of limiting marriage to opposite sex couples is sufficiently important to warrant infringing on the rights of the petitioners. The gain to society from the preservation of the deep-rooted and fundamental legal institution of opposite-sex marriage outweighs the detrimental effect of the law on the petitioners.[172]

He went on to say that equality rights can be overridden by Section 1 of the Canadian Charter. Judge Pitfield dismissed other arguments, ruling that, for same-sex couples, the freedoms of expression or association, as well as mobility rights and rights of liberty and security, are not infringed by the ban on marriage.[173]

Other provincial courts have given Canada a limited time to amend the definition of marriage or they will declare exclusion of GBLTQ illegal. The Ontario Court in June 2003 went even further choosing to declare the prohibition of same-sex marriage unconstitutional effective immediately. The stakes are high, but much good can come at this stage in the struggle. It all depends on how openly and democratically the process goes forward. A rights-based, court-led process is likely to benefit the same-sex marriage side the most. Here the "compact" majority may well acquiesce, less than fully informed about the impact of the GBLTQ paradigm on society, and apathetic under the misguided assumption that the decision will have little impact on their lives or on subsequent generations. On the other hand, an informed democratic-based process will likely benefit the anti-same-sex marriage side. To orthodox onlookers, there is an imperative need to defend the remaining heterosexual "cultural space," indeed, to re-establish secure boundary markers for protection of: (1) heterosexual marriage; (2) natural pro-creation; and (3) the orthodox heterosexual family. Here a "No" to same-sex marriage symbolically accomplishes all three. Other legal clarifications to a no decision will put in place these protections. Not doing so will only serve to prolong the family crisis witnessed over the past forty years.

For the GBLTQ and radical feminists, in as much as they have made redefinition of marriage a central political goal, its achievement may accomplish four things: (1) promote the option of less promiscuity; (2) start a new round of court challenges for bisexual marriage (threesome unions); (3) start a new round of court challenges for lesbian couples' rights to reproductive technology, including cloning, and the establishment of these technology-based family models; and (4) give GBLTQ a court-based sense of equality and sameness, in spite of the unnaturalness of the lifestyle for reproduction and the persistence of very negative and dangerous ecological consequences.

Alternatively, a decision to not change the definition or a decision to establish a unique marriage name and law, will symbolize rejection of the notion of "sameness." Without achieving this claim to sameness, the best societal resolution then becomes one of pragmatic "cooperation," which falls well short of the GBLTQ wish of heart-felt "acceptance." And without genuine acceptance of the GBLTQ lifestyle by the majority, the homosexual adherents remain separated and ever burdened with cognitive dissonance. There is much at stake for all concerned. One needs to ask, why has the GBLTQ strategy changed 180 degrees from separation to inclusion? And why are they prepared to risk so much of their movement's political capital on winning access to an institution so few intend to use?

For many GBLTQ activists and political strategists the struggle, of necessity, has had to reverse itself. The movement started as an expression of desire to create a separate "safe space" for sexual fulfillment. In the "joy-of-sex," "free love," or "liberation" era of the 60s and 70s, the majority of GBLTQ and radical feminists did not care one iota about what the heterosexual majority did as long as they left them alone. Nor at that time would any self-respecting homosexual claim interest in the heterosexual "patriarchal" institution of marriage. Indeed as we have seen, feminists were trying to win heterosexual women away from men and over to lesbianism. Isolation was the order of the day. Bisexuality was seen as a sign of immaturity and compromised sexuality. In those initial pleasure-filled days the movement's self-esteem stood autonomously on its own free sex foundation. During this era the majority of GBLTQ and radical feminists did not see themselves as the "same" and most did not wish to be viewed as the same. Many saw GBLTQ culture and community as superior to an institutionally and culturally *oppressive* heterosexual society. The entire history portrayed in the previous chapters is one of separation from and rejection of the majority status quo. As long as this pleasure-based foundation existed with manageable ecological consequences the GBLTQ lifestyle did not need a sustainable philosophy or any acceptance by the majority to maintain the movement's self-esteem.

Then came AIDS and the deaths of hundreds of thousands of homosexuals, changing everything, particularly the movement's self-esteem. After all, what rational movement (other than one totally in denial; totally given over to *eros*; or both) can sustain itself with a mean life expectancy for males of forty-something, death of peers everywhere, the constant need to take preventative medications and measures to avoid contracting a fatal disease, and the fear that these ultimately will fail. With each sexual act, adherents face the cognition that HIV and AIDS could cross the physical boundaries of their body. With each death of a friend or acquaintance the notion of "naturalness" and "sameness" seems unbelievable. So what rational political options are left for the minority movement in the era of AIDS.

The status quo may be called the old "separateness strategy." It does allow for avoidance of the issue of proclaiming a sustainable philosophy of life, upon which genuine heterosexual acceptance might be found. But as GBLTQ hope for a magic bullet (in the form of an AIDS vaccine or some pharmaceutical cure) fades out of sight the status quo becomes untenable. Moreover, in light of a resurgence of AIDS and STD victims, the secure notion of safe sex (based on the Condom Code) is equally indefensible. Thus, the only relief from the self-image problem is a switch from the "separateness" to a "sameness" strategy. Here the dissonance logic continues to say that the problem is heterosexual homophobia and not the GBLTQ lifestyle. When heterosexuals end their fear of the free love lifestyle the GBLTQ self-image will be fine. The inclusion of GBLTQ in the definition of marriage will help "legislate" this desired acceptance.

Notice the ownership of the societal discrimination problem, particularly in light of forty years of attacking heterosexual institutions. The GBLTQ need not accept the separate space they have created, rather the majority must embrace them – lifestyle, culture, values, behavior, ecological consequences and all. Even if the heterosexual majority could embrace the GBLTQ community in unconditional acceptance, this would not alter the ecology of free love sex and the incompatibility of homosexuality with perpetuation of the species. Parliament is misinformed believing that somehow legislating "sameness" will end the clash of cultures and beliefs. Leaving theistic-based values and common morality aside, what parents would not be disappointed, if not angered, to see their offspring enter the politics, lifestyle and ecology of the GBLTQ community? Taking deliberate legislative action to reduce this potentiality by saying "No" to same-sex marriage is surely a constitutional right; anything less is reverse discrimination. Moreover, in this case the reverse discrimination affects some 97 per cent of society for the intended benefit of only a small fraction of the remaining 3 per cent. The disproportionate nature of this issue, particularly given the protections already in place for sustaining GBLTQ culture and union, is senseless. The macro-consequence of a "sameness" decision by government will be a further split of society into fundamentalists and liberationists. This decision has tremendous implications for what Diana Alstad (quoted in Chapter 7) calls the "planetary battle," the "morality wars," and the morality "battle for peoples minds." As this struggle progresses, the choices are becoming polarized. Inclusive, middle of the road doctrines and ideologies (as studied in Chapter 6) become untenable, if ever they had legitimacy.

Consider that a special definition of union for the GBLTQ (as a unique minority) would better adapt legislation to the range of interests and values held within the community. A fundamental difference being the limited value the minority places on marriage fidelity. Notwithstanding that the only full protection from AIDS and STDs is lifelong fidelity with one partner, no where in all my readings, save Gabriel Rotello, did I find a hint of support for virtuous sex or the need to reinvent GBLTQ culture in the era of AIDS. On the contrary this book is compelling testimony to the unrelenting desire of liberationists (GBLTQ and feminists) to convert the last societal and institutional space for ethical sex over to the free love ethos.

Eric Marcus, espouses this paradoxical notion of the union of marriage and free love, in *The Male Couple's Guide: Finding a Man, Making a Home, Building a Life*. Here he promotes promiscuity and monogamy in the same breath:

Agreement on the fundamental rules of the relationship from the start is essential whether, for example, the rules allow for sex outside the relationship every other Thursday or establish a code of monogamy. If you can't agree on the fundamentals, whether that agreement is spoken or unspoken, you're in trouble. Unless you can find a way to accommodate each other's convictions about how a relationship should be conducted, you're bound for major, ongoing, relationship-threatening conflicts.[174]

Here is the crux of the matter. Marcus sees the need for "fundamental rules" of conduct to avoid relationship conflicts, although the culture to which he speaks has a rock-solid aversion to such rules and any form of behavioral discrimination. Historically, the institution of heterosexual marriage has been predicated upon near universal tenets anchored in theistic faiths such as Christianity. The cultural rules and boundaries of conduct have been clear up until the last 40 years. The whole ethos of the liberation movement, which won the societal space in which the GBLTQ culture now exists, was one of moral freedom, no rules, and no absolute rights or wrongs (no-judgments). The collateral impact of that struggle on heterosexual marriage and family has been studied and found to be mostly negative. Using Marcus' words, when there is no "way to accommodate each other's convictions about how a relationship should be conducted," you are bound for major "conflicts." This will be the result when both cultures are under one definition of marriage. Such an all-encompassing term becomes so inclusive as to be meaningless and misleading. The action would be tantamount to legislating a term that decrees the "Pivot of Civilization" is the same as the "Rivet of Life." The two world paradigms can have equal status before the law of the land, but they are anathema to each other. Gay union, however it may come to be described, can be equal in governmental dealings and authenticity, but it can never be the same as heterosexual marriage. The two cultures are literally toxic to each other. What is needed from government for both societal groups is recognition of their equality with protection of their uniqueness? Here, separate and newly clarified definitions offer the best chance at achieving a cooperative, respectful communal balance.

The separate GBLTQ definition of union will allow for the freedom and beliefs desired by its constituents. Here Marjorie Garber upholds Margaret Sanger's ideology and explains the bisexual notion of marriage by quoting from the Diary of John Cheever:

All marriages are unorthodox in their own ways. Some admit their unorthodoxy more directly than others, and some, often to their own cost, keep secrets. But marriage is an institution, and sexual desire, though we like to think of it as directly and unproblematically linked to 'love and marriage,' is a willful, inconsistent, and often ungovernable entity. How can a structure, like marriage, contain a force, like eroticism? Imperfectly, if at all. We might say that all marriages are bifurcated between the wild and the tame, between the adventurous and the routine, between passion and obligation. Bisexual marriages only make explicit, literal, and racy what is emotionally the case for any long-range commitment that is tied to a structure. The 'choice' between a male and female lover seems more extreme, more extravagant, more transgressive, perhaps, than the other kinds of choices, fantasized and acted-upon, that confront partners in every marriage. But precisely because partners in bisexual marriages have to face the paradoxes of their desires, they have sometimes come to terms with themselves, their partners, and their marriages in a particularly thoughtful way. What these bisexual marriages exemplify is less the paradox of bisexuality than the imperfect fit between the stability of marriage and the unruliness of sexual desire.[175]

In her own way Garber describes a zero-sum relationship between marriage and infidelity. There is no such thing as free love – psychologically or biologically. I keep raising the lessons from Emma Goldman's sex life. The fact that significant numbers of heterosexuals breach their marriages by infidelity should not be heralded as reason to redefine the institution as inclusive of pre-planned and negotiated promiscuity (Thursday nights-only) or permissive to impromptu liaisons. Moreover, the studies and observations already raised show that the intimacy of bi-sexual and homosexual relationships is no less dependent on fidelity than for heterosexuals.

Along the line of Garber, Marcus writes:

Relationships change, circumstances change, people change. Men who entered relationships planning to be monogamous may not find that the arrangement suits them. Men who started a relationship agreeing to nonmonogamy may find over time that that arrangement isn't working out. That's why it's important to leave the door open to discussion about the ground rules of your relationship. Any change in your original joint agreement has to be a mutual decision. For example, you can't decide alone to make your relationship monogamous; you have to make a commitment together. If at some point in your relationship, you and your partner decide monogamy is not working for you – or even if it is working – you may choose to experiment with monogamy. However, if you're going to try sex outside your relationship, wait until you feel your relationship is secure and strong to weather a storm, in the event that an outside excursion together or alone causes one.[176]

This description is not marriage. Who ever heard of experimenting with monogamy? Marcus sees no commitment to the institution or the sanctity of marriage vows and all the values and familial implications behind them. Where everything is negotiable, nothing is secure. What marriage counselor would advise a couple, now secure in their relationship to then start trying sex outside?

The sad fact is there are many and not all are homosexual. Indeed, futurists contend that we have got lots of marrying time. With the advent of puberty at an ever-younger age on the one end and with Viagra and "treatable" menopause extending sexual activity on the other, our sexual lives are lasting longer. Given the new biology, both natural and pharmacologically induced, marriage at twenty-five can mean a sixty-year active commitment. With almost twice the time to be adults, some ask "should we insist on an entire lifetime of marriage – especially when active parenting only absorbs twenty years?" Or perhaps, given changing biological and social realities, a series of two, three, possibly even four marriages might make more sense. A 1996 report by the World Future Society foresees "serial marriages" as the wave of the future:

Almost surely there will continue to be people who have three, four or five spouses, without any intervening widowhood.[177]

In 1999, Barbara Ehrenreich predicted that in the twenty-first century:

...there will be renewable marriages, which get reevaluated every five to seven years after which they can be revised, re-celebrated or dissolved with no or at least fewer hard feelings.[178]

Sounds like a familiar story – the forecast for a 30 hour workweek and the disappearance of marriage in the 80s.

Sociologists call this remarriage model of revolving spouses "conjugal succession," however, most people refer to it as serial monogamy, and many think it's inevitable. The book *Next: Trends for the Near Future* predicts:

Among the results of our diminished attention span will be the growth of serial life partners...Already many Baby Boomers are admitting that the institution of marriage doesn't work for most people their age.[179]

In an era in which people entering the workforce are likely to have five or six careers over a span of five or more decades, we'd be naïve to assume that one's shifting needs will be met by a single life partner. Given the unprecedented rate of change in our world, people now live multiple 'life spans.' And the recently announced breakthroughs in cellular research suggest that one's 'productive' years might soon extend far beyond what the average person experienced during the 20th century. Will second, third, and even fourth families become increasingly common? Will movement from one 'life' to the next be prepared for and celebrated? [180]

Futurist Sandy Burchsted estimates that people may eventually marry an average of four times over the course of a lifetime. According to Burchsted:

...within the next one hundred years marriage will come to be seen as a 'conscious, evolutionary process' that begins with the 'ice-breaker marriage.' Ice-breaker mar-

riages (basically starter marriages) last no longer than five years, during which couples learn to live with a partner and divorce without stigma 'once disillusionment sets in.' The second marriage is the 'parenting marriage,' which lasts fifteen to twenty years and ends when the children are grown up and gone. This is followed by the 'self-marriage,' in which one seeks self-actualization without the burden of raising a family. Finally, there's the 'soulmate connection' marriage for the twilight years, which is an equal partnership of spirituality and marital bliss.[181]

Don't say ever again that GBLTQ "marriage" will not impact the traditional marriage model and its related family unit.

Thankfully, in spite of the soothsayers, the reality is that orthodox marriage is on the increase. In a 2000 Roper poll, "protecting the family" ranked number one among fifty-seven values that Americans hold dear.[182] In a 2000 poll 50 per cent of Americans say that they're optimistic about the institutions of marriage and family, up from 41 per cent in 1995.[183] At the Beverly LaHaye Institute's 2000 forum, *Marriage in the New Millenium*, "social theorist Francis Fukuyama cited anecdotal evidence pointing to women's return to the home in what he described as "well-to-do, professional, middle-class families," and a change in the post feminist cultural biases opposing such choices. The causes behind these changes are certainly open for debate, but evidence suggests that we are in the throes of what historian Ann Douglas has called a "retro quiver."[184] I call it a clash of worldviews for guiding the future of North American society, in which the rhetoric, false ideologies, and dangers of sex liberation have become more evident. People are taking a second look at the direction of societal change.

In opposition to LaHaye's claims, social critic Gertrude Himmelfarb contends that as "people move in and out of families at will," friends will gain equal ground with blood relatives, and obligations will be voluntarized rather than taken as givens. She explains:

This is parentage, and 'alternative lifestyles.' The 'family of choice' is defined not by lines of blood, marriage, or adoption, but by varieties of relationships and habitations among 'autonomous,' 'consensual' adults and their offspring.[185]

Here we see the repackaged ideology of the 60s communal lifestyle, discredited by Alice Rossi in the previous Chapter. What child needs "voluntarized," "autonomous," or "consensual" parents?

In *She Works He Works*, Rosiland C. Barnett and Caryl Rivers uphold the dual-income marriage and family-style as a great triumph over the earlier traditional (they call Ozzie and Harriet style) family. They say:

It is imperative that those of us in the two-earner lifestyle have been as good or better parents – not worse ones. We are already raising a generation of children in two-earner families; if we really want them to be stressed, let's tell them that what we are doing is all wrong, that what we should be doing was what their grandparents did in the 1950s, and that that's the ideal they, too, should aspire to.[186]

Regardless of Barnett and Rivers' wishes, the future-parenting model may well be shaped by the next generation's thinking:

But the actual facts about what is good for real American couples and their families today may well be drowned out by the clamor of what we call the 'new nostalgia,' a combination of longing for the past and fear of change. It not only feeds the guilt that can tie individuals in knots, but can be a major stumbling block to the creation of corporate and government policies that will help, not hinder working families. The new nostalgia has already calcified in politics, in the media, in a spate of books that tell us we must retreat to the past to find solutions for the future.[187]

Barnett and Rivers refer to their search of the media in the past five years, which revealed some 15,000 references in the press to either the breakup or the decline of the American Family, "a chorus that is relentless." They ask, "Do you believe that the decline of the family is absolute fact?" They conclude, "Many Americans do."[188] As a result, they ask, "What position of lofty perfection is the family declining from?" But this line of argument sidesteps current problems and ends in a fruitless debate of interpreting stylized Puritan family life, Victorian marriage, and post WWII *Leave It To Beaver* home life. What we really need to focus on are the legitimate ailments. Barnett and Rivers carve up the family crisis into orthodox criticisms (right) and liberationist complaints (left):

Right: divorce, unwanted pregnancy, STDs, AIDS, suicide, drugs, parenting deficit...

Left: incest, wife beating, and sexual abuse of children.[189]

Again, like the hetero-homo dialogue, we see the debate on two separate tracks, articulating a trade-off – "less divorce" and "more wife-beating." The fact the debate continues along these lines is an insult to all. Where is the proportion and rationalization in this debate? It is true that some wives are beaten, but most are not. The ones that are not are in sound heterosexual marriages. How does addressing wife abuse in unhealthy marriages translate into deriding lifelong monogamous marriages? Are there really informed people who would argue that a Biblical marriage model is not optimum for spousal relationships and parenting? Obviously there are, but these critics seldom attack the model for parenting, rather they reject the monogamous fidelity foundation to its success and place scant significance on nurturing. Liberationists apply a self-centered logic, which says because some, perhaps even a majority, find the practice of fidelity burdensome, society should erase fidelity from the moral marriage code. Liberationist philosophers who argue against the traditional family framework refuse to acknowledge successful marriages and the incompleteness of their own replacement institutional philosophies, which have been playing out in society over the past 40 years.

Indeed, their strategy reversal from separation to demanding inclusion in the heterosexual marriage definition is a comprehensive admission of the failures of their variant models. The notions of the inevitability of marriage evolution, the irreversibility of feminist gains, and the very idea of a patriarchal-liberation trade-off need to be challenged. The confidence behind feminist convictions rests more with the belief that the "compact majority" lacks the will and insight to act in its own interest then in the self-evident truthfulness of the tenets behind their liberation movement. For the enlightenment of the "moral majority," let's look at some more pros and cons of GBLTQ marriage for society at large.

If your child or your child's best friend turns out to be gay, does that mean none of the arguments for fidelity and non-premarital sex applies to them? Are you obliged to give your son or daughter permission to be promiscuous? Is your child now somehow incapable of integrity? Do you turn the kid out of the house as depraved and a scandal to the family[190] or renovate a room for his or her sexual self-expression and experimentation? Wallace argues that given the decision taken to act upon homosexual urges, genuine sexual fidelity is not dependent on orientation. Bathhouses for gays are just as bad as brothels for straights. Writes Wallace (and I support her counsel on this point):

Integrity is a universal norm. Fidelity is a norm applicable to everyone, straight and gay alike.[191]

However, she also contends:

We do not control the power to bless or refuse to bless homosexual unions: Partners in any matrimonial alliance bless one another, and they are blessed by God. As a community we have only the power publicly or communally to teach and support the moral value of honorable and committed sexual fidelity and just as powerfully and clearly to oppose the travesties of promiscuity, predatory, exploitive sexuality...Orientation is not the distinction that matters. Fidelity is.[192]

Here she joins the ranks of other gay and pro-gay Christians upholding Bailey's notion of the God-given invert, who should be accepted and encouraged to live out a lifelong monogamous homosexual relationship in *true* Christian fashion. Again life is not so tidy and categorical, even if Scripture could be ignored. What is the definition of fidelity in bisexual relationships? Does Wallace rule out the ménage-á-trois? Is the bisexual orientation "a distinction that matters" in her liberal view of marriage? If I can be faithful in an agreement with two sex partners, can I not be faithful in a relationship with three, five, a dozen, if all agree to the "open" marriage?

Furthering her pro-gay stance, Wallace writes:

Acknowledging faithful and committed homosexual unions can threaten family life and the stable nurture of children only if we are led thereby, as a society, to regard marriage with greater casualness than we already do. But I'm not sure that greater casualness is possible when adultery is widely described as 'commonplace' or as a 'minor sexual misbehavior.' The crucial task before us in these days is to reflect seriously on how we can help each other to sustain fidelity within matrimony and to teach sexual ethics to our children.[193]

Here two wrongs hardly make a right! Acknowledging the GBLTQ threat, she brushes it away by diagnosing marriage as already broken and beyond hope. Who says adultery is commonplace? Not factual statistics. Who claims it is a minor sexual misbehavior? Not Christians. Not the moral majority. What sexual ethics shall we teach our children is an excellent question.

Like Wallace, Andrew Sullivan makes a similarly deceptive argument for GBLTQ marriage. He writes:

Gay marriage is not a zero-sum game. Because they have no choice but to be homosexual, they are not choosing that option over heterosexual marriage, and so they are not sending any social signals that a heterosexual family life should be denigrated.[194]

This is simply untrue. Under a regime of sexual liberation impacting gays and straights, infidelity has been amplified, if not fully fueled by 40 years of having gay and lesbian lifestyles pushed in our "face." With the fidelity-monogamy taboo breached, many men can now fulfill the paramount dream of most non-Christian men everywhere: they can have the nubile years of more than one young woman. Whether a straight man takes these young women at one time, staying married and having mistresses, or whether he marries two or more young women in succession, or whether he merely lives with young women without marriage, makes little difference to the social consequences. The man is no less effectively a polygamist, or more specifically a polygynist, than if he had maintained a harem. To suggest that the radical (lesbian) feminist attack on marriage and the advent of gay multipartner infidelity has not "denigrated" the institution of marriage and the family is audacious.

The obvious victims of this breakdown of monogamy are the women who must grow old alone when their husbands leave. Here a reflection upon the fate of Alfred Kinsey's mother, described in Chapter 4, brings the travesty home. But they are only the first of the victims. The removal of restrictions on sexual activity does not bring equality and community. It brings ever more vicious sexual competition. The women become "easier" for the powerful to get – but harder for others to keep. Divorces become "easier" – except on divorced older women. Marriages become more "open" – open not only for the partners to get out, but also for the powerful to get in.[195] Monogamy is egalitarian in the realm of love. It is a mode of rationing. It means to put it crudely – one to a customer. Competition is intense enough even so, because of the sexual inequality of human beings. But under a regime of monogamy there are limits. One may covet one's neighbor's wife or husband, one may harbor sexual fantasies, but one generally does not act on one's lusts. One does not abandon one's own wife when she grows older, to take a woman who would otherwise go to a younger man. One does not raid the marriages of others. Thus a balance is maintained and each generation gets its only true sexual rights: the right to a wife or husband and the possibility of participating in the future of the race through children. A society is essentially an organism. We cannot simply exclude a few million women from the fabric of families, remarry their husbands to younger women, and quietly return to our businesses as if nothing has happened. What has happened is a major rupture in the social system.[196] The growth in single moms because boyfriends will not marry is a parallel manifestation of the negative impact of sexual liberation.

The impact of GBLTQ sexual rights and freedoms has also negatively affected some of its own members. Many homosexuals, like heterosexuals, have sufficient discipline and self-control to avoid the slipperiest slopes, the most sordid pits. Many live a decorous and civilized existence. Many others have now been shaken by the threat of AIDS to reject or abandon the wild side of the gay scene. These men are not helped by attempts to move the bathhouse into the midst of society, to make the homosexual circuit more open and accessible. They are not helped by AIDS hysteria and gay protests and parades, campus dances and demonstrations. They do not benefit from demands for rights and quotas that seem designed to flush them out of the closet and onto the street where they can be exploited by the gay-rights brigade. They want to live their lives quietly and productively and safely, and most of them are knowledgeable and sensible enough not to want to inflict their lifestyle on others.[197]

Norman Podhoretz believes that men by nature tend to be promiscuous, and they have only become monogamous when women force them to settle down in exchange for the comforts and pleasures of a stable home and the delights and the troubles, the challenges and the anxieties, that together constitute the rich fascination of fathering and raising children. It is because homosexuals have no women to restrain them that they are generally so promiscuous (whereas lesbians, being women, do tend toward monogamy), and because they are so promiscuous they are doomed to an endless series of anonymous and loveless encounters – not to mention the risk of disease and early death. Homosexuals of a conservative disposition have come to acknowledge this, and they hope to cure it through the legalization of same-sex marriage. Here is an unusually succinct statement of their hope, taken from the jacket of William N. Eskridge, Jr's *The Case For Same-Sex Marriage:*

Whether because of the biology of masculinity or the furtiveness of illegality, gay men have been known for their promiscuous subcultures. Promiscuity has encouraged a cult of youth worship and has contributed to the stereotype of homosexuals as people who lack a serious approach to life. It is time for gay America to mature, and there can be no more effective path to maturity than marriage.[198]

And yet Andrew Sullivan, who in his book *Virtually Normal* makes the same argument as Eskridge, qualifies non-promiscuity with the proviso that the need for "extramarital outlets" should be recognized by both parties in a same-sex marriage. Why, he asks, should the "varied and complicated lives" of gay men be constrained by a "single, moralistic model?" It would seem, then (with individual exceptions noted and acknowledged), that it still takes a woman to domesticate a man, not another man. This means that same-sex marriage will in all probability not spell an end to promiscuity and an embrace of fidelity even among those homosexuals who will avail themselves of the right (and by all indications, they are likely to be few in number). After all, Mark Steyn remarks in a brilliant little piece about Sullivan's book in the *American Spectator*:

A grisly plague has not furthered the cause of homosexual monogamy, so why should a permit from a town clerk?[199]

In an essay for the *New Republic*, titled "The Politics of Homosexuality," editor Andrew Sullivan, links the right to marry with the right to serve as defining categories of citizenship. "If the military ban deals with the heart of what it is to be a citizen," he wrote, "the marriage ban deals with the core of what it is to be member of civil society." And since "the heterosexuality of marriage is civilly intrinsic only if understood to be inherently procreative; and that definition has long been abandoned in civil society," the prohibition of gay marriage functions solely as a sign of public disapproval. Emotionally, Sullivan contends:

Marriage is characterized by a kind of commitment that is rare even among heterosexuals. That many gays and lesbians have formed and will continue to form such long-term attachments is clear, and the question of whether all gay people want to live in committed relationships is hardly relevant. To give them the right to do so legally does not diminish the incentive for heterosexuals to do the same.[200]

Sullivan asks, "Why, in other words, should gay marriage threaten straight marriage, unless, as an institution, it is already threatened?" Here he joins author Catherine Wallace. Once more, this line of thinking perpetuates a cognitive error originated among radical feminists. In propagandizing the patriarchal myth, they chose to ignore the ample evidence of happy, monogamous and fruitful heterosexual marriages – some half of all unions. When marriages are weakened, it is not by application of orthodox values.

If gay people are denied that marriage bond, says Sullivan, their committed relationships are inherently unequal, socially as well as in the eyes of the law:

Their relationships are given no anchor, no end point, no way of integrating them fully into the network of family and friends.[201]

Why can they not settle for a unique union defined within their community? Sullivan uses the metaphor of an "*anchor*" or point of integration. Faced with waves of disease, the emotional floods resulting from the vagaries of multipartnerism and the lack of a hierarchical family structure, the adaptation of GBLTQ marriage is needed for an entirely new and different purpose. Using marriage as an *anchor* in a cultural sea of free love is an ironic ending testimony to the liberation movement. When Sullivan contends same-sex marriage will not negatively impact heterosexual marriage and when he demands inclusion as a right to citizenry, he ignores all that the GBLTQ and feminist movements have stood for over four decades.

Even for those who seek marriage as a hedge against the ecology of homosexuality, the promise is not great. As explained in Chapter 6 – "Replacing the Leviticus Code With The Condom Code," going from one partner to just two a year is enough to sustain the AIDS epidemic. Moreover, Frank Browning writes:

Indeed, by 1990, researchers had discovered through behavioural studies that unattached gay men were significantly less likely to expose themselves to HIV through risky sex than were men in serial monogamous relationships. Apparently then, the reduction in the number of sexual mates has nothing to do with the prevention of viral transmission.[202]

According to Martin Weinberg et al., authors of *Dual Attraction*:

Although most of the bisexuals interviewed were in a significant relationship or looking for one, nonmonogamy was a common aspect of these relationships. It took various forms: swinging, sexual triads, group sex parties, multiple involved partners, casual sex with friends, and anonymous sex at such places as gay bathhouses or through pick-ups at gay or lesbian bars. These multiple relations were not just for sexual gratification but were often crucial for sustaining a sense of one's self as bisexual. Indeed, bisexuals often actively sought partners of both sexes for this reason.[203]

Given that Emma Goldman, pioneer of the free sex philosophy, could not master her jealousy, it would be worthwhile to see how well bisexuals might cope within some GBLTQ notion of (free sex) marriage. Weinberg writes:

Even though they characterized their relationships as open, only about a quarter believed that their partners were free of jealousy. Ten per cent said that there was substantial jealousy, about 20 per cent that it was 'moderate,' and just under a half that it existed 'only a little.' Primary partners were reportedly more jealous of an 'outside' partner of their own sex. The logic goes that a person of the opposite sex would not compete in the same way, in theory satisfying a different set of needs for their partner[204] :

For example, a man speaks of his female partner:

Well, she feels she could be replaced by another female, whereas with men she knows I'm interested just in sex and not any kind of emotional thing. (M)

A man whose primary relationship was with a male:

It's okay with him for me to see women. However, with a man he would have trouble understanding that. He would find it more threatening. (M)[205]

Another man about his female partner:

I don't know if the term 'jealous' is correct here. She just felt at a complete loss having to compete with a male! (M)[206]

The other side of the jealousy issue was how the bisexuals Weinberg interviewed dealt with their primary partners' other relationships. He records:

I don't know all the details, but he's very attractive, and I'm sure he's getting laid fairly often. (M)

He sees Tom. He goes to the baths occasionally. He says he's having sex with women too. I just do not know more than that. He does not tell me. (F)

She varies a lot in her sexual interest in other people. It is really important that she always have the option to relate to other people. There have been times when she has related to a large number of people; there have been times when she was relatively monogamous and I was not. Presently, she is involved with another man and another woman. (M)[207]

Most of those Weinberg interviewed believed that their partners' outside sexual relationships were more casual and anonymous than "involved." This belief helped to prevent jealousy from arising. Thus, close to half said that they were not jealous at all of their partner's outside sexual activities. When jealousy arose it was usually over a sense of insecurity – if the partner was perceived to be younger or more attractive. Jealousy was more easily managed if they were both nonmonogamous.[208]

Twenty per cent of those interviewed had ground rules limiting how emotionally involved each could become with outside partners. A number of such ground rules were mentioned, most of which dealt with the fear of replacement:

...Christiana has usually maintained that she wants ours to be the primary relationship we have only with each other. This means that if we become involved enough with another person, so that there is a danger of replacing our relationship, then we must choose to limit or eliminate the outside relationship. In this way, we have full security, and trust, that our relationship will come first. (F)[209]

The "time deficit" takes on new dimensions in bisexual relationships. Half of those Weinberg interviewed said that they had ground rules for the allocation of time between their significant partners and their outside partners. No mention of quality time with children! Weinberg writes:

We have ground rules for how much time we spend together. We spend one night a week together, Wednesday, and we spend Saturday night and all day and night Sunday together. We have three nights officially where we are together, but we may be with other people socially. Usually, though, we spend six nights a week together. I find it a lot better to know that Steve and I have a particular night together, because I don't worry then about the nights he is with others. (F)[210]

We need to check in. We consult each other's calendars. We let each other know what nights we will be home, what are our plans for the week, who's coming over for dinner, etc. Just kind of let each other know what is happening. (M)[211]

For some, not only was it important to have a schedule, but also to be decisive about it and stick to it. It was important that the time spent together be "quality" time. That is, when they're together they must really be together; they must be sober and not watch TV, etc. Weinberg concludes, "An open relationship clearly required partners to cope with issues of time and energy management."[212] However, assuming the open "primary" relationship can be managed, the couple still has to deal with handling the "secondary" partners. Here meeting outside partners followed two general policies:

Knowing someone minimizes jealousy...If unknown, the mind can run wild. I tend to make goddesses or gods out of these people and meeting them reduces them to human beings. (F)

She really should meet him (the secondary partner). She doesn't want to, although I know she'd enjoy him. (F)[213]

Despite the time and energy given to negotiating rules for open relationships, Weinberg found that even when they existed and were agreed on, they were not always followed. Rules concerning time allocation were broken most often. Those with an established time schedule cited certain problems: e.g., when something spontaneous happened or unforeseen circumstances arose or if they forgot or lost track of time. Others simply did not take the rules seriously. In the words of two interviewees:

If I'm turned on to somebody I go ahead regardless of the rules; I break them whenever I choose.[214]

Close to half of those who reported having ground rules said that the rules had changed over time. The major reason cited was that the rules had to be adapted to changing circumstances. Some reported that rules developed in the first place because the primary partner found out about their outside relationships, making negotiations necessary. Others reported a jealousy problem when ground rules weren't followed – and additional rules were made to deal with this. Rules changed too when the primary partner became settled in a particular outside relationship or when a desire for more intimacy occurred within the primary relationship, or when need for more nonmonogamy grew.[215]

Against this description of the complications of multipartner sexual exploits, it is little surprise that some in the GBLTQ community are repudiating free sex ideology and trying traditional monogamy and fidelity. Even Eric Marcus, who says, "freedom is a good thing;" who supports "self-defined partnerships" – "what ever works best;" and who says, "there is no requirement to follow what society or one's church dictates," believes monogamy has merit. He discovered in his conversations with homosexuals that several people said they just couldn't cope with the emotional rigors of a nonmonogamous relationship.[216]

One of the most common sources of conflict in lesbian couples is this issue of monogamy versus nonmonogamy. Most often, problems arise when one partner wants to open up the relationship and the other does not. This frequently happens when two women have been together for several years, and one partner feels restless, bored with the relationship, less turned on to her lover than before, and attracted to others. Says Toder:

The potential growth of the individual and even of the couple that can result from outside affairs must be balanced against the potential loss of trust and safety in the primary relationship. In addition, there can be some less-than-healthy reasons for wanting to open up the couple relationship: new affairs can be a way to avoid dealing with problems in the primary relationship, to keep from making a commitment to the relationship, or to distract yourself from a boring job or frustrations in your work. By putting the bulk of your energy into numerous emotional involvements, you may be putting off the expression of your creativity in some other form and you may be avoiding confronting a feeling of emptiness and meaninglessness in your life.[217]

Why do so many open relationships cause problems? Toder writes:

The main reason is that many of us have been naïve about just how emotionally complicated nonmonogamy can be. Sex and love go together for most women in our culture. Even what is intended to be a relatively casual and unthreatening affair can quickly evolve into an intense and complex emotional involvement. Believing they should be able to handle nonmonogamy, women have acted according to theory without having a realistic idea of their needs, the extent to which they would suffer from jealousy, and their personal limitations in dealing with potentially ambiguous, frustrating, or complex situations. Furthermore, we women have been socialized to believe that our self-esteem comes primarily from our relationships with other people… These relationships can occupy most if not all of our time, and her sense of worth and identity may come to depend on the success or failure of many relationships instead of one! The point is that nonmonogamy does not guarantee a strong sense of self and independence, just as monogamy does not automatically mean an overwhelming dependence on your partner or a severe limitation on your freedom and growth as an individual.[218]

Are there other reasons why GBLTQ seek marriage? According to psychotherapist Dr. Betty Berzon, specialist in gay and lesbian issues, some gays or lesbians just wish to prove a point to themselves:

It's important to find a partner so others (and you) will know that you can do it. Searching is boring – all that small talk, game playing, insincerity, superficiality. Searching is risky. You can get set up, ripped off, done in by strangers who don't know or care about you.[219]

What Berzon raises here as a reason for seeking long-term relationships does not equate to "sameness" with heterosexual marriage.

Very few GBLTQ have been fortunate enough to have had homosexual parents who could model for them the ideal gay or lesbian relationship. Lacking marriage manuals, parental guidance, and models of conjugal bliss, they have had to wing it. According to Nancy Toder, author of the article "Lesbian Couples: Special Issues":

Many lesbians are afraid to commit themselves to a relationship, not only because of a general fear of making commitments but also because of a more specific fear: That they are indeed gay. For those who have not fully accepted a lesbian identity, making a firm commitment to another woman cements the notion that they are actu-

ally adopting a lesbian lifestyle and must formulate a lesbian identity. This is no small step, particularly in our first same-sex love affair. In response to our fear, we may deny the implications of the relationship ('I'm not a lesbian, I just happen to be in love with this person and this person just happens to be a woman') or generally not believe in the viability of the relationship.[220]

Similar to Berzon's point, the issues of commitment Toder raises argue for "union" but do not constitute "sameness." She writes:

I believe the core of this issue is a question of family. When a woman marries a man, they become family to each other. The question is: When does a same-sex lover become family? Is it when you fall in love? Live together? Buy a house together? Raise a child together? Is it when your blood family accepts your lover as a family member? We have no rules by which to answer these basic questions.[221]

William N.. Eskridge Jr. argues in favor of a "menu" of marriage arrangements, from which members of the GBLTQ could select their preference. He writes:

If some couples crave the commitment and legal benefits of marriage while other couples prefer a less formal arrangement, one possible response would be for the American legal system to offer couples a menu of choices for their unions. Couples could choose (1) to marry, with the accompanying benefits and obligations; (2) to register as domestic partners, entitled to spousal treatment with respect to some economic benefits (such as health care) and decision rules (such as presumption of guardianship) but not limited by rules of divorce and sexual exclusivity; or (3) to order their relationships contractually or quasi-contractually, as through agreements to enter certain economic relationships (such as lease) as a joint enterprise. Under a menu approach such as this one couples could better tailor their status to the particular needs of their relationship. A couple who wanted legal reinforcement for their lifelong commitment could choose marriage while a couple who wanted to ease into commitment could choose domestic partnership, with marriage as a possibility in the future.

Perhaps all couples should be offered this or a broader range of options. States could adopt domestic partnership laws, and employers could adapt their spousal benefits policies to cover domestic partners (or be required to do so by state law). States could also allow same-sex marriage. Families would flourish along different dimensions of interpersonal commitment.[222]

Rightly, Eskridge goes on to conclude this scenario is not a likely one. Of those seeking a long-term relationship, most would jump to full marriage over domestic partnership, and if need be backslide to an appropriate "menu" alternative. He writes:

The large majority of us feel as Genora Dancel does, 'I want to be able to say at the end of my life that I had loved somebody really well for a long time.'[223] *Gay and lesbian partners want a level of commitment that domestic partnership does not provide. More deeply, lesbian and gay couples desire a link to the larger historical community, something marriage (in all its troubled richness) provides and just-concocted domestic partnerships does not. Marriage involves collective participation….The pomp, gravity, and religiosity of marriage might appall the avant-garde, but they lend the institution an air of sanctification that is meaningful to its participants.*[224] *[my underline]*

Given that GBLTQ space has "just been concocted" over the past 40 years, why isn't the novel domestic partnership enough? Eskridge appeals to the longstanding traditions of marriage, ignoring the fact the institution has never been intended for same-sex couples. What a reversal from the marriage bashing days of WITCH and SCUM. However, not all GBLTQ activists support the repositioning of marriage goals. The thought of emphasizing GBLTQ sameness to married heterosexuals in order to obtain this right "terrifies" Paula L. Ettelbrick.[225] She sees marriage as co-opting gays and declawing gay liberation. In rebuttal, says William Eskridge:

The evolution of American family law will surely not stop with the recognition of same-sex marriage.[226]

He further believes that married GBLTQ will not assimilate and disappear as Ettelbrick suggests. Instead, Eskridge explains how concepts of marriage will be re-defined:

Initially, it seems unlikely that married gay couples would be just like married straight couples. For, example, same-sex couples are less likely to follow the traditional bread-winner-housekeeper division in their households.[227]

Nor would the gay and lesbian culture cease to be distinctive. One feature of our experience has been an emphasis on 'families we choose,' anthropologist Kath Weston's felicitous phrase.[228]

Such families are fluid alliances independent of ties imposed by blood and by law. Often estranged from blood kin, openly gay people are more prone to rely on current as well as former lovers, close friends, and neighbors as their social and emotional support system. Include children in this fluid network and the complexity becomes more pronounced.[229]

Because same-sex couples cannot have children through their own efforts, a third party must be involved: a former different-sex spouse, a sperm donor, a surrogate mother, a parent or agency offering a child for adoption. The family of choice can and often does include a relationship with this third party. Gay and lesbian couples are pioneering novel family configurations, and gay marriage would not seriously obstruct the creation of the larger families we choose.[230]

Again, Eskridge's description is not "sameness." At the end of this chapter we will look at the lesbian lobby for human cloning and the potential that biogenetic engineering has to "*seriously obstruct*" family and future generations.

To many, marriage, by definition, has got to be different-sex. Throughout human history, according to religious tradition and as a matter of natural law, marriage has been tied to procreative sexuality, which is a monopoly held by different-sex couples. Under this definitional objection, the state cannot recognize something that is an impossibility:

The Minnesota Supreme Court in Baker v. Nelson (the first legal challenge to the same-sex marriage bar) began its constitutional discussion with the premise that 'the institution of marriage as a union of man and woman, uniquely involving the procreation and rearing of children, is as old as the book of Genesis.' As Baker's reference to Genesis reflects, judges rejecting same-sex marriage have also relied on the nation's religious heritage. The District of Columbia Superior Court's decision in Dean v. District of Columbia quoted passages from Genesis, Deuteronomy, Matthew, and Ephesians to support its holding that 'societal recognition that it takes a man and a woman to form a marital relationship is older than Christianity itself.'[231]

Natural law theorists writing for secular as well as religious audiences maintain that the Judeo-Christian vision of marriage is consistent with the vision of marriage held by Plato, Aristotle, Plutarch, and other leading philosophers who viewed marriage as natural and viewed non-procreative sexuality as anti-marriage and unnatural.[232] Finnis maintains that this consensus bespeaks an underlying human truth: marriage is the union for both procreative and spiritually unitive goals, and it is impossible for these goals to be fulfilled by a same-sex couple.[233]

Without rehashing the evidence and arguments put forward in Chapters 5, 6 and 7 (i.e. the "orthodox" Christian position regarding GBLTQ lifestyle), the following will look at what "gay Christian" churches are doing and saying about same-sex marriage. Reverend Elder Troy D. Perry, of Universal Fellowship of Metropolitan Community Churches, Los Angeles, uses this "Service of Holy Communion" for GBLTQ marriage:

Dearly beloved, we are gathered together here in the sight of God and in the face of this company to join together these two (women/men) in Holy Union; which is an honorable estate, instituted of God, and therefore is not by any to be entered into unadvisedly or lightly; but reverently, discreetly, advisedly, soberly, and in the fear of God. Into this holy estate these two persons present come now to be joined. If any person can show us cause why they may not be joined together, let them speak or else hereafter forever hold their peace...For be well assured, that if any persons are joined together otherwise than as God's word does allow, their union is not binding. Let us pray...

[Name], do you promise, with God's help, to live together with [Name] in Union. Will you love (her/him) comfort (her/him) honor and keep (her/him) in sickness and in health so long as there is love?

We are reminded in Scripture of the story of two women who confess their love to one another. In the Hebrew Scriptures we read the story of Ruth and her words to Naomi when she said, 'In-treat me not to leave thee or to return from following after thee; for whither thou goest, I will go; and where thou lodgest, I will lodge; thy people shall be my people and thy God my God. Where thou diest, will I die, and there will I be buried; the Lord do so to me, and more also, if ought but death part thee and me.' Ruth [mother-in-law] and Naomi [daughter-in-law] stuck together through great adversity. They travelled a long distance to stay together, looked after each other when they were hungry and protected each other from danger. They expressed their love through physical affection in kissing and holding each other (Ruth 1:9, 11). They respected family and community customs and still retained the integrity of their love.

In 1978, Kate Millett said in Los Angeles; '...I would like us to act with the memory and the power of our passion, all the power of our many loves, all the times, you made it and it was good. This is your experience – be proud of it. It is what has made you alive, what had made your life even happen, so that you didn't almost live, so that you didn't not live. This even, through all the tortuous tunnels of love. How really difficult it has been to survive against, to maintain this love against, all that pressure – all that pressure in the other person, in ourselves, in the great world around us, strangling us. This has been our energy, our force, our strength, our power. They had made it hell, and we made it beautiful. Never forget the nights of your love and the days of working for its freedom, its expansion to fill the world with roses of those moments out of time. An army of lovers make a revolution. If a revolution is music ultimately, and not war, an army of lovers not only can't fail, but they could convert revolution into music, into the power of Eros. In fact what was it we wanted to bring into this place, if it wasn't love.'[234]

In this MCC "Service of Holy Communion" we see counterfeit Christianity – the unholy mix of text-proofed Scripture with chosen feminist rhetoric. Moreover, the radical and unscriptural interpretation of Ruth and Naomi's relationship cannot go unnoticed. After years of blurring the gender boundaries, the kiss between a mother and daughter-in-law (a recently widowed daughter-in-law at that) becomes the Scriptural legitimacy for gay and lesbian marriage. When using Biblical text this way, it is prudent in the ceremony not to mention the fact that Ruth soon remarries to another man.

According to Reverend Jim Sandmire, one of the pioneers of the Metropolitan Community Church, the Holy Union ceremony is "to be taken very, very seriously." Sandmire requires that couples who come to him for a *Holy Union* had to have lived together for at least a year:

The reason for that is that we – gay people – have no social institutions that keep gay people together, so it's important to surround this event with as much caution, care, and concern as we can.[235]

But orthodox marriage has never been the endorsement of a proven sexually satisfying love. It has been the conversion of an initial attraction into a biological and social commitment. The very essence of that commitment is having children and creating a flourishing family. We have already seen the statistics on cohabitation and its negative impact on marriage. What should be out of the question for

Christians, Sandimore makes essential as a pre-condition of marriage. He tosses the unequivocal prohibition on pre-marital sex aside, advocating cohabitation in its place. For *Reverend* Sandmire, monogamy is not a "religious" requirement before, during or after *Holy Union*:

I don't personally believe a relationship must be monogamous to be successful...I will say that it is often more difficult to have an open relationship. I think if you're going to have an open relationship you undertake certain kinds of responsibilities for each other that you don't necessarily undertake if you are in a monogamous relationship. What I say to people is, 'It is not my business to delve into what kind of relationship you are going to have in that respect. It is my business to make sure that you both understand it.' The whole concept of truthfulness...Once I come to the conclusion that this relationship is a healthy one, I explain what kind of planning has to be done. I also make it clear to them that I am dead serious about the Holy Union.[236]

What Sandmire describes as "Holy Union" is more appropriately called "Rev. Sandmire's union." The authority for such a union can neither be found in the Bible, Torah or Koran. Where the Christian prohibition on "adultery" comes into this "nonmonogamous" or "open" *Holy Union* is less than clear. Surprisingly, the term is in the MCC lexicon. *Reverend* Sandmire explains that for couples who choose a *Holy Union* with MCC, counseling includes a discussion of what happens in the event they decide to have *Holy Union* and then later decide to end the relationship. Later, "if convinced that the couple entered into their relationship in good faith and tried to save it in good faith" the MCC may decide that it is in the best interest of both parties that the relationship be dissolved:

We will then issue a dissolution of the vows, which simply means the couple is released from them. The document is signed and the Holy Union is taken off the church records. We point out that if you fail to do that and then enter into another relationship, you have committed adultery in the biblical sense. We get pretty heavy about it. And you will not be joined in a Holy Union ceremony by an MCC minister ever again.[237]

One is left pondering what "good faith" means in a "nonmonogamous" marriage. Moreover, what does "enter into another relationship" mean in an "open" Holy Union? Clearly, even gay religious marriage is challenged by the power of positive sex ethos. Many in GBLTQ do not support GBLTQ marriage rights. Equality for Gays and Lesbians Everywhere (EGALE) Canada, has evidenced a split over its strategy to bring same-sex marriage challenges before the courts. Ken Popert, executive director of *Pink Triangle Press* (publishers of the homosexual newspaper *Xtra*) said in *Capital Xtra*:

...their [EGALE] agenda has recently become too focused on same-sex marriages at the cost of other issues affecting the gay and lesbian community.[238]

According to Popert, only a small percentage of gay men want anything to do with marriage. He believes relationships in homosexual society cannot be held to the standards of heterosexuality. Jane Rule, author of *Desert of the Heart*, wrote an article in *BC Bookworld*, in which she said:

To be forced back into the heterosexual cage of coupledom is not a step forward, but a step back into state-imposed definitions of relationship. With all that we have learned, we should be helping our heterosexual brothers and sisters out of their state-defined prisons, not volunteering to join them there.[239]

Managing editor of *Xtra West*, Gareth Kirby, also weighed into the battle against same-sex marriages. In an article for his paper, dated September 6, 2001, he expressed the hope that EGALE looses the fight for equality rights in marriage. His conclusion is based on the view that legal marriage is contrary to what the homosexual movement has always been about, and that legal same-sex marriages would cause permanent damage to the gay culture, not to mention heterosexual marriage. He writes:

...The case wasn't even formally launched and some in our community were already mouthing the same old hierarchical crap that social conservatives have always shoved down our throats: length of involvement is some sort of gauge of commitment, or purity, or love, or respectability, or 'marriage-like' state, living together is better than living apart and marriage requires people to live together.

...In our culture, we haven't created the same hierarchy as has heterosexual culture. We know that love has many faces, and names, ages, places to f..., positions to f...in, and so on. We know that a 30-year relationship is no better than a nine-week, or nine-minute, fling – it's different, but not better. Both have value. We know that the instant intimacy involved in that perfect 20-minute f...in Stanley Park can be a profoundly beautiful thing. We know a two-year relationship where people live apart is a beautiful, absolutely as beautiful as a 30-year relationship where people live together. We know that the people involved in an open relationship can love each other as deeply as the people in a closed relationship...All these things are part of the spectrum of love. And love, in gay culture, is a spectrum, not a hierarchy. That's our culture.[240]

In much of straight culture, love is stuck in a hierarchy. The ceremony, the piece of paper, the government recognition, the tax benefits, the high cost of exit – these are intended to create an aura around marriage that suggests it's better than the alternatives.

Marriage belongs to heterosexual culture and we should respect that. It's a ceremony tying a woman and a man together (though I would argue that marriage inherently puts a woman in a subservient position).

Straight culture encourages its members to find all their needs (lover, best friend, confidante, roommate, vacation partner, parent of their children), in one person, with predictable strains and horrible endings. Gay men and lesbians tend to divvy out the emotional ties between different people – lover(s), roomies, f…buddies, best friends, 'sister(s)' and ex-lovers who become key members of our support network.

Valuing honesty and honoring lust, we almost always open up our relationship to sex with other people after a few years. A recent federally-funded health study of Vancouver gay men found that only two per cent were in long-term relationships. A similar study of straights would, no doubt, have found some 80 per cent or more in long-term relationships.

If we win access to this marriage snake-pit, it will begin the erosion of the culture that we've worked three decades to build. We've spent so long building our culture, and fighting for the freedom to live our lives as we really are, that we sometimes forget to pause to savor what we've made. And, though it has its flaws as do all cultures, it really is quite beautiful…

Instead of demanding that the courts and government lock us into the same straight-jacket that so many straights are in, we would do better to notice that so very many straights are learning from our culture, are rejecting and leaving marriage.

Why would we want to join a club that celebrates something that doesn't work for many of the participants when we already have something better? It's absurd to push for equal treatment under the law when it would mean settling for something that is inferior to our own arrangements and yet suffers a serious superiority complex.

…And they're out of touch with what our movement is about at its heart – freedom, not equality. Building a better world, not settling for equal treatment in the same world. Loving relationships, not hierarchy.[241]

The core paradox in the GBLTQ claim to marriage rights has thus been spelled out by Gareth Kirby. Marriage is an institution loaded with values and associated boundaries and hierarchies. GBLTQ culture by contrast is fundamentally anti-boundary and anti-monogamy. The historical intent and application of marriage has been one of structure, boundaries and commitment. This section ends with a metaphor for the space provided by faithful monogamous lifelong heterosexual marriage. Kim Camp, in *She's Twelve Going On Twenty* writes:

A study was done years ago, observing schoolchildren during recess. The researchers found that if there was not a fence around their playground, children stayed in the middle of the schoolyard, not venturing far a field. When a fence was present, they ventured out to the fence line and enjoyed the entire play area. Boundaries gave them – and give to us – freedom, because they provide a sense of safety.[242]

Christians, other faith-based peoples and family-oriented secularists cannot stand by as the institution of marriage gets watered down to where there are no recognizable boundaries, behind which love, commitment and family can flourish.

Alternative GBLTQ Union

The term perversion is devoid of objective meaning,...expressive of visceral disapproval but nothing rational...Cogent arguments can easily be made for characterizing as sexual perversions (1) voluntary sexual abstinence, celibacy, or retention of virginity past puberty; and (2) long-term monogamy (more than about four years), especially by males. Much more important: what is wrong with, or objectionable about, engaging in, a good, enjoyable sexual perversion (by any definition) as long as it is consensual for all persons involved? Obviously nothing! Such enjoyment is clearly subsumed under the guaranteed, inalienable right to pursuit of happiness given to us by our nation's birth certificate, the Declaration of Independence, and which is the basic, bedrock, unifying American ethical and moral principle, which defines America and provides the very raison d'etre for this country. That clearly includes homosexuality, however characterized. Let us have more and better enjoyment of more and better sexual perversions (consensually engaged in) by more and more people. Individually, collectively, societally, culturally, and nationally, we will all be better off.[243]

Orthodox Christians need to be primed for the possibility that a predominantly secular political and judicial system (confronted by the GBLTQ lobby and encouraged by liberal "pro-gay Christians") may very well choose a path, which leads even farther away from a genuine Christian worldview, to embracing a fully secular and humanist model. It is an inescapable fact that the social-political-judicial trends over the past forty years have been heading in that direction. Many adherents of the "Pivot of Civilization" philosophy, will not see the marriage issue as a societal crossroads, but rather perceive marriage redefinition as the final victory in a chain of "post-Christian era" cultural and sexual reformations. And perhaps this perspective is closer to the truth. Redefining marriage to include GBLTQ and broadening the institution's philosophical foundation to embrace sexual revolution tenets would herald a willful national decision to bury the last vestiges of religious-cultural influence on government in favor of imposed secularism. Humanists across North America would be elated over totally expunging religious influence upon the state (see next Chapter). The Charter of (Individual) Rights and Freedoms would henceforth usurp God in real and symbolic importance to the state. And for those theistic-faith peoples, who refuse to concede such a separation, imagine their cognitive discord. On one hand they submit to: (1) a constitution which literally acknowledges God's supreme authority; (2) a cash system proclaiming literally "In God we trust;" (3) a national anthem literally claiming God's existence; and (4) an oath of allegiance literally before God. On the other hand, our national laws on the *sacred* right of heterosexual marriage now directly contradict the beliefs of the overwhelming majority who claim faith in an Almighty God or whose religion holds same-sex marriage an abomination – Christians, Jews, Muslims and Sikhs.

From the Christian perspective such a national-level departure from God's design would not bode well. Do we really want to conduct another social experiment and see what the fallout will be 10, 20, or 30 years down the line? As mentioned in the Introduction, history will repeat itself, if we choose not to learn from it's lessons. Remember what life was like in Rome and Athens before Christianization and the perverse travesty of Gnosticism in the early centuries of Christianity. The links between the values imbedded in the current "Pivot of Civilization" worldview and this pagan past are alarming. In the Christian worldview truth and light come from Christ illuminating the darkness. Take Christ away and the darkness returns. At this crossroads there is no room for Christian apathy or acquiescence towards attempts to change the definition of marriage.

The authors of *Dual Attraction* asked the question: What is the ideal sociosexual arrangement. Would it be organized as a ménage-á-trois, group sex, communal marriage, or some other unconventional arrangement? Would it be a heterosexual marriage with outside same-sex partners? A core homosexual relationship with outside opposite-sex partners? Some other arrangement? Weinberg writes of the potential marriage variants:[244]

I'd like to have a long-term committed relationship with a woman, and I'd like to have outside relationships with men. (M)

Ideally, I would like a marriage with some woman. And perhaps, having a man involved in some way with the two of us. But in a secondary way to the marriage. (F)

A group of two males and two females where all had equal attraction to each other, who were all bisexual, and all functioned as a family. (M)

A closed group of perhaps eight or ten men and women who would live together – sharing work, emotions, sexuality, meals....There may be primary relationships, but everyone would relate sexually and emotionally in whatever groupings they choose. (M)

The fact that my wife and I would choose to be together would make our marriage stronger – the sense of being tested with a third party and not wanting to separate makes our tie stronger...There would be someone else in our lives who could be there. (M)

Armistead Maupin, probably the most successful gay writer ever published, told Frank Browning, author of *The Culture of Desire: Paradox and Perversity in Gay Lives Today*, that "Sex is the reason this liberation movement came about." According to Browning, Maupin's ire seems directed not so much at censorious, uncomprehending heterosexuals but at certain gays who, during the eighties, seemed set on desexing gay life, recasting gay people as just another community of polite American consumers for whom sex acts are merely incidental, private behaviors.[245] The parks and the bathhouses have been places of freedom and fraternity in Maupin's life, places where the cares and duties of the day dissolved, where barriers of class and education and profession might temporarily evaporate. "I have learned," he says with a chuckle, "that you could tell the difference between a nice guy and a bastard in the dark."[246]

During 1989 and 1990, Tom Stoddard, then executive director of Lambda Legal Defense and Education Fund, and Paula Ettelbrick, Lambda's legal director, conducted a series of public dialogues about gay marriage and domestic partnership. In the debate, Ettelbrick opposes gay marriage; Stoddard supports it. Stoddard argues that the right to marry is a classic American civil liberties matter. Any two human beings should have the right to participate in a union officially recognized by the state. And while marriage should not be held as a higher ideal of relationship, given the privileged place it does hold in society, people who choose to enter into it and maintain the legal responsibilities it confers should not be denied it.[247]

Ettelbrick, upholding original radical feminist analysis, opposes marriage as oppressive and discriminatory, an intrusion of state authority into individual relationships. "We have in this country a system of haves and have-nots along marriage lines. Those who marry get a lot – not just health insurance, but all kinds of government benefits, from housing to immigration rights to family discount rates, even bereavement leave." Rather than bring gay people into the marriage system, Ettelbrick would eliminate the preferential treatment granted to married people. If gay men and lesbians were given the right to marry, she fears, a replication would occur of the discriminatory two-tier system already existing among married and unmarried straight couples; legalized gay marriage, then, would make gays who don't marry outlaws among outlaws. Consider, she suggests, gay extended families that include a number of sexual partners, or those in which long-term primary relationships include both sexual and nonsexual partners. Or consider the gay man with a lover who chooses to have a child with a lesbian who also has a lover, the four then organizing themselves into a committed parenting family. "I don't know that any of us are ready to push for more than two people getting married," Ettelbrick suggests. "If you have two women and two men who are raising that child, assuming that one of the men is the biological father and one of the women is the biological mother of the child, you still have two individuals in that family unit who do not relate legally to the child." The broad nature of gay relationships – some sexual, some mentoring, some fraternal, some utilitarian – commonly involves more than two individuals. A movement to bring lesbians and gay men into the existing marriage system would almost certainly curtail ongoing experimentation with new extended families that recreate the complex emotional and practical support systems that existed in extended families of pre-industrial times.[248]

Ettelbrick's paradoxical argument is intriguing. First, she disparages orthodox marriage of all its ills, which many straights claim came about from forty years of gay liberation and radical feminism. Second, after the GBLTQ denigrating marriage all these years, she has the temerity like Dalma Heyn, to advocate that heterosexuals could learn how to fix (their) marriages and families from GBLTQ liberation experience and free sex experimentation. Through the freedom of exclusion, the very people who have historically been cast outside the legal and moral traditions of family are now advancing models for a resuscitated modern family. According to this line of thinking, the modern nuclear family has become a pressure cooker:

The financial necessity that both parents work combined with the lack of child-rearing support from extended family members has forced couples to rely on childcare services, reducing intimacy between parents and children. Counseling once provided by elder relatives must now be bought at prices that further deplete family resources. Wives have no time to develop friendships with other women, nor hus-

bands with other men. Friendships developed at work are always subject to manipulations of career ambition. Might there be something useful that nuclear heterosexuals could borrow from emerging gay households to alleviate their own stresses?[249]

Ettelbrick asks:

If people were truly liberated regardless of what they were, could that help but restructure other people's lives in a broader context?[250]

Not easily baffled, Frank Browning remains doubtful about the basis upon which these regenerative families are establishing themselves. He asks:

Where do they find their grounding? For whom do they exist? Is the yearning for these new-made families born of essentially private motives, for maximizing of personal happiness? Or do they provide niches of solidarity from which gay Americans can assert their sense of citizenship?[251]

Responding to his own confusion over GBLTQ variant families, he writes:

Deep into her argument, Ettelbrick made her position clear: 'The norm in this society should be recognizing families in the way they are self-defined.' Even in a Utopia where there was no prejudice against homosexuals, Ettelbrick would give society no authority to sanction, to reward, or even to approve one set of family relations over another. Ettelbrick's families would be created solely for the maximum happiness of their individual members. If living in a family made it easier for an individual to participate in public life, she seems to say, that might be a nice social dividend, but it would not be able to shape tax policies, housing programs, or educational services to reward one family arrangement over another. The families Ettelbrick foresees would find their raison d'etre in the same radical individualism that Robert Bellah found everywhere he turned in writing Habits of the Heart.[252]

One should commend Ettelbrick for her frankness; however, the clearest of intentions frequently have unintended consequences. In *Families We Choose*, anthropologist Kath Weston looked closely at how "kinship networks" grew out of gay sexual and friendship relations. Like Robert Bellah, she discovered that most people place pre-eminent value on their right to order their own social space. Asked what she did with all that free choice, one of Weston's informants answered, "I create my own traditions." Writes Browning:

The response is painfully oxymoronic, for tradition is by definition that which is handed down, from one generation to the next, from an earlier era to a later era. To alter, reshape, adapt tradition: these choices we have. We are free to choose who keeps house, who rears the child, who is the primary breadwinner. Unlike habit, which is individual, tradition is a way of living that is collectively established. Unlike convention, which is a contemporary agreement on the rules of behavior, tradition derives its authority from history. It's a tradition in Sicily to eat goat on Easter;

it's the current convention in the Mafia to use Uzis to wipe out uncooperative judges. The notion that one individual can create tradition reflects a naïve arrogance that perhaps only a self-reinvented Californian could express. A more tempered, and perhaps more social, response to Weston's question might have been to say that gay people have pushed open a social space through which individuals are searching for new kinds of family roles and relationships, and that out of the search, some as yet unknowable traditions will emerge. Among bourgeois heterosexual Americans, and especially among heterosexual American men, roles are usually separated by impermeable boundaries: brother, father, son, buddy, and colleague. Gay people, however, do seem to enjoy greater fluidity in their relations as they explore a continuum ranging from lust to love to nurture to mentorship to friendship in the search for a new kind of family.[253]

On balance Browning wonders whether by making sex ordinary, even recreational, some have learned to reform it into a tool for building diverse forms of comradeship. He ponders:

By stealing sex away from the restrictive laws of marriage, by acknowledging its myriad meanings, gay men may have shown how lust contributes to the bonds of friendship. By devaluing the taboo of sex among friends, they may have begun to shine more light on the complex and various ways intimacy can be arranged in emerging gay families. This is not to deny that lust without constraint can be abusive, callous, selfish, and ignoble; the point is that only through the persistent exploration of love and lust and nurturing, gay people have helped to open up the territory of family meanings. Individual gays and lesbians may not be able to create new 'traditions' of mateship and friendship in family life. But their determination to find a new sort of family may well provide vital models for the remaking of all families, straight and gay.[254]

Browning acknowledges that traditional marriage forbids sex with friends (and non-friends for that matter) and that the GBLTQ has created a new unique social space. He also cites a true story around Reed Grier, which highlights the need for some unique and alternative solution to the marriage and family needs of the GBLTQ. The following scenario is toxic to lifelong monogamous marriage and traditional family values:

As I listened to my friend's confession of emotional insularity, I couldn't help but think of something Reed Grier had told me about the passing of his gay family. A day or two after his dearest companion, David, died, Reed 'crawled into bed' with David's lover, Don. Four years later, shortly after Reed's second lover, Ron, died. Reed found himself having sex with Ron's nurse. At first it startled me that Reed should have sought sex in the midst of mourning; it seemed a confirmation of the criticism that gay men are stuck in their sexual obsessions. Yet neither of these single acts in the midst of mourning reflected anything we usually consider obsessive. With Don, the sex seemed to be about ritual bonding, a declaration that even in the midst of an epidemic that had infected every member of these two men's family, they were still alive. In his relations with Ron's nurse, Reed found comradeship and nurturing. Like many gay men who are able to blend sex with friendship, who occasionally use sex as a form of bonding not unlike an intense game of racketball...[255]

"No matter how gay people feel about domestic partnership and gay marriage," says Browning, "most share a core belief: Our friends are our family." "Yet if friendship is to offer more than escape from solitude, it must carry the weight of family, supply the security of solidarity that Reed...seeks." Here Browning asks, "How do we understand its fundamental character?"[256]

In his book, *The Male Couple's Guide: Finding A Man, Making A Home, Building A Life* Marcus gives us insight into what a *separate* concept of GBLTQ union might entail:

(1) Sex with other partners is allowed, but must be kept secret. (2) Sex with other partners is allowed, but must be discussed. (3) Sex is not permitted with mutual friends. (4) Only anonymous sexual encounters are permitted. (5) Sex is permitted only when one partner is out of town. (6) Sex with other partners is not permitted at home. (7) Sex with other partners is permitted at home, but not in the couple's bedroom. (8) Outside sex is permitted, but only when both partners choose a third to join them.[257]

Again, differentiating GBLTQ marriage from heterosexual marriage, Marcus adds:

Once you've set rules, leave room for discussion to adjust the boundaries should you find that the original rules aren't working in practice.[258]

The choice for the heterosexual majority is: (1) to concede to the inclusion of GBLTQ relationships in the institution of marriage and move all of society one huge bound toward the "culture of desire" (Pivot of Civilization ideology); or (2) use this so-called "equal rights" challenge to reaffirm the boundaries which separate the culture of desire space from protected heterosexual space for monogamous and potentially procreative marriage.

The choice for the GBLTQ minority is: (1) to reject all moves toward "sameness," "morality," and equal inclusion in the institution of marriage by sticking with their original radical feminist patriarchal analysis and their original strategy of creating a separate space for a free love homosexual lifestyle; or (2) the GBLTQ can concede to its own activists who now advocate monogamy (in the face of AIDS) and symbolic reunification with the heterosexual majority for GBLTQ self-esteem. Again this appears to be a zero-sum, lose-lose conflict dynamic between combatants.

An obvious way to reshape the clash to a win-win dynamic with promise of sustainable cooperation (which is different than acceptance) is to entrench two separate spaces and allow the GBLTQ to define union as they wish between partners of the same sex. This homosexual union would be differentiated by a unique title, be applicable to GBLTQ relationships, be flexible enough to include all GBLTQ diversity, be both pro-monogamy and nonmonogamy without paradox, and not be "straight" marriage. In this era of AIDS and heightened awareness of STDs, all should see some merit in the advocacy of "true" monogamy through GBLTQ union.

The uniqueness of traditional matrimony against a background of radical feminism, GBLTQ free sex culture, and multipartnerism begs for a well differentiated heterosexual marriage definition and the necessary accompanying legislative provisions. In closing this section and chapter, I wish to return to the BC court challenge by Shane McCloskey for his right to marry Dave Shortt. McCloskey, sees the wrongdoing as discrimination. He argues "sameness" and apparently sees no differentiation in the GBLTQ culture evidenced over these hundreds of pages. His claim to marriage stands on a rampant notion of individualism and personal rights. Like the strategy of the Calgary Birth Control Association (CBCA), I described at the start of the book, no mention is made of the value system accompanying McCloskey's challenge – "We just do rights." The issue thus becomes one of equating heterosexual marriage (a millennium-plus-year-old institution with fundamental underlying values) with another social experiment of GBLTQ marriage, derived from a culture which values liberation, social anarchy and boundary destruction. Little wonder the presiding judge ruled that:

The gain to society from the preservation of the deep-rooted and fundamental legal institution of opposite-sex marriage outweighs the detrimental effect of the law on the petitioners.

That Judge Pitfield's interpretation is not gay-bashing, homophobic or otherwise unfairly discriminatory is evidenced in a separate Supreme Court ruling handed down on December 19, 2002, discriminating against heterosexual petitioners. In this case the highest court in Canada ruled that the Province of Nova Scotia is not acting unconstitutionally when it discriminates between married couples and common-law couples. The petitioners unsuccessfully argued that the Nova Scotia Matrimonial Property Act (MPA) was violating the Charter of Rights and Freedoms for failing to include common-law couples with the definition of "spouse." The majority ruling noted that:

The exclusion from the MPA of unmarried cohabitating persons of the opposite sex is not discriminatory within the meaning of Section 15 (1) of the Charter.

The justices noted that some couples intentionally choose not to marry and thus imposing on them the obligations of marriage "nullifies the individual's freedom to choose alternative family forms and to have that choice respected by the state." According to many pro-family advocates, the current onslaught of legislation to permit GBLTQ couples rights normally reserved to married couples stems from previous faulty decisions granting common-law couples the rights of married couples. It now seems incredulous that the state sees no problem in differentiating common law heterosexuals from married heterosexuals, but may refuse to differentiate gay and lesbian couples from married heterosexual couples. Applying zero-sum logic to this issue, it is clear that "If everything is marriage, then nothing is marriage."

Clones: Alternative Family Planning

All women who bear children are committing, literally and symbolically, a blood sacrifice for the perpetuation of the species...In this sense, female sacrifice in patriarchal and prescientific culture is concretely rooted in female biology...Perhaps the myth and reality of female (and male) sacrifice will cease when intrauterine biological reproduction ceases – or when the function is not assigned to one sex only....

Perhaps either of these events would occur more quickly if women were to control the means of production and reproduction – in this case, the scientific investigation of contraception, extrauterine birth, and uterus implantation; the economic means to insure the eventual success of such research; and the political, legal, and religious authority to publicize and enforce the research findings.'[259]

Phyllis Chesler, 1972

Sex-changing teen wants to be mom and dad – A teenage boy undergoing a sex change operation plans to freeze his sperm so he can father a child after he becomes a woman...'I'd like to have children one day, so I am having my sperm frozen before the operation'...'That way it can be used to fertilize the egg of a surrogate mom. So I could be a mom one day, even though, biologically, I will be the baby's father as well.'[260]

George Gilder writes in his book *Men and Marriage*, that biogenetic engineering "is emerging year by year to become a major force in the definition and prospects of the two sexes, of masculinity and femininity."[261] New technology makes it technically possible, for the first time in human history, to change the very essence of sexuality. Gilder expresses concern over the direction all this technology is leading – in vitro or test-tube fertilization; extracorporeal gestation (artificial womb); and cloning. Yet this seemingly innocent practice [in vitro], which will ultimately help millions of childless couples to have babies, also poses many perplexing problems. Dr. [Leon R.] Kass maintains that many of the women who can be helped by this technique also could be given a permanent cure by surgery on their oviducts (particularly if this operation is promoted as lavishly as the fertilization projects). Test-tube conception also potentially reduces the demand to adopt children. It advances the day when parents will be able to choose the gender of their child, either ordering a fetus of the preferred sex or aborting all undesired ones. And by circumventing the act of love, in vitro conception takes another small step toward dislodging sexual intercourse from its pinnacle as both the paramount act of love and the only act of procreation. It thus promotes the trend toward regarding sex as just another means of pleasure, and weakens the male connection to the psychologically potent realm of procreation.[262]

In addition, the process offers human uses far beyond the circumvention of sterility. It makes possible the disconnection between motherhood and pregnancy. Since the fertilized ovum does not have to be placed in the body of the real 'mother,' it can be handed out to any willing woman – for pay. Writes Gilder:

This is not a far-fetched idea using artificial insemination, a woman in Michigan has already rented her womb to a friend, borne a child fathered by the friend's husband, and delivered it to the wife. The family has received thousands of inquiries from others.[263]

With in vitro techniques rather than artificial insemination, a much more attractive result – full genetic offspring – could be achieved by such means. New, more partial and detached forms of motherhood become possible for busy or preoccupied women. The very role of mother and the profound biological tie with her child – enacted in the women's most intense sexual experiences in childbirth – become optional. This development threatens to diminish further the perceived and felt authority of the basic connections of human life.[264]

If artificial wombs were achieved, the state could assume increasing control over the genetic future of the race. With government controlling production and reproduction, the dreams of the humanist social planner could at last be fulfilled (examined at the end of Chapter 4). Kass quotes C.S. Lewis's powerful tract, *The Abolition of Man*:

If any one age really attains, by eugenics and scientific education, the power to make its descendants what it pleases, all men who live after it are patients of that power. They are weaker, not stronger....The real picture is that of one dominant age...which resists all previous ages most successfully and dominates all subsequent ages most irresistibly, and thus is the real master of the human species. But even within this master generation (itself an infinitesimal minority of the species) the power will be exercised by a minority smaller still. Man's conquest of nature, if the dreams of scientific planners are realized, means the rule of a few hundreds of men over billions upon billions of men. There neither is nor can there be any simple increase in power on man's side. Each new power won by man is a power over man as well.[265]

Concludes Gilder:

Few things ever happen much as predicted. Lewis's vision of a centralized power of reproduction might well give way to a messy proliferation of eugenic experiments and enterprises proceeding over centuries. But the long-run social implications remain dire for the human species as we know it.[266]

In 1986, Gilder described the nature of the change resulting from reproductive technologies:

Although some analysts have predicted the liberation of women or the redundancy of males, the technology in fact most profoundly threatens women. Ultimately the womb could become obsolete. Not only could the female body become a strange combination of otiose spaces and appendages, not only could the man's become the exemplary, utilitarian physique, but the power of women over men could gradually pass away. First with time, her sexual powers would decrease. For if we break the tie between sexual intercourse and procreation, destroy childhood memory of the nurturing and omnipotent mother, banish the mystique of the breasts and the womb and of the female curves and softness, we could remove as well the special attraction of heterosexual love. We may liberate men to celebrate, like the ancient Spartans or the most extreme homosexuals today, a violent, misogynistic, and narcissistic eroticism.[267]

Who wants to move toward ancient Greek and Roman sexism? Nine years after Gilder's *Men and Marriage*, gay author Jonathan Ned Katz wrote *The Invention of Heterosexuality*. He described the future from the gay perspective:

The fall of the old reproductive ethic also eliminates one rationale of the distinction between homosexual and heterosexual. With most of the western world, Christian fundamentalists and the great majority of Catholics regularly employing pleasure enhancers (euphemistically, 'birth control'). Few people now, except the Pope, judge the quality of heterosexual relationships by their fecundity.

As D'Emilio and Freedman describe it, since the early nineteenth century, when the reproductive moorings of sexual relationships came loose for the urban middle class, many Americans have had to grapple, in self-conscious way, with the meaning and purpose of sexual relations. Now, the 'near universality of birth control' highlights the separation of the procreative from the erotic.

Today, the meaning of sexuality no longer seems to reside, self-evidently, within our bodies or in nature, but depends on how we use it. Striking discoveries by biologists of reproduction, and the development of new reproductive technologies, upset 'age-old certainties about the natural connection between sex and procreation.' Whatever ideas about sexuality most Americans hold in theory, the majority now commonly act as if there's no necessary link between 'making love and making babies.'...even the supposedly immutable 'sex act' underwent redefinition in ways that weakened a male monopoly over the nature of sex. The variety of erotic acts hailed in today's heterosexual handbooks also weakens the old heterosexual monopoly over the definition of sex.[268]

Gilder further describes the impact of a "bio-technocracy":

The ultimate pattern that might unfold if the new bioengineering technology is devoted heavily to the agenda of 'women's liberation,' is not that women might be released from pregnancy, but that the men would be released from marriage, and thus from the influence of female sexuality. The male physique, far inferior to the woman's in a sexual society, would become superior in a sexual-suicide society in which the state manages reproduction. The women's breasts and womb would lose their uses. The male body would become the physical ideal and lend symbolic authority to the male command of other instruments of power. The technocracy, a dominantly male creation in the first place, would remain in the hands of a male minority.[269]

The system of marriage that tames men and evokes their love is the chief obstacle to this technocratic future. If marriage endures, the realm of the state and the development and use of the technology can be limited, while the maintenance of human individuality can be assured. If the family should widely break down, then the world of artificial wombs, clones, and child-development centers can become an important reality rather than a laboratory curiosity. Norman Mailer was thus most profound when he defined the movement of women's liberation as the fifth column of the technocracy. He might have added that it is also the fifth column of true patriarchy: the sterile solidarity.[270]

Here Katz' writing verifies Gilder's thinking:

Today's public destabilizing of heterosexual tradition is also clear in the rise of divorce and the creation of new families....By the 1980s the 'traditional two-parent family with children accounted for only three-fifths of all living arrangements.' The idea and reality of the 'family' is pluralizing before American's astonished eyes. Lesbian couples and gay male partners bring up their children from former marriages, or adopt children; single heterosexual women impregnate themselves with the help of an obliging male and a turkey baster, as do numbers of lesbians.

'As Americans married later, postponed childbearing, and divorced more often, and as feminists and gay liberationists questioned heterosexual orthodoxy,' say D'Emilio and Freedman, 'non-marital sexuality became commonplace and open.' Another traditional distinction between hetero- and homosexuals vanishes.[271]

Leon Kass argues:

...that the breakdown of the family threatens to destroy our sense of continuity with the past and the future, as it is the family through which we acquire links to the past as well as a commitment to the future. He sees this trend as one that de-personalizes society. Parenthood means less than in past generations and results in ready acceptance of abortion of unwanted children. In part because of concerns for population and the cost of raising children, but also due to changing conceptions of the family, parents are opting to have fewer or no children. The technology of the pill, and other birth-control methods has made this goal of limited families feasible....In any case, changing values regarding the centrality of the family to human existence have helped create an atmosphere (or another manifestation of it at least) in which traditional parent-child relationships are more easily defined from an individualistic perspective.[272]

Charles Frankel also views the notion of altruistic genetic improvements to society with skepticism:

Despite the great social programs to fight poverty, improve housing, and remove urban problems, the ills of society are perceived by most as getting worse instead of better...on the right, people can look with sympathy on eugenics, envisaging the program's being tried on others, not on themselves. And on the left, biomedicine speaks to the hope, ever rising from the ashes, that the human race can still be made over by proper planning.[273]

As the "gender gap" between women and men narrows, says Katz, so does the sexual orientation gap. The convergence of heterosexuality and homosexuality becomes ever more apparent. The instability of homosexual relationships (unsupported by law and the dominant culture) no longer serves to distinguish them essentially from the many heterosexual relationships destabilized by divorce.[274] There would be no reason for the hetero/homo division if heteros did not stand above homos in a social hierarchy of superior and inferior pleasures. If homosexuals were to win society-wide equality with heterosexuals, there would be no reason to distinguish them. The homo/hetero distinction would be retired from use, just as it was once invented. For Gilder, the question is whether male and female sexual nature will prevail:

More than ever before, society needs today a real feminist movement that asserts the primacy of female nature in marriages and families. Just as women tame the barbarians of each generation of men, women can save sexuality from the male barbarians of specialization who would specialize reproduction. While eschewing a Luddite effort to stop the progress of knowledge, a real woman's movement can rebuke social planners of Marxism, who have been widely thwarted in their efforts to create a 'new society' but are now proposing to engineer a 'new man.'[275]

Katz asks a rhetorical question, "With the abolition of the heterosexual system, the terms heterosexual and homosexual can become obsolete. Then what?" He replies to this question:

Then, after all the put-down peoples unite to enhance the pleasure of their short shift on earth, we will finally become a nation, not only founded, but actually operating according to principles of 'life, liberty, and the pursuit of happiness,' Of those three 'traditional values, the happiness pursuit is 'the real joker in the deck' – in the words of Gore Vidal. The pursuit of happiness, Vidal adds, 'was a revolutionary concept in 1776. It still is.' For the pursuit of happiness, and the achievement of a few earthly joys, require the end of the mean society and the private greed principle, the making of a new pleasure system. I take my stand here with the pleasure party. But the happiness pursuit is a 'traditional value' not limited in appeal to the party of eros.[276]

The lack of concept of family in this post-heterosexual society, enlightened in its pursuit of *pleasure*, as Gilder, Kass and many others argue is no small cause for concern. In New York, a pro-cloning group sprang up, the Clone Rights United Front, whose members included gay men and lesbians who wanted to clone themselves. According to Gina Kolata, the lesbians envisioned taking a cell from one woman and implanting it in an egg from another, thus creating a baby without the presence of a man.[277] Cloning is their only way of obtaining children without a heterosexual dipoid (one set of male and one set of female chromosomes). In mammals, new embryos cannot be created by placing two sperm nuclei or two egg nuclei in a single egg because of the phenomenon of genomic imprinting – nuclei of both sexes are needed:

This phenomenon, whereby the parent puts his or her own stamp on the gene, according to the parent's sex, is called genomic imprinting. Its existence is surprising; it is not what a century of genetics studies had led biologists to expect. It came to light largely through experiments in nuclear transfer (many by Azim Surani at the Institute of Animal Physiology at Babraham, Cambridge) in which mammalian zygotes were given two female pronuclei or two male pronuclei. Such zygotes can develop as far as the blastocyst stage, but if they are implanted into a uterus, they soon fail. The embryos with an all-paternal genome develop a fine placenta but no proper embryo, while those with an all-maternal genome begin by making a good-looking embryo but only a poor placenta. For this reason parthenogenesis in mammals – development of a whole new animal from an unfertilized egg – really does seem 'biologically impossible,' even though it is common enough in other animals, including many vertebrates. In the absence of divine intervention, virgin birth for mammals is not an option. Both a male and a female genome must be present.[278]

Ian Wilmut admits that in cases where reproduction by sex is out of the question: when one person alone seeks to reproduce, without a sexual partner; or when two partners either fail to produce gametes at all or produce incompatible gametes – as in the case of homosexual partners, cloning is the only option. The procedure would be different by the sex of the end parent. Male homosexual couples might conceivably be cloned with the aid of egg donors and surrogate mothers, while female couples could be far more independent; indeed, cloning would allow the dream of some extreme feminists, of reproduction without males. Says Wilmut:

One member of a lesbian couple might provide the cytoplasm; next time around they could reverse the procedure. Of course by such means, a lesbian couple could produce only daughters. A woman could clone herself precisely if one of her own nuclei was introduced into one of her own enucleated oocytes. Many combinations could be imagined.[279]

In December 16, 2002, a poll from Johns Hopkins University revealed that 76 per cent of Americans are against scientific efforts to clone humans. The poll finds that among those who approve of human cloning, there's a clear difference between men and women – 26 per cent of men favor cloning and only 11 per cent of women approve.[280] David P. Gushee studied the claims made by the pro-cloning lobby and found a number of factors at play:

Market forces. The sprawling biotech industry, already doing $80 billion in business in the United States alone, would not be awash in money were there not a demand for its innovations. These products and services include stem cells, gene therapies and enhancements, and, one day, perhaps soon, clones. Biotech firms promise what people want—health, pain relief, reproduction, longevity, and success.[281]

Worldview dynamics. This leads us to a still deeper reality: beneath both economic practice and moral fragmentation lies the foundation of worldview. Among those who press most aggressively for unrestrained development of biotech advances –

including nonscientists—worldviews and philosophies such as naturalism, atheism, utilitarianism, and scientific utopianism reign. Much of our culture's élite lives without a working hypothesis of God. Assuming we dwell alone in the universe, they believe we must simply keep improving life until the next comet hits.

Libertarian ideology—which stresses individualism, privacy, moral relativism, unlimited choice-making, and autonomy—folds neatly into these godless worldviews. It holds that no one should deny himself anything that will bring self-realization and is not immediately harmful to another.

Hence a powerful contingent argues for the largely unrestrained pursuit of biotechnology as a matter of personal (including reproductive) liberty. This quest is driven by a utopian dream: overcoming our species' limits through human power and scientific progress.

Some suggest triumphantly that our species is about to evolve right past homo sapiens to what New Republic senior editor Gregg Easterbrook calls homo geneticus. One enthusiast has said that future generations will look back on our time as 'the point in history when human beings gained the power to seize control of their own evolutionary destiny.'[282]

Gushee discusses "secular bioethics" from the perspective articulated in 1979 by the National Commission in their *Belmont Report*.[283] This report set out three bioethics principles: respect for persons (called autonomy), justice, and beneficence (called utility). The idea of autonomy, an increasingly popular appeal in this postmodern age, is one in which people's personal experiences and values play a most important role in determining what is right and true for them. According to this justification, we ought to respect people's autonomy as a matter of principle. People's beliefs and values are too diverse to adopt any particular set of them as normative for everyone. Society should do everything possible to enhance the ability of individuals and groups to pursue what they deem most important. There are many forms that autonomy justifications can take. However, for John F. Kilner, four stand out as particularly influential in discussions of human cloning:

'Personal freedom.' There is a strong commitment in many countries, the United States in particular, to respecting people's freedom. This commitment is rooted in a variety of religious and secular traditions. Respect for people entails allowing them to make important life decisions that flow from their own personal values, beliefs, and goals, rather than coercing them to live by a burdensome array of social requirements.

'Reproductive choice.' Reproductive decisions are especially private and personal matters. They have huge implications for one's future responsibilities and well being. Social intrusion in this realm is particularly odious.

'Scientific inquiry.' A high value has long been placed on protecting the freedom of

scientific inquiry. More knowledge and better understanding enhance our capacity to make good decisions and accomplish great things in the world.

'Destiny Justification.' ...there is a ...type of proposed justification for human cloning which moves us more explicitly into the realm of theological reflection: the destiny justification. While other theological arguments against cloning have been advanced in the literature to date, many of them are somehow related to the matter of destiny. According to this justification, it is part of our God-given destiny to exercise complete control over our reproductive process. In fact, Richard Seed, in one of his first in-depth interviews after announcing his intentions to clone human beings commercially, made this very argument.[284]

According to Kilner, an autonomy-based justification of human cloning is no more acceptable than a utility-based justification from a theological perspective. Some Christian writers, such as Allen Verhey, have helpfully observed that autonomy, understood in a particular way, is a legitimate biblical notion. As he explains, under the sovereignty of God, acknowledging the autonomy of the person can help ensure respect for and proper treatment of people made in God's image. There is a risk here, however, because the popular ethics of autonomy has no place for God in it. It is autonomy "over" God, not autonomy "under" God. The challenge is to affirm the critical importance of respect for human beings, and for their freedom and responsibility to make decisions that profoundly affect their lives, but to recognize that such freedom requires God. More specifically, such freedom requires the framework in which autonomy is under God, not over God, a framework in which respecting freedom is not just wishful or convenient thinking that gives way as soon as individuals or society as a whole have more to gain by disregarding it. It must be rooted in something that unavoidably and unchangeably 'is." In other words, it must be rooted in God, in the creation of human beings in the image of God.[285] Much more will be said on this in the last chapter, "Theistic Boundaries to Rights and Choice."

When utility is our basis for justifying what is allowed in society, people are used, fundamentally, as mere means to achieve the ends of society or of particular people. It may be appropriate to use plants and animals in this way, within limits. Accordingly, most people do not find it objectionable to clone animals and plants to achieve products that will fulfill a purpose – better milk, better grain, and so forth. However, it is demeaning to "use" people in this way. For example, cloning a child who dies to remove the parents' grief forces the clone to have a certain genetic makeup in order to be the parents' replacement child, thereby permanently subjecting the clone to the parents' will. The irony of this last situation, though, is that the clone will not become the same child as was lost – both the child and the clone being the product of far more than their genetics. The clone will be demeaned by not being fully respected and accepted as a unique person, and the parents will fail to regain their lost child in the process.[286]

As the U.S. National Bioethics Advisory Commission's report has observed (echoed more recently by the report of the President's Council on Bioethics), human cloning:

...invokes images of manufacturing children according to specification. The lack of

acceptance this implies for children who fail to develop according to expectations, and the dominance it introduces into the parent-child relationship, is viewed by many as fundamentally at odds with the acceptance, unconditional love, and openness characteristic of good parenting.[287]

Genetic screening, re-engineering and sex selection are other technological ways that are reshaping the family. Human Genetics Alert, an independent watchdog, and Alternative India Development, which promotes gender equality, called for a ban on all methods of sex selection. Called the Ericsson Technique, it separates male, Y-bearing sperm from female X-bearing sperm by filtration, exploiting the fact that male sperm swim faster. The woman is then artificially inseminated with the chosen batch of sperm. The clinics charge $2,500 for sperm sorting and claim the method is 94 per cent accurate for boys and 81 per cent for girls.[288] "This shows what happens if we have no rules to control the free market," said David King, director of Human Genetics Alert. Alternative India Development said: "Girl children's right to be born live is nipped in the bud by the misuse of sex-determination and sex-selection technologies." Chris Bailey, director of the London Gender Clinic, said that they had been offering sperm sorting for ten years. "Its completely legal in this country." "We have a lot of interest from the Punjabi community."[289] "There are no hard-and-fast rules; there is no legislation," said Arthur Wisot, the executive director of the Center for Advanced Reproductive Care in Redondo Beach, California. "This whole area of medicine is totally unregulated. We don't answer to anyone but our peers."[290]

Against this biogenetic controversy, it will surprise few that in general, a doomsday mentality pervades Canadian attitudes toward the inevitability of cloning humans. Canadians do not want it, but feel powerless to prevent human cloning. Marc Ledger, president of Ledger Marketing, comments:

It's very rare to have such a strong response on the subject. Usually Canadians are much more divided, but essentially people are afraid that we're going to lose control over human cloning.[291]

When asked for their views on the cloning of human beings, known as reproductive cloning, 88.9 per cent of respondents said they were against such a project. Another 2.8 per cent said they didn't have an answer or refused to respond.[292] However, support for cloning rose sharply in the poll when it was linked to embryonic stem-cell research for transplants and treatment of incurable diseases. In Canada, 55.4 per cent of those surveyed said they would support cloning for such scientific purposes, known as therapeutic cloning, while 40.8 per cent were against such research.[293]

Trying to balance these conflicting interests a draft Canadian bill would not prohibit human cloning, only the implantation of cloned embryos. The wording allows scientists to create embryos for stem-cell research. As discussed before, the embryologist prefers to think in a cognitive paradigm whereby he is manipulating sub-human lives which are only "racing to become embryos."

A range of witnesses aired diverse views on the bill before the National Commons Health Committee. Old rivals, REAL Women and Lesbian Mothers Association faced-off against each other. Gwendolyn Landolt, national vice-president of

REAL Women of Canada, called on the government to halt all research with embryos and also ban surrogate motherhood. Mona Greenbaum, a coordinator for Lesbian Mothers Association of Quebec, told the committee lesbians who want to begin families should have the same access to government fertility clinics that heterosexual, married women currently have in several other provinces. Lawrence Soler, government relations director for the Juvenile Diabetes Research Foundation of Canada, pleaded the case for embryonic stem cell research to help find a cure for diabetes. Christian agencies argued it was morally wrong to take one life, even that of an embryo, in order to help another life through medical research.[294]

University of Chicago medical ethics professor Leon Kass, named as head of a new bioethics commission, summarizes the overwhelming case against cloning:

Cloning is a form of experimentation on a nonconsenting subject. Attempts on animals reveal extremely high failure rates, resulting in many disabilities and deformities. No ethical scientist would attempt human cloning at current odds.

Cloning threatens human identity and individuality by permitting the intentional genetic replication of a person whose life is already in process. The clone, says Kass, 'will not be fully a surprise to the world; people are always likely to compare his doings in life with those of his alter ego.'

Cloning turns procreating into manufacturing by enabling the advance selection of a total genetic blueprint. Things are made, but people are begotten. In cloning, that boundary line is erased (although a form of baby manufacturing has been underway since in vitro fertilization began, Kass rightly notes).

Cloning is an act of despotism that perverts parenthood by turning children into genetically engineered possessions intended to fulfill parental wants. Some argue that many children are already brought into the world for reasons other than the sheer desire to welcome new life. But we must reject treating children, however they are born, as commodities or as instruments to other ends.[295]

Other considerations raised by Gushee include:

...Cloning would mark the first instance of humans reproducing through asexual replication, radically altering the nature of procreation and eliminating dual genetic origin in the cloned. Notre Dame law professor Kathleen Kaveny has shown how dramatically cloning would confuse family lines and relations.

If made available solely by the market based on ability to pay, cloning would contribute to distributive injustice. It would weaken marriage and the relationships between men and women by further eroding the link connecting marriage, sex, and childbearing—likely extending the practice of assisted reproduction among homosexuals.

Cloning would contribute to our epidemic narcissism by enabling self-creation without any involvement of another person. The potential for multiple self-cloning could create a household freak show. It could bring more children into the world who lack the benefit of two parents. The sly might try to clone others without their consent; or, conversely, famous people and corporate interests might market highly desired genotypes to those seeking (in vain) to guarantee successful offspring.[296]

It is easy to envision a split between what Princeton University molecular biologist Lee M. Silver creatively labels the GenRich and the Naturals—those who would be able to buy genetic excellence and those who would not.[297] In a scene in *GATTACA*, a young couple at a fertility clinic must select one of their four genetically typed embryos, which have been vetted for traits such as myopia and obesity. A boy would be nice to provide a playmate for their young son, but (in a scene deleted from the final film) they would also like to ensure that they can have grandchildren. "I've already taken care of that," the doctor nonchalantly replies. The couple is thus assured of having a healthy, heterosexual son, but cannot afford the optional extras – genes for heightened musical or mathematical ability. The film also raises the possibility of tampering with the human anatomy, whether by adding an extra finger for a concert pianist or enhancing other appendages ("Beautiful piece of equipment – I don't know why my folks didn't order one like that for me!") In *Remaking Eden*, Princeton University geneticist Lee Silver goes even further, speculating that 1,000 years from now, the human race may have split into two separate species, the GenRich and the Naturals, unable to interbreed.[298]

'Welcome to CLONAID™ – the first human cloning company!' CLONAID was founded in February 1997, by Raël, the leader of the Raelian Movement, an international religious organization, which claims that a human extraterrestrial race, called the Elohim, used DNA and genetic engineering, to scientifically create all life on Earth.[299]

Few might be surprised that the Raelian religion's original symbol was the Star of David with a Swastika inserted in its center. The Raelians believe that the Star of David represents infinite space. Raelians claim that the swastika originally framed by the Star of David represents infinity of time, and trace its origins to Sanskrit and Buddhist symbols, to the Chinese character for temple, and to ancient catacombs, mosques, and synagogues. In 1991, the Raelians abandoned the swastika and replaced it with "a swirling image of a galaxy surrounded by the Star of David."[300] Their own web site notes:

Because of the nature of sensual meditation, many non-Raelians believe that the Raelian religion is simply about sex, a point that is illustrated by the headline of a news article in the Ottawa Citizen (6 March 1995) stating 'Sex, Extra-Terrestrials Focus of Church.'

Brigitte Boisselier, director of CLONAID, says the real issue for CLONAID and Raelianism is freedom of choice in creating life:

There is demand for such cloning, especially among infertile and gay couples, as well as middle-aged single women who want to have a baby.[301]

Today, nobody will tell you that you shouldn't mix your genes with this person or that person, you have the right to choose. So if you choose not to mix your genes but have a baby with only your genes because you're a 45-year-old single woman, why should people tell you not to do that?[302]

Almost a year and a half later, as president of CLONAID, Boisselier announced the birth of a third baby – a boy, born of a surrogate mother, in Japan. The DNA for the baby – she didn't know his name – was obtained from the dead son of a couple – whom she refused to identify – after he died 18 months previous in an accident. Says Boisselier in response to media disgust:

I believe this is a love story. I'm talking about the love of the parents. The parents are happy; this is what matters.

Boisselier said the parents of the dead child who's DNA was used for the cloning called CLONAID. "We rushed over there and had time to take cells, to culture them, to develop them."[303] Because the mother was 41 years old, it was decided that there was a risk of miscarriage and a surrogate mother was chosen to carry the baby. Boisselier said the second cloned baby girl, born to a lesbian couple in Holland on January 3, 2003, was doing well. So far none of the couples had paid for the treatment. The first 20 cloned babies, according to Boisselier, were being funded by two investors who were hopeful of being cloned themselves. After the 20th baby, the many thousands of couples who want cloned babies will be expected to pay. Says Boisselier:

This is how the investors see this, as a capital risk investment.[304]

PART FIVE

PIVOT OF CIVILIZATION
OR
RIVET OF LIFE?

Cursed is the one who trusts man, who depends on flesh for his strength and whose heart turns away from the Lord (Jeremiah 17:5).

Once upon a time there was a wheel tapper called Fred.

And he tapped all the wheels on all the trains that came into the station.

And they changed five hundred and twenty-seven wheels.

And then one day they found out

Fred's hammer was cracked![1]

One worldview, with all its premises, values, philosophies, tenets, truths, adherents and behaviors, is cracked.

Which One?

CHAPTER NINE

THEISTIC BOUNDARIES TO RIGHTS AND CHOICE

Whereas Canada is founded upon the principles that recognize the supremacy of God...

The above quote is part of the first line of the preamble to the Canadian Charter of Rights and Freedoms. Note the Charter does not say God under the supremacy of parliament, the courts or the individual; nor does it say God under the supremacy of academia or science; nor does the Charter recognize the supremacy of an *unknown* God. The Canadian Government, until relatively recently, was not operating in a vacuum regarding the meaning and interpretation of God. For more than a century, until the late 1960s, the theology underpinning the laws of the Land was unequivocally Judeo-Christian. A few manifestations of this imperative included: swearing-in on the Bible to give witness, a Christian Parliamentary Prayer, Christian Crosses as Remembrance Day cenotaphs and memorial wreaths, and civic holidays acknowledging Christmas and Easter. Children in public schools collectively said the Lord's Prayer; many had a number of chances at being one of the three wise men or the Virgin Mary in annual Christmas pageants; and most received a Gideon's New Testament on entry into the fourth grade.

But that was then, and this is now. In between have been a "sexual revolution" and the realization of an essentially humanist-secularist agenda of liberation legislations, leading towards what then Justice Minister Pierre Elliott Trudeau called "The Just Society." The impact of Government policies over this period was to radically reduce the significance of Christianity in the affairs of state and the social lives of Canadian citizens. We are now in the "post-modern era," which is thought by secularists, humanists, and many social planners, to be the dawn of religious estrangement or at least a time of religious homogenization, where Witchcraft, Gnosticism, Raelianism, and Spiritual Humanism, are to have equal state emphasis along with "world religions" like Christianity, Judaism, Islam and others. The state's conception of the God underpinning the Charter of Rights and Freedoms has withered from theistic clarity to pantheistic ambiguity. In just four decades, the Bible as the Nation's descriptive reference for God has been diluted in a sea of spiritual equivalency and all but sunk by state sponsored secularism.

The following text titled "Resolution to Combat Religious Influence," taken from the Canadian humanist web site, offers a substantial explanation for the ideological source behind much of this erosion and revision:

The Humanist Association of Canada is a national association that includes humanists, atheists, agnostics, rationalists, freethinkers, and non-church-affiliated people....We believe that Canada could be a model for many countries on how to develop a free and democratic society composed of many different ethnic, religious, and philosophical groups living in harmony. We believe strongly in the separation of church and state and the neutrality of the state in matters of religion....Many current practices are undemocratic and unfair....We believe in a secular school system for all. People who want to send their children to private or religious schools should assume all the costs themselves. Another example is the recitation of prayers at official public functions. These are unacceptable....Although unsuccessful, many of our members signed a petition to have the reference to God removed from the preamble of the Canadian Constitution. This petition was read out in Parliament by MP Svend Robinson on June 8, 1999.[1]

While masquerading as supporters of freedom of religion, humanists really uphold no respect for the legitimacy of religious faith. Worse, while clamoring against public prayer and for expunging God from state and public institutions, they and like-minded activists, have shown no reservation entering our public schools to preach on homosexuality (in Mary's classroom experience, teaching gay-gene theory), knowing that what they tell students is not science and what they say is contrary to the religious faiths of a significant number of students. Indeed, in Mary's example, the public school teacher said, "the guest speaker was only giving her personal beliefs."

Furthermore, over the past forty years, the state has outlawed virtually any form of Christian activity as part of the public school program. Before this ruling, schools regularly excused dissenters from organized religious events or made efforts to recognize other faith celebrations, as demographically appropriate. Now the state sees "non all-inclusive" religious celebrations, such as Christmas and Easter, as discriminatory, even if only one of several hundred students is of a different faith.

So why rehash what we already know and have grown accustomed to? The fact is that reality has come a full circle. The predominantly secular school systems must now excuse dissenting Christians from special events such as the Calgary Birth Control Association presentation: "Have Courage Oppose Homophobia." No doubt with equal sincerity to the teachers in the earlier "Christian era," Mary's teacher offered my daughter the option of not attending the next CBCA presentation. The sad irony of this example is that the very proponents, who demanded no preferential (discriminating) treatment of students on the basis of religion, now ignore the religious beliefs of the same students the human rights legislation was to protect. The social policy hypothesis seems to be, that people who are against homosexuality, uphold flawed religious beliefs. More important, same-sex marriage legislation will institutionalize this humanist tenet.

As witnessed above, and in the following, the categorization of all religions as equal and protected by law, has allowed secularists to twist a tenet – religious freedom – into state sponsored and enforced religious silence. Better no public worship than offend one atheist or another citizen's religion. Better to leave one's religious beliefs outside Parliament than to advocate your spiritual convictions over those of another. To promote the removal of God from the Charter of Rights and Freedoms is a direct insult to theists and the multi-millions of Canadian Christians, who have over the history of this Nation asked Jesus Christ to keep the country strong and free. The very action by Robinson and some humanists constitutes reverse discrimination. The following humanist notion of spirituality (taken from a link found on the Jesus Seminar web site) makes a further mockery of religion and pokes fun at theistic believers:

You can become an ordained member of the Spiritual Humanist clergy for FREE right now! As a legally ordained clergy member you can legally perform religious ceremonies and rituals like weddings, funerals, benedictions, etc.

All humans have an inalienable right and duty to practice their own religious traditions. Spiritual Humanism allows everyone to fuse their individual religious practices onto the foundation of scientific humanist inquiry. We accept people from any religious background and recognize the validity of all peaceful religious practices and behaviors as being helpful and necessary in developing the spiritual nature of humanity.

If you agree that Religion must be based on Reason, you can be ordained right now for free, and still be able to practice your own religious traditions by simply clicking the button below: 'Ordain Me.'"[7]

There is something terribly aberrant in a free and democratic society, where the overwhelming religion is Christianity, and yet the state enforces its notion of "religious freedom" by outlawing the use of words like "Jesus Christ," "Holy Bible," "Scripture" and other obvious Christian liturgy at public spiritual events such as Remembrance Day or a memorial service for the World Trade Center disaster. This state-sponsored notion that putting down Christian liturgy somehow enhances overall religious freedom is flawed spiritually and intellectually. Christians declare Jesus Christ the be God in the flesh! Denying public worship of Jesus Christ serves only humanist interests.

Is the God of the Charter Real?

In a literal sense (when God means God), there is something incredibly ludicrous and unfortunate about Canada declaring our rights and principles anchored upon the supremacy of God and then proposing government legislation (such as same-sex marriage) contrary to that very authority. We can cast a wide religious net, which includes all time-honored theistic faiths, and the reactions are the same – a marriage is and should remain between one man and one woman. As explained in Chapters 5 and 6, pro-gay theology is a relatively novel phenomenon, which has no standing outside post-modern liberation thinking. The improvised theology draws no authority from the Bible, Torah, or Koran, and when adopted by previously orthodox denominations, results in church conflict and disunity.

Theists must see the same-sex marriage challenge as an affront to God-fearing faiths and in direct opposition to a long-standing Constitutional convention of the supremacy of God. This proposed social experiment with marriage, if implemented, would significantly alter the theistic basis upon which our Constitution and Charter are based. Earlier in the previous chapter, I asked the question, why would the GBLTQ movement risk so much of their political capital on a rights-based fight, which in the end will directly affect only a few homosexuals; to which many homosexuals are opposed; and that if lost, would have catastrophic impact on the self-image of all GBLTQ. In response, I said earlier that the catalyst was low self-esteem and the temptation of penetrating the last exclusively heterosexual societal space. To these motivations can now be added the goal of furthering anti-Christian ideology. The challenge by GBLTQ for the right to same-sex marriage draws considerable energy from the humanist-secularist-liberationist wish to end the legitimacy of God in the ordering of our Confederation or in the United States, the Union. Where a direct petition to remove God from the Charter failed, the enactment of same-sex marriage legislation would symbolically, and perhaps even lawfully (in the Supreme Court's eyes), achieve the same objective. Diana Alstad framed this struggle of worldviews during the earlier fight over abortion:

I view the abortion fight as the frontline in America of a much larger battle, the planetary battle that I call 'the morality wars.' This is a battle for people's minds over 'Who has the right to decide what's right?' and 'What gives them the right to do so?' It's between the forces of the old and the new…[3]

Regrettably in this "planetary battle," many mainline denominations have not just split up but some have crossed sides. The United Church of Canada (UCC) has all but expunged the divinity of Jesus Christ from their theology to uphold new and enlightened pro-gay beliefs. Like Rev. Dr. John Shelby Spong and Robert Funk's Jesus Seminar, many UCC ministers now have no reservations about demoting Jesus Christ – thinking of Him as an equal to Gandhi, or removing His name from public usage altogether. Rev. Wayne Hillier, senior minister at Chalmers United Church, Kingston, Ontario, relates his role in removing Christ from the Parliamentary Prayer. In his 1994 Easter Service he said the following as part of his sermon:

Some time ago I was invited by our local Federal Member of Parliament, Peter Milliken (who happens also to be a member of the United Church of Canada and who exercises that membership by being a faithful worshipper in this congregation), to compose and submit to a parliamentary committee, that he was then chairing, a prayer that I thought might be offered with integrity, by a larger number of parliamentarians than the long-standing existing prayers clearly allowed….I worked hard at composing such a prayer. I considered it a high privilege to be asked and I took my task very seriously. Here is the prayer:

O eternal Spirit, creator of all life that enriches, sustainer of all truth that abides, we come this day, seeking as representatives of this diverse country of Canada, your guiding blessing. As we strive in our varied ways to fulfill our duties, deepen our commitment to persons of vision and integrity. As we labor in this House of Commons, for the sake of the common good, strengthen our resolve to be open to a patience that can endure the strain of waiting; a hope that can rise above frustration; and a courage that can confront the truth. So may this House be blessed with members from all sides and religions who will think wisely and do justly, and love mercy. Amen.

Surprised by the reaction, Hillier comments on the prayer's reception:

Little did I realize (nor I suspect did M.P. Peter Milliken), that this draft prayer would invite such a reaction on the part of the other MP's as well as a larger number of writers of letters to newspaper editors across the land. The reaction was so strong, especially on the part of other Christians who were incensed with the wider reference to God as the 'eternal Spirit,' that the prayer never really had a chance.[4]

Changing the theology behind the laws and Constitution of our Nation has enormous implications. Are we a God-fearing country or a God-less country? Regardless of your personal convictions, you should be able to see the spiritual tragedy and intellectual suicide of an ordained Christian minister, professing salvation through the death and resurrection of Jesus Christ, and then having the casualness to drop any reference to the Savior from prayer, and then to remove all familiar Scriptural terminology for God, Christ's Father (Father Almighty, God Almighty, Lord Almighty, or Heavenly Father), from state religious lexicon. The crowning travesty is to ask that all religions be blessed. After all Christ said:

I am the way and the truth and the life. No one comes to the Father except through me (John 14:6). And I will do whatever you ask in my name, so that the Son may bring glory to the Father. You may ask me for anything, and I will do it (John 14: 13-14).

Humanists, Gnostics, agnostics, atheists and secularists must have applauded Hillier's all-inclusive pluralist prayer. From their perspective a universal, serves all religions type-of-God is only a symbolic God, almost as good as declaring an *unknown* God. In the space of forty years, the God of the Constitution and Charter thus changes from a specific relational God to a token multi-faith God. Taking Jesus Christ out of the prayer lexicon and attempting to address some all-inclusive eternal spirit defiles the God of Scripture. When praying, Christ said, "Our Father in heaven, *hallowed* be Your name" (Matthew 6:9). And God commanded in Exodus 20:7:

You shall not misuse the name of the Lord your God, for the Lord will not hold anyone guiltless who misuses his name.

The final revised Parliamentary version succeeded in eliminating all reference to Jesus Christ, and commences with "Almighty God."[5] Subsequent petitions by angry Christians carried little persuasion:

Mr. Peter Adams (Peterborough, Lib.): Mr. Speaker, I have a petition from residents of the city and county of Peterborough. Whereas the name of our Lord, Jesus Christ, in the Lord's Prayer has been included in the historic parliamentary prayer of the House of Commons since 1867, and whereas Canada was founded and built on the principles of Christianity and the large majority of Canadians profess the Christian faith, therefore the petitioners call on the House of Commons to close the parliamentary prayer with the words: 'Through Jesus Christ our Lord, Amen' and reinstate the Lord's Prayer at the conclusion of the opening prayer.[6]

Mr. Brooke Taylor: Mr. Speaker, I beg leave to table a petition on behalf of over 100 folks here. The prayer of the petition states, "We, the undersigned are protesting the decision to remove all references of Jesus Christ from the sermons of Armed Forces chaplains. We feel that this is an insult both to the Christian faith and to Christians everywhere." Mr. Speaker, I have affixed my name to the petition.[7]

Most Canadians supported the respect given Canadian Sikhs, by allowing this cultural and religious minority to wear turbans publicly as police and as members in the military. This state policy was seen as granting freedom of religion, by allowing Sikhs to differentiate themselves and sustain their beliefs through a visible and unique headdress. With such government policy, it seems extraordinary, that Jesus Christ, the ultimate focus of Christian faith, had to be expunged from public liturgy. The real benefactors from the muzzling of Christians are not members of other theistic faiths, but humanists and atheists.

We cannot approve national policies that support both humanists and Christians. At this point in the analysis, it should be clear that there is no defendable mix or compromise between the two worldviews. There may be civilized respect and cooperation, but never sameness. And this should be the guiding principle for legislative equality in same-sex marriage. There needs to be a definition that separates GBLTQ marriage from heterosexual marriage. They are not the same. The founding principles behind the societal *space* for heterosexuals are entirely different, and at odds, with the principles and conventions underpinning GBLTQ *space*. The God of GBLTQ space cannot be the same as the God of the Charter. Bear with me as I explain.

In September 2003, Johnnie Bowls, 27, and William Hill, 26, were interviewed for an article on the issue of gay marriage. These two gay men have been joined together in *holy union* about three years and would like to be legally married. The article reads:

Q. If God asked you to justify your belief that gay marriage is right, what would you say to him?

Bowls: God has never created any imperfect beings, so there's nothing wrong with me. There is nothing wrong with him. We're together, we love each other and that's it.

Hill: God is love. My connection to God is very strong. And I know that He would want whatever was best for me. And if this is not the best for me then I would know. God blessed me with Johnnie.[8]

From where do Bowls and Hill draw their theologies? If we are serious about the supremacy of God (and many are not), we cannot simply articulate theology in empty terms, generalities and pleasant platitudes. In Bowl's theology there are no imperfect beings. We are implicit gods incarnate. There is never anything wrong with how people act and relate, as long as they love each other. This thinking is closer to Gnosticism (where we are already redeemed) than Christianity. It bears repeating, the Apostle Paul said:

All scripture is given by the inspiration of God, and is profitable for doctrine, for reproof, for correction, for instruction in righteousness: That the man of God may be perfect, thoroughly furnished unto all good works (2 Timothy 16-17).

Ironically, the "no imperfect beings" theology of Bowls is the opposite conclusion to the more common gay religious theory. Donald Faris explains the different emphasis (and therefore different God) of common gay theology:

The thought seems to be, no one is perfect. It is the relationship that counts...The gospel according to this logic is not 'repent, believe, and obey,' but, 'accept yourself.' A simple surrender to one's own self-centeredness and immaturity is the goal; the new obedient life in Jesus Christ is a detour to be avoided.[9]

In Hill's theology, man determines what is right and best. When God is love, there is no need to be concerned with a Creator's will or judgment. Neither Bowls nor Hill is speaking of the Judeo-Christian God – the Holy God who would not be mocked. The God who killed 24,000 over the sin of a few days of sexual immorality with Moabite women (Numbers 25:1-10), notwithstanding that the Jewish men and Moabite women likely loved and respected each other. This God had little patience with those who would worship any deity. If Hill or his partner should die of AIDS at the average age of 42, what is one to say in regard to Hill's statement: "And if this is not the best for me then I would know." Without revisiting all that was said in Chapters 5 and 6, Hill cannot also be speaking of the Christian God for practical reasons. Even Darwinists would have to concede the need for Wellness doctrine and the Condom Code is a recent evolutionary phenomenon, only required because of failure to follow the Leviticus Code or similar guidance. What God calls people from the safety and healthy ecology of the Leviticus Code into a lifestyle "cursed" by disease and co-dependence on pharmaceutical and medical technologies?

We have seen that the Gnostics fervently believed in an *unknown* God, one that would never intervene in their lives, nor call them to account for their actions. As a consequence libertine Gnostics felt no compulsion to do other than what they pleased. Surely, if the Charter of Rights and Freedoms had intended Gnostic values to be included in the founding principles of the Nation, the lawyers would have added "*unknown* God" somewhere.

Perhaps Hill draws his convictions from the Darwinist Rev. Dr. John Shelby Spong or the Jesus Seminar. [Bowls cannot because Spong follows Darwinism and believes humankind is a "work-in-progress" and not "perfection."] If this proves true, Hill is still basing his theology on a different God than the deity referenced in the Charter. Otherwise it wouldn't be crucial to "reconstruct" God, as Spong wishes, or to demote Christ by declaring 75 per cent of Scripture false, as the Jesus Seminar claims. The supreme God in our Charter is real. Jesus Christ has never been a phenomenon of psychological projection and the God of the Charter is certainly not *humankind finding its self-consciousness* as Spong contends. And why does it matter to humanists that we reformulate the tenets of Christianity or redefine God in non-theistic terms? Spong answers:

We reimage God to keep the world from enduring the pain of a continuing reliance on a theistic deity….That same theistic God is quoted by people who want to impose their definitions of homosexuality or their values in the right-to-life movement on everyone else. So it matters how one thinks of God.[10]

Yes, it matters how one thinks of God. The difference can result in a lifetime of frustration and divine silence (such as witnessed in Spong's personal testimony) or a life brimming with Godly significance and providence (as witnessed by millions of Christians). The difference can separate a blessed nation from one not set apart. In the eyes of those who respect God and place faith in the Charter of Rights and Freedoms under the supremacy of God, there can be little doubt as to the consequence of a decision in favor of same-sex marriage, particularly for those upholding Jesus Christ as Lord. The zero-sum dynamic was summarized earlier as follows:

The Christian homosexual position when carefully examined can be exposed for what it is at its very core: an attack upon the integrity, sufficiency, and authority of Scripture, which for the Christian church is an attack upon the very nature of our Holy God.[11]

Again, we must ask, from where do Bowls and Hill draw their theology? Perhaps they are looking toward the future, as did Carl Sagan. But the God of the Charter cannot be part of Sagan's religion, since it has yet to develop:

A religion old or new, that stressed the magnificence of the universe as revealed by modern science, might be able to draw forth reserves of reverence and awe hardly tapped by the conventional faiths. Sooner or later, such a religion will emerge.[12]

Perhaps they cling to a god of the Eugenics Movement:

Evolution is the development of the energy of the universe in such a way that it has an increasing ability to consciously control itself and the universe around it. It is a progressive change from the unconscious to the conscious. We are the universe trying to comprehend itself. Man is the corporeal manifestation of the universe trying to control its own destiny. Man is God in the process of coming into existence.[13]

If they take faith in the God of Charles Darwin, this is still a different God than the God of the Canadian Charter. Darwin sees no practical manifestations of divine revelation in his scientific theology:

Darwin was obviously no traditional Christian, believing in an immanent God who intervenes constantly in His creation. Most accurately, perhaps, Darwin is characterized as one held to some kind of 'deistic' belief in a God who works at a distance through unbroken law: having set the world in motion, God now sits back and does nothing.[14]

Perhaps Bowls and Hill are unwitting adherents to Gnosticism. If this proves true, they are still worshipping a different God than that referenced in the Charter:

The cardinal feature of Gnostic thought is the radical dualism that governs the relation of God and world....The deity is absolutely transmundane, its nature alien to that of the universe which it neither created nor governs and to which it is the complete antithesis....The world is the work of lowly powers.[15]

The Christian Apostle Paul warned that the basis of sin is the refusal to acknowledge "God as God." False worship, half-hearted reverence or a symbolic respect is wrong:

This is the root of sin and thus is the root of the life that is displeasing to God, which ultimately results in death.[16]

Mentioned before, but it bears repeating, Andrew Holleran, a homosexual, explains how he sees the issue of gay theology and gay-Christian worship:

There can be no commerce between, no conflation of, these two things. Fellatio has nothing to do with Holy Communion. Better to frankly admit that you have changed gods, and are now worshipping Priapus, not Christ.[17]

Michael Swift, in *Gay Community News* proclaims our young sons as the focus of idolatry in gay liberation worship:

All laws banning homosexuality will be revoked...Be careful when you speak of homosexuals because we are always among you....the family unit...will be abolished....All churches who condemn us will be closed. Our only Gods are handsome young men.[18]

Gay author Michelangelo Signorile describes a tryst in which his partner addresses the same god as Michael Swift:

Last year I spent a couple of grueling weeks on assignment in Hawaii. One night in a Waikiki gay bar I met your classic gay hunk: tall and masculine, with a buzzed haircut, razor-sharp cheekbones, a body of granite, and a Texas drawl. I'll make you see God tonight, he promised, trying to coax me to go home with him. It didn't take much for me to realize I needed a religious experience; we went to his place.[19]

Armistead Maupin testifies to his God:

In the baths, he found remarkable qualities of communication with men whose names he never knew, men with whom he did not even have sex, with whom he embraced and then moved on, all of which left him with a nearly religious feeling. 'I felt very close to God,' he says. Then, perhaps mindful that our conversation is being recorded for radio broadcast, he breaks the mood and adds, 'My friends say that's because I was always on my knees.'[20]

The forthright and seldom politically correct Rev. Dr. Spong portrays the theological premise behind common liberation theology:

When we unravel the theological tomes of the ages, the make up of God becomes quite clear. God is a human being without human limitations who is read into the heavens. We disguised this process by suggesting that the reason God was so much like a human being was that the human beings were in fact created in God's image. However, we now recognize that it was the other way around. The God of theism came into being as a human creation. As such, this God, too, was mortal and is now dying.[21]

A savior who restores us to our pre-fallen status is therefore pre-Darwinian superstition and post-Darwinian nonsense....the Jesus portrayed in the creedal statement 'as one who, for us and for our salvation, came down from heaven simply no longer communicates to our world. Those concepts must be uprooted and dismissed.[22]

According to Spong's thinking, the God of our Charter needs to be defined as *self-aware humankind*. Here is one of the crucial boundary lines in this apocalyptic "planetary battle" for the source of right and wrong, good and evil. Marriage is redefined inclusive of GBLTQ only by replacing theism with either Gnosticism or humanism. As explained earlier the two have much in common and the views of Spong and Funk are hardly isolated ideas. In considering "Homosexual Liberation Theologies," Faris observed that some "feminist" forms of theology reject Christian tradition in light of highly selective Gnostic variations. Not surprisingly, some followers of these variations include worship of the mother goddess. He writes:

They welcome homosexuality as an attack on what they see as the male dominated 'family'...Having dethroned God and rejected the Lordship of Christ, this type of feminist theologian believes that, in sexual matters, all we need is 'love.'

It is ludicrous to believe that the Creator of the universe, in guiding the biblical authors, was ignorant concerning the things we know about homosexuality through modern biology, psychology, sociology, and so forth. To deny scriptural statements about homosexuality on these grounds is to completely deny God's superintendence in the authorship of Scripture.[23]

As explained in Chapter 6 (on reorientation), there cannot be two *holy* Gods, one blessing GBLTQ behavior and another liberating homosexuals from a lifestyle they pray to escape. The Apostle Paul referred to this paradox, writing of the devil and his works:

The god of this age has blinded the minds of unbelievers, so that they cannot see the light of the gospel of the glory of Jesus Christ (2 Corinthians 4:4).

Homosexual liberation theology is undermined and its adherents demoralized by the testimony of other homosexuals *liberated* from years of gay and lesbian relationships. You will have to decide which witness is telling the truth. An ex-lesbian writes:

Homosexuality is a dead end. While I was so busy gratifying the desires of my flesh it was impossible for God to give me the desires of my heart. Now He is free to do so. I have dated several young men in the past year, and have enjoyed each date. There has been fellowship and sharing about the Lord Jesus Christ. In addition I have a joy I could not experience before. I can once again look forward to getting married.

God wants the best for us. Let's not settle for second best.[24]

Some ex-gays write:

We felt called by God out of homosexuality into what for us was a far better life. At different times and in different ways, almost all of us turned to God in our turmoil, and felt this simple truth deep in our hearts: Homosexuality was wrong for us, and God would lead us out of the pain if we turned to him.

This became a powerful motivator in our lives. Coupled with the fact that for the majority of us, being gay just didn't work, a spiritual hope of eventual peace offered a tiny, flickering light at the end of a tunnel. We walked toward it.[25]

We have found that the path out of unwanted homosexuality is a profoundly spiritual one. Some of us experienced this as a significant religious conversion or spiritual enlightenment where we felt God's deep love for us and guidance for our lives. Others experienced it as the spiritual peace that comes from emotional healing, from loving and forgiving ourselves and others, from breaking down walls that have long prevented us from accepting the love of others, and from learning to really trust God, sometimes for the first time in our lives. This peace, joy and connection to God grew as we began to heal emotionally, build brotherly relationships with other men, surrender all forms of lust, and embrace a new identity as a heterosexual man.[26]

Rather than trying to STOP destructive behaviors and thought patterns, they sought to proactively REPLACE them with new, healthier ones: rather than fighting lust, we learned to surrender it to a Higher Power, asking God to do for us what we could not do for ourselves.[27]

The state redefines marriage only by making a laughing stock of the supreme theistic God of our Constitution. If judicial interpretation of the Charter supports a redefinition of marriage to include gays, lesbians, transsexuals and queers, the Charter cuts itself loose from its intended spiritual anchor. If the legal precedence to embrace GLTQ orientations inside marriage is established, what possible judicial logic could then draw a line to the exclusion of "B" – bisexuals. When the millenniums old institution of heterosexual marriage is arbitrarily revised to include GLTQ, the inclusion of bisexuals is just an interpretation away. At some later date when society has evolved and is ready, discrimination against licensing "loving" and "committed" threesomes will be raised.

The likeness of same-sex legislation to opening Pandora's Box can not be missed. Beyond what has already been said, is the additional issue of where the new "sameness-discrimination" legal boundary would then be determined. Politicians advocating same-sex legislation, contend the Supreme Court will interpret the law so that churches do not have to marry or ordain homosexuals against their denomination's religious convictions. However, such assurances lack credibility in light of historic human rights interpretations. What wise judicial application of the Charter, says to Catholic School Boards, you must allow openly gay students to come to the graduation prom as a couple, but it is perfectly alright to refuse GBLTQ marriage and ordination within your church, in accordance with Catholic theology? When the owner of a print shop refuses to accept a customer's brochure because he has determined its homosexual content is against his religious conviction, the state has already concluded that he has violated the customer's human rights. Which is a worse "technical" violation of rights, to force the customer to find another compliant printer or to refuse to marry a gay couple, given that same-sex "marriage" is a Constitutional right.

To tell a society it is illegal to discriminate on the basis of sexual orientation in all schools, clubs, associations and most places of gathering; to then declare that same-sex marriage is legal and the same in all respects to heterosexual marriage; and then determine that religious denominations may be exempt from conducting homosexual marriage, makes a mockery of theism. In effect, a state that recognizes same-sex marriage, has legislated a religion based on Darwinism in place of the Nation's founding theism. In zero-sum dynamics, which most agree describes this situation, one side gains at the loss of the other. If this comes to pass, we should not be surprised. Our response to the same-sex marriage challenge is really a litmus test for the extent of secularization of the country. Once again, Sir Julian Huxley explained why rampant secularism might happen:

It is because the concept of a Creator-God interferes with our sexual mores. Thus, we have rationalized God out of existence. To us, He has become nothing more than the faint and disappearing smile of the cosmic Cheshire cat in Alice in Wonderland.[28]

Before Canada or the United States decides on the issue of same-sex marriage, each Government should have to rule on whether the God of the Constitution, Oath of Allegiance, National Anthem, Charter of Rights and Freedoms, Parliamentary Prayer, and national currency is real. Perhaps Huxley and Robinson are right, God has become only "the faint and disappearing smile of the cosmic Cheshire cat." If the state believes this to be true, it should have the integrity to say as much. Orthodox Christians and other theists have a right to know whether the state (including the Supreme Court Justices) believes that God is real. Legislation of same-sex marriage should result in a court challenge on the definition of God and the legal interpretation of God's supremacy in the affairs of state. If the state response is "God is not real," as the Humanist Society contend and hope, then we are an atheist country. If the state upholds its traditional tenet that God is real, then theists have a legitimate right to ask, "what God calls for same-sex marriage? From where did this pro-gay and gay theology come?" Neither Canada nor the United States was founded in a theological vacuum. Before we decide to throw out the old, let us at least intellectually, if not spiritually, validate what our *real* God wants.

Your Choice – Your Voice

If the teachings of Charles Darwin, Emma Goldman, Margaret Sanger, Alfred Kinsey, Henry Morgentaler, Carl Sagan, Richard Dawkins, Peter Singer, Kate Millett, Diana Alstad, Dalma Heyn, John Spong, Robert Funk, Carl Jung and the like are true, mankind needs to rid itself of the encumbrance of Christianity. These people are singularly united in their denial of the divinity and authority of Jesus Christ. To them Jesus Christ as God incarnate is a colossal hoax and the traditional Christian tenets based on Christ's teachings are false. Humankind can only move towards an anarchist-humanist utopia through raised self-consciousness and the throwing-off of religiosity. A complete political victory of their ideological views would expunge God from all public and civil acknowledgements. On the other hand, if the teachings of Jesus Christ are true, the beginnings of chaos and endless misery in our society are found in the potpourri of ideas and movements under the label "Pivot of Civilization" – radical feminism, GBLTQ and free sex liberation, anarchism, humanism and secularism to mention a few. These movements and ideologies keep people from seeking a different utopia (God's Kingdom). In the next section you will see some of the summarized consequences of your paradigm choice. This same-sex marriage challenge will either result in a moral and spiritual victory for the "supremacy of God," or result in a legislative (perhaps judicial) failure to honour the "authority of God."

Without the foundation of our Constitution anchored in God, anything becomes permissible and anything goes. Brigitte Boisselier says there is demand for cloning, "especially among infertile and gay couples, as well as middle-aged single women who want to have a baby." For her the real issue is freedom of choice. Individuals should be able to do "What they want, when they want and how they want." This atheistic ethos is counter to the founding theistic principles of our Charter. The appeal only makes sense when the supreme Creator is silenced. Boisselier says:

Today, nobody will tell you that you shouldn't mix your genes with this person or that person, you have the right to choose. So if you choose not to mix your genes but have a baby with only your genes because you're a 45-year-old single woman, why should people tell you not to do that?[29]

Similarly Katha Pollitt contends:

If single women can have sex in their homes, the respect of friends and interesting work, they don't need to tell themselves that any marriage is better than none. Why not have a child on one's own? Children are a joy; many men are not.[30]

Marjorie Garber writes:

Marriage used to be a prelude to childbearing, now the child often comes either before or instead of the marriage.[31]

Kate Millett prophesizes:

With the transformation of the means of production into collective property, the monogamous family will cease to be the economic unit of society. The care and education of children becomes a public matter.'...There is something logical and even inevitable in this recommendation, for so long as every female, simply by virtue of her anatomy, is obliged, even forced, to be the sole or primary caretaker of childhood, she is prevented from being a free being. The care of children, even from the period when their cognitive powers first emerge, is infinitely better left to the best trained practitioners of both sexes who have chosen it as a vocation, rather than to harried and all too frequently unhappy persons with little time nor taste for the work of educating minds, however young or beloved. The radical outcome of Engels' analysis is that the family, as that term is presently understood, must go.[32]

Who says so? From whom do these people draw authority to take such stands? What justifiable theology underpins their thinking? The answer is none. These arguments are anti-theistic to the core. And why shouldn't a God-fearing society say "No" to unfettered individualism and hedonism? Can society afford not to say "No?"

Alice Rossi warns that the radical (lesbian) feminist goal is "total freedom of choice in sex partners throughout one's life." Like the double standard in the men they accuse, liberated women are now to model the free sex male pattern – early initiation, sexual diversity, casual and promiscuous sex. For a married woman not to enjoy sex with men other than her husband, or in some quarters, not to be bisexual is to be out of step with the times. Quoted earlier, Rossi says:

The ideology claims that conquest of sexual jealousy...could be the greatest advance in human relations since the advent of common law...The increased frequency and incidence of swinging and swapping...could then be viewed...as [presaging] a new era in sexual and interpersonal relationships.[33]

Moreover, Rossi concludes that in the so-called "post-nuclear family," "variant family" era, the adult can turn parenthood on and off and exchange children as well as sexual partners at will. She warns:

In reality, the counterculture parents are obviously trying to rear children without having to be bothered by them.[34]

One's response to these issues of private and public civil liberties of course depends on one's worldview. I have framed this book to bring the reader to face a choice between two mutually exclusive paradigms, which are called "Pivot of Civilization" and "Rivet of Life." One of these worldviews is a tapestry of lies. For those who choose not to make a choice, your "vote" will default to the "Pivot of Civilization" platform. Brigitte Boisselier would like nothing better than society to remain neutral, ignorant or otherwise manipulated into silence, so that CLONAID and its clients can do as they please. Activists for same-sex marriage also hope for societal acquiescence. Given the extent of information presented, neutrality is no longer a cognitively valid option. It amounts to opting for denial. Furthermore, in the spiritual battle for our hearts and minds, a *sincere* and *kind neutrality* amounts to joining the ranks of the congregation at the Church in Laodicea. Once again, this is what Jesus Christ thought of the uncommitted and compromised:

I know your deeds, that you are neither cold nor hot. I wish you were either one or the other! So, because you are lukewarm – neither hot nor cold – I am about to spit you out of my mouth...you don't realize that you are wretched, pitiful, poor, blind and naked. I counsel you to buy from me...salve to put on your eyes, so you can see (Revelation 4:15-18).

Having read this far one can make at least an intellectual choice if not a spiritual choice between world paradigms. To simplify decision-making the paradigms of choice are summarized in the next section. What follows are a number of sub-issues presented with alternative choices. Thus, in manageable increments you can choose what you believe and what you prefer to see happen in the future. Each issue will allow for a clear choice. Based on the sum of these incremental issues and decisions a complete vision of your philosophical worldview may be drawn.

Twenty-Four Questions of Philosophy and Belief

Circle either "Pivot of Civilization" or "Rivet of Life" to indicate the choice which best reflects your opinion:

1. There is a revealed God who is the Creator of the universe. The cosmos did not will itself into existence, nor was its creation an accident. The Constitution and Charter of Rights and Freedoms are founded upon the "principles that recognize the supremacy of God," our Creator, a distinct relational and spiritual entity, apart from humankind.

Do you agree?

Pivot of Civilization – Disagree. *Rivet of Life – Agree.*

2. There is a revealed God who created life on earth. Life did not start as the result of a "frozen" accidental event of near zero probability, nor is life the result of transplantation by another evoluntionary alien species.

Do you agree?

Pivot of Civilization – Disagree. *Rivet of Life – Agree.*

3. There is a revealed God who created humankind with a spiritual likeness and moral character. Human beings are not the evolutionary chance result of primates who choose to forage for hard nuts in nearby savannas. Our existence is not "mindless and ungoverned." Life is not meaningless. The human condition is not solitary, poor, nasty, brutish, and short (a tiny element of Nature's grandeur). Mankind's

purpose and destiny is not to maximize fleshly pleasure until the next comet hits earth. We are to honour our Creator.

Do you agree?

Pivot of Civilization – Disagree. *Rivet of Life – Agree.*

4. There is no "gay gene," no "lesbian gene," no "transgender gene," no "bisexual gene." GBLTQ lifestyle is a choice:

The idea that people are born into one type of sexual behavior is foolish.' ... The move towards 'biologizing' homosexuality isn't the result of a scientific consensus, but a political consensus by those eager to label people gay or straight. Homosexuality is a behavior, not a condition....[35]

There is no strong evidence to date to conclude that lesbians are biologically sexed or gendered any differently than heterosexual women, and no strong evidence to suggest that lesbianism is rightly understood as gender inversion or perversion....From their research with women who made transitions from heterosexuality to lesbianism, they [Kitzinger and Wilkinson] concluded that 'adult women who make such transitions are no more driven by biology or subconscious urges than they are when, for instance, they change jobs; such choices could be viewed as influenced by a mixture of personal re-evaluation, practical necessity, political values, chance, and opportunity.'[36]

Human beings were intended to be biologically male and female. The species is intended to be heterosexual in nature. A future in which the distinction between homosexual and heterosexual becomes blurred or obsolete is an ungodly and unnatural prospect.

Do you agree?

Pivot of Civilization – Disagree. *Rivet of Life – Agree.*

5. The AIDS epidemic was brought on by the unnatural (unsafe) ecology of multipartnered promiscuous anal sex. The notion that governments, in an age of bio-power, are obliged to find techno-pharmaceutical solutions, to what are essentially elective lifestyle health risks, amounts to a public policy of consequence avoidance and co-dependent intervention – a classic technological fix. When Wellness doctrine works it suspends, but does not repeal the law of reaping what you sow. The Condom Code is statistically certain to fail and thus AIDS infection rates remain high. AIDS is not an ecological threat to adherents of the Leviticus Code. When sex education policies promote the Condom Code over the Leviticus Code, they bring unwanted pregnancy, disease and death upon our children. Sounder public health can be found in a zero cost shift in sexual moral values, than can be obtained through any investment in medical science.

Do you agree?

Pivot of Civilization – Disagree. *Rivet of Life – Agree.*

6. Human beings should have intrinsic (God-given) value and entitlement to live as members of our species. Their continued existence ought to count for something regardless of whether they are useful, convenient or pleasant; despite whether they are unborn, just born or are one hundred years old. How we care for the disadvantaged and defenseless reflects on the righteousness of society. On the other hand, a person's worth should be based solely on societal function and merit. The state's collaboration in the death of a human zygote, embryo, fetus, baby, child, adolescent, adult, or senior citizen is ethical depending on the utility of the death to society. To move toward humanistic utopia (improvement of the species), humankind is better off as a society, when we stop using bio-power to sustain the lives of the physically, mentally and genetically weak.

[Ironically, proponents of this latter humanistic, survival of the fittest, cost-benefit ethos choose not to apply the philosophy in the case of AIDS. Instead, all of the state's bio-power should be directed towards AIDS healthcare intervention because high-risk sexual behavior is an individual's Constitutional right.]

Which do you want?

Pivot of Civilization – Function and merit. Rivet of Life – Intrinsic worth.

7. Abortion does not empower women, but rather unshackles promiscuous men from any responsibility in the event of their lover's pregnancy. Abortion is not liberating, but is really an act of oppression upon women and the unborn:

'Millions of women have ordered their lives around' abortion. That we have willingly ordered our lives around a denigrating surgical procedure – accepted it as the price we must pay to keep our life plans intact—is an ominous sign...More insidiously, abortion advocacy has been poisonous to some of the deeper values of feminism.[37]

....I am not impressed or persuaded by those who express concern for the low-income woman who may find herself carrying an unplanned pregnancy and for the future of the unplanned child...because the fact remains that in this affluent nation of ours, pregnant cattle and horses receive better health care than pregnant poor women. The poor cry out for justice and we respond with legalized abortion.[38]

The act of abortion, in other than life-threatening circumstance, is a denial of God's dominion in the baby's and mother's lives. Abortion is fundamentally an act of self-centered control – the ordering of one's life around technology to avoid the natural consequences of sexual intercourse.

Do you agree and do you want more or fewer abortions?

Pivot of Civilization – Disagree and more. Rivet of Life – Agree and fewer.

8. Dalma Heyn's feminist model for the average young woman:

...comfortable with independence, employment, autonomy, and multiple sexual relationships. She began having sex, according to the newest Kinsey Institute Report, between the (median) ages of sixteen and seventeen. If she marries at the age of twenty-seven, then, she will have been making love – with one man or several, simultaneously or serially, alone or cohabiting – for a decade. She is used to pleasure as to pleasing, and envisions having both in equal measure in an egalitarian marital relationship.[39]

Do you want teens experimenting in sex earlier or later, more or less or not at all?

Pivot of Civilization–Earlier and more. Rivet of Life–Later and less or not at all.

9. *Do you want more or less sexual promiscuity before and outside marriage?*

Pivot of Civilization – More. *Rivet of Life – Less.*

10. Society still pays lip service to the notion that divorce is aberrant:

Mommies and Daddies should stay together. They always should. They shouldn't never break up. Not never. I don't know why, but I know. They shouldn't. And I don't want to have kids when I'm big. Cause. Not never.[40]

Do you want more or fewer lifelong monogamous heterosexual marriages?

Pivot of Civilization – Fewer. *Rivet of Life – More.*

11. It is unlikely that same-sex marriage, however it is defined, will bring about needed moral and ecological lifestyle changes among gays. If the AIDS plague with hundreds of thousands of young deaths has not curbed needless multipartnerism and high-risk sex, a marriage certificate from town hall is unlikely to bring needed transformation.

Do you agree?

Pivot of Civilization – Disagree. *Rivet of Life – Agree.*

12. The level of sexually transmitted disease in society is a barometer of the level of promiscuous sex. Technology and Wellness doctrines are inadequate buffers against the ecological consequences of free sex.

Do you agree?

Pivot of Civilization – No. Rivet of Life – Yes.

13. The anarchist ideology underpinning free sex, sex positive ethos is clear:

Applying these insights to our own society, it is clear that teenagers should not only have ample access to a private room where they can be undisturbed with their sexual partners, but that parents should actively encourage such behavior for the sake of their child's health and happiness (while, of course, encouraging the knowledge and use of contraceptives and safe sex in general as well as respect for the other person involved in the relationship)....[41]

Do you want children taught free sex ethos and Wellness doctrine more or less or not at all?

Pivot of Civilization – More. Rivet of Life – Less or not at all.

14. Eskridge contends one feature of GBLTQ experience has been an emphasis on "families we choose."[42] Such families are *fluid alliances independent* of ties imposed by blood and by law. Often *estranged* from blood kin, openly gay people are more prone to rely on current as well as former lovers, close friends, and neighbors as their social and emotional support system. Include children in this fluid network and the complexity becomes more pronounced.[43] Gertrude Himmelfarb contends that as "people move *in and out* of families at will," friends will gain equal ground with blood relatives, and obligations will be *voluntarized* rather than taken as givens. This is parentage in alternative lifestyles. The "family of choice" is defined not by lines of blood, marriage, or adoption, but by "*varieties of relationships and habitations*" among "*autonomous,*" "*consensual*" adults and their offspring.[44] Because same-sex couples cannot have children through their own efforts, a *third party* must be involved: a former different-sex spouse, a sperm donor, a surrogate mother, a parent or agency offering a child for adoption. Gay and lesbian couples are *pioneering novel family configurations*, and gay marriage would not seriously obstruct the creation of the larger families we choose.[45]

Do you want more or fewer children raised in one gender parenting environments, often with anonymous biological roots, indeed, consensual voluntary parenting?

Pivot of Civilization – More. Rivet of Life – Fewer.

15. The evidence that marital disruption and father absence contribute to educational under performance is clear.

One-parent children, on the whole, show lower achievement in school than their two-parent peers. Among all two-parent children 30 per cent were ranked as high achievers, compared to 17 per cent of one-parent children. At the other end of the scale the situation is reversed. 23 per cent of two-parent children were low achievers – while fully 38 per cent of the one-parent children fell into this category.[46]

We have come to the conclusion that a constructive, supportive, warmly-related father precludes the possibility of a homosexual son....[47]

For most children the partial or complete loss of a father produces long-lasting feelings of betrayal, rejection, rage, guilt and pain. According to CLONAID, there is a demand for cloned babies, especially among middle-aged single women.

Do you want more or fewer children raised by single parents?

Pivot of Civilization – More. *Rivet of Life – Fewer.*

16. According to Bentley Glass, the outgoing president of the American Association for the Advancement of Science, population control policies will demand families limit their size to no more than two children. In this era, parents will want to be sure that those children are perfect. He says, "Science will come to the rescue." He goes on to predict:

No parents in that future time will have a right to burden society with a malformed or a mentally incompetent child. Just as every child must have the right to full educational opportunity and a sound nutrition, so every child has the inalienable right to sound heritage.[48]

Glass predicts that parents will have their fetuses screened for a myriad of genetic defects, and will abort those fetuses that are imperfect or will use gene therapy to change the genes of their unborn children. He predicts that young people, at an age when their sperm and eggs would be the healthiest, will store their gametes for use when they are older. He predicts that embryos that are especially desirable, because of their perfect genetic inheritance, might be frozen for use by couples who want ideal babies, a process he called "embryo adoption." And he had no serious qualms about advocating these eugenic practices.[49] Glass says:

The Golden Age toward which we move will soon look tawdry as we no longer see endless horizons. We must, then, seek a change within man himself. As he acquires more fully the power to control his own genotype and direct the course of his own evolution, he must produce a Man who can transcend his present nature.[50]

Gnostic theology proclaims:

'When you make the two one, and when you make the inmost as the outermost and the outer as the inner and the above as the below, and when you make the male and female into a single unity, so that the male will not be only male and the female will not be only female, when you create eyes in the place of an eye, and create a hand in the place of a hand, and a foot in the place of a foot, and also an image in the place of an image, then surely will you enter the kingdom.' (Gnostic gospel, Thomas 22)

The heterosexual system of marriage that tames men and evokes their love is the chief obstacle to this technocratic future. If marriage endures, the realm of the state and the development and use of the technology can be limited, while the maintenance of human individuality can be assured. If the family should widely break down, then the world of artificial wombs, clones, and child-development centers can become an important reality rather than a laboratory curiosity.

Do you want more or less biogenetic intervention in the pro-creation process?

Pivot of Civilization – More. *Rivet of Life – Less.*

17. *Do you seek the advent of artificial wombs and a humanistic, eugenic and genetic utopia?*

Pivot of Civilization – Yes, yes, yes. Rivet of Life – No, no, no.

18. One of the pillars of the abortion and biogenetic intervention argument is called the "Destiny Justification" – it is part of our God-given destiny to exercise complete control over our reproductive processes. Richard Seed, in one of his first in-depth interviews after announcing his intentions to clone human beings commercially, made this very argument.[51]

Do you want cloning?

Pivot of Civilization – Yes. *Rivet of Life – No.*

19. Saghir and Robins' found that 63 per cent of lesbians wished they were boys or men, compared with seven per cent of heterosexual women and that the attitude persists into adulthood. They observed:

Lesbians see their social and domestic roles as being incompatible with those of other women. They behave more competitively and are oriented toward career and accomplishments with little interest in raising children or in domestic pursuits.[52]

Not surprising, feminists campaigned against alimony on the explicit grounds that its elimination would flush women out of the home and into the workforce where they belonged. Feminist sociologist Jesse Bernard says:

The revocation of the old promise that marriage meant 'assured support as long as they live' may be one of the best things that could happen to women....They would learn that marriage was not the be-all and end-all of their existence.[53]

But when women are forced to think in terms of lifelong work histories, there is a cost to be paid, and they and their children pay it.

Sexual politics is highly dangerous and diversionary, and may even provide good soil for fascist, demagogic appeals based on hatred...we cannot permit the image of women to be developed by the homosexual.[54] *- Betty Friedan*

> *Do you want more emphasis on home nurturing and parenting or more on careerism and feminism (the masculinization of the female gender)?*
>
> *Pivot of Civilization – Careerism and feminism*
> *Rivet of Life – Nurturing and Parenting.*

20. Frederica Mathewes-Green, member of Feminists For Life:

We can affirm and value the male instinct to protect his family. We can respect the man who exhibits character, strength and fidelity by accepting responsibility for the well-being of his mate and his children.[55] *...Some feminists aren't going to like hearing talk about male and female instincts, or the need of women to be protected by men. Feminist theory sometimes fails to describe reality. Biology has its own logic. Women have a primal bond with their children; were it not so, the human race could not survive....Most women want to provide this care, but they need the assistance of their mates, because it is an arduous task. Male-bashing was a lot of fun, but it's gotten out of hand. Our expectations of men with respect to relationships and responsibilities has plummeted to zero.* [56]

> *Do you want more clarity and affirmation of the male and female genders or do you want a society of fluid, ambiguous androgynous sexes?*
>
> *Pivot of Civilization – Androgyny. Rivet of Life – Clarity and affirmation.*

21. Homosexual reorientation is a scientific fact and it is not a hate crime to advocate such deliverance. Since there is one truth before God, our Creator cannot be blessing GBLTQ sexual behavior on one hand and blessing deliverance from homosexuality on the other. One reality is false. Both science and orthodox Christianity declare unwanted homosexuality can be overcome. GBLTQ have a Constitutional right to access ministries and medical health agencies which support reorientation.

> *Do you agree?*
>
> *Pivot of Civilization – Disagree. Rivet of Life – Agree.*

22. *Do you approve of public schools (under a mantra of discouraging scapegoating), teaching gay-affirming programs to the detriment and discrimination of student's with theistic religious beliefs?*

> *Pivot of Civilization – Yes. Rivet of Life – No.*

23. Lesbians and gays have fought a separation strategy over the past forty years and have developed novel theologies, ideologies and morals to support their newly won societal space. This culture has little in common with traditional marriage and

family values. To equate both segments of society as the "same" is just wrong. Margaret Small wrote in the 70s:

Lesbians are outside of the reality which heterosexual ideology explains. Lesbians therefore have the potential for developing an alternative ideology, not limited by heterosexuality.

Heterosexual ideology limits our vision of any alternative sexed, erotic community...You have to create the space that stands outside of all the boundaries of heterosexuality – assumptions about the family, about marriage, about motherhood, about housework, about childrearing, about rape, about illegitimacy, about spinsterhood – about everything that has to do with the relationships between men and women. To stand outside of heterosexual ideology and to develop an alternative way that male-female relationships could exist is an incredibly creative act.[57]

To now legislate both segments into the same definition of marriage is to make the term "marriage" so broad as to become meaningless. Saying "No" to same-sex marriage is the best and perhaps only opportunity to stop the secular-humanist rout in the "planetary battle" for what is right and wrong, good and bad, and who has the right to say so.

Do you agree?

Pivot of Civilization – Disagree *Rivet of Life – Agree.*

24. People have a legitimate right to be concerned about the mental, physical and spiritual future of society. Under current conditions and trends finding personal and familial peace and security is only going to become more difficult. As issues and options come to a head, society will fragment even more between two polarized worldviews for *hope* and *security*: Those who follow the "What I want, when I want, how I want" ethos will place their safety and future in the hands of the *technocracy* – the logical progression of technological, bio-medical and pharmaceutical fixes to support a gender-free, sexually-liberated society; a self-evolutionary society. Still many more will turn to theistic religion. Increasing fundamentalization of theistic faith members of society will likely result in reaction to perceived and actual expanded influence of individualism, libertinism, liberalism, humanism and secularism. Indeed, this phenomenon is happening already as spirituality becomes a higher priority in people's lives. Nearly two thousand years ago the Apostle Peter described the freedom and security dynamic this way:

This is love for God: to obey his commands. And his commands are not burdensome, for everyone born of God overcomes the world. This is the victory that has overcome the world, even our faith. Who is it that overcomes the world? Only he who believes that Jesus is the Son of God (1 John 5:6).

The Word of God calls humankind out of man-made security. The following extract from the writings of theologian Rudolf Bultmann offers a concise portrayal of the futility of man-made security:

The scientific worldview engenders a great temptation, namely, that man strives for mastery over the world and over his own life. He knows the laws of nature and can use the powers of nature accordingly to his plans and desires. He discovers more and more accurately the laws of social and of economic life, and thus organizes the life of the community more and more effectively...[58]

Thus modern man is in danger of forgetting two things: first, that his plans and undertakings should be guided not by his own desires for happiness and security, usefulness and profit, but rather by obedient response to the challenge of goodness, truth and love, by obedience to the commandment of God which man forgets in his selfishness and presumption; and secondly, that it is an illusion to suppose that real security can be gained by men organizing their own personal and community life. There are encounters and destinies which man cannot master. He cannot secure endurance for his works. His life is fleeting and its end is death. History goes on and pulls down all the towers of Babel again and again. There is no real, definitive security, and it is precisely this illusion to which men are prone to succumb in their yearning for security.[59]

What is the underlying reason for this yearning? It is the sorrow, the secret anxiety which moves in the depths of the soul at the very moment when man thinks that he must obtain security for himself. It is the word of God which calls man away from selfishness and from the illusory security which he has built up for himself. It calls him to God, who is beyond the world and beyond scientific thinking. At the same time, it calls man to his true self. For the self of man, his inner life, his personal existence is also beyond the visible world and beyond rational thinking. The Word of God addresses man in his personal existence and thereby it gives him freedom from the world and from the sorrow and anxiety which overwhelm him when he forgets the beyond. By means of science men try to take possession of the world, but in fact the world takes possession of men. We cannot see in our times to what degree technology brings with it terrible consequences. To believe in the Word of God means to abandon all merely human security and thus to overcome the despair which arises from the attempt to find security, an attempt which is always in vain.[60]

Genuine freedom is not subjective arbitrariness. It is freedom in obedience. The freedom of subjective arbitrariness is a delusion, for it delivers man up to his drives, to do in any moment what lust and passion dictate. This hollow freedom is in reality dependence on the lust and passion of the moment. Genuine freedom is freedom from the motivation of the moment; it is freedom which withstands the clamor and pressure of momentary motivations. It is possible only when conduct is determined by a motive which transcends the present moment, that is, by law. Freedom is obedience to a law of which the validity is recognized and accepted, which man recognizes as the law of his own being. This can only be a law which has its origin and reason in the beyond. We may call it the law of spirit or, in Christian language, the law of God.[61]

Do you want to see the monotheistic God of our Charter of Rights and Freedoms expunged from the state or replaced by an unknown god, a symbolic pantheistic entity, self-conscious humankind or a post-Darwinian construct?

Pivot of Civilization – Yes. *Rivet of Life – No.*

Pivot of Civilization or Rivet of Life?

From an intellectual and political perspective there are now only three options or courses of action the reader can take. As discussed early in this book, God either exists in a tangible way or the universe is empty of divine revelation (including the Gnostic unknown God). You can decide in favor of the Pivot of Civilization worldview, or you can decide in favor of the Rivet of Life worldview, or you can make no decision. From a spiritual perspective, the options are much more complicated, however, the unity among the world religions on this issue of same-sex marriage should itself be an indicator of the perceived attack upon the supremacy of God. Here Muslims, Sikhs, etc. need not convert to Christianity, to approve of the values behind the Rivet of Life. All theistic faiths can find intellectual and political unity with the Christian over the previous twenty-four points of philosophy and belief.

Before continuing to the next section, please make a decision on the worldview you hold as truth by placing your initials by your choice:

Pivot of Civilization ________. No decision________.

Rivet of Life ________.

Respecting Each Other's Space – A Last Hope Paradigm Shift

How we see things is largely governed by the beliefs and values we hold. The worth in a paradigm shift comes when our perception is brought nearer to the truth and as a consequence we are appropriately forced to confront and revise or reaffirm our common assumptions and beliefs. The following real case, which should be titled "Straights are Homophobic, but Lesbians Against Transgendered Males Just Need Their Space," will help demonstrate the effect and promise of a paradigm shift. Place yourself in the position of a Supreme Court judge and decide this public (societal) need versus individual rights conflict. There is a final lesson here for policy on same-sex marriage.

Eight transgender activists, members of a Chicago group called "Camp Trans Planning Committee" and the Boston and Chicago chapters of Lesbian Avengers, were asked to leave the lesbian Michigan Womyn's Music Festival (MWMF) 2000. The expulsion followed a demonstration by transgender activists at the kitchen area during dinner on Saturday evening. Activists held signs proclaiming themselves as "boy.FTM (female-to-male)," "intersex," "drag queen," and "transwoman." They called for festival attendees to join them in their protest and passed out stickers in support of transgender inclusion. Their action was a challenge to the MWMF's express policy, which declares the Festival to be "womyn-born-womyn space" and requests the "transsexual community to respect and support this intention." The Festival further declared that they will not question anyone's gender at the Festival, but that individuals who self-declare as "male-to-female transexuals or female-to-male transexuals now living as men" will be denied admission or asked to leave if on Festival land.[62]

In a press release from www.camptrans.com the expulsion was viewed as "turning a new page in the escalating conflict over the policy's application" and as "the first time the 'womyn-born-womyn' policy had been used against trannie boys, boydykes, FTM's, Lesbian Avengers and young gender-variant women." Reporters on the scene observed festival staff saying to activists, "If you do not identify as womyn-born-womyn, the policy is clear." When challenged repeatedly by activists to clarify their policy, the staff stated:

We have been clear about what this festival is about. It is for womyn-born-womyn. Those of you who are not womyn-born-womyn, who identify as transexual, not as transgender, we are asking you to leave.

Excerpts from Michigan Womyn's Music Festival's statements on the transgender issue are as follows:

The Festival is womyn-born-womyn space. That means it is an event intended for womyn who were born and who have lived their entire life experience as female – and who currently identify as a woman.

Just as we call upon the transexual community to support womyn-born-womyn space, we encourage support and respect the transexual community. As a community, we in Michigan are committed to fighting prejudice and ignorance of all kinds; we do not want to see transphobia fostered here or anywhere. Claiming one week a year as womyn-born-womyn space is not in contradiction to being trans-positive and trans-allies. In the year 2000, the queer community enjoys such rich diversity. We believe there is room for all affinity groups to enjoy separate and supportive space, and also to come together in broader alliances to fight prejudice that affects all of us. We are strong enough to hold our incredible diversity in mutual respect and support.

Lisa Vogel, Festival producer, had this to say:

....we stand by as allies with the trans community and refuse to be forced into false dichotomies that equate being pro-womyn-born-womyn space with being anti-trans. We believe the greater queer community is strong enough to support separate space for all affinity groups. There are times all oppressed communities need separate spaces, even away from our allies.[63]

Camp Trans gave a press release:

More than 60 gender activists from Camp Trans Planning Committee, Boston and Chicago chapters of Lesbian Avengers plus Transexual Menace, supportive attendees and renowned activist Dana Rivers gathered across the road from the Festival this year to do outreach and education on what they viewed as discriminatory policy being unfairly applied.... Said one activist, 'Vogel's policy towards transexuals is now the same as the US military's towards homosexuals. But 'Don't Ask, Don't Tell' only works when the target group collaborates by remaining silent. Well we aren't silent. We don't identify as 'womyn-born-womyn' – we don't know what it even means or why it should be used against us or our trannie friends.[64]

Radical feminist and lesbian, Jennie Ruby, writes:

The transgender movement is wreaking havoc among lesbians, liberals and other social progressives. It is the most radical thing going – but it is really an insidious form of paralyzing liberalism....I know these are strong statements, but the Transgender movement has been taken to heart by so many lesbians, feminists, and progressives, there is such dogma surrounding it, and there is such a taboo on challenging it, that I am unwilling to fudge even a little on how dangerous it is to feminism and women. Look at what happened at the Michigan Womyn's Music Festival last year. Apparently, pre-operation male-to-females (mtfs) entered the festival and disrobed by the showers where women were also naked preparing to shower. If these wannabe 'women' had any real understanding of what it is to be a woman in patriarchy they would have respected, not violated, women's space, and they would have understood the horrific violation it would be for a woman to be confronted with a strange naked biological male, penis and all, when she herself is unclothed and vulnerable.[65]

Asks Ruby:

How in the world has this come about? And how is it that so many well meaning lesbians have bought into the arguments for inclusion of mtfs at Michigan? Clearly, trans people, (like all people) deserve basic human rights, such as access to jobs, health insurance, respectful treatment, and freedom from living in fear of hate crimes and violence. But do mtfs, at any stage of transition, have the right to be at the Michigan Womyn's Music Festival?[66]

She responds to her own line of questioning:

First, one of the ways transgender mtf activists have managed to confuse lesbians who know that there is something wrong with letting men, however altered, into Michigan is through framing their position as one of identity. The argument is that they are, in some fundamental way, really a woman inside a male body. That is their identity. It is taken as a given that one must not question another person's assertion of his or her own identity. But what does it mean to 'be' a man or a woman? Radical feminists...are the only ones arguing that being a man or a woman is a matter of profound socialization (not of biological or hormonal origin). However, many (but not all) transgender people explain themselves in essentialist terms [the cause of human behavior is innate essences].

But an intellectual slight of hand occurs over this matter of identity explaining oneself in this way neatly avoids dealing with the political implications of one's identity. If identity is held as a given, it is off limits to criticism or analysis. Identity politics is a stealth maneuver that demands, in the name of tolerance, that others do not challenge my politics.[67] *Rather than accepting that a person just is transgender as a matter of identity, I believe it is imperative to examine the politics of being mtf. I maintain that there are politics inherent in the choice to be mtf, that is, there are ways of looking at the world, at gender, at identity, and at power relations in that choice. Yet identity politics disallows political analysis or criticisms of identities which are profoundly political.*

Leslie Feinburg, in Trans Liberation, admits "s/he" has heard transwomen being criticized for 'taking up too much space or being overbearing because they were socialized as men,' yet s/he says that it is 'prejudiced' for nontrans people to make this observation...In this manner, the power implications of taking up too much space are ruled exempt from critique. ..as a radical feminist, I believe that gender does not reside for the most part in our bodies – it resides in our heads, where gender socialization occurs. So for mtfs to focus on physically passing as women rather than on overcoming unwitting vestiges of internalized masculinity and power and control sidesteps the real problems with gender – how we come to feel and think inside.

The transgender movement, by dwelling so much on freedom of choice to identity as whatever gender you want, takes our eyes of the consequences of choices and the way our choices are structured by oppressive forces, in short, it does nothing to eliminate a system based on power and privilege. Such a system values competition over connection, control over cooperation, aggression over compassion and individualism over interdependence. Freeing people from gender roles means they are free to hold whatever values they choose including the values of power: they can be controlling, disconnected from others, or aggressive if they want to. The liberation movement I want to join is to dismantle the underlying cultural values of power as embodied in patriarchy, not to liberate people to be free from the constraints of gender roles.[68]

I believe that women's space is a powerful strategy, which is evident because it is so virulently attacked both from without (right wing) and from within (the glbt movement). It seems to me that just when women finally eek out an infinitesimal amount of space to experience one measly week away from patriarchal culture, to begin to try to even the score of five thousand years of patriarchy, the refrain has suddenly become how unfair it is not to be inclusive. There is a lot of liberal rhetoric about nondiscrimination, diversity, and inclusion just at the time when we have started to make a little headway.[69]

I would order the Michigan Womyn's Music Festival to include open transgendered and transexual people ( )

I would uphold the Michigan Womyn's Music Festival decision to exclude open transgendered and transexual people ( )

Please take a decision before continuing.

One should see in this Womyn's dilemma the hypocrisy of now demanding inclusion into traditional heterosexual "marriage space" while demanding boundary lines for their own protection. I agree with Ruby, the paradox for adherents to "sameness" or an "all inclusive equality" is that real differences are white-washed in cognitive denial. Some anatomical males think they are the same as some anatomical females by the terminology and ideology of orientation. Some GBLTQ think their notion of marriage and family is the same as heterosexual marriage and family. The earlier examples of the incompatibility of the Lesbian Caucus of the National Action Committee on the Status of Women and REAL Women representatives at national women's meetings stands as testimony that the two cannot become one.

How did you vote? If you can put the male-to-female transgendered and transexuals into the women's showers, you will likely have little reservation legislating GBLTQ union into sacred heterosexual marriage space.

There is little need for a separate decision over same-sex marriage. If you chose Rivet of Life as your worldview, this paradigm is incompatible with an inclusive definition. The position on same-sex marriage is therefore no. If you chose Pivot of Civilization, you likely want one all-inclusive definition of marriage, although a significant number of adherents to sexual liberation do not support same-sex marriage. They see the reversal, after forty years of condemning heterosexual marriage, as a misguided attempt at mainstreaming GBLTQ culture, and as jeopardizing the hard won queer space and culture, not to mention the hypocrisy of the strategy change itself. Unfortunately and ironically, these people have also been silenced and isolated by the same GBLTQ rights-based strategy, which attempts to avoid talk of philosophy and aggregate consequences. Given the legacy of fabrication, contradiction, errors of commission and omission, wishful thinking, and denial, associated with the secular paradigm of what I want, when I want, how I want, one should not be surprised to find that these people can say no to male-to-female transsexuals at the Michigan Womyn's Music Festival (for all the reason's Ruby raises) and yet say yes to GBLTQ "marriage." You do not have to be one of them.

A Christian Closing Prayer

Dear Heavenly Father,

We acknowledge your sovereignty (as God Almighty), in our lives, over our families, and over our Nation. We come before you alarmed for the future of our children and our Country. Anti-Christian activists call our concern misapprehended "homophobia." We strongly disagree. We see homosexual liberation as a direct attack upon the truth and force of Your Word, and the same-sex marriage challenge as an assault upon heterosexual marriage, the heterosexual family and Your supremacy in the Charter-related affairs of state.

We acknowledge how very far our society has drifted, willfully and in unpremeditated ways, from your wish. We are now victims of a secular form of constitutional idolatry, which places the inviolability of individual rights and freedoms ahead of Your Word and the collective welfare of society. Our judiciary has become pro-secular and pro-pluralist. In their eyes Christianity fits into the general "pigeon hole" of religions, no different before the law than Gnosticism; and increasingly less relevant than humanism. We pray to You to open the eyes of our politicians and judiciary to the hypocrisy and travesty of claiming our Constitution and Charter before You, asking in our anthem that You "keep our land," and then setting legislation against Your will and the collective wishes of virtually all theistic faiths. We wish that each elected member and judge might understand the full depth and breadth of the issues before him (or her). May they recognize and appreciate Your will and fear Your judgment.

We acknowledge that GBLTQ marriage and the advent of genetic engineering have created another crossroads of choice either toward or away from Your design. We pray for a separate definition of GBLTQ union and for protection from cloning. Furthermore, we see that the protective values and boundaries behind which Biblical (orthodox) families are to prosper have been weakened or destroyed, all but the last tenet of sanctified heterosexual marriage. We regret public policies that foster the early independence of our children from family values and religious beliefs. We regret policies and programs that suggest abortion is other than the willful killing of innocent babies. We regret the manifest adultery and fornication in our society. We regret the toxic effect of heterosexual unfaithfulness upon the institution of life-long monogamous marriage. We confess the rampant breakdown of marriage, the ease of divorce, and our unholy response of repeated remarriage. We weep over the havoc perpetrated on children of divorce. We are drowning in our self-made sea of shameful pornography. We are functionally and morally confused in an era of radical feminism, gender "fluidity," and sexual liberation. We regret that much of society and some professed Christian denominations have declared GBLTQ lifestyle blessed and homosexual ecology natural and healthy, in spite of disease, early deaths, and the contrary teaching of Holy Scripture. Open their eyes to see, we pray.

We lay this all at Your feet, including all the errors and deceptions that have contributed to this unholy crisis, starting with the notions that homosexuality is genetic and that life's true values are captured in the "Pivot of Civilization" as explained by Margaret Sanger. Open our eyes in all these areas to the truth. We ask in grace that You heal our Nation. We ask that this moral-ethical crossroads be turned to the good. May the state clarify its definition of "God." May clear boundaries be set to protect our families from anti-Christian influences and the harm of amoral scientific advances.

Above all may Christians unify in spirit, purpose, hope and ACTION. Fill us to the brim with the Holy Spirit. Raise up millions of prayer warriors. Purify Your Church.

We pray for the conviction and either restoration or elimination of all churches guilty of conduct and principles similar to the compromised church of Laodicea. May we take strength and confidence in Your sovereign power and truth. May we hold firm to Your Word and bring light and love to the lost. Lest we not forget that the grace granted each of us is more than enough to redeem and sanctify anyone from the bondage of a bathhouse cubical. May more receive the grace granted us.

We denounce all forms of verbal and physical abuse, especially toward GBLTQ. Replace hate with humility and hypocrisy with righteousness. We ask for forgiveness when our response to the GBLTQ community has been other than a caring and steadfast witness for Jesus Christ. We pray for their mutual respect.

We lift up all ex-gay outreaches such as Exodus International. Thank You for these reborn ex-gay warriors. Bless and empower them to Your glory. We lift up God-fearing organizations like REAL Women, praying for their great anointing in this time of turmoil. May Christian women and men everywhere be called to defend Your Word and the Biblical family.

Praise You for the faith and conviction shown by Mary in her response to the guest speaker presentation on abuse, and the role her action has played in the creation of this book.

Finally, we pray that all would at least come to support the Rivet of Life worldview, if not commit themselves fully to Christ.

We ask this all in Jesus Christ's awesome name.

APPENDIX 1 – LETTER TO HIGH SCHOOL

3 January 2001

Dear Mrs. XXXX,

Before the Christmas break Mary gave me the attached Guest Speaker Evaluation and Response for a presentation given on Sexual Assault by XXXX. I commend Mary for her insight and comments regarding the presentation. We both appreciated the grading and feedback. From your note, I understand that you have a full presentation planned on a subject related to homosexuality, later in the year. Mary told me you have asked her if she would like to be absent from that presentation. I thank you for your sensitivity to different perceptions on such matters. As Mary's father, I respectfully request a brief reply to the following questions and comments, either by letter or telephone, which ever is more convenient. Your response to these background comments and queries may help clarify some concerns I have related to teaching content and policy at XXXX.

I well realize that a sponsoring teacher often has limited control over what a guest speaker says in front of her class. Please accept this letter in good faith, from an interested parent. I am not an authority on sexuality or psychology. By career, I am an engineer, now teaching a number of subjects at college level. Prior to Mary bringing home the Guest Speaker Evaluation, I had read "A Strong Delusion: Confronting the Gay Christian Movement," by Joe Dallas, Eugene Oregon, Harvest House, 1996. More recently, I have read "Homosexuality and the Politics of Truth," by Jeffery Satinover, Grand Rapids, Hamewith Books, 1999. Both books I recommend.

In preparing these papers I have tried to reference all direct material quotes. If I have missed a reference for anything you wish supported, feel free to ask. Please accept my apology in advance for the length of the attachment, but I hope you will find the reading informative and principle-centered in tone and content.

I look forward to hearing from you.

Sincerely,

Carman Bradley

Five Questions Concerning Teaching Content and School Board Policy on Homosexuality

(1) "Being gay is not a matter of choice, rather it is part of your genes. The only 'choice' is whether or not you practice it." To many this is an unsubstantiated claim and a Gay rights 'political' statement. Is this tenant of the Gay Rights Movement actually School doctrine?

Comment: To the extent that homosexuals have been victimized, society needs to be educated to reach out in compassion for their suffering and struggles. Addressing this need was likely one of the objectives of your Guest Speaker presentation on Sexual Abuse. [I will comment further on fostering awareness and compassion at the end of these questions]. A Gay political agenda defined as 'born this way', on the other hand, follows the dictum that the desired ends justify all means, including distortion of the facts. The Gay Rights agenda over the past twenty years has been to shape a new consensus in favor of normalizing homosexual practice by promoting four propositions:

a. biologically, homosexuality is an innate, genetically determined aspect of the body;
b. psychologically, homosexuality is irreversible;
c. morally, the homosexual has little choice in behavior; and
d. sociologically, homosexuality is normal, akin to the social variances of race.

Public acceptance of the first three propositions is fundamental to achieving the last. K.E. Ernulf, in "Biological Explanation, Psychological Explanation, and Tolerance of Homosexuals: A Cross-National Analysis of Beliefs and Attitudes, " Psychological Reports 65, 1989, pp 1003-10, indicated that people who believed that homosexuals are 'born that way' held significantly more positive attitudes toward homosexuals than subjects who believed that homosexuals 'choose to be that way' or 'learn to be that way'.

Born this way. William Byne and Bruce Parsons from Columbia University reviewed 135 prior research studies, reviews, books and academic summaries. In "Human Sexual Orientation: The Biological Theories Reappraised," Archives of General Psychiatry 50, No3, they wrote (abstract):

Recent studies postulate biological factors [genetic, hormonal] as the primary basis for sexual orientation. However, there is no evidence at present to substantiate a biologic theory, just as there is no evidence to support any singular psychosocial explanation. While all behavior must have an ultimate biologic substrate, the appeal of current biologic explanations for sexual orientation may derive more from dissatisfaction with the current status of psychosocial explanations than from a substantiating body of experimental data. Critical review shows the evidence favoring a biologic theory to be lacking. In an alternative model, temperamental and personality traits interact with the familial and social milieu as the individual's sexuality emerges. Because such traits may be heritable or developmentally influenced by hormones, the model predicts an apparent non zero heritability for homosexuality without requiring that either genes or hormones directly influence sexual orientation per se.

A balanced or fair presentation of the 'born this way' theory must address the contradictory evidence:

a. identical twin experience does not show a statistical basis for genetic homosexuality;

b. Psychiatrist, Jeffery Satinover, in Homosexuality and the Politics of Truth points out: "To whatever extent that homosexuality is significantly and directly genetic – and thus homosexuals would mostly discover their 'orientation' before marriage – its presence in the population would shrink from one generation to the next. Unless it was continuously 'redeveloped' by some non-heritable cause or causes, intrauterine or otherwise, it would eventually disappear." The fact that the incidence of homosexuality does not appear to be declining – a point Gay activists emphasize – is thus itself an argument against its being directly genetically determined;

c. Dr. Satinover: "What did the psychoanalysts learn that activists want us to forget? That in the lives of their homosexual patients there was unusually often an emotional mismatch between the child and same-sex parent or opposite-sex parent; or sexual abuse; and most often the rejection of a child by same-sex peers...A consensus occurs over the developmental events and sequences that lead to the habitual use of anxiety-reducing, self-soothing behaviors, including homosexuality. Quite often an individual will use more than one outlet. Thus, for example, homosexuality is commonly associated with both promiscuity and alcoholism or drug use." L. S. Doll, "Self-Reported Childhood and Adolescent Sexual Abuse Among Adult Homosexual/Bisexual Men," Child Abuse and Neglect 16, No6, 1992, pp 855-64, observed that: "1001 adult homosexual and bisexual men attending sexually transmitted disease clinics were interviewed regarding potentially abusive contacts during childhood and adolescence. Thirty-seven per cent of participants reported that they had been encouraged or forced to have sexual contact before age 19 with an older or more powerful partner; 94 per cent occurred with men. Median age of the first contact was 10; median age difference between partners was 11 years. Fifty-one per cent involved use of force; 33 per cent involved anal sex.";

d. The "1990 Kinsey Institute New Report on Sex," confirms that sexual orientation is not necessarily fixed, and may change throughout a person's life span: "Some people have consistent homosexual orientation for a long period of time, then fall in love with a person of the opposite sex; other individuals who have had only opposite sex partners later fall in love with someone of the same sex;" and

e. USA Today reported on April 15, 1993, a survey of 3,321 American men indicated that 2.3 per cent of them had engaged in homosexual behavior in the past ten years, but less than half, only 1.1 per cent, reported being exclusively homosexual;

Homosexuality is very poorly defined. The use of the one term creates the false impression of a uniform gay condition or culture. It obscures the reality of a complex set of variable mental, emotional, and behavioral states that are caused by differing proportions of numerous influences. The desire to shift to a biological basis for explaining homosexuality appeals primarily to those who seek to undercut the vast amount of clinical experience confirming that homosexuality is significantly changeable.

Homosexuality is Irreversible. If homosexuality was once a taboo, what is taboo now is the notion that homosexuals can be healed, if they want to be. In 1994, the Board of Trustees of the American Psychiatry Association (APA) decided to consider altering the code of ethics. The proposed change (presented by a man who is a prominent and vocal Gay activist psychiatrist and chairman of the APA's Committee on the Abuse and Misuse of Psychiatry) would make it a violation of professional conduct for a psychiatrist to help a homosexual patient become heterosexual even at the patient's request. The proposal read, " The APA does not endorse any psychiatric treatment which is based either upon a psychiatrist's assumption that homosexuality is a mental disorder or a psychiatrist's intent to change a person's sexual orientation." According to APA members closely involved, a turning point in the battle in the APA Assembly, came when therapists who help homosexuals change – and a large number of ex-homosexuals – made it clear that if the resolution passed, they would file a lawsuit against the APA and reopen the original basis on which homosexuality was excluded from the list of mental illness diagnoses.

Schwartz and Masters in "The Masters and Johnson Treatment Program for Dissatisfied Homosexual Men [men who wish to change]," American Journal of Psychiatry 141, pp 173-81, reported a five year follow-up success rate of 65 per cent for a sample of 67 patients. An average of 50 per cent success rate has been sustained in 14 other documented studies totaling 622 patients.

Morally the Homosexual has Little Choice in Behavior. The scientific study of man often inspires resistance, dread and revulsion, for its end point is the destruction of the very idea that there is choice in human existence. 'Free will' cannot but be illusions of human subjectivity that are ultimately reducible to other, prior causes. Most people walk away from this notion. However, Gay activists do not want to find any freedom and choice involved in their way of life, and they are fiercely determined to prove that there is no way out either. Thus the debate is lined up in the reverse way of most debates over the medical bases of human behavior. People usually resist the idea that their behavior is driven by unchangeable, biological factors, as in the feminist arguments over the differences between men and women, or in the firestorm over the genetics of IQ and a potential correlation to racial groupings. But in the case of homosexuality, many people rush to embrace scientific research, however flimsy the evidence that seems to reduce this behavior not only to prior causes, but even to the end that there is no choice involved at all. One should see the fallacy in the claim that homosexuality is not immoral because it is supposedly genetic.

Genetics strongly predisposes individuals toward alcoholism. And yet no genes specifically code for it. Of interest in comparing alcoholism to homosexuality is the fact that alcoholism is estimated, according to Dr. Satinover, to be between 50-60 per cent heritable; homosexuality probably considerably less. Yet even greater risk for alcoholism does not lead to the conclusion that alcoholics are not responsible for controlling, changing, or stopping their behavior.

Homosexuality is Normal. On December 15, 1973, the Board of Trustees of APA, concluding months of negotiations with Gay activists, voted to delete homosexuality altogether from the Diagnostic and Statistical Manual (DSM). Opposition from several psychiatrists immediately followed. A referendum on the Board's decision was called for the APA Assembly. Out of 10,000 voting members, nearly 40 per cent opposed normalizing homosexuality. Dr. Ronald Bayer, in Homosexuality and American Psychiatry: The Politics of Diagnosis, New York, Basic Books, 1981, pp 3-4, recounted the events: "The entire process, from the first confrontation organized by gay demonstrators to the referendum demanded by orthodox psychiatrists, seemed to violate the most basic expectations about how questions of science should be resolved. Instead of being engaged in sober discussion of data, psychiatrists were swept up in political controversy. The result was not a conclusion based on an approximation of the scientific truth as indicated by reason, but was instead an action demanded by the ideological temper of the times."

The APA did not state that homosexuality is normal. The resolution that the APA Trustees voted on agreed that only clearly defined mental disorders should be included in the DSM, and that if homosexuals felt no 'subjective distress' about their sexuality and experienced no 'impairment in social effectiveness or functioning', then their orientation should not be labeled as a disorder. According to Bayer, pp 128, the psychiatrist who authored the resolution, in fact, flatly denied that the APA was thereby saying homosexuality was normal.

The APA decision did not necessarily reflect the views of American psychiatrists. A survey conducted by the journal Medical Aspects of Homosexuality in 1979 (six years after the APA decision) asked 10,000 psychiatrists if they felt homosexuality "usually represented a pathological adaptation". Sixty-nine per cent of the respondents said "yes," and 60 per cent said homosexual men were less capable of "mature loving relationships" than heterosexual men.

(2) The 'homosexual orientation' or 'homosexual identity' does not itself cause medical problems; only typical homosexual behaviors can. What steps does XXXX take to portray the health risks of a Gay lifestyle?

Comment: Newsweek, 19 September, 1994, pp 50-51 showed that 31 per cent of the gay subjects had engaged in unprotected anal sex. The Los Angeles Times, 3 September 1995, "Young Gays Straying Into Unsafe Sex," Sec A, p3, indicated that 50 per cent of the gay 15 to 22-year-olds surveyed had recently engaged in high risk sex, and 10 per cent of them were already infected with AIDS virus. In February 1996, the National Cancer Institute reported that gay men between the ages of 18 and 25 show the highest rate of HIV infection, despite the fact that they came of age long after 'safe sex' campaigns were established. E.L. Goldman, "Psychological Factors Generate HIV Resurgence in Young Gay Men, Clinical Psychiatry News, October, 1994, reports that "30 per cent of all 20-year-old gay men will be HIV positive or dead of AIDS by the time they are age 30" because they are resuming 'unsafe sex'. This means that the incidence of AIDS among 20 to 30-year-old homosexual men is roughly 430 times greater than among the heterosexual population at large. According to the National Gay-Lesbian Health Foundation, drug and alcohol problems are three times greater among homosexuals than heterosexuals. Various reports depict significant promiscuity (multiple partners over a lifetime) above the figures found for heterosexual men. Ironically, in the current political atmosphere the notion that homosexuality is dangerous must appear inflammatory.

(3) During teaching on homosexuality, is any effort made to portray the heterosexual family unit as the optimum model for raising children?

Comment: Nil. This should be self evident.

(4) Could you outline when formal teaching about homosexuality is given to students over their time with the Calgary Board of Education? What are the objectives of the education at each stage?

Comment: E.O. Lauman, in The Social Organization of Sexuality: Sexual Practices in the United States, Chicago, University of Chicago Press, 1994, p 295, makes it clear that the vast majority of youngsters who at some point adopt homosexual practices later give them up. However, these young people are the very ones told by educators to treat homosexuality as equally good – and safe – as heterosexuality. Sponsors of early education in homosexuality and behavior try to assure parents that they 'don't recruit,' because homosexuality is not a choice. So we can relax. They say special instruction on homosexuality and sex education will not confuse our kids about their own sexual identity. A Minnesota Adolescent Health Survey of 1992, which surveyed 34,706 students in Minnesota secondary schools showed how common it is for uncertainty about one's sexuality in early adolescence to resolve itself by the later teens: 25.9 per cent of 12-year-olds were unsure whether they were heterosexual or homosexual, whereas only five per cent of the 17-year-olds surveyed were similarly unsure. In other words, children between the ages of 12 and 17 are often uncertain about their sexual preferences. E.L. Pattullo, former director for the Center of Behavioral Sciences at Harvard University is concerned: "It's a good bet that substantial numbers of children have the capacity to grow in either [a homosexual or heterosexual] direction. Such young waverers, who until now have been raised in an environment overwhelmingly biased toward heterosexuality, might succumb to the temptations of homosexuality in a social climate that was entirely evenhanded in its treatment of the two orientations. Pattullo in "Revolt in Queens," The American Spectator, February 1993, Vol 29, No2, p 29, quotes from a well known American lesbian columnist, Donna Minkowitz: "I'm much more comfortable with the notion of 'recruiting' than I am with the guesstimate that restricts same-sex passion to a fixed percentage of the population...In a world without the heterosexual imperative, maybe kids would try on different forms of sexuality as they now try on musical styles, career choices, and haircuts."

(5) When teaching about homosexuality, is there any discussion on how this subject is viewed by Christians, Jews and students of other religions?

Comment: One can teach about the differing views of rightful conduct without proselytizing. Perhaps the most well known text in the world is the Holy Bible. For a significant portion of the global population the Bible is the point of reference for wisdom on God's Word in relations with Him and with other men and women. As evident from Mary's Guest Speaker Evaluation, those Christians in your class will relate what you teach to what they believe. Similarly for Jewish, Muslim and other faith kids; they will see this issue in light of their beliefs. For homosexuality to be seen as 'normal' in their eyes, this belief gap must be bridged. There is much the Christian Church needs to improve regarding dynamics with individuals and elements of society, particularly in the case of homosexuals. Like the Gay community, the Christian community is not one uniform group. It includes extremists, activists and misguided faithful. Yet true believers may not over look God's Word.

The Bible verses that mention same-sex contact are often referred to, in the Gay-Christian Movement as 'the clobber passages.' That cleverly puts the person using them in a negative light: he's not just quoting the Bible – he's clobbering people with it. However, to simply quote a Scripture is not to clobber anyone. For ease of reference some of the applicable Scripture on homosexuality is: Genesis 1:27-28, 2:18-24 – Creation/Created Intent; Genesis 19:4-9 – Destruction of Sodom; Leviticus 18:22, 20:13 – Levitical Law: "Do not lie with a man as one lies with a woman; that is detestable, 18:22." The Apostle Paul writing on the natural and the unnatural, Romans 1:24-27: "Therefore God gave them over in the sinful desires of their hearts to sexual impurity for the degrading of their bodies with one another. They exchanged the truth of God for a lie, and worshipped and served created things rather than the Creator – who is forever praised. Amen. For this reason God gave them over to degrading passions; for their women exchanged the natural function for that which is unnatural and in the same way also the men abandoned the natural function of the women and burned in desire toward one another, men with men committing indecent acts and receiving in their own persons the due penalty of their error."

An unwavering belief among conservative Christians is that homosexuals, like all sinners, need to repent. Having accepted Christ and repented of their sin, Christ will enable them by His grace to lead godly lives without indulging in homosexual practices. It was – and is – vital to the Gay Christian Movement's success that it convince everyone, especially its critics, that homosexuality simply cannot be repented of, any more than skin color. Gay activist and Dean of America's largest gay church, Mel White, is quoted in a article by Randy Frame, "Seeking a Right to the Rite," Christianity Today, 4 March 1996, Vol. 40, No3, p.66, "if you don't see the premise [that God created homosexuality] then gay marriage looks ridiculous, if not insane." But to be seen as created by God, the traditional understanding of homosexuality must be discredited. Activists claim "scientific information, social changes, and personal experience are the greatest forces for change in the way we interpret the Bible." Yet social change and personal experiences are irrelevant to truth; Jesus

Christ, who is the same yesterday, today, and forever (Hebrews 13:8) cared little about social trends. Mel White's two primary messages in his public appearances are clear: the Religious Right is homophobic and must be stopped, and anyone promoting the idea that homosexuality can be overcome must be silenced. Another serious problem the Gay Christian Movement faces has to do with sexual ethics. Scripture gives clear guidelines for sexual behavior: intercourse before marriage is forbidden, marriage must be monogamous, and divorce is permissible only in the event of fornication or abandonment by an unbelieving spouse.

Conclusion. At the heart of an enduring understanding and compassion for others must be honest and open dialog and effective communication. I believe our youth would be best served by educating them towards empathy for others and towards making sound informed sexuality choices themselves, by being presented with a balanced view of the issues surrounding homosexuality in society. Respect for a person's individual rights is not, as Gay activists would wish, identical with accepting his or her political claims for equality in all areas of life. This subject is far too complex to be pigeon-holed under the topic 'Born Gay' and students are much more articulate.

ENDNOTES

INTRODUCTION

[1] NARTH, www.narth.com/docs/narthresponse.html, 2/22/01.

[2] Jeffrey Weeks, *Invented Moralities: Sexual Values in an Age of Uncertainty* (New York: Knopf, 1995), p.141.

[3] Valerie Lehr, *Queer Family Values: Debunking the Myth of the Nuclear Family* (Philadelphia: Temple University Press, 1999), p.15.

[4] CBCA, www.cbca.ab.ca/aboutcbca_philosophy.html, 7/8/03.

[5] CBCA, pamphlet "Sexual Health and Choice," cited from *Be Yourself* by PFLAG, 1994.

[6] Germaine Greer, *Sex and Destiny: The Politics of Human Fertility* (London: Picador, 1985), p.219.

[7] www.positive.org/JustSayYes/birthcontrol.html, 7/8/03.

[8] Cited by Howard Bloom, *Global Brain* (New York: John Wiley & Sons, 2000), from *Don Juan*, George Bernard Shaw.

[9] Robert M. Baird & M. Katherine Baird Ed., *Gash Homosexuality: Debating the Issues* (Amherst New York: Prometheus Books, 1995), p.25.

[10] Ibid., p.27.

[11] Ibid.

[12] John Boswell, *Christianity, Social Tolerance and Homosexuality* (Chicago: University of Chicago Press, 1980), p.117.

[13] Ibid., p.8.

[14] Ibid.

[15] Frank Browning, *The Culture of Desire* (New York: Crown Publishers, 1993), p.96.

[16] Joe Dallas, *A Strong Delusion: Confronting the "Gay Christian" Movement* (Eugene Oregon: Harvest House, 1996), p.37. Quote by Kristi Hamrick, Press Secretary, Family Research Council.

[17] Denis Stairs, *The Diplomacy of Constraint: Canada, the Korean War, and the United States* (Toronto: University of Toronto Press, 1974), pp. 297 and 298.

[18] Gina Kolata, *Clone* (New York: William Morrow and Company, 1998), pp.14 and 15.

[19] Karla Mantilla, "Abortion, power, and the morality wars," *Off Our Backs,* Washington, February 1999. An interview with co-author Diana Alstad, "Abortion and the Morality Wars: Taking the Moral Offensive."

PART 1

[1] Jennie Ruby, "Men in ewe's clothing: The stealth politics of the transgender movement," *Off Our Backs*, Washington, April 2000.

[2] Alfred C. Kinsey, Wardell B. Pomeroy, and Clyde E. Martin, *Sexual Behavior in the Human Male* (Philadelphia: W. B. Saunders Company, 1953), p.661.

CHAPTER 1

[1] Carol Gilligan, *In a Different Voice* (Cambridge Massachusetts: Harvard University Press) 1982), p.64.

[2] Ibid., p.67.

[3] Gabriel Rotello, *Sexual Ecology: Aids and the Destiny of Gay Men* (New York: Dutton, 1997), p.12.

[4] Quoted from *The Mismeasure of Desire: The Science, Theory, and Ethics of Sexual*

Orientation by Edward Stein, in book review by Michael Hemmes, "The cause of affection," *Lambda Book Report*, Washington, March 2000.

[5] Henry Cloud and John Townsend, *Boundaries* (Grand Rapids, Michigan: Zondervan Publishing House, 1992), p.33.
[6] Howard Bloom, *Global Brain* (New York: John Wiley & Sons, 2000), pp.49 and 62.
[7] Cloud and Townsend, p.34.
[8] Randy Shilts, *And The Band Played On* (New York: St. Martin's Press, 1987), p.315.
[9] Cloud and Townsend, p.85.
[10] Ibid., p.42.
[11] Ibid., p.43.
[12] Martin S. Weinberg, Colin J. Williams, Douglas W. Pryor, *Dual Attraction: Understanding Bisexuality* (New York: Oxford Press, 1994), pp.77 and 79.
[13] Ibid, pp.100 and 101.
[14] Ibid., p.79.
[15] Ibid., p.83.
[16] Robert E. Penn, *The Gay Men's Wellness Guide* (New York: Henry Holt, 1997), p.237.
[17] Ibid., pp.196 – 199.
[18] Ibid., pp.236 and 237.
[19] Rotello, p.45.
[20] Ibid, p.46.
[21] Cindy Patton, *Sex & Germs* (Montreal:Black Rose Books, 1986), p.18.
[22] Rotello, p.9.
[23] Ibid.
[24] CNN.com, "U.N.: HIV cases on the rise worldwide," November. 27, 2002.
[25] Patricai Pearson, *National Post*, 30 Jul. 2001, "Watch out for the Viagra generation."
[26] Patton, p.9.
[27] Ibid., p.135.
[28] Ibid., pp.9 and 10.
[29] Bernard Asbell, *The Pill* (New York: Random House,1995), p.7.
[30] Mary Vallis, *National Post*, Mar. 27, 2002, "Cervical Cancer tied to use of birth control." Women had to be on the pill for more than ten years.
[31] Tom Blackwell, *National Post,* Feb. 14 2002, "Syphilis making a comeback."
[32] John J. McNeill, *The Church and the Homosexual* (Mission Kansas: Sheed Andrews and McMeel, 1976), pp.159 and 160.
[33] Ibid., pp.4 and 5.
[34] Catherine Dunphy, *Morgentaler: A Difficult Hero* (Toronto: Random House, 1996), p.62.
[35] David Black, *The Plague Years: A Chronicle of AIDS the Epidemic of Our Times* (New York: Simon and Schuster, 1985), p.135.
[36] Denis Altman, *The Homosexualization of America, The Americanization of the Homosexual* (New York: St. Martin's Press, 1982), p.xi.
[37] Shilts, p.239.
[38] Black, p.169.
[39] Ibid., p.177.
[40] Ibid., p.178.
[41] Larry Kramer, *Reports from the holocaust: the story of an AIDS activist* (New York: St. Martin's Press, 1994), p.xxvii.
[42] Ibid., p.335.
[43] Rotello, p.89.
[44] Ibid.
[45] Ibid., p.70.
[46] Shilts, p.147.
[47] Ibid., p.56.

[48] Heather Sokoloff, *National Post*, 30 Nov. 2001, "AIDS, HIV on rise among gay men, study suggests."
[49] Black, p.159.
[50] Michelangelo Signorile, *Life Outside* (New York: HarperCollins, 1997), p.4.
[51] Altman, p.2.
[52] Black, p.136.
[53] Rotello, p.62.
[54] Shilts, p.19.
[55] Ibid., p.15.
[56] Altman, p.21.
[57] Shilts, p.306.
[58] Altman,p.79.
[59] Shilts, p.19.
[60] Ibid.
[61] Ibid., p.89.
[62] Ibid., p.69.
[63] Rotello, pp.93 and 94.
[64] Ibid., p.98.
[65] Ibid., p.97.
[66] Shilts, p.245.
[67] Ibid., p.260.
[68] Black, p.182.
[69] Shilts, p.307.
[70] Ibid., p.422.
[71] Ibid., p.464.
[72] Ibid., p.498.
[73] Ibid., p.378.
[74] Ibid.
[75] Ibid.
[76] Mark Blasius, *Gay and Lesbian Politics: Sexuality and the Emergence of a New Ethic* (Philadelphia: Temple University Press, 1994), p.209 (Quoted in a book review by Shane Phelan, "Queer liberalism?" *The American Political Review*, Menasha, June 2000.
[77] Ibid., p.137.
[78] Ibid., p.152.
[79] Ibid., p.151.
[80] Shane Phelan, "Queer liberalism?" *The American Political Review*, Menasha, June 2000.
[81] Kramer, *Reports from the Holocaust, p.34.*
[82] Ibid., p.174.
[83] Ibid., p.46.
[84] Ibid., p.351.
[85] Ibid., p.180.
[86] Ibid., p.179.
[87] Ibid., p.395.
[88] Shilts, p.3.
[89] Rotello, p.23.
[90] Ibid.
[91] Ibid., p.24
[92] Ibid.
[93] Ibid., p.25.
[94] Black, p.95.
[95] Ibid., p.96.
[96] Ibid., p.98.

[97] Ibid., p.99.
[98] Rotello, p.27.
[99] Ibid., pp.27 and 28.
[100] Ibid., p.28.
[101] Ibid.
[102] Ibid., pp.29 and 30.
[103] Ibid., pp.30 and 31.

CHAPTER TWO

[1] Marcia Cohen, *The Sisterhood* (New York: Fawcett Columbine, 1988), p.232.
[2] Jonathan Ned Katz, *The Invention of Heterosexuality* (New York: Dutton, 1995), p.156.
[3] www.apa.org/books/4318830s.html, 4/30/02.
[4] Ibid.
[5] Lillian Faderman, *Odd Girls and Twilight Lovers: A History of Lesbian Life in Twentieth-Century America* (New York: Penguin Books, 1991), p.207.
[6] Sheila Jeffreys, *Anticlimax: A Feminist Perspective on the Sexual Revolution* (London: Women's Press, 1990), p.299.
[7] William H. Chafe, *Women and Equality: Changing Patterns in American Culture* (New York: Oxford University Press, 1977), p.133.
[8] Ibid., pp.133 and 134..
[9] Ibid., p.134.
[10] Ibid., pp.136 and 137.
[11] Ibid., p.77.
[12] Cynthia Eller, *The Myth of Matriarchal Prehistory* (Boston: Beacon Press, 2000), p.73.
[13] Ibid., p.74.
[14] Judith Butler cited in Rosaland C. Morris, "All Made Up: Performance and Theory and the New Anthropology of Sex and Gender," *Annual Review of Anthropology 24* (1995), pp.572 and 573.
[15] Denise E. M. Riley, *"Am I That Name?" Feminism and the Category of "Women" in History* (Minneapolis: University of Minnesota Press, 1988), pp 1, 2 and 112.
[16] Ibid., pp.2 and 3.
[17] Daphne Patai, *Heterophobia: Sexual Harassment and the Future of Feminism* (Lanham Maryland: Rowman & Littlefield, 1998), p.132.
[18] Ibid., p.133.
[19] Ibid.
[20] Ibid., p.233.
[21] Katz, p.150.
[22] Ibid.
[23] Patai, pp.134 and 135.
[24] Sonia Johnson, *Wildfire: Igniting The She/*volution (Albuquerque, New Mexico, Wildfire Books, 1989), p.249.
[25] Ibid., p.251.
[26] Ibid., pp.251 and 252.
[27] Janice Raymond, *A Passion for Friends: Toward a Philosophy of Female Affection* (Boston: Beacon Press, 1986), p.35, cited with Johnson, *Wildfire,* p.255.
[28] Ibid.
[29] Ibid., p.46.
[30] Ibid., p.254.
[31] Gloria Steinem, *Wonder Woman* (New York: Holt, Rhinehart, and Winston, and Warner Books, 1972), n.p.
[32] Chesler, p.284.
[33] Helen Diner, *Mothers and Amazons: The First Feminine History of Culture*, ed. and trans. By J. P. Lundin (New York: Julian Press, 1965), n.p.

[34] Martha Ann and Dorothy Myers Imel, *Goddesses in World Mythology* (Santa Barbara, California: ABC-Clio, 1993), p.v.
[35] Ibid., p.14.
[36] Ibid., pp.14 and 15.
[37] Eller, p.184.
[38] Ibid., p.185.
[39] Sarah Taylor, "'Brothers'in Arms? Feminism, Poststructuralism and the 'Rise of Civilization.'" In *Writing the Past in the Present,* ed. Frederick Baker and Julian Thomas, (Lampeter England: St. David's University, 1990), p.37.
[40] Eller, pp.185 and 186.
[41] Eller, p.74.
[42] Doris Darvasi, "Zero Toleranz," *The REAL News*, www.getset.com/realwomen/news9612.html, 2/15/01.
[43] Cecilia Forsyth, "Discrimination Against REAL Women At Federal Conference," www.realwomenca.com/html/newsletter/2000_Jan_Feb/Article_1.html, 2/15/01.
[44] Katz, p.150.
[45] "The National Action Committee on the Status of Women – Canadian Women Calling for Change," www.poetic-justice.com/essays/nac.html, 2/20/01.
[46] Gloria Steinem, *Moving Beyond Words* (New York: Simon & Schuster, 1994), pp.228 and 229
[47] Ibid, p.228.
[48] Ibid.
[49] National Foundation for Family Research and Education, "Miss Smith Goes to New York," www.nffre.org/html/commentaries/msgny.html, 2/16/01.
[50] Eller, p.187.
[51] Patai, p.232.
[52] Jill Vickers, Pauline Rankin and Christine Appelle, *Politics as if Women Mattered* (Toronto: University of Toronto Press, 1993), p.75.
[53] Judith Shulevitz, "Outside Agitator," *The New York Times*, May 9, 1999.
[54] Ibid.
[55] Chafe, pp.136 and 137.
[56] Betty Friedan, *The Feminine Mystique* (New York: Laurel Book Dell Publishing Co., 1983), p.384.
[57] Anonymous, "Now Lesbian Summit: Feminist strategies/lesbian issues," *Off Our Backs*, Washington, June 1999.
[58] Friedan, p.384.
[59] Ibid., p.386.
[60] Ibid., p.389.
[61] Ibid.
[62] Ibid., p.390.
[63] Ibid., p.388.
[64] Toby Marotta, *The Politics of Homosexuality* (Boston: Houghton Mifflin Company, 1981), p.244.
[65] Ibid., pp.244 and 245.
[66] Cohen, p.232.
[67] Ibid., p.233.
[68] Kate Millett, *Sexual Politics* (New York: Simon & Schuster, 1990), p.62
[69] Cohen, p.235.
[70] Ibid., p.238.
[71] Ibid.
[72] Ibid.
[73] Ibid.
[74] Ibid., p.242.
[75] Ibid., p.243.

[76] Ibid., p.246.
[77] Ibid.
[78] Ibid., p.248.
[79] Ibid., p.249.
[80] Ibid.
[81] Ibid., p.250.
[82] Ibid.
[83] Ibid., pp.250 and 251.
[84] Germaine Greer, *Sex and Destiny: The Politics of Human Fertility*, pp.198 and 199.
[85] Phyllis Chesler, *Women & Madness* (New York: Avon Books, 1972), p.46.
[86] Ibid.
[87] W. H. Masters and Virginia Johnson, "Orgasm, Anatomy of the Female," in *Enclyclopedia of Sexual Behavior*, ed. By A. Ellis and A. Abarbanel (New York: Hawthorn Books, 1961), Vol. 2, p.792.
[88] W. H. Masters as quoted by Dr. Mary Jane Sherfey, "The Evolution and Nature of Female Sexuality in Relation to Pyschoanalytic Theory," *The Journal of the American Psychoanalytic Association*, Vol. 14, January 1966, no. 1 (New York: International Press), p.792.
[89] Sherfey, op. cit., p.117.
[90] Chesler, p.47.
[91] Adrian Forsyth, *A Natural History of Sex* (Buffalo, New York: Firefly Books, 2001), p.11.
[92] Ibid.
[93] Ibid., p.19.
[94] Ibid., p.20.
[95] Ibid.
[96] Ibid., p.108.
[97] Ibid.
[98] Ibid., p.109.
[99] Ibid., p.110.
[100] Ibid., p.111.
[101] Ibid., pp.111 and 112.
[102] Ibid., p.112.
[103] Jane J. Mansbridge, *Why We Lost the ERA* (Chicago: Chicago Press, 1986), p.103.
[104] Ibid.
[105] "The National Action Committee on the Status of Women – Canadian Women Calling for Change," www.poetic-justice.com/essays/nac.htm, 2/20/01.
[106] Ibid.
[107] REAL Women of Canada, "Our View," www.realwomenca.com/html/our_view.html, 2/15/01.
[108] Ibid.
[109] Mansbridge, pp.174 and 175.
[110] Ibid., p.98.
[111] Ibid., p.99.
[112] Ibid.
[113] Ibid.
[114] Ibid.
[115] Ibid., p.100.
[116] Ibid., p.101.
[117] Phyllis Schlafly, *Phyllis Schlafly Report* 5, no. 7 (February 1972), pp. 3 and 4.
[118] Representative Henry J. Hyde, Illinois House of Representatives, May 16, 1972, p.202.
[119] *CBS/New York Times* poll, cited in Keith T. Poole and L. Harmon Zeigler, "The Diffusion of Feminist Ideology," *Political Behavior* 3 (1981), p.244.
[120] Mansbridge, p.105.

[121] Ibid.
[122] Ibid.
[123] Ibid., p.107.
[124] Ibid., pp.107 and 108.
[125] Ibid., p.108.
[126] Ibid., p.115.
[127] Ibid., pp.108 and 109.
[128] Ibid., p.109.
[129] Ibid., p.112.
[130] Ibid.
[131] Cited by Richard F. Lovelace in *Homosexuality and the Church* (USA: Fleming H. Revell Company, 1978), p.46. Sally Gearhart and William R. Johnson, eds. *Loving Men/Loving Women: Gay Liberation and the Church* (San Francisco: Glide, 1974), pp. 9 and 16.
[132] Ibid.
[133] Ibid.
[134] Katz, p.149.
[135] Ibid., pp.149 and 150.
[136] Chesler, p.240.
[137] Ibid., pp.240 and 241.
[138] Ibid., p.241.
[139] Ibid.
[140] Johnson, p.59.
[141] Ibid., pp.61 and 62.
[142] Ibid., pp.62 and 63.
[143] Howard Bloom, *The Lucifer Principle* (New York: Atlantic Monthly Press), p.147.
[144] Ibid.
[145] Ibid., p.148.
[146] Ibid.
[147] Ibid., p.149.
[148] Ibid., p.150.
[149] Ibid., p.152.
[150] " 'Bosom friends' fill Anne books, professor says," *Calgary Herald*, Final Edition, May 26, 2000, p.A4.
[151] Greg I. Bahnsen, *Homosexuality: A Biblical View* (Grand Rapids, Michigan: Baker Book House, 1978), p.6.
[152] Patai, p.143.
[153] Marilyn Frye, "Wilful Virgin, or Do You Have to be a Lesbian to be a Feminist?" in *Wilful Virgin: Essays in Feminism, 1976-1992* (Freedom, California: Crossing Press, 1992), p136.
[154] Ibid., p.132.
[155] Ibid.
[156] Patai, p.130.
[157] Faderman, p.212 .
[158] Karen DeCrow, interview by Jack Kammer, in his *Good Will toward Men: Women Talk Candidly about the Balance of Power between the Sexes* (New York: St. Martin's Press, 1994), p.58.
[159] Jeffreys, pp. 300 and 301.
[160] Patai, p129, quoted from Marilyn Frye, *Wilful Virgin.*
[161] Valerie Solanas, *SCUM Manifesto* (New York: Olympia Press, 1968), p.3.
[162] Ibid., pp.41 and 43.
[163] Victor Bockris, *The Life and Death of Andy Warhol* (New York: Bantam, 1989), p.236. Alkinson in 1974 characterized Solans's *SCUM Manifesto* as "the most important feminist statement written to date in the English language." Quoted by Alice Echols, *Dar-*

ing to Be Bad: Radical Feminism in America, 1967-1975 (Minneapolis: University of Minnesota Press, 1989), p.174.

[164] Majorie Garber, *VICEVERSA* (New York: Simon & Schuster, 1995), p.341.

[165] Patai, pp.106 and 107.

[166] Ibid., p.105.

[167] Ibid., pp.44 and 45.

[168] Jane Gallop, *Feminist Accused of Sexual Harassment* (Durham: Duke University Press, 1997), pp. 85 and 86.

[169] Patai, pp.108 and 109.

[170] Ibid., pp.110 and 112.

[171] Ibid., p.112.

[172] Judith Grant, *Fundamental Feminism: Contesting the Core Concepts of Feminist Theory* (New York: Routledge, 1993), p.36.

[173] Weinberg et al., pp.118 and 119.

[174] Garber, p.21.

[175] Ibid., p.22.

[176] Weinberg et al., p.21.

[177] Ibid., pp.22 and 23.

[178] Ibid., pp.23 and 74.

[179] Ibid., p.34.

[180] Ibid., p.35.

[181] Ibid.

[182] Ibid.

[183] Ibid., p.117.

[184] Ibid.

[185] Ibid., p.280.

[186] Ibid., p.282.

[187] Jennifer Baumgardner and Amy Richards, *Manifesta: young women, feminism, and the future*, (New York: Straus and Giroux, 2000), pp.21 and 22.

[188] Ibid., pp.22 and 23.

[189] Ibid., p.78

PART 2

[1] Greer, *Sex and Destiny: The Politics of Human Fertility*, pp. 128 and 129.

CHAPTER 3

[1] Margaret Sanger, *Pivot of* Civilization, taken from www.pro-life.net/sanger/pivot_fw.htm, 3/2/01. Chapter VI, p.6.

[2] "Dabate on Birth Control: Mrs. Sanger and W. Russell and Shaw vs.Roosevelt on Birth Control," ed. By E. Haldeman-Julius (Girard, Kansas: Haldeman-Julius Company, n.d.), p.13.

[3] Margaret Sanger, *Pivot of* Civilization, Chapter I, p.1.

[4] "Carl Sagan's *Demon Haunted World: Science as a Candle in the Dark*," www.visi.com/~markg/haunted.html, 4/18/01.

[5] Peter Singer, *Practical Ethics*, 2nd Edition (Cambridge: Cambridge University Press, 1993), p.331.

[6] Ibid., pp.122 and 125.

[7] *The Feminist Papers: From Adams to de* Beauvoir, ed. by Alice S. Rossi, (New York: Columbia University Press, 1973), p.31.

[8] Ibid.

[9] Ibid., p.33.

[10] Ibid., p.34.

[11] Barbara Ehrenreich, *The Hearts of Men: American Dreams and the Flight from* Commitment (Garden City, New York: Anchor Press/Doubleday, 1983), p.7.
[12] Sanger, *The Pivot of Civilization*, Chapter 2, p.3.
[13] Ehrenreich, p.7.
[14] Emma Goldman, *Living My Life* (New York: Alfred A. Knopft, 1934), p.173.
[15] Garber, *VICEVERSA*, p.75.
[16] Bonnie Haaland, *emma goldman: Sexuality and the Impurity of the State* (New York: Black Rose Books, 1993), p.ix.
[17] Emma Goldman, essay "Minorities Versus Majorities," www.spunk.org/texts/writers/goldman/sp000063.txt, 3/27/01.
[18] Ibid.
[19] Emma Goldman, *Anarchism: What it Really Stands For*, transcribed from the book *Anarchism and other Essays* (New York: Dover Publications, 1969), n.p.
[20] Ibid., n.p.
[21] Ibid.
[22] Ibid., p.21.
[23] Candice Falk, *Love, Anarchy, and Emma Goldman* (New York: Holt, Rinehart and Winston, 1984), p.217.
[24] Ibid, p.21.
[25] Haaland, p.xi.
[26] Theresa Moritz and Albert Moritz, *The World's Most Dangerous Woman: A New Biographyof Emma Goldman* (Toronto: Subway Books, 2001), p.17.
[27] Falk, p.21.
[28] Ibid., pp.24 and 25.
[29] Ibid., p.30.
[30] Ibid., p.79.
[31] Alice Wexler, *Emma Goldman in Exile* (Boston: Beacon Press, 1989), pp.11 and 12.
[32] Haaland, p.xii.
[33] Ibid., p.xiv.
[34] Falk, p.80.
[35] Ibid., p.104.
[36] Ibid.
[37] Wexler, p.87.
[38] Wexler, p.112
[39] Ibid.
[40] Ibid.
[41] Haalnad, p.32.
[42] Ibid., p.38.
[43] Ibid.
[44] Ibid., pp.38 and 39.
[45] Ibid., p.39.
[46] Ibid.
[47] Ibid.
[48] Ibid., p.41.
[49] Ibid., p.42.
[50] Falk, p.203.
[51] Ibid., p.217.
[52] Ibid., pp.224 and 225.
[53] Ibid., p.225.
[54] Ibid., p.291.
[55] Ibid., p.222.
[56] Ibid., p.243.
[57] Sanger, *The Pivot of Civilization*, Chapter 12, p.4.

[58] Madelaine Gray, *Margaret Sanger: A Biography of the Champion of Birth Control* (New York: Richard Marek Publishers, 1979), p.16.
[59] George Grant, *Grand Illusions: The Legacy of Planned Parenthood* (Brentwood, Tennesse: Wolgemuth & Hyatt, 1988), p.44.
[60] "Who was Margaret Sanger?" www.all.org/issues/pp04a.htm, 3/2/01.
[61] Grant, p.44.
[62] "Who was Margaret Sanger?" www.all.org/issues/pp04a.htm, 3/2/01.
[63] Grant, p.45.
[64] Ibid., p.47.
[65] Ibid., p.48.
[66] Joseph Finder, *Red Carpet* (Fort Worth: American Bureau of Economic Research, 1983), pp.17-19.
[67] Gray, pp.58 and 59.
[68] Grant, p.49.
[69] "Who was Margaret Sanger?" www.all.org/issues/pp04a.htm, 3/2/01.
[70] Albert Gringer, *The Sanger Corpus: A Study In Militancy*, unpublished masters thesis, Lakeland Christian College, 1974, Appendix iv., pp.473-502.
[71] Cited in Allan Chase, *The Legacy of Malthus: The Social Costs of the New Scientific Racism* (New York: Alfred Knopf, 1977), p.6.
[72] Grant, p.53.
[73] Ibid.
[74] Sanger, *The Pivot of Civilization*, Chapter 9, p.8.
[75] Ibid., Chapter 10, p.1.
[76] "Who was Margaret Sanger?" www.all.org/issues/pp04a.htm, 3/2/01.
[77] Sanger, *The Pivot of Civilization*, Chapter 10, p.5.
[78] Grant, pp.55 and 56.
[79] Gray, pp.408, 429 and 430.
[80] Ibid., pp.227 and 228.
[81] Grant cites PPFA recommended literature as Wardell B. Pomeroy, *Boys and Sex* (New York: Dell Publishing, 1968, 1981), pp.43-57.
[82] Sanger, *The Pivot of Civilization*, Chapter 10, p.3.
[83] Ibid., Chapter 12, p.3.
[84] John W. Whitehead, *The End of Man* (Westchester, Illinois: Crossway Books, 1986), pp.166 and 167.
[85] G.K. Chesterton, *Eugenics and Other Evils* (London: Cassell, 1922), p.151.
[86] Grant cites *Birth Control Review*, 3:5, (May, 1919), and 5:11, (November, 1921).
[87] David Kennedy, *Birth Control in America: The Career of Margaret Sanger* (New Haven, Connecticut: Yale University Press, 1970), pp.281-288.
[88] Grant, p.93.
[89] Grant cites "Celebrating Seventy Years of Service," 1986 Annual Report, Planned Parenthood Federation of America, p.3.
[90] Grant cites Stan E. Weed, "Curbing Births, Not Pregnancies," *Wall Street Journal*, October 14, 1986; Jacqueline Kasun, *Teenage Pregnancy: What Comparisons Among States and Countries Show* (Stafford, Virginia: American Life League, 1986); Charles Murray, *Losing Ground* (New York: Basic Books, 1984); Barrett Mosbacker, *Teen Pregnancy and School-Based Health Clinics* (Washington, D.C.: Family Research Council, 1987).
[91] A.L. Thornton, "U.S. Statistical Survey: A Reanalysis of the 1980 Census Figures for Population Distribution and Composition," *Demographics Today*, March, 1983, p.62.
[92] www.eugenics.net/papers/quotes.html, 3/2/01.
[93] James H. Jones, *Alfred C. Kinsey: A public/Private Life* (New York: W.W. Norton & Company, 1997), p.13.
[94] Ibid., p.14.
[95] Ibid., p.4.

[96] Ibid., p.22.
[97] Ibid., p.23.
[98] Ibid., pp.81 and 82.
[99] Ibid.
[100] Ibid., p.84.
[101] Ibid., p.37.
[102] Ibid., pp.87 and 88.
[103] Ibid., p.101.
[104] Ibid., p.100.
[105] Ibid., p.243.
[106] Ibid., p.245.
[107] Ibid.
[108] Ibid., p.257.
[109] Ibid.
[110] Ibid.
[111] Ibid., p.258.
[112] Ibid., p.278.
[113] Ibid., p.285.
[114] Ibid., p.307.
[115] Ibid.
[116] Ibid., p.308.
[117] Ibid., p.375.
[118] Ibid., p.384.
[119] Ibid., p.602.
[120] Ibid.
[121] Ibid., p.480.
[122] Ibid., p.328.
[123] Ibid., p.393.
[124] Ibid., p.607.
[125] Ibid.
[126] Ibid., pp.613 and 614.
[127] Ibid., pp.518 and 519.
[128] Ibid., p.519.
[129] Ibid.
[130] Ibid., p.531.
[131] Ibid., p.519.
[132] Ibid., p.520.
[133] Ibid., p.523.
[134] Ibid., p.520.
[135] Ibid., pp.549 and 550.
[136] Ibid., p.576.
[137] Ibid., p.577.
[138] Ibid., p.578.
[139] Ibid., p.579.
[140] Ibid., p.579.
[141] Ibid., pp.582 and 583.
[142] Ibid., p.587.
[143] Ibid., p.660.
[144] Ibid., pp.738 and 739.
[145] Ibid., p.739.
[146] Ibid.
[147] Jonathan Eig, "Sex by the numbers," *Chicago*, Chicago, July 1998.
[148] Ibid.
[149] Ibid.

[150] Catherine Dunphy, *Morgentaler: A Difficult Hero* (Toronto: Random House, 1996), p.8.
[151] Ibid., p.10.
[152] Ibid., p.9.
[153] "Humanist Association Information," www.infoweb.magi.com/~godfree/humhist.html, 2/21/01.
[154] Dunphy, pp.13 and 14.
[155] Ibid., p.17.
[156] Ibid., p.18.
[157] Ibid., pp.22 and 23.
[158] Ibid., p.34.
[159] Ibid., p.37.
[160] Ibid., p.45.
[161] Ibid., p.56.
[162] Ibid., p.62.
[163] Ibid., p.63.
[164] Ibid., p.66.
[165] Ibid., p.62.
[166] Ibid., p.68.
[167] Ibid., p.70.
[168] Ibid., p.71.
[169] Ibid., p.73.
[170] Ibid., p.75.
[171] Ibid., p.78.
[172] Ibid.
[173] Ibid., p.81.
[174] Ibid.
[175] Ibid., p.84.
[176] Ibid., p.100.
[177] Ibid.
[178] Ibid., p.104.
[179] Ibid., p.204.
[180] Ibid., p.322.
[181] Ibid., p.327.
[182] Ibid., p.106.
[183] Ibid., p.107.
[184] Ibid., p.126.
[185] Ibid., p.141.
[186] Ibid., p.150.
[187] Ibid., p.165.
[188] Ibid.
[189] Ibid., p.211.
[190] Ibid., p.212.
[191] www.eugenics.net/papers/quotes.html, 3/2/01.
[192] Hoeller, p.224.
[193] Kurt Rudolph, *Gnosis: The Nature and History of Gnosticism,* trans. by Robert McLachan Wilson, (Edinburgh: T & T Clark Limited, 1983), p.19.
[194] Kevin Davies, *Cracking the Genome* (New York: The Free Press. 2001), p.224.
[195] Ibid., p.225.
[196] Ibid.
[197] Ibid., p.225.
[198] Kolata, pp.230 and 231.
[199] *Clones and Clones*, ed. by Martha C. Nussbaum and Cass R. Sunstein (New York: W.W. Norton, 1998), p.55. Cited in Wilmut, p.281.

[200] Gina Kolata. *Clone* (New York: William Morrow and Company, 1098), p.228.
[201] Kolata, p.168.
[202] Richard Dawkins, *The Blind Watchmaker* (London: Penguin Books, 1991), p.10.
[203] Steve Grand, *Creation: Life and How We Make It* (London: Weidenfeld & Nicolson, 2000), pp.5 and 6.
[204] Ibid., p.6.
[205] Ibid., pp.24 and 25.
[206] Kolata, p.23.
[207] Ibid., p.24.
[208] Ian Wilmut, Keith Campbell, and Colin Tudge, *The Second Creation: Dolly and the Age of Biological Control* (New York: Farrar, Straus and Giroux, 2000), p.27.
[209] Michael Higgins, "Clonaid implores media to tell both sides of the story," *National Post*, 24 January 2003, p.A1.
[210] Ibid.
[211] Wilmut et al., p.251.
[212] Dianne N. Irving, "Legally Valid Informed Consent, " *Lifeissues.net,* www.lifeissues.net/writers/irv/irv_14legalconsent1.html, 12/20/02.
[213] Ibid.
[214] Ibid.
[215] Peter Kreeft, "Human personhood begins at fertilization," www.all.org/issues/eg08.htm, 3/2/01.
[216] Ibid.
[217] Ibid.
[218] Ibid.
[219] Ibid.
[220] Ibid.
[221] Ibid.
[222] Dianne N. Irving, "Legally Valid Informed Consent, " *Lifeissues.net,* www.lifeissues.net/writers/irv/irv_14legalconsent1.html, 12/20/02.
[223] Wilmut, p.39.
[224] Ibid., p.273.
[225] Dianne N. Irving, "What is 'Bioethics'?" *Lifeissues.net*, www.lifeissues .net/writers/irv/irv_36whatisbioethics01.html, 12/20/02.
[226] Ibid.
[227] Ibid.
[228] Ibid.
[229] Ibid.
[230] Ibid.
[231] Kolata, p.76.
[232] Ibid.
[233] Robert H. Blank, *The Political Implications of Human Genetic Technology* (Boulder, Colorado: Westview Press, 1981), p.25.
[234] Ibid., p.22.
[235] Ibid., p.23.
[236] Kolata, p.77.
[237] Terry Golway, "Life in the 90's," *America,* New York, September 12, 1998.
[238] Kolata, pp.77 and 78.
[239] Golway, "Life in the 90's."
[240] Kolata, p.81.

CHAPTER 4

[1] R.C. Sproul, *Not a Chance: The Myth of Chance in Modern Science and Cosmology* (Grand Rapids, Michigan: Baker Books, 1994), p.3. Cited in Hanegraaff, p.61.

[2] Editorial "Spiritual suicide," *Calgary Herald*, August 3, 2003.
[3] Bahnsen, p.9.
[4] N.T. Wright, *The Challenge of Jesus: Rediscovering Who Jesus Was and Is* (Downwers Grove, Illinois: Intervarsity Press, 1999), pp.82 and 83.
[5] Stephen W. Hawking, *A Brief History of Time: From the Big Bang to Black Holes* (New York: Bantam Books, 1988), p.174.
[6] Michael White and John Gribbon, *Stephen Hawking* (London: Penguin, 1992), p.168. Taken from *A Brief History of Time.*
[7] Michael White, *Acid Tongues and Tranquil Dreamers* (New York; William Morrow, 2001), pp. 130 and 131.
[8] Steven Weinberg, *The First Three Minutes: A Modern View of the Origin of the Universe*, 2nd ed. (New York: Basic Books, 1988).
[9] Ibid., p.32.
[10] Ibid., p.8.
[11] Ibid., p.5.
[12] Ibid., p.8.
[13] Ibid, p.9.
[14] Ibid., p.28.
[15] Ibid., p.30.
[16] Ibid., p.180.
[17] Ibid., p.79.
[18] Ibid., p.102.
[19] Ibid., pp.105 and 106.
[20] Isaac Asimov, "In the Game of Energy and Thermodynamics You Can't Even Break Even," *Journal of Smithsonian Institute* (June 1970): p.6. As quoted in Fred Heeren, *Show Me God*, revised edition, (Wheeling, Illinois: Day Star, 1997), pp.128 and 129. Found in Hanegraaf, p.83.
[21] Don Stoner, *A New Look at an Old Earth* (Paramount, California: Schroeder, 1992), p.106. Although discovery of the equivalence between matter and energy ($E = mc^2$) is universally attributed to Albert Einstein, not all sources agree. See Fred Hoyle and Chandra Wickramasinghe, C. *Evolution from Space* (New York: Simon & Schuster, 1981), p.10.
[22] Francis Weston Sears, *Mechanics, Heat, and Sound* (Reading Massachusetts: Addison-Wesley, 1950), p.10. Cited in Stoner, p.106.
[23] Robert Jastrow, C., *God and the Astronomers* (New York: W.W. Norton and Company, 1978), p.47. Hubble calculated that the "Big Bang," must have occurred about two billion years ago. Later refinements corrected this estimate to some fifteen billion years. Cited in Stoner, p.106.
[24] See Weinberg, *First Three Minutes*, pp.153 and 154. Cited in Stoner, p.108.
[25] Wilmut et al., *The Second Creation*, p.17.
[26] Hunter, *Darwin's God*, p.24.
[27] National Academy of Sciences, *Science and Creationism: A view from the National Academy of Sciences,* 2nd, ed. (Washington, D.C.: National Academy Press, 1999), p.19. Cited in Hunter, Darwin's God, p.25.
[28] Crick published the panspermia proposal in his *Life Itself: It's Origin and Nature* (New York: Simon and Schuster, 1981). See also *Time*, New York, 102, 10 September 1973, p.53. Cited in Ian Taylor, *In the Minds of Men: Darwin and the New World Order* (Toronto, TFE Publishing, 1991), pp.195 and 196.
[29] Taylor, *In the Minds of Men*, pp.195 and 196.
[30] Ibid., p.200.
[31] Bernard Lovell, *In The Centre of Immensities*, (London: Hutchison, 1979), p.83. Cited in Taylor, *In the Minds of Men*, pp.201 and 202.
[32] Fred Hoyle, The big bang in astronomy," *New Scientist*, London 92, 19 November 1981, p.571. Cited in Taylor, *In the Minds of Men*, p.202.

[33] Michael Denton, *Evolution: A Theory in Crisis* (Bethesda, Maryland: Alder & Alder, 1986), p.250. Cited in Hanegraaff, p.71.
[34] Davies, pp.33 and 34.
[35] Ibid., pp.56 and 57.
[36] Taylor, *In the Minds of Men*, p.196.
[37] Fred Hoyle and C. Wickramasinghe, *Evolution From Space* (London: J.M. Dent, 1981). Cited in Taylor, *In the Minds of Men*, pp.202 and 203.
[38] Taylor, *In the Minds of Men*, pp.202 and 203.
[39] James F. Coppedge, *Evolution: Possible or Impossible?* (Northridge, California: Probability Research In Molecular Biology, 1993), pp.110 and 114. Cited in Hanegraaff, pp.71 and 72.
[40] Davies, p.113.
[41] Ibid.
[42] Ibid., p.115.
[43] "Supporting Evidence: Science & Future (7)," "Evolution: a myth," www.rael.org.html, 1/7/03.
[44] "Embarrassing Questions for the Evolutionists," www.rael.org.html, 1/7/03.
[45] Dawkins, *The Blind Watchmaker*, p.5.
[46] Stephen J. Gould, "The Panda's Thumb," in *The Panda's Thumb* (New York: W.W. Norton, 1980), p.20. Cited in Hunter, *Darwin's God* , p.47.
[47] Hunter, *Darwin's God* ,p.49.
[48] Ibid.
[49] Stebbins, p.46.
[50] Charles Darwin, *The Origins of the Species*, 6th ed. (1872; repr. London: Collier Macmillan, 1962), p.93. Cited Hunter, p.56.
[51] Ibid.
[52] Ernst Mayr, *Toward a New Philosophy of Biology* (Cambridge, Massachusetts: Harvard University Press, Belknap Press, 1988), p. 208. Cited in Hunter, p.53.
[53] Ernst Haeckel, Natürliche schöpfungsgeschichte Berlin 1876. Translation revised by E. Ray Lankester under the title *The History of Creation* 2 Vols. (New York: D. Appleton, 1876). Cited in Taylor, *In the Minds of Men*, p.190.
[54] Brian Mason, "Organic matter from space," *Scientific American* 208, March 1963, p.45. Cited in Taylor, *In the Minds of Men*, p.183.
[55] Alvan Ellegard, *Darwin and the General Reader* (Stockholm: Göteberg Press, 1958), p.88. Cited in Taylor, *In the Minds of Men*, p.183.
[56] Taylor, *In the Minds of Men*, p.183.
[57] Ibid.
[58] Further details may be found in Brian Mason's book *Meteorites*, (New York: John Wiley, 1962), p.95. Cited in Taylor, *In the Minds of Men*, p.183.
[59] J.H. Lawless et al., "Organic matter in meterorites," *Scientific American* 226, June 1972, p.38. Cited in Taylor, *In the Minds of Men*, " p.184.
[60] Taylor, *In the Minds of men*, pp.191 and 192.
[61] Davies, p.14.
[62] Tim M. Berra, *Evolution and the Myth of Creationism* (Stanford, California: Stanford University Press, 1990), p.22.
[63] Hunter, p.21.
[64] William R. Fix, *The Bone Peddlers* (New York: Macmillan, 1984), p.285. Cited in Hanegraaf, p.94.
[65] Stephen Jay Gould, *Ontogeny and Phylogeny* (Cambridge, Massachusetts: Bellknap Press, 1977), n. 430. Cited in Hanegraaf, p.94.
[66] Ian T. Taylor, *In the Minds of Men*, 3d ed. (Toronto: TFE Publishing, 1991), p.274. Cited in Hanegraaf, p.94.
[67] Ibid., p.276. Taylor writes: "[Haeckel] had added 3-5 mm to the head of Biscoff's dog

embryo, taken 2 mm off the head of Ecker's human embryo, reduced the size of the eye 5 mm, and doubled the length of the posterior." Cited in Hanegraaf, p.95.

[68] Walt Brown, *In the Beginning: Compelling Evidence for Creation and the Flood*, 6th ed. (Phoenix: Center for Scientific Creation, 1995), p.45. Cited in Hanegraaf, p.95.

[69] Henry M. Morris, *Scientific Creationism*, public school edition (San Diego: C.L.P. Publishers, 1981), p.77. Cited Hanegraaf, p.95.

[70] Ibid., pp.75 to 78.

[71] Carl Sagan, *The Dragons of Eden* (New York: Random House, 1977), pp.57 and 58. Cited in Hanegraaf, pp.95 and 96.

[72] Ibid., p.197. Hanegraaf, p.96.

[73] Ibid.

[74] Hanegraaf, pp.96 and 97.

[75] Ritter, Robert John, *Biology*, Nelson Canada, Scarborough, 1993, pp.100 and 101.

[76] Hunter, p.25.

[77] Futuyma, *Science on Trial*, 46, 48, 62, 199. Cited in Hunter, p.49.

[78] Hunter, p.22.

[79] Ibid., p.32.

[80] S.R. Scadding, "Do Vestigal Organs Provide Evidence for Evolution?" *Evolutionary Theory* 5, 1981, pp.173-176. Cited in Hunter, p.32.

[81] Hunter, p.33.

[82] Stephen Jay Gould, "The Panda's Thumb," pp.20 and 21. Cited in Hunter, p.48.

[83] Stebbins, p.66.

[84] Ibid., p.79.

[85] Taylor, *In the Minds of Men*, p.161.

[86] Ibid.

[87] Ibid., p.163.

[88] Ibid., p.164.

[89] Ibid., p.166.

[90] Ibid., p.175.

[91] Quoted in Michael J. Behe, *Darwin's Black Box: The Biochemical Challenge to Evolution* (New York; Free Press, 1996), pp.225 and 226. Cited in Hunter, p.47.

[92] Mark Ridley, *Evolution* (Boston: Blackwell Scientific, 1993), p.49. Cited in Hunter, p.44.

[93] Tim M. Berra, *Evolution and the Myth of Creationism* (Stanford, California: Stanford University Press, 1990), p.19. Cited in Hunter, pp.44 and 45.

[94] Hunter, pp.44 and 45.

[95] Florence Raulin-Cerceau et al., "From Panspermia to Bioastronomy: The Evolution of the Hypothesis of Universal Life," *Origins of Life and Evolution of the Biosphere* 28, 1998, pp.597-612. Cited in Hunter, p.37.

[96] See, for example, Jacques Ninio, *Molecular Approaches to Evolution* (Princeton, New Jersey: Princeton University Press, 1983), pp.79-81. Cited in Hunter, p37.

[97] See for example, Leslie E. Orgel, "The Origin of Life – How Long Did It Take?" *Origins of Life and Evolution of the Biosphere* 28, 1998, pp.91-96; Mitchell K. Hobish, "Studies on Order in Prebiological Systems at the Laboratory of Chemical Evolution," *Origins of Life and Evolution of the Biosphere* 28, 1998, p.124. Cited in Hunter, p37.

[98] Hunter, p.38.

[99] Stebbins, pp.17 and 18.

[100] Ibid., p.22.

[101] Ibid.

[102] Ibid.

[103] Ibid., p.27.

[104] Taylor, *In the Minds of Men*, p.167.

[105] Charles Darwin, *Origin of the Species*, p.85. Cited in Taylor, *In the Mind's of Men*, p.167.

[106] Francis Darwin, ed., *Charles Darwin life and letters* 3 Vols, (London: John Murray, 1887), p296. Cited in Taylor, in the Minds of Men, p.167.
[107] Taylor, *In the Minds of Men*, p.167.
[108] Ibid.
[109] Ibid.
[110] Dawkins, *The Blind Watchmaker*, pp.77 and 78.
[111] Ibid., pp.78 and 79.
[112] Ibid., p.81.
[113] Richard B. Goldschmidt, *The Material Basis of Evolution* (New Haven: Yale University Press, 1940), p.395. As quoted in Gish, *Evolution*, 344 and found in Hanegraaff, p.41.
[114] Stephen Jay Gould, *Natural History* Vol. 86, no. 6, 1977, p.22. As quoted in Gish, p.341. Cited in Hanegraaff, p.43.
[115] Gould, *Natural History*, Vol. 86, no. 5, 1977, p.13. As quoted in Gish, p.346. Cited in Hanegraaff, p.44.
[116] "The Genome Doctor," *Christianity Today*, October 1, 2001, Vol. 45, No. 12, p.42. www.christianitytoday.com/ct/2001/012/2.42.html.
[117] Ibid., pp. 362 and 363.
[118] Henry M. Morris, *The Long War Against God* (Grand Rapids, Michigan: Baker Books, 1989), p.18. Cited in Hank Hanegraaff, *The Face That Demonstrates The Farce of Evolution* (Nashville Tenessee: W Publishing Group, 1998), p.19.
[119] Hanegraaf, p.22. Hanegraaf first heard this quote in a sermon by Dr. D. James Kennedy.
[120] Singer, p.169. Cited in Terry Golway, "Life in the 90s."
[121] Dawkins, *The Blind Watchmaker*, p.14.
[122] Ibid., p.227
[123] Ibid., pp.227 and 228.
[124] Rick Gore, "The First Pioneer," *National Geographic*, August 2002
[125] Rick Gore, "The First Pioneer," *National Geographic*, August 2002
[126] G. Ledyard Stebbins, *Darwin to DNA, Molecules to Humanity* (San Francisco: W.H. Freeman and Company, 1982), pp.352-354.
[127] Hunter, *Darwin's God*, p.117.
[128] Ibid., pp.112 and 113.
[129] Ibid., pp.115 and 116.
[130] Stebbins, p.336.
[131] Ibid., pp.340 and 341.
[132] Ibid., p.342.
[133] Davies, pp.175 and 176.
[134] Ibid., p.176.
[135] Élie Metchnikoff, *The Nature of Man*, [1903] reprint (London: G.P. Putnam's Sons, 1907), p.81. Cited in Taylor, *In the Minds of Men*," p.254.
[136] Ibid., p.161.
[137] Ibid., pp.211 and 212.
[138] Ibid., p.212.
[139] Dawkins, *The Blind Watchmaker*, p.228.
[140] John Reader, *Missing Links* (London: Collins, 1981). Cited in Taylor, *In the Minds of Men*, p.227.
[141] Taylor, *In the Minds of Men*, p.228.
[142] Marvin L. Lubenow, *Bones of Contention: A Creationist Assessment of the Human Fossils* (Grand Rapids, Michigan: Baker Books, 1992), pp.40-43. William R. Fix, *The Bone Peddlers: Selling Evolution* (New York: Macmillan, 1984), pp. 12 and 13. Cited in Hanegraaf, p.53.
[143] Ibid., p.43., Hanegraaf, p.53.
[144] Stephen, J. Gould, "Piltdown Revisited," *Natural History*, New York 88, March 1979,

p.86. M. Bowden, *Ape-men: Fact or Fallacy?* (Bromley, United Kingdom: Sovereign Publications, 1977). Cited in Taylor, *In the Minds of Men*, p.235.

[145] Taylor, *In the Minds of Men*, pp.235 and 236.

[146] H. Breuil, "Lefeu l'industrie de Pierre et d'os dans le gisement du 'Sinanthropus' à Chou K'on Tien (The fire and the industry of stone and bone in the layer of Sinanthropus at Chou K'on Tien), *L'Anthropologie*, Paris, 42, March 1932, pp.1-17. Cited in Taylor, *In the Minds of Men*, p.238.

[147] Taylor, *In the Minds of Men*, p.238.

[148] David Pilbeam, *The evolution of man* (London: Thomas and Hudson:1970a), p.176. Cited in Taylor, *In the Minds of Men*, p.239.

[149] Bowden, p.99. Cited in Taylor, *In the Minds of Men*, p.240.

[150] F. Weidenreich, "On the earliest representation of modern mankind recovered on the soil of East Asia," *Peking Natural History Bulletin*, 1939, 13:161. Cited in Taylor, *In the Minds of Men*, p.240.

[151] Taylor, *In the Minds of Men*, p.240.

[152] Marcellin Boule and H.V. Vallois, *Fossil Men* [1921], trans. by M. Bullock., (London: Thames and Hudson, 1957), p.145. Cited in Taylor, *In the Minds of Men*, p.240.

[153] Stebbins, pp.344 and 345.

[154] Davies, p.177.

[155] Ibid.

[156] Ibid., p.178.

[157] Ibid., p.178.

[158] Ibid., p.182.

[159] *Baker's Dictionary of Theology*, p.493.

[160] *Origen: Contra Celsum*, trans. by Henry Chadwick, (London: Cambridge University Press, 1953, 1965), p.xxiv.

[161] Ibid., pp.xxviii and xxix.

[162] Ibid., p.xix.

[163] Ibid., p.xxi.

[164] Ibid., pp.28 and 29.

[165] Ibid., p.32.

[166] Ibid., p.34.

[167] Ibid., p.35.

[168] Ibid., p.37.

[169] Ibid., pp.118 and 119.

[170] Ibid.,pp.235.

[171] Ibid., pp.235 and 236.

[172] *Baker's Dictionary of Theology*, p.389.

[173] Henry Chadwick, *The Early Church* (London: Penguin Books, 1993), p.19.

[174] Ibid., pp.23-33.

[175] Ibid., p.34.

[176] Ibid., p.36.

[177] Kurt Rudolph, *Gnosis: The Nature and History of Gnoticism*, trans. by Robert McLachan Wilson, (Edinburgh: T&T Clark Limited, 1983), p.10.

[178] Ibid., p.61.

[179] Ron Carlson and Ed Decker, *Fast Facts on False Teachings*, (Eugene, Oregon: Harvest House, 1994), pp.80 and 81.

[180] Rudolph, p.19.

[181] Ibid., p.53.

[182] Ibid., p.61.

[183] Ibid., p.254.

[184] Ibid., p.65.

[185] Ibid., p.115.

[186] Ibid., p.116.

[187] Ibid., p.206.
[188] Ibid., p.247.
[189] Ibid., pp.248 and 249.
[190] Ibid., p.249.
[191] Ibid., p.249.
[192] Ibid., p.139.
[193] Ibid., p.139.
[194] Ibid., p.257.
[195] Ibid., p.257.
[196] Ibid., p.257.
[197] Robert L. Wilken, *The Christians as the Romans Saw Them* (London: Yale University Press, 1984), p.20.
[see www.enemies.com/html/newtestament/BARB_phibionites.html].
[198] Henry Chadwick, *The Early Church*, p.42.
[199] Ibid., p.43.
[200] Ibid., p.44.
[201] Ibid.
[202] Ibid.
[203] Ibid., p.46.
[204] Stephen A. Hoeller, *Jung and the Lost Gospels* (Wheaton, Illoinois:The Theosophical Publishing House, 1989).
[205] Ibid., p.232.
[206] Ibid., p.244.
[207] Cornelius G. Hunter, *Darwin's God*, (Grand Rapids, Michigan: Brazos Press, 2001), pp.10 and 11.
[208] Ibid., p.129.
[209] Ibid.
[210] Michael Horton, "The New Gnosticism," *Modern Reformation*, July/August 1995, 4-12. Cited in Hunter, *Darwin's God*, p.129.
[211] Philip J. Lee, *Against the Protestant Gnostics* (Oxford: Oxford University Press, 1987), p.17. Cited in Hunter, *Darwin's God*, p.130.
[212] Hunter, *Darwin's God*, p.131.
[213] Stephen Jay Gould, *Rocks of Ages*, (New York: Ballantine, 1999). p.203. Cited in Hunter, *Darwin's God*, p.149.
[214] Hunter, *Darwin's God*, p.49.
[215] National Academy of Sciences, *Science and Creationism*, p.ix. Cited in Hunter, *Darwin's God*, p.149.
[216] From Joseph Le Conte's "Evolution: It's Nature, It's Evidences, and Its Relation to Religious Thought To the National Academy of Sciences" *Science and Creationism: A View from the National Academy of Sciences*. Hunter, *Darwin's God*, p.149.
[217] Hans Jonas, quoted in Philip J. Lee *Against the Protestant Gnostics* (Oxford: Oxford University Press, 1987), p.16. Found in Hunter, *Darwin's God*, pp.149 and 150.
[218] Howard Bloom, *The American Religion* (New York: Simon & Schuster, 1992), p.22. Cited in Hunter, *Darwin's God*, p.150.
[219] Ibid.
[220] Quoted in Steven Jay Gould, "Nonmoral Nature," in *Hen's Teeth and Horse's Toes* (New York: W.W. Norton, 1983). Cited in Hunter, *Darwin's God*, p.12.
[221] Hunter, *Darwin's God*, p.13.
[222] Ibid.
[223] Ibid., p.14.
[224] Charles Darwin, *Life and Letters of Charles Darwin*, ed. Francis Darwin (London: John Murray, 1887), 2:249. Cited in Hunter, *Darwin's God*, p.16 and 17.
[225] Charles Darwin, *The Autobiography of Charles Darwin* (New York: Harcourt, Brace and Company, 1958), p.90. Cited in Hunter, *Darwin's God*, p.18.

[226] Letter from Charles Darwin to W. Graham, 3 July 1881, *Life and Letters of Charles Darwin*, vol. 1, p. 316, cited in Gertrude Himmelfarb, *Darwin and the Darwinian Revolution* (London: Chatto & Windus, 1959), p.343. As quoted in Henry M. Morris, *Scientific Creationism*, public school edition (San Diego: C.L.P. Publishers, 1981), p.179. Found in Hanegraaff, p.25.

[227] Thomas H. Huxley, Lay Sermons, *Addresses and Reviews* (New York: Appelton, 1871), p.20. Cited in Hanegraaf, p.25.

[228] Aldous Huxley, *Ends and Means* (London: Chatto & Windus, 1938), pp.269, 270, and 273. Cited in Hanegraaf, Chapter 1, endnote 10.

[229] Quoted in Greegg Easter brook, "Science and God: A Warming Trend?" *Science* 277, 1997, p.892. Cited in Hunter, *Darwin's God*, p.153.

[230] Eller, *The Myth of Matriarchal Prehistory*, p.167.

[231] Ibid, p.169.

[232] Elaine Pagels, Adam, *Eve and the Serpent* (New York: Vintage Books, 1988), pp.51 and 52.

[233] Robin Scroggs, *The New Testament and Homosexuality* (Philadelphia: Fortress Press, 1983), p.52.

[234] Vern L. Bullough, *Homosexuality: A History* (New York: Garland STPM Press, 1979), p.56.

[235] Ibid, cited Plato's *Symposium* 178C, 209C.

[236] Scroggs, p.vii.

[237] Ibid., pp.19 and 20.

[238] Ibid., p.50.

[239] Ibid., p.20.

[240] Ibid., p.21.

[241] Ibid., p.22.

[242] Ibid., p.23.

[243] Ibid., p.24.

[244] Ibid., p.25.

[245] Ibid.

[246] Ibid., pp.31 and 32.

[247] Ibid., p.32.

[248] Ibid., p.33.

[249] Ibid., p.35.

[250] Ibid.

[251] Ibid., pp.38 and 39.

[252] Ibid., p.56.

[253] Ibid., p.39.

[254] Ibid., p.41.

[255] Ibid., p.54.

[256] Ibid., p.60

[257] Ibid., p.60.

[258] Ibid., p.61.

[259] Millett, *Sexual Politics*, p.28.

[260] Ann Brown, *Apology to Women: Christian Images of the Female Sex* (Leicester, England: Inter-Varsity Press, 1991), p18.

[261] Brown, pp.41 and 42.

[262] Ibid., p.34.

[263] Ibid., p.36.

[264] "New church service book sparks furore," *Calgary Herald*, Final Edition, October 31, 1999, p.A3.

[265] Brown, p.37.

[266] Ibid., p.38.

[267] Ibid., p.39.

[268] Ibid., p.27.
[269] Ibid., p.28.
[270] Ibid.
[271] Ibid., p.32.
[272] Ibid., pp.33 and 34.
[273] Chadwick, *The Early Church*, p.59.
[274] Ibid., p.85.
[275] Ibid.
[276] Ibid., p.91.
[277] Ibid., p.93.
[278] Ibid., p.83.
[279] Ibid., p.138.
[280] Ibid., p.140.
[281] Ibid., p.143.
[282] Ibid., p.145.
[283] Ibid., p.147.
[284] Ibid., p.148.
[285] Ibid., p.151.
[286] A.N. Wilson, *God's Funeral* (New York: W.W. Norton & Company, 1999), p.43.
[287] Reference lost.
[288] "William Wilberforce, Renewer of Society," www.elvis.rowan.edu/~kilroy/JEK/07/30.html, 4/18/01.
[289] *The Sacramento Bee*, "Suspect in slayings cites 'creators law,'" 1999, p.7A.
[290] Bruce Durost Fish and Becky Durost Fish, *William Tyndale* (Uhrichville, Ohio: Barbour, 2000), p.194.
[291] Ibid., p.197.
[292] Ibid., p.198.
[293] Baird and Baird, p.33.
[294] Ibid., pp.31 and 32.
[295] Anita Bryant, *The Anita Bryant Story* (Old Tappan, New Jersey: Fleming H. Revell Company, 1977), p.39

PART 3

[1] E.L. Pattullo, Letter to Editor, "Letters from Readers," *Commentary*, New York, March 1997.
[2] Norman Podhoretz, "How the gay-rights movement won," *Commentary*, New York, November 1996

CHAPTER 5

[1] Byrne Fone, *Homophobia* (New York: Picador, 2000), p.12. Cited from *The Advocate*, February 4, 1997, p.4.
[2] Daniel A. Helminiak, *What the Bible Really Says About Homosexuality* (San Francisco, California: Alamo Square Press, 1995), pp.32 and 33.
[3] John Shelby Spong, *Why Christianity Must Change or Die* (San Francisco: Harper, 1998), p.160.
[4] Ibid., p.161.
[5] Ibid., p.162.
[6] Ann Phillips, "Letting Go of Loneliness," testimony in *Portraits of Freedom* by Bob Davies with Lela Gilbert (Downers Grove, Illonois: InterVarsity Press, 2001), pp.24-26.

[7] Richard L. Strauss, *Win the Battle for Your Mind* (Wheaton, Illinois: Victor Books, 1980), p.10.
[8] Emil Brunner, *The Divine-Human Encounter* (Philadelphia: Westminster Press, 1943), pp. 22, 26-28.
[9] James P. Hanigan, *Homosexuality: The Test Case for Christian Sexual Ethics* (New York: Paulist Press, 1988), p.18.
[10] Ibid.
[11] Bahnsen, pp.23 and 24.
[12] William J. Bennett, letter to Editor, cited in "Correspondence," *The New Republic,* Washington, February 23, 1998.
[13] Ibid.
[14] Paul Cameron, letter to Editor, cited in "Correspondence," *The New Republic,* Washington, February 23, 1998.
[15] Garber, *VICEVERSA,* p.47.
[16] Ibid., pp.45 and 46.
[17] Ibid., p.47.
[18] Ibid., p.31.
[19] Ibid., p.42.
[20] Ibid., p.42.
[21] Derrick S. Bailey, *Homosexuality and the Western Christian Tradition* (London: Bailey, Longmans, Green and Company, 1955), p.xi.
[22] Ibid., p.155.
[23] Ibid.
[24] Ibid., pp.155 and 156.
[25] Ibid., p.155.
[26] Ibid., p.158.
[27] Ibid., pp.168 and 169.
[28] Ibid., p.169.
[29] Lovelace, p.34.
[30] Scroggs, p.74.
[31] Lovelace, p.100.
[32] Jerry R. Kirk, *The Homosexual Crisis in the Maineline Church* (New York: Thomas Nelson, 1978), p.54.
[33] Scroggs, p.72.
[34] Ibid., p.72.
[35] Ibid., p.81.
[36] Ibid., p.83.
[37] Ibid., p.84 .
[38] Ibid., pp.85 and 86 .
[39] Ibid., p.92.
[40] Ibid.
[41] Ibid., p.93.
[42] Ibid.
[43] Ibid.
[44] Ibid., p.94.
[45] Ibid.
[46] Ibid.
[47] Ibid., p.113.
[48] Ibid., p.114.
[49] Ibid., p.116.
[50] Ibid.
[51] Ibid., p.117.
[52] Ibid.
[53] Ibid., p.131.

[54] Ibid.
[55] McNeill, p.89.
[56] Mark, Jordan, *The Silence of Sodom* (Chicago: University of Chicago Press, 2000), p.248.
[57] Carlson and Decker, p.136.
[58] Ron Rhodes, *The Culting of America* (Eugene: Harvest House, 1994), p.35.
[59] Carlson, pp.137 and 138.
[60] *Positively gay,* ed. by Betty Berzon, Third Edition, (Berkley: Celestial Arts, 2001), p.23.
[61] Ibid., p.213.
[62] Dallas, p.30.
[63] Dallas, p.31.
[64] Mel White, *Stranger at the Gate* (New York: Simon and Schuster, 1994), pp.132 and 133.
[65] Dallas, p.31.
[66] Ibid.
[67] Ibid., p.32.
[68] Ibid., p.33.
[69] Ibid.
[70] Ibid., p.34.
[71] Ibid.
[72] Ibid.
[73] Troy Perry, *Don't Be Afraid Anymore* (New York: St. Martin's Press, 1990), p.7.
[74] Dallas, pp.66 and 67.
[75] Ibid., p.84.
[76] Ibid., p.85.
[77] *Positively gay,* p.222.
[78] Surya Monro, "Theorizing transgender diversity: Towards a social model of health," *Sexual and Relationship Therapy,* Basingstoke, February 2000.
[79] Ibid.
[80] Francis Mark Mondimore, *A Natural History of Homosexuality* (Baltimore, Maryland: Johns Hopkins University Press, 1996), p.184.
[81] Weinberg et al., p.63.
[82] Ibid., p.51.
[83] "The author formerly known as Pat: An interview with Patrick Califia-Rice," *Lambda Book Report,* Washington, June 2000.
[84] Ibid.
[85] Patrick Califia-Rice, "Family Values," *The Village Voice,* New York, June 27, 2000.
[86] Ibid.
[87] Ibid.
[88] Ibid.
[89] Ibid.
[90] Ibid.
[91] Ann Fausto-Sterling, "The five sexes, revisited," *Sciences,* New York, July/August 2000.
[92] Ann Fausto-Sterling, "The Five Sexes," *Sciences*, March/April 1993.
[93] Robin Hawley Gorsline, "Queering Chruch, Churching Queers," *Cross Currents,* New Rochelle, Spring 1999. Gorsline reviews Kathy Rudy, *Sex and the Church: Gender, Homosexuality, and the Transformation of Christian Ethics* (Boston: Beacon Press, 1999).
[94] Ibid.
[95] Ibid.
[96] Lovelace, p.45.
[97] Dallas, pp.99 and 100.

[98] Donald L. Faris, *The Homosexual* Christian – *a Christian Response to an Age of Sexual Politics* (Markham Ontario: Faith Today Publications, 1993), p.93.
[99] Ibid.
[100] Ibid.
[101] Ibid., p.97.
[102] Candace Chellew, "Inerrancy and Insolence," *Whosoever,* www.whosoever.org/v2Issue2/inerrant.html, p.6, 7/26/01.
[103] Candace Chellew, "Living the way of truth," *Whosoever,* www.whosoever.org/v2Issue2/truth.html, pp.1 and 2, 7/26/01.
[104] Frank Browning, *The Culture of Desire* (New York: Crown Publishers, 1993), pp.80 and 81.
[105] Ibid., p.81.
[106] Ibid., pp.81 and 82.
[107] Ibid., p.88.
[108] Ibid.,
[109] Ibid., p.88 and 89.
[110] Mary Renault, *The Charioteer* (London, Longmans, 1953), p 232, cited in Altman, p.45..
[111] Hendrik Ruitenbeek, *Homosexuality: A Changing Picture* (London:Souvenir Press, 1973), p.202.
[112] Garber, *VICEVERSA,* p.345.
[113] Ibid.
[114] Justin, I *Apology* pp.14-16; pp.27-29; 2 *Apology*; Tertullian, *Apology 3*. Cited in Pagels, *Adam, Eve and The Serpent,* p.10.
[115] Garber, *VICEVERSA*, p.346.
[116] Ibid., pp.346 and 347.
[117] Ibid., p.347.
[118] Ibid., p.352.
[119] Weinberg et al., p.214.
[120] Ibid.
[121] Ibid., p.217.
[122] Ibid., p.222.
[123] Unknown.
[124] McNeill, p.95.
[125] Phyllis Chesler, *Women & Madness* (New York: Avon Books, 1972), pp.183 and 184.
[126] *Freetobeme*, "If I think I might be gay or lesbian, shouldn't I try it out to see if I am?" www.freetobeme.com/answers.htm, 2/22/01.
[127] Weinberg et al., p.30.
[128] Ibid., pp.30 and 31.
[129] Ibid., p.48.
[130] Ibid., p.58.
[131] Ibid., p.158.
[132] Ibid., p.286.
[133] Ibid., p.287.
[134] Ibid., p.290.
[135] Ibid., p.291.
[136] Ibid., pp.16 and 17.
[137] Garber, *VICEVERSA,* p.306.
[138] Ibid., p.306.
[139] Ibid., p.307.
[140] Ibid.
[141] Ibid., p.308.
[142] Garber, *VICEVERSA,* p.352.
[143] Ibid., p.354.

[144] Ibid.
[145] Ibid.
[146] H. Montgomery Hyde, *The Trial of Oscar Wilde* (New York: Dover Publications, 1973), p.166
[147] Ibid., p.166.
[148] Ibid., p.163.
[149] Ibid., p.166.
[150] George Woodcock, *Oscar Wilde: The Double Image* (New York: Black Rose Books, 1989), p.231.
[151] Mel White, *Lust: The Other Side of Love* (Old Tappan, New Jersey: Fleming H. Revell, 1978), p.16.
[152] Ibid.
[153] Ibid.
[154] Ibid., p.17.
[155] Ibid., pp.47 and 48.
[156] Ibid., pp.86 and 87.
[157] Fone, p.23.
[158] *Diagnostic and Statistical Manual of Mental Disorders (DSM-IV),* Ameriacn Psychiatric Association, p.527.
[159] Donald L. Faris, *The Homosexual Challenge – A Christian Response to an Age of Sexual Politics* (Markham, Ontario: Faith Today Publications, 1993), pp.54 and 55.
[160] Marshall Kirk and Hunter Madsen, *After the Ball* (Doubleday, 1989), pp367-368. Cited in Faris, p.55.
[161] William Gairdner, *The War Against the Family* (Stoddart, 1992), p. 357. Cited in Faris, p.56.
[162] Michael Swift, *Gay Community News*, February 15, 1987.
[163] 237p.10.
[164] 237p.12.
[165] Paul Waller, letter to the Editor, "Letters from Readers," *Commentary*, New York, May 1997.
[166] Ibid.
[167] Ibid.
[168] John B. Murray, "Psychological profile of pedophiles and child molesters," *The Journal of Psychology,* Provincetown, March 2000. Cited Ames, M.A., and Houston, D.A., "Legal, social, and biological definitions of pedophilia," *Archives of Sexual Behavior,* 19, 1990, pp.333-342. Cited Lenin, S. M., and Stava, L., "Personality characteristics of sex offenders: A review," *Archives of Sexual Behavior,* 16, 1987, pp.57-79
[169] Murray, "Psychological profile of pedophiles and child molesters," n.p.
[170] Ibid.
[171] Ibid, cited Bogaert, A.R., Bezeau, S., Kuban, M., and Blanchard, R., "Pedophilia, sexual orientation, and birth order," *Journal of Abnormal Psychology,* 106, 1997, pp.331-335.
[172] Jan LaRue, "Legitimizing pedophilia opens the doors to predators," *Insight on the News,* Washington, June 14, 1999.
[173] Ibid.
[174] Michael C. Seto, "Paedophiles and Sexual Offences Against Children," *Archives of Sexual Behavior,* New York, June 1999.
[175] Ibid.
[176] Ibid.
[177] Ibid.
[178] Dallas, p.29.
[179] John Shelby Spong, *A New Christianity For a New World* (San Franciso: Harher, 2001), p.57.
[180] Dallas, p.171.

[181] Spong, *A New Christianity For a New World,* pp.3-6.
[182] Ibid., p.49.
[183] Ibid., p.51.
[184] Spong, *Why Christianity Must Change or Die,* pp.57 and 58.
[185] Spong, *A New Christianity For a New World,* pp.59 and 60.
[186] Ibid., p.61.
[187] Ibid., p.82.
[188] Ibid., p.83.
[189] Ibid., p.84.
[190] Ibid., p.115.
[191] Ibid., p.123.
[192] Ibid., pp.123 and 124.
[193] Ibid., p.133.
[194] Ibid., p.147.
[195] Spong, *Why Christianity Must Change or Die,* p.136.
[196] Ibid., p.137.
[197] Ibid., pp.20 and 21.
[198] Ibid., p.99.
[199] John Shelby Spong, *Rescuing the Bible From Fundamentalism* (San Francisco: Harper, 1991), p.125.
[200] Ibid, p.126.
[201] Dallas, p.174.
[202] Spong, *A New Christianity For a New World,* p.149.
[203] Ibid., p.148.
[204] Ibid., pp.153 and 154.
[205] Ibid., p.157.
[206] Ibid., p.164.
[207] Ibid., p.165.
[208] Ibid.
[209] Ibid., pp.214 and 215.
[210] Ibid., p.230.
[211] Spong, *A New Christianity For a New World,* p.150
[212] Dallas, p.196.
[213] *Positively gay*., p.219
[214].Ibid.
[215] Ibid., p.218.
[216] Ibid., p.55.
[217] Eric Marcus, *The Male Couple's Guide: Finding a Man, Making A Home, Building a Life*, Third Edition, (New York: HaperPerennial, 1988), pp.12 and 13.
[218] Ibid., pp.13 and 14.
[219] Larry Kramer, "GAY MEN WILL HAVE TO LIVE BY NEW RULES," *Seattle Post – Intelligencer*, Seattle, Washington, December 14, 1997.
[220] Sheryl Stolberg, "CULTURE: Some flout the orthodoxy of the past decade, saying the freedom to have many partners is the essence of liberation," *The New York Times;* "Promiscuity and AIDS: Gays argue coexistence," *Orange County Register,* Santa Ana, November 23, 1997.
[221] Larry Kramer, "GAY MEN WILL HAVE TO LIVE BY NEW RULES," *Seattle Post – Intelligencer*, Seattle, Washington, December 14, 1997.
[222] Betty Berzon, *Permanent Partners: Building Gay & Lesbian Relationships That Last* (New York: E.P. Dutton, 1988), p.232.
[223] Ibid., pp.232 and 233.
[224] Patton, pp.135 and 136.
[225] Weinberg et al., *Dual Attraction,* pp.240 and 241.
[226] Ibid., p.246.

[227] Ibid.
[228] Ibid., pp.246 and 247.
[229] Ibid., p.248.
[230] Ibid., p.249.
[231] Ibid., p.251.
[232] Ibid., p.252.
[233] Rotello, p.235.
[234] Ibid., p.235.
[235] Ibid., p.236.
[236] Ibid.
[237] Ibid., p.6.
[238] Ibid., pp.9 and 10.
[239] Michelangelo Signorile, *Life Outside The Signorile Report on Gay Men: Sex, Drugs, Muscles, and the Passages of Life* (New York: HarpersCollins, 1997), p.xxxi.
[240] Rotello, p.92.
[241] Ibid., p.100.
[242] Ibid., p.101.
[243] Ibid., pp.101 and 102.
[244] Ibid., p.102.
[245] Ibid., p.103.
[246] Ibid., p.103.
[247] Ibid., pp.103 and 104.
[248] Browning, pp.84 and 85.
[249] Ibid.
[250] Rotello, p.105.
[251] Ibid.
[252] Ibid., p.106.
[253] Ibid., p.107.
[254] Ibid., pp.108 and 109.
[255] John J. McNeill, *The Church and the Homosexual* (Mission Kansas: Sheed Andrews and McMeel, 1976), pp.4 and 5.
[256] Ibid., pp.110 and 111.
[257] Ibid., p.111.
[258] Ibid., p.112.
[259] Ibid., p.116.
[260] Ibid.
[261] Ibid., p.120.
[262] Ibid., p. 121.
[263] Browning, p.84.
[264] Wallace, p.3.

CHAPTER 6

[1] Davies, p.17.
[2] William Consiglio, *Homosexual No More* (Wheaton, Illinois: Victor Books, 1991), p.13.
[3] Bob Davies, *History of Exodus International* (Resource Series: Homosexuality & Society), Exodus International, p.6.
[4] Dallas, p.92.
[5] Ibid., p.93.
[6] Jerry R. Kirk, *The Homosexual Crisis in the Maineline Church* (New York: Thomas Nelson, 1978), p.27.
[7] Erinn E. Tozer, Mary K. McClanahan, "Treating the Purple Menace: Ethical considerations of conversion therapy and affirmative alternatives," *Counseling Psychologist,* College Park, September, 1999.

[8] Ibid., American Psychological Association, Minutes of the Council of Representatives American Psychologist, 30, 1975, p.633.
[9] Ibid.
[10] Ibid.
[11] Ibid.
[12] Ibid.
[13] McNeill, p.121.
[14] Ibid, cited Irving Beiber, *Homosexuality: A Psychoanalytic Study* (New York: Collier, 19560, p.24.
[15] Ibid.
[16] Faris, p103.
[17] Ibid., p107.
[18] NARTH, "What do psychotherapists say about sexual-orientation change?," www.narth.com/docs/narthresponse.html, 2/22/01.
[19] NARTH, "Is there any recent study which suggests that sexual-orientation change is possible?" www.narth.com/docs/narthresponse.html, 2/22/01.
[20] Ibid.
[21] Levinson, S., Heen, W., and Burns, J., "Should Hawaii Allow Same-Sex Marriage?" *The Honolulu Advertiser* , 9 May 1993. B1, B2.
[22] Neil and Briar Whitehead, *My Genes Made Me Do it!* (Lafayette, Louisianna: Huntington House, 1999), p.9.
[23] Ibid.
[24] Ibid., pp.82 and 83.
[25] Ibid., p.188.
[26] Ibid., p.188.
[27] Ibid., p.189.
[28] Malcolm Ritter, "Study: Some Gays Can Go Straight," *Washington Post,* May 9, 2001, www.washingtonpost.com/wp-srv/aponline/20010509/aponline013921_000.htm, 4/5/02.
[29] *FreeToBeMe,* "Aren't you just a bunch of homophobes?" www.freetobeme.com/answers.htm, 2/22/01.
[30] *PeopleCanChange*, www.peoplecanchange.com, 2/22/02.
[31] Ibid
[32] Ibid.
[33] Ibid.
[34] W. Byne M.D., Ph.D., B. Parsons, M.D., Ph.D, "Human Sexual Orientation: The Biologic Theories Reappraised," *Archives of General Psychiatry*, 1993, p. 228.
[35] W.H. Masters, V.E. Johnson, R.C. Kolodny, *Human Sexuality*, 2nd Ed, (Boston: Little, Brown and Company, 1985), pp.411 and 412.
[36] C.A. Trip, *The Homosexual Matrix* (New York: McGraw-Hill, 1975), p.12.
[37] A.A. Ehrhardt, H.F.L. Meyer-Bahlburg, "Effects of Prenatal Hormones on Gender-Related Behavior," *Science*, 1981, p.1316 .
[38] J. Marmor, "Homosexuality: Nature versus Nurture," *The Harvard Mental Health Letter*, October 1985, p.6.
[39] J. Money, "Sin, Sickness or Status? Homosexual Gender Identity and Psychoneuroendocrinology," *American Psychologist*, 42, No. 4, April 1987, p. 398.
[40] E.D. Wilson (1988) *Counseling and Homosexuality*, 42, No.4 (April), p.398 .
[41] K. Painter, "A Biologic Theory for Sexual Preference," *USA Today*, March 1, 1989, p.4D.
[42] *Homosexuals Anonymous Fellowship Services*, www.members.aol.com/HAwebsite/change/change.html, 2/22/01.
[43] W.H. Masters, V.E. Johnson, *Homosexuality in Perspective* (Boston:Little, Brown and Company, 1979).

[44] R. Kronemeyer, *Overcoming Homosexuality* (New York; Macmillan Publishing, 1980), p.7.

[45] Joan Laird, "Gender in lesbian relationships: Cultural, feminist, and constructionist," *Journal of Marital and Family Therapy,* Upland, October 2000.

[46] Ibid.

[47] Gary Goldbaum, Thomas Perdue, Donna Higgins, "Non-gay-identifying men who have sex with men: Formative research results from Seattle, Washington," *Public Health Reports,* Hyattsville, 1996.

[48] Ibid.

[49] Christopher Hewitt, "Homosexual demography: Implications for the spread of Aids" *Journal of Sex Research*, Vol 35, No. 4, Nov 1998.

[50] Alan P. Bell and Martin S Weinberg, *Homosexualities: A Study of Diversity: Among Men and Women* (New York: Simon and Shuster, 1978), pp.57 and 59.

[51] Whitehead, p.17.

[52] Ibid.

[53] Ibid., pp.20 and 21.

[54] Ibid., p.23.

[55] Ibid.

[56] Ibid., p.25.

[57] Ibid., p.29.

[58] Ibid., p.39.

[59] Ibid.

[60] Ibid., p.78.

[61] Ibid., pp.77-79.

[62] Ibid., pp.79 and 80.

[63] Ibid., p.81.

[64] Ibid., p.71.

[65] Ibid., p.82.

[66] A. Karlen, *Sexuality and Homosexuality: A New View* (New York: Norton, 1971), p. 573.

[67] Ibid., pp.572 and 573.

[68] I. Beiber et al., *Homosexuality: A Psychoanalytic Study* (New York: Basic Books, 1962), p.303.

[69] C. Socarides, "Homosexuality is not just an alternative life style," in *Male and Female: Christian Approaches to Sexuality*, R.T. Barnhouse, U.T. Holmes, eds., (New York: Seabury Press, 1976), p.145.

[70] E. Moberly, *Homosexuality: A New Christian Ethic* (Greenwood, South Carolina: Attic Press, 1983), p.2.

[71] S. Wegscheider, *Another Chance: Hope and Health for the Alcoholic Family* (Palo Alto, California: Science and Behavior Books, 1981), p.127.

[72] Ibid., pp.129 and 130.

[73] Ibid., p.130.

[74] Ibid., p.136.

[75] E. Moberly, *Psychogenesis: The Early Development of Gender Identity* (London: Routledge and Keegan Paul Ltd, 1983), p.78.

[76] Hyde, p.166.

[77] Ibid.

[78] Ibid., p.69.

[79] Ibid., p.75.

[80] Ibid., p.70.

[81] Anne Clark Armor, *Mrs Oscar Wilde: A Woman of Some Importance* (London: Sidgwick & Jackson, 1983), p.229.

[82] E. Moberly, *Homosexuality: A New Christian Ethic*, op. cit., p.5.

[83] E.D. Wilson, *Counseling and Homosexuality* (Waco, Texas: Word Books, 1988), op. cit., p. 59.
[84] E. Moberly, *Homosexuality: A New Christian Ethic*, op. cit., p.42.
[85] Whitehead, p.43.
[86] Ibid., p.44.
[87] Ibid., p.97, cited in Vines G., "Genes in black and white," *New Scientist,* July 1995, pp.34-37.
[88] Ibid., p.98.
[89] Ibid., pp.98 and 99.
[90] Ibid., p.52.
[91] Ibid., p.56.
[92] Ibid., p.58.
[93] Ibid., p.59.
[94] Ibid., p.66, cited in Saghir, M.T., Robins, E., *Male and Female Homosexuality, A Comprehensive Investigation* (Baltimore, Maryland: Williams and Wilkins, 1973).
[95] Ibid., cited in Nicolosi, J., *Reparative Therapy of Male Homosexuality* (Northvale, New Jersey: Jason Aronson, 1991).
[96] Ibid., cited in Bell, A.P., Weinberg, M.S., Hammersmith, S.K., *Sexual Preference: Its Development In Men and Women* (Bloomington, Indiana: Indiana University Press, 1981).
[97] Ibid., p.67, cited in Saghir, M.T., Robins, E., *Male and Female Homosexuality, A Comprehensive Investigation.*
[98] Ibid.
[99] Whitehead, p.8.
[100] Ibid., p.68.
[101] Ibid., p.69. Cited in Saia,M., *Counseling the Homosexual* (Minneapolis, Minnesota: Bethany House, 1988).
[102] Ibid., p.69, cited in Moberly, E.R., *Homosexuality, A New Christian Ethic* (Cambridge: James Clarke & Company, 1983).
[103] Ibid., p.70.
[104] *Peoplecanchange*. www.peoplecanchange.com/reparative_therapy_aka_sexual_reorientation_therapy.htm, 4/22/01.
[105] Ibid.
[106] Ibid.
[107] *FreeToBeMe,* www.freetobeme.com/answers.htm, 2/22/01.
[108] Ibid.
[109] Ibid.
[110] Ibid.
[111] Ibid.
[112] Lovelace, p.123.
[113] Ibid., p.138.
[114] Gowland, William, *Militant and Triumphant* (Nashville: Tidings, 1953).

PART 4

[1] Joan Laird, "Gender in lesbian relationships: Cultural, feminist, and constructionist reflections," *Journal of Marital and Family Therapy,* Upland, October 2000.
[2] Greer, *Sex and Destiny: The Politics of Human Fertility,* p.6.

CHAPTER 7

[1] McNeill, pp.130 and 131.
[2] Ibid., p.131.

[3] CBC Ottawa, "Same-sex couples: Ottawa's surprising stat," www.ottawa.cbc.ca, 12/19/02.

[4] Garber, *VICEVERSA,* p.369.

[5] *The Family*, ed. by Alice s Rossi, Jerome Kagan, Tamara K. Hareven, (New York: W.W. Norton & Company, 1978), p.13.

[6] Ibid., p.13.

[7] Ibid.

[8] Sylvia Ann Hewlett, *A Lesser Life: The Myth of Women's Liberation in America* (New York: William Morrow and Company, 1986), p.173.

[9] *The Family*, ed. by Rossi, p.14. Cited J. Lorber, "Beyond Equality of the Sexes: The Question of the Children," *The Family Coordinator,* 24:4, 1975, p.465.

[10] Ibid., p.14.

[11] Sylvia Ann Hewlett, *Creating a Life: Professional Women and the Quest for Children* (New York: Talk Miramax Books, 2002, p.163.

[12] Ibid.

[13] Ibid.

[14] Cynthia R. Daniels, *At Women's Expense: State Power and the Politics of Fetal Rights* (Cambridge Massachusetts: Harvard University Press, 1993), p.179.

[15] Ibid.

[16] *The Family*, ed. by Rossi, pp.14 and 15.

[17] Ibid.

[18] Ibid., p.15.

[19] Ibid.

[20] Ibid., pp.15 and 16.

[21] Ibid., p.16, cited in J. Rothchild and S.B. Wolf, *The Children of the Counterculture* (New York, 1976).

[22] Ibid.

[23] Ibid.

[24] Nancy Gibbs, "Making Time For A Baby," *Time,* Canadian Edition, April 15, 2002, p. 38.

[25] Ibid.

[26] Arlie Hochschild, with Anne Machung, *The Second Shift* (New York: Viking, 1989), p.12.

[27] Ibid.

[28] Ibid., p.13.

[29] Hewlett, *A Lesser Life,* p.180. Cited in Elisabeth Griffith, *In Her Own Right: The Life of Elizabeth Cady Stanton* (New York: Oxford University Press, 1984), p.184.

[30] Ibid., Griffith, op. cit., p.51.

[31] Ibid., cited in Ann Dally, *Inventing Motherhood: The Conseqwuences of an Ideal* (New York: Schocken Books, 1983), p.133.

[32] Ibid., cited in Shulamith Firestone, *The Dialectic of Sex* (New York: William Morrow, 1970), p.203.

[33] Ibid.

[34] Danielle Crittenden, *What Our Mothers Didn't Tell Us* (New York Simon & Schuster, 1999) pp.96 and 97.

[35] Johnson, *Wildfire,* pp.89 and 90.

[36] John F. Conway, *The Canadian Family in Crisis,* Fourth Edition (Toronto: James Lorimer & Company, 2001), p.26.

[37] Ibid.

[38] Ibid.

[39] Ibid., p.28.

[40] Ibid., p.27.

[41] Sylvia Ann Hewlett, *When The Bough Breaks: The Cost of Neglecting Our Children* (New York: Basic Books, 1991), p.41. Cited in Frank F. Furstenberg, Jr., and Christine

Winquist Nord, "Parenting Apart: Patterns of Childrearing after Marital Disruption," *Journal of Marriage and the Family* 47, no. 4, 4 November 1985, p.2.

[42] Ibid., pp.64 and 65.

[43] Conway, p.31.

[44] Ibid., p.33.

[45] Ibid., p.34.

[46] Ibid.

[47] Ibid., p.35.

[48] Ibid., cited *Leader Post*, Regina, 26 August 1985.

[49] James Poniewozik, "The Cost of Starting Families First," *Time* Canadian Edition, April 15, 2002, p. 46.

[50] Conway, p.49.

[51] Ibid., p.50.

[52] Hewlett, *When The Bough Breaks*, p.70.

[53] Ibid., pp.70 and 71. Cited Janet E, Gans and Dale A Blyth, *America's Adolescents: How Healthy Are They?* (Chicago: American Medical Association, 1990), p.40.

[54] Ibid.. Cited John Kass, "Psychiatrists Get Rich, But Do Patients Profit? *Chicago Tribune,* May 29, 1989, p.1.

[55] Ibid., p.71. Cited study by E. Mavis Hetherington reported in Jane E. Brody, "Divorce's Stress Exacts Long-term Toll," *New York Times,* December 13, 1983, p.C5.

[56] Ibid., p.74. Cited "The Changing American Vacation," *Newsweek,* August 28, 1989, p.8.

[57] Ibid. Cited *Mass. Mutual Family Values Study* (Washington, D.C.: Mellman & Lazarus, 1989).

[58] Susan Faludi, *Backlash: The Undeclared War Against American Women* (New York: Crown Publishers, 1991), p.ix and x.

[59] Ibid.

[60] Ibid., p.x.

[61] Ibid., p.xvi.

[62] Ibid., p.xxiii.

[63] Friedan, *The Feminine Mystique,* p.384.

[64] Faludi, p.xix.

[65] Calgary Herald, "Online divorces opposed in U.S." Friday, March 8, 2002, p A6.

[66] Crittenden, p.103.

[67] Warner Troyer, *Divorced Kids* (Toronto:Clarke, Irwin & Company, 1979), p.26.

[68] Troyer, p.15.

[69] Ibid.

[70] Ibid., p.16.

[71] Hochschild, p.249.

[72] Hewlett, *When The Bough Breaks* , p.89.

[73] Ibid., p.91. Cited in Tamar Lewin, "Father's Vanishing Act Called Common Drama," *New York Times,* June 4, 1990, p.A18.

[74] Ibid., p.250.

[75] Hewlett, *When The Bough Breaks,* p.88. Cited *Studies in Marriage and the Family* (U.S. Bureau of the Census, Current Population Reports Series P-23, no. 162, 1989), p.5.

[76] Ibid. Cited Judith S. Wallerstein and Sandra Blakeslee, *Second Chances: Men, Women and Children a Decade After Divorce* (New York: Ticknor & Fields, 1989), p.149.

[77] Troyer, p.26.

[78] Ibid.

[79] Ibid., p.28.

[80] Troyer, p.45.

[81] Ibid.

[82] Ibid., p.46.

[83] Hewlett, *When The Bough Breaks*, p.92.
[84] Ibid.
[85] Ibid.
[86] Ibid. Cited Robert H. Coombs and John Landsverk, "Parenting Styles and Substance Use During Childhood and Adolescence," *Journal of Marriage and the Family i50, no.2, May 1988, pp.473-482*
[87] Ibid. Cited Wallerstein and Blakeslee, *Second Chances,* p.55.
[88] Troyer, p.47.
[89] Ibid., p.33.
[90] Hewlett, *When The Bough Breaks*, p.93.
[91] Troyer, p.146.
[92] Susan Chira, *A Mother's Place* (New York: HarperCollins, 1998), p.188.
[93] Ibid., p.189.
[94] Troyer, p.146.
[95] Ibid., pp.259-261.
[96] *Why Go to Work?,* from the *Ministry in the Marketplace Series*, (Knoxville, Tennessee: Vision Foundation, 1987).
[97] Ibid.
[98] Ibid.
[99] Chris Lindsay, *The Radical.*
[100] Hochschild, p.30.
[101] *Why Go to Work?,* p.24.
[102] Chira, p.165.
[103] Ibid., p.165.
[104] Ibid., p.187.
[105] Ibid.
[106] Scanzoni, *Sex and the Single Eye,* pp.76 and 77.
[107] Millett, *Sexual Politics,* pp.126 and 127.
[108] Hewlett, *A Lesser Life,* p.185.
[109] Ibid.
[110] Ibid.
[111] Ibid.
[112] Ibid.
[113] Ibid.
[114] Ibid.
[115] Ibid., p.186.
[116] Karla Mantilla, "Abortion, power, and the morality wars," *Off Our Backs,* Washington, February 1999.
[117] Ibid.
[118] *National Post*, "More teens lashing out at parents study says," Tom Blackwell, 22 June 2001, p A1,A8.
[119] Ibid.
[120] Radio Bible Class Ministries, "Right & Wrong: A Case For Moral Absolutes," *Discovery Series*, (Grand Rapids, Michigan: Thomas Nelson, 1995),pp.11 and 12.
[121] Mary Pipher, *The Shelter of Each Other: Rebuilding Our Families* (New York: A Grosset/Putnam Book, 1996), p.202.
[122] Greer, *Sex and Destiny,* p.12 and 13.
[123] Ibid., pp.14 and 15.
[124] Greer, *Sex and Destiny,* p.19.
[125] Ibid., p.25.
[126] Susan H. Greenberg, The Rise of the Only Child; Around the globe, birthrates are falling. Growing up without siblings is now the norm in some places. It's good for the planet. So why is everyone so worried? *Newsweek,* New York, April 23, 2001.
[127] Ibid.

[128] Ibid.
[129] *National Post*, "Facing a future with fewer children" Anne Kingston, March 13, 2002, p A15.
[130] Ibid.
[131] Patai, *Heterophobia,* p.10.
[132] Crittenden, p.98.
[133] Ibid., p.96.
[134] Ibid., p.73.
[135] Ibid.
[136] Hewlett, *When The Bough Breaks*, pp.104 and 105.
[137] Ibid. Cited Christopher Lasch, *The Culture of Narcissism: American Life in the Age of Deminishing Expectations* (new York: Warner, 1979), pp.42, 43, 30.
[138] Ibid.
[139] Hewlett, *A Lesser Life,* p.189.
[140] Hochschild, p.25.
[141] *Calgary Herald*, A woman's place is in the boardroom" September 20, 2000, p.A3.
[142] Ibid.
[143] Hewlett, *A Lesser Life,* pp.31 and 32.
[144] Ibid., p.147.
[145] Hewlett, *When The Bough Breaks*, p.85.
[146] Wallave, pp.40 and 41.
[147] Chira, p.155.
[148] Pipher, pp.3 and 4.
[149] Shelley E. Taylor, *The Tending Instinct* (New York:Times Books, 2002), p.54.
[150] Bloom, *The Lucifer Principle,* p.60.
[151] Taylor, *The Tending Instinct,* p.54.
[152] Ibid.
[153] Ibid., p.55.
[154] Ibid. p. 63.
[155] Ibid., pp.63 and 64.
[156] Hewlett, *When The Bough Breaks*, p.19.
[157] Taylor, *The Tending Instict,* p.65.
[158] Ibid.
[159] Ibid., p.71.
[160] Ibid.
[161] Ibid.
[162] Chira, p.x.
[163] Ibid., p.160.
[164] Ibid.
[165] Ibid.
[166] Ibid.
[167] Hewlett, *When The Bough Breaks*, p.15. Cited Victor R. Fuchs, *Women's Quest For Economic Equality* (Cambridge, Massachusetts: Harvard University Press, 1988), p.111.
[168] Ibid., p.15.
[169] Ibid., p.73.
[170] Ibid.
[171] Ibid.
[172] Hochschild, p.8.
[173] Crittenden, p.79.
[174] Ibid., p.80.
[175] Hochschild, p.9.
[176] Ibid., p.7.
[177] Ibid., p.215.
[178] Ibid., pp.214 and 215.

[179] Weiner and Starr, p.164.
[180] Ibid.
[181] Pipher, p.85.
[182] Cloud and Townsend, p.29.
[183] Ibid., pp.169 and 170.
[184] Ibid., p.170.
[185] Ibid., p.177.
[186] Cloud and Townsend, p.231.
[187] Ibid., p.215.
[188] www.flag.blackened.net/intanark/faq/secJ6.html#secj68.
[189] Glorianne M. Leck, "Heterosexual or homosexual? Reconsidering binary narratives on sexual identities in urban schools," *Education and Urban Society,* Thousand Oaks, May 2000.
[190] *FreeToBeMe*, "If I think I might be gay or lesbian, shouldn't I try it out to see if I am," www.freetobeme.com/answers.htm, 2/22/01.
[191] Jones, *Alfred C. Kinsey,* p.689.
[192] Ibid., p.384.
[193] Ibid., p.531.
[194] NARTH, "Then the teen years aren't the best time to 'come out'?" response to "Just the Facts about Sexual Orientation and Youth," www.narth.com/docs/narthresponse.html, 2/22/01.
[195] Ibid.
[196] Ibid.
[197] Ibid.
[198] Ibid.
[199] Ibid.
[200] NARTH, "Recommended Reading for Teenagers? A Closer Look at P-FLAG," www.narth.com/docs/pflag1.html, 2/22/01.
[201] Ibid.
[202] Ibid.
[203] Karla Mantilla, "Abortion, power, and the morality wars," *Off Our Backs,* Washington, February 1999. An interview with co-author Diana Alstad, "Abortion and the Morality Wars: Taking the Moral Offensive."
[204] Ibid.
[205] "Teenage sex:Just say'wait'," *U.S. News & World Report,* Washington, July 26, 1993.
[206] Ibid.
[207] Ibid. Cited Alan Guttmacher Institute. *Sex and America's Teenagers* (New York: Alan Guttmacher Institute, 1994).
[208] "Teenage sex:Just say'wait'," *U.S. News & World Report,* Washington, July 26, 1993.
[209] Anonymous, "Sexual backlash," *The American Enterprise,* Washington, July/August 1998.
[210] Scott Stossel, "The sexual counterrevolution," *The American Prospect,* Princeton, July/August 1997.
[211] "Choosing Virginity," *Newsweek*, December 9, 2002, p.61.
[212] "Teenage sex:Just say'wait'," *U.S. News & World Report,* Washington, July 26, 1993.
[213] Rebecca Hagelin, "Abstinence-only sex ed," *WorldNetDaily,* December 17, 2002. Planned Parenthood, for example, recently fought the nomination of Kentucy obstetrician-gynecologist David Hager to the Food and Drugs Advisory Committee, partly (according to Rebecca Hagelin) for his advocacy of abstinence-only sex-ed. The teachers' union in New Jersey, cancelled three workshops on sex ed at its convention when organizers learned the three presenters – all distinguished physicians – favored the abstinence-only approach.
[214] "Choosing Virginity," *Newsweek*, December 9, 2002, p.63.
[215] "The Battle Over Abstinence," *Newsweek,* December 9, 2002, p.71.

[216] Julia A. Ericksen, "Sexual liberation's last frontier," *Society,* New Brunswick, May/June 2000.

[217] "Netherlands – Age of Consent," www.ageofconsent.com/netherlands.htm, 12/21/01.

[218] Andrew Gimson, "The minority it's ok to hate," *The Spectator,* London, December 30, 2000.

[219] "Age of Consent – Protection For Our Kids," *The R.E.A.L. WOMEN of BC Newsletter,* www.getset.com/realwomen/news198.html, 2/15/01.

[220] Crittenden, p.33.

[221] Ibid.

[222] Ibid.

[223] Ibid., p.34

[224] Ibid.

[225] Ibid., p.35.

[226] Ibid.

[227] Scott Stossel, The sexual counterrevolution," *The American Prospect,* Princeton, July/August 1997.

[228] Ibid.

[229] Ibid.

[230] Ibid.

[231] The Medical Institute for Sexual Health, "Medical Updates: Frequently Asked Questions," www.medinstitute.org/medical/index.htm.

[232] Bridget Maher, "The Way It Was Meant to Be," *Interlife,* www.frc.org/ie/important/important0201a.html, 2/22/01.

[233] Laumann and Gagnon, p.364.

[234] Ibid., pp.365-368.

[235] REAL Women of BC, "Campaign aimed at Young People not working," www.getset.com/realwomen/news1198.html.

[236] Ibid.

[237] Ibid.

[238] "Teenage sex:Just say'wait'," *U.S. News & World Report,* Washington, July 26, 1993.

[239] Ibid.

[240] Ibid.

[241] Ibid.

[242] Cited by Larry V. Crutchfield in "The early church fathers and abortion," www.all.org/issues/ab99x.htm, 3/2/01. Clement of Alexandria Christ the Educator 2.10 (in Fathers, 23:173, 174).

[243] Wendy Murray Zoba, "Abortion's untold story," *Christianity Today*, Carol Stream, April 27, 1998.

[244] Feminists For Life of America, "Feminist History," www.feministsforlife.org/history/foremoth.htm, 3/5/01.

[245] 1026

[246] "Human Life in the Womb," www.all.org/issues/abfetal.htm.

[247] FFLA, "In Hebrew, 'Uterus' Means 'Compassion',"reprinted from Janet Podell, *The American Feminist*, Summer 1995, www.feministsforlife.org/taf/1995/summer/hebrew.htm, 3/5/01.

[248] FFLA, "Fighting for Pro-life Medical Students: Dr. Pamela E. Smith," reprinted from Dorothy Pauch, *The American Feminist, Fall 1997,* www.feministsforlife.org/taf/1997/fall/pamsmith.htm, 3/5/01.

[249] Wendy Murray Zoba, "Abortion's untold story," *Christianity Today,* Carol Stream, April 27, 1998

[250] FFLA, "The Bitter Price of Choice," reprinted from Frederica Mathewes-Green, *SisterLife, Winter 1990,* www.feministsforlife.org/FFL_topics/after/pricchoc.htm.

[251] Benjamin J. Stein, "A golden age for thugs," *The American Spectator,* Bloomington, May 1998.

[252] Mantilla, "Abortion, power, and the morality wars."
[253] Ibid.
[254] Zorba, "Abortion's untold story."
[255] Wendy Shalit, "Whose choice?" *National Review,* New York, May 18, 1998.
[256] Ibid.
[257] Ibid.
[258] Karen Birchard, "Irish abortion-debate protagonists sit and talk," *The Lancet,* London, October 3, 1998.
[259] FFLA, an interview with author Frederica Mathewes-Green by FFLA President Rosemary Bottcher, "Real Choices," www.feministsforlife.org/taf/1994/winter/realchc.htm, 3/5/01.
[260] Ibid.
[261] Ibid.
[262] Ibid.
[263] Ibid.
[264] "From the Mailbox," www.w-cpc.org/post-abortion/mailbox.html, 3/2/01.
[265] Ibid.
[266] Mantilla, "Abortion, power and the morality wars."
[267] David Whitman, "The untold story," *U.S. News & World Report,* Washington, December 7, 1998.
[268] FFLA, "Graciela Olivarez (1928-1987)," reprinted from Mary Krane Derr, *The American Femminist,* Summer 1998, www.feministsforlife.org/history/herstory/golivare.htm, 3/5/01.
[269] Ibid.
[270] www.rachelsvineyard.org and www.afterabortion.org.
[271] Ibid.
[272] Ibid.
[273] Ibid.
[274] Ibid.
[275] Ibid.
[276] Ibid.
[277] Ibid.
[278] Ibid.
[279] Ibid.
[280] Ibid.
[281] Ibid.
[282] "What is post abortion syndrome?" www.all.org/issues/abhow08.htm, 3/2/01.
[283] Mantilla, "Abortion, power, and the morality wars."
[284] Ibid.
[285] Forsyth, *A Natural History of Sex,* p.70.
[286] Ibid., p.71.
[287] Ibid., p.72.
[288] Ibid., p.73.
[289] Ibid., p.78.
[290] Ibid., p.79.
[291] Davies, pp.13 and 14.
[292] Evangelical Fellowship of Canada, "Rights of the Unborn," *National Affairs,* www.efc-canada.com/issues/life/abunborn.html, 2/21/01.
[293] Kreeft, www.all.org/issues/eg08.htm, 3/2/01.
[294] *Lifeissues.net,* James P. Lucier, "Population Control Numbers Favor The Pro-life Side," *The Pro-life Infonet,* December 17, 2002.
[295] Ibid.
[296] Gloria Steinem, *Revolution From Within* (Boston: Little, Brown and Company, 1992, 1993), p.65.

CHAPTER 8

[1] Nicholas Wade, "On our faithless belief in monogamy," *The New York Times*, 21 May 2001.

[2] *Positively gay*, ed. by Betty Berzon, p.66.

[3] Wallace, p.36.

[4] Eric Marcus, *The Male Couple's Guide*, p.14.

[5] Radio Bible Class Ministries, *Discovery Series*, "Singleness: The Misunderstood World of Single Adults," (Grand Rapids, Michigan: Thomas Nelson, 1993, p.10. Cited Carolyn Koons and Micheal J. Anthony, *Single Adult Passages* (Baker, 1991).

[6] Berzon, Permanent Partners, p.14.

[7] Ibid., p.14.

[8] Browning, *The Culture of Desire*, p.79.

[9] Ibid., p.80.

[10] George Gilder, *Men and Marriage* (Gretna, Louisiana: Pelican Publishing Company,1987),p.70.

[11] Ibid.

[12] Ibid.

[13] Ibid., p.63. Cited Jesse Bernard, *The Future of Marriage* (New York: World Publishing Company, 1972), pp.295-316.

[14] Ibid., p.36. Cited Bernard, *The Future of Marriage.*

[15] Ibid.

[16] Ibid., pp.63 and 64. Cited Morton Hunt, *Sexual Behavior in the Seventies* (Chicago, Illinois: Playboy Press, 1974) and John Leo, "Sex in the 80s," *Time*, 8 April 1984, pp.74-83.

[17] Pamela Paul, *The Starter Marriage and the Future of Matrimony* (New York: Villard, 2002), p.84. Cited Leon R. Kass, "The End of Courtship," *Public Interest* 126, Winter 1997, p.39.

[18] Ibid., pp.84 and 85.

[19] Leon Kass, "Courtship's End: Men and Women Are Paying a High Price for Their Individualism," *Chicago Tribune Magazine*, 9 February 1998, p.10-13. Found in Martha Ruppert *The Dating Trap* (Chicago: Moody Press, 1995), p.22.

[20] Rupert, p.22.

[21] James Dobson, "Complete Marriage and Family Reference Guide," Family.org, www.family.org/docstudy/solid/a0007412.html, 5/13/02.

[22] William Cutrer and Sandra Glahn, "How Far Is OK to Go Before Marriage? (Part 2 of 5)," Family.org, www.family.org/married/romance/a0020147.cfm, 5/13/02.

[23] Letha Scanzoni, *Sex and the Single Eye* (Grand Rapids, Michigan: Zondervan Publishing House, 1968), pp.66 and 67. Cited Harvey Cox, *The Secular City* (New York: The Macmillan Company, 1965), p.210.

Ibid., p 67. Cited Robert R. Bell, *Premarital Sex in a Changing Society* (Englewood Cliffs, New Jersey: Prentice-Hall, 1966), pp.72 and 73.

[24] Ibid.

[25] William Cutrer and Sandra Glahn, "How Do We Make Love Once We Are Able to Love Sex? (Part 4 of 5)," Family.org, www.family.org/married/romance/a0020149.cfm, 5/13/02.

[26] Ibid.

[27] Paul, *The Starter Marriage*, p.50. Cited Barbara Dafoe Whitehead, "The Plight of the High Status Woman," *Atlantic Monthly*, December 1999, p.120.

[28] Ibid. Cited Ilene Rosenzweig, "A Bachelorette Fears Maiking a Commitment," *New York Times*, 14 February 2000, p.4.

[29] Ibid., p.53.

[30] Ibid., p.71. Cited Nancy Ann Jeffrey, "The New Economy Family," *Wall Street Journal*, 8 September 2000, section W, p.1.

[31] Paul., *The Starter Marriage*, pp.59 and 60. Cited Barbara Ehrenreich, "Why It Might Be Worth It (to Have an Affair)," in Deborah Chasman and Catherine Jhee, eds., *Here Lies My Heart: Essays on Why We Marry, Why We Don't, and What We Find There* (Boston: Beacon Press, 1999), p.6.
[32] Ibid., p.59.
[33] Ibid., p76. Cited Stephanie Coontz., *The Way We Really Are: Coming to Terms with America's Changing Families* (New York: Basic Books, 1997), p.37.
[34] Radio Bible Class Ministries, *Discovery Series*, "Singleness: The Misunderstood World of Single Adults," (Grand Rapids, Michigan: Thomas Nelson, 1993, p.9.
[35] Paul, *The Starter Marriage*, p.79. Cited "Generation X Revisited," *Yankelovich Monitor*, 5 April 2000.
[36] Ibid.
[37] Ibid., p.86. Cited Katie Roiphe, *Last Night in Paradise: Sex and Morals at Century's End* (New York: Little, Brown, 1997), pp.28 and 29.
[38] Ibid., p.87. Cited Sharon Begley, *Newsweek*, 8 May 2000, p.52.
[39] Ibid. Cited from Valli Herman-Cohen, "I Do' It My Way," *Los Angeles Times*, 28 January 2000, p.E1.
[40] Ibid., p.231. Cited Kass, "The End of Courtship."
[41] Ibid., p.231. Cited Kass, "The End of Courtship."
[42] Wallace, *For Fidelity*, p.52.
[43] Ibid., pp.52 and 53.
[44] Ibid., pp.68 and 69.
[45] Ibid., p.139. Cited Monica Davey, "Perspective: On the Record: David Popenoe, Co-director of the National marriage Project," *Chicago Tribune*, 1 August 1999, section 14, p.1.
[46] Ibid., p.140.
[47] Ibid., p.144. Cited Margot Hornblower, "Great Xpectations," *Time*, 9 June 1997, p.58.
[48] Ibid., p.145.
[49] Ibid. Cited from Teresa Castro Martin and Larry L. Bumpass, "Recent Trends in Marital Disruption," *Demography* 26, no.1, February 1989, p.37.
[50] Ibid., p.147.
[51] Ibid., p.151. Cited Kari Jensen Gold, "Opinion," *First Things*, November 1992, p.9.
[52] Ibid., p.153. Cited Alex Kuczynski, "Between the Sexes, It's World War III Out There," *New York Times*, 19 July 1998, section 9, p.1.
[53] Ibid., Cited Myriam Miedzian and Alisa Malinivich, *Generations: A Century of Women Speak About Their Lives* (New York: Atlantic Monthly Press, 1997), p.223.
[54] Ibid., p.156. Cited David Popenoe and Barbara Dafoe Whitehead, "The State of Our Unions: The Social Health of Marriage in America," *National Marriage Project*, 2000, p.8.
[55] Ibid., p.157. Cited David Popenoe and Barbara Dafoe Whitehead, "The State of Our Unions," *National Marriage Project*, 2001.
[56] Ibid. Cited Valli Herman-Cohen, "'I Do' It My Way," *Los Angeles Times*, 28 January 2000, p.E1.
[57] Ibid.
[58] Ibid., p.158. Cited Popenoe and Whitehead, "State of Our Unions," 1999.
[59] Ibid., p.232.
[60] Ibid., p.233.
[61] Dalma Heyn, *Marriage Shock: The Transformation of Women into Wives*, (New York: Villard, 1997), p.xii.
[62] Ibid., pp.xii and xiii.
[63] Ibid., p.xvi.
[64] Ibid., p.17.
[65] Ibid., p.19.
[66] Ibid., p.20.

[67] Ibid., p.22.
[68] Ibid., p.23.
[69] Ibid., p.164.
[70] Ibid., p.165.
[71] Ibid., pp.174 and 175.
[72] Ibid., p.175.
[73] Ibid., p.194.
[74] Ibid.
[75] Ibid., p.194.
[76] Greer, *Sex and Destiny*, p.116.
[77] Ibid, p.40.
[78] Ibid., p.131.
[79] Ibid., p.130.
[80] Gilder, p.ix.
[81] Ibid., p.x.
[82] Ibid., p.ix.
[83] Ruppert, *The Dating Trap*, pp.138 and 139.
[84] Ibid., p.139.
[85] Mark Lee, *Creative Christian Marriage*, (Glendale, California: Regal Books, 1977), p.45. Cited Alexander Comfort, "Swinging Future," *Time Magazine*, January 8, 1973, p.35.
[86] Ibid.
[87] Ibid.
[88] Paul, *The Starter Marriage*, p.29.
[89] Ibid.
[90] Ibid, p.9.
[91] Wallace, *For Infidelity*, pp.83 and 84.
[92] Paul, *The Starter Marriage*, p.9.
[93] Ibid.
[94] Ibid., p.10. Cited *2000 Roper Reports*00-1, Q63X.
[95] Ibid. Cited 1999 *Yankelovich Monitor*, Table 165 (54 per cent).
[96] Ibid., pp.10 and 11.
[97] Ibid, p.11.
[98] Ibid. Cited Jackie Calmes, "Americans Retain Puritan Attitudes on Matters of sex," *Wall Street Journal*, 5 March 1998, p.A12.
[99] Ibid., p.12.
[100] Ibid.
[101] Ibid., p.31.
[102] Ibid., p.15.0
[103] Ibid. Cited Sara Terry, "The Unexpected Consequences of 'Living Together'," *Christian Science Monitor*, 10 April 2000, p.1.
[104] Ibid.
[105] Evangelical Fellowship of Canada, "The Contribution of Marriage," *National Affairs*, www.efc-canada.com/billc23.htm, 2/21/01. Cited Nicole Marcil-Gratton, *Growing up with Mom and Dad? The intricate family life courses of Canadian children* (Ottawa: 1998), p.9.
[106] Cheryl Wetzstein, "American birthrate rises," *Insight on the News*, Washington, May 15, 2000.
[107] Ibid.
[108] Julia Steiny, "EDWATCH – Life without father brings only pain," *Providence Journal*, Providence, Rhode Island, August 12, 2001.
[109] Adam Phillips, *Monogamy* (New York: Pantheon Books, 1996), pp.69,81 and 121.
[110] Paul, *The Starter Marriage*, p.74.
[111] Ibid., p.81.

[112] Wallace, *For Fidelity*, p.61.
[113] Ibid., p.67.
[114] Ibid., pp.67 and 68.
[115] Paul, *The Starter Marriage*, p.xii.
[116] Ibid. Cited 1999 *Yankelovich Monitor*, Table 140.
[117] Ibid., p.xiii. Cited American Dialogue/TBWA Chiat/Day "Talking Beauty" poll, July 1995.
[118] Ibid. Cited Blum and Weprin Associates, *New York Times Magazine* poll, March 2000.
[119] Ibid., "Time to repaint the Gen X Portrait," *Yankelovich Monitor*, 12 October 1998.
[120] Ibid. Cited *Roper Reports* 00-1, Q.63X.
[121] Ibid. Cited 1999 *Yankelovich Monitor*, Table 165 (54 per cent).
[122] Ibid.
[123] Ibid. Cited *Roper Reports* 1998, 98-6, Q-79.
[124] Ibid. Cited *General Social Survey*, University of Chicago.
[125] Ibid., p.xiv. Cited *Yankelovich Monitor*, 29 march 1999.
[126] Ibid., p.xvii. Cited U.S. Bureau of the Census, "Marital Status," March 1998 Update.
[127] Ibid., p.18. Cited "'M' Is For Mother, not Marriage," *American Demographics*, May 2000, p.7.
[128] Wallace, *For Fidelity*, p.17.
[129] Ibid., p.18.
[130] Ibid., p.20.
[131] Ibid., p.127.
[132] Paul, p.90. Cited Francine Prose, "Why Confidence Soars After Marriage," *Redbook*, February 1999, p.84.
[133] Ibid. Cited Ira Matathia and Marian Salzman, *Next: Trends for the Near Future* (New York: Overlook Press, 1999), p.399.
[134] Brown, *Apology to Women*, p.162.
[135] Ibid., pp.162 and 163.
[136] Ibid., p.163.
[137] Ibid., p.164.
[138] Ibid., p.165.
[139] Ibid., p.166.
[140] Ibid., p.167.
[141] Paul, p.216.
[142] Ibid., p.217.
[143] Ibid.
[144] Gilder, p.15. Cited Robert Briffault and Bronislaw Malinowski, *Marriage: Past and Present* (Boston: Porter Sargent, 1956), p.50.
[145] Ibid. Cited Margaret Mead, *Male and Female: A Study of the Sexes in a Changing World* (New York: Morrow, 1949), p.195.
[146] Ibid, Briffault and Malinowski, *Marriage Past and Present*, p.79.
[147] Focus on the Family, www.family.org.
[148] Radio Bible Class Ministries, "What Is the Promise of Marriage?" *Discovery Series* (Grand Rapids, Michigan: Thomas Nelson, 1992), p.9.
[149] Ibid., pp.15 and 16.
[150] Radio Bible Class Ministries, "What Will Make My Marriage Work?" *Discovery Series* (Grand Rapids, Michigan: Thomas Nelson, 1986), p.11.
[151] David Boehi, Brent Nelson, Jeff Schulte and Lloyd Shadrach, *Preparing for Marriage* (Ventura, Claifornia: Gospel Light, 1997), p.94.
[152] Rupert, *The Dating Trap*, pp.152 and 153.
[153] Ibid., p.153.
[154] Ken Nair, *Discovering the Mind of a Woman* (Nashville, Tennessee: Thomas Nelson, 1995), p.43.
[155] Ibid., p.45.

[156] Ibid., p.61.
[157] Ibid., p.112.
[158] Ibid., p.119.
[159] Ibid., p.166.
[160] Eric Marcus, *Together Forever: Gay and Lesbian Marriage* (New York: Anchor Books, 1998), p.xii.
[161] Paul, p.224. Cited Lynn Darling, "For Better and Worse," in Deborah Chasman and Catherine Jhee, eds., *Here Lies My Heart: Essays on Why We Marry, Why We Don't, and What We Find There* (Boston: Beacon Press, 1999), p.180.
[162] Ibid., p.242. Cited Gallagher, *Abolution of Marriage*, p.31.
[163] Ibid., p.245.
[164] Joe Woodward, "Religions unite over sex and the family," *Calgary Herald*, 20 February, 2001, pp.A1 and A2.
[165] Ibid.
[166] William N. Eskridge, Jr., *The Case for SAME-SEX MARRIAGE* (New York: The Free Press, 1996), p.51.
[167] Ibid., p.61.
[168] Ibid., p.65
[169] Tom Arnold, "B.C. court says no to gay marriage," *National Post*, Thursday 4 October 2001, p.A1.
[170] REAL Women of B.C., "Petter Cultivating Conjugal Relations With EGALE?!" *The R.E.A.L. WOMEN of B.C. Newsletter*, www.getset.com/realwomen/, 2/5/01. By Laurie Geschke, originally published in the Maple Ridge/Pitt Meadows News.
[171] Ibid.
[172] Tom Arnold, p.A1.
[173] Ibid.
[174] Eric Marcus, *The Male Couple's Guide*, p.22.
[175] Garber, *VICEVERSA*, pp.418 and 419.
[176] Eric Marcus, *The Male Couple's Guide*, p.46.
[177] Paul, p.251.
[178] Ibid.
[179] Ibid.
[180] Ibid., pp.251 and 252.
[181] Ibid., p.252. Cited Ira Matathia and Marian Salzman, *Next: trends for the Near Future* (New York: Overlook Press, 1999), p.396.
[182] Ibid., p.253.
[183] Ibid. Cited the Report Reports 2000 Annual Presentation, Roper Starch Worldwide.
[184] Ibid., p.254.
[185] Ibid., p.257.
[186] Rosalind C. Barnett and Caryl Rivers, *She Works/He Works* (San Francisco: Harper, 1996), p.10.
[187] Ibid., p.11.
[188] Ibid., p.14.
[189] Ibid., p.18.
[190] Wallace, *For Fidelity*, p.14.
[191] Ibid., p.49.
[192] Ibid., p.50.
[193] Ibid.
[194] Andrew Sullivan, quoted in "In defense of gay politics: Confessions of a pastoralist," by David S. Toolan, *America*, New York, September 23, 1995.
[195] Gilder, pp.57 and 58
[196] Ibid., pp.58 and 59
[197] Ibid., p.75
[198] Taken from the jacket of Eskridge, *The Case for Same-Sex Marriage*.

[199] Norman Podhoretz, "How the gay-rights movement won," *Commentary*, New York, November 1996.
[200] Garber, *VICEVERSA*, p.372.
[201] Ibid.
[202] Browning, pp.84 and 85.
[203] Weinberg et al., *Dual Attraction*, p.107
[204] Ibid., p.108.
[205] Ibid.
[206] Ibid., p.109.
[207] Ibid.
[208] Ibid.
[209] Ibid., p.111.
[210] Ibid.
[211] Ibid.
[212] Ibid., p.112.
[213] Ibid.
[214] Ibid.
[215] Ibid., p.113.
[216] Marcus, *Together Forever*, p.73.
[217] Berzon, ed., *Positively gay*, pp.100 and 101.
[218] Ibid., p.101.
[219] Ibid., p.79.
[220] Ibid., p.98.
[221] Ibid.
[222] Eskridge, *The Case for SAME-SEX MARRIAGE*, p.78.
[223] Ibid., p.79.
[224] Ibid.
[225] Ibid., p.80.
[226] Ibid., p.80.
[227] Ibid., p.81.
[228] Ibid.
[229] Ibid.
[230] Ibid., p.80.
[231] Ibid., p.90.
[232] Ibid., p.91.
[233] Ibid.
[234] Ibid., p.194.
[235] Eric Marcus, *The Male Couple's Guide*, p.216.
[236] Ibid., p.217.
[237] Ibid., p.218.
[238] REAL Women of Canada, "Homosexual Lobby Group EGALE Hits Turbulence," *REALity*, www.realwomenca.com/html/newsletter/2002_Jan_Feb/Article_7.html, 4/23/01. Ken Popert quoted in *Capital Extra*, November 9, 2001.
[239] Ibid.
[240] Ibid.
[241] Ibid.
[242] Kim Camp, *She's Twelve Going On Twenty* (Nashville, Tennessee: Word Publishing, 2000, p.223.
[243] Franklin E. Keny, letter to the Editor, "Letters from readers," *Commentary*, New York, March 1997.
[244] Weinberg et al., *Dual Attraction*, pp.77 and 79.
[245] Browning, *The Culture of Desire*, p.80.
[246] Ibid.
[247] Ibid., pp.151 and 152.

[248] Ibid., p.153.
[249] Ibid., pp.153 and 154.
[250] Ibid., p.154.
[251] Ibid.
[252] Ibid., pp.154 and 155.
[253] Ibid., p.155.
[254] Ibid., p.157.
[255] Ibid., p.156.
[256] Ibid., p.157.
[257] Eric Marcus, *The Male Couples Guide*, pp.43 and 44.
[258] Ibid., p.44.
[259] Chesler, *Women & Madness*, p.31.
[260] "Sex-changing teen wants to be mom and dad," *Calgary Herald*, Wednesday, December 12, 2001, p.A6 .
[261] Gilder. *Men and Marriage*, p.179.
[262] Ibid., p.181.
[263] Ibid., p182.
[264] Ibid.
[265] C.S. Lewis, *The Abolition of Man* (New York: Macmillan, 1976). Cited in Gilder, Men and Marriage, p.182.
[266] Gilder, *Men and Marriage*, pp.182 and 183.
[267] Ibid., p.183.
[268] John D'Emilio and Estelle Freedman, "Dialoque of the Sexual Revolutions: A Conversation with John D'Emilio and Estelle Freedman," Mass, 2, pp.338, 339, 358. Cited in Katz, *The Invention of Heterosexuality*, p.184.
[269] Gilder, *Men and Marriage*, p.184.
[270] Ibid., p.185.
[271] D'Emilio and Freedman, p.331. Cited in Katz, *The Invention of Heterosexuality*, p.185.
[272] Blank, p.33.
[273] Ibid.
[274] Katz, *The Invention of Heterosexuality* , p.185.
[275] Gilder, *Men and Marriage*, p.185.
[276] Gore Vidal, "The Tree of Liberty: Notes on Our Patriarchal State," *The Nation*, August 27/September 3, 1990, 1,pp. 202 and 204. Cited in Katz *The Invention of Heterosexuality*, p.190.
[277] Kolata, p.35.
[278] Wilmut et al., p.128.
[279] Ibid., p.287.
[280] "Poll: Americans Opposed To Cloning," Lifeissues.net, www.lifeissues.net/news.php?newsID+00002337&topic, 12/20/02.
[281] David, P. Gushee, "Opposing Forces," *Christianity Today*, October 1, 2001, Vol. 45, No. 12, p.34. www.christianitytoday.com/ct/2001/012/1.34.html.
[282] Ibid.
[283] Irving, "What is 'Bioethics'?"
[284] John F. Kilner, "Human Cloning," www.cbhd.org/resources/aps/kilner_02-11-15.htm.
[285] Ibid.
[286] Ibid.
[287] Ibid., see National bioethics Advisory Commission, Cloning Human Beings: Report and Recommendations of the National Bioethics Advisory Commission, June 1997, p.69.
[288] Richard Woodman, "UK campaigners demand baby sex selection ban," *Lifeclinic*, www.lifeclinic.com/healthnews/article_view.asp?story+23409, 12/20/02.
[289] Ibid.
[290] Kolata, p.11.

[291] Michelle MacAfee, "Cloning worries 88.9% of Canadians, poll finds," *National Post*, 20 August 2001, p.A4.
[292] Ibid.
[293] Ibid.
[294] "Cloning," *Calgary Herald*, 27 November 2001, p.A2.
[295] Gushee, "A Matter of Life and Death."
[296] Ibid.
[297] Gushee, "Tinkering with Genes."
[298] Davies, pp.228 and 229.
[299] CLONAID, www.clonaid.com, pp.1
[300] www.rael.org/int/english/index.html.
[301] Michelle MacAfee, "Cloning worries 88.9% of Canadians, poll finds," *National Post*, 20 August 2001, p.A4.
[302] Ibid.
[303] Michael Higgins, "Clonaid implores media to tell both sides of the story," *National Post*, 24 January 2003, p.A1.
[304] Ibid.

PART 5

[1] Robert I. Pate, "U.S. Army Reserve Components – Peacetime Assessment and Management to Meet Mobilization Requirements." *Military Research Program Paper*, U.S. Army War College, Carlisle, Pennsylvania, 22 May 1975, p. 4.

CHAPTER 9

[1] www.canada.humanists.net/news.html, 4 October 2003
[2] "Spiritual Humanism," www.spiritualhumanism.org, 12/13/02.
[3] Mantilla, "Abortion, power, and the morality wars."
[4] Rev. C. Wayne Hilliker, "What Makes or Breaks Prayer?," Chalmers United Church, Kingston Ontario, April 17, 1994.
[5] House of Commons, Routine Proceedings [025], 18 February 1994
[6] House of Commons, Routine Proceedings [214], 8 June 1995.
[7] Hansard, 8 April 2002.
[8] James A. Fussell, "Gay Q&A," *Calgary Herald*, September 21, 2003, p. A11.
[9] Donald L. Faris, *The Homosexual Christian – a Christian Response to an Age of Sexual Politics* (Markham Ontario: Faith Today Publications, 1993), p.93.
[10] Spong, *A New Christianity For a New World*, p.230.
[11] Dallas, p.171.
[12] www.members.aol.com/Jainster/quote or www.swanmore.freeola.com, 05/09/03.
[13] www.eugenics.net/papers/quotes.html, 3/2/01.
[14] Hunter, *Darwin's God*, p.131.
[15] Hans Jonas, quoted in Philip J. Lee *Against the Protestant Gnostics* (Oxford: Oxford University Press, 1987), p.16. Found in Hunter, *Darwin's God*, pp.149 and 150.
[16] Scroggs, p.116.
[17] Mark, Jordan, *The silence of Sodom* (Chicago: University of Chicago Press, 2000), p.248.
[18] Michael Swift, *Gay Community News*, February 15, 1987.
[19] Michelangelo Signorile, *Life Outside The Signorile Report on Gay Men: Sex, Drugs, Muscles, and the Passages of Life* (New York: HarpersCollins, 1997), p.xxxi.
[20] Frank Browning, *The Culture of Desire* (New York: Crown Publishers, 1993), pp.80 and 81.
[21] Spong, *Why Christianity Must Change or Die*, p.49.
[22] Ibid., p.99.

[23] Dallas, p.174.
[24] Jerry R. Kirk, *The Homosexual Crisis in the Maineline Church* (New York: Thomas Nelson, 1978), p.27.
[25] PeopleCanChange, www.peoplecanchange.com, 2/22/02
[26] Ibid.
[27] FreeToBeMe, www.freetobeme.com/answers.htm, 2/22/01.
[28] Hanegraaf, p.22. Hanegraaf first heard this quote in a sermon by Dr. D. James Kennedy.
[29] Michelle MacAfee, "Cloning worries 88.9% of Canadians, poll finds," *National Post*, 20 August 2001, p.A4.
[30] Garber, *VICEVERSA*, p.369
[31] Ibid.
[32] Millett, *Sexual Politics*, pp.126 and 127.
[33] *The Family*, ed. by Rossi, pp.14 and 15.
[34] Ibid.
[35] K. Painter, "A Biologic Theory for Sexual Preference," *USA Today*, March 1, 1989, p.4D.
[36] Joan Laird, "Gender in lesbian relationships: Cultural, feminist, and constructionist," *Journal of Marital and Family Therapy*, Upland, October 2000.
[37] FFLA, "The Bitter Price of Choice," reprinted from Frederica Mathewes-Green, *SisterLife*, Winter 1990, www.feministsforlife.org/FFL_topics/after/pricchoc.htm.
[38] FFLA, "Graciela Olivarez (1928-1987)," reprinted from Mary Krane Derr, The American Femminist, Summer 1998, www.feministsforlife.org/history/herstory/golivare.htm, 3/5/01.
[39] Dalma Heyn, *Marriage Shock: The Transformation of Women into Wives* (New York: Villard, 1997), p.xii.
[40] Troyer, p.15.
[41] www.flag.blackened.net/intanark/faq/secJ6.html#secj68.
[42] Eskridge, *The Case for SAME-SEX MARRIAGE*, p.81.
[43] Ibid.
[44] Paul, p.257.
[45] Eskridge, *The Case for SAME-SEX MARRIAGE*, p.80.
[46] Hewlett, *When The Bough Breaks*, p.93.
[47] I. Beiber et al., *Homosexuality: A Psychoanalytic Study* (New York: Basic Books, 1962), p.303.
[48] Kolata, p.76.
[49] Ibid.
[50] Ibid.
[51] John F. Kilner, "Human Cloning," www.cbhd.org/resources/aps/kilner_02-11-15.htm.
[52] Whitehead, p.67, cited in Saghir, M.T., Robins, E., *Male and Female Homosexuality, A Comprehensive Investigation.*
[53] Crittenden, p.98.
[54] Cohen, p.250.
[55] FFLA, an interview with author Frederica Mathewes-Green by FFLA President Rosemary Bottcher, "Real Choices," www.feministsforlife.org/taf/1994/winter/realchc.htm, 3/5/01.
[56] Ibid.
[57] Katz, pp.149 and 150.
[58] Rudolf Bultman, *Jesus Christ and Mythology* (New York: Charles Scribner's Sons, 1958), p.39.
[59] Ibid., p.40.
[60] Ibid.
[61] Ibid.
[62] Karla Mantilla and Lisa Vogel, "Michigan: Transgender controversy…and right-wing attacks," *Off Our Backs*, Washington, October 2000.

[63] Ibid.

[64] Ibid.

[66] Karla Mantilla and Jennie Ruby, "Men in ewe's clothing: The stealth politics of the transgender movement," *Off Our Backs*, Washington, April 2000.

[66] Ibid.

[67] Ibid.

[68] Ibid.

[69] Ibid.

ISBN 141201900-1

9 781412 019002